Using German Vocabulary

This textbook provides a comprehensive and thematically structured vocabulary for students of German. Designed for all but the very beginning levels of undergraduate study, it offers a broad range of vocabulary, and is divided into twenty manageable units dealing with the physical, social, cultural, economic and political world.

The word lists are graded into three levels that reflect difficulty and likely usefulness, and are accompanied by extensive exercises and activities, designed to reinforce work done with the lists, and to increase students' competence in using the vocabulary. Suitable for both classroom teaching and private study, the exercises also make use of authentic German texts, enabling students to work with the vocabulary in context. Clearly organized and accessible, *Using German Vocabulary* is designed to meet the needs of a variety of courses at multiple stages of any undergraduate programme.

SARAH M. B. FAGAN is Associate Professor of German at the University of Iowa. She has published articles on German and English in journals such as *Linguistic Inquiry*, *Die Unterrichtspraxis* and the *Journal of Germanic Linguistics*, of which she is also Review Editor. Her previous book, *The Syntax and Semantics of Middle Constructions: A Study with Special Reference to German* (1992), was published in Cambridge University Press's acclaimed series 'Cambridge Studies in Linguistics'.

Companion titles to *Using German Vocabulary*

Using German Vocabulary

SARAH M. B. FAGAN

CAMBRIDGE
UNIVERSITY PRESS

PUBLISHED BY THE PRESS SYNDICATE OF THE UNIVERSITY OF CAMBRIDGE
The Pitt Building, Trumpington Street, Cambridge, United Kingdom

CAMBRIDGE UNIVERSITY PRESS
The Edinburgh Building, Cambridge, CB2 2RU, UK
40 West 20th Street, New York, NY 10011–4211, USA
477 Williamstown Road, Port Melbourne, VIC 3207, Australia
Ruiz de Alarcón 13, 28014 Madrid, Spain
Dock House, The Waterfront, Cape Town 8001, South Africa

http://www.cambridge.org

First published 2004

Printed in the United Kingdom at the University Press, Cambridge

Typeface Ehrhardt 10.5/12 pt.   *System* LaTeX 2$_\varepsilon$ [TB]

A catalogue record for this book is available from the British Library

Library of Congress Cataloguing in Publication data
Fagan, Sarah M. B.
Using German vocabulary / Sarah M. B. Fagan.
   p.   cm.
Includes bibliographical references and index.
ISBN 0 521 79700 4 (pbk.)
1. German language – Vocabulary.   I. Title
PF3445.F34   2004
438.2′42 – dc22   2003055902

ISBN 0 521 79700 4 paperback

Contents

Acknowledgments

This project has benefited from the help and generosity of many people.

I would like to thank all the copyright holders who have so graciously allowed me to reproduce their texts in this book.

For their help in the earlier stages of this project, I would like to thank my research assistants, Linnea McKay, Anne Schreiber and Ann Wilke. My thanks also go to Günter Nold for sharing with me his ideas on vocabulary exercises. I am grateful to Wolfgang Ertl and Gert Webelhuth for providing native-speaker clarification of some issues of meaning and usage that could not be resolved with standard reference works.

I owe special thanks to Kate Brett, who sparked my interest in this project and provided valuable help along the way, including useful feedback on drafts of early chapters. I am grateful to Jean H. Duffy, who willingly shared her book, *Using French Vocabulary,* as a model. My final thanks go to Rosemary Williams, for her careful copyediting, and to my editors, Helen Barton and Andrew Winnard, who have helped see this project through to completion.

Abbreviations and symbols

adj. decl.	adjective declination
art.	article
AU	Austrian German
Bav.	Bavarian
Brit.	British
CH	Swiss German
coll.	colloquial
dial.	dialect
elev.	elevated language
etw	etwas
euph.	euphemistic
fig.	figurative
hum.	humorous
jmd	jemand
jmdm	jemandem
jmdn	jemanden
jmds	jemandes
lang.	language
N	Northern German
naut.	nautical
o.s.	oneself
pej.	pejorative
pl.	plural
poet.	poetic
S	Southern German
s.o.	someone
sb's	somebody's
sl.	slang
sth	something
W	West German
✓	answer key provided

Introduction

Goals

Using German Vocabulary aims to offer a comprehensive, thematically structured vocabulary textbook for all but the very beginning levels of undergraduate instruction in German. The individual units treat topics that expose students to a broad range of vocabulary dealing with the physical, social, cultural, economic and political world. Vocabulary is graded into three levels that reflect frequency, difficulty and degree of usefulness. Exercises and activities are provided to reinforce and aid acquisition. The range of topics covered and the levels of competence addressed allow the book to be integrated into the curriculum in a variety of courses at multiple stages of any undergraduate program.

Because first-year German textbooks typically include a list of vocabulary to learn in each chapter, the acquisition of vocabulary during the first year of college-level instruction in German is relatively straightforward. After the first year, however, it becomes more difficult for instructors and students alike to deal with vocabulary in a systematic manner. Instruction at the intermediate and advanced levels tends to centre around authentic texts in the target language. The vocabulary that students acquire at these levels is thus limited in large part to the vocabulary that occurs in these texts. *Using German Vocabulary* is a tool for dealing systematically with vocabulary acquisition beyond the first year of instruction.

The past decade has seen the publication of a number of German language textbooks that seek to address the issue of vocabulary acquisition beyond the beginning stages of language learning. Some provide thematically organized word lists; others provide thematically organized vocabulary exercises; only two recently published textbooks offer thematically organized word lists together with reinforcement exercises (James and James 1991 together with Müller and Bock 1991; Lübke 1998). *Using German Vocabulary* sets itself apart from these in the level of sophistication of vocabulary presented, in the grading of this vocabulary into three levels, and in the variety and extensiveness of accompanying exercises and activities.

The acquisition of vocabulary is a cumulative process, involving multiple stages that range from passive recognition to active production (Nation 2001; Stoller and Grabe 1993). Different learning strategies contribute in different ways to this process. One strategy, learning from word cards, is an efficient way of learning large numbers of words in a relatively short time (Nation 2001:302). The word lists in *Using German Vocabulary* are intended as a useful source of vocabulary for the production of word cards. Two other important vocabulary learning strategies, using word parts (prefixes, bases, suffixes) and dictionary use, can contribute to the speed in which learners increase the size of their vocabulary (Nation 2001:263–281). *Using German Vocabulary* provides a special chapter on "Words and word formation" that discusses the structure of German words and addresses the issue of dictionary use. Various exercises in the twenty main units promote the awareness of word parts; many exercises and activities in these units involve dictionary use. The exercises in *Using German Vocabulary* are not limited to the word level of vocabulary acquisition. Authentic target language texts, for example, provide various opportunities for students to work with vocabulary in context. As the discussion of the various exercise types below shows, the exercises in each unit are designed to offer students a variety of ways in which to understand as well as use German vocabulary.

Using German Vocabulary is designed for classroom as well as individual use. Because of the range of topics covered, it can be used in a variety of courses as a primary or supplementary text. It also lends itself to self-study. An answer key is provided for a number of exercises in each unit, and the correct answers to many exercises are relatively easy to determine.

Structure and organization

The vocabulary in this book has been organized thematically into twenty units. Each unit presents vocabulary that centres on several related topics. Unit 11, for example, covers the topics of leisure and sport; unit 12 deals with tourism, travel and transport. Each broad topic within a given unit is divided into subtopics in order to provide units for acquisition that are manageable in size and to provide groupings of vocabulary that are semantically and pragmatically more coherent. In unit 9, for example, the broad topic of the visual and performing arts is further subdivided into the subtopics of painting and sculpture, music, dance, theatre, cinema and film, and photography.

Within each subtopic, the ordering of vocabulary items is intended to highlight the structural, semantic and pragmatic relationships among words in order to facilitate the acquisition process. For example, words like *Gemüsegarten* 'vegetable garden' and *Obstgarten* 'orchard', which have the form *-garten* 'garden' in common, are listed together to show structural similarities. Synonyms like *Bibliothek* 'library' and *Bücherei* 'library' and antonyms like *bestehen* 'pass' and *durchfallen* 'fail' are grouped close together to bring out the semantic relationships between lexical items. Words for objects that tend to occur together in everyday life, words like *Hammer* 'hammer' and *Nagel* 'nail', for example, are placed together to capitalize on natural associations. The order of items presented here should not be viewed as somehow definitive or static, however. There are many ways in which lexical items can be grouped together and ordered; this book presents just one. Furthermore, because the lists are intended as the basis for the construction of word cards, the order in which vocabulary items appear should be viewed as only temporary. (See the section below on tips for vocabulary learning.)

The vocabulary in each unit is graded into three levels. The first level contains more common, general-purpose terms as well as terms that are of relatively high frequency. The complexity and difficulty of vocabulary items increases in the second and third levels, so that the third level contains more terms that are technical in nature, semantically complex, marked in the sense that they belong to formal or colloquial registers, etc. Exercises corresponding to the three levels of vocabulary follow the word lists in each unit.

Criteria of selection

Using German Vocabulary includes more than just the most frequent vocabulary items in a given subject area. Because one goal of this textbook is to expose students to useful words they might not otherwise have been exposed to, less frequent but nevertheless useful vocabulary items are included in the word lists. Vocabulary items have been gathered from various sources, including specialized dictionaries and textbooks. Regional variation in vocabulary (primarily north–south differences) is noted; frequently encountered regional variants are listed together with their equivalents in the standard language. Vocabulary items that belong to the colloquial language as well as those that belong to elevated speech are included in the lists.

In dividing the vocabulary in each unit into three levels, an attempt was made to keep the number of entries in each level roughly the same. For this reason, the three levels should be viewed as representing a continuum of increasing complexity and difficulty rather than as three distinct levels of lexical proficiency.

There will inevitably be vocabulary items that one might expect to occur in these lists but that do not. If the lists were to be kept manageable in size, it was not possible to include every potentially relevant and useful lexical item. When words needed to be cut because of length considerations, compound nouns were among those that were typically excluded. The German language contains many compound nouns; the productivity of compound formation is in fact one of the distinctive features of the language (Durrell 2002:476). Because many German compounds are transparent in meaning to native speakers of English, they could be excluded without major loss of coverage. For example, a compound like *Gartenweg* 'garden path', which is composed of the words *Garten* 'garden' and *Weg* 'path', can be understood as well as produced if one knows the words *Garten* and *Weg*, and for this reason it was not included in the word lists. A compound like *Bürgersteig* 'pavement', however, is not transparent in the same way (the meaning 'pavement' cannot be determined directly from the meanings of *Bürger* 'citizen' and *Steig* 'steep path') and for this reason was not excluded from the lists. Because of the natural connections among the various topics and subtopics in this book, many lexical items could have occurred in more than one unit, but do not in order to avoid repetition and conserve space. The word *Spionage* 'spying, espionage', for example, would be appropriate under the categories of law, war, and politics and international relations. Instead of repeating this item in all three categories, it has been put only in the category of politics and international relations.

Exercises

The exercises that follow the word lists in each unit are intended for individual as well as classroom use. They are designed to aid and reinforce the acquisition of the vocabulary in the lists by helping students move from the passive stages of vocabulary acquisition to the active stages, that is, from recognizing and understanding vocabulary to using it appropriately in discourse.

The exercises also provide students with examples of vocabulary in use. Each unit contains at least one authentic German-language text per exercise level that is used as the basis for an exercise. The sentences used for the sentence-completion exercises are based on authentic text. The English sentences that students are asked to translate into German are also based on attested German sentences. Thus the results of such translation exercises mirror authentic text. It is suggested that some texts should be translated orally.

The following list presents the most common types of exercises that occur in *Using German Vocabulary* along with ways in which each exercise type aids acquisition. These exercises all reinforce the work done with word cards. To the extent that students use dictionaries to complete these exercises, they also promote dictionary use, which has been shown to help students learn vocabulary and understand and produce text (Luppescu and Day 1993; Knight 1994).

Exercise	Benefit
Matching words and definitions	Strengthens the form–meaning connection; exposes learners to German-language definitions.
Solving crossword puzzles	Strengthens the form–meaning connection; exposes learners to German-language definitions.
Matching associated words	Helps in understanding the full meaning of a word by focusing on its relationship to other words; helps in recalling a word or its meaning in appropriate contexts.
Building complex words	Helps learners retain knowledge about new complex words; strengthens knowledge about stems, affixes and word formation that can be used to learn words not previously encountered.
Filling word part tables	Reinforces knowledge about new complex words; reinforces knowledge about relationships among related vocabulary items.
Categorization of vocabulary	Helps integrate vocabulary knowledge with knowledge of subject matter.
Finding opposites or synonyms	Helps in understanding the full meaning of a word by focusing on its relationships to other words.
Completion of proportions	Helps reinforce and establish relationships among lexical items.
Differentiation of similar forms	Highlights differences between words that are similar in form; helps learners avoid common pitfalls.
Providing definitions	Strengthens the form–meaning connection.

Identification of multiple meanings	Extends the learner's knowledge of individual lexical items; raises the learner's awareness of polysemy.
Matching collocates	Helps in acquiring the type of knowledge about words that can lead to fluent, native-like speech.
Sentence completion	Provides the opportunity to put vocabulary items in context; brings the learner closer to the production of entire sentences with new vocabulary items.
Translation of English or German idioms	Extends the learner's use of vocabulary items; raises the learner's awareness of the potential lack of a one-to-one correspondence between English and German idioms.
Translation of sentences into German	Provides the opportunity for learners to use vocabulary productively to produce sentence-level discourse; allows learners to focus on grammatical issues involved in vocabulary use.
Translation of German texts into English	Provides exposure to vocabulary in context; provides practice in determining meaning from context.
Summarizing German texts	Tests comprehension of vocabulary in context; provides the opportunity for learners to use vocabulary productively in text-level discourse.
Composition	Encourages learners to use vocabulary productively in text-level discourse.

Tips on learning vocabulary

Word cards. Put the words from the word lists on to small cards that can easily be carried around. Put the German word on one side (with gender and plural formation for nouns and principal parts for strong verbs) and the English translation on the other (native-language translations have been shown to be more effective than target-language translations; see Laufer and Shmueli 1997). Supplement the translations with pictures when possible, as this can improve learning (Nation 2001:304–305). Work with the cards first by looking at a German word and recalling its meaning; then work with the cards by looking at meanings and producing the German forms. Work with sets of cards that are manageable in size; use smaller sets for more difficult words. Change the order of the words as you work with them so that you can learn to recall each word independently. Because words that are similar in form and meaning can be more difficult to learn together than separately (Laufer 1989; Nation 2000; Tinkham 1997; Waring 1997) you should avoid including related words in the same set. For words that are difficult to remember, use a mnemonic link. For example, link the word to the sound of a word in English or German; note the meaning of part(s) of the word (for *Frühstück* 'breakfast' take the first part, *früh* 'early', and think of something like "an early bird at breakfast"); link the word to the situation in which it appeared (Cohen 1990:25–27). Say each word aloud as you work with it, as this can improve long-term memory (Ellis 1997). Work with your word cards on a regular (daily) basis.

Exercises. After you have learned the words in the word lists from one level in a given unit, complete the corresponding exercises. These exercises will reinforce the vocabulary you have learned and help you use this vocabulary. They will expose you to new vocabulary as well as help you identify the vocabulary that you need to review. Redo the exercises periodically to check and reinforce your long-term memory. Use dictionaries to help you complete the exercises; consult both bilingual and monolingual dictionaries. The Wortschatz-Lexikon (http://wortschatz.uni-leipzig.de) is an excellent online source for information about usage. It provides millions of sentence examples for German vocabulary and therefore contains much information about use that is not available in printed dictionaries.

Additional reading. Find additional texts related to the subject matter of the unit you are working on. Online newspapers and magazines are excellent sources of text that are easily accessible. Some of the many sites that are currently available are the following: FOCUS Online (http://focus.msn.de), FAZ.NET (http://www.faz.net), FRANKFURTER RUNDSCHAU online (http://www.fr-aktuell.de), GEO.de (http://www.geo.de), SPIEGEL ONLINE (http://www.spiegel.de), STERN (http://www.stern.de), SÜDDEUTSCHE ZEITUNG (http://www.sueddeutsche.de), DIE WELT online (http://www.welt.de), DIE ZEIT (http://www.zeit.de/).

Bibliography

Vocabulary acquisition

Cohen, Andrew D. 1990. *Language learning: insights for learners, teachers, and researchers.* New York: Newbury House Publishers.

Ellis, Nick. C. 1997. 'Vocabulary acquisition, word structure, collocation, word-class, and meaning.' In Schmitt and McCarthy, 122–39.

Huckin, Thomas, Margot Haynes, and James Coady. 1993. *Second Language Reading and Vocabulary Learning.* Norwood, NJ: Ablex Publishing Corporation.

Knight, Susan. 1994. 'Dictionary use while reading: the effects on comprehension and vocabulary acquisition for students of different verbal abilities.' *Modern Language Journal* 78:285–99.

Laufer, Batia. 1989. 'A factor of difficulty in vocabulary learning: deceptive transparency.' *AILA Review* 6:10–20.

Laufer, Batia and Karen Shmueli. 1997. 'Memorizing new words: does teaching have anything to do with it?' *RELC Journal* 28:89–108.

Luppescu, Stuart, and Richard R. Day. 1993. 'Reading, dictionaries and vocabulary learning.' *Language Learning* 43:263–87.

Nation, I. S. P. 2000. 'Learning vocabulary in lexical sets: dangers and guidelines.' *TESOL Journal* 9,2:6–10.

Nation, I. S. P. 2001. *Learning Vocabulary in Another Language.* Cambridge University Press.

Schmitt, Norbert and Michael McCarthy (eds.). 1997. *Vocabulary: Description, Acquisition and Pedagogy.* Cambridge University Press.

Stoller, Fredricka L., and William Grabe. 1993. 'Implication for L2 vocabulary acquisition and instruction from L1 vocabulary research.' In Huckin *et al.*, 24–45.

Tinkham, Thomas. 1997. 'The effects of semantic and thematic clustering on the learning of second language vocabulary.' *Second Language Research* 13:138–63.

Waring, Robert. 1997. 'The negative effects of learning words in semantic sets: a replication.' *System* 25:261–74.

General vocabulary books

Apelt, Mary L. 1995. *Wortschatz und mehr: Übungen für die Mittel- und Oberstufe.* (Deutsch üben 9.) Ismaning: Verlag für Deutsch.

Buscha, Annerose, and Kirsten Friedrich. 1996. *Deutsches Übungsbuch: Übungen zum Wortschatz der deutschen Sprache.* Munich: Langenscheidt.

Ferenbach, Magda, and Ingrid Schüßler. 2001. *Wörter zur Wahl.* Stuttgart: Klett.

Forst, Gabriele, Veronika Schnorr, Martin Crellin and Adelheid Schnorr-Dümmler. 1995. *Mastering German Vocabulary: A Thematic Approach.* Hauppauge, NY: Barron's.

James, Carol L., and Charles J. James (trans.). 1991. *Basic German Vocabulary: A Learner's Dictionary Divided into Subject Categories with Example Sentences*. Berlin: Langenscheidt.

Lübke, Diethard. 1998. *Wortschatz Deutsch: Learning German Words*. Ismaning: Verlag für Deutsch.

Müller, Jutta, and Heiko Bock. 1991. *Basic German Vocabulary: Workbook*. Berlin; Munich: Langenscheidt. (Companion workbook to James and James 1991.)

Remanofsky, Ulrich. 1991. *Zertifikatstraining Deutsch: Wortschatz*. Ismaning: Hueber.

Saunders, Joy. 1998. *German Vocabulary Handbook*. Princeton, NJ: Berlitz Publishing Company.

Weermann, Eva Maria. 2001. *Vocabulary Builder: German*. Hauppauge, NY: Barron's.

Wilkin, Susan, Cornelia Schnelle and Valerie Grundy (eds.). 2000. *Oxford German Wordpack*. Oxford University Press.

Weiss, Edda. 1999. *Schaum's Outline of German Vocabulary*. New York: McGraw-Hill.

Specialized vocabulary books

Apelt, Mary L. 1990. *German–English Dictionary: Art History, Archaeology*. 2nd edn. Berlin: E. Schmidt.

Barber, Josephine. 1985. *German for Musicians*. Bloomington: Indiana University Press.

Bathelt, Claudia, Kay Hollingsworth and Caroline Haydon. 2001. *PONS Bürowörterbuch: Englisch–Deutsch, Deutsch–Englisch*. Stuttgart: Klett.

Baumgartner, Peter. 2002. *Wörterbuch moderne Wirtschaft mit Anwendungsbeispielen*. Erlangen: Publicis.

Bock, Hanne, Gisela Frey and Ian Bock (comp.). 1997. *Elsevier's Dictionary of European Community / Company / Business / Financial Law: In English, Danish, and German*. Amsterdam: Elsevier.

Britt, Christa, and Lilith Schutte. 1995. *Wiley's English–German, German–English Business Dictionary*. New York: J. Wiley.

Collin, P. H. 1998. *PONS Fachwörterbuch Recht: Englisch–Deutsch, Deutsch–Englisch*. 2nd edn. Stuttgart: Klett.

Collin, P. H., A. Ivanovic and Dorothee Lantemann. 1991. *PONS Fachwörterbuch Marketing: Englisch–Deutsch, Deutsch–Englisch*. Stuttgart: Klett.

Collin, P. H., Rupert Livesey, Liz Greasby and Eberhard Schick. 2000. *PONS Fachwörterbuch Medizin: Englisch–Deutsch, Deutsch–Englisch*. Revised edn. Stuttgart: Klett.

Collin, P. H., Rupert Livesey, Anke Kornmüller, Sigrid Janssen and Liz Greasby. 2001. *PONS Fachwörterbuch Wirtschaft: Englisch–Deutsch, Deutsch–Englisch*. Stuttgart: Klett.

Collin, P. H., Rupert Livesey and Dorthee Lantermann. 1996. *PONS Fachwörterbuch Touristik, Hotellerie, Gastronomie: Englisch–Deutsch, Deutsch–Englisch*. Stuttgart: Klett.

Collin, P. H., Eva Sawers and Rupert Livesey. 1990. *PONS Fachwörterbuch Druck- und Verlagswesen: Englisch–Deutsch, Deutsch–Englisch*. Stuttgart: Klett.

Collin, S. M. H., Eva Torkar and Rupert Livesey. 1993. *PONS Fachwörterbuch Bank- und Finanzwesen: Englisch–Deutsch, Deutsch–Englisch*. Stuttgart: Klett.

Collin, S. M. H., Eva Torkar, Rupert Livesey and Armin Mutscheller. 1997. *PONS Fachwörterbuch Datenverarbeitung: Englisch–Deutsch, Deutsch–Englisch*. 2nd edn. Stuttgart: Klett.

Deliiska, Boriana, and P. Manoilov. 2001. *Elsevier's Dictionary of Computer Science: In English, German, French and Russian*. Amsterdam: Elsevier Science.

Desinger, Bernd, Hans Walter Frischkopf, Ulrich Scheck and Helfried W. Seliger. 1999. *Basiswissen Wirtschaftsdeutsch: Stoffgebiete und Fachwortschatz*. Munich: Iudicum.

Dietl, Clara-Erika, Egon Lorenz, Wiebke Buxbaum and Walter Bonhoeffer. 2000–. *Wörterbuch für Recht, Wirtschaft und Politik*. Vol. 1, *Englisch–Deutsch*. 6th edn. Munich: C. H. Beck.

Eichborn, Reinhart von. 1983. *Cambridge–Eichborn German dictionary: Economics, Law, Administration, Business, General*. Cambridge University Press.

Ferretti, Vittorio. 1996. *Wörterbuch der Datentechnik: Englisch–Deutsch, Deutsch–Englisch*. Berlin: Springer.

Flory, Peter, and Bernd Froschauer. 1995. *Grundwortschatz der Rechtssprache: Deutsch–Englisch, Englisch–Deutsch*. 2nd edn. Neuwied: Kriftel; Berlin: Luchterhand.

Gerstner, Angela. 2002. *Fachwörterbuch der Logistik, Mikroelektronik und Datenverarbeitung: Deutsch–Englisch*. 2nd edn. Erlangen: Publicis.

Gerstner, Angela, and Jens Kiesel. 2002. *Fachwörter der Logistik, Produktionsplanung und -steuerung Deutsch–Englisch*. Berlin: Siemens; Erlangen: Publicis.

Good, Colin. 1995. *Newspaper German: A Vocabulary of Administrative and Commercial Idiom*. Cardiff: University of Wales Press.

Hammer, Wilfried. 1997. *Wörterbuch der Arbeitswissenschaft: Begriffe und Definitionen*. Munich: Hanser.

Hartley, Paul, and Gertrud Robins. 1996. *Manual of Business German: A Comprehensive Language Guide*. New York: Routledge.

Hartley, Paul, and Gertrud Robins. 1997. *German/English Business Glossary*. London: Routledge.

Head, David, and J. Coveney. 1999. *Harrap German Business Management Dictionary*. Edinburgh: Harrap.

Head, Peter, and Rolf Speetzen. 1998. *Wörterbuch für Marketing und Media: Deutsch–Englisch, English–German*. Frankfurt am Main: Media-Micro-Census.

Herd, E. W., and August Obermayer. 1992. *A Glossary of German Literary Terms*. 2nd edn. Dunedin: Department of German, University of Otago.

Keitz, Saiedeh von, and Wolfgang von Keitz. 1992. *Dictionary of Library and Information Science: English/German, German/English*. 2nd edn. Weinheim: VCH.

Kleiner, Herbert E. 1995. *Dictionary of Military Technology: English–German*. Munich: Verlag Kleiner.

Kohlschmitt, Albert. 2002. *PONS Fachwörterbuch Umwelt: Englisch–Deutsch*. Stuttgart: Klett.

Korff, Malte. 2000. *Kleines Wörterbuch der Musik*. Ditzingen: Reclam.

Kraetschmer, Kurt. 1991. *Deutsch–Englisches Wörterbuch der Datenkommunikation*. Vienna: Edition Praesens.

Kucera, Antonín. 2002. *Wörterbuch der exakten Naturwissenschaften und der Technik*. 2nd edn. Wiesbaden: Brandstetter.

Leuchtmann, Horst. 1998. *Wörterbuch Musik: Englisch–Deutsch, Deutsch–Englisch*. 5th edn. Stuttgart: J. B. Metzler.

Mack, Roy, Bettina Mikhail and Michel Mikhail. 1996. *Wörterbuch der Veterinärmedizin und Biowissenschaften: Deutsch–Englisch, Englisch–Deutsch mit einem viersprachigen Anhang, Latein–Deutsch–Englisch–Französisch*. 2nd edn. Berlin: Blackwell Wissenschafts-Verlag.

Markov, A. S. 1984. *Dictionary of Scientific and Technical Terminology: English, German, French, Dutch, Russian*. The Hague: Nijhoff.

Merrifield, Doris Fulda. 1994. *Deutsche Wirtschaftssprache für Amerikaner*. 3rd edn. New York: John Wiley & Sons, Inc.

Mohr, Arno. 2001. *Sozialwissenschaftliches Wörterbuch: Englisch–Deutsch, Deutsch–Englisch*. Munich: Oldenbourg.

Mühle, Peter. 1992. *Wörterbuch der Holzwirtschaft. Englisch–Deutsch, Deutsch–Englisch*. Wiesbaden: O. Brandstetter.

O'Flanagan, Rory, and Ruth Irle. 2001. *Wörterbuch Personal- und Bildungswesen: Deutsch–Englisch*. 3rd edn. Weinheim: Wiley.

Owen, Linda R. (ed.). 1991. *Prähistorisches Wörterbuch: Fachwörterbuch zur Ur- und Frühgeschichte, Deutsch / Englisch, English / German*. Tübingen: Verlag Archaeologica Venatoria.

Pollert, Achim, Bernd Kirchner and Javier Morato Polzin. 2001. *Duden: Das Lexikon der Wirtschaft. Grundlegendes Wissen von A bis Z*. Mannheim: Dudenverlag.

Rehahn, Jens Peter. 1999. *Langenscheidts Fachwörterbuch Telecommunication: Englisch–Deutsch, Deutsch–Englisch*. Berlin; New York: Langenscheidt.

Renouard, Horst E. von. 2002. *Fachwörterbuch elektronische Medien und Dienste*. 2nd edn. Berlin: Springer.

Routledge. 1997. *Routledge German Dictionary of Business, Commerce, and Finance*. London: Routledge.

Routledge. 1999. *German Dictionary of Computing: German–English / English–German*. London: Routledge.

Schmitt, Peter A. 1992. *PONS Fachwörterbuch der Kfz-Technik: Englisch–Deutsch, Deutsch–Englisch*. 2 vols. Stuttgart: Klett.

Seibicke, Wilfried. 1983. *Duden: Wie sagt man anderswo? Landschaftliche Unterschiede im deutschen Sprachgebrauch*. 2nd edn. Mannheim: Bibliographisches Institut.

Seubel, Magdalena, and Neil Morris (eds.). 2001. *The Oxford German Business Dictionary*. Oxford University Press.

Shaw, Gisela. 1995. *Pocket Dictionary of Business German*. London: Hodder & Stoughton.

Stephens, Alan, Eckhard Böhle and Rupert Livesey. 1992. *PONS Fachwörterbuch Landwirtschaft: Englisch–Deutsch, Deutsch–Englisch*. Stuttgart: Klett.

Wilhelm, Petra. 1994. *Dictionary of Communication Design*. Berlin: Springer.

Grammar and usage

Dodd, Bill, Christine Eckhard-Black, John Klapper and Ruth Whittle. 1996. *Modern German Grammar: A Practical Guide*. London: Routledge.

Drosdowski, Günther, and Peter Eisenberg (eds.). 1998. *Duden: Grammatik der deutschen Gegenwartssprache*. 6th edn. Mannheim: Dudenverlag.

Dudenredaktion. 2001. *Duden: Richtiges und gutes Deutsch. Wörterbuch der sprachlichen Zweifelsfälle*. 5th edn. Mannheim: Dudenverlag.

Durrell, Martin. 1992. *Using German: A Guide to Contemporary Usage*. Cambridge University Press.

Durrell, Martin. 2002. *Hammer's German Grammar and Usage*. 4th edn. Chicago: McGraw-Hill.

Strutz, Henry. 1997. *1001 Pitfalls in German*. 3rd edn. Hauppauge, NY: Barron's.

Dictionaries

Betteridge, Harold T. 2001. *Cassell's German–English, English–German Dictionary*. Rev. edn. London: Continuum.

Dudenredaktion. 2000. *Duden: Bildwörterbuch der deutschen Sprache*. 5th edn. Mannheim: Dudenverlag.

Dudenredaktion. 2001. *Duden: Das Stilwörterbuch*. 8th edn. Mannheim: Dudenverlag.

Dudenredaktion and Oxford University Press. 1994. *Oxford–Duden Bildwörterbuch Deutsch und Englisch*. 2nd edn. Mannheim: Dudenverlag.

Hecht, Dörthe, and Annette Schmollinger (eds.). 1999. *PONS Basiswörterbuch Deutsch als Fremdsprache: Das einsprachige Lernerwörterbuch zum neuen Zertifikat Deutsch*. Stuttgart: Klett.

Morris, Neil, and Roswitha Morris (eds.). 2000. *Oxford Starter German Dictionary*. Revised edn. Oxford University Press.

Ruoff, Arno. 1990. *Häufigkeitswörterbuch gesprochener Sprache: Gesondert nach Wortarten, alphabetisch, rückläufig-alphabetisch und nach Häufigkeit geordnet*. (Idiomatica, vol. 8.) Tübingen: Niemeyer.

Scholze-Stubenrecht, Werner (ed.). 2001. *The Oxford–Duden German Dictionary: German–English, English–German*. 2nd rev. edn. Oxford University Press.

Terrell, Peter, Veronika Schnorr, Wendy V. A. Morris and Roland Breitsprecher. 1999. *Collins German–English, English–German Dictionary: Unabridged*. 4th edn. New York: HarperCollins.

Wahrig, Gerhard. 2000. *Deutsches Wörterbuch*. 7th edn. Edited by Renate Wahrig-Burfeind. Gütersloh: Bertelsmann Lexikon.

Synonyms

Bulitta, Erich, and Hildegard Bulitta. 2003. *Wörterbuch der Synonyme und Antonyme: Sinn- und sachverwandte Wörter und Begriffe sowie deren Gegenteil und Bedeutungsvarianten*. Frankfurt am Main: Fischer.

Durrell, Martin. 2000. *Using German Synonyms*. Cambridge University Press.

Farrell, Ralph Barstow. 1977. *Dictionary of German Synonyms*. 3rd edn. Cambridge University Press.

Latzel, Sigbert. 1995. *Lernschwierigkeiten mit deutschen Synonymen*. Parts I and II. Heidelberg: Groos.

Müller, Wolfgang (ed.). 1997. *Duden sinn- und sachverwandte Wörter: Synonymwörterbuch der deutschen Sprache*. 2nd edn. Mannheim: Dudenverlag.

False Friends

Barnickel, Klaus-Dieter. 1992. *Falsche Freunde: Ein vergleichendes Wörterbuch Deutsch–Englisch*. Heidelberg: Groos.

Breitkreuz, Hartmut. 1991. *False Friends: Stolpersteine des deutsch–englischen Wortschatzes*. Reinbek bei Hamburg: Rowohlt Taschenbuch Verlag.

Dretzke, Burkhard, and Margaret I. Nester. 1990. *Student's Guide to False Friends, New Friends and Old Friends*. Berlin: Cornelsen.

Heringer, Hans Jürgen. 2001. *Fehlerlexikon*. Berlin. Cornelsen.

Parkes, Geoff, and Alan Cornell. 1993. *German–English False Friends: Reference and Practice*. Southampton: Englang.

Slang

Graves, Paul G. 1994. *Streetwise German: Speaking and Understanding Colloquial German*. Lincolnwood, IL: NTC Publishing Group.

Strutz, Henry. 2000. *Dictionary of German Slang and Colloquial Expressions*. Hauppauge, NY: Barron's.

Wippermann, Peter (ed.). 2000. *Duden Wörterbuch der Szenesprachen*. Mannheim: Dudenverlag.

Words and word formation

Word formation

Some words in German are simple, consisting of a single unit of meaning, e.g. *Blut* 'blood'. Other words are complex, and are made up of more than one unit of meaning, e.g. *blutarm* (*blut* 'blood' + *arm* 'poor') 'anaemic'. The meaning of a word in German can often be determined from the meaning of its parts, and German words are often more transparent than words in English in this regard; compare German *Blut, bluten, blutarm, Blutung* and *Bluter* with English *blood, bleed, anaemic, haemorrhage* and *haemophiliac*. Knowing some basic facts about German word formation can therefore be of great help in expanding your vocabulary in German.

This description of word formation in German briefly discusses two of the main ways in which complex words are formed from simple words: (1) prefixation and suffixation, and (2) compounding. This is followed by a discussion of the formation of complex nouns, adjectives, verbs and adverbs that presents the basic meanings of the most important prefixes and suffixes involved in the formation of these word classes.

Prefixation and suffixation

Prefixes and suffixes are units of meaning that typically cannot stand on their own, but are added to the beginning of an existing word or word root (in the case of a prefix) or to the end of a word or word root (in the case of a suffix) to form a new word:
Prefixation: *un-* + *gleich* 'equal' = *ungleich* 'unequal'
Suffixation: *schreib* 'write' + *-ung* = *Schreibung* 'spelling'
Many complex words in German are formed with more than one prefix or suffix:
un- + *Freund* + *-lich* + *-keit* = *Unfreundlichkeit* 'unfriendliness'
ver- + *klein* + *-er* + *-ung* = *Verkleinerung* 'reduction'

Suffixation often involves umlauting the vowel of the word to which the suffix is attached:

Buch 'book' + *-lein* = *Büchlein* 'little book'

Arzt 'doctor' + *-in* = *Ärztin* 'woman doctor'

Suffixation is particularly important in the formation of complex nouns; prefixation is of particular importance in the formation of complex verbs.

Some suffixes and prefixes are productive; they are used repeatedly to create new words. The *-er* suffix that derives nouns from verbs, for example, is highly productive: *Lackierer* 'painter', *Denker* 'thinker', *Untergeher* 'loser'. Other suffixes and prefixes are no longer productive, but many words can still be found in the language that contain these prefixes and suffixes. The suffix *-e*, for example, can be found in many nouns like *Enge* 'narrowness' (from *eng* 'narrow') and *Länge* 'length' (from *lang* 'long'), but this suffix is not being used to create new nouns. The prefixes and suffixes that are discussed below include those that are productive as well as those that are well represented in the lexicon of German.

Some prefixes and suffixes are of foreign origin; they are found in words that were borrowed at some point into the German language (e.g. the suffix *-ität* in words like *Anonymität* 'anonymity') or are themselves borrowed and used to create new words (e.g. the prefix *super-* 'ultra' in words like *superschnell* 'ultra-fast'). Because many prefixes and suffixes of foreign origin are well represented in the German language, they are included in the discussion below.

Compounding

Compounding is the formation of a complex word out of two or more existing words:

Haus 'house' + *Tür* 'door' = *Haustür* 'front door'

Leben 'life' + *Mittel* 'means' + *Geschäft* 'store' = *Lebensmittelgeschäft* 'food(stuffs) store', 'grocer's'

The individual words that make up a compound word can themselves be complex (formed by the processes of suffixation and/or prefixation):

Arbeiter (*arbeit* + *-er*) 'worker' + *Vorstadt* (*vor-* + *Stadt*) 'suburb' = *Arbeitervorstadt* 'worker's suburb'

A 'linking' element is often added between the individual words that make up a compound word, e.g. *-e-*, *-en-*, *-er-*, and *-s-* in the following words:

Schwein+e+braten 'roast pork'

Tasch+en+messer 'pocket knife'

Kind+er+wagen 'pram', 'baby carriage'

Einbildung+s+kraft 'imagination'

Although these linking elements look like plural or case endings in some instances, they are best viewed as semantically empty elements.

15

Because the use of linking elements in compounds is often unpredictable, it is best to learn a compound together with its link.

The formation of nouns

Suffixation

Most suffixes that form nouns are linked to a particular gender and thus determine the gender of the word to which they are attached: for example, *-ung* (feminine; *die Wohnung* 'apartment'), *-chen* (neuter; *das Spielchen* 'little game'), *-er* (masculine; *der Verkäufer* 'seller').

-chen (neuter) forms diminutives (from nouns); umlaut is typically added to the stressed vowel, e.g.:
das Haus ➔ *das Häuschen* 'little house'
der Vogel ➔ *das Vögelchen* 'little bird'

-e (feminine) (i) forms nouns denoting an instrument or an action (from verbs), e.g.:
pfeifen ➔ *die Pfeife* 'pipe' (instrument)
spülen ➔ *die Spüle* 'sink' (instrument)
suchen ➔ *die Suche* 'search' (action)
einreisen ➔ *die Einreise* 'entry' (action)

(ii) forms nouns denoting an abstract quality (from adjectives); umlaut is added to the stressed vowel; e.g.:
blau ➔ *die Bläue* 'blue', 'blueness'
gut ➔ *die Güte* 'goodness'

-(er)ei (feminine) (i) forms nouns denoting the place where something is kept, produced, done, etc. (from nouns, often nouns with the suffix *-er*), e.g.:
die Karte ➔ *die Kartei* 'card file'
die Auskunft ➔ *Auskunftei* 'information bureau'
der Bäcker ➔ *die Bäckerei* 'bakery'

(ii) forms nouns denoting a repeated, often annoying action (from verbs); typically with the full form of the suffix, *-erei*; e.g.:
sticken ➔ *die Stickerei* 'embroidery'
fragen ➔ *die Fragerei* 'continued bothersome questioning'

-er (masculine) (i) forms nouns denoting the person or instrument performing the action described by a verb (from verbs), e.g.:
prüfen ➔ *der Prüfer* 'tester' (person)
verteidigen ➔ *der Verteidiger* 'defender' (person)
entsaften ➔ *der Entsafter* 'juice extractor' (instrument)
zubringen ➔ *der Zubringer* 'shuttle' (instrument)

(ii) forms nouns denoting the inhabitant of a place (from place names), e.g.:
Österreich ➔ *der Österreicher* 'Austrian'
Berlin ➔ *der Berliner* 'Berliner'

(iii)   forms nouns denoting a person who belongs to a profession (mainly from compound nouns), e.g.:
die Eisenbahn ➜ *der Eisenbahner* 'railway worker'
der Fußball ➜ *der Fußballer* 'soccer player', 'footballer'

(iv)   forms nouns denoting people belonging to a profession, a group, etc. (from nouns ending in *-ik* or with *-ik* added or substituted for another suffix), e.g.:
die Komik ➜ *der Komiker* 'comedian'
der Alkohol ➜ *der Alkoholiker* 'alcoholic'
die Satire ➜ *der Satiriker* 'satirist'

-*eur* (masculine)   forms nouns denoting the person who performs the action described by a verb (from verbs ending in *-ieren*), e.g.:
hypnotisieren ➜ *der Hypnotiseur* 'hypnotist'
kommandieren ➜ *der Kommandeur* 'commander'

-*heit*, -(*ig*)*keit* (feminine)   forms nouns denoting an abstract quality (typically from adjectives); *-keit* is typically added to adjectives ending in *-bar*, *-ig*, *-lich* and *-sam*; *-igkeit* is typically added to adjectives ending in *-haft*, *-los* and *-e* (which is then deleted), e.g.:
gesund ➜ *die Gesundheit* 'health'
frech ➜ *die Frechheit* 'impertinence'
sichtbar ➜ *die Sichtbarkeit* 'visibility'
erblich ➜ *die Erblichkeit* 'heritability'
ernsthaft ➜ *die Ernsthaftigkeit* 'seriousness'
müde ➜ *die Müdigkeit* 'tiredness'

-*ik* (feminine)   (i)   forms nouns that are collective (denote a group of entities), often with the 'linking' sound *-at-* (from nouns), e.g.:
das Symbol ➜ *die Symbolik* 'symbolism'
das Problem ➜ *die Problematik* 'problems'
A number of these are formed from nouns ending in *-ist*, e.g.:
der Germanist ➜ *die Germanistik* 'German studies'
der Publizist ➜ *die Publizistik* 'mass communications'

(ii)   forms nouns that are related to adjectives ending in *-isch* (from word roots that cannot be used alone), e.g.:
drast- ➜ *die Drastik* 'graphicness' (*drastisch* 'graphic')
kom- ➜ *die Komik* 'comic effect' (*komisch* 'comical')

-*in* (feminine)   forms nouns that denote a person or animal as feminine (from nouns); umlaut is typically added to the stressed vowel, e.g.:
der Arzt ➜ *die Ärztin* '(female) doctor'
der Storch ➜ *die Störchin* '(female) stork'

-(*at*)*ion* (feminine)	forms nouns that are similar in meaning to a verb (mainly from verbs ending in *-ieren*), sometimes with the addition of *-at-*, e.g.: *explodieren* ➔ *die Explosion* 'explosion' *demonstrieren* ➔ *die Demonstration* 'demonstration'
-*ismus* (masculine)	forms nouns denoting economic, political, philosophical, literary, etc. theories and movements (from nouns and adjectives), e.g.: *der Patriot* ➔ *der Patriotismus* 'patriotism' *ideal* ➔ *der Idealismus* 'idealism'
-*ist* (masculine)	forms nouns that denote people (typically from nouns); many have corresponding nouns that end in *-ismus*, e.g.: *der Humor* ➔ *der Humorist* 'humorist' *der Terror* ➔ *der Terrorist* 'terrorist' (*der Terrorismus*)
-*ität* (feminine)	forms nouns that denote characteristics and states (primarily from adjectives), e.g.: *naiv* ➔ *die Naivität* 'naivety' *respektabel* ➔ *die Respektabilität* 'respectability'
-*lein* (neuter)	forms diminutives (from nouns); umlaut is added to the stressed vowel, e.g.: *der Bach* ➔ *das Bächlein* 'rivulet' *der Zweig* ➔ *das Zweiglein* 'little branch'
-*ler* (masculine)	forms nouns referring to a person by profession, place of residence or characteristic (primarily from nouns); often pejorative, e.g.: *der Sport* ➔ *der Sportler* 'athlete' *das Dorf* ➔ *der Dörfler* 'villager' *der Profit* ➔ *der Profitler* 'profiteer'
-*ling* (masculine)	(i) forms nouns denoting the person who is the object of an action (from verbs), e.g.: *finden* ➔ *der Findling* 'foundling' *prüfen* ➔ *der Prüfling* 'examinee' (ii) forms nouns denoting a person with a particular characteristic (from adjectives); often pejorative, e.g.: *feig(e)* ➔ *der Feigling* 'coward' *weich* ➔ *der Weichling* 'weakling'
-*nis* (mainly neuter; some feminine)	forms nouns that denote something that carries out an action or is the result of an action (mainly from verbs), e.g.: *hemmen* ➔ *das Hemmnis* 'obstacle, hindrance' ('something that hinders') *ersparen* ➔ *das Ersparnis* 'savings' ('something that is saved')

-(*at*)*or* (masculine)	forms nouns denoting the person or instrument performing the action described by a verb (mainly from verbs), e.g.: *agitieren* ➜ *der Agitator* 'agitator' *isolieren* ➜ *der Isolator* 'insulator'
-*schaft* (feminine)	forms nouns that are collective (denote a group) or denote a state (primarily from nouns), e.g.: *der Bauer* ➜ *die Bauernschaft* 'farmers', 'farming community' *der Freund* ➜ *die Freundschaft* 'friendship'
-*tum* (mainly neuter)	is used to form nouns that denote characteristic qualities, a group or a territory (typically from nouns referring to persons), e.g.: *der Beamte* ➜ *das Beamtentum* 'civil service mentality; civil servants' *der Fürst* ➜ *das Fürstentum* 'principality'
-*ung* (feminine)	forms nouns that refer primarily to the action of a verb, also to the result of the action (from verbs), e.g.: *landen* ➜ *die Landung* 'landing' *verfilmen* ➜ *die Verfilmung* 'filming', 'film (version)'

Prefixation

With the exception of the prefix *ge-* (see below), the following prefixes are used to form nouns from nouns; they do not change the gender of the noun to which they are attached.

Erz- 'arch', 'ultra' (augmentative; intensive)	*der Feind* ➜ *der Erzfeind* 'arch enemy' *der Reaktionär* ➜ *der Erzreaktionär* 'ultra-reactionary'
Fehl- 'false', 'incorrect', 'wrong', 'bad'	*der Start* ➜ *der Fehlstart* 'false start' *die Diagnose* ➜ *die Fehldiagnose* 'incorrect diagnosis' *die Investition* ➜ *die Fehlinvestition* 'bad investment'
Ge- (i)	forms neuter nouns that denote a repeated or drawn-out action (from verbs); often pejorative in meaning; often with the suffix *-e*, e.g.: *jammern* ➜ *das Gejammer(e)* 'bellyaching' *ächzen* ➜ *das Geächze* 'groaning, groans'
(ii)	forms collective nouns (from nouns), with umlaut of the stressed vowel (*e* also changes to *i*); only weakly productive; mainly neuter, e.g.: *die Mauer* ➜ *das Gemäuer* 'walls; ruin' *der Berg* ➜ *das Gebirge* 'mountain range'
Grund- 'basic', 'essential', 'fundamental'	*die Frage* ➜ *die Grundfrage* 'fundamental issue' *der Kurs* ➜ *der Grundkurs* 'basic course'

Haupt- 'main'	*die Darstellerin* → *die Hauptdarstellerin* 'female lead' *das Thema* → *das Hauptthema* 'main topic; main theme'
Miss- indicates the opposite or a negative (similar to English *mis-*)	*der Erfolg* → *der Misserfolg* 'failure' *die Achtung* → *die Missachtung* 'disregard' *der Brauch* → *der Missbrauch* 'abuse; misuse'
Mit- 'co-', 'fellow'	*die Begründerin* → *die Mitbegründerin* 'female co-founder' *der Bewohner* → *der Mitbewohner* 'fellow occupant'
Neben- 'secondary', 'incidental', 'additional', 'neighbouring'	*die Bemerkung* → *die Nebenbemerkung* 'incidental remark' *die Beschäftigung* → *die Nebenbeschäftigung* 'second job' *das Zimmer* → *das Nebenzimmer* 'adjoining room'
Nicht- 'non'	*der Fachmann* → *der Nichtfachmann* 'non-expert' *der Schwimmer* → *der Nichtschwimmer* 'non-swimmer'
Riesen- 'enormous', 'giant', 'tremendous'	*der Hunger* → *der Riesenhunger* 'enormous hunger' *der Schritt* → *der Riesenschritt* 'giant stride'
Rück- 're-', 'return', 'back'	*der Kauf* → *der Rückkauf* 'repurchase' *die Fahrkarte* → *die Rückfahrkarte* 'return ticket' *der Blick* → *der Rückblick* 'look back' *Rück-* is used with many nouns that are related to verbs beginning with *zurück-* (cf. *der Rückkauf* above and *zurückkaufen* 'buy back', 'repurchase'). The full form *zurück-* is sometimes retained when the noun ends in *-ung* (*zurückhalten* → *die Zurückhaltung* 'reserve').
Schein- 'illusory', 'not real'	*die Welt* → *die Scheinwelt* 'illusory world' *der Friede* → *der Scheinfriede* 'phoney peace'
Un- denotes the opposite; something abnormal; augmentation and intensification	*der Sinn* → *der Unsinn* 'nonsense' *das Wetter* → *das Unwetter* '(thunder)storm' *die Menge* → *die Unmenge* 'enormous amount'
Ur- 'first', 'original'	*die Aufführung* → *die Uraufführung* 'first performance, showing' *die Fassung* → *die Urfassung* 'original version'

The formation of adjectives

Suffixation

-abel (less often -ibel)

forms adjectives from verbs ending in *-ieren*; similar in meaning to English *-able* and *-ible*, e.g.:
akzeptieren ➔ *akzeptabel* 'acceptable'
disponieren ➔ *disponibel* 'available'

-al, -ell

forms adjectives from nouns; similar in meaning to English *-al*, e.g.:
das Fundament ➔ *fundamental* 'fundamental'
das Experiment ➔ *experimentell* 'experimental'
With the exception of *formal* 'concerning form' and *formell* 'excessively stressing form', there is essentially no difference in meaning between *-al* and *-ell* (*-al* tends to be used as the form in compounds; cf. *Experimentalphysik* 'experimental physics' and *experimentell* 'experimental').

-ant, -ent

typically forms adjectives from verbs ending in *-ieren*; similar in meaning to English *-ant* and *-ent*, e.g.:
tolerieren ➔ *tolerant* 'tolerant'
existieren ➔ *existent* 'existent'

-ar, -är

typically forms adjectives from nouns; conveys the meaning 'concerning', 'relative to', e.g.:
das Atom ➔ *atomar* 'atomic, nuclear'
der Muskel ➔ *muskulär* 'having to do with muscles'

-bar

forms adjectives, typically from verbs; similar in meaning to English *-able* and *-ible*; very productive, e.g.:
waschen ➔ *waschbar* 'washable'
wiederverwenden ➔ *wiederverwendbar* 'reuseable'

-en, -ern

forms adjectives from nouns denoting a material; the adjective conveys the meaning that the noun it modifies is made of that material; umlaut is typically added to a word when the *-ern* variant is used, e.g.:
das Metall ➔ *metallen* 'metal'
der Stahl ➔ *stählern* 'steel'

-haft

forms adjectives, typically from nouns; conveys the meaning 'like' or 'with', e.g.:
der Roboter ➔ *roboterhaft* 'robotlike'
der Schmerz ➔ *schmerzhaft* 'painful'

-ig

forms adjectives mainly from nouns; conveys the meaning 'having' or 'like'; umlaut is often used, e.g.:
die Narbe ➔ *narbig* 'scarred'

der Riese ➔ *riesig* '(like a) giant'

This suffix is often used to form adjectives from phrases consisting of an adjective or numeral followed by a noun, e.g.:

zwei Jahre ➔ *zweijährig* 'having a duration of two years'; 'two years old'

kurze Beine ➔ *kurzbeinig* 'short-legged'

-isch is a productive suffix used to form adjectives primarily from nouns; it sometimes occurs with umlaut. It has various functions, including the following:

(i) forms adjectives from nouns denoting people or animals and conveys the meaning 'like'; often pejorative, e.g.:

der Hund ➔ *hündisch* 'doglike, servile'

das Kind ➔ *kindisch* 'childish'

(ii) forms adjectives from foreign words, e.g.:

der Dämon ➔ *dämonisch* 'demonic'

die Biologie ➔ *biologisch* 'biological'

(iii) forms adjectives from proper names and geographical names, e.g.:

Homer ➔ *homerisch* 'Homeric'

das Mittelmeer ➔ *mittelmeerisch* 'Mediterranean'

-(at)iv forms adjectives primarily from nouns (many ending in the suffix *-ion*, which is deleted); conveys the meaning 'having'; similar to English *-ive*, e.g.:

die Aggression ➔ *aggressiv* 'aggressive'

der Instinkt ➔ *instinktiv* 'instinctive'

-lich is an important adjectival suffix (often with umlaut) with a number of functions, including the following:

(i) productively forms adjectives from nouns; conveys the meaning 'concerning', 'like' or 'with', e.g.:

der Herbst ➔ *herbstlich* 'autumn', 'autumnal'

die Leidenschaft ➔ *leidenschaftlich* 'passionate'

(ii) when *-lich* is used with expressions that denote a period of time, the resulting adjective indicates the frequency of an action (not duration or age, like the suffix *-ig*, for which see above), e.g.:

der Tag ➔ *täglich* 'daily'

zwei Stunden ➔ *zweistündlich* 'every two hours'

(iii) although no longer productive (and replaced by the suffix *-bar*), there are many adjectives in *-lich* from verbs. In these adjectives, *-lich* is similar in meaning to English *-able* and *-ible*, e.g.:

begreifen ➔ *begreiflich* 'understandable'

bewegen ➔ *beweglich* 'moveable'

(iv) forms adjectives from other adjectives to indicate a lesser degree of the characteristic expressed by that adjective, e.g.:

alt ➔ *ältlich* 'oldish'

grün ➔ *grünlich* 'greenish'

-los		forms adjectives from nouns; conveys the meaning 'without', e.g.:

-los forms adjectives from nouns; conveys the meaning 'without', e.g.:
der Grund ➔ *grundlos* 'groundless'
das Haar ➔ *haarlos* 'hairless'

-mäßig forms adjectives primarily from nouns, with the following general meanings:
  (i) 'like'; typically formed from nouns denoting people or animals, e.g.:
der Held ➔ *heldenmäßig* 'heroic'
der Löwe ➔ *löwenmäßig* 'lion-like'
  (ii) 'in accordance with', 'as required by', e.g.:
der Fahrplan ➔ *fahrplanmäßig* 'according to schedule'
das Recht ➔ *rechtmäßig* 'lawful', 'rightful', 'legitimate'
  (iii) 'with respect to', e.g.:
das Gefühl ➔ *gefühlsmäßig* 'based on emotion'
das Alter ➔ *altersmäßig* 'according to age'

-os, -ös forms adjectives, typically from nouns; conveys the meaning 'with', sometimes 'like', e.g.:
die Religion ➔ *religiös* 'religious'
das Mysterium ➔ *mysteriös* 'mysterious'

-sam this suffix is only weakly productive, with the following basic functions:
  (i) forms adjectives from verbs; conveys the meanings of possibility (similar in meaning to English *-able* and *ible*) and inclination, e.g.:
biegen ➔ *biegsam* 'flexible', 'malleable'
arbeiten ➔ *arbeitsam* 'hard-working'
  (ii) forms adjectives from nouns; conveys the meaning 'with', e.g.:
die Ehre ➔ *ehrsam* 'respectable'
die Sitte ➔ *sittsam* 'well-behaved'

Prefixation
The following prefixes form adjectives from other adjectives.

erz- intensifies adjectives that have a negative sense, e.g.:
dumm ➔ *erzdumm* 'extremely stupid'
reaktionär ➔ *erzreaktionär* 'ultra-reactionary'

in- (il-, im-, ir-) is used with multisyllabic words of foreign origin to express negation, e.g.:
aktiv ➔ *inaktiv* 'inactive'
legal ➔ *illegal* 'illegal'

un- negates the adjective to which it is attached or expresses the opposite of that adjective, e.g.:
schuldig ➔ *unschuldig* 'not guilty'
vorsichtig ➔ *unvorsichtig* 'careless'

If the base adjective already has an opposite, the form with *un-* expresses a negative rather than an opposite (i.e. an intermediate point on the scale formed by the base and its opposite), e.g.:
sauber 'clean', *unsauber* 'not clean', 'untidy', *schmutzig* 'dirty'

-ur intensifies the meaning of the adjective to which it is prefixed, e.g.:
alt ➔ *uralt* 'very old'
deutsch ➔ *urdeutsch* 'totally German'

The formation of verbs

Suffixation
Although suffixation does not play as important a role in the formation of German verbs as does prefixation (see below), there are several suffixes that are nevertheless important:

-eln forms verbs from nouns; usually with umlaut; conveys two basic types of meaning:
(i) 'bring into a specific form', e.g.:
die Falte ➔ *fälteln* 'pleat'
der Haufen ➔ *häufeln* 'heap up'
(ii) expresses iterative, diminuative meaning, e.g.:
der Frost ➔ *frösteln* 'shiver'
das Werk ➔ *werkeln* 'putter around'

-igen forms verbs from nouns meaning to give (grant) someone something; often in combination with the suffix *be-*, e.g.:
die Pein ➔ *peinigen* 'torment'
die Gnade ➔ *begnadigen* 'pardon', 'reprieve'

-ieren (variants are -isieren and -ifizieren) is used to form verbs primarily from bases of foreign origin, e.g.:
French *arranger* 'arrange' ➔ *arrangieren* 'arrange'
das Exempel ➔ *exemplifizieren* 'exemplify'
Only a few *-ieren* verbs are formed from native bases, e.g.:
der Buchstabe ➔ *buchstabieren* 'spell'
das Amt ➔ *amtieren* 'hold office'

Prefixation
The major way of forming complex verbs in German is by the addition of prefixes. There are three types of prefixes: separable, inseparable and variable.
(1) Separable prefixes are not always attached to the verb stem. They are always stressed and often function syntactically like independent words. The prefix *ein-*, for example, is separable; cf. *'einsteigen* 'get in' in *Sie stieg in den Bus ein* 'She got in the bus'. (The symbol ' is used here to mark stress; it precedes a stressed syllable.)

(2) Inseparable prefixes are always attached to the verb stem and are always unstressed. The prefix *be-*, for example, is inseparable; cf. *be'steigen* 'climb; mount' in *Er bestieg das Pferd* 'He mounted the horse'. (3) Variable prefixes function as both separable and inseparable prefixes. The prefix *über-*, for example, is separable in *'übersetzen* 'ferry over' (*Er setzte uns ans andere Ufer über* 'He ferried us over to the other bank'); in *über'setzen* 'translate' it is inseparable (*Sie übersetzte das Buch* 'She translated the book').

The major separable, inseparable and variable verbal prefixes in German are listed below with their basic properties and meanings.

Separable prefixes

Most separable prefixes also occur as independent words (prepositions, adverbs, nouns, adjectives). Simple (non-compound) separable prefixes are often related to prepositions (cf. the prefix *ein-* and the preposition *in*) and are often identical in form to prepositions (cf. *aus-* and *aus*). Separable prefixes are also formed from nouns, adjectives and adverbs:

(i)   nouns: *der Teil, teilnehmen* 'take part'
(ii) adjectives: *gut, gutmachen* 'make good'
(iii) adverbs: *wieder, wiedergeben* 'give back', 'return'

Although verb forms (infinitives and past participles) were treated orthographically as separable prefixes prior to the spelling reform of 1998, they no longer are:

kennenlernen (old spelling), *kennen lernen* (new spelling) 'get to know'
verlorengehen (old spelling), *verloren gehen* (new spelling) 'get lost'

The following list contains only common, simple separable prefixes (it does not contain compound prefixes, many of which are common; these are often formed from adverbs, e.g., *zurück* 'back', as in *zurückbleiben* 'stay behind', *zurücknehmen* 'take back', etc.). Although some of these prefixes form verbs from word classes other than verbs, only the prefixation of verbs is considered here.

ab-

(i)   expresses distancing, separation, removal, e.g.:
fahren ➜ *abfahren* 'leave', 'depart'
brechen ➜ *abbrechen* 'break off'
(ii) expresses the meaning 'down'
setzen ➜ *absetzen* 'put down'
werten ➜ *abwerten* 'devalue', 'put down'
(iii) conveys the ending or completion of a process, e.g.:
drehen ➜ *abdrehen* 'turn off', 'finish shooting (e.g. a film)'
blühen ➜ *abblühen* 'fade'

an-

(i)   expresses the idea of approaching or connecting, e.g.:
fliegen ➜ *anfliegen* 'approach', 'come in to land'
binden ➜ *anbinden* 'tie up', 'tether'
(ii) conveys the beginning or partial carrying-out of an action, e.g.:
spielen ➜ *anspielen* 'begin (to play)'
braten ➜ *anbraten* 'brown'

auf-   (i)   expresses the meaning 'up', e.g.:
               blicken ➔ *aufblicken* 'look up'
               springen ➔ *aufspringen* 'jump up'
          (ii)   conveys the notion of opening, e.g.:
               brechen ➔ *aufbrechen* 'break open'
               reißen ➔ *aufreißen* 'tear open'
          (iii) signals the (often sudden) beginning of a process, e.g.:
               blitzen ➔ *aufblitzen* 'flash', 'flare up'
               brüllen ➔ *aufbrüllen* 'let out a roar'
          (iv)   expresses the elimination of an object, e.g.:
               brauchen ➔ *aufbrauchen* 'use up'
               essen ➔ *aufessen* 'eat up'

aus-   (i)   expresses the meaning 'out', e.g.:
               atmen ➔ *ausatmen* 'breathe out', 'exhale'
               wandern ➔ *auswandern* 'emigrate'
          (ii)   signals the end of an action or the end (elimination) of an object, e.g.:
               reifen ➔ *ausreifen* 'ripen fully'
               radieren ➔ *ausradieren* 'rub out', 'wipe out'

ein-   (i)   conveys the meaning 'in', 'into', e.g.:
               steigen ➔ *einsteigen* 'get in'
               strömen ➔ *einströmen* 'stream in'
          (ii)   signals the beginning of an action, e.g.:
               schlafen ➔ *einschlafen* 'fall asleep'
               arbeiten ➔ *einarbeiten* 'get used to work'

los-   (i)   expresses distancing, separation, removal, e.g.:
               reißen ➔ *losreißen* 'tear off'
               kriegen ➔ *loskriegen* 'get off', 'get rid of'
          (ii)   signals the (sudden) beginning of a process, e.g.:
               fahren ➔ *losfahren* 'set off'
               lachen ➔ *loslachen* 'burst out laughing'

mit-   expresses the meaning 'together' or 'along', e.g.:
          arbeiten ➔ *mitarbeiten* 'cooperate'
          singen ➔ *mitsingen* 'sing along'

nach-   expresses the notion of following in both a physical and temporal sense, e.g.:
          eilen ➔ *nacheilen* 'hurry after (somebody)'
          liefern ➔ *nachliefern* 'supply later'

vor-   (i)   conveys the meaning 'forward', e.g.:
               beugen ➔ *sich vorbeugen* 'bend forward'
               fahren ➔ *vorfahren* 'drive forward; drive ahead'

(ii)   expresses the temporal notion 'in advance', e.g.:
       arbeiten → *vorarbeiten* 'work in advance'
       schlafen → *vorschlafen* 'stock up on sleep'

(iii) conveys the meaning of presenting something, e.g.:
       lesen → *vorlesen* 'read aloud'
       tragen → *vortragen* 'perform; present'

zu-

(i)   expresses the meaning 'to' or 'towards', e.g.:
       fahren → *zufahren* 'head towards (somebody or something)'
       flüstern → *zuflüstern* 'whisper (something) to (somebody)'

(ii)   expresses the meaning of closing, e.g.:
       drehen → *zudrehen* 'shut'
       kleben → *zukleben* 'seal'

Inseparable prefixes

be-

(i)   derives verbs from verbs. *Be-* often changes the syntactic properties of
       the verbs to which it is attached. It can convert a verb without an object
       into a verb with an accusative object, e.g.:
       lachen 'laugh' → *jemanden belachen* 'laugh at someone'
       It can convert a verb with a dative or prepositional object into a verb
       with an accusative object, e.g.:
       jemandem dienen 'serve someone' → *jemanden bedienen* 'wait on
       someone', 'serve someone'
       auf eine Frage antworten 'answer a question' → *eine Frage beantworten*
       'answer a question'
       When a verb has two objects, the prefixation of *be-* is often associated
       with a 'shift' in objects. A verb with a dative object and an accusative
       object, for example, can be converted into a verb with an accusative
       object and a prepositional object, e.g.:
       jemandem etwas liefern 'deliver something to somebody' → *jemanden mit
       etwas beliefern* 'supply somebody with something'
       Some verbs are not changed syntactically by the addition of *be-*, but
       rather semantically; *be-* adds the meaning of intensification to these
       verbs (also to verbs that are altered syntactically), e.g.:
       fragen 'ask' → *befragen* 'examine'
       fühlen 'feel' → *befühlen* 'run one's hands over'

(ii)   derives verbs from nouns (sometimes with the addition of the suffix
       -ig); these verbs express the meaning of providing with something, e.g.:
       die Nachricht → *benachrichtigen* 'inform (provide with news)'
       das Licht → *belichten* 'expose (film)', 'light'

(iii) forms verbs from adjectives (sometimes with the addition of the suffix
       -ig); these verbs express the meaning of giving somebody or something
       the quality expressed by the adjective, e.g.:
       frei → *befreien* 'make free'
       rein → *bereinigen* 'clear up'

ent-	(i)	derives verbs from nouns and adjectives to convey the meaning of removal, e.g.:

        die Waffe ➔ *entwaffnen* 'disarm'
        mutig ➔ *entmutigen* 'discourage'

    (ii)   forms verbs from verbs to convey several different meanings, including the following:

       1. undoing or reversing, e.g.:
          falten ➔ *entfalten* 'unfold'
          spannen ➔ *entspannen* 'relax; loosen'
       2. 'away from', e.g.:
          kommen ➔ *entkommen* 'escape (get away)'
          reißen ➔ *entreißen* 'snatch away from'
       3. 'begin' (these verbs are felt to belong to elevated speech), e.g.:
          brennen ➔ *entbrennen* 'flare up'
          schlafen ➔ *entschlafen* 'fall asleep'

er-   (i)   forms verbs from verbs to express the beginning of an action, e.g.:
        blühen ➔ *erblühen* 'blossom'
        zittern ➔ *erzittern* 'begin to shake', 'begin to tremble'
        This prefix also forms verbs from verbs to express the reaching of the end of an activity or the achievement of a goal, e.g.:
        frieren ➔ *erfrieren* 'freeze to death'
        arbeiten ➔ *erarbeiten* 'gain by working'

    (ii)   forms verbs from adjectives; conveys the meaning 'become' or 'make', e.g.:
        müde ➔ *ermüden* 'become tired'
        warm ➔ *erwärmen* 'make warm'

miss-   forms verbs from verbs to express negation or the meanings 'wrong' or 'bad', e.g.:
        achten ➔ *missachten* 'disregard'
        brauchen ➔ *missbrauchen* 'misuse', 'abuse'
        In the verb *missverstehen* 'misunderstand', *miss-* is stressed (because of the following unstressed prefix, *ver-*); it is separated from the verbal stem in the 'infinitive plus *zu*' form: *misszuverstehen* 'to misunderstand'.

ver-   is a common prefix with a variety of functions, including the following:
    (i)   forms verbs from adjectives; conveys the meaning 'become' or 'make', e.g.:
        alt ➔ *veralten* 'become old'
        edel ➔ *veredeln* 'ennoble'
    (ii)   forms verbs from nouns; conveys the meaning 'provide with', e.g.:
        das Gift ➔ *vergiften* 'poison'
        das Gold ➔ *vergolden* 'gold-plate', 'gild', 'paint gold'

(iii) forms verbs from verbs to express a number of different meanings, including the following:
1. completion of an action, e.g.:
   heilen ➔ *verheilen* 'heal up'
   brauchen ➔ *verbrauchen* 'use up'
2. a mistaken action, e.g.:
   schlucken ➔ *sich verschlucken* 'choke'
   salzen ➔ *versalzen* 'put too much salt on'
3. intensification, e.g.:
   helfen ➔ *verhelfen* 'help (somebody) achieve (something)'
   zweifeln ➔ *verzweifeln* 'despair'

zer- forms verbs mainly from verbs; conveys the following meanings:
(i) 'into small pieces', e.g.:
   reißen ➔ *zerreißen* 'tear to pieces'
   schneiden ➔ *zerschneiden* 'cut up'
(ii) 'damage', e.g.:
   fressen ➔ *zerfressen* 'eat away; corrode'
   kochen ➔ *zerkochen* 'overcook'

Variable prefixes

A small number of prefixes can function as both separable and inseparable prefixes. When they are separable, they are stressed; when they are inseparable, they are unstressed. In many cases a verb stem will appear with both the separable and inseparable variant of the prefix (cf. *'übersetzen* 'ferry over' and *über'setzen* 'translate', discussed above). In these cases, the two variants are typically associated with a difference in meaning; they are often associated with syntactic differences as well (cf. *eine Jacke 'unterziehen* 'put a cardigan on underneath' and *sich einer Operation unter'ziehen* 'undergo an operation'). Sometimes a verb will appear with either the separable variant (*'durchhalten* 'survive', 'see through') or the inseparable variant (*unter'brechen* 'interrupt'), but not both.

In general, a verb with the inseparable variant of a prefix tends to have a more abstract meaning than its counterpart with the separable variant. For example, *durch'schauen* means 'see through' in the sense of 'not be fooled by' (*Er durchschaute unseren Plan* 'He saw through our plan'), whereas *'durchschauen* means literally (physically) to 'see (look) through' (*Sie schaute durch das Fenster durch* 'She looked through the window').

Although some variable prefixes are used to form verbs from word classes other than verbs (e.g., *das Garn* ➔ *um'garnen* 'ensnare', 'beguile'; *müde* ➔ *über'müden* 'overtire'), the derivation of variable-prefix verbs from nouns and adjectives is not addressed explicitly in the discussion below.

durch-

conveys the meaning 'through', whether inseparable or separable.

(i) Many verbs with *durch-* are separable only, e.g.:

fallen ➔ '*durchfallen* 'fall through', 'fail'

führen ➔ '*durchführen* 'carry out'

(ii) A few verbs with *durch-* are inseparable only, e.g.:

denken ➔ *durch'denken* 'think through'

leben ➔ *durch'leben* 'experience'

(iii) Many verb stems occur with both variants of *durch-* (inseparable and separable). The separable variant often means 'all the way through' ('from one end to the other'); the inseparable variant, on the other hand, while still conveying the meaning of penetration, lacks the sense of an endpoint, e.g.: '*durchstechen* 'stick (something) through (something)' vs. *durch'stechen* 'pierce'

'*durchziehen* 'pass or pull through' vs. *durch'ziehen* 'pervade; traverse'

über-

forms predominantly inseparable verbs; expresses several different meanings, including the following:

(i) 'over' in various senses, e.g.:

kochen ➔ '*überkochen* 'boil over'

sehen ➔ *über'sehen* 'overlook'

werfen ➔ '*überwerfen* 'throw on (clothes)'

(ii) conveys the sense of exceeding something (a boundary, an amount, etc.), e.g.:

schätzen ➔ *über'schätzen* 'overestimate'

schreiten ➔ *über'schreiten* 'cross; exceed'

um-

(i) separable *um-* verbs tend to convey a change of direction or state, e.g.:

drehen ➔ '*umdrehen* 'turn around'

gruppieren ➔ '*umgruppieren* 'rearrange'

(ii) inseparable *um-* verbs tend to have the meaning of encircling or surrounding, e.g.:

fassen ➔ *um'fassen* 'embrace', 'enclose'

segeln ➔ *um'segeln* 'sail round', 'circumnavigate'

Verb stems that occur with both separable and inseparable *um-* exhibit the same semantic differences noted above, e.g.:

'*umbauen* 'rebuild' vs. *um'bauen* 'enclose'

'*umstellen* 'rearrange' vs. *um'stellen* 'surround'

unter-

(i) both inseparable and separable *unter-* convey the meaning 'under', e.g.:

drücken ➔ *unter'drücken* 'suppress'

gehen ➔ '*untergehen* 'sink, go down'

(ii) inseparable *unter-* conveys the meaning 'too low', e.g.:

bieten ➔ *unter'bieten* 'undercut'

treiben ➔ *unter'treiben* 'play things down'

(iii) When a verb stem occurs with both separable and inseparable *unter-*, the separable variant typically conveys the meaning 'under', while the inseparable variant tends to have a more figurative meaning, e.g.:
'*unterbinden* 'tie (on) underneath' vs. *unter'binden* 'stop'
'*unterhalten* 'hold underneath' vs. *unter'halten* 'entertain'

wider- functions primarily as an inseparable prefix, with the following basic meanings:

(i) 'against' (only the inseparable variant), e.g.:
stehen ➔ *wider'stehen* 'resist'
streben ➔ *wider'streben* 'oppose'

(ii) 'back', e.g.:
rufen ➔ *wider'rufen* 'retract'
hallen ➔ '*widerhallen* 'echo'

The formation of adverbs

Suffixation is the most important process in the derivation of complex adverbs in German. The following adverbial suffixes are among the most productive.

-halber forms adverbs from abstract nouns; conveys the meaning 'because of', e.g.:
der Anstand ➔ *anstandshalber* 'for the sake of politeness'
das Interesse ➔ *interessehalber* 'out of interest'

-maßen forms adverbs from participles; it is always used with the linking sounds *-er-*. Conveys the meaning 'as is', e.g.:
bekannt ➔ *bekanntermaßen* 'as is well known'
erwiesen ➔ *erwiesenermaßen* 'as has been proved'

-weise (i) is used to form adverbs from nouns to convey the meaning 'in the form/manner of', 'as', e.g.:
die Andeutung ➔ *andeutungsweise* 'in the form of a hint'
das Beispiel ➔ *beispielsweise* 'for example'

(ii) used to form adverbs from nouns denoting quantities and measurements to convey the meaning 'by the' or 'in', e.g.:
das Kilo ➔ *kiloweise* 'by the kilo', 'in kilos'
der Monat ➔ *monatsweise* 'by the month'

(iii) forms adverbs from adjectives and participles, always with the linking sounds *-er-*; similar in function to the adjectival suffix *-ly* in English, e.g.:
eigenartig ➔ *eigenartigerweise* 'strangely enough'
lächerlich ➔ *lächerlicherweise* 'ridiculously enough'

Tips on dictionary use

You will want to have more than just a paperback dictionary or an abridged version. It will also be very useful to have a monolingual (German–German) dictionary as well as one that is bilingual (German–English and English–German).

(1)   Familiarize yourself with the format of a typical dictionary entry. Find the section (generally at the beginning of the dictionary) that explains the different kinds of information that are included in each entry and the way in which this information is presented. For example, where in an entry is the pronunciation of a word given? What phonetic symbols are used to convey the pronunciation of a word, and where in the dictionary are these symbols explained? How is the gender of a noun indicated? How can one tell if a verb is regular or irregular? Exercises at the end of this chapter will help you determine the kinds of information you should expect to find in a dictionary entry and where in the entry you can find it.

(2)   When searching for the German translation for an English word or phrase, you will need to read though an entire entry to find the appropriate translation. A word in English may have more than one meaning, and these different meanings may be expressed by different words in German. To cite a well-known example, a very general sense of the English verb *know* is 'be aware of', 'have knowledge about'. This sense is typically translated with German *wissen*: *Ich weiß, wo sie wohnt* 'I know where she lives.' But *know* also means 'be acquainted with', which is typically rendered by German *kennen*: *Ich kenne ihn schon seit Jahren* 'I've known him for years.' There are also idiomatic phrases in English that contain the verb *know*. These phrases are very often translated with neither *wissen* nor *kennen*: 'for all I know' = *ich könnte mir gut denken*; 'you know' (as a conversational filler) = *na ja*; *nicht (wahr)*.

(3)   Keep in mind that you often cannot translate an English phrase into German by translating each word in that phrase separately. For example, although the English preposition *for* can be translated with German *für*, the preposition *auf* must be used to translate the English phrase *wait for*: 'Wait for me!' = *Warte auf mich!*

(4)   To most quickly find the correct translation of a phrase in English, look up the semantically most specific word in the phrase. You will quickly find the German equivalent of *take offence*, for example, if you look up the word *offence*. Remember that you cannot expect to produce an acceptable translation for *take offence* if you combine the first German word in the entry for *offence* with the translation of *take* (*nehmen*): *take offence* is rendered in German as *gekränkt* (*beleidigt*; *verärgert*) *sein*, not as **Kränkung nehmen* (an asterisk

is used to indicate that a word or phrase is unacceptable or ungrammatical).

(5) Some words typically occur together (collocate) with other words. In English, for example, the word *great* is used with the word *interest* to express the notion of 'big' (*take a great interest in something*); the word *large*, while also expressing the notion 'big', does not collocate with *interest* (**take a large interest in something*). It is important to note these cooccurrence patterns, some of which can be found in bilingual dictionary entries. Monolingual dictionaries are especially useful in this regard. The *Duden Stilwörterbuch*, in particular, is an excellent source for collocation patterns. The entry for *Interesse* 'interest', for example, includes the following adjective–noun collocations: *geringes* (*kein, lebhaftes, offenkundiges*) *Interesse*; *mit großem* (*besonderem*) *Interesse*. It also provides noun–verb collocations: *Interesse an einer Sache haben* (*nehmen*).

(6) Take the time to browse regularly through your dictionary and follow the many paths and connections you encounter.

a. Take note of the different expressions and idioms in which a particular word can be found. Many simple words have long entries that contain much useful information. In the entry for *Hand*, for example, you can learn useful expressions like *jemandem die Hand geben* 'shake somebody's hand'; you can also learn idioms like *weder Hand noch Fuß haben* 'make no sense'.

b. Look at the neighbouring entries for a given word, which are often formed from the same root (*das Malbuch* 'colouring book', *malen* 'paint', *der Maler* 'painter', *die Malerarbeit* 'painting and decorating' *die Malerei* 'painting', *die Malerin* '(woman) painter', *malerisch* 'picturesque').

c. Look up the cross references that you encounter in an entry; these will lead you to additional useful information. Some dictionaries, for example, refer the reader to tables and charts that provide grammatical information relevant to a particular entry.

d. Look up the synonyms and antonyms of a word, which are often given in an entry. A monolingual dictionary will automatically provide this information. By looking up a word in a German–German dictionary, you will have the opportunity to learn new words and expressions in addition to learning the meaning of the word you look up.

When you make connections like these between words (morphological, semantic, etc.) and learn words in phrases, it is easier to enlarge your vocabulary than if you approach words in isolation.

Exercises

Word formation

Identify the prefixes and suffixes in the following words and then use information about the meaning of these prefixes and suffixes (provided above) to make an educated guess about the meaning of the entire word. Note that some of these words are compounds.

A. Nouns
1. *die Briefschreiberin*
2. *die Fehlplanung*
3. *das Geklopfe*
4. *die Grundregel*
5. *die Hübschheit*
6. *die Rasenpflege*
7. *die Scheinschwangerschaft*
8. *die Stabilität*
9. *die Urquelle*
10. *das Zäunlein*

B. Adjectives
1. *dicklich*
2. *lückenhaft*
3. *mondlos*
4. *rangmäßig*
5. *unlösbar*

C. Verbs
1. *abreißen*
2. *anreißen*
3. *aufkratzen*
4. *beschatten*
5. *entkleiden*
6. *überheizen*
7. *um'mauern*
8. *verdünnen*
9. *zerteilen*
10. *zuknöpfen*

D. Adverbs
1. *eimerweise*
2. *gesundheitshalber*
3. *klugerweise*
4. *konsequentermaßen*
5. *probeweise*

Dictionary use

By looking up the answers to the following questions, you should become familiar with how your dictionary's entries are organized, the kind of information you should expect to find in your dictionary, and the way you should go about finding that information.

1. Provide the gender, genitive ending and plural form for the following words:
   a. *Bagger*
   b. *Schwefel*
   c. *Kasten*
   d. *Pustel*
   e. *Löwe*
   f. *Niederlande*
   g. *Herz*

2. Provide the principal parts of the following verbs (3rd person singular present, simple past, present perfect, e.g. *gehen: geht, ging, ist gegangen*):
   a. *harren*
   b. *bergen*
   c. *fliehen*
   d. *umkommen*
   e. *durchleuchten*

3. Consider the pronunciation of the underlined portions of each of the words below. Which of the words following it in parentheses contains the same sound?
   a. *Band<u>age</u>* (*Staat, Stadt, Bett*)
   b. *<u>J</u>och* (*Boot, Post, Stadt*)
   c. *<u>G</u>elee* (*Gott, Journal, kennen*)
   d. *Sa<u>chs</u>e* (*Buch, mich, backen*)
   e. *Sl<u>u</u>m* (*gut, dumm, Stadt*)

4. Are the following verbs transitive, intransitive or reflexive?
   a. *militarisieren* 'to militarize'
   b. *einsetzen* 'to start'
   c. *flößen* 'to raft', 'to float'
   d. *beschweren* 'to complain'
   e. *engagieren* 'to be/become committed'

5. Translate the following phrases:
   1. to review a book
   2. to make a decision
   3. to go on a date with somebody
   4. to draw a conclusion
   5. to take something into consideration

Unit 1

Towns and buildings

Level 1

Towns

Stadt, die (¨e)	town, city
Großstadt, die (¨e)	large city
Hauptstadt, die (¨e)	capital (city)
städtisch	municipal, town/city, urban
Ort, der (-e)	place, town
Vorort, der (-e)	suburb
Umgebung, die (-en)	surrounding area, environs
Dorf, das (¨er)	village
Straße, die (-n)	street
Autobahn, die (-en)	motorway
Schild, das (-er)	sign
Kreuzung, die (-en)	crossroads, intersection
Ampel, die (-n)	traffic light
Weg, der (-e)	path, way
Park, der (-s)	park
Brücke, die (-n)	bridge
Bürgersteig, der (-e)	pavement
Gehweg, -steig, der (-e; S)	pavement
Bushaltestelle, die (-n)	bus stop
Straßenbahn, die (-en)	tram
U-Bahn, die (-en)	underground, tube
U-Bahn-Station, die (-en)	underground/tube station
S-Bahn, die (-en)	commuter line, suburban line
Sehenswürdigkeit, die (-en)	sight, place of interest

Public buildings and gardens

Rathaus, das (¨er)	city hall
Gericht, das (-e)	court
Gerichtsgebäude, das (-)	courthouse
Polizeirevier, das (-e)	police station
Feuerwache, die (-n)	fire station
Krankenhaus, das (¨er)	hospital
Einwohnermeldeamt, das (¨er)	residents' registration office
Fremdenverkehrsbüro, das (-s)	tourist information office
Bibliothek, die (-en)	library
Bücherei, die (-en)	library
Denkmal, das (¨er)	monument
Schloss, das (¨er)	castle
Burg, die (-en)	(fortified) castle
Kirche, die (-n)	church
Dom, der (-e)	cathedral
Gartenanlage, die (-n)	park, gardens
Zoo, der (-s)	zoo

Vergnügungspark, der (-s)	amusement park
Schwimmbad, das (¨er)	swimming pool

Shops

Geschäft, das (-e)	shop
Laden, der (¨)	shop
Kaufhaus, das (¨er)	department store
Supermarkt, der (¨e)	supermarket
Drogerie, die (-n)	chemist's shop, drugstore
Apotheke, die (-n)	pharmacy
Bäckerei, die (-en)	bakery
Konditorei, die (-en)	cake shop, pastry shop
Restaurant, das (-s)	restaurant
Café, das (-s)	café
Gasthaus, das (¨er)	inn
Bar, die (-s)	bar
Kneipe, die (-n)	pub
Lokal, das (-e)	pub
Eisdiele, die (-n)	ice-cream parlour
Reformhaus, das (¨er)	health food store
Feinkostgeschäft, das (-e)	delicatessen
(chemische) Reinigung, die (-en)	(dry) cleaners

Domestic buildings

Wohnung, die (-en)	flat, apartment, home, lodging
Eigentumswohnung, die (-en)	condominium
Einfamilienhaus, das (¨er)	detached house
Reihenhaus, das (¨er)	terraced house
Wohnblock, der (-s)	block of flats
Hochhaus, das (¨er)	high-rise
Wolkenkratzer, der (-)	skyscraper
Terrasse, die (-n)	patio
Hof, der (¨e)	(back)yard, courtyard
Einfahrt, die (-en)	drive
Tor, das (-e)	gate

Zaun, der (¨e)	fence
Mauer, die (-n)	wall

Features of buildings

Tür, die (-en)	door
Schloss, das (¨er)	lock
Schlüssel, der (-)	key
etw abschließen	to lock (up) sth
Klingel, die (-n)	(door)bell
Decke, die (-n)	ceiling
Wand, die (¨e)	wall
Balkon, der (-s or -e)	balcony
Treppe, die (-n)	staircase; (flight of) stairs
Stufe, die (-n)	stair, step
Aufzug, der (¨e)	lift
Lift, der (-e or -s)	lift
Fenster, das (-)	window
(Fuß)boden, der (¨)	floor
(Dach)boden, der (¨)	attic
Dachkammer, die (-n)	attic
Schornstein, der (-e)	chimney
Kamin, der (-e)	fireplace
Feuerstelle, die (-n)	hearth
Heizung, die (-en)	heating; heater
Klimaanlage, die (-n)	air conditioning (system)
Gang, der (¨e)	corridor
Flur, der (-e)	corridor; (entrance) hall
Diele, die (-n)	hall(way)
Keller, der (-)	cellar
Garage, die (-n)	garage

Buying, selling and renting property

Unterkunft, die (¨e)	accommodation
etw mieten	to rent sth
Mieter(in), der/die (-/nen)	tenant
Untermieter(in), der/die, (-/nen)	subletter
etw vermieten	to rent out sth
Vermieter(in), der/die (-/nen)	landlord/landlady

Mietshaus, das (¨er)	block of (rented) flats	Umzug, der (¨e)	move
		umziehen	to move
Mietvertrag, der (¨e)	rental agreement	Wohngemeinschaft, die (-en)	group sharing a house/flat
Miete, die (-n)	rent		
Kaution, die (-en)	deposit	Wohnungsinhaber(in), der/die (-/nen)	householder
möbliert	furnished		
geräumig	spacious	Eigenheimbesitzer(in), der/die (-/nen)	homeowner
einschließlich	including		

Level 2

Towns

Platz, der (¨e)	town square
Marktplatz, der (¨e)	marketplace
Zentrum, das (Zentren)	centre
zentral	central
Fußgängerzone, die (-n)	pedestrianized zone
Altstadt, die (¨e)	old (part of the) town
Stadtmitte, die (-n)	city centre
Innenstadt, die (¨e)	inner city
Brunnen, der (-)	fountain; well
Friedhof, der (¨e)	cemetery
Radfahrweg, der (-e)	cycle lane
Fußgängerüberweg, der (-e)	pedestrian crossing
Zebrastreifen, der (-; coll.)	zebra crossing
Anlage, die (-n)	park, facility, installation, plant
Grünanlage, die (-n)	green space, park
Hafen, der (¨)	harbour, port
Einkaufs-, Geschäftsviertel, das (-)	shopping district
Wohnviertel, das (-)	residential area
Städter(in), der/die (-/nen)	town-dweller, city-dweller
Vorstädter(in), der/die (-/nen)	suburbanite

Shops

Schaufenster, das (-)	shop window
Selbstbedienungsladen, der (¨)	self-service shop
Kettenladen, der (¨)	chain store
Waschsalon, der (-s)	laundrette, Laundromat
Tabakwarenhandlung, die (-en)	tobacconist's shop
Schreibwarengeschäft, das (-e)	stationer's
Antiquariat, das (-e)	antiquarian/ secondhand bookshop
Antiquitätenladen, der (¨)	antique shop
Flohmarkt, der (¨e)	flea market
Trödelmarkt, der (¨e)	flea market

Domestic buildings

Wohnsiedlung, die (-en)	housing development
freistehend	detached
Zweifamilienhaus, das (¨er)	two-family house, duplex
nebenan	adjoining
benachbart	neighbouring
Fertighaus, das (¨er)	prefab house
Parzelle, die (-n)	lot, plot
etw (zu etw) umbauen	to convert sth (into sth)
das Gebäude befindet sich im Umbau	the building is being rebuilt/converted

Features of buildings

Erdgeschoss, das (-e)	ground floor
Obergeschoss, das (-e)	upper floor, second floor

Stock, der (-)	floor, storey	Eingang, der (¨e)	entrance
Etage, die (-n)	floor, storey	Ausgang, der (¨e)	exit
Stockwerk, das (-e)	floor, storey	Notausgang, der (¨e)	emergency exit
im zweiten/dritten Stock	on the third/fourth floor	Feuer-, Brandleiter, die (-n)	fire escape
Dach, das (¨er)	roof	Saal, der (Säle)	hall, auditorium
(Dach)ziegel, der (-)	tile	Speisekammer, die (-n)	pantry
Ziegeldach, das (¨er)	tiled roof		
Fensterladen, der (- or ¨)	shutter	Abstellraum, der (¨e)	storeroom
		Allzweckraum, der (¨e)	utility room
Rollladen, der (- or ¨)	rolling shutter		
Rouleau (Rollo), das (-s)	(roller) blind	Waschküche, die (-n)	laundry
		Rohrleitung, die (-en)	plumbing
Dachfenster, das (-)	skylight	elektrische Leitungen, pl.	wiring
Scheibe, die (-n)	pane		
Fensterbank, die (¨e)	windowsill; window ledge	Gegensprechanlage, die (-n)	intercom
Guckloch, das (¨er)	spy-hole	etw einbauen	to build sth in, fit sth
Schiebetür, die (-en)	sliding door	Neubau, der (-bauten)	new building
Falltür, die (-en)	trapdoor		

Level 3

Towns

Fahrbahn, die (-en)	roadway	Stadtteil, der (-e)	district, area of a city
Ausfahrt, die (-en)	exit	Bezirk, der (-e)	district
Vorfahrt, die (no pl.)	right of way, priority	Kreis, der (-e)	district
		Gemeinde, die (-n)	community, municipality
Einbahnstraße, die (-n)	one-way street		
Gasse, die (-n)	lane, narrow street, street (AU)	Bevölkerung, die (-en)	population
		Bewohner(in), der/die (-/nen)	resident
Allee, die (-n)	avenue		
Ringstraße, die (-n)	ring road	Einwohner(in), der/die (-/nen)	inhabitant
Bundesstraße, die (-n)	A road; main road		
Landstraße, die (-n)	B road, country road	Einheimische(r), der/die (adj. decl.)	local inhabitant
Umgehungsstraße, die (-n)	bypass	Feuerwehr, die (-en)	fire department
		Müllabfuhr, die (-en)	rubbish collection (service)
Unterführung, die (-en)	underpass		
		Altpapiersammlung, die (-en)	waste paper collection
Tunnel, der (-)	tunnel		
Siedlung, die (-en)	subdivision, development	Kläranlage, die (-n)	water treatment plant

Müllverbren-nungsanlage, die (-n)	waste incineration plant
Bauplatz, der ("e)	building site

Features of buildings

Isolierung, die (-en)	insulation, lagging, soundproofing
Täfelung, die (-en)	panelling
Geländer, das (-)	railing, banister
Treppenhaus, das ("er)	stairwell
Treppenabsatz, der ("e)	landing
Dachrinne, die (-n)	gutter
Dachgesims, das (-e)	eaves
Dachvorsprung, der ("e)	eaves
Abflussrohr, das (-e)	downspout, drainpipe
Giebel, der (-)	gable
Säule, die (-n)	column
Doppelfenster, das (-)	double-glazed window
Fensterrahmen, der (-)	window frame
Flügelfenster, das (-)	casement window
ein-, zweiflügeliges Fenster	single/double casement window
Schiebefenster, das (-)	sash window, sliding window
Gaube (Gaupe), die (-n)	dormer (window)
Panoramafenster, das (-)	picture window
Buntglasfenster, das (-)	stained glass window
Fensterrose, die (-n)	rose window
Fassade, die (-n)	outside, exterior, façade
(weiße) Tünche, die (-n)	whitewash
getüncht	whitewashed
Rauputz, der (no pl.)	roughcast

etw verputzen	to plaster, roughcast sth
Fachwerk, das (no pl.)	half-timbered construction
Portal, das (-e)	portal
Turm, der ("e)	tower
Kirchturm, der ("e)	steeple
Kirchturmspitze, die (-n)	spire
Glockenturm, der ("e)	bell tower
Türmchen, das (-)	turret
Bogen, der (-; S, AU: ")	arch
Gewölbe, das (-)	vault

Buying, selling and renting property

Immobilien, pl.	property, real estate
Makler(in), der/die (-/nen)	house agent
Provision, die (-en)	commission
jmdm ein Haus vermitteln	to locate a house for s.o.
Zimmervermittlung, die (-en)	housing agency
Notar(in), der (-e/nen)	solicitor (dealing with conveyancing); notary public
Kaufvertrag, der ("e)	purchase agreement, contract
Nebenkosten, pl.	additional expenses
Hypothek, die (-en)	mortgage
eine Hypothek aufnehmen	to take out a mortgage
Zinssatz, der ("e)	interest rate
Verkäufermarkt, der ("e)	seller's market
Käufermarkt, der ("e)	buyer's market
etw pachten	to lease sth
jmdm etw verpachten	to lease sth to s.o.
Eigentumsüber-tragung, die (-en)	conveyancing

Household

Level 1

Furniture

Möbel, das (-)	piece of furniture
Küchenmöbel, das (-)	piece of kitchen furniture
Tisch, der (-e)	table
Schreibtisch, der (-e)	desk
Nachttisch, der (-e)	bedside table
Couchtisch, der (-e)	coffee table
Esstisch, der (-e)	dining table
Essgruppe, die (-n)	dining set
Stuhl, der (¨e)	chair
Schaukelstuhl, der (¨e)	rocking chair
Sessel, der (-)	armchair, easy chair
Couch, die (-s or -en) or der ([e]s; CH)	couch, sofa
Sofa, das (-s)	sofa
Bank, die (¨e)	bench
Schrank, der (¨e)	cabinet, cupboard
Bett, das (-en)	bed
Regal, das (-e)	set of shelves
Regalbrett, das (-er)	shelf
Bücherschrank, der (¨e)	bookcase
Kommode, die (-n)	chest of drawers
Schublade, die (-n)	drawer
Garderobe, die (-n)	coat rack, closet
Schirmständer, der (-)	umbrella stand

Soft furnishings

Vorhang, der (¨e)	curtain
Gardine, die (-n)	(sheer) curtain
Store, der (-s)	net curtain
Kissen, das (-)	cushion, pillow
Kopfkissen, das (-)	pillow
Kissenbezug, der (¨e)	cushion cover, pillowcase
Sofakissen, das (-)	scatter cushion
Matratze, die (-n)	mattress
(Bett)decke, die (-n)	blanket, comforter

Steppdecke, die (-n)	quilt
Heizdecke, die (-n)	electric blanket
Betttuch, das (¨er)	sheet
Bettlaken, das (-; N)	sheet
Bettwäsche, die (no pl.)	bed linen
Bettzeug, das (no pl.)	bedclothes
Tagesdecke, die (-n)	bedspread
Federbett, das (-en)	duvet
Bettbezug, der (¨e)	duvet cover
Tischtuch, das (¨er)	tablecloth, table linen
Serviette, die (-n)	napkin

Lighting

Licht, das (-er)	light
Lichtschalter, der (-)	light switch
Lampe, die (-n)	lamp
Leselampe, die (-n)	reading lamp
Hängelampe, die (-n)	hanging lamp
Deckenlampe, die (-n)	ceiling lamp
Stehlampe, die (-n)	standard lamp, floor lamp
Kronleuchter, der (-)	chandelier
Lampenschirm, der (-e)	lampshade
Glühbirne, die (-n)	light bulb
Leuchtstofflampe, die (-n)	fluorescent lamp
Taschenlampe, die (-n)	torch, flashlight
Kerze, die (-n)	candle
Petroleumlampe, die (-n)	oil lamp

Kitchenware

Topf, der (¨e)	saucepan, casserole
Kochtopf, der (¨e)	(cooking) pot
Topfdeckel, der (-)	lid
Pfanne, die (-n)	skillet, pan
Bratpfanne, die (-n)	frying pan

Geschirr, das (-e)	kitchenware, crockery, dishes	(etw) aufräumen	to tidy up (sth)
		(etw) sauber machen	to clean (sth)
Teller, der (-)	plate	Besen, der (-)	broom
Tasse, die (-n)	cup	Besenschrank, der (¨e)	broom cupboard
Untertasse, die (-n)	saucer		
Schüssel, die (-n)	bowl	(etw) fegen	to sweep (sth)
Schale, die (-n)	shallow bowl	Mopp, der (-s)	mop
Glas, das (¨er)	glass	etw moppen	to mop (sth)
Weinglas, das (¨er)	wine glass	Schwamm, der (¨e)	sponge
Becher, der (-)	glass, tumbler, mug		
Besteck, das (-e or [coll.] -s)	place (cutlery) setting; utensils	etw aufwischen	to wipe/mop sth up; wipe/wash sth
Messer, das (-)	knife	Eimer, der (-)	bucket, pail
Gabel, die (-n)	fork	Lappen, der (-)	(cleaning) cloth
Löffel, der (-)	spoon	Putzmittel, das (-)	cleaner
Kochlöffel, der (-)	wooden spoon	Staub, der (no pl.)	dust
Flasche, die (-n)	bottle	Tuch, das (¨er)	dust cloth, duster
Thermosflasche, die (-n)	thermos	(etw) staubsaugen	to vacuum (sth)
		(etw) abwaschen	to wash (sth) up
Kanne, die (-n)	pot, jug, pitcher	(etw) spülen	to wash (sth)
Kaffekanne, die (-n)	coffee pot	(etw) abtrocknen	to dry (sth)
Hackbrett, das (-er)	chopping board	Abwaschtuch, das (¨er)	dish cloth (for washing)
Dosenöffner, der (-)	can opener		
Flaschenöffner, der (-)	bottle opener	Geschirrtuch, das (¨er)	dish towel (for drying)
Korkenzieher, der (-)	corkscrew	Spülmittel, das (-)	dishwashing liquid
Zuckerdose, die (-n)	sugar bowl		
Butterdose, die (-n)	butter dish	Papierhandtuch, das (¨er)	paper towel
Brotkorb, der (¨e)	bread basket		
		Papierkorb, der (¨e)	waste-paper basket

Cleaning

Schmutz, der (no pl.)	dirt	Sack, der (¨e)	sack, bag
dreckig	dirty, filthy	etw wegwerfen	to throw sth away

Level 2

Furniture

Einrichtung, die (-en)	furniture, furnishing	Wandschrank, der (¨e)	closet; built-in cupboard
etw einrichten	to furnish sth		
Einbaumöbel, das (-)	piece of built-in furniture	Hängeschrank, der (¨e)	wall cupboard
Einbauschrank, der (¨e)	built-in cupboard, wardrobe	Schrankwand, die (¨e)	wall, shelf unit
begehbarer Einbauschrank	walk-in cupboard	Raumteiler, der (-e)	room divider

Kleiderschrank, der (¨e)	clothes closet
Etagenbett, das (-en)	bunk bed
Bettcouch, die (-s or -en) or der ([e]s; CH)	bed settee
Frisierkommode, die (-n)	dressing table
Hocker, der (-)	stool
Wäscheschrank, der (¨e)	linen cupboard
Klapptisch, der (-e)	folding table
Klappstuhl, der (¨e)	folding chair
Drehstuhl, der (¨e)	swivel chair
Stapelstuhl, der (¨e)	stacking chair
Hochstuhl, der (¨e)	high chair
Lehnsessel, der (-)	recliner
Sitzsack, der (¨e)	beanbag

Domestic appliances

Gerät, das (-e)	appliance, device
Herd, der (-e)	oven, stove
Elektroherd, der (-e)	electric oven
Gasherd, der (-e)	gas oven
(Back)ofen, der (¨)	oven
Mikrowelle, die (-n)	microwave (oven)
Mikrowellenherd, der (-e)	microwave oven
Kühlschrank, der (¨e)	fridge
Tiefkühlschrank, der (¨e)	freezer
Tiefkühlfach, das (¨er)	freezer compartment
Tiefkühltruhe, die (-n)	(chest) freezer
Geschirrspüler, der (-)	dishwasher
Spülmaschine, die (-n)	dishwasher
Waschmaschine, die (-n)	washing machine
Trockner, der (-)	dryer
Wäscheschleuder, der (-)	spin dryer
Bügelbrett, das (-er)	ironing board

Bügeleisen, das (-)	iron
Staubsauger, der (-)	vacuum cleaner
Wecker, der (-)	alarm clock
Kaffeemaschine, die (-n)	coffee maker
Kaffeemühle, die (-n)	coffee grinder
Mixer, der (-)	blender
Rührmaschine, die (-n)	mixer
Handrührmaschine, die (-n)	hand mixer
Küchenmaschine, die (-n)	food mixer/processor
Toaster, der (-)	toaster
Waffelautomat, der (-en)	electric waffle iron
Waage, die (-n)	scale

Kitchenware

Kessel, der (-)	kettle
Wasserkessel, der (-)	tea kettle
Flötenkessel, der (-)	whistling kettle
Krug, der (¨e)	jug
Wasserkrug, der (¨e)	water jug
Pfeffermühle, die (-n)	peppermill
Salzstreuer, der (-)	salt pot
Essgeschirr, das (-e)	dinner set
Kaffeegeschirr, das (-e)	coffee set
Set, das (-s)	place mat
Untersetzer, der (-)	coaster
Kerzenleuchter, der (-)	candlestick
Gedeck, das (-e)	place setting
Essteller, der (-)	dinner plate
Suppenteller, der (-)	soup plate
Dessertteller, der (-)	dessert plate
Kuchengabel, die (-n)	dessert fork
Teelöffel, der (-)	teaspoon
Esslöffel, der (-)	soup spoon, dessert spoon, tablespoon
Dessertlöffel, der (-)	dessert spoon
Sieb, das (-e)	sieve
Abtropfsieb, das (-e)	colander

Teesieb, das (-e)	tea strainer
Kuchenform, die (-en)	cake tin
Tortenform, die (-en)	gateau/tart/pie tin
Backblech, das (-e)	baking sheet
Springform, die (-en)	spring form tin
Kurzzeitmesser, der (-)	timer
Eieruhr, die (-en)	egg timer
Reibe, die (-n)	grater
Schäler, der (-)	peeler
Kartoffelstampfer, der (-)	potato masher
Abtropfständer, der (-)	dish drainer
Abtropfbrett, das (-er)	drain board
Alufolie, die (-n)	aluminium foil
Butterbrotpapier, das (no pl.)	greaseproof paper
Wachspapier, das (no pl.)	waxed paper
Frischhaltefolie, die (-n)	plastic wrap

Cleaning

Gummihandschuh, der (-e)	rubber glove
Topfkratzer, der (-)	scouring pad
etw scheuern	to scour sth
Scheuertuch, das (¨er)	cleaning rag
etw abspritzen	to spray sth down; spray sth off
etw von/aus etw wischen	to wipe sth from sth
etw schrubben	to scrub sth
etw polieren	to polish sth
Poliermittel, das (-)	polish
etw bohnern	to wax sth [floor]
Bohnerbesen, der (-)	floor polisher
Bohnerwachs, das (no pl.)	floor polish
Teppichkehrmaschine, die (-n)	carpet sweeper

Fleckenentferner, der (-)	stain remover
Luftverbesserer, der (-)	air freshener
Bleichmittel, das (-)	bleach
etw bleichen	to bleach sth
Abfall, der (¨e)	waste, refuse
Abfalleimer, der (-)	dustbin
Biotonne, die (-n)	bio-waste container
Müll, der (no pl.)	rubbish, garbage, refuse
Müllbeutel, der (-)	rubbish bag
Mülltonne, die (-n)	rubbish bin

Tools

Werkzeug, das (-e)	tool, toolset
Werkzeugkasten, der (¨)	tool box
Hammer, der (-)	hammer
Nagel, der (¨)	nail
Kopf, der (¨e)	head
Schraubenzieher, der (-)	screwdriver
Schraube, die (-n)	screw
Zange, die (-n)	pliers
Kneifzange, die (-n)	pincers
Bohrer, der (-)	drill
Schraubenschlüssel, der (-)	wrench
Leiter, die (-n)	ladder
Steckdose, die (-n)	electrical socket
Stecker, der (-)	plug
Verlängerungskabel, das (-)	extension lead
Feuerlöscher, der (-)	fire extinguisher
Farbe, die (-n)	paint
etw streichen	to paint sth
frisch gestrichen!	wet paint
Streichbürste, die (-n)	paintbrush
Farbroller, der (-)	paint roller
Sand-, Schmirgelpapier, das (no pl.)	sandpaper
etw schmirgeln	to sand sth

| Rutscher, der (-) | sander | Bügelsäge, die (-n) | hacksaw |
| Säge, die (-n) | saw | Feile, die (-n) | file |

Level 3

Furniture

Garnitur, die (-en)	suite
eine dreiteilige Garnitur	a three-piece suite
Polstermöbel, das (-)	piece of upholstered furniture
Polsterung, die (-en)	upholstery (padding)
Polsterstoff, der (-e)	upholstery fabric
Geschirrschrank, der (¨e)	dresser, china cabinet
Anrichte, die (-n)	dresser
fahrbarer Anrichtetisch	serving trolley
Laufrolle, die (-n)	caster
Ausziehtisch, der (-e)	extending table
Einlegebrett, das (-er)	leaf
Satz Tische, der (¨e)	nest of tables
Beistelltisch, der (-e)	occasional table
Schreibtisch mit Rollverschluss, der (-e)	roll-top desk
Liege, die (-n)	day bed; divan
Korbmöbel, das (-)	piece of wicker furniture
Rohrstuhl, der (¨e)	cane chair
Bettgestell, das (-e)	bedstead

Floors and walls

Fußbodenbelag, der (¨e)	flooring, floor covering
Teppich, der (-e)	carpet, rug
langfloriger Teppich	shag pile/long-pile carpet
Perserteppich, der (-e)	Persian carpet
Orientteppich, der (-e)	Oriental rug
Berberteppich, der (-)	Berber carpet
Teppichboden, der (¨)	wall-to-wall carpet
etw verlegen	to lay sth
Bettvorleger, der (-)	bedside rug
Läufer, der (-)	runner
Fußmatte, die (-n)	doormat
Parkett, das (-e)	parquet floor
Parkettboden, der (¨)	parquet floor
Fliesenboden, der (¨)	tile floor
Bretterboden, der (¨)	wooden floor
Vinyl, das (no pl.)	vinyl
Linoleum, das (no pl.)	linoleum
Tapete, die (-n)	wallpaper
etw tapezieren	to wallpaper sth
Wandbehang, der (¨e)	wall hanging

Plumbing and bathroom

Spülbecken, das (-)	(kitchen) sink
Wasserhahn, der (¨e)	tap, faucet
Warmwassergriff, der (-e)	hot tap
Kaltwassergriff, der (-e)	cold tap
Mischbatterie, die (-n)	(mixer) tap
Toilette, die (-n)	toilet
WC, das (-s)	toilet
Klosett, das (-s)	toilet
Klo, das (-s; coll.)	loo, john
Klosettbecken, das (-)	toilet bowl
Klosettdeckel, der (-)	toilet lid
Klosettbrille, die (-n)	toilet seat
Spülhebel, der (-)	flushing handle
spülen	to flush
Wasserkasten, der (¨)	water tank

Bidet, das (-s)	bidet
Badewanne, die (-n)	bathtub
Waschbecken, das (-)	washbasin, sink
Überlauf, der (¨e)	overflow
Duschkabine, die (-n)	shower cabinet
Handdusche, die (-n)	shower attachment
Duschwanne, die (-n)	shower base
Toilettenpapierhalter, der (-)	toilet paper holder
Handtuchhalter, der (-)	towel rail
Seifenschale, die (-n)	soap dish
Spiegelschrank, der (¨e)	mirrored bathroom cabinet
Hausapotheke, die (-n)	medicine chest
Personenwaage, die (-n)	bathroom scales
Bademaatte, die (-n)	bath mat

Kitchenware

Käseglocke, die (-n)	cheese cover
Saftpresse, die (-n)	juice extractor
Zitronenpresse, die (-n)	lemon squeezer
Dampfkochtopf, der (¨e)	pressure cooker
Dämpfer, der (-)	steamer
Schmortopf, der (¨e)	casserole dish
Kasserolle, die (-n)	saucepan
Stielkasserolle, die (-n)	saucepan
Tablett, das (-s or -e)	tray
Bratenplatte, die (-n)	meat dish
Käseplatte, die (-n)	cheese board
Tranchiermesser, das (-)	carving knife
scharf	sharp
stumpf	blunt
Tortenheber, der (-)	cake server
Salatbesteck, das (-e or [coll.] -s)	salad servers
Vorlegebesteck, das (-e or [coll.] -s)	(set of) serving cutlery
Vorlegegabel, die (-n)	serving fork

Suppenschöpflöffel, der (-)	soup ladle
Suppenterrine, die (-n)	soup tureen
Soßenlöffel, der (-)	gravy ladle
Soßenschüssel, die (-n)	gravy boat
Sektglas, das (¨er)	champagne glass
Römer, der (-)	a kind of wine glass
Kognakschale, die (-n)	brandy glass
Trichter, der (-)	funnel
Mörser, der (-)	mortar
Stößel, der (-)	pestle
Fleischwolf, der (¨e)	mincer
Nussknacker, der (-)	nutcracker
Tauchsieder, der (-)	immersion heater

Tools

etw an etw schrauben	to screw sth to sth
eine Schraube (in etw) hineindrehen	to drive a screw (into sth)
eine Schraube herausdrehen	to remove a screw
eine Schraube anziehen	to tighten a screw
Gewinde, das (-)	thread
Schraubenbolzen, der (-)	bolt
Schraubenmutter, die (-n)	nut
etw an etw mit Bolzen befestigen	to bolt sth to sth
Sicherung, die (-en)	fuse
Sicherungskasten, der (¨)	fuse box
durchbrennen	to blow
Haarlineal, das (-e)	straightedge
Messwinkel, der (-)	square
Holzhammer, der (-)	mallet
Hobel, der (-)	plane
Angel, die (-n)	hinge (door)
Scharnier, das (-e)	hinge (box)

Lackfarbe, die (-n)	gloss paint	Grundierung, die (-en)	undercoat
Glanzfarbe, die (-n)	gloss paint	Lösungsmittel, das (-)	paint thinner
Anstrich, der (-e)	coat of paint		
Satinoberfläche, die (-n)	satin finish	Lötlampe, die (-n)	blowtorch
		Lötkolben, der (-)	soldering iron

Gardens

Level 1

Garden parts and features

Garten, der (¨)	garden, yard
Rasen, der (-)	lawn
Hecke, die (-n)	hedge
Gartenmöbel, das (-)	piece of garden furniture
Gartenbank, die (¨e)	garden bench
Gartenschirm, der (-e)	sunshade
Blumenbeet, das (-e)	flowerbed
Blumenkasten, der (¨)	window box
Gemüsegarten, der (¨)	vegetable garden, kitchen garden
Obstgarten, der (¨)	orchard
Gartenteich, der (-e)	garden pond

Gardening

im Garten arbeiten	to garden
etw pflanzen	to plant sth
etw anbauen	to grow sth
etw säen	to sow sth
Samen, der (-)	seed
etw graben	to dig sth
etw kultivieren	to cultivate sth
(etw) jäten	to weed (sth)
etw harken	to rake sth
etw (be)gießen	to water sth
etw bewässern	to irrigate, water sth
etw pflücken	to pick sth
blühen	to blossom, bloom
wachsen	to grow
welken	to wilt
(etw) mähen	to mow (sth)
etw ernten	to harvest sth

Plants

Pflanze, die (-n)	plant
Rose, die (-n)	rose
Pfingstrose, die (-n)	peony
Tulpe, die (-n)	tulip
Osterglocke, die (-n)	daffodil
Narzisse, die (-n)	narcissus
Stiefmütterchen, das (-)	pansy
Veilchen, das (-)	violet
Zinnie, die (-n)	zinnia
Studentenblume, die (-n)	marigold
Gänseblümchen, das (-)	daisy
Löwenmäulchen, das (-)	snapdragon
Petunie, die (-n)	petunia
Geranie, die (-n)	geranium
Nelke, die (-n)	pink, carnation
Chrysantheme, die (-n)	chrysanthemum
Lilie, die (-n)	lily
Schwertlilie, die (-n)	iris
Sonnenblume, die (-n)	sunflower

Level 2

Garden parts and features

Schrebergarten, der (¨)	allotment garden
Steinplatte, die (-n)	flagstone
Kiesweg, der (-e)	gravel path
Sonnenuhr, die (-en)	sundial
Gartenzwerg, der (-e)	garden gnome
Spalier, das (-e)	trellis
(Wand)spalierbaum, der (¨e)	(wall) espalier
Regentonne, die (-n)	water barrel
Gartenlaube, die (-n)	summer house
Treibhaus, das (¨er)	hothouse
Pflanzentisch, der (-e)	potting table, bench
Frühbeet, das (-e)	forcing bed
Geräteschuppen, der (-)	tool shed
Komposthaufen, der (-)	compost heap
Vogelscheuche, die (-n)	scarecrow

Garden tools

Spaten, der (-)	spade
Pflanzkelle, die (-n)	trowel
Gartenbesen, der (-)	lawn rake
Harke, die (-n)	rake
Rechen, der (-; S)	rake
Heugabel, die (-n)	pitchfork
Baumschere, die (-n)	tree pruner
Baumsäge, die (-n)	pruning saw
Heckenschere, die (-n)	hedge trimmer
Rosenschere, die (-n)	pruning shears
Obstpflücker, der (-)	fruit picker
Rasenmäher, der (-)	lawn mower
Handrasenmäher, der (-)	hand mower

Grasfangkorb, der (¨e)	grassbag
Rasenlüfter, der (-)	lawn aerator
Gartenschlauch, der (¨e)	garden hose
Schlauchwagen, der (-)	hose reel
Rasensprenger, der (-)	sprinkler
Gießkanne, die (-n)	watering can
Schubkarren, der (-)	wheelbarrow

Plants

Krokus, der (- or -se)	crocus
Schneeglöckchen, das (-)	snowdrop
Maiglöckchen, das (-)	lily of the valley
Hyazinthe, die (-n)	hyacinth
Phlox, der or die (-e)	phlox
Flammenblume, die (-n)	phlox
Forsythie, die (-n)	forsythia
Viburnum, das (no pl.)	viburnum
Schneeball, der (¨e)	snowball bush
Hortensie, die (-n)	hydrangea
Begonie, die (-n)	begonia
Klematis, die (-)	clematis
Dahlie, die (-n)	dahlia
Gladiole, die (-n)	gladiolus
Mohn, der (-e)	poppy
Fingerhut, der (¨e)	foxglove
Platterbse, die (-n)	sweet pea
Gartenwicke, die (-n)	sweet pea
Lavendel, der (-)	lavender
Efeu, der (no pl.)	ivy
Orchidee, die (-n)	orchid

Level 3

Gardening

Sämling, der (-e)	seedling
Zwiebel, die (-n)	bulb
Trieb, der (-e)	shoot
Spross, der (-e)	shoot
Stiel, der (-e)	stem, stalk
Dorn, der (-en)	thorn
Grashalm, der (-e)	blade of grass
etw stutzen	to clip, prune, trim sth
etw verpflanzen	to transplant sth
etw umpflanzen	to transplant/repot sth
Vermehrung, die (-en)	propagation
Ableger, der (-)	layer
Ausläufer, der (-)	runner
Steckling, der (-e)	cutting
Wurzel, die (-n)	root
Knospe, die (-n)	bud
etw veredeln	to graft sth

Plants

Alpenveilchen, das (-)	cyclamen
Amaryllis, die (Amaryllen)	amaryllis
Tuberose, die (-n)	tuberose
Tränende(s) Herz, das (-en)	bleeding heart
Azalee, die (-n)	azalea
Geißblatt, das (no pl.)	honeysuckle
Bartnelke, die (-n)	sweet William
Funkie, die (-n)	hosta
Herzlilie, die (-n)	hosta
Kapuzinerkresse, die (-n)	nasturtium
Löwenzahn, der (¨e)	dandelion
Distel, die (-n)	thistle
Brennnessel, die (-n)	stinging nettle
Akelei, die (-en)	columbine
Prachtscharte, die (-n)	blazing star
Kornblume, die (-n)	corn flower
Hahnenfuß, der (no pl.)	buttercup
Schafgarbe, die (-n)	yarrow
(Edel)lupine, die (-n)	lupin
Aloe, die (-n)	aloe
Vergissmeinnicht, das (-e)	forget-me-not
Seerose, die (-n)	water lily
Ziergras, das (¨er)	ornamental grass
Glyzine (Glyzinie), die (-n)	wisteria
Magnolie, die (-n)	magnolia

Exercises

Level 1

1. Was passt zusammen? ✓

> a. das Bier vom Fass, b. die Erdbeertorte, c. der Herrenmantel, d. der Koch,
> e. vitaminreiche Kost, f. Pillen (pl.), g. das Speiseeis, h. das Vollkornbrot,
> i. die Zahnpasta

1. die Apotheke
2. die Drogerie
3. die Bäckerei
4. die Konditorei
5. die Eisdiele
6. das Restaurant
7. die Reinigung
8. das Lokal
9. das Reformhaus

2. Welches Wort hat die gleiche oder eine ähnliche Bedeutung? ✓

1. der Bürgersteig   6. der Lift
2. der Freizeitpark   7. die Dachkammer
3. die Bücherei   8. die Diele
4. die Kathedrale   9. die Couch
5. das Geschäft   10. das Betttuch

3. Assoziationen. Was passt wo?

> etw aufwischen, dreckig, die Feuerstelle, die Gänseblümchen, die Heizdecke,
> der Kamin, die Klimaanlage, der Lappen, die Osterglocke, etw pflücken,
> der Staub, die Tulpe

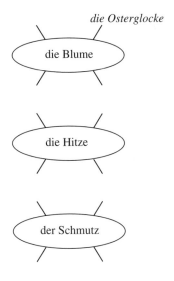

die Osterglocke

die Blume

die Hitze

der Schmutz

4. In jedem Satz fehlt ein Wort. ✓

> Ampel, anbauen, Gartenbank, jäten, Kissen, Obstgarten, Schaukelstuhl,
> Schublade, Sehenswürdigkeit, Veilchen

1. Auf den Bürgersteigen _____ sie Unkraut.
2. Speisepilze kann man selber _____.
3. Er sitzt mit seinen alten Freunden auf der _____ im sonnigen Innenhof.
4. Sie pflückten im _____ ein paar Äpfel.
5. Ich legte dem Kranken ein _____ unter den Kopf.
6. Er verbringt den Tag im _____ unter einem Berg wollener Decken.
7. Sie legte die Wäsche in die _____.
8. Eines Tages im Frühling findet sie das erste _____.
9. Du bist bei Rot über die _____ gefahren!
10. Die meistbestaunte Pariser _____ ist der Eiffelturm.

5. Welches Verb passt? ✓

a. abschließen, b. aufräumen, c. anschalten, d. besichtigen, e. decken, f. fegen,
g. gießen, h. graben, i. leeren, j. mähen, k. säen, l. spülen, m. unterschreiben,
n. zahlen

1. den Rasen	8. den Tisch
2. Samen (pl.)	9. das Licht
3. die Tür	10. das Geschirr
4. den Boden	11. den Schreibtisch
5. die Stadt	12. den Papierkorb
6. die Miete	13. die Pflanzen (pl.)
7. den Mietvertrag	14. das Loch

6. Welches Wort passt nicht? ✓
1. die Klingel, die Kerze, das Schloss, der Schlüssel
2. das Federbett, die Kommode, die Kneipe, der Nachttisch
3. der Besen, die Glühbirne, der Kronleuchter, die Taschenlampe
4. die Bettwäsche, das Putzmittel, der Schwamm, das Spülmittel
5. die Hecke, die Mauer, die Umgebung, der Zaun
6. das Fenster, die Gardine, das Regal, der Vorhang
7. die Kanne, das Messer, die Schüssel, der Topf
8. der Becher, die Kaffeekanne, die Tasse, das Weinglas
9. das Blumenbeet, das Löwenmäulchen, die Pfingstrose, das Stiefmütterchen

7. Suchen Sie eine andere Bedeutung.

1. das Gericht	6. der Hof
2. der Gang	7. das Tor
3. die Kreuzung	8. das Hackbrett
4. die Bank	9. der Löffel
5. die Nelke	

8. Was bedeuten die Wendungen?
1. alle Brücken hinter sich abbrechen
2. hinter Schloss und Riegel sitzen
3. einen Streit vom Zaun brechen
4. zwischen Tür und Angel
5. an die Decke gehen
6. das ist die halbe Miete
7. nicht alle Tassen im Schrank haben
8. es steht auf des Messers Schneide
9. jmdm einen Korb geben
10. es gießt wie aus Eimern
11. wer weiß, was uns noch alles blüht
12. keine Rose ohne Dornen

9. Falsche Freunde. Ergänzen Sie die Tabelle.

Deutsch	Englisch	Deutsch	Englisch
der Stuhl			stool
der Store			store
die Allee			alley
die Ampel			ample
die Kaution			caution
das Klosett			closet
der Mixer			mixer
der Herd			herd

10. Übersetzen Sie ins Englische.

Streit unter Mietern und Nachbarn

Darf der Kinderwagen im Hausflur stehen? Darf eine Satellitenschüssel am Balkon angebracht werden? Wo kann die Wäsche getrocknet werden? Kann der Vermieter das Rauchen im Haus verbieten? Darf nachts gebadet werden? Kann der Vermieter den Hund verbieten? Wie lange darf der Besuch bleiben? Wann darf der Nachbar Klavier spielen? Solche Alltagsfragen rund um die Mietwohnung stehen im Mittelpunkt einer neuen Informationsbroschüre des Deutschen Mieterbundes (DMB): „Mieterrechte und Mieterpflichten". Auf 100 Seiten werden nicht die „großen" mietrechtlichen Themen, wie Kündigung, Mieterhöhung und Nebenkosten abgehandelt, sondern hier werden die Probleme beschrieben, die in allen Mehrfamilienhäusern regelmäßig Ärger auslösen und immer wieder zu Gerichtsprozessen führen. In der neuen Broschüre „Mieterrechte/Mieterpflichten" erfahren Mieter, was sie in der Wohnung dürfen und was nicht, wozu sie die Erlaubnis des Vermieters benötigen, aber auch, welche Rechte und Pflichten Nachbarn haben. Die entsprechenden mietrechtlichen Gesetze, unzählige Vertragsklauseln und viele Gerichtsurteile wurden dafür ausgewertet.   DMB

Ratgeber hilft gegen Stress beim Umzug

Es könnte eigentlich jedem schon einmal bei einem Umzug passiert sein: Erst ist die Straße zugeparkt, dann passt das Sofa nicht durch das Treppenhaus, und am Ende sind alle Kisten voll, die Wohnung aber nicht leer. Umziehen? Kann in Stress ausarten. Dabei ginge es auch anders. Wie, das weiß der Autovermieter National Car Rental: Für alle, die mit Kind und Kegel von A nach B wollen, hat das Unternehmen den Umzugsratgeber „Alles im grünen Bereich" entwickelt und damit ganz offensichtlich eine Marktlücke geschlossen. Die Broschüre geht jetzt in die zweite, neu bearbeitete Auflage.

Auf zwölf Seiten, die in Zusammenarbeit mit dem Deutschen Mieterbund entstanden, werden viele Fragen aufgegriffen, die sich bei einem Umzug stellen und bereits im Vorfeld zu beachten sind. Was sollte in einem Übergabeprotokoll festgehalten werden, und wo bekommt man so ein Formular überhaupt her? Wie gelangen Waschmaschine und Computer ohne nennenswerte Schäden ans Ziel? Und wie passt der ganze Kram eigentlich in ein Fahrzeug? Die Broschüre „Alles im grünen Bereich" gibt jedoch nicht nur nützliche Tipps für die Umzugsvorbereitung und den Tag X, sondern auch für die Zeit danach: wie sich etwa lästige Behördengänge vermeiden lassen. Wer wissen will, welche Papiere man benötigt, um ein Auto umzumelden, für den lohnt es sich, einen kurzen Blick in das Heft zu werfen. Und auch, dass man nach einem Umzug einiges an Steuern sparen kann, dürfte kaum Allgemeinwissen sein.

NCR

FRANKFURTER RUNDSCHAU, Samstag, 9. Juni 2001, Nr. 132/23, S. A9

Level 2

1. Welches Wort hat die gleiche oder eine ähnliche Bedeutung? ✓

1. das Einkaufsviertel
2. der Flohmarkt
3. die Etage
4. die Feuerleiter
5. das Möbel
6. die Spülmaschine
7. der Abfall
8. die Harke
9. der Phlox
10. die Platterbse

2. Was bedeuten die folgenden Zusammensetzungen?

1. das Industrieviertel, das Ladenviertel, das Hafenviertel, das Neubauviertel
2. der Privatweg, der Friedhofsweg, der Grasweg, der Waldweg
3. das Hutgeschäft, das Sportgeschäft, das Weihnachtsgeschäft, das Spielwarengeschäft
4. das Nachbarschaftshaus, das Gotteshaus, das Bürohaus, das Spukhaus
5. das Schlafzimmerfenster, das Schiebefenster, das Kirchenfenster, das Rundfenster
6. der Eckschrank, der Aktenschrank, der Werkzeugschrank, der Panzerschrank
7. der Brotteller, der Frühstücksteller, der Kupferteller, der Pappteller

3. Ergänzen Sie. ✓

1. mieten – der Mieter : vermieten – _____
2. die Stadt – die Städterin : die Vorstadt – _____
3. der Kaffee – die Kaffeekanne : das Wasser – _____
4. der Peffer – die Pfeffermühle : das Salz – _____
5. der Kuchen – die Kuchenform : das Plätzchen – _____
6. der Schraubenzieher – die Schraube : der Hammer – _____
7. etw polieren – das Poliermittel : etw bohnern – _____
8. die Streichbürste – etw streichen : das Schmirgelpapier – _____
9. die Rührmaschine – die Handrührmaschine : der Rasenmäher – _____

4. Was passt zusammen? ✓

a. das Butterbrotpapier, b. der Drehstuhl, c. der Feuerlöscher,
d. der Fleckenentferner, e. der Gartenschlauch, f. die Gießkanne,
g. der Klapptisch, h. der Rasenmäher, i. der Rasensprenger, j. die Reibe,
k. die Säge, l. das Scheuertuch, m. das Set, n. die Schiebetür, o. das Sieb,
p. die Vogelscheuche

1. Mähmaschine für Rasen
2. in Gärten ausgestellte Gestalt zum Verscheuchen der Vögel
3. Gefäß zum Begießen von Pflanzen
4. Gartengerät, das den Rasen beregnet
5. Gartenspritze
6. zusammenklappbarer Tisch
7. Stuhl mit drehbarer Sitzfläche
8. seitlich verschiebbare Tür
9. Tischdeckchen für ein Gedeck
10. Gefäß mit feinen Löchern
11. grober Lappen zum Reinigen
12. Küchengerät zum Reiben von Gemüse
13. fettundurchlässiges Papier
14. Fleckenreiniger
15. Druckgerät zum Bekämpfen von Bränden
16. Werkzeug zum Zerschneiden von Holz und Metall

5. Ordnen Sie.

> das Antiquariat, der Bohrer, der Gartenzwerg, der Komposthaufen, der
> Selbstbedienungsladen, der Schraubenschlüssel, das Spalier, die Steinplatte,
> die Tabakwarenhandlung, das Verlängerungskabel, der Waschsalon, die Zange

Geschäft	Werkzeug	Garten

6. Was passt nicht? ✓
1. -kessel: Flöten-, Tee-, Waage-, Wasser-
2. -stuhl: Hoch-, Klapp-, Kuchen-, Stapel-
3. -bett: Deckel-, Doppel-, Etagen- Wasser-
4. -geschirr: Camping-, Ess-, Kaffee-, Tor-
5. -gabel: Deserteur-, Heu-, Kuchen-, Telefon-
6. -dose: Butter-, Puder-, Stecken-, Zucker-
7. -uhr: Armbinde-, Eier-, Kirchen-, Sonnen-
8. -beet: Blumen-, Früh-, Rot-, Tulpen-
9. -schere: Hecken-, Nagel-, Rosen-, Zigaretten-
10. Bügel-: -brett, -eisen, -teller, -wäsche

7. Wie heißt das Adjektiv? ✓
1. im Zentrum
2. mit Möbeln eingerichtet
3. viel Raum bietend
4. so beschaffen, dass man es begehen kann
5. so beschaffen, dass man es zusammenklappen kann
6. so beschaffen, dass man es verschieben kann
7. so beschaffen, dass man es drehen kann

8. In jedem Satz fehlen ein oder zwei Wörter. ✓

> Allzweckraum, Dachfenster, Fertighaus, Fußgängerüberweg, Fußgängerzone,
> Gegensprechanlage, Raumteiler, Speisekammer, Tiefkühlfach, Wohngemeinschaft

1. Sie machten einen Bummel durch die _____.
2. Er lebt mit seinem Bruder und einem Freund in einer _____.
3. Die Goethestraße kann an einem _____ mit Ampel sicher überquert werden.
4. Hagel beschädigte Hausdächer und durchschlug _____.
5. Im Untergeschoss soll ein _____ mit Tischtennisplatten eingerichtet werden.
6. Die vorsichtige 80jährige fragte über die _____, wer an der Tür sei.
7. Die Sitzecke am Fenster ist das Wohnzimmer, hinter dem _____ steht das Bett.
8. Die kürzere Bauzeit und der feste Preis sprechen durchaus für ein _____.
9. In der _____ fanden sie Süßigkeiten, im _____ gefrorene
   Hähnchen.

9. Wie heißen die Zusammensetzungen? ✓

~~Suppen–~~	mühle	1. *der Suppenteller*
Bleich–	verbesserer	2.
Kaffee–	herd	3.
Einbau–	sieb	4.
Luft–	~~teller~~	5.
Elektro–	leuchter	6.
Abtropf–	eimer	7.
Staub–	möbel	8.
Abfall–	mittel	9.
Kerzen–	sauger	10.

10. Übersetzen Sie ins Englische.

Warme Stofffarben fürs Schlafgemach

Fernöstliche Weisheiten inspirieren immer mehr Bundesbürger auch bei der
Einrichtung ihrer Wohnung. Insbesondere Feng Shui, die 6000 Jahre alte
chinesische Lehre von der Kunst des harmonischen Wohnens, findet derzeit
große Beachtung. Der Stoffhersteller drapilux hat die wichtigsten Feng
Shui-Tipps für das Schlafzimmer zusammengestellt:

- Weich fließende Stoffe spielen im Schlafgemach eine ganz entscheidende
  Rolle. Sie sorgen für harmonische Schwingungen. Die Fenster sollten
  deshalb großzügig mit Gardinen und Dekorationsstoffen ausgestattet
  werden. Das gilt erst recht dann, wenn Jalousien vorhanden sind, die eine
  kühle Abstrahlung haben, was durch zugezogene Vorhänge aufgefangen
  werden kann.

- Vor allem wenn das Bett nahe am Fenster oder der Tür steht, sind nach Feng Shui Himmelbetten oder Baldachine empfehlenswert. Sie verbessern die Schlafqualität und vermitteln Geborgenheit.
- Bei der Auswahl von Möbeln für das Schlafzimmer sollten Einrichtungselemente mit runden, organischen Formen bevorzugt werden. Scharfe Ecken und Kanten haben eine negative Ausstrahlung.
- Warme, aktivierende Farben wie Rot, Grün und Gelb sollten die Farbgestaltung des Schlafraumes dominieren. Grau- und Schwarztöne wirken deprimierend.

Susanne Preuß

FRANKFURTER RUNDSCHAU, Samstag, 19. Mai 2001, Nr. 116/20, S. A8

11. Lesen Sie den folgenden Artikel.

So wird der Balkon zum Wohnraum

Während der Sommermonate ist es die pure Verschwendung wertvoller Wohnfläche: ein Balkon, der höchstens mal zum Wäschetrocknen oder als Abstellplatz für leere Getränkekästen genutzt wird. Dabei lassen sich kleine Balkons schon mit wenigen Accessoires in einen behaglichen Zusatzraum der Wohnung verwandeln. Mit geschickter Gestaltung kann dann das Sonnenbad auf dem Liegestuhl bereits zur perfekten Einstimmung auf den Sommerurlaub werden. Das einfachste Mittel gegen graue Balkon-Tristesse: sorgfältig ausgewählte Pflanzen, die für natürliche Wohlfühl-Atmosphäre sorgen. Hängende Gefäße dekorieren den Balkon mit üppigem Grün oder farbiger Blumenpracht, ohne dass Standfläche am Boden verloren geht. Dabei lässt sich sogar das Angenehme mit dem Nützlichen verbinden: Neben Rankpflanzen und Blumen können in Hängekübeln, Terrakotta-Gefäßen oder Balkonkästen auch Küchenkräuter gedeihen.

Die Pflanzenpracht gedeiht am besten an einem Standort, an dem täglich für mehrere Stunden die Sonne scheint. Allerdings empfiehlt sich trotzdem die Installation einer effektiven Beschattung. Viele Pflanzen verkraften nämlich die intensive Mittagssonne im Hochsommer nicht. Im Fachhandel werden spezielle Klemmkassetten-Markisen für den Balkon, unter anderem von markilux, angeboten. Sie lassen sich einfach mit Hilfe von zwei Klemmpfosten montieren. Bei einem Umzug können die Klemmkassetten-Markisen problemlos mitgenommen werden. Von der Beschattung profitieren natürlich nicht nur die Pflanzen, sondern auch die Menschen. Selbst bei Südausrichtung bleibt ein markisengeschützter Balkon während des ganzen Tages ein wohltuender Aufenthaltsort. Wenn der Platz knapp ist, lassen sich alternativ zum Liegestuhl auch mit Klappmöbeln im Handumdrehen Sitzplätze im Freien schaffen.

Susanne Preuß

FRANKFURTER RUNDSCHAU, Samstag, 16. Juni 2001, Nr. 137/24, S. A7

a. Vokabelübung. Welches Wort im Artikel hat die gleiche oder eine ähnliche Bedeutung? ✓
   1. rein
   2. Traurigkeit
   3. Kletterpflanze
   4. sich gut entwickeln
   5. modisches Zubehör
   6. gemütlich
   7. befestigen

b. Schriftliche Übung. Fassen Sie den Artikel in einem Absatz zusammen.

Level 3

1. Wie heißt das Gegenteil? ✓

1. die Überführung
2. der Eingang
3. die Einfahrt
4. der Käufermarkt
5. etw pachten
6. der langflorige Teppich
7. der Kaltwassergriff
8. eine Schraube hineindrehen
9. das scharfe Messer

2. Was passt zusammen? ✓

a. der Dorn, b. das Einlegebrett, c. die Hypothek, d. der Makler, e. die Schraubenmutter, f. die Soßenschüssel, g. der Stößel, h. der Suppenschöpflöffel, i. die Treppe

1. der Mörser
2. der Soßenlöffel
3. der Ausziehtisch
4. die Suppenterrine
5. der Schraubenbolzen
6. das Geländer
7. die Immobilien (pl.)
8. die Rose
9. der Zinssatz

3. Übersetzen Sie ins Deutsche.
1. village street, mountain road, main street, shopping street, connecting road
2. control tower, city hall tower, television tower
3. bedroom furniture, office furniture, all-purpose furniture, school furniture
4. kitchen table, card table, conference table, dinner table, operation table
5. dance floor, cement floor, stone floor

4. Welches Wort hat die gleiche oder eine ähnliche Bedeutung? ✓
1. der Bezirk
2. das Dachgesims
3. die Anrichte
4. der Parkettboden
5. die Toilette
6. die Kasserolle
7. die Glanzfarbe
8. der Trieb
9. etw verpflanzen

5. Suchen Sie die 26 Planzen, die in der Tabelle versteckt sind (waagerecht und senkrecht). ✓

O	H	E	R	Z	L	I	L	I	E	R	A	L	Ö	B
G	L	A	D	I	O	L	E	A	K	E	L	E	I	R
H	O	L	A	V	E	N	D	E	L	O	P	F	R	E
Z	I	N	N	I	E	R	I	Z	E	S	E	E	F	N
D	A	H	L	I	E	S	S	I	N	E	N	U	O	N
I	M	S	T	A	F	Ö	T	E	N	E	V	I	R	N
K	A	P	U	Z	I	N	E	R	K	R	E	S	S	E
L	G	Ä	L	A	V	E	L	G	R	O	I	L	Y	S
E	N	U	P	L	E	L	Ü	R	O	S	L	U	T	S
M	O	H	E	E	C	K	G	A	K	E	C	P	H	E
A	L	O	E	E	T	E	Ü	S	U	I	H	I	I	L
T	I	S	H	O	R	T	E	N	S	I	E	N	E	Ä
I	E	E	L	Ö	W	E	N	Z	A	H	N	E	E	U
S	C	H	N	E	E	G	L	Ö	C	K	C	H	E	N
F	T	R	Ä	N	E	N	D	E	S	H	E	R	Z	O

6. Was passt nicht? ✓

1. -straße: Bundes-, Einbahn-, Land-, Sack-
2. Fenster-: -laden, -rahmen, -panne, -rose
3. -vertrag: Blau-, Kauf-, Miet-, Pacht-
4. -teppich: Berber-, Decken-, Gebets-, Perser-
5. -becken: Klosett-, Schwimm-, Spül-, Wasch-

7. Was passt zusammen? Ergänzen Sie den Artikel. ✓

1. dort wird Schmutzwasser gereinigt	a. Bettvorleger
2. langer, schmaler Teppich	b. Feuerwehr
3. Straße, die um den Stadtkern verläuft	c. Gasse
4. dreieckige Abschlusswand des Satteldachs	d. Gaube
5. Beseitigung von Müll	e. Giebel
6. Fenster zum Aufschieben	f. Kläranlage
7. Mannschaften und Geräte zur Brandbekämpfung	g. Läufer
8. dort wird Müll verbrannt	h. Tapete
9. Wandverkleidung aus Papier	i. Müllverbrennungsanlage
10. ausgebautes, rechteckiges Dachfenster	j. Ringstraße
11. kleiner Teppich vor dem Bett	k. Schiebefenster
12. kleine, enge Straße	l. Müllabfuhr

8. In jedem Satz fehlt ein Wort. ✓

Badewanne, Dachrinne, Glockenturm, Grashalm, Hausapotheke, Korbmöbel,
Nebenkosten, Panoramafenster, Teppichboden, Tünche

1. Der Blick durch die großen _____ des Wohnzimmers ist traumhaft.
2. Hier genügt eine Regentonne, in der das Wasser aus der _____ aufgefangen wird.
3. Die Glocke im restaurierten _____ wird nun wieder jeden zweiten Sonntag zum Gottesdienst läuten.
4. Die weiße _____ ist schmutziggrau und der Beton bröckelt.
5. Der Vermieter kann keineswegs alle Ausgaben für das Haus als _____ an die Mieter weitergeben.
6. Die meisten Körbe und _____ sind importiert.
7. Den _____ ließen sie von Handwerkern verlegen.
8. Ich gehe jetzt nach Hause und setze mich in eine warme _____.
9. In der _____ sollte Verbandszeug nicht fehlen.
10. Hier wächst kein einziger_____.

9. Aufsatz. Wählen Sie ein Thema.
1. Beschreiben Sie Ihr Elternhaus.
2. Beschreiben Sie den Garten Ihrer Großmutter.
3. Beschreiben Sie Ihr Traumhaus.

10. Lesen Sie den folgenden Artikel.

Guter Rat für die Altbau-Sanierung ist kostenlos

Eine gebrauchte Immobilien kann trotz Charme teure Tücken haben / Bau-Experten helfen am FR-Lesertelefon

Wenn es um die Frage nach dem idealen Wohnen geht, sind sich die Deutschen (fast) einig: Das eigene Haus soll es sein, natürlich mit eigenem Garten, in ruhiger Lage, schöner Landschaft und nahe am Arbeitsplatz. Ein Neubau allerdings muss es nicht mehr unbedingt sein. Viele bevorzugen ein schönes altes Haus. Damit der Erwerb einer gebrauchten Immobilie nicht zum Albtraum wird, müssen Interessenten allerdings viele Punkte beachten. Zum Beispiel wird die Finanzierung einer Bestandsimmobilie von staatlicher Seite nicht wie ein Neubau gefördert. Außerdem können versteckte Bauschäden immense Kosten nach sich ziehen.

Die *Frankfurter Rundschau* veranstaltet deswegen zusammen mit der Bausparkasse Wüstenrot eine Leseraktion. Joachim Exler, Thomas Holzinger und Hans Sacher, drei ausgewiesene Experten, werden am kommenden Dienstag zwischen 17.30 Uhr und 19 Uhr am *FR*-Lesertelefon kostenlos Ratschläge und Tipps rund um Kauf und Sanierung von gebrauchten Immobilien geben.

Alte Häuser, so lautet oft die Vorstellung, sind solide gebaut, strahlen Charme aus und versprechen behagliches Wohnen. Sie bieten vielfach einen dauerhaften Wert für gutes Geld. Das stimmt leider nicht immer. Denn auch schöne und behaglich aussehende Häuser können Tücken haben: Nicht alle Wände sind solide gebaut. Außenputz kann locker, Innenputz feucht sein. Dachbalken sind manchmal morsch oder vom Hausbock befallen. Auch Decken, Treppen, Türen und Fenster können schadhaft sein. Nicht zu vergessen die Heizungsanlage, die sanitären Einrichtungen und die Elektroinstallation, die den Wert eines Gebäudes mitbestimmen. Bei feuchten Mauern und Schwammbildung ist Vorsicht geboten. Wüstenrot rät deshalb, vor Abschluss eines Kaufvertrages ein „Verkehrswertgutachten" einzuholen. Die Industrie- und Handelskammern helfen bei der Suche nach einem Sachverständigen.

Ein solches Wertgutachten – die Kosten sind vergleichsweise gering – bewahrt Althausfreunde davor, „die Katze im Sack" zu kaufen. Außerdem dient dieses Gutachten dem mitfinanzierenden Kreditinstitut als Nachweis dafür, bis zu welcher Höhe das Haus beleihbar ist.

Ist das Haus dann gekauft, sind oft erhebliche Renovierungsaufwendungen nötig. Auch darauf wird das Verkehrswertgutachten hinweisen. Der Hauskäufer tut gut daran, für den zusätzlichen Renovierungsaufwand vorzusorgen, und zwar in technischer wie in finanzieller Hinsicht. Zunächst sollte man einen Architekten einschalten. Mit ihm zusammen überlegt man die Modernisierungsziele, plant die nötigen Baumaßnahmen und kalkuliert die Kosten.

Der Hauseigentümer wird dann zusammen mit seinem Bausparkassenfachmann klären, welche Eigenmittel er für das Modernisierungsvorhaben zur Verfügung stellen kann oder will, wie viele Fremdmittel er aufnehmen muss und ob und welche Mittel aus Förderungsprogrammen der öffentlichen Haushalte zur Verfügung stehen. In vielen Fällen wird es zweckmäßig sein, einen Steuerberater hinzuzuziehen. Denn steuerliche Fragen spielen bei jeder Finanzierung eine erhebliche Rolle.

Dann ist der Architekt wieder am Zuge. Er wird sein Wissen in Sachen „Genehmigungsverfahren" einbringen, denn die Anforderungen der örtlichen Bauvorschriften sind vielfältig: Standsicherheit, Schall- und Wärmedämmung, Brandschutz, Dachneigung, Fenstergröße, Wohnungszuschnitt, Wohnungsnutzung, Lage der Treppe, Schornsteinquerschnitt, Art der Toilette und des Bades, Anzahl der Feuerstellen, Heizungsart – das sind Stichworte, hinter denen genehmigungspflichtige Maßnahmen stehen. Auch eine Änderung der äußeren Gestaltung durch einen neuen Anstrich, durch Verputzen oder Verfugen ist überwiegend genehmigungspflichtig.

Sind die Modernisierungsziele abgesteckt, die baurechtlichen Hürden genommen, ist das nötige Geld verfügbar, dann wird der Architekt die zweckmäßige Reihenfolge der Maßnahmen und den Zeitplan festlegen. Wenn dann die eingeholten Kostenvoranschläge kritisch verglichen worden sind, dürfen die gewählten Handwerker anrücken und Hammer, Maurerkelle und Pinsel schwingen.   kmk

Frankfurter Rundschau, Samstag, 26. Mai 2001, Nr. 121/31, S. A7

a. Vokabelübung. Wie heißt das Wort (die Wendung) auf Englisch?

1. der Albtraum
2. die Sanierung
3. die Bausparkasse
4. behaglich
5. die Tücke
6. der Dachbalken
7. morsch
8. der Sachverständige
9. die Katze im Sack
10. das Verkehrswertgutachten
11. beleihbar
12. genehmigungspflichtig

b. Schriftliche Übung. Fassen Sie den Artikel zusammen.

Unit 2

The physical world

Level 1

Mountains

Berg, der (-e)	mountain
Gebirge, das (-)	mountain range, mountains
Bergkette, die (-n)	mountain range
Mittelgebirge, das (-)	low mountains
Hochgebirge, das (-)	high mountains
gebirgig	mountainous
Hügel, der (-)	hill
Alpen, pl.	Alps
Tal, das (¨er)	valley
Stein, der (-e)	stone
Gestein, das (-e)	rock(s)

Woodlands and plains

Wald, der (¨er)	forest
Wäldchen, das (-)	grove
Waldland, das (¨er)	woodland
Urwald, der (¨er)	jungle
Dschungel, der (-), das (-), or die (-n)	jungle
Regenwald, der (¨er)	rainforest
Baum, der (¨e)	tree
Stamm, der (¨e)	trunk
Rinde, die (-n)	bark
Saft, der (¨e)	sap
Zweig, der (-e)	twig
Ast, der (¨e)	branch
Wipfel, der (-)	treetop
Eiche, die (-n)	oak
Ahorn, der (-e)	maple
Tanne, die (-n)	fir
Kiefer, die (-n)	pine
Linde, die (-n)	linden
etw fällen	to fell, cut sth down

Water

Wasser, das (- or ¨)	water
Wasserfall, der (¨e)	waterfall
Süßwasser, das (no pl.)	fresh water
Salzwasser, das (no pl.)	salt water
fließen	to flow
Fluss, der (¨e)	river
Bach, der (¨e)	creek, brook, stream
Strom, der (¨e)	large river
Strömung, die (-en)	current
Meer, das (-e)	sea
Meeresspiegel, der (no pl.)	sea level
See, die (-n)	sea
Ozean, der (-e)	ocean
See, der (-n)	lake
Teich, der (-e)	pond
Strand, der (¨e)	beach
Sand, der (-e)	sand
Ufer, das (-)	bank, shore
Küste, die (-n)	coast
Insel, die (-n)	island

Halbinsel, die (-n)	peninsula
Festland, das (no pl.)	mainland
tief	deep

flach	shallow
Brunnen, der (-)	well, fountain, spring water

Level 2

Mountains

Pass, der (¨e)	pass
Spalt, der (-e)	crevice
Höhle, die (-n)	cave
Gipfel, der (-)	peak, summit
Spitze, die (-n)	top
Höhe, die (-n)	height, altitude
Fels, der (-en)	rock
Felsen, der (-)	rock
Felsbrocken, der (-)	boulder
felsig	rocky
Felswand, die (¨e)	cliff
Felsvorsprung, der (¨e)	ledge
Berg-, Erdrutsch, der (-e)	landslide

Woodlands and plains

Ebene, die (-n)	plain
Tiefebene, die (-n)	lowland plain
Flachland, das (no pl.)	lowland, plains
Tiefland, das (¨er; also -e)	lowlands
Strauch, der (¨er)	shrub
Dickicht, das (-e)	thicket
Farn, der (-e)	fern
Moos, das (-e)	moss
Laubbaum, der (¨e)	deciduous tree
Nadelbaum, der (¨e)	coniferous tree
Fichte, die (-n)	spruce
Zeder, die (-n)	cedar
immergrün	evergreen
Nadel, die (-n)	needle
Zapfen, der (-)	cone
Eichel, die (-n)	acorn

Lichtung, die (-en)	clearing
Blöße, die (-n)	clearing
Unterholz, das (no pl.)	undergrowth

Water

Kanal, der (¨e)	canal
Nebenfluss, der (¨e)	tributary
Quelle, die (-n)	source
Mündung, die (-en)	mouth, estuary
Ebbe, die (-n)	low tide
Flut, die (-en)	high tide
Hochwasser, das (-)	high tide or water; flood
Überschwemmung, die (-en)	flood
etw überschwemmen	to flood sth
über die Ufer treten	to flood
Sturzflut, die (-en)	flash flood
Welle, die (-n)	wave
Flutwelle, die (-n)	tidal wave
Schaum, der (¨e)	foam
Gischt, der (-e) or die (-en)	foam, surf, spray
Brandung, die (-en)	surf
Schlamm, der (-e or ¨e)	mud, silt
schlammig	muddy
Sumpf, der (¨e)	marsh, swamp, quagmire
Leuchtturm, der (¨e)	lighthouse
Düne, die (-n)	sand dune
Deich, der (-e)	dyke
Damm, der (¨e)	dam
Stausee, der (-n)	reservoir, artificial lake

Level 3

Mountains

steil	steep
Steilwand, die (¨e)	steep rock face
schroff	sheer
Anhöhe, die (-n)	rise, elevation, knoll, hill
Ausläufer, pl.	foothills
Bergrücken, der (-)	mountain ridge
Tafelberg, der (-e)	mesa, flat-topped mountain
Hochebene, die (-n)	plateau
Hochland, das (¨er; also -e)	highlands
Hang, der (¨e)	slope
Gefälle, das (-)	slope, incline
Schlucht, die (-en)	ravine
Abgrund, der (¨e)	precipice, abyss
Geröll, das (-e)	scree, talus

Woodlands and plains

Grasland, das (no pl.)	grassland
Prärie, die (-n)	prairie
Heide, die (-n)	heath
Esche, die (-n)	ash
Ulme, die (-n)	elm
Holunder, der (-)	elder
Pappel, die (-n)	poplar
Zitterpappel, die (-n)	aspen
Espe, die (-n)	aspen
Birke, die (-n)	birch
Buche, die (-n)	beech

Wacholder, der (-)	juniper
Lorbeer, der (-en)	laurel
Trauerweide, die (-n)	weeping willow
Liguster, der (-)	privet
Ebenholz, das (no pl.)	ebony
Palme, die (-n)	palm
Stechpalme, die (-n)	holly
Mistel, die (-n)	mistletoe

Water

Flussaue, die (-n)	flood plain
Klamm, die (-en)	gorge
Kap, das (-s)	cape
Bucht, die (-en)	bay, cove
Golf, der (-e)	gulf
Moor, das (-e)	bog
Torf, der (-e)	peat
Böschung, die (-en)	embankment
Schwemmkegel, der (-)	levee, riverside embankment
Furt, die (-en)	ford
Landzunge, die (-n)	promontory
Tümpel, der (-)	pond
Strudel, der (-)	whirlpool, eddy
Dünung, die (-en)	swell
(Korallen)riff, der (-e)	(coral) reef
Alge, die (-n)	alga
Seetang, der (no pl.)	kelp, seaweed
Lagune, die (-n)	lagoon
Haff, das (-s or -e)	lagoon [on the Baltic]

The animal world

Level 1

Mammals

Tier, das (-e)	animal
Säugetier, das (-e)	mammal
Haustier, das (-e)	pet
zahm	tame

etw zähmen	to tame sth
Hund, der (-e)	dog
Junge(s), das (adj. decl.)	puppy, cub, kitten
Fell, das (-e)	coat of fur

Katze, die (-n)	cat, feline
Kätzchen, das (-)	kitten
Kater, der (-)	tomcat
Pferd, das (-e)	horse
Hase, der (-n)	hare
Kaninchen, das (-)	rabbit
Ratte, die (-n)	rat
Maus, die (¨e)	mouse
Eichhörnchen, das (-)	squirrel
Fuchs, der (¨e)	fox
Hirsch, der (-e)	deer, red deer, stag
Hirschkuh, die (¨e)	hind
Reh, das (-e)	deer, doe
Wildschwein, das (-e)	wild boar
Wolf, der (¨e)	wolf
Bär, der (-en)	bear
Eisbär, der (-en)	polar bear
Waschbär, der (-en)	raccoon
Elefant, der (-en)	elephant
Rüssel, der (-)	trunk
Stoßzahn, der (¨e)	tusk
Herde, die (-n)	herd
Giraffe, die (-n)	giraffe
Zebra, das (-s)	zebra
Löwe, der (-n)	lion
Tiger, der (-)	tiger
Affe, der (-n)	monkey
Nilpferd, das (-e)	hippopotamus
Nashorn, das (¨er)	rhinoceros
Kamel, das (-e)	camel
Höcker, der (-)	hump
Wal, der (-e)	whale
ein Tier füttern	to feed an animal
Futter, das (no pl.)	feed
Hundefutter, das (no pl.)	dog food
Rasse, die (-n)	breed
Schnauze, die (-n)	muzzle, snout
Maul, das (¨er)	mouth [of animals]
Schwanz, der (¨e)	tail
Pfote, die (-n)	paw

Birds

Vogel, der (¨)	bird
Feder, die (-n)	feather
Daune, die (-n)	down (feather)
Flügel, der (-)	wing
Klaue, die (-n)	claw
Schnabel, der (¨)	beak
Spatz, der (-en)	sparrow
Taube, die (-n)	dove
Specht, der (-e)	woodpecker
Kuckuck, der (-e)	cuckoo
Schwalbe, die (-n)	swallow
Krähe, die (-n)	crow
Schwan, der (¨e)	swan
Storch, der (¨e)	stork
Adler, der (-)	eagle
Eule, die (-n)	owl
Uhu, der (-s)	eagle owl
Pinguin, der (-e)	penguin
Pelikan, der (-e)	pelican
Möwe, die (-n)	seagull
Fischreiher, der (-)	heron
Kanarienvogel, der (¨)	canary
Papagei, der (-en)	parrot
Wellensittich, der (-e)	budgie [Australian parrot]
Vogelkäfig, der (-e)	bird cage
Sitzstange, die (-n)	perch

Reptiles and amphibians

Kriechtier, das (-e)	reptile
Schlange, die (-n)	snake
Giftschlange, die (-n)	poisonous snake
Eidechse, die (-n)	lizard
Chamäleon, das (-s)	chameleon
Frosch, der (¨e)	frog
Kaulquappe, die (-n)	tadpole
Kröte, die (-n)	toad
Schildkröte, die (-n)	turtle
Rückenschild, der (-e)	carapace
Alligator, der (-en)	alligator
Krokodil, das (-e)	crocodile

Fish

Fisch, der (-e)	fish
(etw) fischen	to fish (for sth)

etw angeln	to fish for sth; catch sth
Forelle, die (-n)	trout
Hering, der (-e)	herring
Karpfen, der (-)	carp
Lachs, der (-e)	salmon
Hecht, der (-e)	pike
Thunfisch, der (-e)	tuna
Aal, der (-e)	eel
Hai, der (-e)	shark
Fischgräte, die (-n)	fishbone

Molluscs, crustaceans and other deep-sea fauna

Muschel, die (-n)	mussel; shell
Kammmuschel, die (-n)	scallop
Klaffmuschel, die (-n)	clam
Auster, die (-n)	oyster
Krabbe, die (-n)	crab, shrimp, prawn
Garnele, die (-n)	shrimp, prawn
Flusskrebs, der (-e)	crayfish
Hummer, der (-)	lobster
Schnecke, die (-n)	snail
Nacktschnecke, die (-n)	slug
Schwamm, der (¨e)	sponge

Insects and worms

Insekt, das (-en)	insect
Fliege, die (-n)	fly
Mücke, die (-n)	midge, gnat
Stechmücke, die (-n)	mosquito
Biene, die (-n)	bee
Käfer, der (-)	beetle
Marienkäfer, der (-)	ladybird
Maikäfer, der (-)	May bug
Schmetterling, der (-e)	butterfly
Motte, die (-n)	moth
Spinne, die (-n)	spider
Heuschrecke, die (-n)	grasshopper, locust
Ameise, die (-n)	ant

Ameisenhaufen, der (-)	anthill
Kakerlak, der (-en)	cockroach
Küchenschabe, die (-n)	cockroach
Floh, der (¨e)	flea
Wurm, der (¨er)	worm
Regenwurm, der (¨er)	earthworm

Animal behaviour

(etw) fressen	to eat (sth) [of animals]
fliegen	to fly
kriechen	to creep, crawl
krabbeln	to crawl
pfeifen	to sing
(etw) stechen	to bite, sting (sth)
Mückenstich, der (-e)	mosquito bite
summen	to buzz
miauen	to meow
schnurren	to purr
bellen	to bark
Gebell, das (no pl.)	barking
Wauwau, der (-s)	bow-wow
knurren	to growl [dog, lion]
jmdm (or jmdn) ins Bein beißen	to bite s.o. in the leg
wiehern	to neigh
meckern	to bleat

Protection and hunting

vom Aussterben bedroht	threatened with extinction
ausgestorben	extinct
bedrohte Tierart, die (-en)	endangered species
Jagd, die (-en)	hunting, shooting
auf die Jagd gehen	to go hunting, shooting
Falle, die (-n)	trap
eine Falle für ein Tier legen/(auf)stellen	to set a trap for an animal
etw (in/mit einer Falle) fangen	to trap sth (in/with a trap)

Level 2

Mammals

Jagdhund, der (-e)	hunting dog, hound
Apportierhund, der (-e)	retriever
Blindenhund, der (-e)	guide dog
Schäferhund, der (-e)	sheep dog
Deutscher Schäferhund	German shepherd, Alsatian
schottischer Schäferhund	collie
Pudel, der (-)	poodle
Dackel, der (-)	dachshund
Leine, die (-n)	leash
Halsband, das (¨er)	collar
Maulkorb, der (¨e)	muzzle
Napf, der (¨e)	bowl [for animal's food]
Hundekuchen, der (-)	dog biscuit
einen Hund abrichten	to train a dog
Hundehütte, die (-n)	kennel, doghouse
Mieze(katze), die (-n; child lang.)	kitty
Meerschweinchen, das (-)	guinea pig
Hamster, der (-)	hamster
Wüstenspringmaus, die (¨e)	gerbil
Kaninchenbau, der (-e)	rabbit burrow
(Kaninchen)stall, der (¨e)	(rabbit) hutch
Fuchsbau, der (-e)	fox den
Fuchswelpe, der (-n)	fox cub
Kitz, das (-e)	fawn, kid
Ren(tier), das (-e)	reindeer
Elch, der (-e)	elk
Geweih, das (-e)	set of antlers
Biber, der (-)	beaver
Biberbau, der (-e)	beaver's lodge
Igel, der (-)	hedgehog
Stachelschwein, das (-e)	porcupine
Stachel, der (-n)	spine
Maulwurf, der (¨e)	mole
Maulwurfshügel, der (-)	molehill
(Riesen)panda, der (-s)	(giant) panda
Hermelin, das (-e)	ermine
Nerz, der (-e)	mink
Zobel, der (-)	sable
Pelz, der (-e)	fur
Beutelratte, die (-n)	opossum
Beutel, der (-)	pouch
Känguru, das (-s)	kangaroo
Fledermaus, die (¨e)	bat
Mähne, die (-n)	mane
Tatze, die (-n)	paw [of large animals]
Kralle, die (-n)	claw
Höhle, die (-n)	cave, den [of wild animal]
Löwenhöhle, die (-n)	lion's den
Leopard, der (-en)	leopard
Gepard, der (-e)	cheetah
Luchs, der (-e)	lynx
Puma, der (-s)	mountain lion
Pavian, der (-e)	baboon
Schimpanse, der (-n)	chimpanzee
Gorilla, der (-s)	gorilla
Robbe, die (-n)	seal
Walross, das (-e)	walrus
Otter, der (-)	otter
Pottwal, der (-e)	sperm whale
Atemloch, das (¨er)	blow hole
Delphin, der (-e)	dolphin
Tümmler, der (-)	porpoise

Birds

Brieftaube, die (-n)	homing pigeon
Rotkehlchen, das (-)	robin
Kardinal, der (¨e)	cardinal
Fink, der (-en)	finch

Distelfink, der (-en)	goldfinch
Stieglitz, der (-e)	goldfinch
Kleiber, der (-)	nuthatch
Zaunkönig, der (-e)	wren
Drossel, die (-n)	thrush
Amsel, die (-n)	blackbird
Nachtigall, die (-en)	nightingale
Lerche, die (-n)	lark
Grasmücke, die (-n)	warbler
Rabe, der (-n)	raven
Eichelhäher, der (-)	jay
Elster, die (-n)	magpie
Star, der (-e)	starling
Eisvogel, der (¨)	kingfisher
Falke, der (-n)	falcon
Habicht, der (-e)	hawk
Fasan, der (-e or -en)	pheasant
Rebhuhn, das (¨er)	partridge
Pfau, der (-en)	peacock
Flamingo, der (-s)	flamingo
Geier, der (-)	vulture

Fish

Salzwasserfisch, der (-e)	saltwater fish
Süßwasserfisch, der (-e)	freshwater fish
Seezunge, die (-n)	sole
Butt, der (-e)	flounder
Heilbutt, der (-e)	halibut
Steinbutt, der (-e)	turbot
Barsch, der (-e)	perch
Kabeljau, der (-e or -s)	cod

Molluscs, crustaceans and other deep-sea fauna

Weichtier, das (-e)	mollusc
Krebstier, das (-e)	crustacean
Krustentier, das (-e)	crustacean
Perlmuschel, die (-n)	pearl oyster
Perlmutter, die (no pl.)	mother-of-pearl
Perle, die (-n)	pearl

Tintenfisch, der (-e)	cuttlefish, squid, octopus
Qualle, die (-n)	jellyfish
Seestern, der (-e)	starfish

Insects and worms

Grille, die (-n)	cricket
Libelle, die (-n)	dragonfly
Wespe, die (-n)	wasp
Hornisse, die (-n)	hornet
Hummel, die (-n)	bumble-bee
Raupe, die (-n)	caterpillar
Seidenraupe, die (-n)	silkworm
Glühwürmchen, das (-)	firefly, glow-worm
Leuchtkäfer, der (-)	firefly
Mistkäfer, der (-)	dung beetle
Termite, die (-n)	termite
Zecke, die (-n)	tick
Schwalbenschwanz, der (¨e)	swallowtail
Weberknecht, der (-e)	daddy-long-legs [spider]

Animal behaviour

ein Netz spinnen	to spin a web
flattern	to flutter [wings; intransitive]
schweben	to hover
nisten	to nest
Nest, das (-er)	nest
Nistkasten, der (¨)	nesting box
brüten	to brood
piepen	to cheep, chirp
gackern	to cluck
etw picken	to peck sth
etw beriechen	to sniff at sth
etw beschnüffeln	to audibly sniff at sth
aufspüren	to track down
fauchen	to hiss [cat]
zischen	to hiss [goose, snake]
brüllen	to bellow [cow], roar [lion], trumpet [elephant]
brummen	to growl [bear]
quiek(s)en	to squeak, squeal

Protection and hunting

Naturpark, der (-s)	wildlife reserve
Naturschutzgebiet, das (-e)	wildlife sanctuary
die Jagd auf Federwild	shooting game birds
Großwildjagd, die (-en)	big-game hunting
Beute, die (no pl.)	bag
Walfang, der (¨e)	whaling
Walfänger, der (-)	whaler [ship]
Walfänger(in), der/die (-/nen)	whaler [person]

Level 3

Mammals

Insektenfresser, der (-)	insectivore
Nagetier, das (-e)	rodent
Beuteltier, das (-e)	marsupial
Rüsseltier, das (-e)	proboscidian
Huftier, das (-e)	ungulate
Wiederkäuer, der (-)	ruminant
Raubtier, das (-e)	carnivore
Hundeartige, pl.	Canidae
Herrentier, das (-e)	primate
Perserkatze, die (-n)	Persian cat
Siamkatze, die (-n)	Siamese cat
getigerte Katze	tabby cat
streunend	stray (adj.)
Schnurrhaar, das (-e)	whisker
eine Katze sterilisieren	to spay a cat
Wurf, der (¨e)	litter
mit Stammbaum	pedigree (adj.)
Promenadenmi- schung, die (-en; coll., hum.)	mongrel
Dogge, die (-n)	mastiff
Deutsche Dogge	Great Dane
Boxer, der (-)	boxer
Terrier, der (-)	terrier
Pekinese, der (-n)	Pekinese
Spitz, der (-e)	spitz
Eskimohund, der (-e)	husky
Windhund, der (-e)	greyhound
Afghane, der (-n)	Afghan hound
Bernhardiner, der (-)	St Bernard
Vorstehhund, der (-e)	pointer
Bluthund, der (-e)	bloodhound
Schweißhund, der (-e)	bloodhound
Dalmatiner, der (-)	Dalmatian
Rhesusaffe, der (-n)	rhesus monkey
Orang-Utan, der (-s)	orangutan
Wiesel, das (-)	weasel
Dachs, der (-e)	badger
Stinktier, das (-e)	skunk
Büffel, der (-)	buffalo
Hyäne, die (-n)	hyena
Schakal, der (-e)	jackal
Mungo, der (-s)	mongoose
Ameisenbär, der (-en)	anteater
Faultier, das (-e)	sloth

Birds

Zugvogel, der (¨)	migratory bird
Raubvogel, der (¨)	bird of prey
Greifvogel, der (¨)	diurnal bird of prey
flugunfähiger Vogel	flightless bird
Ruderfüßer, der (-)	web-footed bird
Ruderfuß, der (¨e)	webbed foot
Schwimmfuß, der (¨e)	webbed foot
Watvogel, der (¨)	wader
Singvogel, der (¨)	songbird
Schwarm, der (¨e)	flock
Schar, die (-en)	flock
Brut, die (-en)	brood
Regenpfeifer, der (-)	plover
Wachtel, die (-n)	quail
Moorhuhn, das (¨er)	grouse
Seeschwalbe, die (-n)	tern
Fischadler, der (-)	osprey

Strauß, der (-e)	ostrich
Beo, der (-s)	mynah bird
Kakadu, der (-s)	cockatoo
Ara, der (-s)	macaw
Muskelmagen, der (¨)	gizzard
(Feder)schopf, der (¨e)	crest
Gelege, das (-)	clutch of eggs

Reptiles and amphibians

Waran, der (-e)	monitor lizard
Leguan, der (-e)	iguana
Gecko, der (-s)	gecko
Natter, die (-n)	adder, viper
Ringelnatter, die (-n)	grass snake, garter snake
Klapperschlange, die (-n)	rattlesnake
Schlangenbiss, der (-e)	snakebite
Schlangenhaut, die (¨e)	snakeskin
Boa, die (-s)	boa
Kobra, die (-s)	cobra
Lurch, der (-e)	amphibian
Salamander, der (-)	salamander
Molch, der (-e)	newt

Fish

Wels, der (-e)	catfish
Bartfäden, pl.	barbels
Schellfisch, der (-e)	haddock
Stör, der (-e)	sturgeon
Sprotte, die (-n)	sprat
Elritze, die (-n)	minnow
Seepferdchen, das (-)	sea horse
(Stech)rochen, der (-)	(sting)ray
Schwertfisch, der (-e)	swordfish
Flosse, die (-n)	fin, flipper
Schwanzflosse, die (-n)	tail fin
Kieme, die (-n)	gill
Schuppe, die (-n)	scale
Schwarm, der (¨e)	shoal
Fischbrut, die (-en)	fry

Molluscs, crustaceans and other deep-sea fauna

Wellhornschnecke, die (-n)	whelk
Strandschnecke, die (-n)	winkle
Schneckenhaus, das (¨er)	snail shell
Fühler, der (-)	tentacle, feeler
Seeigel, der (-)	sea urchin
Seegurke, die (-n)	sea cucumber
Rankenfüßer, der (-)	barnacle

Insects and worms

wirbellos	invertebrate (adj.)
Schmeißfliege, die (-n)	bluebottle
Stubenfliege, die (-n)	housefly
Eintagsfliege, die (-n)	mayfly
Bremse, die (-n)	horsefly
Wanze, die (-n)	bedbug
Kokon, der (-s)	cocoon
Puppe, die (-n)	pupa
Larve, die (-n)	grub, larva
Made, die (-n)	maggot
Ohrwurm, der (¨er)	earwig
Blattlaus, die (¨e)	aphid
Skorpion, der (-e)	scorpion

Animal behaviour

sich in etw verwandeln	to metamorphose into sth
schwärmen	to swarm
Bienenschwarm, der (¨e)	swarm (of bees)
quaken	to quack [duck]; croak [frog]
krähen	to crow
krächsen	to caw
zwitschern	to chirp
gurren	to coo
schreien	to hoot
kreischen	to screech

kollern	to gobble		
sich mausern	to moult		
sich an etw krallen	to dig claws/talons into sth [cat, bird]		
die Krallen zeigen	to bare/unsheath claws		
brünstig werden/sein	to come into/be in heat		
rossig werden/sein	to come into/be in heat [mare]		
läufig werden/sein	to come into/be in heat [dog]		
rollig werden/sein	to come into/be in heat [cat]		

Protection and hunting

Tierrechte, pl.	animal rights
Tierrechtler(in), der/die (-/nen)	animal rights supporter
Tierbefreiungsfront, die (-en)	animal liberation front
Tierschutzverein, der (-e)	animal protection society
Tierschützer(in), der/die (-/nen)	animal protectionist
Tierversuch, der (-e)	animal experiment
tierische(s) Produkt, das (-e)	animal product
Robbenfang, der (¨e)	seal hunting

Weather

Level 1

General

Wetter, das (no pl.)	weather
Wetterkarte, die (-n)	weather map
Wetterlage, die (-n)	weather situation
Temperatur, die (-en)	temperature
Grad, der (-e)	degree
10 Grad Wärme/Kälte	10 degrees above/below freezing
Celsius (no art.)	centigrade, Celsius
Fahrenheit (no art.)	Fahrenheit
sinken	to fall
steigen	to rise

Sunshine

Sonne, die (-n)	sun
sonnig	sunny
scheinen	to shine
warm	warm
Wärme, die (no pl.)	warmth
heiß	hot
Hitze, die (no pl.)	heat
schwitzen	to sweat
trocken	dry
bei klarem Wetter	on a clear day

Clouds

Wolke, die (-n)	cloud
wolkig	cloudy
wolkenlos	clear
bedeckt	overcast
halbbedeckt	partly cloudy
Wolkendecke, die (-n)	cloud cover
Nebel, der (-)	fog
neblig	foggy, misty
dichter Nebel	thick fog
nebeln	to be foggy, misty

Rain

Regen, der (-)	rain
regnen	to rain
Regenwetter, das (no pl.)	rainy/wet weather
regnerisch	rainy
nass	wet
feucht	damp
Tropfen, der (-)	drop
Schauer, der (-)	shower
Regenbogen, der (-; S, AU, CH ¨)	rainbow

Snow and ice

Schnee, der (no pl.)	snow
schneeig	snowy
Schneefall, der (¨e)	snowfall
schneien	to snow
Eis, das (no pl.)	ice
eiskalt	icy cold
frisch	chilly
Kälte, die (no pl.)	cold
Frost, der (¨e)	frost
frostig	frosty
frieren	to freeze
schmelzen	to melt

Wind and storms

Wind, der (-e)	wind
windig	windy, breezy

Brise, die (-n)	breeze
wehen	to blow
blasen	to blow
Sturm, der (¨e)	storm, gale
stürmisch	stormy
stürmen	to storm
Unwetter, das (-)	storm
Gewitter, das (-)	storm, thunderstorm
Blitz, der (-e)	(flash of) lightning
es blitzt	there is (a flash of) lightning
Donner, der (-)	(clap of) thunder
Donnerschlag, der (¨e)	clap/peal of thunder
donnern	to thunder

Level 2

General

Wettervorhersage, die (-n)	weather forecast
voraussichtlich	probably
unverändert	unchanged
veränderlich	changeable
Mistwetter, das (no pl.; coll.)	lousy weather
Durchschnittstemperatur, die (-en)	average temperature
Tagestemperatur, die (-en)	day temperature
Höchsttemperatur, die (-en)	highest temperature
Tiefsttemperatur, die (-en)	lowest temperature
Wind-Kälte-Faktor, der (-en)	wind chill factor
Niederschlag, der (¨e)	precipitation
Niederschlagsgebiet, das (-e)	area of precipitation
Klima, das (-s or -te)	climate
klimatisch	climatic

Sunshine

Sonnenschein, der (no pl.)	sunshine
strahlen	to beam
Sonnenstrahl, der (-en)	sunbeam
heiter	fine, bright, fair
Aufheiterung, die (-en)	bright period
aufklaren	to clear [sky]; clear up [weather]
Warmfront, die (-en)	warm front
Hitzenwelle, die (-n)	heat wave, hot spell
glühend heiß	blazing hot
tropisch	tropical

Clouds

sich bewölken	to cloud over, become overcast
bewölkt	cloudy
dicht/stark bewölkt	heavily overcast
der Himmel ist leicht bewölkt	there is only light cloud cover
Gewitterwolke, die (-n)	storm cloud, thundercloud

Schatten, der (-)	shade
Dunst, der (¨e)	haze, mist
dunstig	misty
Nebelhorn, das (¨er)	foghorn
Nebelscheinwerfer, der (-)	fog lamp

Rain

Regenfall, der (¨e)	fall of rain
heftige Regenfälle	heavy rains
Dauerregen, der (-)	steady rain
verregnet	rainy, wet
nieseln	to drizzle
Nieselregen, der (-)	drizzle
in Strömen regnen	to pour down
(in Strömen) gießen (coll.)	to pour down
Regenguss, der (¨e)	downpour
regenarm	with little rain
regenreich	with high rainfall
regenfrei	without rain

Snow and ice

Schneeflocke, die (-n)	snowflake
schneebedeckt	snow-covered, snow-capped
Schneematsch, der (no pl.)	slush
schneeglatt	slippery with packed snow
Schneeglätte, die (no pl.)	slippery, packed snow
Glatteis, das (no pl.)	ice, black ice
Schneeregen, der (no pl.)	sleet

strenger/klirrender Frost	hard/crisp frost
hageln	to hail
Hagel, der (no pl.)	hail
Hagelkorn, das (¨er)	hailstone
Schneewehe, die (-n)	snowdrift
Schneegestöber, das (no pl.)	snow flurry
Schneeverhältnisse, pl.	snow conditions
Pulverschnee, der (no pl.)	powder snow
zufrieren	to freeze over
Gefrierpunkt, der (no pl.)	freezing point
Kaltfront, die (-en)	cold front
Kältewelle, die (-n)	cold spell
tauen	to thaw
Tauwetter, das (no pl.)	thaw
Tau, der (no pl.)	dew

Wind and storms

Windstoß, der (¨e)	gust of wind
leichter Windstoß	puff of wind
ein leichter Wind kommt auf	a breeze has sprung up
ein heftiger Wind	a gale
Gewitterfront, die (-en)	storm front
es gewittert	it's thundering
gewitt(e)rig	thundery
Gewitterneigung, die (no pl.)	likelihood of thunderstorms
Hagelschauer, der (-)	hail storm

Level 3

General

Wetterkunde, die (no pl.)	meteorology
Witterungsverhältnisse, pl.	weather conditions
Luftdruck, der (no pl.)	barometric pressure

Hoch, das (-s)	high
Tief, das (-s)	low
Tiefdruckgebiet, das (-e)	depression
Ausläufer eines Tiefs, der (-)	trough

Ausläufer eines Hochs, der (-)	ridge	niederschlagsfrei	without precipitation
Luftströmung, die (-en)	air stream	regendicht	rainproof
		es regnet sich ein	it's raining steadily
		eingeregnet	rain-bound
		Landregen, der (-)	steady rain
		anhaltender Regen	continuous rain

Sunshine

sonnenbeschienen	sunlit
sonnenüberflutet	sun-drenched
sonnenarm	with little sunshine
schwül	sultry, muggy
es ist drückend heiß	the heat is stifling
Affenhitze, die (no pl.; coll.)	scorcher
Hitzefrei haben	to have time off from school/work because of excessive heat
transpirieren (elev.)	to perspire

Snow and ice

Graupelregen, der (no pl.)	sleet
Graupel, die (-n)	small hailstone
es graupelt	soft hail is falling
(Rauh)reif, der (no pl.)	hoarfrost
rieseln	to fall gently/lightly
Harsch, der (no pl.)	frozen snow
harschen	to freeze over
Kältesturz, der (¨e)	sudden drop in temperature
Kälteeinbruch, der (¨e)	sudden onset of cold weather
Lawine, die (-n)	avalanche

Clouds

Bewölkung, die (-en)	cloud (cover)
Bewölkungsauflockerung, die (-en)	breaking up of the cloud cover
Bewölkungszunahme, die (no pl.)	increase in the cloud cover
Nebelschwaden, pl.	swathes of mist
Wolkenfetzen, der (-)	wisp of cloud
trüb	dull, dismal, grey, overcast
düster	dark; gloomy; cheerless
verhangen	overcast

Wind and storms

brausen	to roar
toben	to rage
sich legen	to die down, subside
nachlassen	to let up, die down
Orkan, der (-e)	hurricane
Taifun, der (-e)	typhoon
Wirbelsturm, der (¨e)	cyclone
Wirbelwind, der (-e)	whirlwind
Tornado, der (-s)	tornado
Auge, das (-n)	eye (of a storm)
Bö, die (-en)	gust, squall
böig	gusty
in Böen orkanartig	gusting to hurricane force
Gegenwind, der (-e)	headwind
Passatwind, der (-e)	trade wind
Föhn, der (-e)	warm, dry wind
Sturmtief, das (-s)	deep low
Flaute, die (-n)	calm
Windstille, die (no pl.)	calm

Rain

sprühen	to drizzle
Sprühregen, der (-)	drizzle, fine rain
Wolkenbruch, der (¨e)	cloudburst
wolkenbruchartig	torrential
Platzregen, der (-)	downpour, cloudburst
prasseln	to pelt down
Niederschlag, der (¨e)	rainfall
vereinzelte Niederschläge, pl.	scattered showers
niederschlagsarm	with low precipitation

Exercises

Level 1

1. Wie heißt das Gegenteil? ✓

1. das Mittelgebirge
2. das Salzwasser
3. tiefes Wasser
4. wild
5. der Kater
6. die Temperatur steigt
7. sonnig
8. die Hitze
9. frieren
10. trocken

2. Welches Wort hat die gleiche oder eine ähnliche Bedeutung? ✓

1. der Dschungel
2. die See
3. das Reptil
4. etw fischen
4. die Küchenschabe
5. blasen
6. das Unwetter

3. Wie heißt das Adjektiv? ✓

1. das Gebirge	
2. die Sonne	
3. die Wärme	
4. die Hitze	
5. die Wolke	
6. der Nebel	
7. der Regen	
8. der Schnee	
9. der Frost	
10. der Wind	
11. der Sturm	

4. Was passt zusammen? ✓

a. bellen, b. die Feder, c. der Höcker, d. der Rückenschild, e. der Rüssel, f. schnurren, g. stechen, h. summen, i. wiehern

1. der Elefant
2. die Katze
3. der Vogel
4. das Pferd
5. die Biene
6. die Stechmücke
7. der Kamel
8. der Hund
9. die Schildkröte

5. Ordnen Sie.

der Aal, der Affe, der Ast, die Auster, die Eiche, das Eichhörnchen, der Hai, die Kiefer, die Küste, das Reh, der Schwamm, der Stamm, der Strand, der Tiger, das Nashorn, der Zweig

Baum	Säugetier	Ozean

6. Erklären Sie den Unterschied.

1. die Rinde, das Rind
2. der Wal, der Wald
3. der See, die See
4. der Käfer, der Käfig
5. der Wipfel, der Gipfel
6. der Teich, der Teig
7. das Fell, der Fels
8. der Fall, die Falle

7. Ergänzen Sie. ✓

1. essen – fressen : der Mund – _____
2. die Kuh – muhen : die Katze – _____
3. der Hund – die Schnauze : der Vogel – _____
4. der Käfer – krabbeln : die Schnecke – _____
5. die Kuh – das Kalb : der Hund – _____
6. der Regen – regnen : der Schnee – _____
7. der Berg – das Hochgebirge : der Fluss – _____
8. der See – der Teich : der Fluss – _____
9. der Ozean – die Küste : der Fluss – _____
10. der Ahorn – der Baum : die Taube – _____
11. die Katze – das Kätzchen : der Frosch – _____

8. Was bedeuten die Wendungen?

1. aus einer Mücke einen Elefanten machen
2. mir fällt ein Stein vom Herzen
3. schlank wie eine Tanne
4. reden wie ein Wasserfall (coll.)
5. der große Teich (hum.)
6. wie Sand am Meer
7. da liegt der Hase im Pfeffer (coll.)
8. wo die Füchse sich gute Nacht sagen
9. ein Wolf im Schafspelz sein
10. wie ein Bär schlafen
11. weiß der Kuckuck (coll.)
12. wie ein Spatz essen
13. Eulen nach Athen tragen

14. sei kein Frosch! (coll.)
15. der Hecht im Karpfenteich sein
16. jmdm einen Floh ins Ohr setzen (coll.)

9. Übersetzen Sie ins Englische.

Die F.A.Z.-Wetterinformationen: Heute
In Mitteleuropa überwiegend sonnig und weitgehend trocken. Allerdings in
den Vogesen und Alpen einzelne gewittrige Schauer. In Portugal, Spanien und
Norditalien meist sonnig, in Süditalien und auf dem Balkan heiter bis wolkig
mit einzelnen Schauern. Auch in Rumänien und der Ukraine einzelne
Regenfälle oder Schauer, in Russland meist heiter und trocken.

Frankfurter Allgemeine Zeitung, Samstag, 26. Mai 2001, Nr. 121, Seite 22

Tierkunde: Blutrünstige Miezen

**Katzen gehorchen auch nach mehreren Tausend Jahren der
Haustierhaltung ihrem Urtrieb. Dass ihr Jagdinstinkt nun eine Gefahr
für die heimische Tierwelt darstellt, belegt ein Gutachten der
britischen Mammal Society.**

Laut einer britischen Studie fallen jährlich über 250 Millionen Tiere des
Königreiches den Raubzügen streunender Katzen zum Opfer – darunter auch
Exemplare seltener Kleintierarten. Die britische Mammal Society hat nichts
gegen Katzen – doch aufgeschreckt durch neue Erkenntnisse zum
Raubverhalten des Heim-Tigers empfiehlt sie deren Besitzern, ihre Katze
nachts im Haus zu halten oder zur Warnung potenzieller Beute mit einem
lautstarken Glöckchen oder einem elektronischen Pieper auszustatten.
Nach dem von der Gesellschaft herausgegebenen Bericht "Look What The
Cat Brought In" erlegten die fast tausend Katzen, deren Halter gebeten
worden waren, fünf Monate lang jedes angeschleppte Beutetier zu notieren,
insgesamt mehr als 14 000 Säugetiere, Vögel, Reptilien und Amphibien.
Rechnet man diese Ergebnisse auf die gut acht Millionen Hauskatzen hoch,
die in Großbritannien leben – in Deutschland sind es 6,3 Millionen –, ergibt
sich eine Zahl von jährlich über 250 Millionen Opfern.
Zwar wurden Katzen vor allem ihrem Ruf als Mäusefänger gerecht: Mäuse
rangieren ganz oben auf der Beuteliste, einschließlich der seltenen
Wasserspitz-, Schwimm- und Schlafmäuse; für letztere – für den Menschen
völlig harmlose Nager – könnte die Hauskatze allerdings einen der wichtigsten
Fressfeinde darstellen. Unter den Vögeln mussten Spatzen am häufigsten ihr
Leben lassen. Und selbst Lurche, Eidechsen und größere Tiere wie
Kaninchen, Eichhörnchen, Wiesel und Hermeline wurden erlegt. Für die
selteneren unter den Beutetieren bedeutet die Bejagung durch Hauskatzen
eine nicht zu unterschätzende Gefährdung des Artbestandes. Ratten hingegen
wurden von den Katzen meist verschmäht – wegen deren heftiger
Gegenwehr.

GEO MAGAZIN, Nr. 4/April 2001, S. 229

Level 2

1. Welches Nomen passt? ✓

1. der Gepard	a. für die Jagd abgerichteter Hund
2. die Höhle	b. Hunderasse mit krausem Fell
3. der Hundekuchen	c. dicke Schnur
4. der Jagdhund	d. Hartgebäck für Haushunde
5. die Kralle	e. Pfote von großen Tieren
6. die Leine	f. langer Haarwuchs an Kopf und Hals mancher Tiere
7. die Mähne	g. Schüssel
8. der Napf	h. Behausung wilder Tiere
9. der Pudel	i. scharfer Zehennagel von manchen Säugetieren
10. die Tatze	j. Katze und schnellstes Raubtier

2. Welches Wort hat die gleiche oder eine ähnliche Bedeutung? ✓

1. die Blöße
2. die Überschwemmung
3. der Schaum
4. der Damm
5. der Gipfel
6. der Collie
7. der Dachshund
8. das Opossum
9. der Distelfink
10. das Krebstier
11. der Leuchtkäfer
12. der Naturpark

3. Wie heißt das Nomen? ✓

1. felsig	
2. schlammig	
3. klimatisch	
4. dunstig	
5. schneeglatt	
6. gewitterig	

4. Wie heißt das Gegenteil? ✓

1. die Ebbe
2. der Laubbaum
3. die Mündung

4. Salzwasserfisch
5. regenarm
6. die Tiefsttemperatur
7. aufklaren
8. stark bewölkt
9. die Warmfront

5. Wie heißt die Tierwohnung der folgenden Tiere? ✓

1. der Hund
2. das Kaninchen
3. der Fuchs
4. der Biber
5. der Löwe
6. der Maulwurf
7. der Vogel
8. die Ameise

6. Was passt zusammen? ✓

a. das Atemloch, b. der Beutel, c. das Geweih, d. das Netz, e. die Perlmutter,
f. der Stachel

1. das Känguru
2. die Perlmuschel
3. der Elch
4. der Igel
5. der Pottwal
6. die Spinne

7. Falsche Freunde. Ergänzen Sie die Tabelle.

Deutsch	Englisch	Deutsch	Englisch
der Ahorn			acorn
der Mist			mist
der Rain			rain
der Rat			rat
die Bank			bank
die Welle			well
der Igel			eagle
der Fink			fink
der Butt			butt

8. Suchen Sie die 30 Tiere, die in der Tabelle versteckt sind (waagerecht und senkrecht). ✓

E	T	Ü	M	M	L	E	R	H	S	T	A	R	S	M	E
Z	E	C	K	E	S	C	H	O	P	I	L	Ä	N	A	I
W	Ü	S	T	E	N	S	P	R	I	N	G	M	A	U	S
E	R	H	B	R	E	C	U	N	K	T	R	H	C	L	V
B	B	A	R	S	C	H	M	I	A	E	A	E	H	W	O
E	R	B	A	C	N	I	A	S	B	N	S	I	T	U	G
R	F	I	U	H	Ü	M	R	S	E	F	M	L	I	R	E
K	L	C	N	W	N	P	V	E	L	I	Ü	B	G	F	L
N	A	H	B	E	R	A	B	E	J	S	C	U	A	A	L
E	M	T	Ä	I	C	N	E	A	A	C	K	T	L	M	E
C	I	S	R	N	E	S	H	N	U	H	E	T	L	S	R
H	N	E	I	C	H	E	L	H	Ä	H	E	R	N	E	Ö
T	G	T	I	H	E	R	M	E	L	I	N	O	N	L	N
R	O	T	K	E	H	L	C	H	E	N	R	O	B	B	E
I	T	E	Ä	N	K	E	R	F	A	L	K	E	T	T	R
S	C	H	W	A	L	B	E	N	S	C	H	W	A	N	Z

9. In jedem Satz fehlt ein Wort. ✓

Aufheiterung, beschnüffeln, brüllt, Durchschnittstemperatur, flattert, Glatteis, Nieselregen, piepen, Schneegestöber, Tauwetter, Walfang, Wettervorhersage

1. Heuschrecken zirpen, und hier und da _____ eine Elster von Steinhaufen zu Steinhaufen.
2. Wir haben seit gestern alle Arten Regen erlebt: _____ , Sprühregen, Platzregen, Schauerregen, Dauerregen.
3. Auf allen Flughäfen werden bald Drogenhunde die Urlauber bei der Einreise _____ .
4. Der finnische Langläufer kämpfte sich mit gesenktem Kopf durch das dichte _____ .
5. Die Umweltorganisation Greenpeace hat den japanischen und norwegischen _____ kritisiert.
6. 43 Prozent der Befragten achten vor einer Reise auf die _____ .
7. Die Forscher errechneten, dass im vergangenen Jahr die weltweite _____ ein halbes Grad über normal lag.
8. Vorhersage: im Osten und Süden zunehmende _____ und nur noch im Alpenraum einzelne Niederschläge.

9. Die Wände waren so dünn, dass man dahinter jeden Vogel ———————————— hören konnte.

10. Schneefälle und ———————————— haben am Montag auf deutschen Straßen die Autofahrer ins Rutschen gebracht.

11. Er ———————————— wie ein Ochse.

12. Die Wetterexperten sagen jetzt mildes ———————————— mit reichlich Regen voraus.

10. Wie heißen die Zusammensetzungen? ✓

~~Schnee-~~	schauer	1. *die Schneeverhältnisse*
Wind-	punkt	2.
Gewitter-	horn	3.
Hagel-	flut	4.
Gefrier-	~~verhältnisse~~	5.
Kälte-	front	6.
Nebel-	rutsch	7.
Pulver-	welle	8.
Sturz-	stoß	9.
Erd-	schnee	10.

11. Übersetzen Sie ins Englische.

Bald Walfleisch auf japanischen Märkten?

TOKIO, 15. Juni (AP). Japan will nach Angaben eines Zeitungsberichtes das Fleisch von Walen, die sich in den Netzen verfangen, zum Verkauf freigeben. Den Tieren müsse nach Plänen des Landwirtschaftsministeriums lediglich eine DNA-Probe zu Forschungszwecken entnommen werden, berichtete die Tageszeitung „Asahi" am Freitag. Japan hat den kommerziellen Walfang vor mehr als zehn Jahren eingestellt und lässt seither die Jagd nach Walen offiziell nur noch zu Forschungszwecken zu. Wenn sich Wale in Netzen verfangen und noch leben, müssen sie bislang wieder freigelassen werden. Viele in Netzen gestrandete Wale enden nach Angaben der Zeitung „Asahi" jedoch in Restaurants, Schätzungen zufolge sind jährlich mehr als 100 Tiere betroffen. Die internationale Walfangkommission hat Japan erlaubt, eine begrenzte Zahl von Walen zu Forschungszwecken zu jagen. Japan will damit nach eigenen Angaben die Wanderungen, Ernährungsgewohnheiten und die Zahl der Wale erforschen. Umweltgruppen und viele Staaten, darunter die Vereinigten Staaten und Großbritannien, halten dies jedoch nur für einen Vorwand, um die Jagd weiter betreiben zu können. Walfleisch gilt in Japan als Delikatesse. Nach Schätzungen werden allein in diesem Jahr rund 600 Wale von japanischen Walfängern getötet.

Frankfurter Allgemeine Zeitung, Samstag, 16. Juni 2001, Nr. 137, S. 9.

12. Lesen Sie den folgenden Text.

Leben im Extrem
Von der Kunst, die Wasserarmut in der Wüste zu überlisten

Mehr als 1/3 der Landfläche unserer Erde besteht aus Wüsten,
Wüstensteppen oder Trockensavannen (nicht gerechnet die beiden
Polargebiete). Diese nahezu vegetationslosen Gebiete hatte der Astronaut Neil
Armstrong vor Augen, als er aus dem All berichtete, dass die Landmassen
"ganz überwiegend braun" erscheinen. Ein Kriterium ist für das Phänomen
Wüste entscheidend: die Aridität, der Mangel an Wasser. In ariden Gebieten
ist die Verdunstung größer als der Niederschlag.

Das scheinbare Paradoxon erklärt sich durch Grundwasser, das an die
Oberfläche gelangt und dort verdunstet. Dabei fällt sogar Regen – nur kommt
davon kaum etwas auf dem Boden an. Denn in der Wüste sind "Geisterregen"
besonders häufig – die Tropfen verdunsten beim Fall durch die heiße Luft,
noch bevor sie die Erde erreichen.

16 Prozent der Weltbevölkerung leben in den 21 Trockengebieten der Erde,
meist in deren Randzonen. So gut wie unbewohnt sind die hyperariden
Kernräume, in denen im Durchschnitt weniger als 25 Millimeter Niederschlag
pro Jahr fallen. Tatsächlich können manche Gebiete 40 Jahre lang ohne Regen
sein, bis überraschend die statistische Niederschlagsmenge aller Trockenjahre
wolkenbruchartig auf die Erde stürzt.

In dieser extrem lebensfeindlichen Umwelt vermögen nur hoch
spezialisierte Tier- und Pflanzenarten zu bestehen. Akazien in der Sahara zum
Beispiel bohren ihre Wurzeln auf der Suche nach Grundwasser bis zu 50
Meter tief. Ohne Wurzeln kommt dagegen die kugelförmige *Bromelie
Tillandsia* latifolia aus. Sie zieht ihre Feuchtigkeit aus der nebligen Luft der
Atacama-Wüste, durch die der Wind die Pflanze treibt.

In vielen Wüsten herrscht neben Wassermangel extreme Hitze. Bis zu 52
Grad Celsius im Schatten erreicht die Temperatur in der Sahara, denn dort
brennt die Sonne ohne einen Wolkenfilter auf die Erde. Andererseits wird
ohne Wolkendecke die Wärme nicht am Boden gehalten, und das ist der
Grund für den häufigen Nachtfrost. Die maximale Schwankung zwischen
Tag- und Nachttemperatur beträgt 68 Grad Celsius.

Da es keinen Schatten spendenden Pflanzenbewuchs gibt, leben einige
Flechten in den Poren von Kalkgestein. Dort bekommen sie Licht, sind aber
vor Austrocknung geschützt. Anders die Flechte *Ramalina maciformis*, die
sogar auf glühend heißen Steinen überlebt: Sie würde erst bei 85 Grad Celsius
eingehen.

Unter den Säugetieren ist das Kamel auf besonders spektakuläre Weise an
die Wüste angepasst. Einen halben Monat kann es ohne zu trinken im heißen
Sommer durch die Sahara ziehen. Findet es dann eine Wasserstelle, schluckt
das Höckertier gleich 200 Liter in nur einer Viertelstunde. Noch wesentlich
länger vermögen einige Pflanzen ohne Wasser zu überleben. Und manche
Ephemeren hatten schon 300 Jahre ihres Daseins als Samen verbracht, ehe
Forscher sie zum Leben erweckten. Solche "Kurzzeit-Pflanzen" wachsen,
blühen und sterben innerhalb weniger Tage. Übrig bleiben neue Samen.

Wer nicht ohne Wasser gedeihen kann, der speichert es. Einige Sträucher
haben insgesamt 600 Kilometer lange Wurzelstränge, die weit verzweigt auf

etwa 1000 Quadratmetern jeden Tropfen Regenwasser aufsaugen. Auch Kakteen sind potente Wasserspeicher. Der Saguaro-Kaktus zum Beispiel sammelt in seinem dehnbaren "Stamm" und den Verzweigungen bis zu 8000 Liter. Damit kann er sich zwei trockene Jahre lang über Wasser halten.

Ausgerechnet die fast 9 Millionen Quadratkilometer große Sahara dient einem anderen Ökosystem als Quell des Lebens. Jährlich exportiert die größte Wüste der Welt Abermillionen Tonnen Staub mit den Passatwinden westwärts. Über den Urwäldern von Südamerika regnen etwa 13 Millionen Tonnen pro Regenzeit als Dünger ab. Es ist eine regelmäßige Dusche mit Kalium, Phosphor und Kalzium, ohne die der tropische Regenwald nicht lebensfähig wäre.

GEO MAGAZIN, Nr. 4/März 2000

a. Vokabelübung. Wie heißt das Wort auf Englisch?
1. die Wasserarmut
2. die Wüste
3. die Aridität
4. die Verdunstung
5. das Grundwasser
6. der Wolkenfilter
7. der Wasserspeicher

b. Schriftliche Übung. Fassen Sie den Text zusammen.

Level 3

1. Was passt zusammen? ✓

a. das Beuteltier, b. der flugunfähige Vogel, c. der Greifvogel, d. das Herrentier, e. Hundeartige, f. das Nagetier, g. das Raubtier, h. der Ruderfüßer, i. das Rüsseltier, j. der Wiederkäuer

1. der Elefant   6. der Strauß
2. das Stachelschwein   7. der Büffel
3. der Pelikan   8. der Löwe
4. die Dogge   9. der Rhesusaffe
5. das Känguru   10. der Habicht

2. Welches Wort hat die gleiche oder eine ähnliche Bedeutung? ✓

1. die Espe   7. schwitzen
2. der Teich   8. bedeckt
3. der Pointer   9. nieseln
4. der Bluthund   10. sich legen
5. der Ruderfuß   11. der Zyklon
6. der Schwarm [Vögel] 12. die Windstille

3. Welches Wort passt nicht? ✓

1. das Gelege, der Muskelmagen, die Seeschwalbe, der Wurf
2. die Kieme, der Schakal, die Schuppe, der Stör
3. der Afghane, der Bernhardiner, der Dalmatiner, der Salamander
4. die Birke, die Bucht, die Esche, der Holunder
5. die Anhöhe, der Abgrund, die Schlucht, das Tal
6. das Haff, die Lagune, der See, die Ulme
7. die Mieze, die Perserkatze, das Schnurrhaar, der Windhund
8. die Eidechse, der Leguan, der Mungo, der Waran
9. die Aufheiterung, der Landregen, das Mistwetter, der Regenguss

4. Wie heißt das Gegenteil? ✓

> a. die Bewölkungsauflockerung, b. die Bö, c. heiter, d. das Hochland, e. prasseln,
> f. sonnenarm, g. das Tief, h. die Windstille

1. die Bewölkerungszunahme
2. das Hoch
3. rieseln
4. sonnenüberflutet
5. leichter Windstoß
6. der Wind
7. düster
8. das Tiefland

5. Ergänzen Sie. ✓

1. der Regen – der Schnee : der Tau – _____
2. der Hügel – kleiner Hügel : das Hagelkorn – _____
3. das Gestein – der Bergrutsch : der Schnee – _____
4. die Katze – rollig werden : die Hündin – _____
5. der Zobel – der Pelz : die Schlange – _____
6. die Katze – die Schnurrhaare : der Wels – _____
7. das Pferd – der Schwanz : der Fisch – _____
8. die Schildkröte – der Rückenschild : die Schnecke – _____
9. der Igel – der Seeigel : das Pferd: _____

6. Ordnen Sie.

der Ara, der Beo, die Blattlaus, der Boxer, die Bremse, der Steinbutt, die Elritze,
der Fischadler, das Moorhuhn, der Ohrwurm, der Pekinese, die Promenadenmischung,
der Stechrochen, die Schmeißfliege, der Schwertfisch, die Sprotte, der Spitz, der Terrier,
die Wachtel, die Wanze

Hunde	Vögel	Fische	Insekten

7. Was heißen die Zusammensetzungen?

1. der Bedlingtonterrier, der Bullterrier, der Foxterrier, der Scotchterrier
2. die Angorakatze, die Hauskatze, die Langhaarkatze, die Tigerkatze
3. der Fleischfresser, der Insektenfresser, der Pflanzenfresser
4. der Frühlingssturm, der Sandsturm, der Schneesturm, der Staubsturm
5. die Gaswolke, die Lämmerwolke, die Parfümwolke, die Schneewolke
6. holzarm, schneearm, waldarm, wasserarm

8. In jedem Satz fehlt ein Wort. ✓

gurren, kollert, krähen, Kokon, Krallen, Maden, quaken, Robbenfang, Tierrechtler, Tierversuch, Torf

1. Deutsche Hähne _____ kikeriki, englische Hähne cock-a-doodle-do.
2. In den Bäumen zwitschern die Vögel, am Tümpel _____ die Frösche.
3. Dort nisten die Tauben; man hört sie _____ .
4. Der Truthahn _____ , das Zicklein meckert.
5. Der kleine Panther zeigte seine Zähne und _____ .
6. Für radikale _____ sind Fleischesser Mörder.
7. Viele Bewohner Grönlands leben vom Wal- und _____ .
8. Seine Arbeitsgruppe will eine Creme entwickeln, die im _____ getestet werden kann.
9. Diese _____ sind beliebtes Vogelfutter.
10. Seidenraupen spinnen aus Seide einen _____ um sich herum.
11. _____ gehört ins Moor und wird als Bodenverbesserungsmittel stark überschätzt.

9. Suchen Sie eine andere Bedeutung. Was passt zusammen? ✓

a. die Brut, b. der Dachs, c. die Eintagsfliege, d. der Hang, e. die Hyäne, f. die Puppe, g. der Schwarm, h. der Strudel

1. kurzlebige Sache
2. Kinderspielzeug
3. jmd, für den man schwärmt
4. Mehlspeise mit eingerolltem Obst
5. Gesindel
6. unerfahrener, junger Bursche
7. hemmungslos gieriger Mensch
8. Neigung, Vorliebe

10. Was bedeuten die Wendungen?

1. die Puppen tanzen lassen (coll.)
2. seine Fühler ausstrecken

3. wie ein Wiesel laufen
4. eine Natter am Busen nähren
5. jmdn auf die Palme bringen (coll.)

11. Wählen Sie eins der folgenden Themen für eine Pro- und Kontra-Diskussion.
1. der Walfang
2. Tierrechte und Tierversuche
3. der Holzeinschlag und bedrohte Tierarten

12. Lesen Sie den folgenden Textausschnitt.

Dolomiten: Auf Klettersteigen in die Höhe

Viele halten es für großen Unfug, die Berge für Nichtkletterer in Eisen zu verpacken und so begehbar zu machen. Die Dolomiten sind mit ihren 90 Klettersteig-Routen ein Paradies für Bergbegeisterte. Dank Leitern, Stahlseilen und Eisenklammern sind hier Touren zu 3000 Meter hohen Zielen auch für Anfänger möglich.

Ein Text von Julica Jungehülsing

Luft. Unter meinen Sohlen ist nichts als dünne Luft. Und ein dünner Eisenhaken. <u>Dann kommt ziemlich lange gar nichts und irgendwo gut 100 Meter tiefer eine Geröllhalde.</u> Meine Knie fühlen sich an wie schlappe Gummibälle, mit ausgebreiteten Armen klammere ich mich an Fels und Seil und gebe ein extrem unelegantes Bild ab. Fotograf Guido ist da offensichtlich anderer Meinung: <u>Er turnt in 2500 Meter Höhe auf einem grausam bröselig wirkenden Felsvorsprung herum und richtet seine Kamera auf die Szene.</u> Unten klicken die Karabiner nachsteigender Kletterer, weiter oben wird die Aussicht bestaunt: »Schau mal, wie die Wolken durch die Zinnen ziehen, ist es nicht aufregend schön?« Großartig, ganz bestimmt. <u>Aber ich habe beschlossen, für eine Weile weder in den Abgrund da unten noch über meine Schulter ins Dolomiten-Panorama zu blicken.</u> Der Aufstieg über Felskanten und die senkrecht am Hang verankerten Leitern und Eisenstifte deckt meinen Bedarf an Aufregung vollkommen.

Via Ferrata – Der Weg aus Eisen

Dabei ist es doch bloß ein Klettersteig, über den Fotograf Guido Mangold, Bergführer Roland Pramstaller und ich die 2790 Meter hohe Nordöstliche Cadinspitze bezwingen wollen. Eine der fast 500 durch Stahlseile, Leitern und Krampen gesicherten Alpen-Routen – auch »Vie Ferrate« genannt –, über die richtige Kletterer meist verächtlich die Nase rümpfen. <u>Könner, die allein mit Pickel, Haken und Seil steile Felswände meistern, halten es für »einen großen Schmäh«, die Berge für Nichtkletterer in Eisen zu verpacken.</u> Manche kritisieren die Naturverschandelung, andere, dass künstliche Sicherungen leichtsinnige Halbschuhtouristen in Regionen locken, in denen sie mangels Können, Kraft und Kondition nichts verloren haben.
   Trotzdem: <u>Tausenden von Bergbegeisterten ermöglichen die Steige, sich relativ risikofrei in einer Landschaft aus Scharten, Graten, wilden Wänden zu</u>

bewegen, die sie ohne die präparierten Anlagen nie erleben würden. Und für einige bilden die »Vie Ferrate« eine Art Einstiegsdroge zum wahren Klettern. Reinhold Messner widersprach den Kritikern mit einem anderen Argument: »Ich bin so vielen glücklichen Menschen auf den Steigen begegnet«, sagte der Südtiroler Extrembergsteiger einmal, »dass ich einfach dafür sein muss.«

Vom puren Glücksgefühl sind wir auf den »Via Merlone«-Leitern an der Cadinwand noch ein Stück entfernt. Ich mühe mich damit ab, meine Schnapp-Karabiner immer wieder in den nächsthöheren Seilabschnitt zu hakeln, gleichzeitig tapfer aufzusteigen und nicht darüber nachzudenken, dass der schmale Grat da oben anscheinend ins Leere führt. Macht er dann aber nicht, er bringt uns vielmehr zu einem schottrigen Hang, auf dem sich eine Gruppe junger Polen zum Verschnaufen in der Sonne niedergelassen hat. Ausgezeichnete Idee. Zwar trainiere ich seit Monaten sechsmal pro Woche Kraft und Ausdauer und rauche nur noch jede dritte Zigarette, aber so eine Klettertour ist anstrengender als alles, was ich bisher gemacht habe.

Roland hält jedoch wenig von Atempausen kurz vor dem Gipfel: »Na, kimmst?« – »Nö, lass mal . . .« Wenn ich es recht überlege, brauche ich eigentlich keinen Stempel im Gipfelbuch, und ohnehin sieht das, was mein Bergführer da einen »schönen Kamin nach oben« nennt, in meinen Augen wie eine Höllenscharte aus. Nee Jungs, gewiss nett, euer Gipfel, aber mir reicht's. »Das geht jetzt schon«, sagt Roland – mit der Betonung auf »schon« –, klickt seinen Karabiner in meinen Karabiner und nimmt mich wie ein trotziges Kind sanft, aber bestimmt an Hand und Leine.

Psychogener Höhenschwindel und eine herrliche Sicht

Es geht dann tatsächlich, und der Lohn der Angst ist herrlich. Die Sextener Dolomiten präsentieren sich vom Gipfel aus wie eine Panorama-Postkarte, nur schöner, weil echt. Bilderbuchwolken ziehen hinter der Großen Zinne auf, irgendwo sehr weit unten glitzert blaugrün der Dürrensee, und dann beginnt es ganz sanft und friedlich zu schneien. Im Juli. Guido freut sich über das dramatische Licht, Roland drängt zum Abstieg, weil in der Ferne ein Donner grollt, und ich ertappe mich dabei, etwas debil vor mich hinzukichern.

Ist sie das nun, jene »kritiklose Fröhlichkeit«, vor der Klettersteigkenner und Buchautor Paul Werner gewarnt hat? Sie gilt als Symptom der Höhenkrankheit, anzutreffen ab zwei- bis dreitausend Metern, und geht einher mit Ohrensausen. Nein, mein nervöses Kichern gilt wohl eher der Tatsache, nun wieder mehr als 300 Sprossen senkrecht hinabsteigen zu müssen. Und derlei Aussichten lösen schlimmstenfalls den »psychogenen Höhenschwindel« aus – laut Werner ein »instinkthafter Schutzreflex« oder »ängstlich gefärbtes Unwohlsein«. Der Experte hält das für überwindbar. Meine Seilschaft kennt dergleichen ohnehin nicht: »Das geht jetzt schon«, höre ich nur, womit Bergführer Roland wieder mal recht behält; denn irgendein mitfühlender Wettergott verwandelt den Schnee weiter unten in dichten Nebel. Wie wunderbar: statt messerscharfer Abgründe nur noch graue Suppe, in der Tiefblicke kurz unter den eigenen Fußsohlen enden.

Nie zuvor, darauf wette ich meinen Steinschlaghelm, hat jemandem Linas göttlicher Apfelstrudel im Rifugio Fonda-Savio besser geschmeckt als mir nach geglücktem Abstieg vom Cima Cadin di Nord-Est. Auf dem Marsch von der Hütte zum Auto treibt Roland uns im Bergziegen-Tempo durch sturzbachartigen Regen talwärts, es wird dunkel, die Pfützen sind schlammig, die Steine glitschig. Sei's drum – ich grinse trotz alledem breit vor mich hin: geschafft, überlebt, großartig – mehr davon ...

GEO SAISON, Nr. 7/Juli/August 2001

a. Übersetzen Sic ins Englische die zehn Sätze (Satzteile), die im Text unterstrichen sind.

b. Fragen.
   1. Wer sind Guido, Roland und Julica?
   2. Wie hat sich Julica auf die Klettertour vorbereitet?
   3. Was macht Julica nach dem Abstieg?

c. Schriftliche Übung. Fassen Sie den Text zusammen.

Unit 3

The human body and health

Level 1

General

Haut, die (¨e)	skin
Fleisch, das (no pl.)	flesh
Blut, das (no pl.)	blood
Blutgruppe, die (-n)	blood group
(Blut)kreislauf, der (¨e)	circulation
Durchblutung, die (no pl.)	flow of blood
Muskel, der (-n)	muscle
Nerv, der (-en)	nerve

Head

Kopf, der (¨e)	head
Gesicht, das (-er)	face
Haar, das (-e)	hair
Stirn, die (-en)	forehead
Ohr, das (-en)	ear
Auge, das (-n)	eye
Nase, die (-n)	nose
Wange, die (-n)	cheek
Backe, die (-n)	cheek
Mund, der (¨er)	mouth
Lippe, die (-n)	lip
Zunge, die (-n)	tongue
Zahn, der (¨e)	tooth
Kinn, das (-e)	chin
Hals, der (¨e)	neck, throat

Body

Körper, der (-)	body
Rücken, der (-)	back

Schulter, die (-n)	shoulder
Brust, die (¨e)	chest; breast
Busen, der (-)	bosom, bust
Bauch, der (¨e)	abdomen

Limbs

Arm, der (-e)	arm
Ell(en)bogen, der (-)	elbow
Hand, die (¨e)	hand
Handgelenk, das (-e)	wrist
Faust, die (¨e)	fist
Finger, der (-)	finger
Daumen, der (-)	thumb
Bein, das (-e)	leg
Knie, das (-)	knee
Fuß, der (¨e)	foot
Zehe, die (-n)	toe

Internal organs

Organ, das (-e)	organ
innere Organe, pl.	internal organs
Lunge, die (-n)	lung
Atem, der (no pl.)	breath
(etw) atmen	to breathe (sth)
(etw) ein-, ausatmen	to breathe (sth) in/out
Herz, das (-en)	heart
Leber, die (-n)	liver
Magen, der (- or ¨)	stomach
Niere, die (-n)	kidney

Skeleton

Skelett, das (-e)	skeleton
Knochen, der (-)	bone
Gelenk, das (-e)	joint
Schädel, der (-)	skull
Kiefer, der (-)	jaw
Rippe, die (-n)	rib

Sexual organs

Geschlechtsorgane, pl.	sex organs
Scham, die (no pl.; euph.)	private parts
Penis, der (-se or Penes)	penis
Glied, das (-er)	penis
männliches Glied	penis
Schwanz, der (¨e; coll.)	penis
Scheide, die (-n)	vagina
Kitzler, der (-)	clitoris

Symptoms, ailments and illnesses

krank	sick
Krankheit, die (-en)	disease, sickness, illness
an etw erkrankt sein	to be ill/down with sth
sich erkälten	to catch a cold
Erkältung, die (-en)	cold
erkältet sein	to have a cold
Schnupfen, der (-)	cold
Fieber, das (-)	fever
Fieber haben	to have a fever/temperature
gesund	healthy
Gesundheit, die (no pl.)	health
Grippe, die (-n)	flu
Husten, der (no pl.)	cough
husten	to cough
niesen	to sneeze
verstopft	congested
Virus, das (Viren)	virus
wehtun	to hurt, be sore

jmdn/sich verletzen	to injure sb/o.s.
Verletzung, die (-en)	injury
Wunde, die (-n)	wound
(Knochen)bruch, der (¨e)	fracture
blauer Fleck	bruise
blaue Flecken bekommen	to bruise
Narbe, die (-n)	scar
Blase, die (-n)	blister
Röte, die (no pl.)	redness
jucken	to itch
juckend	itchy
Juckreiz, der (no pl.)	itch
sich etw brechen	to break sth
sich etw verstauchen	to sprain sth
Verstauchung, die (-en)	sprain
jmdn/sich schneiden	to cut sb/o.s.
sich in den Finger stechen	to prick one's finger
bluten	to bleed
Stich, der (-e)	sting, insect bite, stitch
übel	nauseous, queasy
Übelkeit, die (-en)	nausea
Brechreiz, der (no pl.)	nausea
Brechreiz verspüren	to feel nauseous
schwellen	to swell
geschwollen	swollen
Schmerz, der (-en)	pain
schmerzhaft	painful
Kopfschmerzen, pl.	headache
Kofpweh, der (no pl.; coll.)	headache
Migräne, die (-n)	migraine
Halsschmerzen, pl.	sore throat
Ohrenschmerzen, pl.	earache
Bauchschmerzen, pl.	stomachache
Was fehlt Ihnen/dir?	What's the matter?
klagen	to complain
Herzanfall, der (¨e)	heart attack
Herzinfarkt, der (-e)	heart attack, cardiac infarction

Herzstillstand, der (¨e)	cardiac arrest	Ansteckung, die (-en)	infection
Schlaganfall, der (¨e)	stroke	blaues Auge	black eye
(sich) erbrechen	to vomit, be sick	Verstopfung, die (-en)	constipation; blockage
Erbrechen, das (no pl.)	vomiting	deprimiert	depressed
brechen (coll.)	to vomit	Depression, die (-en)	depression
sich übergeben	to vomit	Geisteskrankheit, die (-en)	mental illness
spucken (coll.)	to be sick, throw up, vomit	geisteskrank	mentally ill
Durchfall, der (¨e)	diarrhoea	Nervenzusam-menbruch, der (¨e)	nervous breakdown
zittern	to shiver	Stress, der (-e)	stress
schwitzen	to sweat	Angst, die (¨e)	fear, anxiety
Schweiß, der (no pl.)	sweat	Schock, der (-s or -e)	shock
in kalten Schweiß ausbrechen	to break out in a cold sweat	Schlaflosigkeit, die (no pl.)	insomnia
Krebs, der (-e)	cancer	Schläfrigkeit, die (no pl.)	drowsiness
Lungenentzündung, die (-en)	pneumonia	menstruieren	to menstruate
eine Lungen-entzündung holen	to catch pneumonia	Periode, die (-n)	period
Geschwür, das (-e)	ulcer, growth	Schwanger-schaftsabbruch, der (¨e)	abortion
geschwürig	ulcerous		
ansteckend	infectious, contagious	Abtreibung, die (-en)	abortion

Level 2

General

Blutgefäß, das (-e)	blood vessel	(Augen)lid, das (-er)	(eye)lid
Blutader, die (-n)	vein	Augapfel, der (¨)	eyeball
Halsblutader, die (-n)	jugular vein	Augenbraue, die (-n)	eyebrow
Schlagader, die (-n)	artery	Wimper, die (-n)	eyelash
Sehne, die (-n)	tendon	Nasenloch, das (¨er)	nostril
Achillessehne, die (-n)	Achilles tendon	Speichel, der (no pl.)	saliva
Pore, die (-n)	pore	Schneidezahn, der (¨e)	incisor
		Backenzahn, der (¨e)	molar
		Kehle, die (-n)	throat
Head		Nacken, der (-)	nape of the neck
Gehirn, das (-e)	brain		
Kopfhaut, die (¨e)	scalp		
Ohrläppchen, das (-)	earlobe	**Body**	
Bart, der (¨e)	beard	Rumpf, der (¨e)	torso
Schnurrbart, der (¨e)	mustache	Achsel, die (-n)	shoulder, armpit
		Achselgrube, die (-n)	armpit

Achselhöhle, die (-n)	armpit
Taille, die (-n)	waist
Hüfte, die (-n)	hip
Gesäß, das (-e)	backside

Limbs

Glied, das (-er)	limb
Oberarm, der (-e)	upper arm
Unterarm, der (-e)	lower arm
Armbeuge, die (-n)	inside of one's arm
Zeigefinger, der (-)	index finger
Mittelfinger, der (-)	middle finger
Ringfinger, der (-)	ring finger
kleiner Finger	little finger
Fingerspitze, die (-n)	finger tip
Mittelzehe, die (-n)	middle toe, third toe
große/kleine Zehe	big/little toe
zweite/vierte Zehe	second/fourth toe

Internal organs

Luftröhre, die (-n)	windpipe (trachea)
Speiseröhre, die (-n)	oesophagus
Darm, der (¨e)	intestine(s)
Dünndarm, der (¨e)	small intestine
Dickdarm, der (¨e)	large intestine
Blinddarm, der (¨e)	caecum, appendix
Mastdarm, der (¨e)	rectum
Gallenblase, die (-n)	gall bladder
Harnblase, die (-n)	bladder

Skeleton

Jochbein, das (-e)	cheekbone
Wirbelsäule, die (-n)	spinal column
Schlüsselbein, das (-e)	collarbone
Schulterblatt, das (¨er)	shoulder blade
Brustkorb, der (¨e)	thorax, chest
Brustbein, das (-e)	breastbone (sternum)
Stießbein, das (-e)	tailbone (coccyx)
Hüftbein, das (-e)	hip bone
Kniescheibe, die (-n)	kneecap

Senses

Sinn, der (-e)	sense
Geruchssinn, der (no pl.)	sense of smell
Tastsinn, der (no pl.)	sense of touch
Gefühlssinn, der (no pl.)	sense of touch
Geschmackssinn, der (no pl.)	sense of taste
Sehvermögen, das (no pl.)	sense of sight
Gehörsinn, der (no pl.)	sense of hearing
blind	blind
kurzsichtig	shortsighted, nearsighted
weitsichtig	longsighted, farsighted
schwerhörig	hard of hearing
gehörlos	deaf
taub	deaf
taubstumm	deaf mute

Symptoms, ailments and illnesses

Symptom, das (-e)	symptom
Leiden, das (-)	illness, complaint
an/unter etw leiden	to suffer from sth
eine Krankheit auf jmdn übertragen	to pass a disease on to sb
etw liegt in der Familie	there is a family history of sth
Cholesterin, das (no pl.)	cholesterol
Cholesterinspiegel, der (-)	cholesterol level
Kreislaufstörung, die (-en)	circulatory problem
sich entzünden	to become inflamed
Entzündung, die (-en)	inflammation
ein stechender Schmerz	a stab of pain
ein bohrender Schmerz	a gnawing pain

heftiger Schmerz	severe pain	Koma, das (-s)	coma
zum Platzen voll sein	to feel bloated	im Koma liegen	to be in a coma
sich einen Muskel zerren	to pull a muscle	ins Koma fallen	to go into a coma
		Geschwulst, die (¨e)	tumour
Muskelkater, der (-)	sore muscles		
einen steifen Nacken haben	to have a stiff neck	gutartig	benign
		bösartig	malignant
Muskelriss, der (-e)	torn muscle	Brustkrebs, der (no pl.)	breast cancer
Bluthochdruck, der (no pl.)	high blood pressure		
		Hautkrebs, der (no pl.)	skin cancer
Blutung, die (-en)	bleeding, haemorrhage	AIDS (Aids), das (no pl.)	AIDS
Blutarmut, die (no pl.)	anaemia	Aidskranke(r), der/die (adj. decl.)	person suffering from AIDS
blutarm	anaemic	HIV, der or das (no pl.)	HIV
Blutbild, das (-er)	blood count		
kränklich	sickly	HIV-positiv	HIV-positive
schwer/ernstlich/ unheilbar krank	seriously/critically/ terminally ill	HIV-infiziert	HIV-infected
		Geschlechtskrankheit, die (-en)	sexually transmitted disease
Lebensgefahr, die (no pl.)	critical condition, mortal danger	Kopfläuse, pl.	head lice
durchkommen	to pull through	Nisse, die (-n)	nit
sich von etw erholen	to recover from sth	Akne, die (no pl.)	acne
Bruchstelle, die (-n)	break	Schuppen, pl.	dandruff
Kieferbruch, der (¨e)	fractured jaw	Kahlheit, die (no pl.)	baldness
komplizierter Bruch	compound fracture		
Fissur, die (-en)	hairline fracture	Fußpilz, der (-e)	athlete's foot
Hustenanfall, der (¨e)	coughing fit	Leberflecke, die (-n)	mole
heiser	hoarse	Warze, die (-n)	wart
Schwäche, die (-n)	weakness, faintness	Atembeschwerden, pl.	breathing problems
schwind(e)lig	dizzy		
Schwindel, der (no pl.)	dizziness	Lungenkollaps, der (no pl.)	collapsed lung
Schwindelgefühl, das (-e)	feeling of dizziness	Heuschnupfen, der (no pl.)	hay fever
Ohnmacht, die (-en)	faint	Allergie, die (-n)	allergy
in Ohnmacht fallen/sinken	to faint	allergisch gegen etw sein	to be allergic to sth
zusammenbrechen	to collapse	Ausschlag, der (¨e)	rash
ohnmächtig	unconscious	Kinderlähmung, die (no pl.)	polio
Bewusstlosigkeit, die (no pl.)	unconsciousness		
		Tuberkulose, die (-n)	tuberculosis
bewusstlos	unconscious	Zuckerkrankheit, die (-en)	diabetes
betäubt	drugged		
Überdosis, die (-dosen)	overdose	zuckerkrank	diabetic

übermüdet	overtired	(schwer) herzkrank sein	to have a (serious) heart condition
Ermüdung, die (no pl.)	fatigue	Herzkrankheit, die (-n)	heart condition
sich überarbeiten	to overwork oneself		
angeschlagen	exhausted, under the weather	Herzversagen, das (no pl.)	heart failure
bettlägerig	bed-ridden	Nierenversagen, das (no pl.)	kidney failure
wieder auf die Beine kommen	to get back on one's feet	Syndrom, das (-e)	syndrome
Mandelentzündung, die (-en)	tonsillitis	prämenstruelles Syndrom	premenstrual syndrome
Mumps, der (no pl.)	mumps	Krampf, der (¨e)	cramp, spasm, convulsion
Masern, pl.	measles		
Röteln, pl.	German measles	krampfartig	convulsive, spasmodic
Windpocken, pl.	chicken pox		
Wundstarrkrampf, der (no pl.)	tetanus	Krampfader, die (-n)	varicose vein
		Gelenkentzündung, die (-en)	arthritis
Blutvergiftung, die (-en)	blood poisoning		
Lebensmittelvergiftung, die (-en)	food poisoning	Asthma, das (no pl.)	asthma
		Remission, die (-en)	remission
		remittieren	to go into remission
Nierensteine, pl.	kidney stones	Rückfall, der (¨e)	relapse
Gallenstein, der (-e)	gallstone	einen Rückfall bekommen/erleiden	to relapse
Blinddarmentzündung, die (-en)	appendicitis		
behindert	disabled	Wehen, pl.	labour
Schwerbeschädigte(r), der/die (adj. decl.)	severely disabled person	in den Wehen liegen	to be in labour
		Sonnenstich, der (-e)	sunstroke
		ausgetrocknet	dehydrated

Level 3

Head

Scheitel, der (-)	top of the head	Sehnerv, der (-en)	optic nerve
Trommelfell, das (-e)	eardrum	Gaumen, der (-)	palate
Gehörgang, der (¨e)	auditory canal	weicher/harter Gaumen	soft/hard palate
Schläfe, die (-n)	temple		
Grübchen, das (-)	dimple	Zäpfchen, das (-)	uvula
Sommersprosse, die (-n)	freckle	Wurzel, die (-n)	root
		Krone, die (-n)	crown
Regenbogenhaut, die (¨e)	iris	Zahnschmelz, der (no pl.)	enamel
Pupille, die (-n)	pupil	Gebiss, das (-e)	set of false teeth
Hornhaut, die (¨e)	cornea	Kehlkopf, der (¨e)	larynx
Netzhaut, die (¨e)	retina	Stimmband, das (¨er)	vocal cord

Body

Leib, der (-er)	body
Leiste, die (-n)	groin
Nabel, der (-n)	navel
Kreuz, das (-e)	small of the back
Brustwarze, die (-n)	nipple
Warzenhof, der (¨e)	areola

Limbs

Handteller, der (-)	palm of the hand
Daumenballen, der (-)	ball of the thumb
Fingerglied, das (-er)	phalange
Fingerbeere, die (-n)	finger pad
Handrücken, der (-)	back of the hand
Oberschenkel, der (-)	thigh
Kniekehle, die (-n)	hollow of the knee
Unterschenkel, der (-)	shank
Wade, die (-n)	calf
Ballen, der (-)	ball of the foot
Knöchel, der (-)	ankle; knuckle
Fußrücken, der (-)	instep
Fußsohle, die (-n)	sole of the foot
Ferse, die (-n)	heel

Internal organs

Schilddrüse, die (-n)	thyroid gland
Zungenbein, das (-e)	hyoid bone
Bronchie, die (-n)	bronchial tube
Zwerchfell, das (-e)	diaphragm
Milz, die (-en)	spleen
Bauchspeicheldrüse, die (-n)	pancreas
Wurmfortsatz, der (¨e)	appendix
After, der (-)	anus
Schließmuskel, der (-n)	anal sphincter
Harnleiter, der (-)	ureter

Skeleton

Oberarmbein, das (-e)	humerus
Speiche, die (-n)	radius
Elle, die (-n)	ulna

Handwurzelknochen, der (-)	carpal bone
Mittelhandknochen, der (-)	metacarpal bone
Becken, das (-)	pelvis
Sitzbein, das (-e)	ischium
Schambein, das (-e)	pubis
Kreuzbein, das (-e)	sacrum
Oberschenkelbein, das (-e)	femur
Wadenbein, das (-e)	fibula
Schienbein, das (-e)	shinbone (tibia)
Fußwurzelknochen, der (-)	tarsal bone
Vorfußknochen, der (-)	metatarsal bone
Zehenknochen, der (-)	phalange
Fersenbein, das (-e)	heel bone

Sexual organs

Vorhaut, die (¨e)	foreskin
Hoden, der (-)	testicle
Hodensack, der (¨e)	scrotum
Vorsteherdrüse, die (-n)	prostate gland
Gebärmutter, die (¨)	uterus
Eileiter, der (-)	fallopian tube
Eierstock, der (¨e)	ovary
Gebärmutterhals, der (¨e)	cervix
Schamlippe, die (-n)	labium
Vulva, die (Vulven)	vulva

Symptoms, ailments and illnesses

von etw befallen sein	to be afflicted with sth
Beschwerden, pl.	discomfort
Sodbrennen, das (no pl.)	heartburn
Magenbeschwerden, pl.	stomach trouble
magenkrank	dyspeptic
Magenblutung, die (-en)	gastric haemorrhage

Blutgerinnsel, das (-)	blood clot	Hühnerauge, das (-n)	corn
gerinnen	to clot	Hautausschlag, der (¨e)	eczema
Botulismus, der (no pl.)	botulism	Hautentzündung, die (-en)	dermatitis
Salmonelle, die (-n)	salmonella	Schuppenflechte, die (no pl.)	psoriasis
Leukämie, die (-n)	leukaemia		
Bluterkrankheit, die (no pl.)	haemophilia	Eiter, der (no pl.)	pus
Bluter(in), der/die (-/nen)	haemophiliac	Abszess, der (-e)	abscess
		wunde Stelle, die (-n)	sore, abrasion
Drüsenfieber, das (no pl.)	glandular fever	wundgelegene Stelle, die (-n)	bed sore
Scharlach, der (no pl.)	scarlet fever	etw abschürfen	to graze sth
		Prellung, die (-en)	contusion
Krupp, der (no pl.)	croup	Gürtelrose, die (no pl.)	shingles
Zyste, die (-n)	cyst	schielen	to squint
Polyp, der (-en)	polyp	Astigmatismus, der (no pl.)	astigmatism
Kropf, der (¨e)	goitre		
Herzrhythmusstörung, die (-en)	arrhythmia	Star, der (-e)	group of eye diseases
Herzgeräusch, das (-e)	heart murmur	grauer Star	cataract
		grüner Star	glaucoma
Thrombose, die (-n)	thrombosis	Gerstenkorn, das (¨er)	sty
Embolie, die (-n)	embolism	Bindehautentzündung, die (-en)	conjunctivitis
Arterienverkalkung, die (-en)	arteriosclerosis		
Kehlkopfentzündung, die (-en)	laryngitis	Bakterium, das (Bakterien)	bacterium
Nebenhöhlenentzündung, die (-en)	sinusitis	Milzbrand, der (no pl.)	anthrax
karzinogen	carcinogenic	Pocken, pl.	smallpox
kanzerogen	carcinogenic	Cholera, die (no pl.)	cholera
Magengeschwür, das (-e)	stomach/gastric ulcer	Malaria, die (no pl.)	malaria
		Aussatz, der (no pl.)	leprosy
Blasenentzündung, die (-en)	cystitis	Epidemie, die (-n)	epidemic
Demenz, die (-en)	dementia	Schizophrenie, die (-n)	schizophrenia
Alzheimerkrankheit, die (no pl.)	Alzheimer's disease	schizophren	schizophrenic
		posttraumatisch	post-traumatic
Aphasie, die (-n)	aphasia	sich etw aus-, verrenken	to dislocate sth
Gewebe, das (-)	tissue		
Narbengewebe, das (-)	scar tissue	etw luxieren	to dislocate sth
		Luxation, die (-en)	dislocation
Furunkel, der (-) or das (-)	boil	Bandscheibenvorfall, der (¨e)	slipped disc

Osteoporose, die (-n)	osteoporosis	Skorbut, der	scurvy
Downsyndrom, das	Down's syndrome	(no pl.)	
(no pl.)		Inkontinenz, die	incontinence
Geburtsfehler, der (-)	birth defect	(no pl.)	
Gaumenspalte,	cleft palate	inkontinent	incontinent
die (-n)		Gehirnblutung,	cerebral
Hasenscharte,	hare lip	die (-en)	haemorrhage
die (-n)		Gehirnerschütterung,	concussion
Klumpfuß, der (¨e)	club foot	die (-en)	
Autismus, der (no pl.)	autism	Gehirnhaut-	meningitis
autistisch	autistic	zündung, die (-en)	
(Scheiden)ausfluss,	vaginal discharge	Epilepsie, die (no pl.)	epilepsy
der (no pl.)		epileptisch	epileptic
Fehlgeburt, die (-en)	miscarriage	Lämung, die (-en)	paralysis
Eileiterschwanger-	tubal pregnancy	querschnittsgelähmt	paraplegic
schaft, die (-en)		Querschnittslähmung,	paraplegia
ektopische	ectopic pregnancy	die (-en)	
Schwangerschaft		Keuchhusten, der	whooping cough
(Schwangerschafts)	morning sickness	(no pl.)	
übelkeit, die (-en)		Bronchitis, die	bronchitis
Wochenbettdepression,	post-partum	(Bronchitiden)	
die (-en)	depression	Stechen, das (-)	twinge, sharp pain
Gelbsucht, die	jaundice	pochend	throbbing
(no pl.)		prickelnd	tingling
Rachitis, die (no pl.)	rickets	brennend	tingling

The health service and medicine

Level 1

Medical personnel and specialities		Krankenpfleger(in),	nurse
Medizin, die	medicine	der/die (-/nen)	
(no pl.)		Facharzt, der (¨e);	(medical) specialist
Heilkunde, die	medicine	Fachärztin, die	
(no pl.)		(-nen)	
Arzt, der (¨e); Ärztin,	doctor	einen Facharzt zu	to consult a specialist
die (-nen)		Rate ziehen	
Hausarzt, der (¨e);	family doctor	Kinderarzt, der (¨e);	paediatrician
Hausärztin,		Kinderärztin,	
die (-nen)		die (-nen)	
Doktor(in), der/die	doctor	Kinderheilkunde, die	paediatrics
(-en/nen)		(no pl.)	
Krankenschwester,	(female) nurse	Frauenarzt, der (¨e);	gynaecologist
die (-n)		Frauenärztin,	
		die (-nen)	

Frauenheilkunde, die (no pl.)	gynaecology
Chirurg(in), der/die (-en/nen)	surgeon
Chirurgie, die (no pl.)	surgery
Optiker(in), der/die (-/nen)	optician
Augenarzt, der (¨e); Augenärztin, die (-nen)	eye specialist
Augenheilkunde, die (no pl.)	ophthalmology
Psychiater(in), der/die (-/nen)	psychiatrist
Psychiatrie, die (no pl.)	psychiatry
Kinderpsychiater(in), der/die (-/nen)	child psychiatrist
Apotheker(in), der/die (-/nen)	(dispensing) chemist, druggist

Medical facilities

Krankenhaus, das (¨er)	hospital
Klinik, die (-en)	clinic
Praxis, die (Praxen)	practice, office
Wartezimmer, das (-)	waiting room
Krankenwagen, der (-)	ambulance
Apotheke, die (-n)	chemist's, pharmacy, drugstore

Medical treatment

Medikament, das (-e)	medicine
Mittel, das (-)	medicine
ein Mittel gegen etw	a cure for sth
Droge, die (-n)	drug
gegen etw helfen	to be good for sth, help to relieve sth
Schmerzmittel, das (-)	painkiller
Hustenmittel, das (-)	cough medicine
Tablette, die (-n)	tablet, pill
Schlaftablette, die (-n)	sleeping pill

Pille, die (-n)	pill
die Pille nehmen (coll.)	to be on the pill
Tropfen, pl.	drops
Kondom, das (-e)	condom
Gummi, der (-s; coll.)	johnny, rubber
etw einnehmen	to take sth orally [medicine]
auf nüchternen Magen	on an empty stomach
etw verschreiben	to prescribe sth
etw aufschreiben	to write sth down, prescribe sth
Rezept, das (-e)	prescription
Sprechstunde, die (-n)	consulting hours
Patient(in), der/die (-en/nen)	patient
jmdn untersuchen	to examine sb
Untersuchung, die (-en)	examination, screening
Selbstuntersuchung, die (-en)	self-examination
jmds Temperatur messen	to take sb's temperature
Puls, der (-e)	pulse
jmdm den Puls fühlen	to take sb's pulse
jmdm in den Hals schauen	to look down sb's throat
tief Atem holen	to take a deep breath
die Herztöne/die Lungen abhorchen	to listen to the heart/lungs
eine Urinprobe nehmen	to take a urine specimen
Blutprobe, die (-n)	blood test, blood sample
Behandlung, die (-en)	treatment
jmdn pflegen	to care for sb
Intensivpflege, die (no pl.)	intensive care
jmdn/etw heilen	to cure sb/sth
heilen	to heal
etw verbinden	to bandage, dress sth
Operation, die (-en)	operation

jmdn operieren	to operate on sb	Untersuchungstisch, der (-e)	examining table
Notdienst, der (-e)	emergency services	Rollstuhl, der (¨e)	wheelchair
erste Hilfe leisten	to administer first aid	Hörgerät, das (-e)	hearing aid
jmdn wiederbeleben	to resuscitate sb	Krücke, die (-n)	crutch
Mund-zu-Mund-Beatmung, die (no pl.)	mouth-to-mouth resuscitation		
Herzmassage, die (-n)	heart massage		

Dentistry

Zahnarzt, der (¨e); Zahnärztin, die (-nen)	dentist, dental surgeon
Zahnheilkunde, die (no pl.)	dentistry
Zahnarzthelfer(in), der/die (-/nen)	dental assistant
Zahntechniker(in), der/die (-/nen)	dental technician
Zahnschmerzen, pl.	toothache
Loch, das (¨er)	cavity
in einem Zahn bohren	to drill a tooth
Bohrer, der (-)	drill
einen Zahn plombieren	to fill a tooth
(Zahn)füllung, die (-en)	filling
Plombe, die (-n; coll.)	filling
einen Zahn ziehen	to pull, extract a tooth
Gebiss, das (-e)	dentures
künstliche Zähne, pl.	false teeth

Medical equipment

Hörrohr, das (-e)	stethoscope
Thermometer, das (-)	thermometer
Spritze, die (-n)	syringe
Gummihandschuh, der (-e)	rubber glove
Verband, der (¨e)	bandage, dressing
einen Verband auf die Wunde legen	to dress the wound
Binde, die (-n)	bandage
(Heft)pflaster, das (-)	plaster, bandage, Band-Aid ®; Elastoplast ®
Verband(s)kasten, der (¨)	first-aid kit
Sanitätskasten, der (¨)	first-aid kit
Reiseapotheke, die (-n)	first-aid kit
Krankenbahre, die (-n)	stretcher

Level 2

Medical personnel and specialities

Allgemeinmediz-iner(in), der/die (-/nen)	general practitioner	Orthopäde, der (-n); Orthopädin, die (-nen)	orthopaedic surgeon
Allgemeinmedizin, die (no pl.)	general medicine	Orthopädie, die (no pl.)	orthopaedics
Internist(in), der/die (-en/nen)	house surgeon, internist	Hautarzt, der (¨e); Hautärztin, die (-nen)	dermatologist
innere Medizin	internal medicine	Dermatologie, die (no pl.)	dermatology
Radiologe, der (-n); Radiologin, die (-nen)	radiologist	Geburtshelfer(in), der/die (-/nen)	obstetrician
Radiologie, die (no pl.)	radiology		

Geburtshilfe, die (no pl.)	obstetrics
Hebamme, die (-n)	midwife
Pharmazeut(in), der/die (-en/nen)	pharmacist
Pharmazie, die (no pl.)	pharmaceutics
Notarzt, der (¨e); Notärztin, die (-nen)	emergency doctor
Sanitäter(in), der/die (-/nen)	paramedic
Krankenträger(in), der/die (-/nen)	stretcher-bearer
Arzthelfer(in), der/die (-/nen)	doctor's assistant
Physiotherapeut(in), der/die (-en/nen)	physiotherapist
Physiotherapie, die (-n)	physiotherapy
Psychologe, der (-n); Psychologin, die (-nen)	psychologist
Psychologie, die (no pl.)	psychology
Psychotherapeut(in), der/die (-en/nen)	psychotherapist
Psychotherapie, die (no pl.)	psychotherapy

Medical facilities

(Kranken)station, die (-en)	ward
Intensivstation, die (-en)	intensive-care unit
Röntgenstation, die (-en)	X-ray unit
Operationssaal, der (-säle)	operating room
Genesungsheim, das (-e)	convalescent home
Notaufnahme, die (-n)	emergency room
Blutbank, die (-en)	blood bank
Samenbank, die (-en)	sperm bank

Medical treatment

vorbeugende Medizin, die (no pl.)	preventive medicine
etw diagnostizieren	to diagnose sth
Diagnose, die (-n)	diagnosis
eine Diagnose stellen	to make a diagnosis
Aidstest, der (-s or -e)	AIDS test
Krankenkasse, die (-n)	health insurance organization or company
Krankenversicherung, die (-en)	health insurance
(kranken)versichert sein	to have health insurance
Versichertenkarte, die (-n)	health-insurance card
Krankenschein, der (-e)	health-insurance certificate
jmdn ins Krankenhaus einliefern	to admit sb to the hospital
jmdn entlassen	to discharge sb
Attest, das (-e)	doctor's certificate
Arznei, die (-en)	drug
rezeptpflichtig	available only by prescription
etw ohne Rezept kaufen	to buy sth over the counter
Antibiotikum, das (Antibiotika)	antibiotic
Kapsel, die (-n)	capsule
Spritze, die (-n)	shot, injection
Impfung, die (-en)	vaccination, inoculation
jmdn (gegen etw) impfen	to immunize, vaccinate sb (against sth)
Dosis, die (Dosen)	dosage
Dauertropfinfusion, die (-en)	drip feed
Blutwäsche, die (-n)	dialysis
etw gipsen	to put sth in plaster
etw in Gips legen	to put sth in plaster

den Knochen einrichten	to set the bone	Gipsverband, der (¨e)	plaster cast
etw amputieren	to amputate sth	Druckverband, der (¨e)	pressure bandage
Amputierte(r), der/die (adj. decl.)	amputee	Tourniquet, das (-s)	tourniquet
Röntgenbild, das (-er)	X-ray	(Arm)schlinge, die (-n)	sling
etw röntgen	to X-ray sth	Schiene, die (-n)	splint
das Röntgenbild auswerten	to analyse the X-ray	Röntgengerät, das (-e)	X-ray apparatus
Kur, die (-en)	treatment (at a spa), health cure	Bettpfanne, die (-n)	bedpan
		Schieber, der (-)	bedpan
in Kur gehen	to go to a health resort (for a course of treatment)	Tropf, der (¨e)	IV, dripfeed
		am Tropf hängen	to be on an IV, a drip

Alternative medicine

Krankengymnastik, die (no pl.)	physical therapy	Akupunktur, die (-en)	acupuncture
Diät, die (-en)	diet	homöopatisch	homeopathic
jmdn auf Diät setzen	to put sb on a diet	Homöopath(in), der/die (-en/nen)	homeopath
fasten	to fast		
Beruhigungsmittel, das (-)	tranquillizer	Homöopathie, die (no pl.)	homeopathy
Antidepressivum, das (-va)	antidepressant	Aromatherapie, die (no pl.)	aromatherapy
Gurgelmittel, das (-)	gargle	Naturheilkunde, die (no pl.)	naturopathy
Salbe, die (-n)	salve, ointment		
Creme (Krem, Kreme), die (-s)	cream	Lichttherapie, die (no pl.)	light therapy
		Chiropraktiker(in), der/die (-/nen)	chiropractor

Medical equipment

Injektionsnadel, die (-n)	hypodermic needle	Chiropraktik, die (no pl.)	chiropractic
Tropfer, der (-)	dropper	holistisch	holistic
Tupfer, der (-)	swab		

Level 3

Medical personnel and specialities

Osteopath, der (-en); Osteopathin, die (-nen)	osteopath	Virologie, die (no pl.)	virology
Osteopathie, die (-n)	osteopathy	Hals-Nasen-Ohren-Arzt, der (¨e);	ear, nose and throat
Virologe, der (-n); Virologin, die (-nen)	virologist	Hals-Nasen-Ohren-Ärztin, die (-nen)	specialist

HNO–Arzt, der (¨e); HNO–Ärztin, die (-nen)	ENT specialist
Hals–Nasen–Ohren–Heilkunde, die (no pl.)	otolaryngology
Onkologe, der (-n); Onkologin, die (-nen)	oncologist
Onkologie, die (no pl.)	oncology
Urologe, der (-n); Urologin, die (-nen)	urologist
Urologie, die (no pl.)	urology
Kardiologe, der (-n); Kardiologin, die (-nen)	cardiologist
Kardiologie, die (no pl.)	cardiology
Rheumatologe, der (-n); Rheumatologin, die (-nen)	rheumatologist
Rheumatologie, die (no pl.)	rheumatology
Hämatologe, der (-n); Hämatologin, die (-nen)	haematologist
Hämatologie, die (no pl.)	haematology
Endokrinologe, der (-n); Endokrinologin, die (-nen)	endocrinologist
Endokrinologie, die (no pl.)	endocrinology
Neurologe, der (-n); Neurologin, die (-nen)	neurologist
Neurologie, die (no pl.)	neurology
Anästhesist, der (-en); Anästhesistin, die (-nen)	anaesthetist
Anästhesiologie, die (no pl.)	anaesthesiology
Geriater(in), der/die (-/nen)	geriatrician
Geriatrie, die (no pl.)	geriatrics
Pathologe, der (-n); Pathologin, die (-nen)	pathologist
Pathologie, die (no pl.)	pathology
Sprachtherapeut(in), der/die (-en/nen)	speech therapist
Sprachtherapie, die (no pl.)	speech therapy
Fußpfleger(in), der/die (-/nen)	podiatrist
Fußpflege, die (no pl.)	podiatry

Medical treatment

Linderungsmittel, das (-)	palliative
etw lindern	to alleviate, relieve, ease sth
abschwellendes Mittel	decongestant
Expektorans, das (-ranzien or -rantia)	expectorant
Barbiturat, das (-e)	barbiturate
Steroid, das (-e)	steroid
Sedativum, das (-va)	sedative
jmdn sedieren	to sedate sb
Relaxans, das (Relaxantia or Relaxanzien)	relaxant
mit Vollnarkose/ Lokalanästhesie	under a general/local anaesthetic
Brechmittel, das (-)	emetic
harntreibendes Mittel	diuretic
Naht, die (¨e)	stitch, suture
die Wunde nähen	to stitch up/suture the wound

Gewebsverpflanzung, die (-en)	tissue graft
etw verpflanzen/ transplantieren	to transplant sth
Herzverpflanzung, die (-en)	heart transplant
Laserchirurgie, die (no pl.)	laser surgery
Schlüssellochchir- urgie, die (no pl.)	keyhole surgery
Knopflochchirurgie, die (no pl.)	keyhole surgery
Zäpfchen, das (-)	suppository
Abführmittel, das (-)	laxative
Intrauterinpessar, das (-e)	IUD
Spermizid, das (-e)	spermicide
Abtreibungspille, die (-n)	morning-after pill
Ausschabung, die (-en)	curettage
Gebärmutterhalsab- strich, der (-e)	cervical smear test
Hormonbehandlung, die (-en)	hormone treatment
Ultraschall, der (no pl.)	ultrasound
Sonographie (Sonografie), die (-n)	sonography
Epiduralanästhesie, die (no pl.)	epidural
etw einleiten	to induce sth
Zangengeburt, die (-en)	forceps delivery
sich den Magen auspumpen lassen	to have one's stomach pumped
Elektrokardiogramm (EKG or Ekg), das (-e)	electrocardiogram
Chemotherapie, die (no pl.)	chemotherapy
Strahlentherapie, die (-n)	radiotherapy

Strahlenbehandlung, die (-en)	radiotherapy

Medical equipment

Elektrokardiograph, der (-en)	electrocardiograph
EKG-Gerät, das (-e)	EKG
Defibrillator, der (-en)	defibrillator
Dialyseapparat, der (-e)	dialysis machine
lebenserhaltende Apparate, pl.	life-support system
Spekulum, das (Spekula)	speculum
Skallpell, das (-e)	scalpel
Magenpumpe, die (-n)	stomach pump
Herzschrittmacher, der (-)	pacemaker
Geburtszange, die (-n)	obstetrical forceps
Beatmungsgerät, das (-e)	respirator

Dentistry

Karies, die (no pl.)	caries
Zahnfäule, die (no pl.)	tooth decay
Zahnbelag, der (¨e)	plaque
Zahnstein, der (no pl.)	tartar
Krone, die (-n)	crown
Brücke, die (-n)	bridge
Implantat, das (-e)	implant
Mundspiegel, der (-)	mouth mirror
Kieferorthopäde, der (-n); Kieferorthopädin, die (-nen)	orthodontist
Kieferorthopädie, die (no pl.)	orthodontics
Zahnspange, die (-n)	braces

Exercises

Level 1

1. Zu jedem Bild passt ein Nomen. ✓

a. das Hörrohr, b. der Krankenwagen, c. die Krücken, d. das Heftpflaster,
e. der Rollstuhl, f. der Sanitätskasten, g. die Spritze, h. das Thermometer

1. _____   2. _____   3. _____   4. _____

5. _____   6. _____   7. _____   8. _____

Some images © 2003 www.clipart.com.

2. Welches Wort hat die gleiche oder eine ähnliche Bedeutung? ✓

1. die Wange
2. die Erkältung
3. die Übelkeit
4. Kopfschmerzen
5. der Herzinfarkt
6. sich übergeben
7. die Abtreibung
8. die Medizin
9. die Doktorin
10. die Krankenschwester
11. das Medikament
12. die Pille
13. das Kondom
14. die Binde
15. der Verbandkasten
16. die Füllung
17. die Fraktur

3. Was passt zusammen? ✓

a. die Angst, b. der Bauchweh, c. die Faust, d. das Fieber, e. die Geisteskrankheit,
f. das Gelenk, g. die Grippe, h. die Migräne, i. die Narbe, j. die Nase,
k. die Periode, l. der Stich, m. die Verletzung

1. bewegliche Verbindung zwischen Skelettteilen
2. krankhaft erhöhte Körpertemperatur

3. bildet sich bei der Heilung von Wunden
4. durch Insekt hervorgerufene Verwundung
5. der Leibschmerz
6. große Sorge
7. heftiger Kopfschmerz
8. die Monatsblutung
9. die Psychose
10. körperliche Beschädigung
11. die Influenza
12. die geballte Hand
13. das Riechorgan

4. Welches Verb passt? ✓

> a. abhorchen, b. ausbrechen, c. fühlen, d. holen, e. leisten, f. messen, g. nehmen,
> h. plombieren, i. verspüren, j. ziehen

1. Brechreiz	6. jmds Temperatur
2. in kalten Schweiß	7. die Lungen
3. eine Lungenentzündung	8. erste Hilfe
4. einen Facharzt zu Rate	9. einen Zahn
5. die Pille	10. jmdm den Puls

5. Ordnen Sie.
das Bein, der Daumen, der Ellenbogen, das Gesicht, das Handgelenk, das Herz,
das Kinn, die Leber, die Lunge, der Magen, die Niere, das Ohr, die Stirn,
die Zehe, die Zunge

der Kopf	Glieder	innere Organe

6. Was bedeuten die Wendungen?

1. feuriges Blut haben	6. aus dem hohlen Bauch
2. unter vier Augen	7. kalte Füße bekommen
3. kein Blatt vor den Mund nehmen	8. einen dicken Schädel haben
4. jmdm den Rücken stärken	9. Hals- und Beinbruch!
5. schwach auf der Brust sein (coll.)	10. jmdn auf den Arm nehmen

7. Wie heißt der entsprechende Arzt und die entsprechende Ärztin? ✓
1. die Kinderheilkunde
2. die Frauenheilkunde
3. die Chirurgie
4. die Psychiatrie
5. die Augenheilkunde
6. die Zahnheilkunde

8. Übersetzen Sie ins Deutsche. ✓

1. He gets on my nerves.
2. She was out of breath.
3. He has a skeleton in the closet.
4. He is nothing but skin and bones.
5. She poked him in the ribs.
6. I caught a cold.
7. The doctor looked down her throat.
8. She took a deep breath.

9. Suchen Sie eine andere Bedeutung.

1. die Scham
2. das Glied
3. der Schwanz
4. das Rezept
5. die Blase
6. die Spritze
7. der Kreislauf
8. die Verstopfung

10. Was brauchen Sie . . . ✓

1. wenn Sie husten?
2. wenn Sie an Schlaflosigkeit leiden?
3. wenn Sie Schmerzen haben?
4. bei einem Herzstillstand?
5. wenn Sie Medikamente kaufen müssen?
6. wenn Sie ins Krankenhaus getragen werden müssen?
7. wenn Sie sich den Fuß verstauchen?
8. wenn Sie ein Loch im Zahn haben?

a. die Apotheke, b. die Herzmassage, c. das Hustenmittel, d. die Krankenbahre, e. die Krücken (pl.), f. die Plombe, g. die Schlaftablette, h. das Schmerzmittel

11. Übersetzen Sie ins Englische.

Noten für den Arzt

Patienten sollen künftig im Internet gezielt nach einem kompetenten, freundlichen Arzt suchen können. Unter „www.checkthedoc.de" entsteht derzeit eine Datenbank, in der deutsche Allgemeinmediziner und Fachärzte von ihren Patienten beurteilt werden. Ein Kranker soll sich den Arzt heraussuchen können, der an seinem Wohnort am besten abschneidet. Die Patienten vergeben Schulnoten für fachliche Kompetenz und Freundlichkeit. Außerdem wird die Organisation der Praxis bewertet, beispielsweise wie lange der Arzt seine Patienten im Wartezimmer sitzen lässt. Das Prinzip – Kunden bewerten, Neukunden folgen dem Rat – ist nicht neu: Ähnliche Systeme existieren bereits für Produkte aller Art ...

DER SPIEGEL 40/2001, S. 110

12. Lesen Sie den folgenden Text.

Unfall am 133. Tag

Der erste Kunstherz-Patient ist in kritischem Zustand. Dennoch soll die voll implantierbare Titanpumpe „Abiocor" schon bald auf den Markt kommen.

Jetzt sind es schon fünf. Fünf sterbenskranken Männern in den USA fehlt das eigene Herz.

Chirurgen haben es ihnen herausgeschnitten, als es zum Weiterleben zu schwach war. Jeder dieser Todgeweihten trägt seither eine technisch hoch ambitionierte Maschine in der Brust – das erste voll implantierbare Kunstherz aus Titan und Plastik, 900 Gramm schwer, groß wie eine Pampelmuse. Aus ihren Körpern ragen keine Kabel. Sie tragen nicht, wie ihre gemarterten Vorgänger in den achtziger Jahren, riesenhafte Apparate mit sich herum. Sie haben keinen tastbaren Puls – und sind doch, zumindest bis Ende vergangener Woche, noch am Leben.

Aber was für ein Leben? Vor fast fünf Monaten wurde Robert Tools, 59, in Louisville (Kentucky) als weltweit erstem Patienten das neuartige Kunstherz „Abiocor" eingesetzt (SPIEGEL 28/2001). Zuvor ging es ihm so elend, dass er seinen Kopf nicht vom Kissen heben konnte. Mit dem Maschinenherz in der Brust schien sich Tools hervorragend zu erholen. 30-mal hat der pensionierte Bibliothekar Ausflüge vom Krankenbett gemacht. Er ging speisen mit dem Bürgermeister und fischen mit dem Enkel, und noch Anfang November hatten seine Ärzte ihm in Aussicht gestellt, dass er Weihnachten für einige Tage nach Hause dürfe. Das tun sie jetzt nicht mehr.

Am 133. Tag mit dem neuen Herzen hat Tools einen Schlaganfall erlitten, gefolgt von einer Blutung im Gehirn. Er ist rechtsseitig gelähmt. Er kann nicht sprechen und wird über ein Loch in der Luftröhre beatmet. Eine Lungenentzündung ist hinzugekommen. Nur an manchen Tagen ist er nach Auskunft seiner Ärzte geistig präsent. Seine Familie betet für ihn, die Mediziner halten seinen Zustand für kritisch.

Der Pionierpatient Tools ist, so gesteht sein Operateur Laman Gray ein, wahrscheinlich das Opfer seines Kunstherzens geworden: An den Wänden von Abiocor hat sich wohl ein Blutgerinnsel gebildet, das ins Hirn vorgedrungen ist.

Mediziner wissen schon länger, dass solche Gerinnsel in Kunstherzen entstehen können. Blut verdünnende Mittel sollten das Risiko senken, doch bei Tools wurden sie bald abgesetzt: Sie führten bei ihm zu so starken Blutungen aus der Nase und im Magen, dass nur Transfusionen ihn am Leben hielten.

Wie es Tools Leidensgenossen geht, ist nicht genau bekannt. Der Ex-Reifenhändler Tom Christerson, 70, überlebte in Louisville knapp eine Infektion mit Fieber von 41,6 Grad, die seine Nieren und Leber in Mitleidenschaft zog. Die Namen der übrigen Abiocor-Empfänger in Houston, Los Angeles und Philadelphia werden geheim gehalten. Die Männer sind – angeblich – auf dem Pfad der Erholung, aber Genaues wird nicht verraten. Aus gutem Grund: Der Aktienkurs der Herstellerfirma Abiomed verhält sich umgekehrt proportional zu den Fieberkurven der Herzträger: Er steigt, wenn die Temperatur sinkt; jede schlechte Nachricht über die Kranken kostet Börsenwert ...

Marco Evers

DER SPIEGEL 48/2001, S. 259

a. Vokabelübung. Wie heißt das Wort auf Englisch?

1. das Kunstherz	6. gelähmt
2. sterbenskrank	7. die Luftröhre
3. todgeweiht	8. das Blutgerinnsel
4. implantierbar	9. die Erholung
5. die Blutung	

b. Schriftliche Übung. Fassen Sie den Text in einem Absatz zusammen.

Level 2

1. Wie heißen die entsprechenden Sinne? ✓

1. hören
2. sehen
3. riechen
4. schmecken
5. fühlen

2. Wie heißen ... ✓

die fünf Finger?	die fünf Zehen?
1. der Daumen	1. die große Zehe
2.	2.
3.	3.
4.	4.
5.	5.

3. Welche Definition passt? ✓

a. blind, b. gehörlos, c. kurzsichtig, d. schwerhörig, e. weitsichtig

1. nicht fähig, mit dem Gehör wahrzunehmen
2. nur entfernte Dinge gut erkennen
3. ohne Sehvermögen
4. vermindert hörfähig
5. nur auf kurze Entfernung gut sehend

4. Welches Wort hat die gleiche oder eine ähnliche Bedeutung? ✓

1. die Arterie	7. die Dialyse
2. die Vene	8. die Bettpfanne
3. die Achselgrube	9. die Polio
4. der Tumor	10. bewusstlos
5. die Arthritis	11. der Hals
6. die Droge	

5. Welches Verb passt? ✓

a. fallen, b. gehen, c. hängen, d. legen, e. liegen, f. setzen, g. stellen, h. übertragen, i. zerren

1. eine Diagnose
2. ein Bein in Gips
3. in Kur
4. jmdn auf Diät
5. am Tropf
6. eine Krankheit auf jmdn
7. in Ohnmacht
8. sich einen Muskel
9. im Koma

6. Wie heißt das Gegenteil? ✓
1. krank
2. einatmen
3. der Dickdarm
4. jmdn ins Krankenhaus einliefern
5. der Oberarm
6. gutartig

7. Welches Nomen passt nicht? ✓
1. das Gehirn, die Kopfhaut, der Schädel, das Stießbein
2. die Bruchstelle, der Busen, die Fissur, der Kieferbruch
3. die Kahlheit, Kopfläuse, die Schiene, Schuppen
4. der Augapfel, der Blinddarm, das Lid, die Wimper
5. der Internist, die Hautärztin, die Hebamme, der Radiologe
6. die Kinderpsychiaterin, der Physiotherapeut, die Psychologin, der Psychotherapeut
7. die Achsel, der Ausschlag, die Leberflecke, die Warze
8. der Gehörgang, das Hörrohr, die Luftröhre, die Speiseröhre
9. Masern, der Mumps, Wehen, Windpocken
10. die Krankenbahre, die Krankenkasse, die Krankenversicherung, die Versichertenkarte

8. Wie heißt das Adjektiv? ✓

1.	ohne Bewusstsein
2.	an Blutarmut leidend
3.	körperlichen Schmerz verursachend
4.	krankhaft überempfindlich; auf Allergie beruhend
5.	an Zuckerkrankheit leidend
6.	wie ein Krampf
7.	von Schwindel befallen

9. In jedem Satz fehlt ein Wort. ✓

> Beruhigungsmittel, Brustkorb, Chiropraktikerin, Ermüdung, Gipsverband,
> Homöopathie, Impfung, Intensivstation, Krankengymnastik,
> Lebensmittelvergiftungen, Ohrläppchen, Schlüsselbein

1. Der Patient muss sich bis zu zehnmal täglich in den Finger oder das _____ stechen, um einen Bluttropfen zu gewinnen.
2. Beim Skiurlaub hat er sich bei einem Sturz das _____ gebrochen.
3. Etwa eine Million Menschen in Deutschland nehmen jeden Tag Schlaf- oder _____.
4. Ich atme ganz tief ein und spüre, wie mein _____ sich weitet.
5. Etwa zehn bis vierzehn Tage nach der _____ wirkt der Schutz.
6. Für viele Skifahrer wird die Wintersaison im _____ enden.
7. Sie fährt ihn zur _____ und achtet darauf, dass er seine Medikamente richtig einnimmt.
8. Sie liegt auf der _____ des Krankenhauses im Koma.
9. Am Ende seiner Reise nach Frankreich zeigte der Papst deutliche Anzeichen der _____ .
10. Sie leiden an Botulismus, eine der gefährlichsten _____ .
11. Die _____ hat sich vor allem um meinen Rücken gekümmert.
12. Was bieten nun alternative Heilmethoden wie _____ ?

10. Übersetzen Sie ins Englische.

Gefäßverschluss im Darm

Wird der Blutverdünner Heparin in den Kliniken zu sorglos verabreicht? Bei vielen Patienten führt das Mittel zu gefährlichen Komplikationen.

Ihr Kampf gegen den Tod begann mit einem harmlosen Unfall. Beim Überqueren der Hauptstraße geriet die Rentnerin Helga G. ins Stolpern und stürzte. Mit starken Schulterschmerzen wurde die 71-Jährige im September vergangenen Jahres in das Johanniter-Krankenhaus in Geesthacht bei Hamburg eingeliefert.

In der Klinik diagnostizierten die Mediziner einen Trümmerbruch des rechten Oberarms. Neben Schmerzmitteln verschrieb der aufnehmende Arzt vorsorglich Heparin: ein Medikament, das Gefäßverschlüssen (Thrombosen) vorbeugen soll. Helga G. erhielt das Medikament drei Wochen lang täglich.

Dies wäre besser nicht geschehen: Kaum hatte die Patientin die Klinik verlassen, kam sie erneut ins Krankenhaus – sie musste als Notfall per Hubschrauber eingeflogen werden. Die Rentnerin überlebte nur knapp; die Chirurgen mussten ihren linken Fuß und den Unterschenkel amputieren.

Solche schweren Komplikationen sind durchaus typisch für Heparin, und sie treten keineswegs selten auf. Ursache ist eine allergische Reaktion, die bei manchen Patienten zu ausgerechnet dem führt, was die Heparin-Gabe eigentlich verhindern soll: schwere, sich im ganzen Körper ausweitende Verstopfungen in den Blutgefäßen ...

Zwei Wochen nach ihrer Einlieferung in das Krankenhaus klagte Helga G. über kolikartige Schmerzen im Bauchbereich. Die behandelnden Ärzte tippten auf eine Blinddarmentzündung und öffnete den Bauch der Patientin.

In Wahrheit, stellte sich dabei heraus, hatte sie einen schweren Gefäßverschluss im Dünndarmbereich. Der Darm musste teilweise entfernt werden – eine Komplikation, die auf eine Heparin-Allergie hindeutete. Dennoch erhielt Helga G. auch weiterhin das Blutverdünnungsmedikament. Die Folge: Im Lauf der folgenden Tage verschlechterte sich der Zustand der Patientin immer weiter.

Schließlich fiel Helga G. ins Koma. Um ihr Leben zu retten, mussten die Chirurgen ihren linken, inzwischen schwer thrombotischen Unterschenkel unterhalb des Kniegelenks entfernen ...

[D]as Bundesinstitut für Arzneimittel und Medizinprodukte (BfArM) warnt schon länger vor der gefährlichen Heparin-Allergie. Dennoch hat die Zahl der gemeldeten Zwischenfälle in den vergangenen Jahren stark zugenommen. Seit 1994 sind dem BfArM insgesamt 633 Fälle gemeldet worden, bei 90 Patienten kam es dabei zu Thrombosen. Die Liste ist aber mit Sicherheit unvollständig – der Fall der Helga G. etwa kommt darin noch nicht vor.

Matthias Brendel

DER SPIEGEL 48/2001, pages 246–247

Level 3

1. Welches Wort hat die gleiche oder eine ähnliche Bedeutung? ✓

1. karzinogen
2. die Dementia
3. das Ekzem
4. der Anthrax
5. etw luxieren
6. brennend
7. das Palliativ
8. die Schlüssellochchirurgie
9. die Strahlentherapie
10. die Karies
11. die Iris
12. der Körper
13. die Hämophilie

2. Ordnen Sie.

der Elektrokardiograph, der Defibrillator, der Eierstock, die Gebärmutter, das Herzgeräusch, die Herzrhythmusstörung, der Hodensack, der Kardiologe, die Kniekehle, der Knöchel, der Oberschenkel, die Schamlippe, die Vorhaut, die Wade

das Herz	das Bein	Geschlechtsorgane

3. Welcher Facharzt bzw. welche Fachärztin beschäftigt sich mit . . . ✓

1. Erkrankungen der Harnorgane?
2. Krankheiten alternder Menschen?
3. Viren?
4. Geschwülsten?

5. der schmerzhaften Entzündung von Gelenken und Muskeln?

6. Erkrankungen von Hals, Nase und Ohren?

7. Blut?

8. Drüsen?

4. Was bedeuten die folgenden Zusammensetzungen?

1. der Brustkrebs, der Darmkrebs, der Hautkrebs, der Kehlkopfkrebs, der Leberkrebs, der Lungenkrebs

2. die Darmblutung, die Durchblutung, die Gehirnblutung, die Magenblutung, die Monatsblutung

3. die Bindehautentzündung, die Blasenentzündung, die Gehirnhautentzündung, die Gelenkentzündung, die Hautentzündung, die Lungenentzündung, die Mandelentzündung, die Nebenhöhlenentzündung

4. der Fingerknochen, der Fußwurzelknochen, der Handwurzelknochen, der Mittelhandknochen, der Vorfußknochen, der Zehenknochen

5. Was nehmen Sie ein, . . . ✓

1. wenn die Nase verstopft ist?

2. um das Erbrechen herbeizuführen?

3. um die Harnausscheidung anzuregen?

4. um die Erregbarkeit herabzusetzen?

5. um die Darmentleerung zu beschleunigen?

6. um die Schwangerschaft zu verhindern?

> a. das Abführmittel, b. abschwellendes Mittel, c. die Abtreibungspille, d. das Brechmittel, e. harntreibendes Mittel, f. das Sedativum

6. Ergänzen Sie. ✓

1. die Hand – der Handrücken : der Fuß – _____

2. der Scheitel – der Hals : die Krone – _____

3. der Oberarm – das Oberarmbein : der Oberschenkel – _____

4. die Speiche – die Elle : das Wadenbein – _____

5. die Sprachtherapie – der Sprachtherapeut : die Pathologie – _____

6. das Herz – die Herzverpflanzung : das Gewebe – _____

7. die Zangengeburt – die Geburtszange : die Dialyse – _____

8. der Orthopäde – der Gipsverband : der Kieferorthopäde – _____

9. das Herz – der Herzschrittmacher : die Lunge – _____

7. Wie heißt das entsprechende Adjektiv? ✓

1. der Autismus (jmd, der an Autismus leidet ist . . .)

2. die Inkontinenz

3. die Schizophrenie

4. die Epilepsie

5. die Querschnittslähmung

6. die Depression

7. die Geisteskrankheit

8. Welches Nomen passt nicht? ✓

1. das Hühnerauge, die Hornhaut, die Pupille, der Sehnerv
2. der Kehlkopf, die Kehlkopfentzündung, der Kropf, der Krupp
3. die Brust, die Brustwarze, die Warze, der Warzenhof
4. der After, der Mastdarm, die Milz, der Schließmuskel
5. komplizierter Bruch, die Naht, die Osteoporose, die Rachitis
6. das Intrauterinpessar, das Spermizid, der Ultraschall, die Vasektomie
7. die Antidepressivum, die Epiduralanästhesie, die Lokalanästhesie, die Vollnarkose
8. der Daumenballen, die Fingerbeere, der Handteller, das Kreuzbein
9. der Astigmatismus, der Eiter, das Gerstenkorn, grauer Star

9. Beim Arzt.

1. Es geht Ihnen schlecht. Sie glauben, dass Sie sich eine Grippe geholt haben. Beschreiben Sie dem Arzt bzw. der Ärztin Ihre Symptome.
2. Sie glauben, dass Sie schwanger sind. Erklären Sie dem Arzt bzw. der Ärztin, wie Sie sich fühlen.
3. Sie haben lange in der Sonne gelegen und haben Symptome eines Sonnenstichs. Beschreiben Sie dem Arzt bzw. der Ärztin diese Symptome.
4. Es geht Ihnen elend. Sie glauben, dass Sie an Lebensmittelvergiftung leiden. Beschreiben Sie dem Arzt bzw. der Ärztin Ihre Symptome.

10. Übersetzen Sie ins Englische.

Milzbrand für die CIA
Salmonellen für Clinton

WASHINGTON, 26. Oktober. Neue Milzbrandfunde haben in Washington nun auch das Außenministerium und den Geheimdienst CIA betroffen. In Postverteilungsstellen beider Behörden wurden zumindest „Spuren" der Bakterien entdeckt. Bei einem Mitarbeiter der Poststelle des Außenministeriums wurde inzwischen Lungenmilzbrand diagnostiziert. Bei einem separaten Zwischenfall in New York fanden Beamte des Secret Service in einem an den ehemaligen Präsidenten Bill Clinton adressierten Umschlag, Plastikröhrchen mit Salmonellenbakterien. Clinton, der sich gegenwärtig in Rom aufhält, kam damit in seinem Büro nicht in Berührung ...

Leo Wieland

Frankfurter Allgemeine Zeitung, Samstag, 27. Oktober 2001, Nr. 150, S. 1

11. Lesen Sie die folgenden Auszüge eines Gesprächs mit Heinrich Schoeneich.

„Kinder leiden am meisten"

In München verdient er sein Geld mit Schönheitsoperationen, in Afghanistan versorgt Heinrich Schoeneich Kriegsopfer. Ein Gespräch über zwei Welten

ZEIT: Was hat Sie nach Afghanistan geführt?
SCHOENEICH: Ich gehöre zum Team von Interplast, einer medizinischen Hilfsorganisation, die, übrigens nicht nur in Afghanistan, Kriegsverletzungen,

angeborene Missbildungen und Verbrennungsfolgen versorgt. Ich behandle hauptsächlich Kinder, die leiden am meisten unter Krieg, Armut und Unterversorgung. Natürlich verweigern wir auch keinem Erwachsenen eine notwendige Operation. Aber in Afghanistan behandeln wir 60 bis 70 Prozent Kinder.

ZEIT: Gibt es typische Verletzungen?

SCHOENEICH: In den ersten Jahren waren es zu 70 Prozent Kriegsverletzungen, Minen-, Schrapnell-, Schussverletzungen und Verbrennungen. Als indirekte Kriegsfolge gibt es sehr viele Poliofälle. Zwar wurde auch während der sowjetischen Besatzung regelmäßig geimpft, aber der Impfstoff war unwirksam, weil Stromausfälle die Kühlkette unterbrochen hatten. Seit die Taliban vor drei Jahren ein Waffenverbot verhängt haben, sind die Kriegsverletzungen tatsächlich zurückgegangen.

ZEIT: Was sind jetzt die häufigsten Operationen?

SCHOENEICH: Viele Klumpfüße, Gaumenspalten und hauptsächlich Verbrennungen. Das liegt an den eisigen Wintern in dieser Höhe. Die Leute schlafen in Hütten, in deren Zentrum ein kleiner Ofen steht. Da legen sie sich sternförmig herum und breiten einen Teppich so über sich aus, dass die warme Luft darunter streicht. Immer wieder verursacht herunterfallende Holzglut Brände und schwere Verbrennungen. Die führen zu extremen Verwachsungen. Die Kinder laufen auf narbigen Stümpfen, die aufgebrochen sind und verkrustet mit Schmutz.

ZEIT: Wie sind Ihre Arbeitsbedingungen vor Ort?

SCHOENEICH: Das Krankenhaus ist im Vergleich zum restlichen Land eine Oase. Es liegt abseits des Kriegsgeschehens 65 Kilometer südwestlich von Kabul. Es hat 40 Betten und ist dank seiner umsichtigen Leiterin gut ausgestattet. Wenn unser Team zweimal im Jahr anreist, dann sind bis zu 500 Patienten zu versorgen. Dann werden rundherum Zelte aufgebaut. Leider können wir nicht alle, die kommen, auch operieren.

ZEIT: Trotz Dauereinsatz?

SCHOENEICH: Ja, von morgens sieben bis abends sechs, ohne Mittagspause. Jeden Tag 18 bis 20 Patienten. Beim letzten Mal haben wir zu zweit 180 Kranke operiert. Wobei es mich immer wieder erstaunt, mit welch einfachen Mitteln unsere Anästhesistin auskommt und dass insbesondere alle Operationen ohne große Infektion abgehen. Da kommen die Patienten mit völlig verdreckten Wunden auf den OP-Tisch, und die Wunden heilen ohne Antibiotika.

ZEIT: In München verdienen Sie Ihr Geld mit Schönheitsoperationen, in Afghanistan flicken Sie kriegsversehrte und missgebildete Kinder zusammen. Wie finden Sie sich in zwei so verschiedenen Welten zurecht?

SCHOENEICH: Manchmal muss ich allerdings mein ärztliches Tun in Deutschland infrage stellen. Von Haus aus bin ich plastischer Chirurg. Ich war zehn Jahre an der Uni und habe fast alles gemacht: von der angeborenen Missbildung über Tumorchirurgie, Handchirurgie, Wiederherstellung nach Unfällen bis zur Geschlechtsumwandlung. Mit Schönheitsoperationen verdiene ich das Geld für meine Einsätze in Afghanistan und Birma. Interplast bezahlt nur den Flug, aber kein Gehalt.

Das Gespräch führte Sabine Etzold

DIE ZEIT, 27. September 2001, Nr. 40, S. 32

a. Vokabelübung. (i) Ergänzen Sie den Artikel. (ii) Wie heißt das Wort (die Wendung) auf Englisch?
   1. Schönheitsoperation
   2. Kriegsopfer
   3. Kriegsverletzung
   4. angeborene Missbildung
   5. Unterversorgung
   6. Impfstoff
   7. Verwachsung
   8. Tumorchirurgie
   9. Handchirurgie
   10. Geschlechtsumwandlung

b. Fassen Sie den Text kurz zusammen.

Unit 4

Physical appearance

Level 1

Build

Körperbau, der (no pl.)	build, physique
Figur, die (-en)	figure, physique
dick	fat, thick
dicklich	pudgy
fett	fat
Bauch, der (¨e)	stomach, paunch
einen Bauch ansetzen	to put on a paunch
dickbäuchig	paunchy, pot-bellied
breit	broad
schlank	slender, slim
dünn	thin
mager	thin, gaunt, skinny, scraggy
groß	big, large, great, tall
Größe, die (-n)	height, size
mittelgroß	of average height
von mittlerer Größe sein	to be of average height
klein	small, little, short
ab-, zunehmen	to lose/gain weight
ein Kilo ab-, zunehmen	to lose/gain one kilo
wiegen	to weigh
Gewicht, das (-e)	weight
schwer	heavy
stark	strong
athletisch	athletic

Face

gut/gesund aussehen	to look well
blühend	glowing
blühend aussehen	to look marvellous/the picture of health
jugendlich aussehen	to look youthful
jung aussehend	fresh-faced
älter	elderly
ältlich	rather elderly, oldish
jmdm ähnlich sehen	to resemble sb
sich verändern	to change
ein Gesicht machen/ziehen	to make/pull a face
ein trauriges Gesicht machen	to look sad
ein böses Gesicht machen	to look cross
ein fröhliches Gesicht machen	to look pleasant/cheerful
ein offenes Gesicht	an open face
ein leuchtendes Gesicht	a radiant face
ein strahlendes Gesicht	a radiant face
ein frisches Gesicht	a cheerful face
ein freudiges Gesicht	a delighted face

ein (tod)ernstes Gesicht	a (deadly) serious face	eine feine Nase	a delicate nose
ein blasses Gesicht	a pale face	eine gerade Nase	a straight nose
ein unfreundliches Gesicht	an unpleasant face	eine lange Nase	a long nose
ein erstauntes Gesicht	an astonished face	eine spitze Nase	a pointed nose
ein bekanntes Gesicht	a familiar face	trockene/feuchte Lippen	dry/moist lips
ein längliches Gesicht	a long face	dicke Lippen	thick, swollen lips
ein breites Gesicht	a wide face	dünne Lippen	thin lips
ein schmales Gesicht	a thin face	ein rundes Kinn	a round chin
ein volles Gesicht	a full face	ein spitzes Kinn	a pointed chin
ein zartes Gesicht	a delicate face	bärtig	bearded
ein niedliches Gesicht	a cute face	glattrasiert	clean shaven

eine feine Nase — a delicate nose
eine gerade Nase — a straight nose
eine lange Nase — a long nose
eine spitze Nase — a pointed nose
trockene/feuchte Lippen — dry/moist lips
dicke Lippen — thick, swollen lips
dünne Lippen — thin lips
ein rundes Kinn — a round chin
ein spitzes Kinn — a pointed chin
bärtig — bearded
glattrasiert — clean shaven

ein (tod)ernstes Gesicht — a (deadly) serious face
ein blasses Gesicht — a pale face
ein unfreundliches Gesicht — an unpleasant face
ein erstauntes Gesicht — an astonished face
ein bekanntes Gesicht — a familiar face
ein längliches Gesicht — a long face
ein breites Gesicht — a wide face
ein schmales Gesicht — a thin face
ein volles Gesicht — a full face
ein zartes Gesicht — a delicate face
ein niedliches Gesicht — a cute face
Gesichtsausdruck, der (¨e) — expression
Miene, die (-n) — expression, face
eine ernste Miene — a serious expression
eine freundliche Miene — a kind/friendly expression
Gesichtszüge, pl. — features
feine Gesichtszüge — delicate features
harte Gesichtszüge — severe, hard features
weiche Gesichtszüge — soft, gentle features
fettige/trockene Haut — oily/dry skin
weiche/zarte Haut — soft skin
Gesichtsfarbe, die (-n) — complexion
Hautfarbe, die (-n) — skin colour
dunkle/helle Hautfarbe — dark/light skin colour
(un)gesunde Hautfarbe — (un)healthy skin colour
rot werden — to blush
eine breite Stirn — a broad forehead
eine hohe/niedrige Stirn — a high/low forehead
verschwollene Augen — puffy eyes
buschige Augenbrauen — bushy eyebrows
eine breite Nase — a wide nose
eine schmale Nase — a thin nose

Hair

schönes Haar — nice hair
blondes Haar — blond/fair hair
graues Haar — grey hair
dunkles Haar — dark hair
helles Haar — fair hair
kurzes/langes Haar — short/long hair
das Haar kurz/lang tragen — to wear one's hair short/long
dichtes/dünnes Haar — thick/thin hair
seine Haare fallen (ihm) aus — his hair is falling out
fettiges/trockenes Haar — oily/dry hair
lockiges Haar — curly hair
Dauerwelle, die (-n) — perm
sich eine Dauerwelle machen lassen — to have one's hair permed
das Haar färben — to colour one's hair
das Haar blondieren — to bleach one's hair; dye one's hair blond
Glatze, die (-n) — bald head
eine Glatze haben — to be bald

Posture

(Körper)haltung, die (-en) — posture
eine gute/schlechte Haltung haben — to have good/bad posture
eine aufrechte Haltung — an erect posture

eine gebückte Haltung	a stoop	kurze/lange Finger	short/long finger
		dicke/dünne Finger	fat/thin fingers
in gebückter Haltung	bending forward	einen dicken Finger haben	to have a swollen finger
eine gekrümmte Haltung	a stoop		
in gekrümmter Haltung	stooping	***(Un)attractiveness***	
		schön	beautiful
eine bequeme Haltung	a comfortable posture	bildschön	very beautiful, ravishing
hängende Schultern	drooping/sloping/ round shoulders	unschön	unsightly, ugly, plain [face]
die Schultern hängen lassen	to slouch	hübsch	pretty; nice-looking
		gut aussehend	good-looking, handsome
Limbs		hässlich (wie die Sünde)	ugly (as sin)
kurze/lange Beine	short/long legs		
schöne Beine haben	to have good legs	süß	very pretty
dicke/dünne Beine haben	to have fat/thin legs	niedlich	cute
		(un)attraktiv	(un)attractive
meine Beine sind dick (geworden)	my legs are swollen	eine gute/hübsche Figur haben	to have a good/nice figure

Level 2

Build		kraftvoll	vigorous
fleischig	fleshy	stämmig	stocky, sturdy, burly
beleibt	stout, portly		
wohlbeleibt	corpulent	schmal	slim, slender
dickleibig	corpulent, fat	eine schlanke/schmale Taille haben	to be slim/ narrow-waisted
fettleibig	obese		
mollert (coll., AU)	obese		
vollschlank	full-figured	winzig	tiny
rund	rotund	missgebildet, -gestaltet	deformed
rundlich	chubby, tubby		
kugelrund (hum.)	rotund, plump, tubby	hager	gaunt, thin, lean, scrawny
Bauchansatz, der (¨e)	beginnings of a paunch	abgemagert, -gemergelt	emaciated
Übergewicht haben	to be overweight	verhungert aussehen	to look half-starved
übergewichtig	overweight		
kräftig	well-built, sturdy, hefty	knochig	bony
		nur Haut und Knochen sein (coll.)	to be nothing but skin and bones
muskulös	muscular		
breitschultrig	broad-shouldered		

Face

ein anderes Gesicht aufsetzen/machen	to put on a different face
ein entspanntes Gesicht	a relaxed face
ein bleiches Gesicht	a pale face
ein kreidebleiches Gesicht	a face white as chalk
ein graues Gesicht	an ashen face
ein angespanntes Gesicht	a tense face
ihr Gesicht war vor Sorge angespannt	her face was tense with anxiety
ein wütendes Gesicht machen	to look angry
ein rötliches Gesicht	a ruddy face
ein gerötetes Gesicht	a flushed face
ein hochrotes Gesicht	a bright red face
ein zufriedenes Gesicht machen	to look contented/ satisfied
ein ausdrucksvolles Gesicht	an expressive face
ein ausdrucksloses Gesicht	an expressionless/ impassive face
ein steinernes Gesicht	a stony face
mit versteinertem Gesicht	stony-faced
ein braungebranntes/ gebräuntes Gesicht	a tanned face
ein geschminktes Gesicht	a rouged face
ein regelmäßiges Gesicht	a face with regular features
ein feingeschnittenes Gesicht	a finely shaped face
ein unverwechselbares Gesicht	a distinctive face
ein jungenhaftes Gesicht	a boyish face
ein faltiges Gesicht	a wrinkled face

über das ganze Gesicht strahlen (coll.)	to beam all over one's face; be all smiles
über das ganze Gesicht lächeln	to be all smiles
edle Gesichtszüge	finely shaped features
strenge Gesichtszüge	severe features
ausgeprägte Gesichtszüge	pronounced features
eine liebenswürdige Miene	a kind/charming expression
eine heitere Miene	a cheerful expression
eine besorgte Miene aufsetzen	to put on a worried expression
Teint, der (-s)	complexion
empfindliche Haut	sensitive skin
Pickel, der (-)	pimple
pickelig	pimply
rauhe Haut	rough skin
runz(e)lige Haut	wrinkled skin
glatte Haut	smooth skin
grobe Haut	coarse skin
großporige Haut	large-pored skin
olivbraune Haut	olive skin
hellhäutig	fair-skinned
dunkelhäutig	dark-skinned, swarthy
rosige Haut	rosy skin
rot anlaufen	to turn red
sommersprossige Haut	freckled skin
eine runzlige Stirn	a lined brow
die Stirn runzeln	to frown
eine glatte Stirn	a smooth forehead
(dunkle) Ringe um die Augen	(dark) circles under one's eyes
Schatten unter den Augen	shadows under one's eyes
staunende Augen	bulging eyes [from surprise]
hervortretende Augen	bulging eyes
vorstehende Augenbrauen	prominent eyebrows

vorstehende Backenknochen	prominent cheekbones	sein Haar hinten zu einem Pferdeschwanz zusammenbinden	to tie one's hair back in a ponytail
rotbackig, -bäckig	rosy-cheeked		
eine krumme Nase	a crooked nose	das Haar aufgesteckt tragen	to wear one's hair up
eine edle Nase	a finely shaped nose		
eine scharfe Nase	a sharp nose	sich die Haare aufbinden	to put one's hair up
eine platte Nase	a flat nose		
eine fleischige Nase	a fleshy nose	das Haar im Knoten tragen	to wear one's hair in a bun
breite/schmale Lippen	thick/thin lips	das Haar links/rechts gescheitelt tragen	to wear one's hair parted on the left/right
volle Lippen	full lips		
blasse Lippen	pale lips		
Doppelkinn, das (-e)	double chin	das Haar in der Mitte gescheitelt tragen	to wear one's hair parted in the middle
ein kräftiges Kinn	a strong chin		
ein energisches Kinn	a forceful chin		
		Bürstenschnitt, der (no pl.)	crew cut

Hair

tiefschwarzes Haar	jet-black hair
kastanienbraunes Haar	chestnut hair

Posture

rotbraunes Haar	auburn hair	eine straffe/ strammige Haltung	an erect posture
rotblondes Haar	carroty hair		
kupferrotes Haar	coppery hair	eine krumme Haltung haben	to stoop
angegrautes Haar	greying hair		
silbernes Haar (poet.)	silvery hair	krumm werden	to develop a stoop
schlohweißes Haar	snow-white hair	eine schlaffe Haltung	a slouch
flachsblondes Haar	flaxen hair	eine lässige Haltung	a casual posture
glänzendes Haar	shiny/lustrous hair	den Rücken krümmen	to hunch one's back
seidiges Haar	silky/sleek hair		
feines Haar	fine hair	einen Buckel haben	to be a hunchback
starkes/volles Haar	thick hair	buck(e)lig	hunch-backed
schönes volles Haar	a fine head of hair		
offenes Haar	loose hair		
glattes Haar	straight hair		

Limbs

welliges Haar	wavy hair	kräftige Beine	strong legs
krauses Haar	frizzy hair	wohlgeformte Beine	shapely legs
Krause, die (no pl.)	frizziness, frizzy hair	schlanke Beine	slender legs
das Haar legen	to set one's hair	geschwollene Beine	swollen legs
das Haar in Locken legen	to curl one's hair	rechts-, linkshändig	right-, left-handed
		zarte/schlanke Finger	delicate/slender fingers
ungekämmtes Haar	unkempt hair		
zurückgekämmtes Haar	swept-back hair		

(Un)attractiveness

Pferdeschwanz, der (¨e)	ponytail	hinreißend	enchanting, adorable
		bezaubernd	enchanting

schick	chic	abstoßend	repulsive
auffallend	striking	entstellt	disfigured
appetitlich	attractive	eine entstellende	a disfiguring scar
unappetitlich	unsavoury-looking	Narbe	
unansehnlich	plain		

Level 3

Build

behäbig	stolid and portly	ein verzerrtes	a distorted face
füllig	corpulent, portly [person]; ample, portly [figure]	Gesicht	
		ein undurch- dringliches	an inscrutable face
Fettkloß, der (¨e; coll., pej.)	fatso	Gesicht	
Dickwanst, der (¨e; coll.)	fatso	ein durchgeistigtes Gesicht	a spiritual look
		ein hageres/ eingefallenes	a gaunt face
Fett ansetzen	to put on weight	Gesicht	
zu Fettansatz neigen	to tend to put on weight	ein kantiges Gesicht	an angular face
		mit teigigem Gesicht	pasty-faced
üppig	voluptuous	ein mürrisches	a sullen face
kurvenreich	curvaceous	Gesicht	
pummelig	chubby	ein gelassenes	a serene face
mollig	plump	Gesicht	
schlankwüchsig	of slender/slim build	ein verhutzeltes	a wizened face
rank	lissome	Gesicht	
gertenschlank	willowy	ein	a face streaked with
schlaksig	lanky	tränenverschmiertes	tears
grazil	delicate	Gesicht	
zierlich	slightly built, petite, dainty	ein markantes Gesicht	a striking, distinctive face
verkrüppelt	stunted	Pferdegesicht, das (-er)	horsy face
winzig klein	midget	ein schwermütiges	a melancholic face
mick(e)rig	puny	Gesicht	
dürr	scrawny	ein mürrisches/	to scowl
spindeldürr	skinny	verdrießliches	
spill(e)rig	skinny	Gesicht machen	
flachbrüstig	flat-chested	schmollen	to pout, sulk
vollbusig	full-bosomed, busty, buxom	Schmollmund, der (no pl.)	pout
		einen Schmollmund machen	to pout
### *Face*		Duldermiene, die (-n)	martyred expression
abgespannt aussehen	to look drawn [from tiredness]		
abgehärmt aussehen	to look drawn [from worries]		

mit unbewegter Miene	with an impassive expression; straight-faced	eine gebogene Nase	an aquiline nose
ohne eine Miene zu verziehen	straight-faced	Adlernase, die (-n)	aquiline nose
eine verschlossene Miene	a reserved expression	aufgesprungene Lippen	chapped lips
seine Miene verfinsterte/ verdüsterte sich	his face darkened	rissige Lippen	cracked/chapped lips
		aufgeworfene Lippen	pursed lips
Grimasse, die (-n)	grimace	die Lippen aufwerfen/ schürzen	to purse one's lips
schlaffe/straffe Haut	flaccid/firm skin		
rissige Haut	cracked, chapped skin	die Lippen kräuseln	to pucker one's lips
		ein Kinn mit einem Grübchen	a cleft chin
wettergegerbte Haut	weather-beaten skin	ein fliehendes Kinn	a receding chin
fahle Haut	pale/pallid skin	ein vorspringendes/ vorstehendes Kinn	a prominent/ protruding chin
gelbliche Haut	sallow skin		
makellose Haut	perfect skin	ein markantes Kinn	a prominent chin
fleckige Haut	blotchy skin	ein kantiges Kinn	a square jaw
eine fliehende Stirn	a sloping forehead		
eine gewölbte Stirn	a domed forehead	*Hair*	
eine steile Stirn	a steep forehead	sich lichten	to grow thin [hair]
eine zerfurchte Stirn	a furrowed brow	lichtes Haar haben	to be thin on top
Mandelaugen, pl.	almond eyes	spärliches Haar	thin hair
hohläugig	hollow-eyed	schütteres Haar	thin hair
tiefliegende Augen	deep-set eyes	strähniges Haar	straggly hair
eng zusammenste- hende Augen	close-set eyes	widerspenstiges Haar	fly-away/ unmanageable hair
schlitzäugig (also pej.)	slant-eyed		
verquollene Augen	puffy eyes [esp. from crying]	verstrubbeltes/ strubb(e)liges Haar	tousled hair
		wirres Haar	tangled hair
blutunterlaufene Augen	blood-shot eyes	zerzaustes Haar	tousled/dishevelled hair
Tränensäcke unter den Augen haben	to have bags under one's eyes		
		zottiges Haar	shaggy hair
Pausbacken, pl.	red, chubby cheeks	wuscheliges Haar (coll.)	frizzy hair
pausbackig, -bäckig	chubby-cheeked		
eingefallene Backen	hollow cheeks	Wuschelkopf, der (¨e; coll.)	mop of frizzy hair
eine knollige Nase	a bulbous nose		
eine höckrige Nase	a nose with a bump	lockeres Haar	fluffy hair
Hakennase, die (-n)	hooked nose	angeklatschte Haare	plastered-down hair
Stupsnase, die (-n)	snub/turned-up nose	stumpfes Haar	dull hair
Stumpfnase, die (-n)	pug nose	wallendes Haar	flowing hair
		einen Zopf/Zöpfe tragen	to wear a braid/ braids, plait(s)
stumpfnasig	pug-nosed		

das Haar in Zöpfe flechten	to braid, plait one's hair
Haarbüschel, das (-)	tuft of hair
gespaltene Haarspitzen	split ends
Spliss, der (no pl.)	split ends
das Haar tönen	to tint one's hair
sich Streifen ins Haar färben lassen	to have one's hair streaked
ihr stehen die Haare zu Berge	her hair is standing on end
ihr sträuben sich die Haare	her hair is standing on end

Limbs

krumme Beine	bow legs
krummbeinig	bow-legged
O-Beine, pl.	bow legs
o-beinig	bow-legged
x-beinig	knock-kneed
aufgesprungene Hände	chapped hands
Wurstfinger, pl.	pudgy/stubby fingers
klobige Finger	huge fingers
verkrüppelte Finger	crippled fingers
flinke Finger	nimble fingers
geschickte Finger	dexterous fingers
ungeschickte Finger	clumsy fingers

Gesture and movement

Level 1

General

gehen	to go, walk
fahren	to go [by vehicle], travel, ride
zu Fuß gehen	to go on foot
spazieren gehen/fahren	to go for a walk/drive
mitgehen	to go along, go with
kommen	to come
laufen	to run, walk, go
sich/etw bewegen	to move/move sth
Bewegung, die (-en)	movement
sich umdrehen	to turn around
weggehen	to leave, go away
losgehen	to set off
abfahren	to depart, leave
etw verlassen	to leave sth
ankommen	to arrive
Ankunft, die (¨e)	arrival
jmdm/einer Sache folgen	to follow sb/sth
vorbeigehen	to pass
wandern	to hike
Wanderung, die (-en)	hike
etw reiten	to ride sth [a horse, steed]

die Plätze tauschen	to change places
etw überqueren	to cross sth [street]

Movement forwards and backwards

sich vorwärts bewegen	to move forward
zurückgehen	to go back, return
Rückwärtsbewegung, die (-en)	backwards movement
weitergehen	to go on
nach links/rechts biegen	to turn left/right
schieben	to push, shove
sich durch die Menge schieben	to push one's way through the crowd
jmdn/etw erreichen	to reach sb/sth
Fortschritte machen	to make headway
etw ziehen	to pull sth
marschieren	to march
Marsch, der (¨e)	march, walk, hike
Parade, die (-n)	parade
paradieren	to parade

Movement upwards and downwards

aufstehen	to stand up, get up
hinauf-, hinuntergehen	to go up/down
nach oben gehen	to go up
aufwärts	up(wards)
abwärts	down(wards)
herunterkommen	to come down
steigen	to climb
hinauf-, hinuntersteigen	to climb up, go up/climb down
springen	to jump
Sprung, der (¨e)	jump, leap
sich (hin)setzen	to sit down
fallen	to fall
umfallen	to fall over/down
hinfallen	to fall down
zusammenfallen	to collapse
sich (hin)legen	to lie down

Fast and slow movement

eilen	to hurry
sich beeilen	to hurry
es eilig haben	to be in a hurry
rennen	to run
jagen	to race
nach etwas jagen	to chase after sth
hinter jmdm/etw herjagen	to chase after sb/sth
stürzen	to rush, dash
auf jmdn/etw zustürzen	to rush towards sb/sth
hinein-, hereinstürzen	to burst in
bummeln	to stroll
(auf allen vieren) kriechen	to crawl (on all fours)
herumwandern	to wander around

Movement of the limbs

etw setzen	to set/put sth
etw werfen	to throw/fling sth
etw hochwerfen	to toss sth up
jmdm etw zuwerfen	to toss sth to sb
etw fortwerfen	to fling sth away
etw schieben	to push sth
(etw) stoßen	to punch/kick/butt/dig (sth)
jmdn/etw schlagen	to hit/beat/strike sb/sth
jmdn mit der Faust schlagen	to punch sb
etw kratzen	to scratch sth
jmdm die Hand geben	to shake sb's hand
jmdm winken	to wave one's hand at/to sb
etw reiben	to rub sth
jmdn in die Arme nehmen	to take sb in one's arms
jmdn/etw fangen	to catch sb/sth
jmdn an die/bei der Hand nehmen	to take sb by the hand
Geste, die (-n)	gesture
etw greifen	to take hold of/grasp sth
mit beiden Händen zugreifen	to seize with both hands
etw festhalten	to hold on to sth
sich an jmdm/etw festhalten	to hold on to sb/sth
etw anfassen	to touch/feel/take hold of sth
jmdn anfassen	to take sb's hand
etw drehen	to twist sth
in die Hände klatschen	to clap one's hands
jmdm ins Gesicht schlagen	to slap sb on the face
jmdm (mit der flachen Hand) schlagen	to give sb a slap
jmdm auf die Schulter klopfen	to give sb a pat on the shoulder
herumstehen	to stand around
(etw) rühren	to stir (sth)
etw umrühren	to stir sth

Movement of the head

den Kopf schütteln	to shake one's head
den Kopf drehen	to turn one's head
sich nach etw umdrehen	to turn one's head towards sth
den Kopf heben	to raise one's head
den Kopf beugen/senken	to bow one's head
mit dem Kopf nicken	to nod one's head
Zustimmung nicken	to nod one's agreement
jmdm zunicken	to nod to sb
den Kopf zurückwerfen	to throw/toss one's head back

Leaning and bending

sich auf etw stützen	to lean against sth
sich mit dem Ellbogen auf etw stützen	to lean one's elbow on sth
sich gegen etw lehnen	to lean against sth
sich anlehnen	to lean
sich hinauslehnen	to lean out
sich zurücklehnen	to lean back
sich im Sessel zurücklehnen	to lean back in one's chair

sich bücken	to bend
sich beugen	to bow
sich nach vorn beugen	to bend/lean forward
kippen	to tip over

Impact

gegen etw/einander stoßen	to bump against sth/each other
jmdn anstoßen	to bump into sb
mit jmdm zusammenstoßen	to collide with sb; bump into sb
Zusammenstoß, der (¨e)	collision
etw umstoßen	to knock sth over
gegen etw fahren	to run into sth
jmdn umfahren	to knock sb over/ down [with a vehicle]
einen Unfall haben	to have a crash, an accident
mit etw kollidieren	to collide with sth
Karambolage, die (-n)	crash, collision
(etw) hämmern	to hammer (sth)
mit der Faust an die Tür hämmern	to thump the door with one's fist

Level 2

General

Gang, der (¨e)	walk, gait
Bahn, die (-en)	path, orbit, trajectory
Schritt, der (-e)	step, pace
treten	to step
sich regen	to move
sich rühren	to stir
aufbrechen	to set off, start out
sich (jmdm/einer Sache) nähern	to approach (sb/sth)
jmdm begegnen	to meet sb, run into sb
(jmdm) vorangehen	to go ahead (of sb)

an jmdm/etw vorbeigehen	to pass sb/sth
etw überholen	to pass sth [in a car]
vorbeiziehen	to pass [procession]
sich entfernen	to go away
umkehren	to turn back
die Runde machen	to circulate
tippeln (coll.)	to walk
einem Schlag ausweichen	to dodge a blow
sich vor etw drücken	to dodge sth
etw durchqueren	to cross sth [country]
etw überfliegen	to fly over sth, overfly sth

Movement forwards and backwards

abbiegen	to turn off (e.g. a road)
zurücktreten	to step back
zurückkehren	to return, come back
Rückkehr, die (no pl.)	return
hin	away from me/here
her	towards me/here
hin und her gehen	to walk back and forth
vorankommen	to make progress
sich nach vorn durcharbeiten	to work one's way forward
sich an jmdn wenden	to turn to sb
auf jmdn/etw zugehen	to move towards sb/sth
(an jmdm/etw) vorbeimarschieren	to march past (sb/sth)
Vorbeimarsch, der (¨e)	parade

Movement upwards and downwards

(hinunter-, hinauf)klettern	to climb (down/up)
sich aufsetzen	to sit up
Aufstieg, der (-e)	climb, ascent
etw besteigen	to climb up sth, ascend sth
aufspringen	to jump up; leap to one's feet
auf und ab	up and down
ausrutschen	to slip (and fall)
(etw) hinunterrutschen	to slide down (sth)
auf die Nase fallen (coll.)	to fall flat on one's face
etw hochheben	to lift up sth
zusammenbrechen	to collapse, cave in, crumble
zusammensinken	to collapse, slump
hinab-, niedersinken	to sink down

Fast and slow movement

in Eile sein	to be in a hurry
mach schnell! (coll.)	hurry!
davonlaufen	to run away
die Beine unter den Arm nehmen	to take to one's heels
die Beine in die Hand nehmen	to take to one's heels
abhauen (coll.)	to clear out
auf der Flucht	on the run
sausen	to dash, rush
rasen	to dash/rush/tear along
hetzen	to rush; tear, race, dash
fegen (coll.)	to sweep
spurten	to spurt; sprint, dash
sprinten	to sprint
stürmen	to storm
herumtoben, -tollen	to romp around
seine Schritte beschleunigen/ verlangsamen	to quicken/slow one's pace
schreiten	to stride
stiefeln (coll.)	to stride, hoof it
schlendern	to stroll, saunter
sich im Schneckentempo bewegen	to move at a crawl, a snail's pace

Movement of the limbs

etw treten	to kick sth
jmdm einen Tritt geben/versetzen	to give sb a kick
jmdn boxen	to punch sb
jmdn hauen (coll.)	to belt/clobber/beat sb
jmdm ins Gesicht hauen (coll.)	to hit/belt/slap sb in the face
die Arme verschränken	to cross one's arms
die Beine übereinander schlagen	to cross one's legs
das Bein hochwerfen	to kick [dancer]
gestikulieren	to gesticulate
jmdn packen	to seize, grab hold of
(sich) jmdn/etw schnappen (coll.)	to grab/snatch sb/sth

jmdn kneifen	to pinch sb
Händeschütteln, das (no pl.)	hand-shaking
jmdn umarmen	to hug sb
sich/einander umarmen	to embrace (reciprocal)
etw kneten	to knead sth
jmdm einen Klaps geben	to give sb a slap/smack
mit den Fingern auf den Tisch trommeln	to drum one's fingers on the desk
die Faust ballen	to clench one's fist/fingers
mit dem Fuß stampfen	to stamp one's foot
auf Zehenspitzen gehen	to tiptoe, walk on tiptoe
etw schwenken	to swing/wave sth
etw schwingen	to swing/wave/ brandish/wield sth
etw befühlen	to feel/run one's hands over sth
etw berühren	to touch sth
etw ausstreuen	to scatter sth
sich an jmdn/etw klammern	to cling to sb/sth
sich an etw hängen	to hang on to sth
sich in die Arme fallen	to fall into each other's arms
etw schmeißen (coll.)	to chuck, toss, sling, fling, hurl sth
den Arm beugen	to flex one's arm
das Knie beugen	to bend one's knee
Kniebeuge, die (-n)	knee bend
seine Knie umfassen	to hug one's knees
die Beine strecken	to stretch one's legs
sich dehnen/recken	to stretch

Movement of the head

den Kopf neigen	to incline one's head
den Kopf (ab)wenden	to turn one's head (away)
etw köpfen	to head sth [football]
etw köpfeln (S, AU, CH)	to head sth [football]

den Kopf einziehen	to duck
den Kopf (in die Höhe) recken	to crane one's neck
den Kopf vorstrecken	to crane one's neck forward
blinzeln, zwinkern	to blink, wink
mit den Augen blinzeln/zwinkern	to bat one's eyes

Balance and imbalance

stolpern	to stumble, trip
gegen etw stoßen	to stumble against sth
fest/sicher auf den Beinen	steady on one's feet
unsicher/wackelig auf den Beinen sein	to be unsteady on one's feet
wackeln	to totter
schwanken	to sway
auf etw steigen	to mount sth
etw besteigen	to mount sth

Leaning and bending

sich vorbeugen	to lean forward
sich neigen	to lean, bend
etw anwinkeln	to bend sth [knee, arm]
etw abwinkeln	to bend [arm, leg]
etw krumm machen	to bend sth [finger]
(nieder)knien	to kneel (down)
auf den Knien	on bended knee(s)
sich (vor jmdm) verbeugen	to bow (to sb)
sich (vor jmdm) verneigen (elev.)	to bow (to/before sb)
sich vor Lachen biegen/krümmen	to double up with laughter
sich ducken	to duck

Impact

gegen einander prallen	to knock against each other
gegen/auf/an etw prallen	to hit/collide with sth

zusammenprallen	to collide
gegen etwas krachen	to crash into sth
gegen/auf etw rammen	to ram/crash into sth
Flugzeugunglück, das (-e)	plane crash
Eisenbahnunglück, das (-e)	train crash

sich prügeln	to thump each other
mit der Tür knallen	to bang/slam the door
mit dem Wagen gegen etw knallen	to smash the car into sth
den Hörer auf die Gabel knallen	to slam/bang down the receiver

Level 3

Movement forwards and backwards

drei Schritte vortreten	to take three steps forward
vorrücken	to move forward [also troops]
drängen	to push, press
sich drängen	to crowd, throng, push one's way
drängeln	to push (and shove)
sich nach vorn drängeln	to push one's way to the front
Schubs, der (-e; coll.)	shove
zurückweichen	to draw back, shrink back
sich zurückziehen	to retire, withdraw, retreat
sich schleppen	to drag oneself
im Zickzack laufen	to zigzag
auf jmdn/etw zusteuern	to head for sb/sth
auf etw zuhalten	to head for sth
rückwärts herausfahren	to back out
einen Rückzieher machen	to back out

Movement upwards and downwards

stürzen	to fall, plunge, plummet
ins Zimmer stürzen	to bound into the room
Sturz, der (¨e)	fall

zusammenstürzen	to collapse, cave in
etw ersteigen	to scale sth
Ersteigung, die (-en)	ascent
etw erklettern	to scale sth, climb to the top of sth
sich aufbäumen	to rear up [horse]
aufschrecken	to start
von seinem Stuhl hoch fahren	to start from one's chair
sich plumpsen lassen	to flop down
jmdn zu Boden strecken	to knock sb down; send sb sprawling
herunterkrachen	to crash down
vor Freude hüpfen	to jump for joy
sich (nieder)hocken	to crouch/squat (down)
sich senken	to come down; subside; sink; descend
Senkung, die (-en)	lowering, reduction, subsidence

Fast and slow movement

sich sputen	to hurry
schleudern	to skid
ins Schleudern kommen	to go into a skid
ausreißen (coll.)	to run away
verduften (coll.)	to beat it
huschen	to slip, steal, flit, dart
zurückschrecken	to flinch

traben	to trot	Ohrfeige, die (-n)	slap on the face; box on the ears
im Trab	at a trot		
wandeln	to stroll	jmdm eine Ohrfeige geben	to slap sb's face; box sb's ears
stapfen	to tramp		
latschen (sl.)	to trudge	jmdn ohrfeigen	to slap/hit sb; box sb's ears
trotten	to trudge		
tappen	to come/go falteringly	Schlag mit dem Handrücken, der (¨e)	back-handed slap
schlurfen	to shuffle		
trödeln	to dawdle, loiter	jmdn zu Brei hauen (sl.)	to beat sb's brains in
trippeln	to patter		
zotteln	to saunter, amble	jmdn windelweich/ grün und blau hauen (coll.)	to beat sb black and blue
zockeln, zuckeln	to saunter, amble		
gammeln (coll.)	to laze/loaf about, bum around	in die Pedale treten	to pedal
		jmdm etw entreißen	to grab sth away from sb
krabbeln	to crawl		
		nach etw tappen	to grope for sth
		jmdn/etw streifen	to brush against sb/sth

Movement of the limbs

jmdn/etw im Würgegriff haben	to have a stranglehold on sb/sth	jmdn mit offenen Armen auf- nehmen/empfangen	to welcome sb with open arms
eine Linke/Rechte schlagen	to throw a left/right	etw von etw schnip- pen/schnipsen (coll.)	to flick sth from sth
Spagat machen	to do the splits		
ausschlagen	to kick [horse]	etw betasten	to feel sth [with one's fingers]
scharren	to paw at the ground [horse]	etw verstreuen	to scatter sth, strew sth
an der Tür scharren	to scratch/paw at the door [dog]	etw streicheln	to stroke sth
jmdm die Hand reichen (elev.)	to shake sb's hand		
jmdn in die Arme schließen (elev.)	to take sb in one's arms		

Balance and imbalance

mit den Armen herumfuchteln (coll.)	to wave one's arms around	trippeln	to trip
		torkeln	to stagger, reel
		taumeln	to stagger, sway
die Beine baumeln lassen	to dangle one's legs	wanken	to stagger, sway, totter
jmdn liebkosen	to caress sb	einen Purzelbaum schlagen	to (do a) somersault
jmdn tätscheln	to pat sb		
etw abtasten	to feel sth all over	einen Salto machen	to somersault [sports]
jmdn auf Waffen abtasten	to frisk sb for weapons	schwingen	to oscillate
jmdn zwicken (S; AU)	to pinch sb		

Gait

stolzieren	to strut
stelzen	to strut, stalk
großspurig stolzieren	to walk with a swagger
arrogant auftreten	to walk with a swagger
tänzeln	to prance, skip
hüpfen	to skip
sich in den Hüften wiegen	to sway one's hips
einen wiegenden Gang haben	to have a rolling gait
watscheln	to waddle
über den Onkel gehen	to walk pigeon-toed
onkeln (coll.)	to walk pigeon-toed
lahmen	to be lame
hinken	to limp, hobble
humpeln	to limp, hobble; walk with a limp
trippeln	to mince

Impact

Massenkarambolage, die (-n)	pile-up
etw an die Wand schmettern	to smash sth against the wall
etw zerschmettern	to smash sth to pieces
zurückprallen	to bounce back
von etw abprallen	to bounce off sth
vom Wind geschüttet	buffeted by the wind
von den Wellen hin und her geworfen	buffeted by the waves
jmdn durchrütteln	to shake sb about badly
etw schütteln	to shake/joggle sth
jmdn durchschütteln	to give sb a good shaking [bus]

jmdm einen Schock versetzen	to give sb a jolt
jmdm einen Schreck(en) einjagen	to give sb a jolt

Insidious movement

(sich) schleichen	to creep, sneak, steal
sich stehlen	to steal, creep
aus dem Zimmer schlüpfen	to slip out of the room
jmdm entwischen	to give sb the slip
entschlüpfen	to escape, slip away
sich einschleichen	to steal/sneak/creep in
sich durch etw zwängen	to worm one's way through sth
sich in etw hineindrängen	to worm one's way into sth
etw beschleichen	to creep up on/to sth; steal up to sth, stalk sth

Wriggling movements

sich durch etw schlängeln	to wriggle through sth; worm one's way through sth
sich in etw zwängen	to wiggle into sth
sich aus etw herauswinden	to wriggle out of sth
mit den Hüften wackeln	to wiggle one's hips
sich winden	to writhe
auf dem Stuhl herumrutschen	to wriggle about on one's chair
zappeln	to wriggle, fidget
zappelig sein	to have the fidgets
von etw wimmeln	to be swarming/teeming with sth

Exercises

Level 1

1. Wie heißt das Gegenteil? ✓

1. dick
2. groß
3. abnehmen
4. ein breites Gesicht
5. harte Gesichtszüge
6. dunkle Hautfarbe
7. trockene Haut
8. eine hohe Stirn
9. trockene Lippen
10. ein rundes Kinn
11. dunkles Haar
12. kurzes Haar
13. dünnes Haar
14. trockenes Haar
15. eine gute Haltung haben
16. kurze Beine
17. kurze Finger
18. dicke Finger
19. schön
20. attraktiv

2. Wie heißt das Adjektiv? ✓

a. ältlich, b. bärtig, c. bildschön, d. dickbäuchig, e. fett, f. lockig, g. mager, h. süß, i. todernst

1. sehr schön
2. mit Bart
3. mit einem dicken Bauch
4. dick
5. sehr ernst
6. Locken habend
7. sehr hübsch
8. etwas alt
9. dünn

3. Welches Adjektiv passt nicht? ✓

1. der Körperbau: athletisch, blass, dicklich, kräftig, schlank
2. das Gesicht: frisch, fröhlich, länglich, strähnig, voll
3. die Nase: aufrecht, breit, gerade, lang, spitz
4. das Haar: blondiert, rot, grau, runzelig, schön
5. die Körperhaltung: aufrecht, bequem, gekrümmt, lässig, schlank

4. Welches Wort bzw. welcher Ausdruck hat die gleiche oder eine ähnliche Bedeutung? ✓

1. ein leuchtendes Gesicht
2. der Gesichtsausdruck
3. weiche Haut
4. eine gebückte Haltung
5. hinaufgehen
6. umfallen
7. eilen
8. etw rühren
9. den Kopf beugen

5. Welches Verb passt? ✓

a. geben, b. gehen, c. haben, d. klatschen, e. kriechen, f. machen, g. nehmen, h. schlagen, i. tauschen, j. zurücklehnen

1. zu Fuß
2. die Plätze
3. Fortschritte
4. auf allen vieren
5. jmdn mit der Faust

6. jmdm die Hand
7. jmdn an die Hand
8. in die Hände
9. sich im Sessel
10. einen Unfall

6. In jedem Satz fehlt ein Wort. ✓

anfassen, Arme, beugte, Gesten, klopfte, nicken, schieben, Sprung, schütteln, winken, Zusammenstoß

1. Er begleitete seine Worte mit vielen _____.
2. Wir konnten uns nicht durch die Menge _____.
3. "Dies ist ein kleiner Schritt für einen Menschen, aber ein riesiger _____ für die Menschheit." (Neil Armstrong)
4. Sie _____ ihm zum Abschied.
5. Bei dem _____ wurde eine Autofahrerin schwer verletzt.
6. Kinder können hier Tiere _____ und streicheln.
7. Er _____ ihm auf die Schulter.
8. Einige Zuschauer lachen, andere _____ den Kopf.
9. Seine Kollegen _____ zustimmend.
10. Er _____ sich nach vorn.
11. Er nahm sie in die _____ und küsste sie.

7. Welches Präfix passt? ✓

a. ab, b. an, c. auf, d. fest, e. hinein, f. mit, g. um, h. vorbei, i. zu, j. zusammen

1. Sie ist an ihm _____gegangen, ohne zu grüßen.
2. Sie sind vor zwei Minuten mit dem Zug vom Hauptbahnhof _____gefahren.
3. Als sie sich _____drehte, erkannte ich sie.
4. Heute bin ich vor Sonnenaufgang _____gestanden.
5. Er hat sich am Geländer _____gehalten.
6. Ich habe ihm den Ball _____geworfen.
7. Er ist mit ihm _____gestoßen.
8. Darf ich _____gehen?
9. Bist du gut _____gekommen?
10. Die Mutter hörte das Geschrei der Kinder und stürzte ins Zimmer _____.

8. Was bedeuten die Wendungen?

1. gute Miene zum bösen Spiel machen
2. auf etw Gewicht legen
3. hässlich wie die Nacht
4. Himmel und Hölle in Bewegung setzen

5. jmdm den Marsch blasen (coll.)
6. wen es juckt, der kratze sich
7. tief in die Tasche greifen

9. Nennen Sie je fünf Adjektive bzw. Ausdrücke, die den folgenden Figuren passen. Nennen Sie je zwei, die ihnen nicht passen.

1. Rotkäppchen
2. der Weihnachtsmann
3. Katarina Witt
4. der Präsident bzw. die Präsidentin der Vereinigten Staaten
5. Ihr Deutschlehrer bzw. Ihre Deutschlehrerin

10. Was bedeuten die folgenden Präfixverben?

1. anstoßen, niederstoßen, umstoßen, wegstoßen
2. ausgehen, fortgehen, losgehen, weggehen, weitergehen, zurückgehen
3. aufwerfen, fortwerfen, hochwerfen, niederwerfen, wegwerfen
4. anlehnen, hinauslehnen, vorlehnen, zurücklehnen
5. abfahren, fortfahren, umfahren, wegfahren, zurückfahren

11. Übersetzen Sie ins Englische.

Drei Verletzte nach Zusammenstoß mit LKW

Schwer verletzt wurden mehrere Personen bei einem Zusammenstoß mehrerer Autos auf dem Airportring am Donnerstagmorgen. Ein 21-jähriger Hanauer, der mit einem Lastwagen in Richtung Mörfelden unterwegs war, kollidierte mit zwei entgegenkommenden Fahrzeugen. Zwischen den Toren 26 und 27 stieß der Transporter mit einem Rüsselheimer Opelfahrer (45) und dem Mercedes eines 41-Jährigen aus Otterstadt zusammen. Wie es zu dem Unfall kommen konnte, ist nach Polizeiangaben noch unklar.

Der Hanauer und der Fahrer aus Rüsselsheim mussten schwer verletzt zur stationären Behandlung in ein Krankenhaus gebracht werden. Ein fünfjähriges Mädchen, die als Beifahrerin im Opel saß, wurde bei dem Unfall leicht verletzt. An den Fahrzeugen entstand ein erheblicher Sachschaden. Wegen der Karambolage war der Airportring gestern zwischen 10 und 12.30 Uhr in beide Richtungen gesperrt.

Boris Schlepper

FRANKFURTER RUNDSCHAU, Samstag, 15. September 2001, Nr. 215/37, S. 31

12. Übersetzen Sie ins Englische.

Depression

Wir müssen in die Mitte der Sitzreihe, die schon zur Hälfte besetzt ist. Mit dem rituellen „Entschuldigung!", das durch Lächeln mit Kopfnicken oder „Kein Problem!" quittiert wird, kommen wir aber gut durch; schließlich

handelt es sich um routinierte Theaterbesucher, und bis zum Beginn der
Vorstellung ist noch gut Zeit.

Bloß eine jüngere Frau, an der wir als Letzte vorbei müssen, um zu unseren
Plätzen zu gelangen, schaut mürrisch und verzichtet auf jede
Verzeihungsgeste. Als ich mich neben ihr niederlasse, weht so etwas wie Ekel
herüber. Kurz vor Beginn der Aufführung will noch ein letztes Paar hindurch
und noch weiter in die Mitte der Sitzreihe – „Entschuldigung!", „Kein
Problem!" –: Einen kurzen Augenblick schaut es wirklich so aus, als
verweigere die junge Frau den Durchlass und wolle sitzen bleiben. Sollen sie
doch von der anderen Seite Zugang suchen! So klar denkt sie das nicht; ihr
Hass und Ekel hüllen die anderen Leute in eine Art Fluidum oder Äther, der
alles, was die tun oder lassen, vergiftet. Die anderen Leute stellen eine
Zumutung dar und fordern zu einem Zornesausbruch heraus, den sie auf der
Stelle – es würde ja doch nichts nützen – unterdrückt.

Was jetzt auf der Bühne beginnt, nennt man Tanztheater. An diesem Abend
eine hoch überraschende Folge aus Schwerkunst, Breakdance,
Zirkusnummern und Kabarett. Eine Schwarzafrikanerin kann ihre unglaublich
umfangreichen Hinterbacken so wogen machen, dass sie ein eigenes Tanzstück
aufführen; ein Schlangenmensch bewegt seine Glieder, als wären sie ohne
Knochen – und dann gibt er noch eine Extranummer als
Vogelstimmenimitator! Zur Musik von Vivaldi!

Das Publikum verzichtet auf keine Gelegenheit zum Szenenbeifall und tobt
nach seinen Möglichkeiten mit. Bloß die Frau neben mir bleibt völlig
unbewegt. Gewiss bestärkt sie die lustige Publikumsmasse in ihrem
Ekelgefühl. Ein paar Mal weht ihre Abneigung so dicht herüber, dass ich aufs
Händeklatschen verzichte. Dafür male ich mir genüsslich aus, welchen
Widerwillen die Papiertaschentücher erwecken, mit denen ich mir immer
wieder den Schweiß vom Gesicht wische (je älter ich werde, umso leichter
schwitze ich).

Mit dem Schlussbeifall am Ende der Vorstellung versucht das Publikum
seine eigene Begeisterung noch einmal zu übertreffen. Zum heftigen
Klatschen kommen Bravorufe und eine Art Entzückungsgeheul hinzu. Auch
ich breche gern in dies ekstatische Juhuhen aus, hin und wieder – und die Frau
neben mir, die sich immerhin zurückhaltend am Händeklatschen beteiligt, darf
damit aufhören und sich die Ohren zuhalten … Zuerst zögere ich noch mit
meinem periodischen Heulen; aber dann denke ich: Es kommt ihr doch genau
zupass.

Man kennt diese Zustände von Welthass, Weltekel. Sie begleiten eine
schwere Depression. Wer an ihr leidet, freilich, nimmt an sich selbst nur die
unersättliche innere Leere, den beißenden Verlust wahr. Wie er sich
gleichzeitig in einem unermesslichen Hochmut über die anderen Leute erhebt,
das bemerken nur die anderen Leute.

Michael Rutschky

FRANKFURTER RUNDSCHAU, Samstag, 8. September 2001, Nr. 209/36,
S. 17

Level 2

1. Ordnen Sie.

angegraut, der Bauchansatz, beleibt, der Bürstenschnitt, faltig, flachsblond, gescheitelt, geschminkt, eine heitere Miene, kraus, der Pferdeschwanz, der Pickel, sommersprossig, stämmig, übergewichtig, vollschlank, wütend, zufrieden

Körperbau	Gesicht	Haar

2. Welches Wort bzw. welcher Ausdruck hat die gleiche oder eine ähnliche Bedeutung? ✓

1. korpulent
2. fettleibig
3. missgebildet
4. abgemagert
5. ein braungebranntes Gesicht
6. die Gesichtsfarbe
7. starkes Haar
8. eine straffe Haltung
9. hinreißend
10. hinabsinken
11. sich bewegen
12. sausen
13. herumtoben
14. gegen etw krachen
15. sich vor Lachen krümmen
16. mit den Augen blinzeln

3. Welches Wort passt nicht? ✓

1. breitschultrig, dickleibig, korpulent, wohlbeleibt
2. hager, knochig, fleischig, verhungert
3. großporig, rau, rosig, rotblond
4. edel, fettleibig, krumm, platt
5. abstoßend, appetitlich, niedlich, schick
6. graben, greifen, packen, schnappen
7. schwanken, schwenken, stolpern, wackeln

4. Wie heißt das Gegenteil? ✓

1. ein ausdrucksvolles Gesicht
2. lockiges Haar
3. runzlige Haut
4. dunkelhäutig
5. rechtshändig
6. hin
7. seine Schritte beschleunigen
8. fest auf den Beinen

5. Welche Definition passt? ✓

a. davonlaufen, b. gestikulieren, c. jmdn hauen, d. hetzen, e. sich recken, f. sich rühren, g. schlendern, h. etw schmeißen, i. schreiten, j. tippeln, k. jmdn treffen, l. vorankommen

1. sich sehr beeilen
2. bummeln
3. jmdm begegnen
4. zu Fuß gehen
5. vorwärts kommen
6. sich bewegen

7. langsam und feierlich gehen
8. jmdn prügeln
9. Gesten machen
10. etw werfen
11. sich dehnen
12. weglaufen

6. Welches Verb passt? ✓

a. ausweichen, b. ballen, c. fallen, d. geben, e. hauen, f. machen, g. nehmen,
h. schlagen, i. verschränken

1. auf die Nase
2. die Arme
3. einem Schlag
4. die Beine unter den Arm
5. jmdm einen Tritt

6. jmdn ins Gesicht
7. die Beine übereinander
8. die Faust
9. die Runde

7. Ordnen Sie die folgenden Ausdrücke nach der Größe, Geschwindigkeit usw. ✓

1. dickleibig, fettleibig, rundlich, schmal, winzig
2. angegrautes Haar, graues Haar, schlohweißes Haar, silbernes Haar, tiefschwarzes Haar
3. sich im Schneckentempo bewegen, eilen, rennen, sausen, schlendern, sprinten
4. ein bleiches Gesicht, ein gerötetes Gesicht, ein hochrotes Gesicht, ein kreidebleiches Gesicht
5. glattes Haar, krauses Haar, lockiges Haar, welliges Haar

8. Ergänzen Sie den Artikel und das entsprechende Verb. ✓

Artikel	Substantiv	Verb
1. der	Gang	gehen
2.	Tritt	
3.	Schritt	
4.	Vorbeimarsch	
5.	Aufstieg	
6.	Gestikulation	
7.	Wanderung	
8.	Ankunft	
9.	Parade	
10.	Sprung	
11.	Zusammenstoß	
12.	Rückkehr	
13.	Marsch	

9. In jedem Satz fehlt ein Wort. ✓

> a. aufgesteckt, b. Doppelkinn, c. feingeschnittenen, d. gescheitelt,
> e. kastanienbraunes, f. pickeliges, g. Ringe, h. runzelt, i. strahlt, j. Taille,
> k. versteinertem

1. Sie hört die Vorwürfe mit _____ Gesicht.
2. Die Frau mit dem _____ Gesicht und dem flotten Kurzhaarschnitt ist Jugendmodel.
3. Er _____ über das ganze Gesicht.
4. Sie ist schlank, hat braune Haare und ein _____ Gesicht.
5. Er neigt zu Fettansatz, hat ein rundes Gesicht mit einem _____ .
6. Sie hatte blaue Augen und _____ Haar.
7. Ihr goldblondes Haar trug sie _____ oder zu einem Pferdeschwanz zusammengebunden.
8. Sie trägt das dunkle Haar schulterlang und rechts _____ .
9. Sie hat eine schmale _____ und lange schlanke Beine.
10. Er hat dunkle _____ um die Augen.
11. Jetzt _____ er die Stirn.

10. Übersetzen Sie ins Englische.

Taxi raste mit Tempo 130 in den Gegenverkehr

Mit 130 Stundenkilometern ist ein Taxi auf der Hanauer Landstraße gegen einen entgegenkommenden Kleinlaster geprallt. Zwei Männer wurden bei dem schweren Unfall in der Nacht zum Freitag schwer verletzt, ein dritter Beteiligter erlitt leichte Verletzungen.

Der Taxifahrer raste kurz vor 2 Uhr stadtauswärts durch die Hanauer Landstraße. Auf der nassen Fahrbahn verlor er nach Angaben der Polizei in Höhe der Launhardtstraße die Kontrolle über seinen Wagen und schleuderte auf die Gegenfahrbahn. Dort rammte er einen Kleinlaster, der Richtung Innenstadt fuhr. Polizeibeamte stellten fest, dass die Geschwindigkeitsanzeige in dem Wagen bei 130 Stundenkilometern stehen geblieben war ...

Volker Mazassek

FRANKFURTER RUNDSCHAU, Samstag, 22. September 2001, Nr. 221/38, S. 30

11. Aufsatzthemen.

1. Beschreiben Sie den typischen Amerikaner bzw. die typische Amerikanerin.
2. Beschreiben Sie einen Verwandten bzw. eine Verwandte (Mutter, Großvater, jüngere Schwester).
3. Vergleichen Sie zwei Geschwister. Wie sehen sie aus? Wie unterscheiden sie sich? Wie ähneln sie sich?
4. Beschreiben Sie einen Menschen, den Sie oft sehen aber nicht kennen.

12. Übersetzen Sie ins Englische.

Aus „very welle" von Sabine Marbach

Bestialer Gestank, Brandblasen auf dem Kopf und büschelweise Haarausfall – Katharina Laible musste einiges ertragen, bis die Krause erfunden war. Ihr Mann Karl Nessler hatte sich in den Kopf gesetzt, glattes Haar dauerhaft zu wellen. Versuchsobjekt war Katharina, sein Instrument eine glühende Zange. Am 8. Oktober 1906 gelang dem Schwarzwälder das Unglaubliche: Der erste Dauerwellapparat war erfunden. Die Prozedur dauerte acht Stunden und kostete das Vermögen von 105 Goldmark, bei einem durchschnittlichen Jahreseinkommen von 946 Mark. Damals musste jede Welle einzeln gelegt werden. Die elektrischen Heizer wogen je 900 Gramm und mussten mindestens zehn Minuten gehalten werden.

Die Krause setzte sich dennoch durch. Greta Garbo und Marlene Dietrich machten sie in den 20er Jahren salonfähig. Mit der Erfindung der chemischen Kaltwelle trat sie in den 50er Jahren ihren Siegeszug an. „Die Popularität der Dauerwelle ist eine Wellenbewegung wie die Welle selbst", sagt Eva Richter vom Zentralverband des deutschen Friseurhandwerks (ZV), „mal ist sie großlockig, mal kleinlockig, und dann ist ein paar Jahre wieder glattes Haar modern."

Zurzeit erlebt die Welle einen ungeahnten Aufschwung. Pünktlich zum 95. Geburtstag verhilft ihr ausgerechnet ein Mann im Land der Spaghettifrisuren zu neuem Ansehen. Der japanische Ministerpräsident Junichiro Koizumi wird trotz 12 Milliarden Mark Staatsverschuldung in seinem Land gefeiert wie ein Popstar. Die auffällige, graue Dauerwelle des 59-Jährigen steht für „Veränderung" und das „neue Japan", meinen seine Anhänger. „Ein krauser Kopf – widerborstig, auflehnend", finden seine Gegner.

„Sein Haar zeigt die Freiheit, die er sich nimmt, die Leute sollten auf ihn hören", rät dagegen der ehemalige Kreativdirektor von Vidal Sassoon, Mazayuki Mogi, der seine gut dotierte Stellung in einem Pariser Modehaus vor kurzem aufgab, um an der Aufbruchstimmung in seiner Heimat teilzuhaben. Eines ist für ihn jedenfalls klar: Koizumis Konkurrent Hashimoto trug mit Pomade einen Stil von gestern.

Auch in unseren Breiten wird die künstliche Lockenpracht wieder populär. Glänzte sie in den letzten 20 Jahren nur noch kleingedreht, schlohweiß auf dem Kopf der Dame über 60, sind die Tage der Schnittlauch-Tracht gezählt: Madonna, Claudia Schiffer und Gisèle Bündchen tragen den Schopf wieder „gewickelt". Frauenmagazine propagieren seit Neuestem den Locken-Look. Die Nachfrage in Deutschland hat sich bei Leuten unter 30 Jahren im vergangenen Jahr verdoppelt. „Geben Sie der Dauerwelle noch ein bis drei Jahre", sagt Winfried Löwel, Modeexperte beim ZV, „dann hat sie sich wieder durchgesetzt."...

FRANKFURTER RUNDSCHAU, Samstag, 3. November 2001, Nr. 256/44, Magazin, S. 16

Level 3

1. Welches Adjektiv passt? ✓

a. behäbig, b. pummelig, c. rank, d. schlaksig, e. spindeldürr, f. verkrüppelt, g. zierlich

1. dicklich	5. lang aufgeschossen
2. biegsam, schlank	6. missgestaltet
3. klein und fein	7. beleibt
4. sehr dürr	

2. Wie heißt das entsprechende Substantiv (mit Artikel)? ✓

1. schubsen	
2. stürzen	
3. ersteigen	
4. senken	
5. traben	
6. ohrfeigen	

3. Welches Wort bzw. welcher Ausdruck hat die gleiche oder eine ähnliche Bedeutung? ✓

1. der Fettkloß	10. latschen
2. ein eingefallenes Gesicht	11. zotteln
3. ein melancholisches Gesicht	12. jmdn kneifen
4. schmollen	13. oszillieren
5. verstrubbeltes Haar	14. stelzen
6. gespaltene Haarspitzen	15. über den Onkel gehen
7. ihr stehen die Haare zu Berge	16. jmdm einen Schrecken einjagen
8. krumme Beine	17. jmdn grün und blau hauen
9. auf etw zuhalten	18. blinzeln

4. Welches Wort passt nicht? ✓

1. das Gesicht: abgehärmt, grazil, kantig, teigig, mürrisch
2. das Haar: flink, spärlich, widerspenstig, wuschelig, zottig
3. die Haut: fahl, makellos, schlaff, straff, zerzaust
4. die Stirn: fliehend, gewölbt, runzelig, wallend, zerfurcht
5. die Nase: gebogen, höckrig, knollig, pausbackig, stumpf
6. Augen: blutunterlaufen, füllig, hervortretend, tiefliegend, verquollen
7. Lippen: aufgesprungen, aufgeworfen, kraus, voll, wulstig

5. Welches Präfix passt? ✓

a. ab, b. auf, c. aus, d. durch, e. ein, f. ent, g. nieder, h. ver, i. zurück

1. Die Menge wich ehrfürchtig _____.
2. Das Pferd bäumte sich _____.
3. Der Junge ist von zu Hause _____gerissen.
4. Sie ist _____gekniet und betet.
5. Er hat mir die Zeitung _____rissen.
6. Sie hat ihre Kleider im ganzen Zimmer _____streut.
7. Er konnte den Ball nur _____prallen lassen.
8. In die Rechnung hat sich ein Fehler _____geschlichen.
9. Im Wagen wurden sie tüchtig _____geschüttelt.

6. Wie heißt das Gegenteil? ✓
1. flachbrüstig
2. ein vorspringendes Kinn
3. dichtes Haar
4. angeklatschte Haare
5. o-beinig

7. In jedem Satz fehlt ein Wort. ✓

abgespannt, markantes, Pausbacken, plumpsen, schmerzverzerrtem, sputen, Stupsnase, Tränensäcke, unbewegter, wimmelt, Wuschelkopf, zappelig

1. Selbstsicher mit _____ Miene sprach er mit den Journalisten.
2. Als Erster kam er mit _____ Gesicht auf dem Gipfel an.
3. Er wirkte müde und _____.
4. Sie hatte eine breite Nase und ein _____ Kinn.
5. Sie hat glatte, braune Haare, braune Augen und runde _____.
6. Er hat kurzes, blondes Haar und auffallende _____ unter den Augen.
7. Das kleine Mädchen hat ein offenes Kindergesicht mit Sommersprossen und _____.
8. Der Junge hat einen auffällig dunklen _____.
9. Sie wurde vor Ungeduld ganz _____.
10. Dann lässt sie sich wieder auf ihr Bett _____.
11. Im Bahnhof _____ es von Ankommenden und Abreisenden.
12. Wer in Berlin auf der Suche nach einer großen, sanierten Altbauwohnung in Charlottenburg ist, sollte sich _____.

8. Welches Verb passt? ✓

a. abtasten, b. drängeln, c. empfangen, d. hauen, e. hüpfen, f. reichen, g. schlagen, h. strecken, i. wiegen

141

1. sich nach vorn
2. jmdn zu Boden
3. vor Freude
4. eine Linke
5. jmdm die Hand

6. jmdn auf Waffen
7. jmdn zu Brei
8. sich in den Hüften
9. jmdn mit offenen Armen

9. Wie heißen die Zusammensetzungen? ✓

~~Wurst~~	nase	1. *die Wurstfinger*
Pferde	schütteln	2.
Haken	spitze	3.
Mandel	baum	4.
Hände	~~finger~~	5.
Zehen	mund	6.
Knie	miene	7.
Purzel	gesicht	8.
Dulder	augen	9.
Schmoll	beuge	10.

10. Übersetzen Sie ins Englische.

Funktionierender Bürgermeister a.D.

16 Jahre regierte Eberhard Diepgen Berlin. Nach dem Sturz macht er weiter wie bisher: Gefühle werden »runtergekämpft«. Drei Wochen an der Seite eines Dauerläufers

Von Sven Hillenkamp

Am liebsten wäre Eberhard Diepgen einfach verschwunden. Ohne diesen letzten Gang. »So, jetzt hau ich ab«, hatte er gesagt und um sich geblickt. Er war allein, niemand stand bei ihm. Er lief los, zwischen den Leuten hindurch, die sich in Gruppen unterhielten, Richtung Ausgang.

Der Zoodirektor schneidet ihm den Weg ab: »Noch ein kleiner Spaziergang durch den Zoo?« Der Mann breitet die Arme aus.

»Ja. Gern.«

Da ist ein Zögern gewesen. Etwas ist über Diepgens Gesicht gehuscht, ein Vorhang, und als der Vorhang fort war, ist der Ausdruck ein anderer. Jetzt geht es nicht mehr schnell zum Ausgang, weg von hier im dunklen Fond. Jetzt wird entspannt über die Sandwege geschlendert, der kürzlich gestürzte Regierungschef und ein Zoodirektor, der eine rote Krawatte mit grünen Eulen umgebunden hat, zu Ehren des neuen Regierungschefs.

Im Berliner Zoologischen Garten feiert man Richtfest für das moderne Pinguin- und Seelöwengehege: ein »Termin Regierender Bürgermeister«, wie Hunderte andere in Diepgens Kalender, die er alle ausgestrichen hat. Nur diesen einen Termin wollte er noch wahrnehmen, obwohl er dort eigentlich nichts mehr zu suchen hat. Warum er das tut? Das weiß Diepgen selbst nicht so genau. »Ich will mal gucken, ob Wowereit kommt.«

Klaus Wowereit, der Nachfolger, kommt nicht. Er hat einen Stellvertreter geschickt, den Justizsenator. »In dieser Stadt kommen und gehen die Senate«, spricht der beschwingt ins Mikrofon, das über der Betongrube aufgestellt ist, »was bleibt, ist die Liebe der Berliner zu ihrem Zoo.«

Mal sehen, ob Wowereit kommt

Diepgen hört zu, mit verschränkten Armen gegen den Wind gelehnt. Er sagt nichts. Es ist, als sei er gar nicht da. Und doch steht er da, neben dem Redner, vor der Grube, lauscht und beobachtet die Gäste. Er hat sich einen zweifelhaften Traum erfüllt. Im Film sieht der so aus: Ein Mann besucht seine eigene Beerdigung. Am 16. Juni führten SPD, PDS und Grüne im Berliner Abgeordnetenhaus bekanntlich durch, was eine Zeitung die »politische Exekution des Eberhard Diepgen« genannt hat.

Manchmal schleicht sich ein unsicheres Grinsen in die Züge des Exekutierten. Er ist sich offenbar der Lächerlichkeit der Situation bewusst. Das Problem ist, dass ihn hier – im Gegensatz zu den bekannten Filmszenen – alle sehen können.

Aus diesem Grund war auch dem Zoodirektor nicht zu entgehen. Da hätte Eberhard Diepgen schon nein sagen müssen. Statt dessen lässt er sich nun über die Wege führen, interessiert sich für Spiegelkarpfen und sagt: »Ich muss mal wieder richtig in den Zoo gehen!«

Der Zoodirektor winkt mit seiner rot-grünen Krawatte. »Extra für den neuen Regierenden!« Er lacht. »Tja, so geht's.« Der Direktor ist wirklich gut gelaunt, es ist ein sonniger Tag. »Wollen Sie mal hören, wie ein Vogel einen ehemaligen Regierenden auslacht?«

»Ja, will ich«, sagt Diepgen.

Es werden zwei Vögel. Zuerst Joachim, ein Kookaburra, dann ein namenloser Schreiseeadler. Die Vögel setzen auf Kommando des Direktors ein, und als Diepgen das Tor erreicht, hört man das Gekrächz immer noch. Kurz vor dem Ausgang, wo der graue BMW wartet, schießt ein Mann in Bermudashorts auf Diepgen zu und ergreift seine Hand. »Schön, Sie zu sehen! Ich bin sehr traurig!«

So war es fast immer auf dem Weg dieses Berufspolitikers. Im letzten Moment, auch wenn Diepgen entscheidungsschwach schien und als »der blasse Eberhard« Hohn über sich ergehen lassen musste, eilte das Volk zu Hilfe. Vier Wahlen hat er in Berlin gewonnen ...

DIE ZEIT, 9. August 2001, Nr. 33, Leben, S. 45

11. Schriftliche Übung. Wählen Sie ein Thema.
1. Beschreiben Sie einen Autounfall.
2. Beschreiben Sie die folgende Szene: Ein Mann holt eine Frau am Flughafen ab.
3. Beschreiben Sie eine traurige (überglückliche, zornige) Person. Beschreiben Sie ihre Gesichtsausdrücke, Gesten, Bewegungen usw.

Unit 5

Personality and human behaviour

Level 1

Virtue and vice, strictness and laxity

Charakter, der (-e)	character, moral courage
Eigenschaft, die (-en)	quality, characteristic
korrekt	correct, right, decent
streng	strict
Strenge, die (no pl.)	strictness, rigour
Anstand, der (no pl.)	decency
anständig	respectable, well behaved
unanständig	improper, immoral
Unanständigkeit, die (no pl.)	impropriety, immorality
Eifersucht, die (no pl.)	jealousy
eifersüchtig	jealous
Lust, die (¨e)	interest, desire, inclination
(un)moralisch	(im)moral
korrupt	corrupt
ein gutes/schlechtes Gewissen haben	to have a clear/guilty conscience
Gewissensbisse, pl.	pangs of conscience

Honesty and dishonesty, trust and distrust

(un)ehrlich	(dis)honest
Ehrlichkeit, die (no pl.)	honesty
direkt	direct
offen	open, direct, candid
Offenheit, die (no pl.)	openness, frankness, candour
treu	loyal, faithful, devoted
Treue, die (no pl.)	loyalty, fidelity
glaubwürdig	credible
taktlos	tactless, indelicate
Taktlosigkeit, die (no pl.)	tactlessness
taktvoll	tactful
ernsthaft	earnest
gerade	honest, upright, upstanding
aufrecht	upright
Verdacht, der (¨e)	suspicion
verdächtig	suspicious

Willpower

Wille, der (no pl.)	will, intention
Willenskraft, die (no pl.)	willpower
weich	soft, soft-hearted
schwach	weak
willensschwach	weak-willed
willensstark	strong-willed, determined
willenlos	weak-willed, spineless

Benevolence and malevolence, generosity and meanness

nett	nice
lieb	kind
fair	fair
mitfühlend	compassionate, sympathetic
menschlich	humane
großzügig	generous
Großzügigkeit, die (no pl.)	generosity
gierig	greedy
Gier, die (no pl.)	greed
schlecht	bad, wicked
schlimm	wicked
schrecklich	terrible, dreadful
böse	evil, wicked
bösartig	malicious
Böswilligkeit, die (no pl.)	maliciousness, malevolence
gemein	mean, nasty
jmdn beleidigen	to insult sb
jmdn verletzen	to hurt sb
lügen	to lie
jmdn ausnutzen	to exploit sb
jmdn retten	to rescue sb
hilfreich, hilfsbereit	helpful
Hilfsbereitschaft, die (no pl.)	helpfulness
Güte, die (no pl.)	goodness
Respekt, der (no pl.)	respect
Achtung, die (no pl.)	respect
Hochachtung, die (no pl.)	great respect, high esteem
selbstsüchtig	selfish
Selbstsucht, die (no pl.)	selfishness

Friendliness and unfriendliness, communicativeness

Freund(in), der/die (-e/nen)	friend
(un)freundlich	(un)friendly
Freundlichkeit, die (no pl.)	friendliness
befreundet sein	to be friends
Bekannte(r), der/die (adj. decl.)	acquaintance
jmds Bekanntschaft machen	to make sb's acquaintance
Kamerad(in), der/die (-en/nen)	companion
Kollege, der (-n); Kollegin, die (-nen)	colleague, workmate
neugierig	nosy, prying
Verhältnis, das (-se)	relationship; affair
liebend	devoted
Kontakt, der (-e)	contact
mit jmdm Kontakt aufnehmen	to make contact with sb
kontaktfreudig	outgoing
jmdn vom Sehen kennen	to know sb by sight

Amiability

sympathisch	likeable
liebenswert	lovable, endearing
liebevoll	loving, affectionate
jmdn faszinieren	to captivate sb
schwierig	troublesome
(wegen etw) Schwierigkeiten machen	to be difficult (about sth)
Streit, der (-e)	quarrel
(mit jmdm) einen Streit anfangen	to pick a quarrel (with sb)
beleidigt sein	to take offence
jmdm auf die Nerven gehen	to get on sb's nerves
jmdn verrückt machen	to drive sb crazy
sich über jmdn ärgern	to be annoyed/angry at sb
dickköpfig	stubborn, pigheaded

Tolerance and intolerance

(in)tolerant (gegen jmdn)	(in)tolerant (of sb)
(In)toleranz, die (no pl.)	(in)tolerance
jmdn tolerieren	to tolerate sb

Vorurteil, das (-e)	prejudice
Vorurteile gegen jmdn/etw haben/hegen	to be prejudiced against sb/sth
vorurteilsfrei, -los	unprejudiced
gefühllos	insensitive
Gefühllosigkeit, die (no pl.)	insensitivity

Good/bad manners

(un)höflich	(im)polite
Höflichkeit, die (no pl.)	politeness
brav	well behaved, good
pünktlich	punctual
gute/schlechte Manieren haben	to be good-/bad-mannered
frech	impertinent, impudent, cheeky
respektlos	disrespectful
laut	noisy
lärmend	noisy
vulgär	vulgar

Good/bad humour

(un)glücklich	(un)happy
Glück, das (no pl.)	happiness, luck
traurig	sad
Traurigkeit, die (no pl.)	sadness
(un)zufrieden	(dis)satisfied, (un)happy
Unzufriedenheit, die (no pl.)	dissatisfaction, unhappiness
enttäuscht	disappointed
Spaß, der (¨e)	fun
spaßig	funny, droll
Humor, der (no pl.)	humour
einen Sinn für Humor haben	to have a sense of humour
humorvoll	with a sense of humour, humorous
froh	happy, glad
fröhlich	cheerful, happy
Witz, der (-e)	joke
witzig	funny

Scherz, der (-e)	joke
scherzhaft	jocular, jovial
amüsant	amusing, entertaining
sich amüsieren	to enjoy o.s., have a good time
sauer sein	to be annoyed
Laune, die (-n)	mood
guter/schlechter Laune sein	to be in a good/bad mood
angenehm	pleasant
sich freuen	to be pleased
etw genießen	to enjoy sth
Freude, die (-n)	happiness, joy, pleasure
lustig	merry, jolly, jovial
heiter	cheerful, happy, light-hearted
klagen	to complain, moan
(über jmdn/etw) schimpfen	to bitch/moan/grumble (about sth)

Stability and instability

ruhig	calm
Ruhe, die (no pl.)	peace, calmness
beruhigt	calmed down
über etw beunruhigt sein	to be worried/disturbed about sth
deprimiert	depressed
nervös	nervous, on edge
Nervosität, die (no pl.)	nervousness, tension
aufgeregt	excited, nervous, flustered, agitated
durcheinander sein	to be confused, be in a state
emotional, emotionell	emotional
Stress, der (-e)	stress
im Stress sein	to be under stress
gestresst	stressed out
launenhaft	moody, temperamental
launisch	moody
ärgerlich	annoyed, angry
verärgert	annoyed

auf jmdn böse sein	to be mad at sb	intelligent	intelligent
wütend (auf jmdn) sein	to be furious, angry (at sb)	schlau	clever, smart, shrewd, cunning
Wut, die (no pl.)	fury, rage	gebildet	educated, learned, well-bred, cultured
zornig	angry	ungebildet	uneducated
verrückt	crazy	kultiviert	cultivated, cultured, refined
wahnsinnig	insane, mad		
Wahnsinn, der (no pl.)	madness	dumm	stupid, dumb
irre	mad, insane	Dummheit, die (no pl.)	stupidity
irrsinnig	mad, crazy, insane	Dummkopf, der (¨e)	idiot, fool
sich beherrschen	to control oneself, keep one's temper	blöd (coll.)	silly, stupid, idiotic
die Beherrschung verlieren	to lose one's temper/self-control	blödsinnig	stupid, idiotic
		Blödheit, die (no pl.)	stupidity
		doof (coll.)	dumb, daft
locker (coll.)	cool	idiotisch	idiotic
		begabt	talented, gifted
Good/poor judgment		minderbegabt	less gifted
vorsichtig	careful, cautious	Begabung, die (-en)	talent, gift
sorgfältig	careful	geschickt	skilful, clever
weise	wise	ungeschickt	clumsy, awkward
Weisheit, die (no pl.)	wisdom	Talent, das (-e)	talent
(un)vernünftig	(ir)rational, (un)reasonable	talentiert	talented, gifted
		untalentiert	untalented
Vernünftigkeit, die (no pl.)	good sense		
kritisch	critical	**Energy and apathy**	
rational	rational	tätig	active
Verstand, der (no pl.)	(common) sense, reason	(in)aktiv	(in)active
		passiv	passive
bei klarem Verstand	rational	kraftvoll	powerful
(un)aufmerksam	(in)attentive, (un)observant	kraftlos	weak, feeble
		aggressiv	aggressive
Aufmerksamkeit, die (no pl.)	attention	lebhaft	lively
		lebendig	lively
sparsam	thrifty	begeistert	enthusiastic
gedankenlos	thoughtless	energisch	energetic
Gedankenlosigkeit, die (no pl.)	absent-mindedness, thoughtlessness	spontan	spontaneous
		fleißig	hard-working, industrious, diligent
sorglos	careless		
Sorglosigkeit, die (no pl.)	carelessness		
		tüchtig	efficient, capable
		apatisch	apathetic
Intelligence and cunning		energielos	sluggish
klug	clever, bright, intelligent, shrewd	faul	lazy, idle
		denkfaul	mentally lazy

gelangweilt	bored
müde	tired, weary

Courage and cowardice

Mut, der (no pl.)	courage
mutig, tapfer	brave, courageous
heroisch	heroic
sich sorgen	to worry
sich Sorgen machen	to worry
besorgt	anxious, worried
unbesorgt	unconcerned
Angst, die ("e)	fear
ängstlich	anxious, apprehensive, timid
Furcht, die (no pl.)	fear
furchtlos	fearless, intrepid
feige	cowardly

scheu	shy
schüchtern	shy, bashful
abergläubisch	superstitious

Modesty and pride

stolz	proud
Stolz, der (no pl.)	pride
(un)bescheiden	(im)modest
Bescheidenheit, die (no pl.)	modesty
arrogant	arrogant
hochnäsig	snooty
selbstbewusst	self-confident, self-possessed
selbstsicher	self-confident
eingebildet	conceited
Einbildung, die (-en)	conceit
snobistisch	snobbish

Level 2

Virtue and vice, strictness and laxity

(un)sittlich	(im)moral
sittenlos	immoral
kein Rückgrat haben	to be spineless
geil	lecherous
Geilheit, die (no pl.)	lechery
Laster, das (-)	vice
lasterhaft	depraved
verdorben	perverted, wicked, depraved
(un)bestechlich	(in)corruptible
schamlos	unashamed
bedenkenlos	unscrupulous
Bedenkenlosigkeit, die (no pl.)	unscrupulousness
schändlich	shameful, disgraceful
Charakterfehler, der (-)	character defect
jmdn (um etw) beneiden	to envy sb (sth)
verlegen	embarrassed
schuldbewusst	conscience-stricken
reuevoll	contrite
selbstgerecht	self-righteous

Selbstgerechtigkeit, die (no pl.)	self-righteousness
gottesfürchtig	God-fearing
moralistisch	moralistic
moralisieren	to moralize

Honesty and dishonesty, trust and distrust

(un)redlich	(dis)honest
Redlichkeit, die (no pl.)	honesty, integrity
(un)aufrichtig	(in)sincere
zuverlässig	reliable
vertrauenswürdig	trustworthy
Vertrauen, das (no pl.)	trust
(in)diskret	(in)discreet
Misstrauen, das (no pl.)	mistrust, distrust
misstrauisch	mistrustful, distrustful
jmdn hereinlegen/ betrügen	to fool sb
Betrug, der (no pl.)	deceit, deception

betrügerisch	deceitful
Täuschung, die (-en)	deception, deceit
jmdn täuschen	to deceive sb
etw verdrehen	to distort sth
etw entstellen	to distort sth
lügnerisch	lying
ausweichend	evasive
scheinheilig	hypocritical
leichtgläubig	credulous, gullible
Leichtgläubigkeit, die (no pl.)	credulity, gullibility
formbar	malleable

Willpower

Entschiedenheit, die (no pl.)	determination, staunchness
Entschlossenheit, die (no pl.)	determination
entschlossen	determined, resolute
unbeirrt, unbeirrbar	unwavering
hartnäckig	obstinate, stubborn, persistent
Hartnäckigkeit, die (no pl.)	obstinacy, stubbornness
zielstrebig	determined
zielbewusst	purposeful, decisive
zielsicher	unerring
unbeugsam	uncompromising, unbending
nachgiebig	soft, compliant
(ir)resolut	(ir)resolute
unschlüssig	irresolute, hesitant
Unschlüssigkeit, die (no pl.)	irresoluteness, hesitancy

Benevolence and malevolence, generosity and meanness

gerecht	fair
kleinlich	mean, petty
schäbig	shabby, mean
grausam	cruel
Bosheit, die (no pl.)	wickedness, malevolence
boshaft	malevolent
übel wollend	malevolent

wohlwollend	benevolent
Wohlwollen, das (no pl.)	benevolence
geizig	mean, miserly, stingy
Geiz, der (no pl.)	miserliness
jmdn (wegen etw) verspotten	to mock/ridicule sb (about sth)
jmdn misshandeln	to mistreat sb
jmdm drohen	to threaten sb
rücksichtsvoll	considerate
Rücksichtnahme, die (no pl.)	consideration
selbstlos	selfless
entgegenkommend	obliging
Entgegenkommen, das (no pl.)	obligingness
Verzeihung, die (no pl.)	forgiveness
versöhnlich	conciliatory
Nächstenliebe, die (no pl.)	charity
Menschenliebe, die (no pl.)	human kindness, philanthropy
Menschenfreundlich-keit, die (no pl.)	philanthropy
menschenfreundlich	philanthropic
blutgierig	bloodthirsty
habgierig	grasping, rapacious
Habgier, die (no pl.)	greed, acquisitiveness
Habsucht, die (no pl.)	greed, acquisitiveness

Friendliness and unfriendliness, communicativeness

enge Freunde, pl.	close friends
dicke Freunde (pl.; coll.)	bosom pals/buddies
sich mit jmdm anfreunden	to make friends with sb
Freundschaft, die (-en)	friendship
mit jmdm vertraut werden	to become friendly with sb
Vertraute(r), der/die (adj. decl.)	close/intimate friend; confidant(e)

zugänglich	approachable
distanziert	distant
Distanz, die (-en)	distance, detachment
zurückhaltend	restrained, reserved
verschlossen	reserved
mit ihr kann man gut auskommen	she is easy to get along with
liebenswürdig	kind, amiable
unliebenswürdig	not very pleasant
barsch	curt
schroff	abrupt, curt, brusque

Amiability

bezaubernd	enchanting, captivating, bewitching
Reiz, der (-e)	charm
(un)gesellig	(un)sociable
verächtlich	contemptuous, derisive
lästig	tiresome, annoying
widerlich	repugnant
unausstehlich	insufferable
unerträglich	unbearable
streitsüchtig	quarrelsome, pugnacious
eigensinnig	obstinate, stubborn
stur	obstinate
starrköpfig (coll.)	pigheaded
starrsinnig	pigheaded
trotzig	defiant
kompromisslos	uncompromising
Spielverderber(in), der/die (-/nen)	killjoy, spoilsport
sich einmischen	to interfere, meddle

Tolerance and intolerance

engstirnig	narrow-minded
spießig	narrow-minded
aufgeschlossen	open-minded
Aufgeschlossenheit, die (no pl.)	open-mindedness
unparteiisch	impartial
Unparteilichkeit, die (no pl.)	impartiality

(un)voreingenommen	(un)biased, (un)prejudiced, (im)partial
Unvoreingenom-menheit, die (no pl.)	impartiality
(un)befangen	(im)partial, (un)biased

Good/bad manners

grob	coarse, rude
rau	rough
roh	brutish, callous, uncouth
Rohheit, die (no pl.)	brutishness, callousness, uncouthness
ordinär	vulgar, common
unverschämt	impudent, impertinent
Unverschämtheit, die (-en)	impudence, impertinence
unanständig	rude
unartig	naughty
ungezogen	naughty, badly behaved, cheeky

Good/bad humour

erfreut	pleased
sonnig	happy
(hoch)beglückt	(blissfully) happy
lebenslustig	full of the joys of life
lebensfroh	full of zest for life
betrübt	sad
Kummer, der (no pl.)	grief, sorrow
Trauer, die (no pl.)	grief
in Trauer sein	to be in mourning
übel gelaunt sein	to be in a bad mood
nicht bei Laune sein (coll.)	to not be in a good mood
Vergnügen, das (-)	pleasure
vergnügt	cheerful
Missvergnügen, das (no pl.)	discontent
missvergnügt	discontented
missmutig	sullen, morose, discontented

bedrückt	despondent, depressed
niedergeschlagen	despondent, dejected
Niedergeschlagenheit, die (no pl.)	despondency
optimistisch/ pessimistisch	optimistic/pessimistic
schwarzseherisch	pessimistic
jmdn necken	to tease sb
jmdn hänseln	to tease sb
jmdn (mit etw) aufziehen (coll.)	to tease sb about sth
Streich, der (-e)	prank
meckern (coll.)	to moan, grouse
Meckerer, der (-; coll.); Meckerin, die (-nen; coll.)	moaner, grumbler, grouser
bitter	embittered
verbittert	bitter
trübsinnig	melancholic, gloomy
schwermütig	melancholic
todunglücklich (coll.)	desperately unhappy
kreuzunglücklich (coll.)	terribly miserable
Missfallen, das (no pl.)	displeasure

Stability and instability

gefasst	composed, calm, collected
Gefasstheit, die (no pl.)	composure, calmness
ausgeglichen	well balanced
nüchtern	sober
Mäßigkeit üben	to exercise/show moderation/ restraint
beständig	constant, steadfast
unbeständig	erratic, inconsistent
exzentrisch	eccentric
angespannt	tense
aufs Höchste angespannt sein	to be highly tense
empfindlich	sensitive, touchy
Empfindlichkeit, die (no pl.)	sensitivity, touchiness

überempfindlich	oversensitive
sensibel	sensitive
reizbar	sensitive, touchy
aufgebracht	outraged, incensed
empört	outraged
rasend	raging, raving, mad
depressiv	depressive
über(be)lastet	under too great a strain
paranoid	paranoid
ausgeflippt (coll.)	freaky, freaked out, flipped out
verzweifelt	desperate, frantic
geisteskrank	mentally ill
geistesgestört	mentally disturbed
übergeschnappt (coll.)	crazy
bekloppt (sl.)	loony, crazy, mad
bescheuert (sl.)	nuts
behämmert (sl.)	loony, crazy, mad
nicht alle Tassen im Schrank haben (coll.)	to not be right in the head
einen Vogel haben (sl.)	to be off one's rocker
brutal	violent
gewalttätig	violent
Hitzkopf, der (¨e)	hothead
hitzköpfig	hot-headed
aufbrausend	quick-tempered, hot-tempered

Good/poor judgment

einsichtig	reasonable, understanding
gesunder Menschenverstand	common sense
Überlegung, die (-en)	thought, reflection
vorherige Überlegung	forethought
Vorausplanung, die (-en)	advance planning
weitblickend	far-sighted
anspruchsvoll	discriminating, demanding
wählerisch	choosy, particular

151

gewissenhaft	conscientious
pflichtbewusst	conscientious, with a sense of duty
zerstreut	absent-minded
schwachköpfig (coll.)	feather-brained
(in)konsequent	(in)consistent
widersprüchlich	inconsistent
nachlässig	careless, negligent
Nachlässigkeit, die (-en)	carelessness, negligence
leichtfertig	careless
Leichtfertigkeit, die (no pl.)	carelessness
rücksichtslos	inconsiderate, thoughtless, reckless
Rücksichtslosigkeit, die (no pl.)	recklessness

Intelligence and cunning

gescheit	clever, sensible
schlagfertig	quick and clever
gelehrt	learned, erudite, scholarly
hochgelehrt	erudite, very learned
geistig	intellectual
hochgeistig	highly intellectual
geistreich	witty, intelligent, ingenious, quick-witted
geistlos	stupid, dull, unimaginative
einfallsreich	imaginative
einfallslos	unimaginative
belesen	well read
(un)fähig	(in)capable, (in)competent
listig	cunning, crafty, wily
hinterlistig	crafty, cunning, deceitful
hinterhältig	underhand, devious
einfältig	simple, naive
unwissend	ignorant, unsuspecting, inexperienced

Unwissenheit, die (no pl.)	ignorance
Unkenntnis, die (no pl.)	ignorance
beschränkt	limited, dim, stupid
zurückgeblieben	retarded

Energy and apathy

leidenschaftlich	passionate
Leidenschaft, die (-en)	passion
stürmisch	tempestuous, passionate
eifrig	eager, enthusiastic, assiduous
übereifrig	overeager
unternehmend	enterprising, active
unternehmungslustig	active
betriebsam	busy
ehrgeizig	ambitious
Trieb, der (-e)	drive, urge, desire
Schwung, der (¨e)	drive, energy
unnachgiebig	relentless, unyielding
schwärmerisch	effusive, wildly enthusiastic
nachlässig	indifferent, apathetic
gleichgültig	indifferent
unbeteiligt	indifferent, uninterested
teilnahmslos	indifferent, apathetic
entschlusslos	indecisive
abgespannt	weary, tired, run down
abgeschlagen	exhausted, tired out
zerschlagen	worn out
erledigt (coll.)	worn out
ruhelos, rastlos	restless

Courage and cowardice

unerschrocken	intrepid, courageous
beherzt	brave, courageous
Mut schöpfen	to take heart
den Mut verlieren	to lose heart
sorgenfrei, sorglos	carefree
unbekümmert	carefree, unconcerned

unbeschwert	carefree	angeberisch	boastful
angsterfüllt	fearful	Angeber(in), der/die (-/nen)	show-off, boaster
angstvoll	apprehensive, fearful		
verängstigt	frightened, scared, intimidated	großtuerisch	boastful, bragging
		wichtigtuerisch	pompous
verschreckt	frightened, scared	großsprecherisch	boastful, boasting
schreckhaft	easily startled, jumpy	protzig (coll.)	showy
Feigling, der (-e)	coward	hochmütig	arrogant, haughty
Feigheit, die (no pl.)	cowardice	Hochmut, der (no pl.)	arrogance
verschüchtert	intimidated	eitel	vain, conceited
eingeschüchtert	intimidated	Eitelkeit, die (-en)	vanity, vainness
furchtsam	timid, timorous	selbstgefällig	self-satisfied, smug
		herablassend	condescending

Modesty and pride

aufgeblasen	puffed up, self-important	Selbstüberschätzung, die (no pl.)	overestimation of one's abilities
		zurückhaltend	self-effacing

Level 3

Virtue and vice, strictness and laxity

tugendhaft	virtuous	lüstern	lecherous, lascivious, lewd, lustful
Tugend, die (-en)	virtue		
keusch	chaste, pure	Lüsternheit, die (no pl.)	lechery
Keuschheit, die (no pl.)	chastity	begehrlich	covetous
ehrenhaft	honourable, respectable	ausschweifend	dissolute
		Ausschweifung, die (-en)	debauchery, dissolution
Ehrenhaftigkeit, die (no pl.)	sense of honour, honourableness	gefräßig	gluttonous, voracious
sittenstreng	highly moral		
asketisch	ascetic, austere	Gefräßigkeit, die (no pl.)	gluttony
gebührend	proper	unersättlich	insatiable
gehörig	proper	verwerflich	reprehensible
Skrupel, der (-)	scruple	verworfen	depraved
Skrupel haben	to have scruples	Verworfenheit, die (no pl.)	depravity
skrupellös	scrupulous		
Skrupellosigkeit, die (no pl.)	unscrupulousness	zügellos leben	to live a life of licentious indulgence
skrupellos	unscrupulous		
verdienstvoll	of outstanding merit	Zügellosigkeit, die (no pl.)	licentiousness
verdient	of outstanding merit		
vergnügungssüchtig	pleasure-hungry	verabscheuenswert, verabscheuenswürdig	detestable, loathsome
Sinnenlust, die (no pl.)	lust		

| liederlich | dissolute, dissipated |
| übel/gut beleumdet sein | to have a bad/good reputation |

Honesty and dishonesty, trust and distrust

rechtschaffen	honest, upright
Rechtschaffenheit, die (no pl.)	honesty, uprightness
wahrhaft	truthful; true, real
(un)wahrhaftig	(un)truthful
offenherzig	open, frank, candid
freimütig	frank, honest, open
heuchlerisch	hypocritical
Heuchelei, die (-en)	hypocrisy
geheimnistuerisch	secretive
verlogen	lying
heimtückisch	insidious
Argwohn, der (no pl.)	suspicion
argwöhnisch	suspicious
Vortäuschung, die (-en)	pretence
verräterisch	treacherous, perfidious
Verrat, der (no pl.)	betrayal
(il)loyal	(dis)loyal
Illoyalität, die (no pl.)	disloyalty

Willpower

beharrlich	persistent, insistent
Beharrlichkeit, die (no pl.)	persistence, insistence
Standhaftigkeit, die (no pl.)	steadfastness
zäh	dogged, tenacious
Zähigkeit, die (no pl.)	doggedness, tenacity
Ausdauer, die (no pl.)	perseverance, persistence, tenacity
ausdauernd	persevering, tenacious, persistent
labil	weak

Benevolence and malevolence, generosity and meanness

großmütig	magnanimous
Großmut, die (no pl.)	magnanimity
karitativ	charitable
Gnade, die (-n)	mercy
gnädig	merciful
mildtätig	charitable
wohltätig	charitable
wohlmeinend (elev.)	well meaning
konziliant	obliging, accommodating
uneigennützig	unselfish, selfless
Uneigennützigkeit, die (no pl.)	altruism
niederträchtig	malicious, vile
Niederträchtigkeit, die (no pl.)	maliciousness, vileness
nachtragend	vindictive
garstig	nasty, naughty
anstößig	offensive
jmdn quälen	to torment sb
unerbittlich	inexorable, pitiless
erbarmungslos	merciless
knauserig (coll.)	mean, stingy
(mit etw) knausern (coll.)	to be stingy (with sth)
knickerig (coll.)	stingy
(mit etw) knickern (coll.)	to be stingy (with sth)

Friendliness and unfriendliness, communicativeness

Gefährte, der (-n); Gefährtin, die (-nen)	companion, partner
Genosse, der (-n); Genossin, die (-nen)	comrade, mate, buddy, pal
Zechgenosse, der (-n); Zechgenossin, die (-nen)	drinking companion
Kumpel, der (-s; coll.)	pal, chum, buddy

Brüderschaft, die (no pl.)	close friendship
mit jmdm Brüderschaft trinken	to agree over a drink to use "du"
Ergebenheit, die (no pl.)	devotion
anhänglich	devoted, affectionate
liebedienernd	fawning
katzenfreundlich	overly friendly
verbindlich	friendly
unverbindlich	detached, impersonal
umgänglich	affable
leutselig	affable
feindselig	hostile
Feindseligkeit, die (no pl.)	hostility, animosity
abweisend	cold
bärbeißig	gruff
brüsk	brusque, abrupt
kurz angebunden	curt, brusque
wortkarg	taciturn
schweigsam	silent, taciturn
gesprächig	communicative, chatty
mitteilsam	communicative, garrulous
überschwenglich	effusive
Anziehungskraft, die (¨e)	attraction, appeal
eine große Anziehungskraft auf jmdn ausüben	to attract sb strongly

Amiability

gutmütig	good-natured
zuvorkommend	obliging
kokett	coquettish
jmdn fesseln	to fascinate, captivate sb
von/über etw entzückt sein	to be delighted by/at sth
unleidlich	tetchy
spitzfindig	oversubtle, hair-splitting
spöttisch	mocking

bissig	vicious
aufdringlich	pushy
störrisch	stubborn, obstinate
kampflustig	belligerent, pugnacious
aufsässig	recalcitrant
prozesssüchtig	litigious
abstoßend	repulsive, repellent

Good/bad manners

gehorsam	obedient
ungeschliffen	unrefined
unflätig	coarse
derb	crude, coarse
ungehobelt	uncouth
obszön	obscene
keck	impertinent, cheeky
unverfroren	insolent, impudent
flegelhaft	loutish, boorish
rüpelhaft	loutish
ungebärdig	unruly
krakeelen (coll.)	to make a row

Good/bad humour

frohsinnig	cheerful
munter	cheerful, merry, perky
putzmunter (coll.)	chirpy, perky
quietschvergnügt (coll.)	really chirpy, chipper
aufgeräumt	jovial
selig	overjoyed
glückselig	blissfully happy
aufgekratzt (coll.)	in high spirits
schelmisch	mischievous, impish
verschmitzt	mischievous
jammern	to moan
Miesepeter, der (-; coll., hum.)	grouch
miesepet(e)rig (coll.)	grouchy
brummig	grumpy, grouchy, sour-tempered
Brummbär, der (-en; coll.)	grouch
Meckerfritze, der (-n; coll.)	bellyacher; grouser

155

Meckerliese, die (-n; coll.)	bellyacher
bockig	petulant
quengelig (coll.)	whining
grantig	grumpy
mürrisch	grumpy, sullen
griesgrämig	grumpy, grouchy
wehmütig	melancholically nostalgic
elegisch	mournful
verdrießlich	morose, sullen

Stability and instability

seelenruhig	calm, as cool as you please
gleichmütig	serene, composed
Gelassenheit, die (no pl.)	calmness, coolness, composure
gelassen	calm, cool, composed
stoisch	stoic
gesetzt	staid
charakterfest	steadfast
standhaft	steadfast, strong
unerschütterlich	unshakeable, imperturbable
entrüstet	indignant, outraged
grimmig	furious
rabiat	violent, furious
fuchsteufelswild (coll.)	livid
jähzornig sein	to have a violent temper
wutentbrannt	infuriated, furious
sich in einen Wutanfall hineinsteigern	to work oneself up into a rage
plemplem (coll.)	nuts
durchdrehen (coll.)	to crack up
durchgedreht (coll.)	nuts
einen Dachschaden haben (coll.)	to be not quite right in the head
hirnverbrannt	crazy
nicht bei Sinnen sein	to be out of one's mind
geistig umnachtet (elev.)	mentally deranged
verhaltensgestört	disturbed
unzurechnungsfähig	of unsound mind

für unzurechnungsfähig erklärt werden	to be certified insane
schrullenhaft, schrullig	quirky
wunderlich	strange, odd
gefügig, fügsam	submissive, compliant
haltlos	insecure
manisch	manic
Hysterie, die (no pl.)	hysteria
hysterisch	hysterical
rasende Eifersucht	insane jealousy

Good/poor judgment

umsichtig	circumspect, prudent, judicious
besonnen	level-headed
urteilsfähig	discerning, discriminating
Urteilsfähigkeit, die (no pl.)	discernment, discrimination
Urteilsvermögen, das (no pl.)	judgment, discernment
wachsam	vigilant
entschlussfreudig	decisive
unbesonnen	impulsive, rash, reckless
Unbesonnenheit, die (no pl.)	rashness
ungestüm (elev.)	impetuous
übermäßig	excessive
kühn	audacious, impudent
verwegen	audacious
Verwegenheit, die (no pl.)	audacity
geistesabwesend	absent-minded
schusselig (coll.)	scatter-brained
kapriziös	capricious
flatterhaft	flighty
wankelmütig	fickle
unberechenbar	unpredictable

Intelligence and cunning

scharfsinnig	perspicacious, astute, sharp-witted

Scharfsinn, der (no pl.) — astuteness, acumen, keen perception
genial — brilliant, inspired
ein genialer Mensch — a genius
Intellekt, der (no pl.) — intellect
durchgeistigt — cerebral
vergeistigt — cerebral, spiritual
begnadet — gifted, blessed
gewitzt — crafty, cunning
gerissen — crafty, cunning
raffiniert — clever, cunning
durchtrieben — cunning, sly
verschlagen — sly, artful
pfiffig — smart, sharp, cute
geistesgegenwärtig — quick-witted
töricht (elev.) — foolish, stupid
dämlich (coll.) — stupid, dumb
unterbelichtet (coll.) — dim
begriffsstützig, begriffsstutzig (AU) — thick

Energy and apathy

beflissen — zealous
pflichteifrig — zealous
regsam — lively, active
arbeitsam — industrious, hard-working
emsig — industrious, busy
rührig — active, enterprising
glühend — ardent
glutvoll — passionate
verzückt — enraptured
lustlos — listless
lahm — dull, lethargic
lasch — limp, listless
schlaff — lethargic, listless
schlapp — worn out, listless, run-down
saft- und kraftlos — washed-out
gerädert (coll.) — tired out
matt — weak, weary
Mattigkeit, die (no pl.) — weakness, weariness
träge — sluggish, lethargic

Trägheit, die (no pl.) — sluggishness, lethargy
nichtsnutzig — good for nothing
tatenlos — idle
Nichtstuer, der (-) — slacker
tranig (coll.) — slow, sluggish
trödelig — slow, dawdling

Courage and cowardice

unverzagt — undaunted
draufgängerisch — daring, audacious
kühn — bold, daring, brave, fearless
tollkühn — daredevil, daring
verwegen — daring, bold
vermessen — bold
waghalsig — foolhardy, daredevil
wagemutig — daring, bold
todesmutig — absolutely fearless
mannhaft — manly, valiant
heldenhaft, -mütig — heroic, valiant
couragiert — courageous
Schneid, der/S, AU: die (no pl.; coll.) — guts, nerve, courage
zag, zaghaft — timid
beklommen — apprehensive, anxious, full of trepidation
bang(e) — scared, frightened
mir ist bang(e) vor jmdm/etw — I am scared/frightened of sb/sth
Angsthase, der (-n; coll.) — scaredy-cat, cowardy custard
gehemmt — inhibited
verklemmt — inhibited

Modesty and pride

dünkelhaft — arrogant, haughty, conceited
Dünkel, der (no pl.) — conceit, arrogance
anmaßend — presumptuous, arrogant
hochfahrend — arrogant
überheblich — arrogant, supercilious

Überheblichkeit, die (no pl.)	arrogance	versnobt	snobbish, snobby
siegesgewiss, –sicher	confident of victory/success	großkotzig (sl.)	pretentious
		hochgestochen	stuck–up
erhobenen Hauptes	with one's head held high	hochtrabend	pompous
		großspurig	flashy, showy
prahlerisch	boastful, bragging	Demut, die (no pl.)	humility
Prahler(in), der/die (-/nen)	boaster, bragger, braggart	demütig	humble

---

Exercises

Level 1

1. Falsche Freunde. Ergänzen Sie die Tabelle.

Deutsch	Englisch	Deutsch	Englisch
brav			brave
Lust			lust
sympathisch			sympathetic
faul			foul
nett			net
dezent			decent
genial			genial
kurios			curious
rationell			rational
sensibel			sensible

2. Wie heißt das Gegenteil? ✓

1. moralisch
2. ein gutes Gewissen haben
3. ehrlich
4. taktlos
5. freundlich
6. gute Manieren haben
7. tolerant
8. zufrieden
9. aufmerksam
10. aktiv
11. kraftvoll

3. Wie heißt das entsprechende Adjektiv? ✓

Substantiv	Adjektiv
1. die Unanständigkeit	
2. die Eifersucht	
3. die Strenge	
4. die Treue	
5. der Verdacht	
6. die Großzügigkeit	
7. die Hilfsbereitschaft	
8. die Selbstsucht	
9. die Gefühllosigkeit	
10. die Nervosität	
11. der Wahnsinn	
12. die Bescheidenheit	

4. Wie heißt das Adjektiv? ✓

a. begeistert, b. doof, c. energisch, d. furchtlos, e. lärmend, f. mutig, g. pünktlich, h. schlau, i. unbegabt, j. unbesorgt, k. vernünftig, l. witzig

1. ohne Furcht
2. ohne Sorgen
3. tapfer
4. voller Energie
5. enthusiastisch
6. ohne Begabung
7. dumm
8. clever
9. rational
10. lustig und geistreich
11. zur rechten Zeit
12. laut

5. Welches Wort passt nicht? ✓
1. schwach, streng, weich, willenlos
2. bescheiden, böse, gemein, schlimm
3. respektlos, tolerant, vorurteilsfrei, vorurteilslos
4. fröhlich, glücklich, heiter, launisch
5. gebildet, eingebildet, kultiviert, weise

6. begabt, feige, geschickt, talentiert
7. apatisch, arrogant, hochnäsig, snobistisch
8. ängstlich, besorgt, schüchtern, tüchtig

6. Welches Wort hat die gleiche oder eine ähnliche Bedeutung? ✓

> a. aufrecht, b. direkt, c. hilfsbereit, d. launenhaft, e. lebhaft, f. schlimm,
> g. verärgert, h. witzig

1. offen	5. spaßig
2. gerade	6. launisch
3. hilfreich	7. ärgerlich
4. schlecht	8. lebendig

7. Was bedeuten die Wendungen?
1. bitte recht freundlich!
2. allen Respekt!
3. nur Mut!
4. meine Güte!
5. ein Glück!
6. viel Spaß!
7. Ruhe, bitte!

8. Welches Verb passt? ✓

> a. anfangen, b. aufnehmen, c. gehen, d. hegen, e. kennen, f. machen, g. verlieren

1. jmds Bekanntschaft
2. die Beherrschung
3. jmdn vom Sehen
4. mit jmdm einen Streit
5. jmdm auf die Nerven
6. Vorurteile gegen jmdn
7. mit jmdm Kontakt

9. In jedem Satz fehlt ein Wort. ✓

> enttäuscht, Gewissensbisse, gierig, glaubwürdig, klug, Laune, liebevolles,
> selbstsicher, unhöflich, Wut

1. Er war außer sich vor _____.
2. Er gibt sich einigermaßen _____: „Angst vor Konkurrenz habe ich nicht."
3. Sie ist _____ und gebildet.
4. Es wäre _____, sie warten zu lassen.
5. _____ isst er einen Teller nach dem anderen leer.

6. Seine Tochter war ein schönes, sensibles und _____ Mädchen.
7. Ich war wirklich _____ und überrascht über ihre Entscheidung.
8. Sie war guter _____.
9. Hinterher empfindet sie _____ und Scham über ihr Verhalten.
10. Den Augenzeugen halte ich für _____.

10. Übersetzen Sie ins Englische.

Mein Idol ist Stefan Raab
Er macht gute Witze und kann auch viel einstecken. Besonders gut hat mir der Boxkampf gefallen, weil er nicht zu feige war, um gegen die Profi-Boxerin Regina Halmich zu boxen. Ich finde auch, der hat einen guten Charakter, und mit seinem Charme verzaubert er die Zuschauer im Studio oder zu Hause am Fernseher. Mit seinen Sprüchen hat er großen Erfolg. Sein Auftreten im Studio ist auch immer sehr witzig. Mit seinen Reportagen über Prominente, oder wenn er sich über Leute lustig macht, bringt er mich immer wieder zum Lachen. Auf seinem Pult hat er Tasten, wo er draufdrückt, und es erscheinen Sprüche oder Melodien. Das finde ich genial! Seine Musik ist auch toll, wie z.B. das Lied *Maschendrahtzaun*.

Benny Muys (12), Willich-Neersen

FRANKFURTER RUNDSCHAU, Samstag, 30. Juni 2001, Nr. 149/26, Magazin, S. 20

Mein Idol ist Joanne K. Rowling
Ich bewundere sie, weil sie zwei Kinder allein erzogen hat, und dabei hatte sie kaum Geld. Als sie die ersten fantasievollen Harry-Potter-Bücher auf Servietten in einer Teestube schrieb, weil sie kein Geld für Papier und Heizöl hatte, hielt sie tapfer durch. Während sie in Hamburg ihr neues Buch vorstellte, habe ich sie getroffen. Daher weiß ich, dass sie sehr ruhig und fröhlich ist. Ihren Erfolg hat sie verdient, denn was sie geleistet hat, ist wirklich toll. Mit ihrer Fantasie hat sie viele Kinderherzen erobert, aber auch Erwachsene lesen ihre Bücher! Mir gefällt besonders Hermine.

Friederike Hauschildt (10 Jahre), Brunsbüttel

FRANKFURTER RUNDSCHAU, Samstag, 17. November 2001, Nr. 268/46, Magazin, S. 14

11. Schriftliche Übung. Beschreiben Sie Ihr Idol.

Level 2

1. Welches Wort hat die gleiche oder eine ähnliche Bedeutung? ✓

1. moral
2. ehrlich
3. jmdn betrügen
4. etw verdrehen
5. unbeirrt
6. irresolut
7. die Habsucht
8. fair
9. reserviert
10. der Charme
11. eigensinnig
12. engstirnig

13. unparteiisch   17. pessimistisch
14. ungezogen   18. jmdn necken
15. sonnig   19. melancholisch
16. traurig   20. brutal

2. Wie heißt das Adjektiv? ✓

1. sehr beglückt   8. ohne Rücksicht
2. sehr unglücklich   9. ohne gute Sitten
3. sehr gelehrt   10. ohne Schamgefühl
4. sehr geistig   11. ohne Kompromisse
5. zu empfindlich   12. ohne Sorgen
6. zu eifrig   13. ohne Teilnahme
7. zu stark belastet

3. Wie heißt das entsprechende Substantiv? Was bedeutet es auf Englisch? ✓

Adjektiv	Substantiv	Übersetzung
1. geil		
2. bedenkenlos		
3. selbstgerecht		
4. leichtgläubig		
5. entschlossen		
6. hartnäckig		
7. geizig		
8. menschenfreundlich		
9. entgegenkommend		
10. unvoreingenommen		
11. unverschämt		
12. niedergeschlagen		
13. empfindlich		
14. nachlässig		

4. Wie heißt das Gegenteil? ✓

1. geistreich
2. fähig
3. vergnügt
4. befangen
5. einfallsreich
6. rücksichtsvoll
7. resolut
8. diskret
9. aufrichtig

5. Welches Verb passt? ✓

a. erregen, b. gewinnen, c. schenken, d. schließen, e. schöpfen, f. sein,
g. spielen, h. üben

1. Mut
2. Mäßigkeit
3. in Trauer
4. jmdm Vertrauen
5. jmds Missfallen
6. Distanz zu etw
7. jmdm einen Streich
8. mit jmdm Freundschaft

6. Wie heißen die Wendungen?

1. Hochmut kommt vor dem Fall
2. eitel wie ein Pfau
3. Feigheit vor dem Feind
4. ich bin Kummer gewohnt
5. stur wie ein Panzer
6. mit nüchternem Kopf
7. Unwissenheit schützt nicht vor Strafe

7. Welches Adjektiv passt am besten? ✓

1. Im Gespräch mit den Damen schämt er sich und errötet.
    a. reuevoll
    b. selbstbewusst
    c. verlegen
2. Der Beamte hat unerlaubte Geschenke angenommen.
    a. bestechlich
    b. verschlossen
    c. vertrauenswürdig
3. Sie sagt bewusst die Unwahrheit.
    a. barsch
    b. lügnerisch
    c. nachgiebig
4. Sie ist freundlich, sehr herzlich und zuvorkommend.
    a. liebenswürdig
    b. reizbar
    c. starrsinnig
5. Er ist ein treuer Freund.
    a. beständig
    b. leichtfertig
    c. wählerisch
6. Er ist ein kluger Kerl.
    a. eingeschüchtert
    b. gescheit
    c. nachlässig

7. Sie findet es schwer, eine Entscheidung zu treffen.
    a. angstvoll
    b. entschlusslos
    c. herablassend
8. Sie ist ein sehr unzufriedener Mensch.
    a. listig
    b. verbittert
    c. pflichtbewusst

8. Welches Wort passt nicht? ✓
1. behämmert, bekloppt, bescheuert, beschränkt
2. gleichgültig, scheinheilig, teilnahmslos, unbeteiligt
3. grob, ordinär, rau, unbeständig
4. bedrückt, sorgenfrei, unbekümmert, unbeschwert
5. angeberisch, großsprecherisch, schwärmerisch, wichtigtuerisch

9. In jedem Satz fehlt ein Wort. ✓

> abgespannt, aufbrausend, dicke, gefasster, glückstrahlend, hinterlistig, leidenschaftliche, weitblickend

1. Sie wird als herzlos, verräterisch und _____ gezeichnet.
2. Sie ist noch _____ von der langen Reise.
3. Sie ist eine _____ Fürsprecherin der Kinder und ihrer Rechte.
4. Er erwies sich als weise und _____.
5. Er beschreibt sich als hitzköpfig, _____ und stur.
6. Mit ruhiger und _____ Stimme hat er es verkündet.
7. Sie freute sich riesig und fiel ihrem Freund _____ um den Hals.
8. Seit der Schulzeit sind sie _____ Freunde.

10. Was passt nicht? ✓
1. -köpfig: dick-, ehr-, hitz-, schwach-, starr-
2. -liebe: Heimat-, Jugend-, Jung-, Menschen-, Nächsten-
3. -gierig: blut-, geld-, hab-, liebe-, neu-
4. ziel-: -bewusst, -gerichtet, -losig, -sicher, -strebig
5. -sam: aufmerk-, betrieb-, einsicht-, spar-, unbeug-

11. Übersetzen Sie ins Englische.

Onkel Noam aus dem Netz

Die Globalisierungsgegner haben einen intellektuellen Guru: den amerikanischen Linguisten Noam Chomsky. Er versteht sich als Dissident – auch innerhalb der politischen Linken seines Landes

von Jörg Lau

Am 15. April 1992 hat die Pressestelle des renommierten Massachusetts Institute of Technology, kurz MIT, eine frohe Botschaft zu verkünden: „Chomsky ist der Zitat-Champion." Die Rede ist von dem Sprachwissenschaftler Noam Chomsky, dem Star der linguistischen Fakultät des bei Boston gelegenen Elitecampus: Professor Chomsky sei die „meistzitierte lebende Person" der letzten zehn Jahre und befinde sich „in der Tat in illustrer Gesellschaft. Die Top Ten der zitierten Quellen im betreffenden Zeitraum waren: Marx, Lenin, Shakespeare, Aristoteles, die Bibel, Plato, Freud, Chomsky, Hegel und Cicero."

Marx und Lenin – und wohl auch Freud – dürften in der Zwischenzeit auf hintere Plätze abgerutscht sein. Noam Chomsky aber, unterdessen 72 Jahre alt, ist heute stärker präsent als je zuvor. Es ist allerdings nicht mehr so sehr der von ihm begründete Strang der „strukturalen Linguistik", der seinen Ruhm ausmacht, sondern sein politischer Aktivismus. Chomsky ist ein Vordenker jenes bunten Patchworks von Globalisierungsgegnern, das sich selbst gerne das „Volk von Seattle" nennt und zum Schrecken aller Gipfeltreffen geworden ist ...

Die USA : Ein Schurkenstaat?
Der Optimismus seiner Sprachphilosophie ist nun aber, so scheint es, in scharfen Widerspruch zu dem tiefschwarzen Pessimismus seiner politischen Analysen geraten. Chomsky ist der einzige Intellektuelle von Rang, der für die eigentlich antiintellektuelle Bewegung der Globalisierungsgegner überhaupt eine Rolle spielt. Das Internet ist die technische Voraussetzung für Chomskys Altersruhm. Dort haben seine Anhänger die größten Teile seines politischen Werks zugänglich gemacht. Das führende elektronische Theorieorgan der radikalen Linken in den USA, *Z Magazine*, pflegt ein Noam Chomsky Archive mit Hunderten von Essays, Interviews, Buchexzerpten und Debattenbeiträgen. Zum Verdruss seiner vielen Gegner, die ihn als die größte Nervensäge der Pax Americana betrachten, ist es unabweisbar, dass Noam Chomsky von seinen zahlreichen Lesern wahrhaft und aufrichtig geliebt wird.

Nun gehört es eigentlich nicht zu den Aufgaben eines kritischen Intellektuellen, derartige Liebesgefühle in seinem Publikum zu erwecken. Sie müssten ihm sogar verdächtig erscheinen. Chomsky jedoch liegen solche Skrupel offenbar fern. Seine Vorträge sind gespickt mit leicht zu merkenden Refrains über die Vereinigten Staaten als Reich des Bösen. Eine Rede anlässlich des Jubiläums *Fünfzig Jahre UN, Weltbank, IMF und Menschenrechtscharta* gipfelte in dem Diktum: „Wir sind ein gewalttätiger, gesetzloser, verbrecherischer Schurkenstaat." Chomskys neuestes Buch ist denn auch dem außenpolitischen Konzept des *rogue state* gewidmet. Es läuft darauf hinaus, den Begriff als bloße machtpolitische Ideologie der USA zu demaskieren – und diese selbst im Gegenzug als den wahren Schurkenstaat hinzustellen ...

Noam Chomsky ist schließlich nicht irgendein verbohrter Spinner, der sich seinem Altersradikalismus überlässt. Durch sein Engagement gegen den Vietnamkrieg war er einst zum Modell für die Unbestechlichkeit eines Intellektuellen durch die Propagandalügen des State Department geworden. Seine Vorlesungen Ende der sechziger Jahre wurden zu Erweckungserlebnissen für die junge Studentengeneration, die sich mit dem Quietismus ihrer akademischen Lehrer nicht mehr abfinden mochte. Chomsky hatte dabei immer zwischen seinen sprachphilosophischen Ansichten und seinem Aktivismus, seiner Theorie und seinen politischen Ansichten unterschieden – was ihm als besondere intellektuelle Redlichkeit ausgelegt wurde. Unvermeidlicherweise aber erglänzte die Chomskysche Linguistik dennoch in der Aura seiner politischen Progressivität ...

DIE ZEIT, 26. Juli 2001, Nr. 31, Feuilleton, S. 29

Level 3

1. Welches Adjektiv passt? ✓

> a. beharrlich, b. ehrenhaft, c. garstig, d. gefräßig, e. gnädig, f. katzenfreundlich, g. verbindlich, h. vergnügungssüchtig, i. verräterisch, j. verwerflich

1. anständig
2. immer neue Vergnügungen suchend
3. unsittlich
4. scheinheilig freundlich
5. auf Verrat zielend
6. hartnäckig
7. böse
8. barmherzig, mild
9. übermäßig viel essend
10. freundlich

2. Wie heißen die Adjektive? ✓

1. sehr vergnügt
2. sehr munter
3. sehr wild
4. sehr kühn
5. voller Tugend
6. voller Dünkel

3. Welches Wort hat die gleiche oder eine ähnliche Bedeutung? ✓

1. gebührend
2. verdient
3. offenherzig
4. mildtätig
5. knauserig
6. wortkarg
7. gesprächig
8. mürrisch
9. gelassen
10. charakterfest
11. fügsam
12. verwegen
13. gewitzt
14. tranig
15. heldenmütig
16. siegessicher
17. leutselig
18. flegelhaft

4. Erklären Sie den Unterschied.

1. skrupellös, skrupellos
2. lustig, lüstern
3. wunderbar, wunderlich

5. Welches Wort passt nicht? ✓

1. bärbeißig, brüsk, keusch, schroff
2. großmütig, karitativ, schäbig, uneigennützig
3. der Genosse, der Kamerad, der Kumpel, der Prahler
4. aufsässig, störrisch, trotzig, verdrießlich
5. dämlich, derb, unflätig, ungehobelt
6. flatterhaft, geistesgegenwärtig, wankelmütig, unberechenbar
7. emsig, pflichteifrig, regsam, waghalsig
8. arrogant, couragiert, hochfahrend, überheblich

6. In jedem Satz fehlt ein Wort. ✓

> aufdringlich, Eifersucht, schelmisch, selig, Sinnen, umnachtet, ungebärdiges,
> unzurechnungsfähig, Wutanfall, zuvorkommend

1. Sie ist nicht bei _____ .
2. Er ist geistig _____ .
3. Sie hat es aus rasender _____ getan.
4. Er hat sich in einen _____ hineingesteigert.
5. Man hat ihn für _____ erklärt.
6. Sie war _____, dass sie das Examen bestanden hat.
7. Er wirkt sehr höflich und _____ gegenüber allen Kunden.
8. Sie haben ein _____ Kind.
9. Er war aggressiv und _____, wenn er getrunken hatte.
10. Das Kind lächelte _____ .

7. Wie heißen die Wendungen?

1. rechtschaffen Hunger haben
2. ich weiß es wahrhaftig nicht
3. ein zähes Leben haben
4. Bangemachen gilt nicht
5. dazu gehört Schneid
6. ein mattes Echo finden
7. ein lahmer Typ
8. ein wachsames Auge auf jmdn haben
9. ruhig und besonnen

8. Schriftliche Übung. Wählen Sie ein Thema.

1. Beschreiben Sie die Charaktereigenschaften eines Freundes bzw. einer Freundin.
   Unterstützen Sie Ihre Aussagen mit Anekdoten.

2. Beschreiben Sie die Charaktereigenschaften des idealen Freundes bzw. der idealen Freundin.

3. Beschreiben Sie eine alte Person, die Sie besonders interessant finden.

9. Lesen Sie den folgenden Text.

Aus „Das Nett-Näpfchen" von Markus Brauck

Die Fernsehnation war ja dabei, als er nach einer Dreiviertelstunde ausufernden Talk-Kampfes zwischen Verona Feldbusch und Alice Schwarzer sein Scheitern eingestand, kokett jammernd wie ein Musterschüler, der seine Hausaufgaben glänzend gemacht hat, sie aber nicht vortragen darf: „Und dabei hatte ich mich doch so schön vorbereitet." Viel hätte nicht gefehlt, und Alice Schwarzer hätte ihm ein Bonbon in den Mund geschoben, „Ist ja gut, mein Junge" gemurmelt und ihm über den Scheitel gestreichelt. Dabei ist Johannes B. Kerner der Letzte, der derzeit Trost braucht. Das Duell der Blubb-Blondine, bei der nur die Haare nicht blond sind, und der Übermutter der Emanzen brachte seiner Show eine Einschaltquote von 30 Prozent – doppelt so viel wie sonst ...

Johannes Baptist Kerner soll für das ZDF werden, was Harald Schmidt für Sat 1 ist und Stefan Raab für Pro 7: der Quotenbringer zur Late Night, das Aushängeschild des Senders, kurz: eine „Marke", von der ZDF-Intendant Dieter Stolte so gern spricht. Und er hat exakt das Profil, das man für Erfolg beim ZDF zurzeit so braucht: Er ist jung, aber ist kein junger Wilder. Und so steht er für die Verjüngung des Senders, ohne am ältlichen Aussehen des Programms etwas zu ändern ...

Passenderweise bringt der Mann mit den hochtrabenden Initialen JBK all die positiven Eigenschaften mit, die Eltern und Großeltern so erfreuen: Er ist bescheiden („Im Mittelpunkt meiner Show stehen die Gäste, nicht ich."), er ist nicht abgehoben (Von Wolfram Siebeck befragt, auf welchen Gegenstand in der Küche er verzichten könne, antwortet er: „Trüffelhobel"). Und er ist nett („Gnadenlos nett", schrieb der *Stern*). Und da alle von allen abschreiben, taucht in beinahe jedem Porträt über ihn sein Satz auf: „Soll ich zum Arschloch mutieren, weil mich alle nett finden?" Das ist entwaffnend. Und das ist, neben seiner Haupteigenschaft Nettigkeit, vielleicht auch schon seine größte Qualität: Er entwaffnet sein Gegenüber. Wenn er jemanden interviewt und wenn er interviewt wird.

So, wie er einem da gegenübersitzt, in der ZDF-Kantine, nicht nur darauf aus, seine Botschaften herüberzubringen, sondern offenbar ehrlich an seinem Gesprächspartner interessiert. Ein Interesse, das nicht gespielt aussieht und womöglich nicht einmal ist. Mühelos nimmt er dem Interviewer das Gespräch aus der Hand und fragt ein bisschen nach dem Leben des anderen, wo es eigentlich um sein Leben gehen soll. Fragt nach, mit diesem „Erzählen Sie mal, so unter uns" -Blick, sagt: „Das ist ja interessant, da müsste ich Sie ja eigentlich einmal in meine Show einladen." Und – schwupps! – sitzt man an Kerners Küchentisch, quasi unter Freunden. Beinahe könnte man der Schmeichelei erliegen, wenn einem da nicht einfiele, dass er die Gabe besitzt, treuherzig Interesse für gänzlich uninteressante Figuren mimen zu können. Also, raus aus der Kuschel-Ecke, und ran zum Angriff. Kerner habe doch eher ein schwaches Bild abgegeben, beim „Gipfeltreffen" von Feldbusch und

Schwarzer, habe zu spät eingegriffen und sei mit seiner Idee, Gemeinsamkeiten zwischen den beiden zu finden, kläglich gescheitert.

Doch ebenso rasch, wie er sich zum Fragesteller aufgeschwungen hat, zieht er sich wieder in die Rolle des Antwortenden zurück. Bleibt freundlich, offen, ehrlich. Und schwer angreifbar. Das sei alles richtig. Er sei auf etwas anderes vorbereitet gewesen. „Zum Schluss war ich ja fast ein bisschen resigniert." Schwarzer und Feldbusch seien bemüht gewesen, mehr zu reden als zuzuhören. Aber was hätte er denn machen sollen? Als Zuchtmeister dazwischengehen?

Natürlich war die Sendung trotzdem ein Erfolg. „Aber wir besaufen uns nicht an der Einschaltquote." Im Fernsehen erreiche man auf kurze Sicht nichts. Und jetzt sei es an der Zeit, dass man wieder aus den Schlagzeilen verschwinde und in Ruhe an der Show weiterarbeiten könne. Wenn einer so redet, ist es das untrügliche Zeichen, dass er ganz oben angelangt ist im Fernsehhimmel: Nun muss er wieder tiefstapeln. „Meine Rolle ist doch nur, die Fragen zu stellen, die man sich vorstellen kann." Und setzt dazu einen Unschuldsblick auf, der sogar Staatsanwälte milde werden lassen könnte ...

FRANKFURTER RUNDSCHAU, Samstag, 7. Juli 2001, Nr. 155/27, S. 22

a. Vokabelübung. Wie heißt das Wort (die Wendung) auf Englisch?
1. ausufern
2. Übermutter
3. blubbern
4. hochtrabend
5. abgehoben
6. gnadenlos nett
7. entwaffnend
8. gespielt
9. treuherzig
10. Kuschel-Ecke
11. kläglich
12. angreifbar
13. Zuchtmeister
14. untrüglich

b. Schriftliche Übung. Beschreiben Sie Johannes Baptist Kerner in Ihren eigenen Worten.

Unit 6

Clothes, accessories and grooming

Level 1

Garments

Kleidung, die (no pl.)	clothes, clothing
Kleid, das (-er)	dress
Kleider, pl.	clothes
Hose, die (-n)	pair of trousers
Hemd, das (-en)	shirt
Jeans, pl. or die (-)	jeans
T-Shirt, das (-s)	T-shirt
Rock, der (¨e)	skirt
Bluse, die (-n)	blouse
(Unter)wäsche, die (no pl.)	underwear
Damenunterwäsche, die (no pl.)	lingerie
Unterhose, die (-n)	pair of (under)pants
Unterhemd, das (-en)	vest, undershirt
Unterrock, der (¨e)	petticoat, slip
Halbrock, der (¨e)	half-slip, waist slip
Büstenhalter (BH), der (-)	bra
Anzug, der (¨e)	suit (for men)
Gürtel, der (-)	belt
Krawatte, die (-n)	tie
Schlips, der (-e; N)	tie
Halstuch, das (¨er)	neckerchief
Kostüm, das (-e)	suit (for women)
Mantel, der (¨)	coat
Regenmantel, der (¨)	raincoat
Jacke, die (-n)	jacket
Strickjacke, die (-n)	cardigan
Hut, der (¨e)	hat
Mütze, die (-n)	cap
Strickmütze, die (-n)	knitted hat
Handschuh, der (-e)	glove
Schal, der (-e or -s)	scarf
Tuch, das (¨er)	scarf
Strumpf, der (¨e)	stocking, sock
Strumpfhose, die (-n)	tights, panty hose
Socke, die (-n)	sock
Schlafanzug, der (¨e)	pyjamas
Pyjama, der, AU and CH: also das (-s)	pyjamas
Nachthemd, das (-en)	nightgown
Bademantel, der (¨)	bathrobe, beach robe
Badehose, die (-n)	swimming trunks
Badeanzug, der (¨e)	swimsuit
Bademütze, die (-n)	bathing cap
sich/jmdn anziehen	to get dressed/dress sb
etw anziehen	to put sth on
etw anprobieren	to try sth on
sich umziehen	to get changed
sich/jmdn ausziehen	to get undressed/undress sb
etw ausziehen	to take sth off
etw tragen	to wear sth

passen	to fit
Kleidergröße, die (-n)	size

Garment details and style

Bund, der (¨e)	waistband
Schnalle, die (-n)	buckle
Reißverschluss, der (¨e)	zip
Hosenschlitz, der (-e)	fly
Bein, das (-e)	leg (of trousers)
Tasche, die (-n)	pocket
kariert	checked
gestreift	striped
(Hals)ausschnitt, der (-e)	neckline
Kragen, der (-; S, AU, CH also ¨)	collar
Kapuze, die (-n)	hood
kurz-, langärmelig	short/long-sleeved
Knopf, der (¨e)	button
Knopfloch, das (¨er)	buttonhole
Armloch, das (¨er)	armhole
secondhand, gebraucht	secondhand, used
bügelfrei	non-iron
waschecht	colourfast

Footwear

Schuh, der (-e)	shoe
Halbschuh, der (-e)	(ankle-high) shoe
Hausschuh, der (-e)	slipper
Stiefel, der (-)	boot
Stiefelette, die (-n)	ankle boot
Gummistiefel, der (-)	rubber boot
Sandale, die (-n)	sandal
Turnschuh, der (-e)	gym shoe, trainer, sneaker
Absatz, der (¨e)	heel
flach	low-heeled
mit flachen/hohen Absätzen	low/high-heeled
Schuhgröße, die (-n)	shoe size
Schuhnummer, die (-n)	shoe size
sich die Schuhe zubinden	to tie one's shoelaces

Care and cleaning

Fleck, der (-en)	stain, spot
etw reinigen	to clean sth, dry-clean sth
Wäsche, die (no pl.)	laundry
Waschpulver, das (-)	laundry detergent
(etw) waschen	to wash (sth)
etw spülen	to rinse sth
etw schleudern	to spin sth
(etw) trocknen	to dry (sth)
(Kleider)bügel, der (-)	hanger
etw aufhängen	to hang sth up
Wäscheklammer, die (-n)	clothes peg
tropfen	to drip
Bügeleisen, das (-)	iron
(etw) bügeln	to iron (sth)
(etw) plätten (N)	to iron (sth)
Schuhcreme, die (-s)	shoe polish
Schuhbürste, die (-n)	shoe brush
Schuhspanner, der (-)	shoe tree
etw putzen	to polish sth

Jewelry and accessories

Schmuck, der (no pl.)	jewelry
Ring, der (-e)	ring
Ohrring, der (-e)	earring
Armband, das (¨er)	bracelet
(Armband)uhr, die (-en)	(wrist)watch
(Hals)kette, die (-n)	necklace
Band, das (¨er)	ribbon
Haarspange, die (-n)	hair slide, barrette
Sonnenbrille, die (-n)	sunglasses
(Hand)tasche, die (-n)	purse, handbag
(Regen)schirm, der (-e)	umbrella
kostbar	valuable; precious
wertvoll	valuable

Grooming

jmdn/sich/etw waschen	to wash sb/o.s./sth
(sich) duschen	to take a shower

(jmdn) baden	to bathe (sb)	sich die Haare bürsten	to brush one's hair
Seife, die (-n)	soap	sich die Zähne putzen	to brush one's teeth
Shampoo, das (-s)	shampoo		
Haarwaschmittel, das (-)	shampoo	Zahnbürste, die (-n)	toothbrush
Waschlappen, der (-)	facecloth, washcloth	Zahnpasta, die (-pasten)	toothpaste
Badetuch, das (¨er)	bath towel	Papiertaschentuch, das (¨er)	tissue, paper handkerchief
jmdn/sich/etw abtrocknen	to dry off sb/o.s./sth	sich die Haare schneiden lassen	to have one's hair cut
jmdn/sich/etw kämmen	to comb sb/o.s./sth's hair	sich rasieren	to shave
Kamm, der (¨e)	comb	sich die Beine rasieren	to shave one's legs
Haartrockner, der (-)	hair dryer	Rasierapparat, der (-e)	razor
Föhn, der (-e)	blow dryer		
die Haare föhnen/mit dem Föhn trocknen	to blow-dry one's hair	Trockenrasierer, der (-)	electric razor
(Haar)bürste, die (-n)	hairbrush	Rasiercreme, die (-s)	shaving cream

Level 2

Garments

Mode, die (-n)	fashion	Wickelrock, der (¨e)	wrap–around skirt
(in) Mode sein	to be in fashion	Hosenrock, der (¨e)	culottes
Pullover, der (-)	pullover, sweater	Plisseerock, der (¨e)	(accordion–)pleated skirt
Pulli, der (-s; coll.)	pullover		
Rollkragenpullover, der (-)	turtleneck sweater	Trainingsanzug, der (¨e)	track suit
Rolli, der (-s; coll.)	turtleneck sweater	Slip, der (-s)	briefs (for men); knickers (for women)
Twinset, das or der (-s)	twin-set		
Weste, die (-n)	vest	Schlüpfer, der (-)	knickers
Lederjacke, die (-n)	leather jacket	Hosenträger, der (-)	suspenders
Anorak, der (-s)	anorak, windbreaker	Hauskleid, das (-er)	house coat
Schultertuch, das (¨er)	shawl	Sakko, der, also (AU only) das (-s)	jacket
Sporthemd, das (-en)	sports shirt	Hosenanzug, der (¨e)	trouser suit
Karohemd, das (-en)	checked shirt	Uniform, die (-en)	uniform
Latzhose, die (-n)	overalls	Kittel, der (-)	smock
Overall, der (-s)	overalls	Arbeitskittel, der (-)	white coat
kurze Hose, die (-n)	pair of shorts	Arbeitsanzug, der (¨e)	overalls
Bermudashorts (Bermudas), pl.	Bermuda shorts	Schürze, die (-n)	apron

Garment details and style

eng anliegend	tight-fitting
bequem geschnitten	loose-fitting
tailliert	waisted; fitted
Schlitz, der (-e)	slit
rückseitiger Schlitz	back slit
Seitenschlitz, der (-e)	side slit
Jackenschlitz, der (-e)	vent
Manschette, die (-n)	(shirt) cuff
Hosenaufschlag, der (¨e)	trouser turn-up
Gesäßtasche, die (-n)	hip pocket
Seitentasche, die (-n)	side pocket
Brusttasche, die (-n)	breast pocket
V-Ausschnitt, der (-e)	V-neck
Rundhalsausschnitt, der (-e)	crew neck
(tief) ausgeschnitten	low-cut
Dekolletee, das (-s)	plunging neckline
tiefer Kleidausschnitt	plunging neckline
rückenfrei	backless
trägerlos	strapless
(Spaghetti)träger, der (-)	(spaghetti) strap
Schulterpolster, das (-)	shoulder pad

Footwear

Schuhband, das (¨er)	shoelace
Schnürsenkel, der (-)	shoelace; bootlace
Schnürschuh, der (-e)	lace-up shoe
Straßenschuh, der (-e)	walking shoe
Rennschuh, der (-e)	track shoe
Pumps, der (-)	pump
Slingpumps, der (-)	sling-back shoe
Lackschuh, der (-e)	patent-leather shoe
Stöckelschuh, der (-e)	stiletto-heeled shoe
stöckeln	to totter (on stilettos)
Schuhanzieher, der (-)	shoe-horn
Schuhlöffel, der (-)	shoe-horn

Jewelry and accessories

Trauring, der (-e)	wedding ring
Siegelring, der (-e)	signet ring
Ohrgehänge, das (-)	pendant earring
Armband mit Anhängern, das (¨er)	charm bracelet
Armreif, der (-e); Armreifen, der (-)	bangle
Anhänger, der (-)	pendant
Medaillon, das (-s)	locket
Halsband, das (¨er)	choker
Edelstein, der (-e)	precious stone, gem
Diamant, der (-en)	diamond
(Zucht)perle, die (-n)	(cultured) pearl
Brosche, die (-n)	brooch
Anstecknadel, die (-n)	pin
Manschettenknopf, der (¨e)	cuff link
Krawattennadel, die (-n)	tiepin

Grooming

Sonnencreme, die (-s)	sunscreen
Lichtschutzfaktor, der (-en)	sun-protection factor
jmdn/sich/etw eincremen (einkremen)	to put cream on sb/o.s./sth
etw färben	to dye, colour sth
Haarfärbemittel, das (-)	hair dye
Lockenwickler, der (-)	curler
Dauerwelle, die (-n)	perm
Frisur, die (-en)	hairstyle
Haarspray, das (-s)	hairspray
Haarteil, das (-e)	hairpiece
Perücke, die (-n)	wig
Binde, die (-n)	sanitary towel
Tampon, der (-s)	tampon
sich frisch machen	to freshen oneself up

sich die Nägel schneiden	to cut one's nails
Nagelfeile, die (-n)	nail file
Nagelschere, die (-n)	pair of nail scissors
Deodorant (Deo), das (-s)	deodorant

Rasierwasser, das (¨)	aftershave
kölnisch Wasser, das (no pl.)	(eau de) cologne
Feuchtigkeitscreme, die (-s)	moisturizer
Schaumbad, das (¨er)	bubble bath

Level 3

Garments

Umstandskleid, das (-er)	maternity dress
Windel, die (-n)	nappy, diaper
Windelhöschen, das (-)	plastic pants
ein Baby windeln	to put a baby's nappy on
Strampelhöschen, das (-)	playsuit
gestrickter Babyschuh	bootee
sich fein machen	to dress up
schick angezogen sein	to be dressy
Abendkleid, das (-er)	evening gown
Ein-, Zweireiher, der (-)	single/double-breasted suit
Smoking, der (-s)	dinner jacket, tuxedo
Frack, der (¨e)	tail coat
Fliege, die (-n)	bow tie
Smokingschleife, die (-n)	bow tie
Hochzeitskleid, das (-er)	wedding dress
Pelzmantel, der (¨)	fur coat
Lederhose, die (-n)	lederhosen
Dirndl, das (-)	dirndl (skirt)
breitrandiger Hut	wide-brimmed hat
Sombrero, der (-s)	sombrero
Filzhut, der (¨e)	felt hat
Lodenhut, der (¨e)	loden hat
Baskenmütze, die (-n)	beret

Schiffermütze, die (-n)	German sailor's cap
Strohhut, der (¨e)	boater
Zylinder, der (-)	top hat
Ledermütze mit Fellklappen, die (-n)	leather cap with fur flaps
Südwester, der (-)	sou'wester
Topfhut, der (¨e)	cloche
Florentinerhut, der (¨e)	picture hat
Schlapphut, der (¨e)	slouch hat

Garment details and style

etw füttern	to line sth
gefüttert	lined
wattiert	quilted; padded
Smokarbeit, die (-en)	smocking
gesmokt	smocked
Aufschlag, der (¨e)	lapel
Revers, das or (AU) der (-)	lapel
ein-, zweireihig	singe/double-breasted
Mieder, das (-)	bodice
Tunnelgürtel, der (-)	drawstring waist
Bügelfalte, die (-n)	crease (created intentionally by ironing)
Abnäher, der (-)	dart
Paspel, die (-n)	piping
Druckknopf, der (¨e)	snap fastener
Haken, der (-)	hook
Öse, die (-n)	eye; eyelet
etw mit etw besetzen	to trim sth with sth

Lederbesatz, der (¨e)	leather trimming
Pelzbesatz, der (¨e)	fur trimming
Spitze, die (-n)	lace
Rüsche, die (-n)	frill
Zopfmuster, das (-)	cable pattern
Stickerei, die (no pl.)	embroidery
Zierstich, der (-e)	decorative stitch
(Vorder)falte, die (-n)	(front) pleat
Kelterfalte, die (-n)	inverted pleat
Hüftweite, die (-n)	hip measurement
Oberweite, die (-n)	bust measurement
Schrittlänge, die (-n)	inside leg measurement

Footwear

Obermaterial Leder	leather uppers
Zunge, die (-n)	tongue
Blatt, das (¨er)	instep
Schaft, der (¨e)	leg (of boot)
Spitze, die (-n)	toe
vorn offen	open-toed
Plateausohle, die (-n)	platform sole
Schuhriemen, der (-)	sandal strap
Slipper, der (-)	slip-on shoe
Pantoffel, der (-n)	backless slipper; mule
Pantolette, die (-n)	mule
Gummisandale, die (-n)	flip-flop
Holzschuh, der (-e)	(wooden) clog

Care and cleaning

Stoff, der (-e)	material
Saum, der (¨e)	hem
Naht, die (¨e)	seam
die Naht ist geplatzt	the seam has split
sich etw aufreißen	to tear sth
Riss, der (-e)	tear
etw länger/kürzer machen	to lengthen/shorten sth
etw enger machen	to take sth in
etw auslassen	to let sth out
(etw) nähen	to sew (sth)

Nähmaschine, die (-n)	sewing machine
etw flicken	to patch sth
etw stopfen	to darn sth
Nadel, die (-n)	needle
Stecknadel, die (-n)	pin
Sicherheitsnadel, die (-n)	safety pin
Faden, der (¨)	thread
Garn, das (-e)	thread; yarn
Zentimetermaß, das (-e)	tape measure

Make-up

Schminke, die (-n)	make-up
sich (leicht/stark) schminken	to put on (a little/a lot of) make-up
die Lippen schminken	to put on lipstick
Lippenstift, der (-e)	lipstick
Wimperntusche, die (-n)	mascara
Lidschatten, der (-)	eye shadow
Lidstrich, der (no pl.)	eyeliner
Grundierungscreme, die (-s)	foundation
Gesichtspuder, der (-)	face powder
sich die Nase pudern	to powder one's nose
Puderdose, die (-n)	powder compact
Rouge, das (-s)	rouge, blusher
Rouge auflegen	to put on rouge
Nagellack, der (-e)	nail polish
sich die Nägel lackieren	to paint one's nails
Nagellackentferner, der (-)	nail polish remover
Parfum, das (-s); Parfüm, das (-e or -s)	perfume

175

Food and drink

Level 1

General

Lebensmittel, pl.	food
Nahrungsmittel, das (–; mainly pl.)	food
jmdn/sich ernähren	to feed sb/o.s.
Guten Appetit!	Enjoy your meal!
satt	full
Speise, die (–n)	dish; food
Vorspeise, die (–n)	appetizer
Gericht, das (–e)	dish
Imbiss, der (–e)	snack
Jause, die (–n; AU)	snack
(jmdm) (irgendwie) schmecken	to taste (somehow) (to sb)
etw schmecken	to taste sth
Geschmack, der (¨e; coll.: ¨er)	taste
Mahlzeit, die (–en)	meal
(etw) essen	to eat (sth)
Essen, das (–)	meal; food; dinner
Frühstück, das (–e)	breakfast
(etw) frühstücken	to eat (sth for) breakfast
Mittagessen, das (–)	lunch
zu Mittag essen	to (have) lunch
Abendessen, das (–)	supper
Abendbrot, das (no pl.; N)	supper

Meat, fish and poultry

Fleisch, das (no pl.)	meat
Rindfleisch, das (no pl.)	beef
Kalbfleisch, das (no pl.)	veal
Schweinefleisch, das (no pl.)	pork
Schinken, der (–)	ham
Lammfleisch, das (no pl.)	lamb
Geflügel, das (no pl.)	poultry

Huhn, das (¨er)	chicken
Hähnchen, das (–)	chicken
Ei, das (–er)	egg
Gans, die (¨e)	goose
Ente, die (–n)	duck
Pute, die (–n)	turkey
Fisch, der (–e)	fish
Fett, das (–e)	fat
fett	fatty
mager	lean
Eintopf, der (¨e)	stew
Soße, die (–n)	sauce, gravy
Fleischerei, die (–en)	butcher's shop
Metzgerei, die (–en; S, CH)	butcher's shop
Schlachterei, die (–en; N)	butcher's shop

Fruit

Obst, das (no pl.)	fruit
Obstsalat, der (–e)	fruit salad
Frucht, die (¨e)	fruit
Apfel, der (¨)	apple
Apfelsine, die (–n)	orange
Orange, die (–n; S)	orange
Zitrone, die (–n)	lemon
Limone, die (–n)	lime
Banane, die (–n)	banana
Pfirsich, der (–e)	peach
Aprikose, die (–n)	apricot
Pflaume, die (–n)	plum
Zwetsche, die (–n)	plum
Zwetschge (S, CH), Zwetschke (AU), die (–n)	plum
Erdbeere, die (–n)	strawberry
Himbeere, die (–n)	raspberry
Heidelbeere, die (–n)	blueberry
(Wein)traube, die (–n)	grape
saftig	juicy

(un)reif	(un)ripe
reifen	to ripen

Vegetables

Gemüse, das (-)	vegetable
Bohne, die (-n)	bean
Erbse, die (-n)	pea
Möhre, die (-n)	carrot
Mohrrübe, die (-n)	carrot
Karotte, die (-n)	(small) carrot
Kartoffel, die (-n)	potato
Erdapfel, der (¨; S, AU)	potato
Kohl, der (-e = kinds of)	cabbage
Kraut, das (no pl.; S, AU)	cabbage
Rotkohl, der (no pl.)	red cabbage
Blumenkohl, der (no pl.)	cauliflower
Karfiol, der (no pl.; S, AU)	cauliflower
Brokkoli, pl.	broccoli
Tomate, die (-n)	tomato
Paradeiser, der (-; AU)	tomato
Tomatenmark, das (no pl.)	tomato purée
Zwiebel, die (-n)	onion
Salat, der (-e)	lettuce; salad
Gurke, die (-n)	cucumber
Spinat, der (no pl.)	spinach
Spargel, der (-)	asparagus
Mais, der (no pl.)	sweet corn
Paprika, der (-s)	sweet pepper
Pilz, der (-e)	mushroom
Champignon, der (-s)	mushroom
Radieschen, das (-)	radish
Rettich, der (-e)	white radish
Radi, der (-; AU, Bav.)	white radish
Meerrettich, der (-e)	horseradish
knackig	crisp

Dairy

Milch, die (no pl.)	milk
Mager-, Vollmilch, die (no pl.)	skim/whole milk
Butter, die (no pl.)	butter
(Speise)eis, das (no pl.)	ice cream
Gefrorene(s), das (adj. decl.; S, AU)	ice cream
Käse, der (no pl.)	cheese
Joghurt (Jogurt), der and (esp. AU and CH) das (-s)	yogurt
Sahne, die (no pl.)	cream
Rahm, der (no pl.; S, CH)	cream
Obers, das (no pl.; AU)	cream

Breads, grains and pasta

Brot, das (-e)	bread
belegtes Brot	(open-faced) sandwich
Butterbrot, das (-e)	slice of bread and butter; sandwich
Stulle, die (-n; N)	slice of bread and butter; sandwich
Brötchen, das (-)	roll
Semmel, die (-n; Bav., AU)	roll
Wecken, der (-; S, AU)	oblong roll
Mehl, das (-e = kinds of)	flour
Reis, der (-e = kinds of)	rice
Nudel, die (-n)	noodle; pasta
Spaghetti, pl.	spaghetti
Scheibe, die (-n)	slice
Schnitte, die (-n; N)	slice
Knäckebrot, das (-e)	crispbread

Pastries, desserts and sweets

Nachtisch, der (-e)	dessert
Mehlspeise, die (-n; AU)	dessert
Kuchen, der (-)	cake
Torte, die (-n)	gateau; tart; pie
Keks, der or das (- and -e)	biscuit
Plätzchen, das (-)	biscuit
Süßigkeit, die (-en)	sweet
Bonbon, der or (AU only) das (-s)	sweet
Schokolade, die (-n)	chocolate
Eier-, Pfannkuchen, der (-)	pancake
Krapfen, der (-)	doughnut; fritter
Berliner, der (-)	jam doughnut

Drinks

Getränk, das (-e)	drink, beverage
Schluck, der (-e)	swallow
ein kleiner/großer Schluck	a sip/a gulp
Trinkwasser, das (no pl.)	drinking water
Mineralwasser, das (¨)	mineral water
Sprudel, der (-)	sparkling mineral water
sprudeln	to be fizzy
Limonade, die (-n)	lemonade; soft drink
Limo, die (-s; coll.)	pop
Cola, das or die (-s; coll.)	Coke ®
Saft, der (¨e)	juice
Kakao, der (no pl.)	cocoa, hot chocolate
(heiße) Schokolade, die (-n)	(hot) chocolate
Kaffee, der (-s = kinds of)	coffee
Tee, der (-s)	tea
Bier, das (-e)	beer
Wein, der (-e)	wine

Rot-, Weißwein, der (-e)	red/white wine
Korken, der (-)	cork
Sekt, der (-e)	sparkling wine, champagne
Schnaps, der (¨e)	schnapps, booze, liquor
Alkohol, der (no pl.)	alcohol
alkoholfrei	nonalcoholic

Cooking

Rezept, das (-e)	recipe
Kochbuch, das (¨er)	cookery book
Zutat, die (-en)	ingredient
(Konserven)dose, die (-n)	can
(etw) kochen	to boil (sth); cook (sth)
etw zum Kochen bringen	to bring sth to a boil
etw vorbereiten	to prepare sth
etw zubereiten	to prepare, make, cook sth
etw würzen	to season sth
etw über/auf etw streuen	to sprinkle sth over/on sth
etw mit etw bestreuen	to sprinke sth with sth
etw schneiden	to slice, cut up sth
etw mischen	to mix sth
Mischung, die (-en)	mixture
etw schlagen	to beat/whisk/whip sth
(etw) braten	to roast/fry/bake (sth)
etw begießen	to baste sth
etw füllen	to stuff sth
Füllung, die (-en)	stuffing
etw räuchern	to smoke sth
(etw) backen	to bake (sth)
(etw) grillen	to grill (sth)
anbrennen	to burn

Level 2

General

etw probieren	to try sth
Portion, die (-en)	portion, serving
haltbar sein	to keep (well)
Essen/Getränke zum Mitnehmen	takeaway food/drinks
Schnellimbiss, der (-e)	fast food
Fertignahrung, die (no pl.)	convenience food
Fertiggericht, das (-e)	ready-to-serve meal
Hauptgericht, das (-e)	main course
Gang, der (¨e)	course
Menü, das (-s)	set menu
vegetarisch	vegetarian
vegan, streng vegetarisch	vegan
Rohkost, die (no pl.)	raw fruits, nuts and vegetables

Meat, fish and poultry

Braten, der (-)	roast
Sauerbraten, der (-)	sauerbraten
Steak, das (-s)	steak
Kotelett, das (-s)	chop; cutlet
Schnitzel, das (-)	cutlet
Wiener Schnitzel, das (-)	Wiener schnitzel
Hamburger, der (-)	hamburger
Hackfleisch, das (no pl.)	minced meat
Fleischklößchen, das (-)	meatball
Speck, der (no pl.)	bacon
Wurst, die (¨e)	sausage; cold cuts
Aufschnitt, der (no pl.)	cold cuts
Salami, die (-s)	salami
Brühwürstchen, das (-)	sausage (heated in boiling water)
Wiener Würstchen, das (-)	wiener
Frankfurter, der (-)	frankfurter
Weißwurst, die (¨e)	veal sausage
Bratwurst, die (¨e)	frying sausage
Rührei, das (-er)	scrambled egg
Spiegelei, das (-er)	fried egg
ein weich/hart gekochtes Ei	a soft/hard-boiled egg
Omelett, das (-e or -s) and (AU, CH: only) Omelette, die (-n)	omelet
Hering, der, (-e)	herring
Rollmops, der (¨e)	roll-mop, pickled herring
(Öl)sardine, die (-n)	sardine (in oil)

Fruit

Kompott, das (-e)	stewed fruit
Back-, Dörrobst, das (no pl.)	dried fruit
Back-, Dörrpflaume, die (-n)	prune
Rosine, die (-n)	raisin
Apfelmus, das (-e; pl. rare)	apple sauce
Bratapfel, der (¨)	baked apple
Johannisbeere, die (-n)	currant
Brombeere, die (-n)	blackberry
Stachelbeere, die (-n)	gooseberry
Preiselbeere, die (-n)	cranberry
Rhabarber, der (no pl.)	rhubarb
(Wasser)melone, die (-n)	(water)melon

Vegetables

Sauerkraut, das (no pl.)	sauerkraut
Pommes frites, pl.	chips, French fries
Bratkartoffeln, pl.	fried potatoes
Geröstete, pl. (adj. decl.; S, AU)	fried potatoes

Rösti, die (no pl.; CH) — fried potatoes

Kartoffelbrei, der (no pl.) — mashed potatoes

Kartoffelmus, das (no pl.) — mashed potatoes

Salzkartoffeln, pl. — boiled potatoes

Pellkartoffel, die (-n) — potato cooked in its skin/jacket

in der Schale gebackene Kartoffel, die (-n) — baked/jacket potato

Kartoffelkloß, der (¨e) — potato dumpling

Kartoffelknödel, der (-; S) — potato dumpling

Kartoffelchips, pl. — potato crisps

Soups

Suppe, die (-n) — soup

Brühe, die (-n) — (clear) soup; stock broth

Mehlschwitze, die (-n) — roux

Suppenwürfel, der (-) — stock cube

Suppengrün, das (no pl.) — herbs and vegetables for soup

Gemüsesuppe, die (-n) — vegetable soup

Tomatensuppe, die (-n) — tomato soup

Zwiebelsuppe, die (-n) — onion soup

Linsensuppe, die (-n) — lentil soup

Spargelcremesuppe, die (-n) — cream of asparagus soup

Ochsenschwanzsuppe, die (-n) — oxtail soup

Dairy

Weich-, Hartkäse, der (no pl.) — soft/hard cheese

Frischkäse, der (no pl.) — cream cheese

(Käse)rinde, die (-n) — (cheese) rind

Streichkäse, der (no pl.) — cheese spread

Schlagsahne, die (no pl.) — whipping cream; whipped cream

Schlag, der (no pl.; AU) — whipped cream

saure Sahne, die (no pl.) — sour cream

Quark, der (no pl.) — curd cheese

Hüttenkäse, der (no pl.) — cottage cheese

Kondensmilch, die (no pl.) — evaporated milk

Dickmilch, die (no pl.) — soured milk

Breads, grains and pasta

Vollkornbrot, das (-e) — whole-grain bread

Weißbrot, das (-e) — white bread

Graubrot, das (-e) — bread made with wheat and rye flours

Schwarzbrot, das (-e) — whole-grain rye bread; pumpernickel

Toastbrot, das (-e) — sliced white bread for toasting

Brezel, die (-n) — pretzel

Brezen, die (-; Bav., AU) — pretzel

Teigwaren, pl. — pasta

Haferflocken, pl. — rolled oats

Müsli, das (-s) — muesli

Puffmais, der (no pl.) — popcorn

knusprig — crisp

altbacken — stale

Pastries, desserts and sweets

Apfeltasche, die (-n) — apple turnover

Apfelstrudel, der (-) — apple strudel

Milchreis, der (no pl.) — rice pudding

Käsekuchen, der (-) — cheesecake

Leb-, Pfefferkuchen, der (-) — gingerbread

Stolle, die (-n) or Stollen, der (-)	stollen	Öl, das (-e)	oil
Tafel Schokolade, die (-n)	bar (slab) of chocolate	Essig, der (-e)	vinegar
		Ketschup (Ketchup), der or das (-s)	ketchup
Lutscher, der (-)	lollipop	Majonäse (Mayonnaise), die (-n)	mayonnaise
etw lutschen	to suck sth		
Eis am Stiel, das (no pl.)	iced lolly, Popsicle	Marmelade, die (-n)	jam
Zuckerwatte, die (no pl.)	candyfloss	Konfitüre, die (-n; CH)	jam

Nuts

Nuss, die (¨e)	nut
etw rösten	to roast sth
Haselnuss, die (¨e)	hazelnut
Walnuss, die (¨e)	walnut
Erdnuss, die (¨e)	peanut
Mandel, die (-n)	almond
gebrannte Mandeln, pl.	sugared roasted almonds
Pistazie, die (-n)	pistachio
Paranuss, die (¨e)	Brazil nut
Kastanie, die (-n)	chestnut

Herbs, spices and condiments

Kraut, das (¨er)	herb
Gewürz, das (-e)	spice; seasoning
Petersilie, die (-n)	parsley
Dill, der (-e; esp. AU), also Dille, die (-n)	dill
Basilikum, das (no pl.)	basil
Schnittlauch, der (no pl.)	chives
Knoblauch, der (no pl.)	garlic
Salz, das (-e)	salt
Pfeffer, der (-)	pepper
Zimt, der (no pl.)	cinnamon
Curry, der or das (no pl.)	curry
Vanille, die (no pl.)	vanilla
Honig, der (no pl.)	honey
Senf, der (-e)	mustard

Drinks

Milchmixgetränk, das (-e)	milk shake
Kaffee mit Milch, der (-s = kinds of)	coffee with milk/cream
schwarzer Kaffee	black coffee
koffeinfrei	decaffeinated, caffeine-free
Filterkaffee, der (-s = kinds of)	filter coffee
Eiskaffee, der (-s = kinds of)	iced coffee
Pulverkaffee, der (-s = kinds of)	instant coffee
Kräutertee, der (-s)	herb tea
Kamillentee, der (-s)	chamomile tea
Pfefferminztee, der (-s)	peppermint tea
Bier vom Fass, das (-e)	draught beer
Lagerbier, das (-e)	lager
Helle, das (adj. decl.; coll.)	light beer
Pils([e]ner), das (-)	pilsner
Exportbier, das (-e)	export-style beer
Weißbier, das (-e)	beer brewed from wheat
prosit! or prost! (coll.)	cheers!
prosten	to say cheers
Zum Wohl!	Cheers!
nüchtern	sober
betrunken	drunk
beschwipst	tipsy
einen Schwips haben	to be tipsy

Cooking

etw schälen	to peel, shell, skin sth
etw knacken	to crack sth
etw in kleine Stücke schneiden	to mince sth
etw in Würfel schneiden	to dice sth
etw klein hacken	to chop sth
etw tranchieren	to carve sth
etw raspeln	to grate sth
etw schnitzeln	to chop up/shred sth
Teig, der (-e)	dough, pastry, batter
Hefe, die (no pl.)	yeast
Hefeteig, der (-e)	yeast dough
etw kneten	to knead sth
aufgehen	to rise
etw umrühren	to stir sth
(etw) rühren	to stir (sth)
etw in etw einrühren	to stir sth into sth
etw (mit etw) vermengen/ vermischen	to mix sth (with sth)
Zucker, der (- = kinds of)	sugar
Puderzucker, der (no pl.)	powdered sugar
Vanillezucker, der (-)	vanilla sugar
Backpulver, das (-)	baking powder
Natriumkarbonat, das (no pl.)	baking soda

Level 3

Meat, fish and poultry

gar	cooked; done
durch	well done
medium	medium
halb durchgebraten	medium rare
englisch gebraten, schwach gebraten	rare
zäh	tough
zart, weich	tender
Wild, das (no pl.)	game
Hirsch-, Rehfleisch, das (no pl.)	venison
Kaninchen, das (-)	rabbit
Bruststück, das (-e)	breast
Keule, die (-n)	drumstick, leg
Rippchen, das (-)	rib
Schweinshachse (S: -haxe), die (-n)	knuckle of pork
Schweineschmalz, das (no pl.)	lard
Leber, die (-n)	liver
Leberkäse, der (no pl.)	meat loaf
Leberwurst, die (¨e)	liver sausage
Leberknödel, der (-)	liver dumpling
Leberpastete, die (-n)	liver pâté

Sardelle, die (-n)	anchovy
Sardellenpaste, die (-n)	anchovy paste
Meeresfrüchte, pl.	seafood
Hummer, der (-)	lobster
Languste, die (-n)	crayfish
Krebs, der (-e)	crab
Garnele, die (-n)	prawn, shrimp
Muschel, die (-n)	mussel
Auster, die (-n)	oyster

Fruit

Mandarine, die (-n)	mandarin orange
Pampelmuse, die (-n)	grapefruit
Ananas, die (- or -se)	pineapple
Kokosnuss, die (¨e)	coconut
Dattel, die (-n)	date
Feige, die (-n)	fig
Schale, die (-n)	peel
Haut, die (¨e)	skin
Stein, der (-e)	stone
Kern, der (-e)	pip

Vegetables

Rübe, die (-n)	turnip
rote Rübe	red beet

Kohlrabi, der (-s) — kohlrabi
Wirsing, der (no pl.) — savoy cabbage
Grünkohl, der (no pl.) — kale
Rosenkohl, der (no pl.) — Brussels sprouts
Mangold, der (-e) — chard
Endivie, die (-n) — endive
Brunnenkresse, die (no pl.) — watercress
Fenchel, der (no pl.) — fennel
Artischocke, die (-n) — artichoke
Aubergine, die (-n) — aubergine, eggplant
Süßkartoffel, die (-n) — sweet potato
Kürbis, der (-bisse) — pumpkin
Lauch, der (-e) — leek
Sellerie, der (-[s]) or (AU only) die (-) — celery
Sojabohnenkeim, der (-e) — bean sprout

Breads, grains and pasta

Weizen, der (no pl.) — wheat
Roggen, der (no pl.) — rye
Gerste, die (no pl.) — barley
Maismehl, das (no pl.) — corn meal
Brotkrümel, der (-) — breadcrumb
Brösel, der or (AU) das (-) — breadcrumb
Spätzle, pl. (S) — spaetzle (kind of pasta)
Spätzli, pl. (CH) — spaetzle (kind of pasta)
Stärkemehl, das (no pl.) — corn starch

Pastries, desserts and sweets

Konfekt, das (no pl.) — confectionery; S, AU, CH: biscuits
Praline, die (-n) — filled chocolate
Lakritze, die (-n) — liquorice
Karamelle, die (-n) — caramel
Sahnebonbon, der or (AU only) das (-s) — toffee

Marzipan, das or (AU) der (-e) — marzipan
Milch-, Zartbitter-schokolade, die (-n) — milk/plain chocolate
Zuckerguss, der (¨e) — icing
Schokoladenguss, der (¨e) — chocolate icing
Sachertorte, die (-n) — sachertorte
Sahnetorte, die (-n) — cake layered with whipped cream
Schichttorte, die (-n) — layer cake
Schwarzwälder Kirschtorte, die (-n) — Black Forest gateau
Biskuit, das or der (-s or -e) — sponge cake

Herbs, spices and condiments

Knoblauchzehe, die (-n) — garlic clove
Estragon, der (no pl.) — tarragon
Oregano (Origano), der (no pl.) — oregano
Lorbeerblatt, das (¨er) — bay leaf
Majoran, der (-e) — marjoram
Rosmarin, der (no pl.) — rosemary
Salbei, der or die (no pl.) — sage
Thymian, der (-e) — thyme
Minze, die (-n) — mint
Kümmel, der (no pl.) — caraway
Kreuzkümmel, der (no pl.) — cumin
Ingwer, der (-) — ginger
Muskatnuss, die (¨e) — nutmeg
Nelke, die (-n) — clove
Olivenöl, das (-e) — olive oil
Weinessig, der (no pl.) — wine vinegar
Balsamessig, der (no pl.) — balsamic vinegar
Süßstoff, der (-e) — artificial sweetener

pikant, würzig	spicy	köcheln	to simmer
scharf	hot, spicy	pochieren	to poach
		etw dämpfen	to steam sth
Drinks		etw dünsten	to steam/braise [meat]/stew [fruit] sth
Most, der (-e)	cider; unfermented fruit juice		
Schorle, die (-n)	spritzer	(etw) schmoren	to braise (sth)
Bowle, die (-n)	alcoholic punch	etw ziehen lassen	to steep/brew sth
kohlensäurehaltig	carbonated	etw sieben	to sift sth
Kohlensäure, die (no pl.)	carbonic acid	etw steif/schaumig schlagen	to whip sth until stiff/to a froth
mit/auf Zimmertemperatur	at room temperature	ein Ei in die Pfanne schlagen	to crack an egg into the pan
trocken	dry	ein Ei in die Suppe schlagen	to beat an egg into the soup
lieblich	sweet		
Spätlese, die (-n)	late vintage	etw panieren	to breadcrumb sth
Auslese, die (-n)	fine wine made from fully ripe grapes	Paniermehl, das (no pl.)	breadcrumbs
Champagner, der (-)	champagne [from Champagne]	die Knochen aus etw lösen	to bone sth
Spirituosen, pl.	spirits	etw entgräten	to fillet/bone sth
Weinbrand, der (¨e)	brandy	Mürb(e)teig, der (-e)	shortcrust pastry
Kognak, der (-s)	brandy, cognac		
Rum, der (-s)	rum	Blätterteig, der (no pl.)	puff pastry
Likör, der (-e)	liqueur		
mit Eis	on the rocks	etw garnieren	to garnish sth
etw pur trinken	to drink sth straight	Garnierung, die (-en)	garnish
Schaum, der (¨e)	head, froth [of beer]		
		Beize, die (-n)	marinade
Cooking		etw marinieren	to marinate sth
sieden	to boil	etw einlegen	to pickle sth
etw leicht kochen lassen	to simmer sth	etw abgießen	to drain sth

---

Exercises

Level 1

1. Ordnen Sie.

die Apfelsine, die Erbse, die Gurke, die Himbeere, der Kohl, der Meerrettich, die Möhre, der Pfirsich, die Pflaume, das Radieschen, der Spargel, die Traube, die Zitrone, die Zwiebel

das Obst	das Gemüse

2. Welches Wort hat die gleiche oder eine ähnliche Bedeutung? ✓

1. das Shampoo
2. der Föhn
3. die Socke
4. der Pyjama
5. secondhand
6. die Schuhnummer
7. wertvoll
8. die Lebensmittel
9. das Gericht
10. der Champignon
11. der Keks

3. Welches Nomen passt? ✓

a. das Armband, b. der Bügel, c. der Handschuh, d. die Kapuze, e. das Kleid, f. der Rock, g. die Schuhcreme, h. die Stiefelette, i. der Waschlappen

1. Unterteil des Kleides
2. Bekleidungsstück für die Hand
3. Oberbekleidungsstück für Frauen
4. am Mantel befestigte Kopfbedeckung
5. halbhoher Stiefel
6. darüber kann man ein Kleidungsstück aufhängen
7. damit putzt man die Schuhe
8. am Arm zu tragendes Schmuckstück
9. Tuch zum Waschen des Körpers

4. Nennen Sie die Zutaten.

1. der Eintopf
2. der Obstsalat
3. belegtes Brot
4. der Kuchen

5. Welches Nomen passt nicht? ✓

1. der Büstenhalter, der Halbrock, das Nachthemd, die Unterwäsche
2. der Kamm, die Kette, die Krawatte, der Kragen
3. der Absatz, das Bügeleisen, der Stiefel, der Turnschuh
4. die Bürste, die Seife, das Waschpulver, die Zahnpasta
5. die Gans, das Huhn, der Krapfen, die Pute
6. das Bier, der Saft, der Sekt, der Sprudel
7. der Bonbon, das Knäckebrot, der Kuchen, die Nudel

6. Was bedeuten die folgenden Zusammensetzungen?

1. der Kinderschuh, der Rollschuh, der Schneeschuh
2. der Gummihandschuh, der Damenhandschuh, der Lederhandschuh
3. das Pulloverhemd, das Nachthemd, das Flanellhemd
4. die Khakihose, die Pyjamahose, die Hochwasserhose
5. die Flaschenbürste, die Nagelbürste, die Klosettbürste

7. Wie heißt das hochdeutsche Wort? ✓

1. der Schlips
2. etw plätten
3. der Erdapfel
4. der Karfiol
5. der Paradeiser
6. der Radi
7. das Kraut
8. die Zwetschge
9. die Orange
10. der Rahm
11. das Gefrorene
12. die Mehlspeise
13. die Stulle
14. die Semmel
15. die Jause
16. die Metzgerei
17. das Abendbrot

8. Übersetzen Sie ins Deutsche. ✓

1. to hit below the belt
2. to tighten one's belt
3. keep your shirt on
4. to pocket (steal) sth
5. to be in s.o.'s pocket
6. to button one's lip
7. to be in s.o.'s shoes
8. old hat
9. at the drop of a hat
10. to give s.o. the boot
11. to scare the pants off s.o.
12. to catch s.o. with his/her pants down
13. that was a close shave
14. it'll all come out in the wash

9. Was bedeuten die Wendungen?

1. das ist Jacke wie Hose (coll.)
2. da geht einem der Hut hoch (coll.)
3. wissen, wo jmdn der Schuh drückt
4. schmutzige Wäsche waschen
5. seine Meinung wie sein Hemd wechseln
6. den Mantel nach dem Wind drehen
7. faule Fische (coll.)
8. nicht die Bohne! (coll.)
9. alles in Butter! (coll.)
10. das ist ein hartes Brot
11. ohne Saft und Kraft (pej.)
12. jmdn/etw durch den Kakao ziehen
13. das ist kalter Kaffee
14. abwarten und Tee trinken! (coll.)
15. jmdm reinen Wein einschenken

10. Welches Verb passt? ✓

> a. sich . . . anstecken, b. aufsetzen, c. aufspannen, d. sich . . . bürsten,
> e. jmdm . . . halten, f. sich . . . umbinden, g. zuziehen

1. den Hut
2. den Schal
3. den Mantel
4. den Schirm
5. den Ring
6. den Reißverschluss
7. die Haare

11. Übersetzen Sie ins Deutsche. ✓

1. food for thought
2. to chicken out
3. to talk turkey
4. neither fish nor fowl
5. to chew the fat
6. to stew over sth
7. to stew in one's own juice

  8. to ride the gravy train
  9. peaches-and-cream complexion
 10. a plum job
 11. to be as like as two peas in a pod
 12. to spill the beans (to s.o.)
 13. to butter s.o. up

12. Übersetzen Sie ins Englische.

Ägypten ist das schöne Land der Fälscher. Schon seit Jahrhunderten leben ganze Dörfer davon, pharaonische Fresken, Statuen und Alabasterkatzen zu kopieren und diese dann als echte Antiquitäten zu verkaufen. Oft wird die Kopie schöner, perfekter und makelloser als das Original. Stilistisch richteten sich die Fälscher oft nach dem Geschmack ihrer Kunden. Daran hat sich bis heute nichts geändert. Nur: Zu den altägyptischen Kulturgütern, die für die internationale Kundschaft gefälscht werden, ist ein neuer Markt hinzugekommen. Internationale Marken werden für den ägyptischen Käufer gefälscht. Gucci für die Dame, Boss für den Herrn und Adidas für alle.

Wer will da noch Originale, wenn die Fälschungen viel billiger sind – und schöner. In der Innenstadt von Kairo, in den schmalen Gassen des Basars (ungefähr 500 Meter von den Ständen mit den nachgemachten Alabasterkatzen) gibt es die unglaublichsten Entwürfe. Braune Plastik-Adiletten zum Beispiel, mit Kupferschnallen und silbernen Logos in den Sohlen. »Unsere Mädchen kleiden sich eben lieber elegant. So derbe Boots, wie sie Touristinnen hier tragen, sind nichts für sie«, erklärt der Hersteller und Verkäufer Onkel Mohammed.

Natürlich bekommt man in besseren Geschäften auch Handtaschen, die den Modellen der Modeschöpfer aus Europa zum Verwechseln ähnlich sehen. Faruk, ein Taschenschuster, lässt sich Kataloge aus Paris und Düsseldorf schicken und kopiert sie dann detailgetreu für »die Gattinnen ausländischer Diplomaten«. Orangefarbene Plastiktäschchen mit Yves-Saint-Laurent-Logo wären unter seinem Niveau. Die gibt es drei Ecken weiter. Dort kann man sich nicht nur aussuchen, welche Farbe die Taschen haben soll. Auch die Marke ist frei wählbar; die Exemplare unterscheiden sich also nur durch das Logo: Gucci, Christian Dior oder Louis Vuitton. Ähnlichkeiten mit dem Originalprodukt? Rein zufällig. »Wir orientieren uns an der internationalen Mode und passen sie dann dem ägyptischen Geschmack an«, sagt Ines Mansour, die in einer der feineren Boutiquen in Kairos Innenstadt für das Design zuständig ist. »Auch bei uns trägt man in diesem Jahr diese länglichen Taschen aus Lackleder, allerdings nicht in so krassen Farbkombinationen wie in Europa. Das gefällt unseren Damen hier nicht.«

Da Ägypten jetzt ein Stückchen dichter an Europa heranrutschen möchte und demnächst ein Assoziationsabkommen mit der EU schließen will, soll mit den Fälschungen bald Schluss sein. Derzeit berät das ägyptische Parlament über ein Markenschutzgesetz. In den vergangenen Monaten ist man bereits an Fälscher und Fake-Geschäfte herangetreten. So könnte es jetzt auch bald Onkel Mohammed an den Kragen gehen. In seiner kleinen Werkstatt näht er jeden Tag ein Paar Latschen aus billigem Leder. Das macht er schon, solange er denken kann. Da er mitbekommen hat, dass die Jugend in Ägypten ganz verrückt danach ist, schreibt er Adidas auf die Sohlen. Er versteht nicht so recht, was die Aufregung um das neue Gesetz soll: »Wenn die nicht wollen, dass ich da Adidas draufschreibe, drucke ich mit der gleichen Schrift einfach was anderes rein. Mohammed zum Beispiel«.

Julia Gerlach

DIE ZEIT, 31. Mai 2001, Nr. 23, S. 67

Level 2

1. Welches Wort hat die gleiche oder eine ähnliche Bedeutung? ✓
1. das Dekolletee
2. das Schuhband
3. der Schuhanzieher
4. die Shorts
5. das Backobst
6. der Kartoffelmus
7. die Nudeln
8. der Pfefferkuchen
9. der Milkshake
10. etw vermischen

2. Wo kann man es kaufen? ✓

der Armreif, die Brezel, die Brosche, das Brühwürstchen, das Deo, die Dickmilch, die Feuchtigkeitscreme, das Haarfärbemittel, das Hackfleisch, der Hartkäse, das Kotelett, das Ohrgehänge, die Perlenkette, der Pumps, saure Sahne, der Schnürschuh, der Speck, das Vollkornbrot

Bäckerei: . . .
Drogerie: . . .
Fleischerei: . . .
Juweliergeschäft: . . .
Milchladen: . . .
Schuhgeschäft: . . .

3. Ergänzen Sie. ✓
1. der Pullover – der Pulli : der Rollkragenpullover – _____
2. die Hose – der Hosenaufschlag : das Hemd – _____
3. der Seitenschlitz – der rückseitige Schlitz : die Seitentasche – _____
4. der Braten – der Sauerbraten : der Hering – _____

5. die Pflaume – die Backpflaume : die Weintraube – _____

6. der Zucker – süß : der Essig – _____

7. die Nuss – knacken : die Banane – _____

4. Falsche Freunde. Ergänzen Sie die Tabelle.

Deutsch	Englisch	Deutsch	Englisch
der Slip			slip
der Slipper			slipper
der Rock			rock
der Biskuit			biscuit
die Bowle			bowl
der Keks			cake
das Kittchen			kitchen
die Konfektion			confection(ery)
das Menü			menu
die Mode			mode
der Most			most
das Rezept			receipt
die Salve			salve

5. In jedem Satz fehlt ein Wort. ✓

Anorak, Hosenträger, Latzhose, Sakko, Schürze, Trainingsanzug,
Twinset, Wickelrock

1. Er trug eine blaue _____ und ein dunkles Hemd.
2. Die Teilnehmer/-innen sollten Sportbekleidung wie _____, Gymnastikschuhe oder Socken und ein Handtuch mitbringen.
3. Es ist ein graufarbiger knöchellanger _____.
4. _____ über dem Hemd gelten auch als kleidsam.
5. Er trägt ein grau-braunes _____, darunter ein braunes Polohemd und eine graue Strickweste.
6. Das klassische _____ mit kurzen oder langen Strickjacken ist auch wieder da.
7. Die Kinder klammern sich an die _____ der Mutter.
8. Sie zog sich langsam den orangefarbenen _____ über ihren Rennanzug.

6. Wie heißen die Zusammensetzungen? ✓

Haar-	schuh	1. *das Haarspray*
Sonnen-	stein	2.
Dauer-	feile	3.
Renn-	wickler	4.
Trau-	welle	5.
Brust-	~~spray~~	6.
Nagel-	wasser	7.
Schaum-	ring	8.
Rasier-	creme	9.
Locken-	tuch	10.
Edel-	tasche	11.
Schulter-	bad	12.

7. Was passt nicht? ✓

1. -beere: Brom-, Eis-, Johannis-, Preisel-
2. -nuss: Erd-, Hasel-, Mandel-, Wal-
3. -suppe: Kittel-, Linsen-, Spargelcreme-, Tomaten-
4. -käse: Frisch-, Hut-, Streich-, Weich-
5. -mus: Apfel-, Fertig-, Kartoffel-, Pflaumen-
6. -brot: Braun-, Grau-, Toast-, Weiß-
7. -kartoffel: Brat-, Brei-, Pell-, Salz-
8. -kaffee: Eis-, Espresso-, Filter-, Pulver-
9. -tee: Beutel-, Kamillen-, Kräuter-, Pfefferminz-
10. -bier: Export-, Lager-, Leicht-, Weiß-

8. Übersetzen Sie ins Englische.

1. Wasser zum Kochen bringen und die Eier darin 10 Minuten hart kochen.
2. Die Zwiebeln und die Knoblauchzehen schälen und zusammen fein hacken.
3. Das Fleisch in gleichgroße Würfel schneiden und diese mit dem Salz bestreuen.
4. Wenn das Fleisch weich ist, die Sahne in das Gulasch rühren und, ohne es kochen zu lassen, noch einmal gut erhitzen.
5. Ganze Keulen und Rücken werden nach einem besonderen Prinzip tranchiert.
6. Die Tomaten waschen und in Achtel schneiden.
7. Die Karotten grob raspeln.
8. Geben Sie die Flüssigkeit fast tropfenweise in die Mehlschwitze.
9. Die Petersilie und das Basilikum waschen, abtropfen lassen und fein schneiden.
10. Aus dem Kartoffelteig mit leicht bemehlten Händen Klöße formen.

9. Beschreiben Sie . . .

1. Ihr Lieblingsgericht.
2. was zu einem Steak passt.

3. die Zutaten eines Omeletts.
4. das Frühstück eines Veganers.
5. ein Essen mit vier Gängen.

10. Übersetzen Sie ins Englische.

Feine Quarktorte

Für den Teig:
Fett für die Form • *250 g Mehl* • *125 g Butter* • *1 Messerspitze Salz* • *30 g Zucker*
• *1 Eigelb* • *2 Essl. Wasser*
Für die Füllung:
1 ungespritzte Zitrone • *3 Eigelbe* • *40 g Butter* • *80 g Speisestärke* •
$^1/_2$ l Milch • *120 g Zucker* • *1 Stange Vanille* • *350 g Quark* • *6 Eiweiße*
Etwa 4350 Kalorien/18 210 Joule insgesamt

Vorbereitungszeit: 5 Minuten. *Zubereitungszeit*: 25 Minuten. *Kühlzeit*: 1 Stunde.
Backzeit: 35–45 Minuten. *Backhitze*: 200° C.

Erforderliche Küchengeräte: Springform (24 bis 26 cm Durchmesser), dünner
Karton oder starkes Papier, Reibe, Sieb, Rollholz, Kasserolle, Schneebesen
oder Rührgerät, Kuchengitter.

Das wird vorbereitet: Die Form ganz wenig einfetten. Von der Zitrone die
Schale abreiben.

So wird's gemacht: Das Mehl auf ein Backbrett sieben, die Butter in Flocken
darüberstreuen und in die Mitte eine Vertiefung drücken. Das Salz, den
Zucker, das Eigelb und das Wasser hineingeben und alles zu einem Mürbteig
kneten. Den Teig 1 Stunde im Kühlschrank kalt stellen. Den Backofen auf
200° C vorhitzen. • Den Mürbteig 3 bis 4 mm dick ausrollen. Die Springform
damit auslegen. Diesen Mürbteig nun 15 Minuten im vorgeheizten Backofen
»blind« backen, d. h. ohne Füllung. Dafür empfiehlt es sich, einen Streifen aus
dünnem Karton oder starkem Papier ringsum vor den Rand zu stellen, damit
er beim Backen nicht herunterrutscht. Der Teig soll ganz hellgelb gebacken
werden. • Für die Füllung die Eigelbe mit der Butter (sie soll etwas weich
sein), der Speisestärke und einigen Löffeln Milch verrühren. Die übrige Milch
mit 60 g Zucker zum Kochen bringen. Die aufgeschnittene Vanillestange und
die abgeriebene Zitronenschale in die kochende Milch geben. Die angerührte
Speisestärke dazurühren und aufkochen lassen. Nun den Quark unter die
heiße Füllcreme geben. Die Eiweiße zu Schnee schlagen, 60 g Zucker
einrieseln lassen und den Eischnee ebenfalls unter die heiße Quark-Füllcreme
ziehen. Das Ganze in die vorgebackene Mürbteigtorte füllen und die Torte im
heißen Ofen 20 bis 30 Minuten backen, bis die Oberfläche schön braun ist.
• Die Torte einige Minuten abkühlen lassen, dann mit der Form auf das Gitter
stürzen und auskühlen lassen. • Die abgekühlte Quarktorte wieder umdrehen
und die Oberfläche mit Puderzucker besieben.

Kochen heute, von Arne Krüger und Annette Wolter, S. 523–524

Level 3

1. Wie heißt das Gegenteil? ✓

1. etw länger machen
2. etw enger machen
3. sich leicht schminken
4. zart (Fleisch)
5. schwach gebraten
6. trocken (Wein)
7. betrunken
8. Kaffee mit Milch
9. ohne Kohlensäure
10. koffeinhaltig
11. frischbacken (Brot)

2. Übersetzen Sie ins Deutsche.

1. fur jacket, sports jacket, jeans jacket, corduroy jacket
2. summer hat, woman's hat, man's hat, bishop's hat
3. housecoat, winter coat, suede coat, loden coat
4. Sunday dress, doll's dress, wraparound dress, knitted dress
5. sports cap, ski cap, woollen cap, chef's hat

3. Welches Verb passt? ✓

> a. auflegen, b. mit Spitze besetzen, c. entgräten, d. lackieren, e. sich … pudern,
> f. schlagen, g. schminken, h. sieben, i. stopfen, j. windeln

1. die Lippen
2. die Nase
3. Rouge
4. die Nägel
5. die Strümpfe
6. das Kleid
7. ein Baby
8. den Fisch
9. das Mehl
10. die Sahne

4. Ordnen Sie.

die Ananas, die Auster, die Dattel, der Estragon, die Feige, der Fenchel, die
Garnele, der Hummer, das Kaninchen, der Kürbis, die Languste, der Mangold, die
Pampelmuse, das Rehfleisch, der Rosmarin, der Salbei, der Thymian, der Wirsing

Gemüse	Kräuter	Meeresfrüchte	Obst	Wild

5. Was passt nicht? ✓

1. Leber-: -käse, -keule, -knödel, -pastete
2. -mehl: Beiz-, Mais-, Panier-, Weizen-
3. -torte: Sacher-, Schicht-, Smok-, Speck-
4. -kohl: Grün-, Rosa-, Rot-, Weiß-
5. -lese: Aus-, Bären-, Spät-, Trauben-
6. Wein-: -brand, -essig, -lese, -zehe
7. -teig: Blätter-, Hefe-, Mürb-, Saum-

6. Was passt zusammen? ✓

1. der Südwester	a. schirm- und randlose Mütze
2. der Sombrero	b. Kreissäge
3. der Florentiner	c. Hut aus Filz
4. die Baskenmütze	d. wasserdichter Leinenhut des Seemanns
5. der Zylinder	e. Glockenhut
6. die Schiffermütze	f. Hut aus Lodenstoff
7. der Topfhut	g. breitrandiger mexikanischer Hut
8. der Filzhut	h. hoher röhrenförmiger Herrenhut
9. der Strohhut	i. blaue Schirmmütze
10. der Lodenhut	k. Damenstrohhut mit flachem Kopf und weiter Krempe

7. Übersetzen Sie ins Deutsche. ✓

1. Simmer the sauce for 4 to 6 minutes.
2. Poached eggs are eaten either on toast with spicy sauces or else in a warm mustard sauce with boiled or mashed potatoes.
3. Pour the sauce over the meat, put on the lid, and braise in the oven for 30 minutes.
4. Crack the eggs into a cup.
5. Sprinkle the corn salad with the parsley.
6. Dice the bacon. Peel and dice the onion.
7. Drain the beans and mix with the diced bacon (bacon dice), the pepper slices, the diced onion, the salt, the pepper, the garlic powder, and the vinegar.
8. Garnish the cucumber salad with the egg slices.

8. Welches Wort passt nicht? ✓

1. das Abendkleid: die Hüftweite, das Mieder, die Oberweite, die Schrittlänge
2. das Baby: gestrickte Babyschuhe, das Strampelhöschen, die Windel, die Wimperntusche
3. der Schuh: das Blatt, der Schaft, die Sohle, die Zunge
4. der Besatz: der Abnäher, der Pelzbesatz, die Rüsche, die Spitze
5. der Verschluss: der Druckknopf, der Haken, die Paspel, der Reisverschluss
6. die Schminke: die Grundierungscreme, der Lidstrich, der Lippenstift, der Zierstich
7. das Jackett: einreihig, gefüttert, der Pantoffel, das Revers
8. die Süßigkeit: die Karamelle, die Lakritze, die Muskatnuss, die Praline
9. der Alkohol: die Bowle, der Most, die Schorle, die Spirituosen

9. Suchen Sie eine andere Bedeutung.

1. der Aufschlag	5. die Muschel
2. die Fliege	6. die Nelke
3. der Krebs	7. die Spitze
4. die Linse	8. der Zylinder

10. Übersetzen Sie Ihr Lieblingsrezept (Vorspeise, Suppe, Salat, Fleischgericht, Fischgericht, Gemüsegericht, Süßspeise, Gebäck) ins Deutsche.

11. Übersetzen Sie ins Englische.

Aus „Königin der Farben" von Petra Mies

Die technischen Fortschritte in der Kosmetik sind rasant, wobei die Forschung von neuen Erkenntnissen aus Luft- und Raumfahrt, Auto-Industrie und Optik profitiert. Seit vier Jahren arbeitet bespielsweise Chanel in internationalen Partnerschaften daran, diese Technologien auf Kosmetik zu übertragen. Geschmacksneutral, geruchsneutral, anti-allergisch und pflegend. Was auf die Haut kommt, soll immer weniger zu spüren sein. Und das Weniger braucht immer mehr High-Tech-Pigmente. Wobei es länderspezifische Vorlieben gibt. In Frankreich störe das Parfum im Lippenstift weniger als etwa in Deutschland, sagt Heidi Morawetz. Der Lippenstift ist das wichtigste Kosmetik-Produkt. Selbst Frauen, die es sonst eher ungeschminkt mögen und Make-up meiden, tragen hin und wieder Lippenstift auf. Weil die farbigen Lippen auch ein blasses Gesicht fröhlicher aussehen lassen. Weil er so sexy sein kann. Und weil er so vielseitig ist. Auf die Wangen aufgetragen und verschmiert, dient er als Rouge-Ersatz. Praktisch ist er überdies: „Ich kann ihn überall aus der Tasche holen, halte mir einen Spiegel vors Gesicht und male mir die Lippen an, das ist doch eine schöne Geste." Und warum machen Männer das nicht? Da lacht die Fachfrau. Einerseits habe das gesellschaftliche Gründe. „Im 18. Jahrhundert beispielsweise haben sich ja Männer und Frauen geschminkt." Andererseits sieht sie den Spieltrieb, die Freude daran, den eigenen Körper mit Kosmetik zu verschönern, als eher weiblich. „Junge Frauen machen das doch stundenlang und probieren schrille Farben aus, aber nicht nur, um den Burschen zu gefallen, sondern auch aus Spaß."

FRANKFURTER RUNDSCHAU, Samstag, 14. April 2001, Nr. 88/15, Magazin, S. 7

12. Lesen Sie den folgenden Essay.

Bitte nicht nur zur Weihnachtszeit

Ich wünschte, es wäre Weihnachten das ganze Jahr. Soziologisch gesehen ein grauenhafter Zustand. Die Familien würden an ihrer unnatürlichen Nähe zerbrechen, durch konventionelle Verpflichtungen verarmen und, die davor flüchten, unter Lawinen begraben und von Taifunen verweht werden. Ökologisch wären endlos verlängerte Weihnachten nicht weniger katastrophal. Wer jemals über die Guanorückstände der Gänse (so was wird natürlich gewogen und statistisch ausgewertet) informiert wurde, kann sich ein Bild machen.

Aber das alles würde wettgemacht durch den Christstollen. Dieses herrliche Backwerk stünde uns an jedem Tag des Jahres zur Verfügung!

Bevor ich mich in Einzelheiten verliere, möchte ich daran erinnern, dass Tag für Tag in deutschen Wohnzimmern, vor allem aber in unseren Cafés und

Konditoreien, mediokre Kuchen, fette Torten und parfümiertes Gebäck zum Segen der Diät-Industrie in ungeheuren Mengen konsumiert werden. Nur Apotheker und Konditoren können sich darüber freuen. Der Feinschmecker aber denkt mit Wehmut an die Weihnachtstage, als zum Nachtisch wie selbstverständlich ein Christstollen auf den Tisch gestellt wurde.

Dieses Backwerk, liebe Freunde, verdiente in unserem Jahresablauf eine ständige Präsenz. Denn es handelt sich um ein ebenso delikates wie originelles Detail der deutschen Küche.

Nicht dass der Stollen den Gesamteindruck unserer Essgewohnheiten entscheidend ändern könnte. Aber mit diesem Ding aus Butter, Zucker und Aromaten haben unsere Urgroßmütter einen bemerkenswerten Beitrag zur Feinschmeckerei geleistet. Egal, ob ihn die Muhmen in Dresden erfunden haben oder ein Bäcker im Odenwald, der Christstollen hat eine herausragende Rolle in der „Deutschen Leitkultur" verdient.

Er schmeckt sanft, buttrig, ist nie zu süß und schmilzt, was allgemein als Vorzug gilt, auf der Zunge. Tut er es nicht, stammt er vermutlich aus einer Fabrik.

Die Konkurrenz unter den Stollenbäckern ist groß, und das kommt der Qualität des mehr oder weniger süßen Kuchens entgegen. Sie müssen und wollen sich unterscheiden, wenn es darum geht, der Beste zu sein. Also hat hier auch die kleine Stadtbäckerei eine Chance. Was heißt Chance! Sie hat einen Vorsprung! Denn die in Massenproduktion gebackenen Stollen aus den Großbäckereien geben sich beim Vergleich sofort zu erkennen. Da ist einmal die Verwendung von Vanillezucker, diese penetrante Zutat aus dem Labor, und das Backpulver.

Dazu ist zu sagen: Wo Backpulver herausschmeckt, wurde schlecht gebacken (das gilt für jegliches Gebäck), und Vanillepulver ist ein Kunstprodukt, das mit einer in Milch gekochten Stange Bourbon-Vanille nicht verglichen werden darf.

Es ist das alte Lied von der Qualität der Zutaten. Beim Christstollen, der sich von Weihnachten bis heute mühelos gehalten hat, können wir Verbraucher eine erfreuliche Entwicklung zur besseren Qualität feststellen. Sogar in Kleinstädten bemühen sich ehrgeizige Konditoren um erstklassige Stollen, wobei es keine Rolle spielt, ob das Rezept »original« Dresdner Herkunft ist oder in Wiesbaden modernisiert wurde.

Insofern gibt sich der Christstollen als typisch deutsch zu erkennen: Sauerkraut, Eisbein, Bratwurst und ähnliche Spezialitäten kümmern sich auch nicht mehr um den ethnologisch korrekten Ahnenpass.

Was mich am Christstollen aber vor allem begeistert, ist nicht das nationale Logo, sondern seine wunderbare, fast einmalige Fähigkeit, jeder Art von Dessertwein zu einer Glanzrolle zu verhelfen. Sie passen alle. Und nicht nur die deutlich süßen. Sogar trockene Weine ohne ausgeprägte Säure tun sich nicht schwer mit einem Christstollen, sofern er nur schwach gesüßt ist. Aber von den Auslesen an gibt es kein Halten bei der Kombination zu diesem saftigen Backwerk. (Mein Gott, ja: Ein Stollen sollte keine Gelegenheit haben auszutrocknen. Also nach dem Anschnitt in Folie verpacken!)

Sie passen alle: die mehr oder weniger süßen Gewürztraminer; der Beaumes-de-Venise, die Moelleux von der Loire und aus dem Gebiet Jurançon; jede deutsche Beeren- und Trockenbeerenauslese; die süßen Bomben aus dem Sauternes und dem Burgenland.

Der erfahrene Weintrinker wird dazu anmerken, dass es nicht gerade ideal sei, wenn eine Speise alles mit sich geschehen lasse und dadurch den Wein zu einer beliebigen Alkoholbeilage degradiere. Das ist richtig – aber zu scholastisch, um den Genießer beirren zu können. So mancher hat eine Flasche alten Madeira im Keller oder eine Trockenbeerenauslese von Kracher (Burgenland).

Als ihm diese Kostbarkeiten geschenkt wurden, hat er sich verzweifelt gefragt, wann und wozu er die denn trinken könne.

Ein Christstollen löst das Problem sofort. Die Mischung aus Rosinen, Mandeln, Zitronat und den anderen Zutaten, die da mit Mehl, Zucker und Eiern eine enge und harmonische Verbindung eingegangen sind, scheint auf solche Weine geradezu gewartet zu haben. Jedenfalls ist dieses weihnachtliche Backwerk mehr als die meisten anderen Dessertkuchen in der Lage, dem süßen oder halbsüßen Wein eine wunderbare Freundschaft zu bieten.

Wenn es den Englischen Kuchen und ähnliche Verwandte ganzjährig gibt, warum sollte diese Auszeichnung dem Dresdner Stollen nicht vergönnt sein?

Sprechen Sie mit Ihrem Konditor. Vielleicht lässt er sich überzeugen!

Wolfram Siebeck

DIE ZEIT, 1. März 2001, Nr. 10, Leben, S. 10

a. Vokabelübung. Wie heißt das Wort auf Englisch?
   1. das Backwerk
   2. konsumieren
   3. der Feinschmecker
   4. delikat
   5. die Essgewohnheit
   6. die Säure
   7. die Kostbarkeit

b. Fragen.
   1. Welche Zutaten brauchen Sie zu einem Stollen?
   2. Was hat der Stollen mit Sauerkraut, Eisbein und Bratwurst gemeinsam?
   3. Was für Weine kann man zum Stollen trinken?

c. Schriftliche Übung. Fassen Sie den Essay kurz zusammen.

Unit 7

Perception

Level 1

Sight

(etw) sehen	to see (sth)
wegsehen	to look away
sich umsehen	to glance around
jmdm in die Augen sehen	to look sb in the eyes
jmdn/etw ansehen	to look at, watch, see sb/sth
(jmdm) zusehen	to watch (sb)
sichtbar	visible
blicken	to look
Blick, der (-e)	look, glance
auf seine Uhr blicken	to glance at one's watch
jmdn/etw anblicken	to look at, watch, see, glance at sb/sth
Anblick, der (-e)	sight
gucken	to look
jmdn angucken (coll.)	to look at sb
schauen (esp. S, AU, CH)	to look
jmdn/etw anschauen (esp. S, AU, CH)	to look at, watch, see sb/sth
jmdn/etw beobachten	to observe sb/sth
Beobachtung, die (-en)	observation
starren	to stare
jmdn/etw anstarren	to stare at sb/sth
jmdn/etw ausmachen	to make out sb/sth
etw unterscheiden	to distinguish sth
scheinen	to shine; appear
Schein, der (no pl.)	light, glow, gleam, glint
hell	light, bright
Helligkeit, die (no pl.)	lightness, brightness, paleness
dunkel	dark
halbdunkel	half-dark, dim
Dunkelheit, die (no pl.)	darkness
Dunkel, das (no pl.)	darkness
sich verdunkeln	to darken
undeutlich	indistinct, hazy, blurred
strahlen	to shine, glow, gleam, sparkle, beam
strahlend	radiant, bright, brilliant
Strahl, der (-en)	ray, beam, streak
blitzen	to flash, sparkle
aufblitzen	to flash, flare

Sound

etw hören	to hear sth
jmdm/einer Sache zuhören	to listen to sb/sth

laut	loud
lautstark	loud
Lärm, der (no pl.)	noise, din, row
lärmen	to make a noise
Geräusch, das (-e)	sound, noise
schweigen	to be silent, say nothing
still	silent
Stille, die (no pl.)	silence, quiet, stillness
leise	quiet, soft, faint
ruhig	calm, quiet
Ruhe, die (no pl.)	rest, peace, silence
donnern	to thunder, boom out, roar
trommeln	to drum
hämmern	to pound, thump
dumpf schlagen	to thud
Schlag, der (¨e)	bang, thud, knock, beating
Klang, der (¨e)	sound, tone
klingen	to sound, ring
klingeln	to ring, go off [alarm clock]
hupen	to sound, hoot, honk
rauschen	to roar, rustle, murmur, swish, hiss
sausen	to buzz, whistle, roar
Krach, der (¨e)	loud noise, racket; crash, bang
krachen	to crash, ring out, creak
pfeifen	to whistle
Pfiff, der (-e)	whistle
klicken	to click

Taste

Geschmack, der (¨e)	taste, flavour
(gut) schmecken	to taste good
etw schmecken	to taste sth
nach etw schmecken	to taste of sth
ohne Geschmack	tasteless
süß	sweet
sauer	sour, pickled
mild	mild, smooth
scharf	hot, pungent
salzig	salty
gesalzen	salted
bitter	bitter, acrid
lecker	delicious, lovely, yummy

Smell

Geruch, der (¨e)	smell, odour, scent, fragrance, aroma
geruchlos	odourless, scentless
(etw) riechen	to smell (sth)
Gestank, der (no pl.)	stench, stink
(nach etw) stinken	to stink (of sth)
stinkend	smelly, fetid
stinkig (sl.)	stinking, smelly
faulig	foul, putrid
frisch	fresh
kräftig	strong, powerful
schwach	faint
zart	delicate
fein	delicate
süßlich	sweetish, slightly sweet
sich verbreiten	to spread

Touch

etw anfassen	to touch sth
sich weich anfühlen	to feel soft
hart	hard, stiff
steif	stiff
glatt	smooth
rutschig	slippery
kratzig	scratchy
kratzen	to be scratchy/itchy
jucken	to itch
rau	rough
pulverig	powdery
kleben	to stick
klebrig	sticky, tacky

Level 2

Sight

jmdn/etw besehen	to have a look at sb/sth
jmdn/etw anglotzen (coll.)	to gawk at sb/sth
sich einer Sache bewusst sein/werden	to be/become aware or conscious of sth
etw merken	to notice sth
jmdn/etw bemerken	to notice sth
jmdn/etw erkennen	to make out, recognize sb/sth
jmdn/etw betrachten	to look at, study, examine sb/sth
jmdn/etw besichtigen	to see, view sb/sth
etw durchblättern	to cast a quick glance at sth; leaf through sth
jmdn/etw fixieren	to fix one's gaze on sb/sth
jmdn (feindselig) fixieren	to stare sb in the face
forschend schauen	to peer, look searchingly
angestrengt schauen	to peer, look with difficulty
(sich) jmdn forschend/prüfend ansehen	to peer searchingly at sb
(sich) etw genau ansehen	to peer searchingly at sth
(sich) jmdn/etw angestrengt ansehen	to peer with difficulty at sb/sth
vorn und hinten Augen haben	to have eyes in the back of one's head
seine Augen überall haben	to have eyes in the back of one's head
die Augen/den Blick auf jmdn/etw heften	to fasten one's eyes/gaze on sb/sth
die Augen von etw nicht abwenden können	not to be able to take one's eyes off sth
kein Auge von jmdm/etw lassen	not to take one's eyes off sb/sth
etw ins Auge fassen	to consider sth
jmdn/etw zu Gesicht bekommen	to set eyes on sb/sth, get a glimpse of sb/sth
keinen Blick von jmdm/etw wenden	not to take one's eyes off sb/sth
jmdm einen Blick zuwerfen	to give sb a look
jmdn/etw mustern	to eye, scrutinize sb/sth
jmdn mürrisch/ verdrießlich ansehen	to scowl at sb
finster	dark
Finsternis, die (-se)	darkness
sich verfinstern	to darken
glühen	to glow
schimmern	to glimmer, gleam, shimmer
Schimmer, der (no pl.)	glimmer, gleam, shimmer
Glanz, der (no pl.)	gleam, shine, sparkle, sheen, gloss, glare
glänzen	to shine, gleam
glänzend	shining, gleaming, dazzling, glistening
glanzlos	dull, lacklustre
Dämmerung, die (-en)	twilight; dusk; dawn
Abenddämmerung, die (-en)	dusk
Morgendämmerung, die (-en)	dawn
leuchten	to shine
aufleuchten	to light up
funkeln	to sparkle, twinkle, glitter, gleam

blass	pale, wan, faint	rascheln	to rustle
verblassen	to fade, pale	knistern	to rustle, crackle
verblasst	faint	tosen	to roar, rage, thunder
trüb	dull, dim		
matt	dull, dim	Getose, das (no pl.)	raging
jmdn finster anstarren	to glower at sb	Getöse, das (no pl.)	din, racket, row
		ohrenbetäubend	deafening
jmdn verächtlich/ herausfordernd anstarren	to glare contempt/defiance at sb	schallen	to sound, ring out, resound
		Schall, der (–e or ¨e)	sound
sich Blicke zuwerfen	to exchange glances	erschallen	to ring out, sound
jmdm mit den Augen/mit Blicken folgen	to follow sb with one's eyes	quietschen	to squeak, squeal, screech, shriek
		poltern	to crash, thump about
blenden	to dazzle, blind		
blendend	dazzling	Gepolter, das (no pl.)	clatter
blinken	to gleam, flash		
aufblinken	to flash	zischen	to fizz, hiss, sizzle, whiz
glitzern	to glitter, twinkle		
jmdm/einer Sache nachsehen	to gaze after sb/sth	knarren	to creak
		knacken	to creak, crackle
jmdn/etw flüchtig sehen	to glimpse sb/sth	klirren	to clink, tinkle, rattle, jangle, crackle, crunch

Sound

verklingen	to fade away	klimpern	to jingle, tinkle
ausklingen	to finish ringing	knirschen	to crunch
abklingen	to die/fade away	rasseln	to rattle
nachklingen	to go on sounding	kreischen	to screech, squeal, shriek
Nachklang, der (¨e)	reverberation, echo		
Echo, das (–s)	echo	brausen	to roar, thunder, ring out
echoen	to echo		
läuten	to ring, go off [alarm clock]	tuten	to hoot, toot, sound

Taste

sich anhören	to sound	schmackhaft	tasty
summen	to hum, buzz	geschmacklos	tasteless
Gesumm, das (no pl.)	buzzing, humming	fade	tasteless, insipid
		wässerig	watery
bumsen (coll.)	to bang, thump	würzig	spicy
Bums, der (–e; coll.)	bang, thud, thump	ungewürzt	unseasoned
knallen	to bang, slam, crack, ring out	sahnig	creamy
		fein	delicate
zuknallen	to slam	delikat	exquisite, delicious
tönen	to sound, ring, resound	köstlich	delicious
		appetitlich	appetizing
ertönen	to sound, ring out		

Smell

duften	to smell
duftend	sweet-smelling, fragrant
Duft, der (¨e)	pleasant smell, scent, fragrance
aromatisch	aromatic
würzig	aromatic
geruchsfrei	unscented
geruchsneutral	unscented
Körpergeruch, der (¨e)	body odour
es riecht verbrannt	there's a burnt smell
parfümiert	scented
lieblich	sweet
streng	pungent
stechend	pungent
scheußlich	terrible
ekelhaft	disgusting, revolting
übel	foul, nasty
schimmelig riechen	to smell mouldy

geruchsempfindlich	sensitive to smells
etw ausströmen	to give off sth
eine Fahne haben	to reek of alcohol

Touch

etw berühren	to touch sth
Berührung, die (-en)	touch, contact
seidig	silky, satiny
sich wie Seide anfühlen	to have a silky feel
stacheln	to prick, prickle
stachelig	prickly
stechen	to prick, sting
kitzeln	to tickle
dornig	thorny
schleimig	slimy
breiig	mushy
schlüpfrig	slippery
poliert	polished
lackiert	lacquered
uneben	uneven
sandig	gritty

Level 3

Sight

jmdn/etw erblicken (elev.)	to catch sight of sb/sth
jmdn/etw erspähen (elev.)	to espy, catch sight of sb/sth
etw sichten	to sight sth
etw wahrnehmen	to perceive, notice sth
einen Schleier vor den Augen haben	to not see clearly
jmdm entgeht etw	sb fails to see sth
etw beaugenscheinigen	to inspect sth
jmdn/etw beaugapfeln (hum.)	to give sb/sth the once over
jmdn/etw beäugen	to eye sb, inspect sth
jmdn/etw in Augenschein nehmen	to take a close look at sb/sth

jmdn mit den Augen/Blicken messen (elev.)	to look sb up and down
seine Augen/Blicke durch ein Zimmer schweifen lassen	to cast one's eyes around a room
jmdn/etw anstieren (coll.)	to stare at sb/sth
jmdn/etw angaffen (coll., pej.)	to gape at sb/sth
Stielaugen machen	to stare goggle-eyed
er machte Stielaugen	his eyes nearly popped out of his head
jmdn mit Blicken durchbohren	to look piercingly at sb
spähen	to peer, peep
Düsterkeit, die (no pl.)	gloom, gloominess, darkness

düster	gloomy, sombre	brummen	to buzz, drone, growl
sich verdüstern	to darken	Gebrumm, das	droning, buzzing,
stockdunkel	pitch-dark	(no pl.)	growling
stockfinster	pitch-dark	Rabatz, der	racket, din
duster (N; coll.)	dark	(no pl., coll.)	
zappenduster (coll.)	pitch-black,	Krakeel, der (no pl.)	row
	pitch-dark	Radau, das	row, racket
schummerig	dim	(no pl., coll.)	
dämmerig	dim, faint, gloomy	quatschen	to squelch
Dämmerlicht, das	twilight	hallen	to reverberate, ring,
(no pl.)			ring out
Zwielicht, das (no pl.)	twilight	Hall, der (no pl.)	reverberation, echo
Geflimmer, das	shimmering,	Nachhall, der (-e)	reverberation, echo
(no pl.)	flickering,	Widerhall, der	echo, reverberation
	twinkling	(no pl.)	
Gefunkel, das (no pl.)	sparkling, twinkling,	widerhallen	to resonate,
	gleaming,		reverberate,
	glittering		resound, echo
Geglitzer, das (no pl.)	glitter(ing)	verhallen	to die away
aus dem	out of the corner of	Gedudel, das	tootling, droning,
Augenwinkel	one's eye	(no pl., coll.)	noise
(heraus)		Geklimper, das	plunking
flirren	to shimmer	(no pl.)	
schillern	to shimmer	plären	to blare out, yell,
grell	glaring, dazzling		shriek, screech,
Grelle, die (no pl.)	glare		howl
Grellheit, die (no pl.)	glare	schmettern	to blare out, bellow
grell leuchten	to glare	pumpern	to thump
verbleichen	to fade, pale	(S, AU; coll.)	
verblichen	faint	rumpeln	to bump and bang
blinzeln	to blink		about
zwinkern	to blink, wink	rumoren	to make a noise, bang
flimmern	to shimmer		about
flackern	to waver, flicker	plätschern	to babble, splash,
			patter, lap

Sound

		glucksen	to gurgle, glug
Heidenlärm, der	unholy/dreadful row,	gluckern	to gurgle, glug
(no pl., coll.)	din, racket	patschen	to splash
Mordskrach, der	terrible din/racket	prasseln	to clatter, crackle
(no pl., coll.)		bimmeln	to ring
Spektakel, der	row, rumpus, racket	surren	to hum, whirr, buzz,
(-; coll.)			purr
Höllenspektakel,	diabolical noise/row	schnurren	to purr, hum, whirr
der (-)		schwirren	to buzz
dröhnen	to boom, roar,	knattern	to rattle, clatter,
	resound, pound		crackle

Taste

deliziös	delectable
gustiös (AU)	appetizing
wohlschmeckend (elev.)	palatable
mundig (elev.)	appetizing, savoury
pikant	piquant, spicy
herb	sharp, tangy, dry [wine]
süffig	smooth [beer]
weich	smooth [whisky]
einen feinen Gaumen haben	to be a gourmet, enjoy fine food
appetitanregend	appetizing
Geschmacksknospe, die (-n)	taste bud
einen üblen Nachgeschmack hinterlassen	to leave a bad taste in the mouth
ranzig	rancid

Smell

wohlriechend (elev.)	fragrant
Bukett, das (-s or -e)	bouquet
Blume, die (-n)	bouquet
(nach etw) dunsten (elev.)	to smell (of sth)
muffeln (S, AU)	to smell musty
muffig	musty, stuffy, stale

moderig	musty
herb	sharp, tangy
säuerlich	sour
berauschend	heady
(etw) schnuppern	to sniff (sth)
an etw schnuppern	to sniff (at) sth
moschusartig	musky
Odeur, das (-s or -e; elev.)	pleasant aroma
Fährte, die (-n)	scent, trail
etw durchziehen	to fill, pervade sth
durchdringend	pungent, pervasive, sharp
betäubend	overpowering
stickig	stuffy, close

Touch

tasten	to feel around, grope
etw spüren	to feel sth
dickflüssig	viscous
zähflüssig	glutinous, viscous, thick
viskos	viscous
leimig	gluey, tacky
sämig	thick, viscous
glitschig (coll.)	slippery
kribbeln	to tickle, tingle
ein kribbeliges Gefühl in der Hand	pins and needles in one's hand

Colour and light

Level 1

Colours

Farbe, die (-n)	colour
schwarz	black
weiß	white
grau	grey
braun	brown
rot	red
gelb	yellow
blau	blue

grün	green
lila	purple
violett	purple, violet
orange	orange
silbern	silver
golden	gold
rosa	pink
rosafarben, -farbig, -rot	pink

pink	shocking pink		
beige	beige		
hell-	light		
dunkel-	dark		
blass-	pale		
tief-	deep		
schwärzlich	blackish		
weißlich	whitish		
grau-, gräulich	greyish		
bräunlich	brownish, browny		
rötlich	reddish		
bläulich	bluish		
gelblich	yellowish		
grünlich	greenish		
farbenblind	colour-blind		
grünblind	suffering from red–green colour-blindness		
bunt	coloured, colourful, multicoloured, spotted		
farbig	coloured		
einfarbig	all one colour		
Schwärze, die (no pl.)	blackness		
Weiße, die (no pl.)	whiteness		
Bläue, die (no pl.)	blueness		
Röte, die (no pl.)	redness, red; blush		
blutrot	blood-red		
buttergelb	butter yellow		
himmelblau	sky-blue, azure		
grasgrün	grass-green		
gefleckt	spotted, speckled, dappled		

Verbs

etw schwärzen	to blacken sth
etw weißen	to whiten sth; whitewash sth
grauen	to become grey; dawn
bräunen	to tan, go brown
etw röten	to make red, redden
sich röten	to turn/become red
blauen	to turn blue
etw bläuen	to dye sth blue
grünen	to turn green; blossom

Expressions

mir wurde schwarz vor den Augen	everything went black
schwarz auf weiß	in writing, in black and white
ein weißes (Blatt) Papier	a blank/clean sheet of paper
er/sie ist weiß geworden	his/her hair has turned white
grau werden	to go grey
einen roten Kopf bekommen	to go red in the face
eine Fahrt ins Blaue	a trip with an unknown destination
grünes Licht geben	to give the go-ahead, the green light
grüne Weihnachten	Christmas without snow
ins Grüne	into the country

Level 2

Colours

blauschwarz	blue-black	schokolade(n)braun	chocolate-coloured
grauschwarz	greyish black	nussbraun	nut-brown, hazel
silberweiß	silvery white	braunrot	brownish red
mausgrau	mouse-grey	rotbraun	reddish brown
steingrau	stone-grey	kastanienbraun	maroon
aschgrau	ash-grey	erdfarben, -farbig	earth-coloured
schwarzbraun	dark brown	khakifarben	khaki(-coloured)
kaffeebraun	coffee-coloured	taupe	taupe
		purpurn	crimson

purpurrot	crimson (red)
purpurfarben, -farbig	crimson
hochrot	bright red
knallrot	bright red, scarlet
flammend rot	flame red, blazing red
feuerrot	fiery red, flaming, scarlet
kirschrot	cherry(-red)
erdbeerfarben	strawberry pink
himbeerrot	raspberry pink
rostrot	rust-coloured, russet
fuchsrot	red, chestnut, ginger, carroty
krebsrot	red as a lobster
weinrot	wine-red, claret
rosenrot	rosy (red)
kupferrot	copper-red, copper-coloured
kupferfarben, -farbig	copper-coloured
blaurot	purple
veilchenblau	violet
königsblau	royal blue
saphirblau	sapphire blue
kobaltblau	cobalt blue
stahlblau	steel-blue
zitronengelb	lemon yellow
honigfarben	honey-coloured
strohgelb	straw-coloured
senffarben, farbig	mustard(-coloured)
maisgelb	corn-coloured
pfirsichfarben	peach-coloured
lachsfarben	salmon pink
pastellfarben	pastel(-coloured)
pastellrosa	pastel pink
oliv(grün)	olive (green)
jadegrün	jade green
seegrün	sea-green
meergrün	sea-green
flaschengrün	bottle-green
gelbgrün	yellowish green
Farbton, der (¨e)	shade, tone, tint
Spur, die (-en)	touch

eine Spur zu grell	a touch too garish
grell	garish, gaudy, loud
kunterbunt	multicoloured
gesprenkelt	speckled
blass	sickly

Verbs

jmdn anschwärzen	to blacken sb's name; inform on sb
ergrauen	to go/turn grey
etw anbräunen	to brown lightly [cooking]
anbräunen	to tan lightly
jmdn verbläuen	to bash/beat up sb
etw begrünen	to plant greenery in/on sth
vergilben	to become yellow
erröten	to turn red, turn pink, blush

Expressions

schwarzarbeiten	to moonlight; do work without paying taxes
schwarzfahren	to travel without paying
schwarzhören	to use a radio without a licence
etw schwarz malen	to paint a black/gloomy picture of sth
der weiße Sport	tennis
der graue Alltag	dull reality
ein Roter (adj. decl.; coll.)	a red [wine]
ein Roter/eine Rote (adj. decl.)	a redhead
die blauen Jungs, pl. (coll.)	the boys in blue [sailors]
die blaue Stunde	the twilight hour
gelbe Seiten, pl.	yellow pages
ein grüner Junge	a greenhorn
grün hinter den Ohren	wet behind the ears

Level 3

Colours

schwarzblau	bluish black, inky blue
kohlschwarz	jet black
pech(raben)schwarz	pitch-black
kohl(pech)-rabenschwarz	jet black, raven, raven-black
schwanenweiß (elev.)	lily-white
anthrazit(farben, -farbig)	charcoal-grey
perlgrau	pearl grey
feldgrau	field-grey
bleigrau	lead-grey
bleifarben, -farbig	lead-coloured, lead-grey
taubenblau	blue-grey, dove-grey
preußischblau	Prussian blue
siena	sienna
rehbraun	russet
sepia	sepia
ockerbraun, -gelb	ochre
ziegelrot	brick-red
korallenrot	coral(-red)
frais(e)	strawberry pink
zinnoberrot	vermilion
karmesin(rot)	crimson
scharlachrot	scarlet
krapprot	madder red
karmin(rot)	carmine (red)
cerise	cerise, cherry
rubinrot	ruby-red, ruby
burgunderrot, -farben	burgundy (red)
aubergine	dark purple
mauve	mauve
malvenfarben, -farbig	mauve
fliederfarben, -farbig	lilac
lavendel(farben)	lavender
bleu	light blue
dottergelb	golden yellow
safrangelb	saffron (yellow)
goldgelb	golden brown
bernsteingelb, -farben	amber(-coloured)
marineblau	navy blue

Hauch, der (-e; elev.)	hint
Stich, der (-e)	tinge, shade
ein Stich ins Rote	a tinge of red
quitte(n)gelb	sickly yellow
schwefelgelb	sulphurous yellow
giftgrün	bilious green
moosgrün	moss-green
lindgrün	lime green
smaragd(grün)	emerald
türkis	turquoise
türkisgrün, -farben	turquoise(-coloured)
marmoriert	marbled
scheckig	spotted, gaudy, blotchy, patchy, dappled [horse]
buntscheckig	spotted, dappled [horse]
getüpfelt	spotted, dotted
irisierend	iridescent

Expressions

in den schwarzen Zahlen sein	to be in the black
da kannst du schreien, bis du schwarz bist	you can shout until you're blue in the face
weiße Mäuse sehen	to see pink elephants
alles grau in grau sehen	to always see the gloomy side of things
in grauer Vorzeit/Ferne	in the dim and distant past/future
heute rot, morgen tot	here today, gone tomorrow
einen blauen Montag machen/einlegen	to skip work on Monday
jmdm das Blaue vom Himmel versprechen	to promise sb the earth/moon
vor Neid gelb werden	to turn green with envy
etw durch eine rosa(rote) Brille sehen	to see sth through rose-coloured spectacles

Materials and textures

Level 1

Cloth

Stoff, der (-e)	material, fabric
Jeansstoff, der (-e)	denim
Wollstoff, der (-e)	woollen fabric
Wolle, die (-n)	wool
wollen	woollen
Baumwolle, die (no pl.)	cotton
Seide, die (-n)	silk
seiden	silk
Kunstseide, die (no pl.)	artificial silk, rayon
Reyon (Rayon), der or das (no pl.)	rayon
Zellwolle, die (no pl.)	rayon
Polyester, der (-)	polyester
Cord (Kord), der (-e)	corduroy
Satin, der (-s)	satin; sateen
Velvet, der (-s)	cotton velvet
Samt, der (-e)	velvet
Waschsamt, der (no pl.)	washable velvet
Flanell, der (-e)	flannel
Leinen, das (-)	linen
Loden, der (-)	loden

Wood

Holz, das (¨er)	wood
Hartholz, das (¨er)	hardwood
Weichholz, das (¨er)	softwood
Anmachholz, das (no pl.)	kindling
(Holz)splitter, der (-)	splinter (of wood)
Bambus, das (-se)	bamboo
Rohr, das (-e)	cane, wicker
aus Rohr geflochtene Stühle	cane/wicker chairs
Kork, der (-e)	cork
Mahagoni, das (no pl.)	mahogany
Teakholz, das (no pl.)	teak

Building materials

Beton, der (no pl.)	concrete
etw betonieren	to surface sth with concrete
eine frisch betonierte Fläche	recently laid concrete
Asphalt, der (-e)	asphalt
etw asphaltieren	to asphalt sth
Ziegelstein, der (-e)	brick
Dachziegel, der (-)	roof tile
Backstein, der (-e)	brick
mauern	to lay bricks
Kreide, die (-n)	chalk

Metal

Metall, das (-e)	metal
metallartig	metallic
Stahl, der (-e or ¨e)	steel
rostfreier Stahl	stainless steel
Gold, das (no pl.)	gold
Silber, das (no pl.)	silver
Bronze, die (-n)	bronze
Eisen, das (no pl.)	iron
Zinn, das (no pl.)	tin; pewter
Kupfer, das (no pl.)	copper
Blei, das (no pl.)	lead

Various

Glas, das (no pl.)	glass
Leder, das (-)	leather
Pappe, die (-n)	cardboard
Plastik, das (no pl.)	plastic
Gummi, das or der (-s)	rubber
gummiartig	rubbery
Wachs, das (-e)	wax
Stroh, das (no pl.)	straw
Seil, das (-e)	rope
Schnur, die (¨e)	string, cord

Level 2

Cloth

Gewebe, das (–)	fabric
Filz, der (–e)	felt
Kamelhaar, das (no pl.)	camel hair
Kaschmir, der (–e)	cashmere
Kaschmirwolle, die (no pl.)	cashmere
Shetlandwolle, die (no pl.)	Shetland wool
Mohär (Mohair), der (–s)	mohair
Frottee, das (–s)	terry towelling
Velours, der (no pl.)	velour
Gabardine, der or die (no pl.)	gabardine
Tweed, der (–s)	tweed
Twill, der (–s or –e)	twill
Köper, der (–)	twill
Popelin, der (no pl.); Popeline, die (no pl.)	poplin
Musselin, der (–e)	muslin
Chintz, der (–e)	chintz
Gaze, die (–n)	gauze
Flor, der (–s)	gauze
Batist, der (–e)	batiste
Baumwollbatist, der (–e)	cotton batiste
Kräuselkrepp, der (no pl.)	crepe
Mako, der or die (–s)	Egyptian cotton
Damast, der (–e)	damask
Voile, der (–s)	voile
Kattun, der (–e)	calico
Jacquard, der (–s)	jacquard

Wood

Sperrholz, das (no pl.)	plywood
Spanholz, das (no pl.)	chipboard
Span, der (¨e)	piece of kindling
Furnier, das (–e)	veneer
Furnierholz, das (¨er)	veneering

Holzbalken, der (–)	beam
wurmstichig	worm–eaten
Wurmloch, das (¨er)	wormhole
Balsaholz, das (¨er)	balsa
Sandelholz, das (¨er)	sandalwood
Ebenholz, das (¨er)	ebony

Building materials

(Ver)putz, der (no pl.)	plaster
etw verputzen	to plaster sth
Gips, der (–e)	plaster
Gipsplatte, die (–n)	plasterboard
Lehm, der (–e)	clay
lehmig	clayey
Ton, der (–e)	clay
Kies, der (–e)	gravel
kieshaltig	gravelly
Granit, der (–e)	granite
Marmor, der (–e)	marble

Metal

Blech, das (–e)	(sheet) metal
Walzblech, das (no pl.)	sheet metal
Wellblech, das (no pl.)	corrugated iron
Gusseisen, das (no pl.)	cast iron
Schmiedeeisen, das (no pl.)	wrought iron
Roheisen, das (no pl.)	pig iron
Messing, das (no pl.)	brass
Versilberung, die (–en)	(silver–)plating
Vergoldung, die (–en)	gold–plating

Various

Kunstleder, das (–)	imitation leather
Wildleder, das (–)	suede
Lackleder, das (no pl.)	patent leather
Tesafilm, der (–e; trademark)	Scotch tape ®, Sellotape ®

Klebeband, das (¨er)	adhesive tape, sticky tape	Zwirn, der (-e)	(strong) thread, yarn
Schaumgummi, der (no pl.)	foam rubber	Kordel, die (-n)	cord
		Edelstein, der (-e)	precious stone
Faden, der (¨)	thread; string	Halbedelstein, der (-e)	semi-precious stone
Bindfaden, der (¨)	string		

Level 3

Cloth

Kammgarn, das (-e)	worsted	astig	knotty
Bouclé (Buklee), das (-s)	bouclé yarn	Knorren, der (-)	gnarl, knot
		knorrig	knotty
Kunstfaser, die (-n)	man-made/synthetic fibre	Intarsia (Intarsie), die (Intarsien)	inlay
Chemiefaser, die (-n)	man-made/synthetic fibre	Spachtel, der (-) or die (-n)	filler
Tüll, der (-e)	tulle	Spachtelmasse, die (-n)	filler
Lamé (Lamee), der (-s)	lamé	Holzschliff, der (no pl.)	wood pulp
Organza, der (no pl.)	organza	nicht abgelagert	unseasoned
Steif-, Schneiderleinen, das (no pl.)	buckram	Grundierfarbe, die (-n)	primer
Vlieseline, die (no pl.; trademark)	interfacing	### *Building materials*	
		Teer, der (-e)	tar
Inlett, das (-s or -e)	ticking	etw teeren	to tar sth
Organdy, der (no pl.)	organdy	teerig	tarry
Ulster, der (-)	heavy, rugged fabric	Makadam, der or das (-e)	tarmac
Manchester, der (no pl.)	heavy corduroy	etw makadamisieren	to tarmac sth
Rips, der (-e)	rep	Schotter, der (-)	gravel
Drill(ich), der (-e)	drill	etw schottern	to gravel sth
Drell, der (-e; N)	drill	Splitt, der (-e)	stone chippings, aggregate
Nessel, der (-)	coarse, untreated cotton cloth	Kalkstein, der (no pl.)	limestone
		Kitt, der (-e)	putty

Wood

Maserung, die (-en)	grain	### *Metal*	
gemasert	grainy	Edelmetall, das (-e)	precious metal
fein gemasert	fine grained	hämmerbar	ductile
Holzbalken mit einer Stärke von 2 auf 4 Zoll	two-by-four	Metallermüdung, die (no pl.)	metal fatigue
Ast, der (¨e)	knot		

etw galvanisieren	to electroplate, galvanize sth	Pergament, das (-e)	parchment
Galvanisierung, die (-en)	electroplating, galvanizing	Glasfaser, die (-n)	fibreglass
Auflage, die (-n)	plating	Tau, das (-e)	rope
mit Silberprägung	embossed in silver	Feuerstein, der (-e)	flint
Email, das (-s); Emaille, die (-n)	enamel	Flint(stein), der (-e)	flint
Draht, der ("e)	wire	Bimsstein, der (no pl.)	pumice (stone)
Maschendraht, der (no pl.)	wire netting	Schmirgel, der (no pl.)	emery
Schlacke, die (-n)	slag	Perlmutt, das or Perlmutter, die (no pl.)	mother-of-pearl
Schrott, der (no pl.)	scrap metal, old iron	Elfenbein, das (no pl.)	ivory

Various

Plastiline, das (-e; trademark)	Plasticine ®	Porzellan, das (-e)	porcelain, china
Vinyl, das (no pl.)	vinyl		

Exercises

Level 1

1. Wie heißt das Verb? ✓
1. etw schwarz machen
2. etw weiß anstreichen
3. etw rot färben
4. etw blau färben
5. grau werden
6. braun werden
7. rot werden
8. blau werden
9. grün werden

2. Wie heißt das Gegenteil? ✓
1. hell
2. laut
3. süß
4. einfarbig
5. das Hartholz
6. die Helligkeit
7. weich

3. Wie heißt das Substantiv? ✓

Adjektiv	Substantiv
1. blau	*das Blau*
2. grün	
3. gelb	
4. rot	
5. rosa	
6. braun	

4. Welches Präfix passt? ✓

1. Der Anblick war so schrecklich, dass sie ———sehen musste.
   a. an-   b. um-   c. weg-   d. zu-
2. Er hat ihn misstrauisch ———gesehen.
   a. an-   b. um-   c. weg-   d. zu-
3. Sie will ———sehen, wie ich das mache.
   a. an-   b. um-   c. weg-   d. zu-
4. Er hat sich mehrmals nach seinem Vater ———gesehen.
   a. an-   b. um-   c. weg-   d. zu-
5. Ich kann das nicht, wenn sie mir ———sehen.
   a. an-   b. um-   c. weg-   d. zu-

5. Welche Farbe passt? ✓

1. gras———————
2. himmel———————
3. blut———————
4. butter———————
5. schnee———————

6. Wie heißt das entsprechende Substantiv? ✓

1. riechen	
2. stinken	
3. blicken	
4. klingen	
5. pfeifen	
6. lärmen	
7. strahlen	
8. schmecken	
9. krachen	

7. Welches Verb passt? ✓

> hämmern, hupen, klicken, klingeln, lärmen, rauschen, schweigen

1. der Wecker
2. der Wind
3. das Feuerzeug
4. das Herz
5. das Auto
6. der Angeklagte
7. die Schüler

8. Farben. ✓

1. Welche Farben hat die deutsche Fahne?
2. Nennen Sie die Grundfarben.
3. Wie heißt das Gegenteil von *blassblau*?
4. Wie nennt man Weihnachtstage ohne Schnee? Mit Schnee?
5. Ich habe es _____ auf _____ bekommen. = Ich habe es schriftlich bekommen.
6. Eine Sanitätsorganisation heißt das _____ Kreuz.
7. Welche Farbe hat ein Veilchen?
8. Welche Farbe hat eine Apfelsine?
9. Eine Uhr aus Gold ist eine _____ Uhr.
10. Der 25. Jahrestag der Hochzeit ist die _____ Hochzeit.

9. Aus welchem Material sind die folgenden Gegenstände? ✓

> a. Bronze, b. Glas, c. Gummi, d. Kupfer, e. Leder, f. Pappe, g. Plastik,
> h. rostfreier Stahl, i. Wachs

1. die Kerze	6. das Centstück
2. der Stiefel	7. die Medaille für den dritten Platz
3. das Besteck	8. die Aktenmappe
4. der Karton	9. der Müllbeutel
5. die Flasche	

10. Ordnen Sie.

Kleidung	Baustelle

der Backstein, die Baumwolle, der Beton, der Cord, der Dachziegel, das Leinen, der Loden, mauern, die Seide, die Wolle

11. Wie heißen die entsprechenden Adjektive und Substantive? ✓

Adjektiv	Adjektiv + -lich	Substantiv
1. schwarz	*schwärzlich*	*die Schwärze*
2. weiß		
3. blau		
4. rot		

12. Wie heißt das Adjektiv? ✓

a. glatt, b. kräftig, c. lecker, d. rau, e. rutschig, f. salzig, g. scharf, h. steif, i. stinkend, j. süßlich, k. zart

1. nach Salz schmeckend
2. wohlschmeckend
3. übel riechend
4. kratzig
5. zum Rutschen bringend
6. etwas süß

7. ganz eben
8. nicht leicht zu biegen
9. intensiv
10. kaum spürbar
11. stark gewürzt

13. Übersetzen Sie ins Deutsche. ✓

1. He has gone completely grey.
2. The boy who is sitting in the wheelchair doesn't want to be stared at.
3. By no means should one observe the solar eclipse unprotected.
4. He glanced impatiently at his watch.
5. The sky darkened before the thunderstorm.
6. Nervously he drummed with his fingers on the table.
7. The putrid smell spread in the corridor.
8. Cheese from pasteurized milk is safer, but unfortunately it doesn't taste like cheese.
9. She went red in the face with excitement.
10. The steps still have to be surfaced with concrete.

14. Übersetzen Sie ins Englische.

Ui, Gold!
Jedes kleine Mädchen will eines Tages ein Kleid aus Gold. Erst lächeln die Eltern nachsichtig. Aber das Mädchen bohrt nach. Es weint und greint, so lange bis ihnen der Kragen platzt. Und dann erklären sie, was einfach nicht stimmt: dass es keine Kleider aus Gold gibt, dass Gold ein Metall ist und kein Stoff zum Nähen. Der Preis dieser infamen Lüge: Die Mädchen wollen jetzt ein Pferd. Dabei wäre ein Spaghetti-Top von Hanro ein adäquater Kleid-Ersatz, viel billiger und pflegeleicht. Und Pferdeäpfel produziert es auch nicht.

Barbara Höfler

FRANKFURTER RUNDSCHAU, Samstag, 27. Oktober 2001, Nr. 250/43, Magazin, S. 15

Innig

In dem Innenstadtcafé war es wie immer voll und laut. Irgendeine peppige Musik wogte durch den Raum und vermischte sich mit den Rauchschwaden, die knapp über den Scheiteln der Gäste schwebten. An fast allen Tischen wurde gegessen und geschwatzt, gelacht und gestikuliert.

An dem einen Tisch, ganz hinten an der Wand in der kleinen Nichtraucher-Nische, war etwas anders. Er hob sich ab von dem lärmigen Geschehen im Lokal am Dom. Das Paar, das sich den kleinen Zweiertisch teilte, war noch jung. 17, 18 vielleicht. Die beiden wechselten weder Blicke noch Worte. Das Schweigen zwischen ihnen war nicht das ein wenig schale eines alten, von vielen Fernsehabenden abgenutzten Ehepaars. Es war auch nicht das leidenschaftliche Verstummen eines Liebespaars nach wüstem Streit. Beide hatten ein Buch in der Hand, in dem sie lasen – unbeeindruckt vom tosenden Lärm um sie herum. Innig. Und ein kecker Sonnenstrahl schien von ihnen unbemerkt die Rauchschwaden über ihren Köpfen zu zerteilen.

Ihre Bastienne

FRANKFURTER RUNDSCHAU, Samstag, 26. Januar 2002, Nr. 22/4, S. 25

Level 2

1. Welche Farbe passt? ✓

1. maus_____
2. schokoladen_____
3. kirsch_____
4. saphir_____
5. zitronen_____
6. jade_____

7. asch_____
8. mais_____
9. kobalt_____
10. feuer_____
11. oliv_____

2. Welches Wort hat die gleiche oder eine ähnliche Bedeutung? ✓

> a. duften, b. fade, c. die Finsternis, d. das Gewebe, e. der Köper, f. der Lehm,
> g. leuchten, h. lieblich, i. meergrün, j. der Nachklang, k. ohrenbetäubend,
> l. schlüpfrig, m. schmackhaft, n. der Schimmer, o. trüb

1. das Dunkel
2. schwacher Glanz
3. glänzen
4. matt
5. das Echo
6. riechen
7. der Stoff
8. der Twill

9. der Ton
10. sehr laut
11. geschmacklos
12. wohlschmeckend
13. süß
14. rutschig
15. seegrün

3. Falsche Freunde. Ergänzen Sie die Tabelle.

Deutsch	Englisch	Deutsch	Englisch
purpurn			purple
die Fabrik			fabric
das Inlett			inlet
delikat			delicate
fade			fade
patent			patent
solide			solid
stark			stark
das Odeur			odour

4. Welches Wort passt nicht? ✓
1. der Baumwollbatist, der Jeansstoff, der Mako, die Zellwolle
2. das Kamelhaar, der Kaschmir, der Kattun, der Mohär
3. das Ebenholz, das Mahagoni, das Sandelholz, das Spanholz
4. das Bügeleisen, das Gusseisen, das Roheisen, das Schmiedeeisen
5. jmdn betrachten, jmdn fixieren, jmdn mustern, jmdn verbläuen
6. funkeln, glitzern, läuten, schimmern
7. ertönen, glühen, klingen, schallen
8. blaurot, erdbeerfarben, knallrot, purpurn

5. Welche Definition passt? ✓

1. schwarzfahren	a. blendend hell
2. jmdn anschwärzen	b. jmdn starr ansehen
3. schwarzbraun	c. dunkel werden
4. grell	d. ein schussartiges Geräusch geben
5. knallen	e. etw verbreiten
6. jmdn anglotzen	f. ohne Fahrkarte fahren
7. etw durchblättern	g. tief dunkelbraun
8. sich verfinstern	h. bleich
9. blass	i. jmdn verleumden
10. etw ausströmen	j. etw flüchtig ansehen

6. Welches Adjektiv passt? ✓

a. blendend, b. fuchsrot, c. geruchsfrei, d. sandig, e. seidig, f. stachelig, g. wässerig, h. wurmstichig

1. die Suppe	5. der Kaktus
2. die Seife	6. das Haar
3. der Stoff	7. das Holz
4. der Boden	8. das Weiß

7. Welches Material passt am besten? ✓

> a. der Edelstein, b. der Filz, c. das Frottee, d. das Furnierholz, e. der Kies, f. das Lackleder, g. das Messing, h. das Schaumgummi, i. die Shetlandwolle, j. der Span, k. der Tesafilm, l. das Wellblech

1. der Schuh	7. der Bademantel
2. der Polster	8. der Pullover
3. die Türklinke	9. das Möbel
4. das Dach	10. das Feuer
5. der Weg	11. der Riß im Papier
6. der Hut	12. der Fingerring

8. In jedem Satz fehlt ein Wort. ✓

> appetitlich, Blick, Dämmerung, errötete, flaschengrün, heftete, Kaschmirwolle, kreischen, lackiert, sahnige, verklingen, zugeknallt

1. Sie _____ ihre Augen auf sein Gesicht.
2. Die _____ war schon angebrochen, als ich in Frankfurt landete.
3. Er wandte keinen _____ von ihr.
4. Ihre Schritte _____ in der Ferne.
5. Er hat die Tür hinter sich _____.
6. Über ihren Köpfen _____ die Möwen.
7. Sie hat eine _____ Muschelsuppe bestellt.
8. In diesem Restaurant gibt es _____ präsentierte und garantiert frische Kost.
9. Ihre Fingernägel sind hellrot _____.
10. Das Wasser ist nicht blau, sondern _____.
11. Sie _____ vor Verlegenheit.
12. Sie trug einen Wintermantel aus _____.

9. Was gehört zusammen? ✓

> a. kitzeln, b. klirren, c. knarren, d. knistern, e. rasseln, f. stechen, g. summen, h. tosen, i. zischen

1. die Biene	6. die Gläser
2. das Papier	7. die Ketten
3. der Wasserfall	8. die Wolle eines Pullovers
4. das Fett in der Pfanne	9. der Dorn
5. die Tür	

10. Übersetzen Sie ins Deutsche. ✓

1. She has eyes in the back of her head.
2. He peered at her searchingly.
3. I didn't set eyes on her.
4. He glowered at me.
5. Your suggestion sounds good.
6. There's something rustling in the straw.
7. The chocolate cake tasted simply delicious.
8. Today I'd like to take a break and enjoy the scent of the roses.
9. Other occupants of the apartment house noticed the pungent odour.
10. He wore a wine-red bomber jacket and white jeans.
11. Palm trees surround pastel-coloured houses.
12. The prettiest shade for lips and nails is a rich (strong) pink.

11. Übersetzen Sie ins Englische.

Der Duft der Welt

Exotische Gewürze gehören zur Weihnachtszeit wie Glühwein und Zimtsterne. In der Hamburger Speicherstadt wurden sie einst gelagert. Ein idealer Ausgangspunkt für eine Reise im Kopf, mit Bildern und Geschichten rund um den Globus, ist das dortige Gewürzmuseum.

Text: Franz Lerchenmüller

... Heute, im Zeitalter der Container, der Warenterminbörsen und Just-in-time-Anlieferung, lagern im Freihafen vornehmlich Teppiche, auch ein paar letzte alteingesessene Kaffee- und Teehändler sind noch da. Die Gewürzimporteure aber haben die Speicherstadt verlassen – der Aufwand ist zu groß: Jede Last muss von Hand zu den einzelnen Stockwerken hochgehievt werden, Gabelstapler und Paletten können in den Räumen nicht eingesetzt werden, die Quadratmeterbelastung wäre zu hoch. Zu teuer also, zu wenig funktional das Ganze.

Und dennoch ist in der Speicherstadt ein Hauch jener Zeit zu spüren, als die Luft noch nach Kaffee und Kardamom roch: Im zweiten Stock des Speichers am Sandtorkai 32 befindet sich seit acht Jahren das Hamburger Gewürzmuseum „Spicy's". Vorbei am „Afghanischen Teppichmuseum" führt die Treppe nach oben zu einer schweren Eisentür. Dahinter grobe Dielen, mächtige Träger, weißgestrichene Backsteinwände. Und ein feiner Duft nach Zimt. Gegründet haben das Museum Uwe Paap und Viola Vierk, beide jahrelang im Gewürzhandel tätig. Vor kurzem hat die blonde Hanseatin das Unternehmen in alleiniger Regie übernommen.

Und, kein Zweifel: Die 350 Quadratmeter mit Fotos, Maschinen, Warenproben und Jutesäcken sind der richtige Ausgangspunkt für eine Reise in die Welt der Gewürze. Eine Reise in die Ferne und in die Vergangenheit, eine Reise im Kopf, mit Bildern und Geschichten.

Auf einem langen Tisch stehen 33 Tonschalen. Über jeder prangt ein Name, der nach Verführung klingt: Cassia-Blüten, Kurkuma-Finger, Cilandro, Schinusstrauch, Ingwer-Flocken. Jetzt sind Fingerspitzen, Augen und Ohren gefragt: Die winzigen Perlen des Schwarzkümmels rieseln fast unhörbar aus der Hand. Schmutziggrüner Lorbeer raschelt grob. Knirscht Koriander, oder knackt er, wenn man ihn zerdrückt? Der dunkelbraune Sternanis, schrundig gekerbt, setzt der Berührung stillen, kantigen Widerstand entgegen.

Die Nase freilich kommt zu kurz: Aus den offenliegenden Gewürzen sind die duftenden ätherischen Öle längst entwichen. Aber wie zum Ausgleich findet sich gleich daneben ein Set von 15 kleinen Fläschchen: Gewürzöle, Extrakt aus gepressten Kräutern. Und was da aus den gläsernen Hälsen steigt, stellt mit der Nase ordentlich was an: Es schmeichelt, betört, umnebelt zunächst, beißt aber bald, betäubt und erschlägt den Geruchssinn: Ingwer zieht bitter hoch, Dill müffelt, Petersilie riecht streng, Koriander stinkt – die Essenz vom Besten ist zu viel des Guten. Und man versteht, warum Duftstoffe in der Natur nur in Spuren vorkommen ...

FRANKFURTER RUNDSCHAU, Samstag, 22. Dezember 2001, Nr. 298/51, Magazin, S. 6–7

Level 3

1. Welche Farbe passt? ✓

> a. anthrazit, b. bleu, c. cerise, d. fliederfarben, e. fraise, f. karmesinrot,
> g. malvenfarben, h. scharlachrot, i. sepia, j. siena

1. kirschrot	6. karminrot
2. erdbeerfarben	7. dunkelbraun
3. mauve	8. rotbraun
4. helllila	9. schwarzgrau
5. hochrot	10. hellblau

2. Welches Wort hat die gleiche oder eine ähnliche Bedeutung? ✓

> a. das Bukett, b. der Drillich, c. flimmern, d. der Flint, e. glitschig, f. gluckern,
> g. die Grellheit, h. gustiös, i. moderig, j. schummerig, k. der Widerhall, l. zähflüssig,
> m. das Zwielicht

1. die Grelle	8. die Blume
2. das Dämmerlicht	9. muffig
3. dämmerig	10. viskos
4. flirren	11. schlüpfrig
5. das Echo	12. der Feuerstein
6. glucksen	13. der Drell
7. appetitlich	

3. Wie heißt das Adjektiv bzw. Substantiv? ✓

1. sehr dunkel
2. sehr schwarz
3. sehr rot
4. sehr duster
5. sehr großer Lärm
6. großer Krach
7. großer Spektakel

4. Welches Wort passt nicht? ✓

1. das Elfenbein, die Intarsia, das Perlmutt, die Schlacke
2. der Makadam, der Schotter, der Schrott, der Splitt
3. der Draht, der Faden, der Kitt, das Tau
4. der Cord, die Kordel, der Manchester, der Rips
5. das Bouclé, das Kammgarn, der Nessel, der Zwirn
6. der Hauch, die Spur, der Stich, der Teer
7. der Pelz, das Pergament, der Schmirgel, das Wildleder
8. das Gebrumm, das Gedudel, das Gepolter, das Gewühl

5. Welches Verb passt? ✓

> a. brummen, b. knattern, c. plätschern, d. prasseln, e. pumpern, f. quatschen,
> g. schmettern, h. surren

1. Kameras
2. Maschinengewehre
3. der Bach
4. der Bär
5. der sumpfige Boden
6. der Hagel
7. das Herz
8. Trompeten

6. Ergänzen Sie die Farben. ✓

1. blei___
2. rubin___
3. moos___
4. dotter___
5. schwanen___
6. marine___
7. kohl___

7. Welches Adjektiv passt am besten? ✓

> a. dickflüssig, b. pikant, c. ranzig, d. stickig, e. süffig, f. weich

1. die Butter
2. das Bier
3. der Whisky
4. die Soße
5. die Luft
6. das Blut

8. In jedem Satz fehlt ein Wort. ✓

> beäugen, Chemiefaser, düster, flackert, gemasertem, knorrig, säuerliche, schweifen,
> spähen, Steifleinen, Tüll, verblichen

1. Die Hosen aus _____ können in der Waschmaschine gewaschen und ohne Bügeln wieder getragen werden.
2. Die neuen Jacken, ohne _____, Futter und Schulterpolster, sind sehr leicht.
3. Sie trug ein bodenlanges, pastellfarbenes Ballkleid aus _____.
4. Die Bäume sind alt und _____.
5. Meine Großeltern hatten eine alte Standuhr aus fein _____ Holz.
6. Die Zukunft sieht _____ aus.
7. Die Farben sind _____.
8. Eine Kerze _____ und wirft Schatten an die Wände.
9. Er richtete sich auf, um über das Gestrüpp zu _____.
10. Die anderen Bewerber _____ ihn misstrauisch.
11. Er lässt seine Blicke durch das Zimmer _____.
12. Der _____ Geruch von Joghurt und Buttermilch hat mich schon als Kind angewidert.

9. Schriftliche Übung. Wählen Sie ein Thema. Achten Sie auf Geräusche, Gerüche, Farben usw.

1. Beschreiben Sie einen Bahnhof voller Menschen.
2. Beschreiben Sie einen Sonnenuntergang am Strand.
3. Beschreiben Sie einen Jahrmarkt.

10. Übersetzen Sie ins Englische.

Aus „Die Farben des Schnees" von Stefanie Bisping

Vor dem Fenster ziehen verschneite Berge vorbei, kleine Inseln und manchmal ein paar Holzhäuser. Das Wetter wechselt in Minutenschnelle. Helles Morgenlicht verdüstert sich im dichten Schneetreiben, bald darauf strahlt die Sonne aus jäh aufgerissenem Himmel. Dann schimmern Berge und Felsen weiß, bläulich und violett, zu ihren Füßen liegt spiegelglatt dunkelblaues Wasser. Kaum etwas dürfte wohl so schwer auf dem Gemüt lasten, dass man beim Anblick dieser einsamen, erhabenen Landschaft nicht ein bisschen frohlocken wollte. Weil es so schön ist, so still und so weit weg von allem. Da vergisst man vieles – sogar, dass man im rauen Seegang der Nacht zuvor um ein Haar aus der Koje gefallen wäre. So stark schlingerte das Schiff.

Die Landungsbrücke klappt hinunter, und hinter tanzenden Schneeflocken schimmert die Stadt Tromsø in verschiedenen Schattierungen von Blau. Noch Anfang des 20. Jahrhunderts sah man hier gelegentlich Trapper mit Eisbären an der Leine durch die Straßen gehen. Es waren Tiere, deren Mütter die Männer oben in Spitzbergen erlegt hatten. Das „Paris des Nordens" nennen Einheimische ihre Stadt. 6500 Studenten, vielen Kneipen und Geschäften sowie der angeblich nördlichsten Brauerei der Welt ist diese Einschätzung zu verdanken. Und: In Tromsø stehen die letzten Ampeln auf den nördlichsten 900 Kilometern norwegischen Bodens. „Tor zur Arktis" ist der passendere Beiname für die Stadt, von der aus Fridtjof Nansen und Roald Amundsen ihre Polarexpeditionen begannen. Vergleiche mit irgendwelchen Metropolen hat sie gar nicht nötig: mit den bunten Holzhäusern auf der Stadtinsel Tromsøya und auf dem Festland jenseits des Tromsøysundes, den eine kilometerlange Brücke überspannt, mit dem märchenhaften Lichterglanz, der die frühe Dämmerung des Winters erhellt ...

Im Herbst wird Schellfisch gefangen, im Winter Dorsch, im Sommer kommen Seelachs und Touristen, die auf die Mitternachtssonne neugierig sind. Knapp 4000 Rentiere weiden im Sommer auf den Hügeln der Insel Mageroya, den Winter verbringen sie auf den Hochebenen des Festlands. Aber auch in der dunklen Jahreszeit sind Tiere da: Schneehasen, Wiesel, Nerze und Lemminge. Doch die lassen sich kaum blicken. Stattdessen sieht man Schnee satt und Menschen, die auf Tretschlitten ihre Einkäufe erledigen, und warmes Licht, das aus roten, gelben und weißen Holzhäusern hinaus in die Kälte scheint.

Von Ende November bis Ende Januar dauert die Polarnacht. Wenn die Sonne zum ersten Mal wieder über den Horizont steigt, wird am Nordkap – wie überall nördlich des Polarkreises – ein Sonnenfest gefeiert. Die Kinder haben schulfrei und malen sich Sonnen in die Gesichter. Von da an geht es zügig voran, schon einen Monat später bleibt es bis zu frühen Nachmittag hell. Dann erst geht die Sonne in dramatischen Farben unter und färbt die tief verschneite Landschaft golden, orange und hellblau, die Dämmerung ist lang und so schön, dass es den Puls beschleunigt. Und da scheint es gar nicht mehr unmöglich, hier zu leben ...

FRANKFURTER RUNDSCHAU, Samstag, 10. November 2001, Nr. 262/45, Magazin, S. 8

11. Lesen Sie den folgenden Artikel.

„Grau erinnert an Grauen"

Farbenstreit im neuen Polizeipräsidium: Der Behördenchef favorisiert gelbe, die Neubauleitung graue Lamellen

Von Hans-Jürgen Biedermann

Über das neue Polizeipräsidium, dem mächtigen Klotz am Alleenring, wird wieder genörgelt. Die Architektur war ja von Anfang an ein Zankapfel. Wegen des anthrazitfarbenen Blendwerks an der Fassade bezeichnen Spötter den Bau als „größtes Mausoleum der Stadt", das so gar nicht dem Leitbild einer bürgernahen Polizei entspreche. Andere Kritiker sprechen von einer „Festung", die sich mit dem Pentagon in der US-Hauptstadt vergleichen lasse. Keine schmeichelhaften Attribute – ein Gebäude als Reizobjekt.

Die Gewerkschaft der Polizei (GdP) setzt jetzt einen drauf und mäkelt auch noch an der Innenausstattung herum. „Farbenstreit im Polizeipräsidium", titelt Heinz Homeyer, der Vorsitzende der Frankfurter Bezirksgruppe, eine GdP-Erklärung.

Es geht um die Lamellenvorhänge an den Fenstern. Deren Farbgebung ist offenbar so wichtig, dass sich sogar die Behördenleitung damit befasst hat. Polizeipräsident Harald Weiß-Bollandt favorisierte nach Rücksprache mit dem Personalrat ein „freundliches Gelb" und bat die Neubauleitung, einen entsprechenden Auftrag zu erteilen. Doch die ignorierte das Ansinnen und hat sich für „Mittelgrau" entschieden. Das hält die Gewerkschaft für einen mittleren Skandal. „Grau erinnert eher an Grauen, schlägt auf die Psyche und wirkt demotivierend", stellt Heinz Homeyer einigermaßen entsetzt fest. Werden die Beamten jetzt zu grauen Mäusen?

Die Neubauleitung selbst darf sich zum grau-gelben Disput nicht äußern. Auskünfte erteilt die vorgesetzte Behörde, das Justizministerium. Dessen Sprecherin Susanne Rothenhöfer kann die Aufregung überhaupt nicht verstehen. Man habe sich doch „von vornherein auf Grau geeinigt". Diese Farbe sei aus Sicht des Arbeitsschutzes „optimal" und von einem „Lichtplaner" ausdrücklich empfohlen worden. Sie passt im Übrigen auch zum Design der Büromöbel.

„Alles grau in grau", stöhnt Heinz Homeyer deshalb und wundert sich über das Farbenverständnis von Architekten und Neubauleitung. „Die halten Graustufen offenbar für Regenbogenfarben."

Auf die Bauleitung ist der Gewerkschafter noch aus einem anderen Grund nicht gut zu sprechen. Er vermutet, sie habe ihre Kontrollfunktion gegenüber den Baufirmen nur unzureichend wahrgenommen, weshalb der Umzugstermin wackele. Tatsächlich wettet derzeit niemand darauf, dass die Möbelwagen im Juni zwischen Friedrich-Ebert-Anlage (Altbau) und Adickesalle (Neubau) pendeln werden. Wenn doch, „dann ziehen wir auf einer Baustelle ein", befürchtet Homeyer. Die Kantine für die mehr als 2000 Bediensteten werde wohl nicht bis zur Jahresmitte fertig. Dann heißt es halt: Brotbüchsen auspacken und Butterstullen futtern.

FRANKFURTER RUNDSCHAU, Samstag, 22. Dezember 2001, Nr. 298/51, S. 8

a. Vokabelübung. Wie heißt das Wort auf Englisch?

1. der Klotz	6. das Reizobjekt
2. nörgeln	7. mäkeln
3. der Zankapfel	8. die Rücksprache
4. das Leitbild	9. das Grauen
5. die Festung	10. die Graustufe

b. Schriftliche Übung. Fassen Sie den Artikel in einem Absatz zusammen.

Unit 8

Shapes and patterns

Level 1

Shapes and lines

Form, die (-en)	form, shape
Linie, die (-n)	line
gerade	straight
Gerade, die (-n)	straight line
krumm	bent, crooked
die krumme/ gekrümmte Linie	curved line
Figur, die (-en)	figure
Kreis, der (-e)	circle
rund	round
Rundung, die (-en)	curve
Kurve, die (-n)	curve, bend, corner
Biegung, die (-en)	bend, curve, twist, turn
gebogen	curved, hooked
Bogen, der (-; ¨ S)	curve, arch, arc, bend
oval	oval
Kugel, die (-n)	ball, sphere
kugelförmig	spherical
Ecke, die (-n)	corner
Dreieck, das (-e)	triangle
dreieckig	triangular
Viereck, das (-e)	square
viereckig	square

Rechteck, das (-e)	rectangle, oblong
rechteckig	rectangular, oblong
Kreuz, das (-e)	cross
Stern, der (-e)	star
Pyramide, die (-n)	pyramid
scharf	sharp
spitz	pointed, sharp
Spitze, die (-n)	tip, top
Seite, die (-n)	side
Punkt, der (-e)	point, spot, dot
flach	flat
unregelmäßig	irregular
ungleichmäßig	irregular
uneben	uneven, bumpy
Grenze, die (-n)	boundary, limit

Patterns

Muster, das (-)	pattern
gemustert	patterned
Streifen, der (-)	stripe, streak
gestreift	striped
kariert	checked
gepunktet	spotted, polka-dot
geblümt	floral [fabric]

Level 2

Shapes and lines

parallel	parallel
Parallele, die (-n)	parallel (line)
Strich, der (-e)	stroke, line
senkrecht	perpendicular
waagerecht	horizontal
kreuzweise	cross-wise
quer	sideways, cross-wise, diagonally
Quadrat, das (-e)	square
quadratisch	square
Rand, der (¨er)	edge, side, rim, brim, margin
kreisförmig	circular
Halbkreis, der (-e)	semicircle
konzentrische Kreise, pl.	concentric circles
Kreisbogen, der (-; ¨ S, AU, CH)	arc
abgerundet	rounded
Knick, der (-e)	sharp bend
diagonal	diagonal
Diagonale, die (-n)	diagonal
schräg	diagonal
(a)symmetrisch	(a)symmetric
das gleichseitige Dreieck	equilateral triangle
das gleichschenklige Dreieck	isosceles triangle
Kegel, der (-)	cone
kegelförmig	conical
konisch	conical
pyramidenförmig, -artig	pyramidal
Würfel, der (-)	cube
Zylinder, der (-)	cylinder

zylindrisch	cylindrical
Pfeil, das (-e)	arrow
kreuzförmig	cruciform
Hakenkreuz, das (-e)	swastika
schmal	narrow
stumpf	dull, blunt
schief	crooked
Winkel, der (-)	angle
Vieleck, das (-e)	polygon
das regelmäßige Vieleck	regular polygon
Umlaufbahn, die (-en)	orbit
Kreisbahn, die (-en)	orbit
Spirale, die (-n)	spiral
spiralförmig, spiralig	spiral
Profilbild, das (-er)	profile
Seitenansicht, die (-en)	profile
Umriss, der (-e)	outline, contours
Schaubild, das (-er)	graph, diagram

Patterns

quer/horizontal gestreift	diagonally/ horizontally striped
Querstreifen, der (-)	diagonal stripe
Nadelstreifen, der (-)	pinstripe
Motiv, das (-e)	motif
gefleckt	spotted
gescheckt	spotted [animal]
getigert	striped
Karo, das (-s)	check
Schild, der (-e)	shield, escutcheon
Wappen, das (-)	coat-of-arms

Level 3

Shapes and lines

Gestalt, die (-en)	form, shape, build
Gestaltung, die (no pl.)	shaping, forming; configuration
Anordnung, die (-en)	arrangement, order, formation
das griechische Kreuz	Greek cross

das lateinische Kreuz	Latin cross	wirbeln	to twirl
Keltenkreuz, das (-e)	Celtic cross	wellig, gewellt	wavy
Andreaskreuz, das (-e)	St. Andrew's cross	zusammengedreht	twisted
David(s)stern, der (-e)	Star of David	Ausbuchtung, die (-en)	bulge
konkav	concave	Wulst, der or die (¨e)	bulge
konvex	convex	Krümmung, die (-en)	curvature
der rechte Winkel	right angle	Labyrinth, das (-e)	maze
der spitze Winkel	acute angle		
der stumpfe Winkel	obtuse angle	*Patterns*	
der gestreckte Winkel	straight angle	Dessin, das (-s)	design, pattern
Kante, die (-n)	edge	mit Blumen/Sternen übersät	studded with flowers/stars
das unregelmäßige Viereck	irregular quadrilateral	mit Nieten verziert	studded [clothing]
Parallelogramm, das (-e)	parallelogram	marmoriert	marbled
Rhombus, der (-ben)	rhombus	Marmorierung, die (-en)	marbling
Trapezoid, das (-e)	trapezoid	gerippt	ribbed; fluted
knollig	bulbous	meliert	mottled
Wölbung, die (-en)	bulge, curve, arch, vault	gesprenkelt	mottled, speckled
sich wölben	to bulge	klecksig	blotchy
gewölbt	arched	getupft	speckled
Schattenriss, der (-e)	silhouette	geädert	veined
Schattenbild, das (-er)	silhouette	Fischgrät(en)muster, das (-)	herringbone pattern
Umlauf, der (¨e)	revolution	Hahnentrittmuster, das (-)	dog's tooth check
sich winden	to wind	Schottenmuster, das (-)	tartan pattern
gewunden	sinuous, tortuous, serpentine		

Size and quantity

Level 1

General

groß	big, large, tall	Breite, die (-n)	width, breadth
Größe, die (-n)	size	Raum, der (no pl.)	space, expanse
klein	little, small	Zwischenraum, der (¨e)	space, gap
Dimension, die (-en)	dimension	Platz, der (¨e)	space, area
hoch	high, tall	kurz	short
Höhe, die (-n)	height, altitude	Menge, die (-n)	quantity, amount
lang	long		
Länge, die (-n)	length	Messgerät, das (-e)	gauge

Bandmaß, das (-e)	tape measure
Waage, die (-n)	scales, balance, weighing machine

Weights and measures

Maß, das (-e)	measurement
Gewicht, das (-e)	weight
Meter, der (-)	metre
Kilometer, der (-)	kilometre
Liter, der or das (-)	litre
Gramm, das (-)	gramme
Kilo(gramm), das (-)	kilo(gramme)
Pfund, das (-e; after numbers -)	pound
Lineal, das (-e)	ruler
Grad, der (-e; after numbers -)	degree
Wert, der (-e)	value
etw messen	to measure sth
wiegen	to weigh
Prozent, das (-e; after numbers -)	per cent

Capacity, volume and quantity

Zahl, die (-en)	number, figure
Gesamtzahl, die (-en)	total number
Summe, die (-n)	sum
Quantität, die (-en)	quantity
Masse, die (-n)	mass, lots
nichts	nothing
wenig	little
ein wenig	a little
fast	almost
voll	full
Hand voll, die (-)	handful
leer	empty
ein bisschen	a little
viel	a lot (of)
genug	enough
wie viel	how much, how many
halb so viel	half as much
mindestens	at least
höchstens	at the most
Ganze(s), das (adj. decl.; no pl.)	the whole thing, everything
ein paar	a couple

mehrere	several, a number of
einige	some, a number of

Portion

Stück, das (-e)	piece, parcel, plot
Teil, der (-e)	part
Hauptteil, der (-e)	major part
Einzelteil, das (-e)	individual/separate part
etw teilen	to divide (up)/share sth
etw schneiden	to slice sth
Portion, die (-en)	portion
Paar, das (-e)	pair
Hälfte, die (-n)	half
Tafel, die (-n)	bar

Accumulation

Haufen, der (-)	heap, pile
ein ganzer Haufen	a whole bunch of
etw häufen	to pile/heap up sth
sich häufen	to mount up, occur increasingly often
Häufung, die (-en)	accumulation; increasing number
Sammlung, die (-en)	collection
Ansammlung, die (-en)	pile, heap; collection
jede Menge	heaps, loads, tons

Distance

hier	here
da	(over) there
dort	(over) there
weit	far, a long way
nah(e)	near, close
Nähe, die (no pl.)	closeness, proximity, vicinity, area near(by)
nächst	next
bei	at, close to
Entfernung, die (-en)	distance

Increase and decrease

größer werden	to become larger
länger werden	to become longer

höher werden	to increase in height	sich vergrößern	to increase, be extended, be enlarged, expand
billiger werden	to decrease in price	Vergrößerung, die (-en)	increase, enlargement, magnification
wachsen	to grow		
zunehmen	to increase, gain weight	etw verstärken	to strengthen/ intensify/increase/ amplify sth
Zunahme, die (-n)	increase, rise		
an Größe/Länge usw. zunehmen	to increase in size/length etc.	Verstärkung, die (no pl.)	strengthening, intensification, increase
abnehmen	to decrease, lose weight, diminish	steigen	to increase, rise
Abnahme, die (-n; pl. rare)	decrease, decline	Steigerung, die (-en)	increase, heightening, intensification
zurückgehen	to disappear, go down, subside, decrease	Anstieg, der (-e)	rise, increase
		etw verbreiten	to spread/ disseminate/ circulate sth
Rückgang, der (no pl.)	drop, fall, decline, decrease		
etw senken	to lower/sink/reduce sth	sich verbreiten	to spread
		Entwicklung, die (-en)	development, expansion, generation
sich senken	to fall, come down, subside, sink, fall		
Senkung, die (-en)	lowering, reduction	Schwellung, die (-en)	swelling
etw vergrößern	to increase/extend/ enlarge/expand sth	etw aufblasen	to blow up/inflate sth
		etw aufpumpen	to pump up/inflate sth

Level 2

General

Rahmen, der (-)	scope, bounds	Fläche, die (-n)	area, surface, side, face
in der Breite	widthways, widthwise	Umfang, der (¨e; pl. rare)	size, extent, perimeter, circumference, girth
etw verbreitern	to widen sth		
sich verbreitern	to widen out, get wider		
Dicke, die (-n)	thickness	Proportion, die (-en)	proportion
Tiefe, die (-n)	depth	in den Proportionen stimmen/nicht stimmen	to be in/out of proportion
niedrig	low, short		
massig	massive, bulky	winzig	minuscule, minute
geräumig	spacious, roomy	Verhältnis, das (-se)	ratio
reichlich Platz	ample room	ein Verhältnis von 3 zu 1	a ratio of 3 to 1
Oberfläche, die (-n)	surface, surface area		

Weights and measures

Milliliter, der or das (-)	millilitre
Zentimeter, der (-)	centimetre
Quadratkilometer, der (-)	square kilometre
etw ausmessen	to measure (out) sth
etw abmessen	to measure off sth, measure up sth
an/bei jmdm Maß nehmen	to take sb's measurements
Durchschnitt, der (-e)	average
durchschnittlich	on average
im Durchschnitt	on average

Capacity, volume and quantity

zahllos	countless
keinerlei	none (at all)
vielerlei	many different, all kinds of
mehrfach	multiple
etwa	about
ungefähr	about, approximately, roughly
beinahe	almost
lediglich	only
zusätzlich	additional
kaum	hardly
knapp	short, scarce
voller	full of
reichen	to be enough
ausreichen	to be sufficient
genügen	to be sufficient
nicht genügend	insufficient
gesamt	whole
insgesamt	altogether
sämtlich	all, every single one
vollständig	complete
Mehrheit, die (-en)	majority
Mehrzahl, die (no pl.)	majority
überwiegend	vast majority of, most
Minderheit, die (-en)	minority
Minderzahl, die (no pl.)	minority
riesig	enormous, huge

gewaltig	enormous, huge
übrig	left over
Rest, der (-e)	remainder, leftover
Minimum, das (-ma)	minimum
Maximum, das (-ma)	maximum
Reichtum, der (¨er)	wealth
Überfluss, der (no pl.)	abundance
Fülle, die (no pl.)	wealth, abundance
Überfülle, die (no pl.)	superabundance
Übermaß, das (no pl.)	excess

Portion

Anteil, der (-e)	share
teilweise	partly; partial; in places
partiell	partial
etw austeilen	to distribute sth
etw verteilen	to space/spread sth out, distribute
Scheibe, die (-n)	disc, slice
Schnitte, die (-n)	slice
Abschnitt, der (-e)	section, segment
(mit jmdm) halbe–halbe machen (coll.)	to go halves (with sb)
Dosis, die (-sen)	dose
Ration, die (-en)	ration

Accumulation

etw häufeln	to heap/pile up sth
etw aufhäufen	to pile sth up, accumulate sth
sich aufhäufen	to pile up, accumulate
Stapel, der (-)	stack, pile
etw (auf)stapeln	to pile up/stack sth
Stoß, der (¨e)	pile, stack
etw türmen	to stack/pile sth up
sich türmen	to be piled up

Distance

Strecke, die (-n)	distance, way
fern	distant, a long way away
entfernt	distant, far, away

weit weg/entfernt	far away	sich vervielfachen	to multiply (several times)
Abstand, der (¨e)	distance	etw/sich verdoppeln	to double sth/double
daneben	next to	etw/sich	to triple sth/triple
drüben	over there	verdreifachen	

Increase and decrease

		etw erhöhen	to raise/increase/heighten sth
etw schwächen	to weaken sth		
etw verengen	to narrow/restrict sth	etw ausbreiten	to spread out sth
sich verengen	to narrow, contract, become constricted	sich ausbreiten	to spread, extend, stretch out
		etw strecken	to stretch sth
etw vertiefen	to deepen/strengthen sth	etw dehnen	to stretch/lengthen sth
sich vertiefen	to deepen, become more intense	Dehnung, die (-en)	stretching, lengthening
etw verkürzen	to shorten sth	an Wert verlieren/gewinnen	to decrease/increase in value
etw verlängern	to lengthen/extend/prolong sth	an Gewicht zunehmen	to increase in weight
Verlängerung, die (-en)	lengthening, extension, prolongation	an Größe verlieren	to decrease in size
		im Preis fallen	to decrease in price
in die Länge/Breite wachsen	to lengthen/broaden out	etw ergänzen	to add to/amplify/amend sth
Zusatz, der (¨e)	addition, additive, addendum	Ergänzung, die (-en)	completion, enlargement, addition
anwachsen	to increase		
etw vervielfachen	to multiply/greatly increase sth	etw zusammenpressen	to compress sth

Level 3

General

im Kleinformat	in miniature	maßstäblich, maßstab(s)gerecht, maßstab(s)getreu	scale, (true) to scale
etw versetzt anordnen	to stagger sth		
der Länge nach	lengthways	Landvermessung, die (-en)	surveying
Ausmaß, das (-e)	size, magnitude, dimensions [pl.]	Landvermesser(in), der/die (-/nen)	surveyor
Abmessung, die (-en)	dimension, measurement	Reichweite, die (-n)	range

Weights and measures

Ausdehnung, die (-en)	extent	Durchmesser, der (-)	diameter
Flächenausdehnung, die (-en)	area	Halbmesser, der (-)	radius
Maßstab, der (¨e)	scale, standard, ruler	Radius, der (-dien)	radius

Fuß, der (no pl.)	foot
Zoll, der (no pl.)	inch
Meile, die (-n)	mile
Yard, das (-s)	yard
Tonne, die (-n)	ton
Gallone, die (-n)	gallon
Pint, das (- or -s)	pint
Unze, die (-n)	ounce
Hektar, der (-)	hectare
Ar, das (-e)	are (= 100 square metres)
Zentner, der (-)	hundredweight

Capacity, volume and quantity

betragen	to be, amount to [so much]
Betrag, der (¨e)	sum, amount
Anzahl, die (-en)	number, amount
zirka (circa)	about, approximately
gering	low, small, little
reichlich vorhanden sein	to be abundant
Unmenge, die (-n)	mass, enormous number
Unmasse, die (-n)	load
Unzahl, die (no pl.)	enormous number
unzählig	innumerable, countless
unzahlbar	uncountable
zahlreich	numerous
beträchtlich	considerable
erheblich	considerable
ansehnlich	considerable
mannigfach	multifarious, manifold
Rauminhalt, der (-e)	capacity, cubic content
Fassungsvermögen, das (-)	capacity
fassen	to hold
spärlich	scanty
dürftig	meagre
kärglich	meagre, sparse
mick(e)rig (coll.)	measly
enorm	enormous

ungeheuer	enormous, tremendous, immense
Vielzahl, die (no pl.)	multitude
Atom, das (-e)	atom
Teilchen, das (-)	particle
Körnchen, das (-)	particle

Portion

Scherbe, die (-n)	fragment, broken piece
Brocken, der (-)	lump, chunk, scrap
Strang, der (¨e)	cord, strand, rope, hank, skein
Strähne, die (-n)	strand, skein, hank
Bruchteil, der (-e)	fraction
Spur, die (-en)	fraction
Prozentsatz, der (¨e)	percentage
bruchstückhaft	fragmentary
fragmentarisch	fragmentary
Fetzen, der (-)	shred, tatter, scrap
etw aufteilen	to divide/split up sth; share out sth
etw einteilen	to divide up sth
etw unterteilen	to (sub)divide sth

Accumulation

etw anhäufen	to accumulate/amass sth
sich anhäufen	to accumulate, pile up
Anhäufung, die (-en)	accumulation, amassing
etw aufschichten	to stack/build/pile sth up
Aufschichtung, die (-en)	stacking, piling up, building
etw in etw stopfen	to cram sth into sth
gerammelt voll sein	to be crammed

Distance

(sich) nähern	to approach
sich entfernen	to move away
Abstand zu jmdm/etw wahren	to keep one's distance from sb/sth
angrenzend	adjoining
dicht	close

Ferne, die (-n)	distance	sich weiten	to widen, dilate, swell
Weite, die (-n)	distance		
weitab	far away	Ausweitung, die (-en)	widening, expansion, spreading

Increase and decrease

umfangreicher werden	to increase in volume	etw ausdehnen	to stretch/expand/ increase sth
an Umfang zunehmen	to increase in volume	Ausdehnung, die (-en)	expansion, extension, expanse
Zuwachs, der (no pl.)	growth, increase	etw in die Höhe treiben	to inflate sth
Wachstum, das (no pl.)	growth	anschwellen	to swell, grow louder, rise, grow
etw vermehren	to increase sth		
sich vermehren	to increase, multiply, reproduce, propagate	Anschwellung, die (-en)	swelling
		aufquellen	to swell up, rise (up)
Vermehrung, die (-en)	increase, multiplying, propagation	sich zusammenziehen	to contract, close up
sich stark vermehren	to proliferate	schrumpfen	to shrink, contract, shrivel, decrease, dwindle
wuchern	to proliferate, run wild, be rampant		
etw blähen	to swell/distend/ billow/fill sth	etw schrumpfen lassen	to cause sth to shrink
sich blähen	to billow out, dilate, puff oneself up	Schrumpfung, die (no pl.)	shrinkage
etw erweitern	to widen/enlarge/ expand sth	etw beeinträchtigen	to restrict/diminish/ impair/reduce sth
sich erweitern	to widen, enlarge, expand	etw vermindern	to reduce/decrease/ lessen/lower sth
Erweiterung, die (-en)	widening, enlargement, expansion	sich vermindern	to decrease, diminish
		Verminderung, die (-en)	reduction, decrease, lessening

Containers

Level 1

Dishes and pots

(See also Unit 1, Kitchenware)

		Büchse, die (-n)	can, tin
		Pappbecher, der (-)	paper cup
		Blumentopf, der (¨e)	flower pot
		Bierkrug, der (¨e)	beer mug, tankard
Glas, das (¨er)	jar, glass		
Teetasse, die (-n)	teacup	Ölkanne, die (-n)	oilcan
Vase, die (-n)	vase	Nachttopf, der (¨e)	chamber pot
Dose, die (-n)	can, tin, jar		

Boxes

Kasten, der (¨)	box, crate
Schmuckkasten, der (¨)	jewelry box
Kiste, die (-n)	box, chest, crate
Schachtel, die (-n)	box
Streichholzschachtel, die (-n)	matchbox
eine Schachtel Zigaretten	a pack of cigarettes
Karton, der (-s)	cardboard box, carton
Box, die (-en)	box
Kassette, die (-n)	box, case, strongbox
Kasse, die (-n)	cash box
Koffer, der (-)	suitcase
Handkoffer, der (-)	small suitcase
Kosmetikkoffer, der (-)	vanity case
Truhe, die (-n)	chest
Pillendose, die (-n)	pillbox

Baskets

Korb, der (¨e)	basket
Handkorb, der (¨e)	small basket
Papierkorb, der (¨e)	wastepaper basket
Einkaufskorb, der (¨e)	shopping basket
Wäschekorb, der (¨e)	laundry basket
Nähkorb, der (¨e)	sewing basket
Hängekorb, der (¨e)	hanging basket

Bottles

Flasche, die (-n)	bottle, baby's bottle
Parfümfläschchen, das (-)	perfume bottle
Weinflasche, die (-n)	wine bottle
Thermosflasche, die (-n)	thermos flask
in Flaschen	bottled

Bags

Tasche, die (-n)	bag, purse, case
Einkaufstasche, die (-n)	shopping bag
Handtasche, die (-n)	handbag
Brieftasche, die (-n)	wallet
Reisetasche, die (-n)	holdall, travelling bag
Tüte, die (-n)	bag, packet, cornet, cone
Papiertüte, die (-n)	paper bag
Plastiktüte, die (-n)	plastic bag
Sack, der (¨e)	sack, bag
Beutel, der (-)	bag, purse, carrier bag, pouch, paper bag
Plastikbeutel, der (-)	plastic bag
Teebeutel, der (-)	tea bag
Mappe, die (-n)	portfolio, briefcase, schoolbag
Schultasche, die (-n)	schoolbag
Schulmappe, die (-n)	schoolbag
Rucksack, der (¨e)	rucksack, backpack
Schlafsack, der (¨e)	sleeping bag

Barrels, buckets, tanks and tubs

Eimer, der (-)	bucket, pail
eimerweise	by the bucket
Fass, das (¨er)	barrel, keg, vat, churn, drum
Bierfass, das (¨er)	keg
Weinfass, das (¨er)	wine cask
Tonne, die (-n)	barrel, cask, drum, trash can
Wanne, die (-n)	tub, reservoir, oil pan
Badewanne, die (-n)	bathtub
Kessel, der (-)	tank
Tank, der (-s or -e)	tank
Becken, das (-)	basin, sink
Spülbecken, das (-)	sink
Waschbecken, das (-)	washbasin

Level 2

General

Behälter, der (-)	container
Container, der (-)	container
Gefäß, das (-e)	container, vessel
etw enthalten	to contain sth
in etw enthalten sein	to be contained in sth
Inhalt, der (-e)	contents

Boxes

Briefkasten, der (¨)	letter box
Karteikasten, der (¨)	file-card box
Nähkasten, der (¨)	sewing box
Zigarrenkiste, die (-n)	cigar box
Sandkasten, der (¨)	sandbox
Kohlenkasten, der (¨)	coal bin, coal box
Pappkarton, der (-s)	cardboard box
Pappschachtel, die (-n)	cardboard box
Milchtüte, die (-n)	milk carton
Milchpackung, die (-en)	milk carton
Saftpackung, die (-en)	juice carton
Eierkarton, der (-s)	egg carton, eggbox
Schuhkarton, der (-s)	shoe box
Hutschachtel, die (-n)	hatbox
Geigenkasten, der (¨)	violin case
Geschenkpackung, die (-en)	gift box
Geldschrank, der (¨e)	safe
Sparbüchse, die (-n)	money box

Bottles

Einwegflasche, die (-n)	non-returnable bottle
Wegwerfflasche, die (-n)	disposable bottle
Pfandflasche, die (-n)	returnable bottle
abgefüllt in	bottled in
Karaffe, die (-n)	carafe, decanter
Wärmflasche, die (-n)	hot-water bottle
Bettflasche, die (-n)	hot-water bottle
Bettwärmer, der (-)	hot-water bottle

Bags

Gefrierbeutel, der (-)	freezer bag
Einkaufsnetz, das (-e)	string bag
Müllbeutel, der (-)	rubbish bag, garbage bag
Mülltüte, die (-n)	bin liner
Schulranzen, der (-)	school satchel
Aktentasche, die (-n)	briefcase, portfolio, organizer
Aktenmappe, die (-n)	briefcase, portfolio
Umhängetasche, die (-n)	shoulder bag
Unterarmtasche, die (-n)	clutch bag
Kosmetiktäschchen, das (-)	vanity bag
Kleidersack, der (¨e)	suit bag
Tabak(s)beutel, der (-)	tobacco pouch
Sandsack, der (¨e)	sandbag, punch-bag
Postsack, der (¨e)	mailbag
Tragetasche, die (-n)	tote bag

Barrels, buckets, tanks and tubs

Kübel, der (-)	bucket, pail
Wasserkasten, der (¨)	water tank
Mülltonne, die (-n)	rubbish bin
Abfalleimer, der (-)	rubbish bin
Eiskühler, der (-)	ice bucket
Milchkanne, die (-n)	milk churn
Henkel, der (-)	handle
Ausguss, der (¨e)	sink
Spüle, die (-n)	sink

Carriers and racks

Brett, das (-er)	shelf
Regal, das (-e)	set of shelves
Handtuchhalter, der (-)	towel rail
Schlüsselring, der (-e)	key ring

Ständer, der (-)	stand	Fahrradständer, der (-)	bicycle rack
Kleiderständer, der (-)	coat stand	Ablage, die (-n)	place to keep/ put sth
Wäscheständer, der (-)	clothes horse	Gepäckablage, die (-n)	luggage rack
Kerzenständer, der (-)	candle holder	Gepäckträger, der (-)	luggage carrier [on bicycle]
Geschirrständer, der (-)	dish rack	Dachgepäckträger, der (-)	roof rack
Schirmständer, der (-)	umbrella stand	Gestell, das (-e)	rack

Level 3

Dishes and pots

(See also Unit 1, Kitchenware)

Pokal, der (-e)	goblet
Kelchglas, das (¨er)	goblet, goblet-shaped glass
Bierseidel, das (-)	beer mug, tankard
Napf, der (¨e)	(small) bowl
Urne, die (-n)	urn
Kanister, der (-)	can
Krügchen, das (-)	cruet

Boxes

Sarg, der (¨e)	coffin
Schatulle, die (-n)	money box, jewelry box
Etui, das (-s)	case
Zigarettenetui, das (-s)	cigarette case
Futteral, das (-e)	case
Stange Zigaretten, die (-n)	carton of cigarettes
Vitrine, die (-n)	glass case
Wahlurne, die (-n)	ballot box
Sammelbüchse, die (-n)	collecting box
Nistkasten, der (¨)	nesting box
Schaukasten, der (¨)	showcase, display case

Federkasten, der (¨)	pencil box
Handschuhfach, das (¨er)	glove compartment
Kummerkasten, der (¨)	suggestion box
Tresor, der (-e)	safe

Baskets

Deckelkorb, der (¨e)	basket with a lid
Henkelkorb, der (¨e)	basket with a handle
Drahtkorb, der (¨e)	wire basket
Tragekorb, der (¨e)	pannier
Reuse, die (-n)	fish trap, weir basket
Weidenkorb, der (¨e)	wicker basket

Bottles

Flakon, der or das (-s)	bottle, flacon
Korbflasche, die (-n)	demijohn
Bouteille, die (-n)	bottle
Pulle, die (-n; coll.)	bottle
Ampulle, die (-n)	ampoule
Flachmann, der (¨er)	hip flask
Glaskolben, der (-)	glass flask
(Glas)glocke, die (-n)	bell jar

Bags

Matchbeutel, der (-)	duffle bag
Matchsack, der (¨e)	duffle bag
Tornister, der (-)	knapsack, satchel

Brotbeutel, der (-)	haversack
Spucktüte, die (-n)	sick-bag
Leichensack, der ("e)	body bag
Airbag, der (-s)	airbag
Sitzsack, der ("e)	beanbag [= seat]
Futterbeutel, der (-)	nosebag
Satteltasche, die (-n)	saddlebag
Kissen, das (-)	sachet

Barrels, buckets, tanks and tubs

Spund, der ("e)	bung, spigot
Zapfen, der (-)	bung, spigot
Faul-, Klärbehälter, der (-)	septic tank

Spülkasten, der (")	cistern [of toilet]
Zisterne, die (-n)	cistern
Entwicklerschale, die (-n)	developing tank
Ölwanne, die (-n)	oil pan
Wasserspeicher, der (-)	tank, reservoir
Trog, der ("e)	trough, tub
Backtrog, der ("e)	dough trough
Bottich, der (-e)	tub, vat
Zuber, der (-)	washtub
Sauerstoffbehälter, der (-)	oxygen tank

Time

Level 1

The day, week and year

Tag, der (-e)	day
heute	today
gestern	yesterday
morgen	tomorrow
Morgen, der (-)	morning
Mittag, der (-e)	midday, noon
Nachmittag, der (-e)	afternoon
Abend, der (-e)	evening
Nacht, die ("e)	night
Mitternacht, die (no pl.)	midnight
Woche, die (-n)	week
Wochenende, das (-n)	weekend
Monat, der (-e)	month
Jahr, das (-e)	year
Jahreszeit, die (-en)	season
Frühling, der (-e)	spring
Frühjahr, das (no pl.)	spring
Herbst, der (-e)	autumn
Winter, der (-)	winter
Sommer, der (-)	summer
Datum, das (-ten)	date
Der Wievielte ist heute? —	What date is today? —

Heute ist der vierte März.	Today is the fourth of March.
Den Wievielten haben wir heute? —	What date is it today? —
Den zehnten November.	The tenth of November.

Clock time

Uhr, die (-en)	watch, clock, hour of the day
Wieviel Uhr ist es?	What time is it?
Wie spät ist es?	What time is it?
Es ist neun Uhr.	It is nine o'clock.
um neun Uhr	at nine o'clock
fünf nach neun	five past nine
zehn nach neun	ten past nine
Viertel nach neun	quarter past nine
zwanzig nach neun	twenty past nine
fünf vor halb zehn	twenty-five past nine
halb zehn	nine-thirty, half past nine
fünf nach halb zehn	twenty-five to ten
zwanzig vor zehn	twenty to ten
Viertel vor zehn	quarter to ten

Sekunde, die (-n)	second
Minute, die (-n)	minute
Stunde, die (-n)	hour

Time phrases

kurz	short(ly)
lange	a long time
jahrelang	for years
früh	early
spät	late
pünktlich	on time
gerade	just
jetzt	now
sofort	right away, now, immediately
dann	then
bald	soon
schon	already
noch	still, yet
oft	often
meistens	mostly, most of the time, usually

gewöhnlich	normally, usually
selten	seldom
immer	always
endlich	finally, at last
Mal, das (-e)	time
jedes Mal	every time, each time
diesmal	this time
einmal	once
manchmal	sometimes
mehrmals	several times
nie	never
niemals	never
nochmals	again, once more
nächst	next
plötzlich	sudden
Augenblick, der (-e)	moment
Moment, der (-e)	moment, minute
Beginn, der (no pl.)	beginning
Schluss, der (¨e)	end, conclusion
seit	since

Level 2

The day, week and year

heute Morgen	this morning
gestern Nachmittag	yesterday afternoon
morgen Abend	tomorrow evening
morgen früh	tomorrow morning
letzte Nacht	last night
übermorgen	the day after tomorrow
vorgestern	the day before yesterday
Vormittag, der (-e)	morning
morgens	in the morning
vormittags	in the morning(s)
mittags	at midday
nachmittags	in the afternoon(s)
abends	in the evening(s)
nachts	at night, in the night
Jahrzehnt, das (-e)	decade
Jahrhundert, das (-e)	century

Jahrtausend, das (-e)	millennium
Kalender, der (-)	calendar
im Januar	in January
am Montag	on Monday
Mitte September	mid–September
Ende Mai	at the end of May
bis	until, by
bis Anfang Februar	until/by the beginning of February
Werktag, der (-e)	weekday, workday
Feiertag, der (-e)	public holiday
Wochentag, der (-e)	weekday

Clock time

| zwei Uhr nachts | two a.m. |
| zwei Uhr nachmittags | two p.m. |

acht Uhr morgens	eight a.m.	kommend	coming, next
acht Uhr abends	eight p.m.	eben	just
zwölf Uhr mittags	12:00 noon	Weile, die (no pl.)	while
zwölf Uhr nachts	12:00 midnight	dauernd	continual, constant
gegen elf	around eleven	(un)regelmäßig	(ir)regular
Sommerzeit, die (no pl.)	summertime, daylight saving time	gleich	right away
		erst	right (now), just (now)
		zuerst	first (of all)

Time phrases

damals	then, at that time	zunächst	first (of all), at first
neulich	recently	zuletzt	finally, last
kürzlich	recently	schließlich	finally, eventually, after all
vor kurzem	recently	spätestens	at the latest
nun	now	jemals	ever
häufig	often, frequent	ein andermal	another time
ab und zu	now and then	irgendwann	sometime, some day
öfter	now and then, every once in a while	vorbei	over
		danach	after that, then
Vergangenheit, die (-en; pl. rare)	past	bisher	until now, up to now
Gegenwart, die (no pl.)	present	vorher	before
		nachher	afterwards
Zukunft, die (no pl.)	future	hinterher	afterwards
		kaum	hardly, scarcely
bereits	already	allmählich	gradually
vergangen	last, past	sobald	as soon as
		ewig	eternally, for ages
		ständig	continual, constant

Level 3

The day, week and year

tagsüber	during the day	gestrig	yesterday's, of yesterday
täglich	daily	heutig	today's, of today
wöchentlich	weekly	morgig	tomorrow's, of tomorrow
monatlich	monthly		
jährlich	yearly	Silvester, das (-)	New Year's Eve
heute in einer Woche	a week from today	Neujahr, das (no pl.)	New Year
Schaltjahr, das (-e)	leap year		
Tagesanbruch, der (¨e)	dawn	### Clock time	
Sonnenaufgang, -untergang, der (¨e)	sunrise/sunset	fünfzehn Uhr fünfundvierzig	15:45
		dreizehn Uhr fünfzehn	13:15
		zwanzig Uhr dreißig	20:30

Viertelstunde, die (-n)	quarter of an hour	darauf	after that, then
		daraufhin	after that, following that, thereupon
Dreiviertelstunde, die (-n)	three quarters of an hour	gegenwärtig	present, current
viertel acht	quarter past seven	damalig	at that time
dreiviertel acht	quarter to eight	vorig	previous, last
ab zehn Uhr	from ten o'clock on	bisherig	up to now, to date, previous
vorgehen	to be fast [clock, watch]	künftig	future
nachgehen	to be slow [clock, watch]	stets	always
		hindurch	throughout
stehenbleiben	to stop [clock, watch]	gleichzeitig	at the same time, simultaneous
Punkt zehn	at ten on the dot		
Zeitzone, die (-n)	time zone	Zeitalter, das (-)	age, historical period

Time phrases

Frist, die (-en)	time period, deadline, grace period	Zeitraum, der (¨e)	(period of) time
		dauerhaft	lasting, durable
kurz-, langfristig	short/long-term	von . . . an	from . . . onward
zuweilen	from time to time, now and then	um . . . herum	around
		soeben	just now
hin und wieder	now and again	vorhin	before that, just a moment ago
gelegentlich	occasional		
neuerdings	recently, of late	bislang	so far, until now
vorläufig	temporary	heutzutage	today, nowadays, these days
vorübergehend	temporary		
des Öfteren (elev.)	on many occasions	eher	earlier, sooner
längst	a long time ago	im Laufe	in the course of
demnächst	soon, in the near future	im Voraus	in advance
		jeweils	currently, at the time
endgültig	once and for all		
rechtzeitig	in time, on time	inzwischen	in the meantime

Exercises

Level 1

1. Zu jedem Bild passt ein Nomen. ✓

a. der Bogen, b. das Dreieck, c. die Gerade, d. der Kreis, e. das Kreuz,
f. das Rechteck, g. der Stern, h. das Viereck

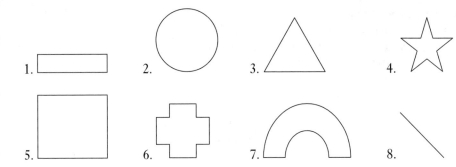

1. ▭   2. ◯   3. △   4. ☆

5. ◻   6. ✛   7. ◠   8. ╲

2. Wie heißt das Gegenteil? ✓

1. gerade	8. etwas
2. groß	9. dort
3. lang	10. die Länge
4. voll	11. der Tag
5. viel	12. früh
6. weit	13. oft
7. zunehmen	

3. Welches Wort hat die gleiche oder eine ähnliche Bedeutung? ✓

a. der Augenblick, b. die Biegung, c. die Büchse, d. einige, e. der Frühling,
f. die Kiste, g. die Menge, h. niemals, i. die Schachtel, j. spitz, k. die
Schulmappe

1. scharf	7. die Box
2. die Kurve	8. die Schultasche
3. die Quantität	9. der Moment
4. mehrere	10. das Frühjahr
5. die Dose	11. nie
6. der Kasten	

4. Was passt zusammen? ✓

a. ein Haufen, b. ein Paar, c. eine Portion, d. eine Sammlung, e. ein Stück,
f. eine Tafel

1. _____ Schuhe
2. _____ Schokolade
3. _____ Eis
4. _____ Kuchen
5. _____ Brennholz
6. _____ von Gemälden

5. Welches Wort passt nicht? ✓

1. der Beutel, der Eimer, der Sack, die Tüte
2. der Bierkrug, der Blumentopf, der Pappbecher, die Teetasse
3. der Hängekorb, der Koffer, die Truhe, die Reisetasche
4. gebogen, kariert, kugelförmig, rund
5. das Bandmaß, das Lineal, der Meter, die Waage
6. die Abnahme, der Anstieg, der Rückgang, die Senkung
7. die Entfernung, die Schwellung, die Steigerung, die Vergrößerung
8. der Abend, die Mitternacht, der Monat, der Nachmittag
9. die Frühe, der Herbst, der Sommer, der Winter
10. die Minute, die Sekunde, die Stunde, die Uhr

6. Die Uhrzeiten. ✓

1. 7.00	
2. 7.05	*fünf nach sieben*
3. 7.10	
4. 7.15	
5. 7.20	
6. 7.25	
7. 7.30	
8. 7.35	
9. 7.40	
10. 7.45	
11. 7.50	
12. 7.55	

7. Welche Definition passt? ✓

1. der Handkoffer	a. Korb für Papierabfälle
2. der Einkaufskorb	b. Korb für Schere, Nadeln, Garne usw.
3. der Handkorb	c. kleiner Koffer für Schminke
4. der Nähkorb	d. Kästchen zum Aufbewahren von Schmuck
5. der Kosmetikkoffer	e. kleiner Behälter für Pillen
6. der Papierkorb	f. Korb zum Tragen von Einkäufen
7. der Picknickkorb	g. großer Korb zum Aufbewahren usw. von Wäsche
8. die Pillendose	h. kleiner Korb mit Henkel
9. der Schmuckkasten	i. kleiner Koffer
10. der Wäschekorb	j. Korb für Picknicksachen

8. Was bedeuten die Wendungen?

1. jmdm einen Korb geben
2. viel auf dem Kasten haben (coll.)
3. eine alte Kiste (coll.)
4. knapp bei Kasse sein (coll.)
5. zur Flasche greifen
6. etw in der Tasche haben (coll.)
7. jmdm auf den Sack gehen (coll.)
8. tief in den Beutel greifen
9. ein Fass ohne Boden

9. Wie heißen die Zusammensetzungen? ✓

Einkaufs–	sack	1. *die Einkaufstasche*
Parfüm–	tüte	2.
Schlaf–	flasche	3.
Bade–	beutel	4.
Papier–	tasche	5.
Bier–	wanne	6.
Thermos–	fläschchen	7.
Spül–	schachtel	8.
Tee–	fass	9.
Streichholz–	becken	10.

10. In jedem Satz fehlt ein Wort. ✓

> gepunktete, Gesamtzahl, gestreiftes, Grenze, Hauptteil, ovales, Pyramide, viereckig, Zwischenraum

1. Sein Leid führt ihn bis an die _____ des Wahnsinns.
2. Der Tisch ist nicht rund, sondern _____.
3. Er ist 1,78 Meter, schlank, hat ein _____ Gesicht, blaue Augen und kurze blonde Haare.
4. Das Prisma hat die Form einer dreiseitigen _____.
5. Er trägt ein blauweiß _____ Hemd mit hohem Kragen und schmaller weißer Krawatte.
6. Der _____ zwischen den beiden Gebäuden soll ebenfalls genutzt werden.
7. Auf der Tanzfläche drehen sich _____ Glockenröcke.
8. Die _____ der Angeklagten erhöhte sich auf 47.
9. Das Krankenhaus hat den _____ der Baukosten getragen.

11. Übersetzen Sie ins Englische.

Aus „Wenn Waltraud ‚in die Himbeeren‘ geht, ist Marmelade angesagt" von Yvonne Holl

Mit dem linken Arm presst Waltraud Wagner den kleinen Weidenkorb an die Brust. So hat sie den rechten frei und schiebt ihn immer wieder in das Blätterdickicht. Wenn sie die Hand hinauszieht, liegen kleine rosa Früchte darin, die Waltraud Wagner in den Korb kullern lässt. Obwohl die Armbewegungen routiniert sind, dauert es eine Weile, bis zumindest der Korbboden bedeckt ist vom süßen Obst. „Himbeeren pflücken dauert am längsten", sagt sie, „weil die so klein sind". Bei Erdbeeren habe man schneller eine größere Menge beisammen und am schnellsten fülle sich ein Sammlerkorb mit Johannisbeeren. „Dafür machen Johannisbeeren daheim mehr Arbeit, weil man die Beeren vom Stiel zupfen muss", beschreibt die Eschersheimerin die Vor- und Nachteile der verschiedenen Beerensorten ...

Um 11 Uhr vormittags hat Waltraud Wagner genug Beeren für mehrere Glas Himbeermarmelade beisammen. Wie die meisten Pflücker, war auch sie früh dran. „Gehen sie mal in der Mittagshitze pflücken, dann wissen sie, warum hier morgens am meisten los ist", sagt Hofbetreiberin Tatjana Schneider. Seit 8 Uhr in der Früh steht sie im Laden auf dem Hof hinter einer großen weißen Waage. Erst wiegt sie die leeren Gefäße der Pflücker. Gerade kommen zwei Frauen aus Bad Homburg. Tatjana Schneider stellt den grünen Plastikeimer auf die Waage, der Zeiger schlägt aus und sie schreibt „300 Gramm" mit einem Marker auf den Plastikrand ...

FRANKFURTER RUNDSCHAU, Samstag, 30. Juni 2001, Nr. 149/26, S. 27

12. Lesen Sie den folgenden Text.

Der Saft zum Sommer

Die Erfrischung im Sommer ist selbst gemachter Johannisbeersaft mit Mineralwasser gespritzt. Zwei Kilogramm der roten Früchte geben ungefähr einen bis eineinhalb Liter Saft. Das Rezept: Die gewaschenen Beeren entstielen, in einem Kochtopf gut zerdrücken und einen Liter Wasser dazugeben. Das Ganze zum Kochen bringen, danach bei mäßiger Hitze ungefähr 20 Minuten weiter köcheln lassen.

Ein Baumwollhandtuch über ein Gefäß spannen, den Fruchtbrei darauf geben und den Saft ablaufen lassen. Reste mit einem Löffel ausdrücken. Einfacher geht es mit einem Haarsieb: Den Fruchtbrei in das Sieb geben und ausdrücken. Den Saft nach Belieben zuckern und etwa fünf Minuten kochen lassen. Bis zu 400 Gramm pro Liter Saft sind möglich. Die heiße Flüssigkeit in heiß ausgespülten Flaschen füllen und sofort mit Gummikappen verschließen. Damit sich der Saft länger hält, sollte er nach dem Öffnen im Kühlschrank aufbewahrt werden. Eine andere Methode ist das Dampf-Entsaften. Sie ist vor allem für größere Mengen von Früchten geeignet ...

Christina Hebel

FRANKFURTER RUNDSCHAU, Samstag, 30. Juni 2001, Nr. 149/26, S. 27

Fragen.

1. Wieviele Johannisbeeren braucht man, um einen Liter Johannisbeersaft zu machen?
2. Was kann man statt eines Baumwollhandtuchs gebrauchen? Was ist ein Vorteil dieser Methode?
3. Wieviel Zucker braucht man, um den Johannisbeersaft zu zuckern?
4. Was muss man tun, bevor man die Beeren zum Kochen bringt?
5. Wie wird der Saft aufbewahrt?
6. Wann gebraucht man einen Entsafter, um Johannisbeersaft zu machen?
7. Wie genießt man den Johannisbeersaft?

Level 2

1. Wie heißt das Gegenteil? ✓

1. waagerecht
2. symmetrisch
3. breit
4. die Höhe
5. die Mehrheit
6. das Minimum
7. an Wert verlieren
8. spitz
9. die Einwegflasche
10. regelmäßig
11. zuerst
12. vorher

2. Zu jedem Bild passt ein Nomen. ✓

a. das gleichschenklige Dreieck, b. der Kegel, c. konzentrische Kreise, d. das Pfeil,
e. das Schaubild, f. das regelmäßige Vieleck, g. der Würfel, h. der Zylinder

1.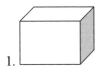
2.
3.
4.

5.
6.
7.
8.

3. Wie heißt das entsprechende Substantiv? ✓

1. parallel
2. diagonal
3. gerade
4. quer gestreift
5. spiralig
6. dreieckig
7. quadratisch

4. Welches Wort hat die gleiche oder eine ähnliche Bedeutung? ✓

a. der Abstand, b. anwachsen, c. ausreichen, d. etw aufstapeln, e. etw austeilen,
f. die Fülle, g. gewaltig, h. kegelförmig, i. kürzlich, j. die Mehrzahl, k. nun, l. schräg,
m. die Seitenansicht, n. teilweise, o. die Umlaufbahn, p. ungefähr, q. vormittags

1. diagonal
2. konisch
3. der Orbit
4. das Profilbild
5. etwa
6. genügen
7. die Mehrheit
8. riesig
9. der Reichtum
10. partiell
11. zunehmen
12. etw verteilen
13. etw aufhäufen
14. die Distanz
15. neulich
16. morgens
17. jetzt

5. Die Uhrzeiten. ✓

1. three a.m.	drei Uhr nachts
2. seven p.m.	
3. nine a.m.	
4. 12:00 midnight	
5. 12:00 noon	
6. three p.m.	
7. six a.m.	
8. nine p.m.	
9. two p.m.	

6. Kreuzworträtsel ✓

senkrecht:
1. Griff
2. Becken mit Abfluss
3. Schachtel aus Pappe
4. zugeteiltes Maß
5. Kasten zum Aufbewahren der Geige
8. Lederbeutel für Tabak
11. Kasten für die Karten/Zettel einer Kartei
15. 1/1000 Liter
18. Spülbecken
19. Übrigbleibendes
20. zugemessene Menge

waagerecht:

6. viereckiges Muster
7. Aktenmappe
9. kurz, eben noch zureichend
10. Safe
12. Gefäß für Schnittblumen
13. Eimer
14. Glasflasche mit Glasstöpsel
16. kleine Kiste für Zigarren
17. Beutel aus Plastik zum Transportieren von Müll
21. Milchpackung
22. abgeschnittene Scheibe
23. km^2

7. Welches Verb passt? ✓

a. fallen, b. machen, c. nehmen, d. stimmen, e. verlieren, f. wachsen, g. zeichnen

1. etw in Umrissen
2. einen Strich durch etw
3. aus dem Rahmen
4. in den Proportionen
5. an jmdm Maß
6. in die Länge
7. an Größe

8. Welcher Ausdruck passt nicht? ✓
1. sich ausbreiten, länger werden, sich verbreitern, sich verengen
2. die Ansammlung, der Stapel, der Stoß, die Strecke
3. der Behälter, der Container, der Inhalt, die Schachtel
4. die Bettflasche, der Bettwärmer, die Thermosflasche, die Wärmflasche
5. der Dachgepäckträger, das Regal, der Wäscheständer, das Waschbecken
6. die Ecke, der Knick, die Kreisbahn, der Winkel
7. jede Menge, lediglich, vielerlei, zahllos
8. die Brieftasche, die Handtasche, die Umhängetasche, die Unterarmtasche
9. der Jahrgang, das Jahrhundert, das Jahrtausend, das Jahrzehnt
10. der Arbeitstag, der Feiertag, der Werktag, der Wochentag

9. Auf Deutsch. ✓
1. tomorrow evening
2. this afternoon
3. yesterday evening
4. last night
5. this evening
6. tomorrow morning
7. tomorrow afternoon
8. the day after tomorrow
9. yesterday morning
10. the day before yesterday

10. In jedem Satz fehlt ein Wort. ✓

> Abfalleimer, Fahrradständer, Fläche, Gepäckablagen, Kerzenständer, Sandkasten, Schirmständer, Schulranzen

1. Die _____ entspricht ungefähr der Größe Vermonts.
2. Im Hof des Hauses ist ausreichend Platz für Fahrräder, aber kein _____.
3. Der Junge mit seinem _____ auf dem Rücken ist wohl auf dem Weg nach Hause.
4. Laut Polizeiangaben war eine brennende Kerze vom _____ auf das Sofa gefallen.
5. Dort steht eine Milchkanne als _____.
6. Die _____ über den Sitzen sind häufig für größere Koffer ungeeignet.
7. Biomüll gehört nicht in den _____, sondern auf den Komposthaufen im Garten.
8. Die Kinder bauen Burgen im _____.

11. Erklären Sie den Unterschied.
1. die Dicke, der Dicke
2. der Schild, das Schild
3. das Wappen, die Waffe
4. die Masse, das Maß
5. der Grad, die Gerade

12. Übersetzen Sie ins Englische.

Aus „Gelber oder blauer Sack – der Kampf um den Abfall" von Matthias
Bartsch

... Es geht, wie so oft beim Thema Müll, um viel Geld. Vier Milliarden Mark
pro Jahr kassiert die Firma DSD jährlich dafür, dass sie in der ganzen
Republik Blechdosen, Joghurtbecher, Milchtüten oder Saftkartons in gelben
Plastiksäcken sammelt und verwertet. Bezahlt wird das vom Verbraucher. Der
muss für jedes Produkt, dessen Verpackung einen „Grünen Punkt" trägt, über
einen höheren Einkaufspreis indirekt Lizenzgebühren an das DSD zahlen.
Knapp 45 Mark kostet das im Schnitt jeden Bundesbürger pro Jahr.
   Von diesem Milliarden-Kuchen will auch Landbell etwas abhaben. Das
Mainzer Unternehmen, das hauptsächlich von einem Mitglied der
Darmstädter Chemie-Familiendynastie Merck finanziert wird, verspricht, die
Verwertungs-Vorgaben der Verpackungsverordnung zwischen 25 und 50
Prozent billiger erfüllen zu können ... Landbell verteilt keine gelben, sondern
blaue Säcke. Und darin werden nicht, wie beim DSD, alle
„Leichtverpackungen" vom Plastik-Milchdöschen bis zum Styropor-Kasten
gesammelt, sondern nur noch „papierfaserhaltige Verpackungen": etwa
Getränkekartons oder Pizza-Schachteln. Daraus kann beispielsweise
Wellpappe hergestellt werden. In der Altpapier-Tonne (oder Sammlung) soll
nur noch „feines" Zeitschriften- und Zeitungspapier landen, das dann relativ
sortenrein an Papier-Recycler (De-Inker) geliefert werden könnte.
   Wiederverwertbares Glas und große Kunststoffverpackungen wie
Shampoo- oder Reinigungsflaschen müssen im Landbell-System von der
Verbrauchern zu Sammel-Containern an zentralen Plätzen gebracht werden.
Blechdosen oder kleine Kunststoffverpackungen (wie Joghurtbecher oder
Abdeckfolien) können dagegen ungespült in die Restmülltonne geworfen
werden. Der teure manuelle Sortier-Aufwand, der beim DSD in eigens
errichteten Sortieranlagen nötig ist, entfällt ...

FRANKFURTER RUNDSCHAU, Samstag, 30. Juni 2001, Nr. 149/26, S. 29

13. Lesen Sie den folgenden Text.

Nach unten durchlässig
Die Mär von der Offenheit des deutschen Schulsystems

Bildung spaltet. Das müssen Tausende Schüler in diesen Tagen erleben.
Während die einen aufs Gymnasium wechseln, ziehen andere nach den Ferien
in die Hauptschule. In kaum einer anderen Nation gliedert sich das
Schulwesen derart streng wie hierzulande, fallen die Entscheidungen über
künftige Lebenschancen so früh.
   „Das ist halb so schlimm", sagt mancher Bildungspolitiker. Schließlich sei
das System hinreichend flexibel. Jede eingeschlagene Schullaufbahn ist
korrigierbar, lautet ein Vers aus dem deutschen Bildungscredo. Aber er trifft
nur die halbe Wahrheit. Wenn überhaupt, dann sind deutsche Schulen vor
allem in eine Richtung durchlässig: nach unten. Das Dortmunder Institut für
Schulentwicklungsforschung (IFS) hat in den nordrhein-westfälischen
Klassen von fünf bis zehn die Zahl der Auf- und Absteigen gezählt und
festgestellt: Auf 100 Schüler, die absteigen, kommen nur fünf Kinder, die in

einen anspruchsvolleren Bildungsgang wechseln. <u>Vor zehn Jahren betrug das Verhältnis noch 20 zu 100, vor zwanzig Jahren sogar 40 zu 100.</u>

Klarer Fall, denkt man, wenn in Städten wie Köln rund die Hälfte der Schüler ins Gymnasium drängt. Da wundert es nicht, dass viele nach ein paar Jahren aufgeben. Aber dieser Verdacht ist falsch, fanden die Dortmunder Schulforscher heraus. Die Zahl der Gymnasialwechsler sinkt in Nordrhein-Westfalen – die Zahl der Absteiger hingegen wächst. Des Rätsels Lösung: <u>Ob viele oder wenige auf dem Gymnasium bleiben, entscheidet nicht allein die Leistung, sondern auch die Zahl der Schüler insgesamt. Als der Pillenknick die Schülerzahl in den achtziger Jahren reduzierte, verringerte sich auch die Zahl der Sitzenbleiber und Schulwechsler am Gymnasium.</u> Zehn Jahre später – die Schülerzahl war auf ihrem Höhepunkt – drehte sich der Trend um: Die Zahl der Absteiger wuchs.

Die Erklärung ist ebenso einfach wie pädagogisch bedenklich. Ist die Schülerzahl groß, fehlen den Lehrern Zeit und Ruhe, sich um jedes Kind zu kümmern. Bei kleineren Klassen dagegen steigen Muße und Motivation, sich gerade den schwächeren Schülern zu widmen. <u>Auch Eigeninteresse mag bei der Fürsorge eine Rolle spielen: Jeder Schüler repräsentiert schließlich auch den Bruchteil einer Lehrerstelle und sichert somit Arbeitsplätze.</u>

<u>Dass Angebot und Nachfrage über den Auf- oder Abstieg mitbestimmen, dies beschädigt erheblich die Illusion von der Gerechtigkeit unseres dreigliedrigen durchlässigen Schulsystems.</u> Nicht nur Leistung und Begabung, auch schlichte Demografie entscheidet über Schulkarrieren.

Bald brechen für die deutschen Schüler wieder bessere Zeiten an. Ab 2004 werden ihre Zahlen sinken. Die Gymnasien werden verstärkt um ihre Klientel werben müssen – und sich besonders gut um jene Schüler kümmern, die sie bereits haben. Statt Schulwechsel heißt das Konzept dann Förderkurse.

Martin Speiwak

DIE ZEIT, 12. Juli 2001, Nr. 29, S. 27

a. Übersetzen Sie ins Englische die Sätze, die im Text unterstrichen sind.
b. Fassen Sie den Text in einem Absatz zusammen.

Level 3

1. Zu jedem Bild passt ein Nomen. ✓

a. das Parallelogramm, b. der rechte Winkel, c. der Rhombus, d. der spitze Winkel, e. der stumpfe Winkel, f. das Trapezoid, g. das unregelmäßige Viereck

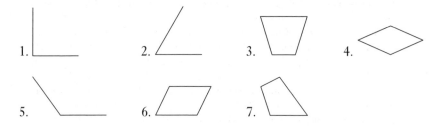

1.   2.   3.   4.

5.   6.   7.

2. Wie heißt das Substantiv? ✓

1. sehr große Menge
2. sehr große Zahl
3. größeres Maß
4. zu große Fülle

3. Wie heißt das entsprechende Adjektiv? ✓

1. gestern	*gestrig*
2. morgen	
3. heute	
4. der Tag	*täglich*
5. das Jahr	
6. der Monat	
7. die Woche	

4. Welches Wort hat die gleiche oder eine ähnliche Bedeutung? ✓

a. die Anhäufung, b. der Betrag, c. die Bouteille, d. bruchstückhaft, e. erheblich, f. die Ferne, g. der Halbmesser, h. kärglich, i. rechtzeitig, j. soeben, k. der Spund, l. stets, m. die Strähne, n. der Tresor, o. ungeheuer, p. vorübergehend

1. beträchtlich
2. enorm
3. der Radius
4. dürftig
5. die Geldsumme
6. der Strang
7. fragmentarisch
8. die Akkumulation
9. die Weite
10. der Geldschrank
11. die Flasche
12. der Zapfen
13. vorläufig
14. ständig
15. pünktlich
16. gerade

5. Was gehört zusammen? ✓

a. das Brett, b. die Entwicklerschale, c. das Etui, d. der Flachmann, e. die Glocke, f. der Kanister, g. der Pokal, h. die Reuse, i. die Schatulle, j. die Spucktüte, k. der Zuber

1. der Schmuck
2. der Wein
3. das Benzin
4. Bücher
5. Brillen
6. Fische
7. der Schnaps
8. der Käse
9. die Wäsche
10. der Film
11. das Flugzeug

6. Welches Wort passt nicht? ✓

1. der Leichensack, der Sarg, der Tragekorb, die Urne
2. die Anschwellung, die Schrumpfung, die Verminderung, die Verringerung
3. der Briefkasten, der Kummerkasten, der Nistkasten, die Wahlurne
4. der Brocken, der Fetzen, die Scherbe, die Vitrine
5. der Kleidersack, der Matschsack, der Postsack, der Sitzsack
6. die Ausdehnung, das Ausmaß, die Größe, der Umlauf
7. sich anhäufen, sich erweitern, sich vermehren, sich vermindern
8. das Schattenbild, der Schattenriss, die Silhouette, der Umriss
9. das Dessin, die Marmorierung, der Maßstab, das Muster

7. Welches Verb passt? ✓

a. anordnen, b. lassen, c. treiben, d. wahren, e. zunehmen

1. Abstand zu etw
2. an Umfang
3. etw in die Höhe
4. etw aufquellen
5. etw versetzt

8. Ordnen Sie die folgenden Ausdrücke nach der Größe, Länge usw. ✓

1. der Fuß, die Meile, das Yard, der Zoll
2. die Gallone, der Liter, das Pint, die Unze
3. das Gramm, das Kilo, das Pfund, der Zentner
4. ansehnlich, spärlich, unzählig
5. der Federkasten, das Handschuhfach, die Mülltonne, die Streichholzschachtel
6. dreiviertel zwei, halb zwei, viertel zwei, zwei
7. gegenwärtig, künftig, vorig
8. demnächst, längst, neuerdings

9. Zeichnen Sie die folgenden Kreuze.

1. das Andreaskreuz
2. das griechische Kreuz
3. das Keltenkreuz
4. das lateinische Kreuz

10. In jedem Satz fehlt ein Wort. ✓

Fischgrätmuster, geädert, Frist, Gestalt, knollige, Krümmung, Labyrinth, melierten, Nieten, wellig, Zeitraum

1. Während er im Wartezimmer sitzt, starrt er die braungrün _____ Wände an.
2. Seine Augen waren rot _____ vor Erschöpfung.
3. Er trägt einen grauen Pullover und ein Jackett mit _____.
4. Er kaufte sich einen Ledergürtel, rundum mit goldfarbenen _____ verziert.

5. Wer weist den Weg heraus aus dem _____ der Gassen?
6. Eine zunehmende _____ der Brustwirbelsäule und ein vorgewölbter Bauch sind weitere Zeichen für Osteoporose.
7. Das Buch ist vor Feuchtigkeit aufgequollen und _____.
8. In mythischen Texten kommt die Göttin auch in _____ einer Kuh vor.
9. Seine _____ Nase ist noch stärker gerötet als sonst.
10. Die neue _____ endet im September 2003.
11. Das Buch behandelt einen _____ von etwa zehn Jahren.

11. Welche Definition bzw. welches Synonym passt? ✓

> a. der Backtrog, b. das Bierseidel, c. der Bottich, d. der Henkelkorb,
> e. das Kelchglas, f. die Pulle, g. der Tornister

1. Flasche
2. großes, offenes Holzgefäß
3. Ranzen aus Segeltuch oder Fell
4. Trog, in dem der Teig vorbereitet wird
5. Korb mit zwei Henkeln
6. Glas in Form eines Kelches
7. Bierkrug

12. Übersetzen Sie ins Englische.

Deutscher Beitrag zum Haushalt soll sinken

BRÜSSEL, 20. Juli (dpa). Der deutsche Bruttobeitrag zum Haushalt der EU soll weiter sinken. Für 2002 sei erstmals das Unterschreiten der Schwelle von 24 Prozent am Gesamthaushalt möglich, berichteten Diplomaten am Freitag in Brüssel am Rande des EU-Haushaltsrates. Nach einem von den Mitgliedsländern mehrheitlich unterstützten Vorschlag wird der deutsche Brottobeitrag im kommenden Jahr 23,7 Prozent des gesamten EU-Budgets von 95,6 Milliarden Euro ausmachen, also 22,2 Milliarden Euro.

Für 2001 hatte der endgültige Anteil Deutschlands noch 25,5 Prozent ausgemacht, 1997 waren es 28,2 Prozent gewesen, 1994 hatte der Anteil 33,3 Prozent betragen. Ein Grund für die Verringerung ist ein Beschluss vom Berliner EU-Gipfel von 1999, wonach der nach der Wirtschaftskraft bemessene Anteil Deutschlands zwar steigt, die Anteile an der Mehrwertsteuer aber sinken. Rund 50 Prozent des EU-Etats werden aus Mehrwertsteueranteilen der Mitgliedsländer bestritten. Da Deutschland auch Zahlungen von der EU erhält, ist letztlich der Nettobeitrag für Brüssel deutlich geringer. Deutschland zahlt in der Regel etwa doppelt so viel in die EU-Kasse ein wie aus Brüssel zurückfließt. Über den Haushalt 2002 wird voraussichtlich noch bis Dezember beraten.

FRANKFURTER RUNDSCHAU, Samstag, 21. Juli 2001, Nr. 167/29, S. 5

© dpa Deutsche Presse-Agentur GmbH

13. Lesen Sie den folgenden Textausschnitt.

Zählen, wieviel Sterne stehen

Die größte Inventur aller Zeiten soll für Überblick im Universum sorgen/Von Ulf von Rauchhaupt

Vom Universum kennen wir erst winzige Ausschnitte. Daher glauben die Kosmologen, ihr Goldenes Zeitalter zu erleben: Mit ihrem Urknallmodell verfügen sie über eine elegante und schlüssige Theorie, die viele Beobachtungen mit den bekannten Naturgesetzen in Einklang bringt. Dennoch offenbaren immer ausgefeiltere astronomische Messungen, dass im Grundverständnis des Universums noch riesige Lücken klaffen (*ZEIT* Nr. 16/01). Nach den neuesten Beobachtungen wird das Schicksal des Alls nämlich von noch unbekannten dunklen Materien und Energien bestimmt, an die sich die physikalische Schulweisheit erst noch gewöhnen muss.

Tröstlich zu wissen, dass man wenigstens den sichtbaren Teil des Universums immer besser kennen lernt. Einfach ist auch das nicht. Das beobachtbare Universum enthält schätzungsweise hundert Milliarden Galaxien verschiedener Typen und Entwicklungsstadien. Hinzu kommen einige Milliarden Sterne unserer eigenen Galaxie, der Milchstraße. Nur ein verschwindender Bruchteil davon ist bislang systematisch vermessen. Der Grund ist einfach: Planvolle Himmelsdurchmusterungen sind nervtötend, sie bringen Astronomen weniger Ruhm ein als die Entdeckung eines Schwarzen Lochs oder eines effektvoll glühenden Staubnebels. Spitzenteleskope, die besonders tief ins All blicken, sind zu schade für kosmische Erbsenzählerei.

Andererseits führt gerade das Sammeln und Ordnen vieler unscheinbarer Einzelfunde oft zu wichtigem Erkenntnisgewinn. Das gilt für die Entschlüsselung der Gene ebenso wie für das Einordnen alter Knochen in verschiedenen Erdschichten, aus denen Paläontologen die Evolution des Lebens herauslesen. Damit haben sie übrigens viel mit den Kosmologen gemeinsam: Auch deren Blick ins All ist „geschichtet", denn die begrenzte Geschwindigkeit des Lichts führt zu einer Überblendung verschiedener Phasen der Vergangenheit. Je entfernter eine Galaxie, desto früher liegt das kosmische Entwicklungsstadium, in dem wir sie sehen.

„Ein kosmisches Genomprojekt"

Den Rekord hält seit wenigen Wochen ein Galaxienembryo – ein so genannter Quasar – im Sternbild Sextant, dessen Licht sich vor etwa 13 Milliarden Jahren auf den Weg machte. Damals waren seit dem Urknall erst ein paar hundert Millionen Jahre vergangen, das Universum besaß gerade mal ein Siebtel seiner heutigen Ausdehnung. Infolge seiner jahrmilliardenlangen Reise durch ein expandierendes All hat sich die einst gleißende ultraviolette Strahlung des Quasars in ein tiefrotes Glimmen verwandelt. Das Ausmaß dieser so genannten Rotverschiebung erlaubt den Rückschluss auf die Entfernung einer Galaxie.

Der winzige Lichtfleck am Rand von Raum und Zeit war kein Zufallsfund, sondern Ergebnis der größten je unternommenen Durchmusterung des sichtbaren Himmels, des Sloan Digital Sky Survey (SDSS). Wenn dieser „Himmelsüberblick" im Jahre 2005 abgeschlossen ist, wird ein Viertel des gesamten Himmels in digitalen Farbfotos im Internet verfügbar sein, ein

Umfang von rund zehntausend Gigabyte. Anfang Juni wurden die ersten 500 Gigabyte ins Netz gestellt (skyserver.fnal.gov). Astronomen sprechen bereits euphorisch vom „kosmischen Genomprojekt" ...

DIE ZEIT, 12. Juli 2001, Nr. 29, S. 27

a. Vokabelübung. Wie heißt das Wort (die Wendung) auf Englisch?
1. winzige Ausschnitte
2. Urknallmodell
3. ausgefeilt
4. riesige Lücken klaffen
5. schätzungsweise
6. ein verschwindender Bruchteil
7. planvolle Himmelsdurchmusterungen

b. Fassen Sie den Text zusammen.

Unit 9

Visual and performing arts

Level 1

Painting and sculpture

Kunst, die (¨e)	art
Kunstwerk, das (-e)	work of art
die schönen Künste, pl.	fine arts
die bildenden Künste, pl.	plastic or visual arts
Künstler(in), der/die (-/nen)	artist
künstlerisch	artistic
Maler(in), der/die (-/nen)	painter
(jmdn/etw) malen	to paint (s.o./sth)
etw abmalen	to paint a copy of sth; paint sth from life
Gemälde, das (-)	painting
Malerei, die (no pl.)	the art of painting
Glasmalerei, die (-en)	stained glass
Pinsel, der (-)	brush
(jmdn/etw) zeichnen	to draw (s.o./sth)
Zeichenblock, der (¨e)	sketch pad
Zeichnung, die (-en)	drawing, sketch
Zeichner(in), der/die (-/nen)	graphic artist
Skizze, die (-n)	sketch
Siebdruck, der (-e)	silk screen
Radierung, die (-en)	etching
etw radieren	to etch sth
etw ätzen	to etch sth

Abdruck, der (-e)	print
Steindruck, der (-e)	lithography, lithograph
Plakat, das (-e)	poster
Abbildung, die (-en)	illustration
etw bebildern	to illustrate sth, decorate sth with pictures
Bild, das (-er)	picture
Abbild, das (-er)	image
Bildhauer(in), der/die (-/nen)	sculptor
bildhauern	to sculpt
etw hauen	to carve sth
Bildhauerei, die (no pl.)	(the art of) sculpture
Skulptur, die (no pl./-en)	the art of sculpture/a work of sculpture
Plastik, die (no pl./-en)	the art of sculpture/a work of sculpture
Büste, die (-n)	bust
Standbild, das (-er)	statue
Ausstellung, die (-en)	exhibition
Einzelausstellung, die (-en)	one-man show
etw ausstellen	to exhibit sth
Meisterwerk, das (-e)	masterpiece
jmdn/etw darstellen	to represent, portray, depict, show s.o./sth

Darstellung, die (-en) — representation, portrayal, depiction

etw schaffen — to create sth

etw gestalten — to design, shape, form, structure sth

Motiv, das (-e) — theme, motif

Einzelheit, die (-en) — detail

Music

Musik, die (-en) — music, piece (of music), score; band

E-Musik, die (no pl.; coll.) — serious music

U-Musik, die (no pl.; coll.) — light music

Musiker(in), der/die (-/nen) — musician

Kammermusik, die (-en) — chamber music

Sinfonie (Symphonie), die (-n) — symphony

Oper, die (-n) — opera

Konzert, das (-e) — concerto; concert

Melodie, die (-n) — melody

Rhythmus, der (-men) — rhythm

Saiteninstrument, das (-e) — stringed instrument

Saite, die (-n) — string

Geige, die (-n) — violin

Geiger(in), der/die (-/nen) — violinist

erster/zweiter Geiger — first/second violin

(etw) geigen — to play (sth on) the violin

(Geigen)bogen, der (-; S: ¨) — bow

Bratsche, die (-n) — viola

Bratschist(in), der/die (-en/nen) — violist

Cello, das (-s) — cello

Cellist(in), der/die (-en/nen) — cellist

Kontrabass, der (¨e) — double bass

Kontrabassist(in), der/die (-en/nen) — double bass player

Holzblasinstrument, das (-e) — woodwind instrument

etw blasen — to blow, play sth

Flöte, die (-n) — flute

Flötist(in), der/die (-en/nen) — flautist

Pikkoloflöte, die (-n) — piccolo

Blockflöte, die (-n) — recorder

Klarinette, die (-n) — clarinet

Klarinettist(in), der/die (-en/nen) — clarinettist

Oboe, die (-n) — oboe

Oboist(in), der/die (-en/nen) — oboist

Fagott, das (-e) — bassoon

Fagottist(in), der/die (-en/nen) — basoonist

Blechblasinstrument, das (-e) — brass instrument

Trompete, die (-n) — trumpet

Trompeter(in), der/die (-/nen) — trumpeter

Horn, das (¨er) — French horn

Hornist(in), der/die (-en/nen) — horn player

Posaune, die (-n) — trombone

Posaunist(in), der/die (-en/nen) — trombone player

Tuba, die (Tuben) — tuba

Tubist(in), der/die (-en/nen) — tuba player

Schlaginstrument, das (-e) — percussion instrument

Triangel, der (-) — triangle

Becken, das (-) — cymbal

Trommel, die (-n) — drum

kleine/große Trommel — snare/bass drum

Trommelschlegel, der (-) — drumstick

Pauke, die (-n) — kettledrum (pl. timpani)

Paukenschlegel, der (-) — timpani stick

Schlagzeuger(in), der/die (-/nen)	drummer, percussionist
Klavier, das (-e)	piano
Klavierspieler(in), der/die (-/nen)	piano player, pianist
Pianist(in), der/die (-en/nen)	(concert) pianist
jmdn/etw begleiten	to accompany s.o./sth
Flügel, der (-)	grand piano
Taste, die (-n)	key
weiße/schwarze Taste	white/black key
Pedal, das (-e)	pedal
Orgel, die (-n)	organ
Organist(in), der/die (-en/nen)	organist
Cembalo, das (-s or -bali)	harpsichord
Cembalist(in), der/die (-en/nen)	harpsichordist
Chor, der (¨e)	choir, chorus; choral piece
Chorist(in), der/die (-en/nen)	chorus member
Chorleiter(in), der/die (-/nen)	chorus leader, choir leader
Sänger(in), der/die (-/nen)	singer
Stimme, die (-n)	voice
Dirigent(in), der/die (-en/nen)	conductor
(jmdn/etw) dirigieren	to conduct (s.o./sth)
Komponist(in), der/die (-en/nen)	composer
(etw) komponieren	to compose (sth)
etw bearbeiten	to arrange, adapt sth
Orchester, das (-)	orchestra
Kapelle, die (-n)	band; (light) orchestra
Streichquartett, das (-e)	string quartet
Solist(in), der/die (-en/nen)	soloist
Solistenkonzert, das (-e)	recital
Band, die (-s)	band [e.g. rock band]
Gitarre, die (-n)	guitar
Gitarrist(in), der/die (-en/nen)	guitarist
Griffbrett, das (-er)	finger board
Tasteninstrument, das (-e)	keyboard instrument
Saxofon, das (-s)	saxophone
Saxofonist(in), der/die (-en/nen)	saxophonist
Schlagzeug, das (-e)	drums
Jazz, der (no pl.)	jazz
Rock, der (no pl.)	rock music
Heavymetal (Heavy Metal), das (no pl.)	heavy metal
Pop, der (no pl.)	pop music
Techno (Tekkno), der or das (no pl.)	techno
Punk(rock), der (no pl.)	punk rock
Rap, der (no pl.)	rap
Blues, der (-)	blues
Reggae, der (no pl.)	reggae
Volksmusik, die (no pl.)	folk music
Volkslied, das (-er)	folk song
Liedermacher(in), der/die (-/nen)	singer-songwriter
(Schall)platte, die (-n)	record
Kassette, die (-n)	cassette
Compactdisc (Compact Disc; CD), die (-s)	compact disc
Aufnahme, die (-n)	recording
Album, das (Alben)	album
Schlager, der (-)	hit
Hit, der (-s)	hit
Song, der (-s)	hit, song, satirical song

Dance

Tanz, der (¨e)	dance
(etw) tanzen	to dance (sth)
Ballett, das (-e)	ballet

Balletttänzer(in), der/die (-/nen)	ballet dancer
Ballerina, die (-nen)	ballerina, ballet dancer
etw choreografieren	to choreograph sth
Choreograf(in), der/die (-en/nen)	choreographer
Choreografie, die (-n)	choreography
Tanzstunde, die (-n)	dance class

Theatre

Theater, das (-)	theatre
Schauspieler(in), der/die (-/nen)	actor/actress
Darsteller(in), der/die (-/nen)	actor/actress
Haupt-, Nebenrolle, die (-n)	principal/supporting role
Kostüm, das (-e)	costume
Bühne, die (-n)	stage
Szene, die (-n)	scene
(Theater)stück, das (-e)	play
Schauspiel, das (-e)	play; drama
Drama, das (-men)	drama
Lustspiel, das (-e)	comedy
Komödie, die (-n)	comedy; farce; comedy theatre
Trauerspiel, das (-e)	tragedy
Tragödie, die (-n)	tragedy
Tragikomödie, die (-n)	tragicomedy
Handlung, die (-en)	action, plot
Akt, der (-e)	act
Aufzug, der (¨e)	act
Pause, die (-n)	intermission
Beifall, der (no pl.)	applause
Beifall klatschen	to applaud
buhen (coll.)	to boo
Theaterkritiker(in), der/die (-/nen)	theatre or drama critic
Zuschauer(in), der/die (-/nen)	member of the audience
Publikum, das (no pl.)	audience; public
Stadttheater, das (-)	municipal theatre

Staatstheater, das (-)	state theatre
Studiobühne, die (-n)	studio theatre
Freilichtbühne, die (-n)	open-air theatre
Inszenierung, die (-en)	production
Vorstellung, die (-en)	performance
Aufführung, die (-en)	performance
Erstaufführung, die (-en)	première [of a production]
Uraufführung, die (-en)	première [of a work]
etw aufführen	to perform, put on, stage sth
spielen	to act
etw einstudieren	to rehearse sth
Kostümprobe, die (-n)	dress rehearsal

Cinema and film

Film, der (-e)	film, movie
Streifen, der (-; coll.)	film, movie
Kino, das (-s)	cinema, movie theatre
Kinocenter, das (-)	multi-screen cinema
Kinoprogramm, das (-e)	film programme; film guide
Filmemacher(in), der/die (-/nen)	filmmaker
Produzent(in), der/die (-en/nen)	producer
Regisseur(in), der/die (-e/nen)	director
Regie, die (no pl.)	direction
Regie führen	to direct
einen Film drehen	to shoot a film
(etw) filmen	to film (sth)
Star, der (-s)	star
Drehbuch, das (¨er)	screenplay
Drehbuchautor(in), der/die (-en/nen)	screenplay writer
Dramaturg(in), der/die (-en/nen)	script editor
Dokumentarfilm, der (-e)	documentary
Kulturfilm, der (-e)	documentary

Zeichentrickfilm, der (-e)	cartoon	Fotografie, die (-n)	photograph
		Fotografie, die (no pl.)	photography
Gruselfilm, der (-e)	horror film		
Kriminalfilm, der (-e)	crime film, thriller	Fotograf(in), der/die (-en/nen)	photographer
Ausstattungsfilm, der (-e)	spectacular (film)	(etw) fotografieren	to photograph sth; take photographs
Schocker, der (-)	sensational film, shocker	etw aufnehmen	to photograph sth
Pornofilm, der (-e)	porn film		
Kinokasse, die (-n)	cinema box office	fotogen	photogenic
Kinokarte, die (-n)	cinema ticket	Fotoapparat, der (-e)	camera
Nachmittagsvorstel-lung, die (-en)	matinee	Foto, der (-s)	camera
		Kamera, die (-s)	camera
Kinobesucher(in), der/die (-/nen)	cinemagoer	Schwarzweißfilm, der (-e)	black and white film
Bildwand, die (¨e)	(projection) screen	Farbfilm, der (-e)	colour film
Leinwand, die (¨e)	screen	Diapositiv, das (-e)	slide
Breitwand, die (¨e)	wide screen	Negativ, das (-e)	negative
Filmkritiker(in), der/die (-/nen)	film critic	etw abziehen	to print sth
		Glanzabzug, der (¨e)	glossy print
		auf mattem Papier abgezogen sein	to have a matt finish

Photography

Foto, das, CH: die (-s)	photo	etw vergrößern	to enlarge sth
		Vergrößerung, die (-en)	enlargement
Lichtbild, das (-er)	photograph		

Level 2

Painting and sculpture

Museum, das (-seen)	museum	Kunstsammler(in), der/die (-/nen)	art collector
Sammlung, die (-en)	collection	Original, das (-e)	original
Erwerb, der (-e)	acquisition	etw signieren	to sign sth
Galerie, die (-n)	gallery	Signatur, die (-en)	signature
Galerist(in), der/die (-en/nen)	art dealer, gallery owner	Fälschung, die (-en)	forgery, fake
		etw fälschen	to forge sth
Kunsthändler(in), der/die (-/nen)	art dealer	etw datieren	to date sth
		Leinwand, die (¨e)	canvas
Kunsthandel, der (no pl.)	art trade, art market	etw aufspannen	to mount, stretch sth
Auftrag, der (¨e)	commission		
in Auftrag geben	to commission	Staffelei, die (-en)	easel
Versteigerung, die (-en)	auction	Palette, die (-n)	palette
		Palettenmesser, das (-)	palette knife
Gebot, das (-e)	bid	Malspachtel, der (-) or die (-n)	spatula
(etw) bieten	to bid (sth)		

Atelier, das (-s)	studio	Blatt, das (¨er)	sheet of music
Ateliermalerei, die (no pl.)	painting done indoors	(etw) vom Blatt spielen/singen	to sight-read (sth)
Freilichtmalerei, die (no pl.)	plein-air, open-air painting	lippensynchron singen	to lip-synch
Bildnis, das (-se)	portrait	gastieren	to give a guest performance
Porträt, das (-s)	portrait		
Porträt sitzen	to sit for one's portrait	Gastspiel, das (-e)	guest performance
		Tournee, die (-n)	tour
posieren	to pose	auf Tournee	on tour
eine Pose einnehmen	to pose	vorsingen, -spielen	to audition
jmdm Modell stehen	to model for sb	Probe, die (-n)	rehearsal
jmdm Modell sitzen	to sit for sb	eine Probe abhalten	to rehearse
Aktmodell, das (-e)	nude model	(etw) proben	to rehearse (sth)
Akt, der (-e)	nude	Akkordeon, das (-s)	accordion
Grafik, die (no pl./-en)	graphic arts/work of graphic art	Mundharmonika, die (-s or -ken)	harmonica
Grafiker(in), der/die (-/nen)	graphic artist	Dudelsack, der (¨e)	bagpipes
		Glocke, die (-n)	bell
gegenständlich	representational	Hackbrett, das (-er)	dulcimer
abstrakt	abstract	Harfe, die (-n)	harp
anschaulich	concrete, vivid, graphic	Harfenist(in), der/die (-en/nen)	harpist
Wandgemälde, das (-)	mural	(ein Lied) harfen	to play (a song on) the harp
Deckengemälde, das (-)	ceiling mural		
		Laute, die (-n)	lute
Landschaft, die (-en)	landscape	Lautenist(in), der/die (-en/nen)	lutanist
Seelandschaft, die (-en)	seascape	Wiegenlied, das (-er)	lullaby
Stillleben, das (-)	still life	Hymne, die (-n)	hymn
		Weihnachtslied, das (-er)	Christmas carol

Music

(etw) üben	to practise (sth)
Klavierstunde, die (-n)	piano lesson
Klavierunterricht, der (no pl.)	piano lessons, piano instruction
Klavierstimmer(in), der/die (-/nen)	piano tuner
etw stimmen	to tune sth
verstimmt	out of tune
Stimmgabel, die (-n)	tuning fork
absolutes Gehör	perfect pitch
(etw) nach dem Gehör singen	to sing (sth) by ear
richtig/falsch singen	to sing in/out of tune

Dance

Tanzsaal, der (-säle)	dance hall; ballroom
Tanzboden, der (¨)	dance floor
Tanzfläche, die (-n)	dance floor
Gesellschaftstanz, der (¨e)	ballroom dance; ballroom dancing
Tanzpartner(in), der/die (-/nen)	dance partner
Tanzschritt, der (-e)	dance step
Walzer, der (-)	waltz
Tango, der (-s)	tango
Foxtrott, der (-e or -s)	foxtrot
Foxtrott tanzen	to foxtrot

Rumba, der or die (-s)	rumba	Garderobe, die (n)	dressing room; cloakroom
Salsa, der (-s)	salsa	Garderobenmarke, die (-n)	cloakroom ticket
Ballettschule, die (-n)	ballet school	Zuschauerraum, der (¨e)	auditorium
Ballettratte, die (-n; coll.)	ballet pupil		
Balletttruppe, die (-n)	ballet company; corps de ballet	Rang, der (¨e)	circle
		erster/zweiter/dritter Rang	dress circle/upper circle/gallery
Rundtanz, der (¨e)	round dance	Parkett, das (-e)	stalls, parquet
Polka, die (-s)	polka	Loge, die (-n)	box
Modetanz, der (¨e)	popular dance	Reihe, die (-n)	row
Twist, der (-s)	twist	Sitzplatz, der (¨e)	seat
twisten	to (do the) twist	Platzanweiser(in), der/die (-/nen)	usher
Volkstanz, der (¨e)	folk dance		

Theatre

Regisseur(in), der/die (-e/nen)	director	Programmheft, das (-e)	programme
Intendant(in), der/die (-en/nen)	manager and artistic director	Orchestergraben, der (¨)	orchestra pit
Dramaturg(in), der/die (-en/nen)	literary and artistic director	Operette, die (-n)	operetta, comic opera
Inspizient(in), der/die (-en/nen)	stage manager	Pantomime, die (-n)	pantomime
Bühnenarbeiter(in), der/die (-/nen)	stagehand	Kabarett, das (-s or -e)	cabaret
Bühnenbild, das (-er)	(stage) set	Einakter, der (-)	one-act play
Bühnenbildner(in), der/die (-/nen)	stage or set designer	Perücke, die (-n)	wig
		Schminke, die (-n)	make-up
Bühnenmaler(in), der/die (-/nen)	scene-painter	sich/jmdn/etw schminken	to put make-up on o.s./sb/sth
Charge, die (-n)	small character part	Maskenbildner(in), der/die (-/nen)	make-up artist
Chargenspieler(in), der/die (-/nen)	character actor/actress	Kostümentwurf, der (¨e)	costume design
ausverkauft	sold out	Kostümbildner(in), der/die (-/nen)	costume designer
Spielplan, der (¨e)	programme		
Abonnement, das (-s)	season ticket; subscription [newspaper]	Vorhang, der (¨e)	curtain; curtain call
		einen Vorhang bekommen	to get a curtain call
Abonnent(in), der/die (-en/nen)	season-ticket holder; subscriber [newspaper]	vor den Vorhang treten	to take a curtain call
		sich verbeugen	to bow
etw abonnieren	to have a season ticket/subscription for sth		

Cinema and film

Vorfilm, der (-e)	supporting film
Hauptfilm, der (-e)	main feature
Kurzfilm, der (-e)	short; short film
Spielfilm, der (-e)	feature film

etw verfilmen	to make a film of sth	Filmfestspiele, pl.	film festival
Verfilmung, die (-en)	film version	etw subventionieren	to subsidize sth
auf die Leinwand bringen	to film	Kinoverbot bekommen	to be banned in cinemas
Leinwandgröße, die (-n; coll.)	famous film star	Filmzensur, die (no pl.)	film censorship
Knüller, der (-)	blockbuster		
Filmkamera, die (-s)	film camera		

Photography

Dunkelkammer, die (-n)	darkroom
etw entwickeln	to develop sth
Sucher, der (-)	viewfinder
Auslöseknopf, der (¨e)	shutter release button
Objektiv, das (-e)	lens
Fischaugenobjektiv, das (-e)	fisheye lens
Weitwinkelobjektiv, das (-e)	wide-angle lens
Teleobjektiv, das (-e)	telephoto lens
Blitzgerät, das (-e)	flash (unit)
etw fokussieren	to focus sth
Dreibein, das (-e)	tripod
Stativ, das (-e)	tripod
Filmrolle, die (-n)	roll of film
Filmkassette, die (-n)	film cassette or cartridge

(Dia)projektor, der (-en)	(slide) projector
Vorführraum, der (¨e)	projection room
Filmvorführer(in), der/die (-/nen)	projectionist
Literaturfilm, der (-e)	literary film
Problemfilm, der (-e)	serious film
Liebesfilm, der (-e)	romantic film
Vor-, Nachspann, der (-e)	opening/final credits
Ausstattung, die (-en)	décor and costumes
mit Untertiteln	with subtitles
Originalfassung, die (-en)	original version
Originalton (O-Ton), der (no pl.)	original sound

Level 3

Painting and sculpture

etw auffrischen	to brighten up, touch up, restore sth
etw restaurieren	to restore sth
Buntstift, der (-e)	coloured pencil, crayon
Kreidestift, der (-e)	chalk
Kohlestift, der (-e)	stick of charcoal
Pastellstift, der (-e)	pastel (crayon)
Malkasten, der (¨)	paint box
Farbtube, die (-n)	tube of paint
Ölfarbe, die (-n)	oil paint or colour
Firnis, der (-se)	varnish
Temperafarbe, die (-n)	tempera colour

Wasserfarbe, die (-n)	watercolour
Aquarellfarbe, die (-n)	watercolour
Aquarell, das (-e)	watercolour [painting]
aquarellieren	to paint in watercolours
Fixiermittel, das (-)	fixative
Acrylfarbe (Akrylfarbe), die (-n)	acrylic paint
Federzeichnung, die (-en)	pen drawing, pen sketch
lavierte Federzeichnung	wash drawing, pen-and-wash drawing

etw lavieren	to wash sth	(etw) meißeln	to chisel, carve (sth)
Transparentpapier, das (-e)	tracing paper	Ton, der (-e)	clay
		tönern	(made of) clay
Pauspapier, das (-e)	tracing paper	Holz, das (¨er)	wood
etw pausen	to trace sth	hölzern	wooden
Dessin, das (-s)	design, drawing	Beitel, der (-)	chisel
Entwurf, der (¨e)	design, plan, conception	Metall, das (-e)	metal
		metallen	(made of) metal
Anordnung, die (-en)	arrangement	Marmor, der (-e)	marble
Aufbau, der (no pl.)	structure, construction, composition	marmorn	(made of) marble
		Bronze, die (-n)	bronze
		bronzen	(made of) bronze
Vordergrund, der (no pl.)	foreground	etw bronzieren	to bronze sth
		etw gießen	to cast, found sth
Hintergrund, der (¨e)	background	Abguss, der (¨e)	casting, cast copy
Deckfarbe, die (-n)	body colour, opaque colour	Gipsabguss, der (¨e)	plaster cast
		Gipsmodell, das (-e)	plaster model
Lasurfarbe, die (-n)	transparent colour	Flachrelief, das (-s or -e)	low relief
Fondfarbe, die (-n)	background colour		
Helldunkel, das (no pl.)	chiaroscuro	Basrelief, das (-s or -e)	bas-relief
Clair-obscur, das (no pl.)	chiaroscuro	Hochrelief, das (-s or -e)	high relief
etw schattieren	to shade sth	Hautrelief, das (-s or -e)	high relief
Anschauungsrichtung, die (-en)	direction of viewing		
		Fresko, das (-ken)	fresco
Frontalperspektive, die (-n)	frontal depiction, frontal perspective	## Music	
Froschperspektive, die (-n)	worm's-eye view	Musikwissenschaft, die (no pl.)	musicology
Beschauer(in), der/die (-/nen)	viewer	musizieren	to make music
		Fingersatz, der (ë)	fingering
Betrachter(in), der/die (-/nen)	viewer, observer	(Musik)note, die (-n)	(musical) note
		ganze/halbe Note	semibreve/minim; whole/half note
Betrachtungspunkt, der (-e)	viewpoint, point of station	Viertel-, Achtelnote, die (-n)	crotchet/quaver; quarter/eighth note
einansichtig	having only one viewing point		
Fluchtpunkt, der (-e)	vanishing point	Sechzehntelnote, die (-n)	semiquaver (sixteenth-note)
Diagonale, die (-n)	diagonal (line)		
Horizontale, die (-n)	horizonal (line)	punktierte Note	dotted note
Vertikale, die (-n)	vertical (line)	punktierte halbe Note	dotted minim
Stein, der (-e)	stone		
Steinblock, der (¨e)	block of stone	Viertel-, Achtelpause, die (-n)	crotchet/quaver (quarter/eighth) rest
steinern	(made of) stone		
Meißel, der (-)	chisel		

ganze/halbe Pause	semibreve/minim (whole/half) rest	steppen	to tap dance
(Musik)noten, pl.	written music, copy, part	Steppeisen, das (-)	tap
		Limbo, der (-s)	limbo
Notenständer, der (-)	music stand	Flamenco, der (-s)	flamenco
Bass-, Violinschlüssel, der (-)	bass, treble clef	Kastagnette, die (-n)	castanet
		Bauchtanz, der (¨e)	belly dance
		bauchtanzen	to belly dance
Takt, der (-e)	measure (bar), time, beat		

Theatre

Auftakt, der (-e)	upbeat	Bühnenanweisung, die (-en)	stage direction
Niederschlag, der (¨e)	downbeat	Auftritt, der (-e)	entrance (on stage); scene
taktmäßig	in time		
Taktstock, der (¨e)	baton	auftreten	to appear on stage, enter
Taktbezeichnung, die (-en)	time signature		
		Abgang, der (¨e)	exit (off stage)
Zweihalbetakt, der (-e)	two–two time	abgehen	to exit
		„X ab"	'exit X'
Dreivierteltakt, der (-e)	three–four time	rechts vom Schauspieler	stage right
Sechsachteltakt, der (-e)	six–eight time	links vom Schauspieler	stage left
Kreuz, das (-e)	sharp	nach vorn	downstage
B, das (-)	flat	nach hinten	upstage
Auflösungszeichen, das (-)	natural (sign)	hinter der Bühne	backstage
		Dialog, der (-e)	dialogue
Tonartvorzeichnung, die (-en)	key signature	Monolog, der (-e)	monologue
		beiseite (sprechend)	aside
Dur, das (no pl.)	major (key)	Besetzung, die (-en)	casting; cast
Moll, das (no pl.)	minor (key)	etw besetzen	to cast sth
Dur-, Mollakkord, der (-e)	major/minor chord	Kulisse, die (-n)	piece of scenery
		Kulissen, pl.	scenery, wings
Dreiklang, der (¨e)	triad	Kulissenwechsel, der (-)	scene change
Oktave, die (-n)	octave		
Satz, der (¨e)	movement	Versatzstück, das (-e)	set piece, (moveable) piece of scenery

Dance

Ballettröckchen, das (-)	tutu	Bühnenausstattung, die (-en)	stage property, props
Spitzenschuh, der (-e)	ballet shoe	Beleuchtung, die (-en)	lighting
Ballettschuh, der (-e)	ballet shoe	Beleuchter(in), der/die (-/nen)	lighting technician
Trikot, das (-s)	leotard		
Spitzentanz, der (no pl.)	toe dance	Rampenlicht, das (-er)	footlight
Stepptanz, der (¨e)	tap dance	Scheinwerfer, der (-)	spotlight
		der eiserne Vorhang	safety curtain

263

Souffleur, der (-e), Souffleuse, die (-n)	prompter
Souffleurkasten, der (¨)	prompt box
Stichwort, das (¨er)	cue
Lampenfieber, das (no pl.)	stage fright
Festspiel, das (-e)	festival production; pl.: festival
Festspielhaus, das (¨er)	festival theatre

Cinema and film

einen Film vorführen/zeigen	to screen a film
Vorführung, die (-en)	screening
Ausschnitt, der (-e)	clip
einen Film herausbringen	to release a film
Filmverleih, der (-e)	distribution company
Stummfilm, der (-e)	silent film
Tonfilm, der (-e)	sound film; talkie
Soundtrack, der (-s)	soundtrack
Geräuscheffekt, der (-e)	sound effect
etw synchronisieren	to dub sth
nicht synchron	out of sync
Specialeffect (Special Effect), der (-s)	special effect
Atelieraufnahme, die (-n)	studio shot
Außenaufnahme, die (-n)	exterior shot; location shot
Außenaufnahmen drehen	to shoot on location
Innenaufnahme, die (-n)	interior shot
aus dem Off	from off camera
Fahrt, die (-en)	tracking shot
Großaufnahme, die (-n)	close-up
Totale, die (-n)	long shot
Halbtotale, die (-n)	medium shot
Blende, die (-n)	fade
Ein-, Ausblendung, die (-en)	fade-in/out

Kameramann, der (-leute)	cameraman
etw montieren	to edit sth
Cutter(in), der/die (-/nen)	editor
Verschnitt, der (-e)	outtake
Statist(in), der/die (-en/nen)	extra, supernumerary
Statistenrolle, die (-n)	walk-on part
Komparse, der (-n); Komparsin, die (-nen)	extra, supernumerary
Stuntman, der (-men)	stunt man
Stuntwoman, die (-women)	stunt woman

Photography

Kleinbildkamera, die (-s)	35 mm camera
digitale Kamera	digital camera
(einäugige) Spiegelreflexkamera	(single-lens) reflex camera
Zeitrafferkamera, die (-s)	time-lapse camera
Blende, die (-n)	aperture, f-stop, diaphragm
bei/mit Blende 8	at (an aperture setting of) f/8
die Blende schließen	to stop down
abblenden	to stop down
aufblenden	to increase the aperture
Blendenautomatik, die (-en)	automatic aperture control
Belichtungszeit, die (-en)	exposure time
Belichtungsautomatik, die (-en)	automatic exposure control
Belichtungsmesser, der (-)	light meter
Autofokus, der (-)	autofocus
Schärfentiefe, die (no pl.)	depth of focus
etw kolorieren	to colourize sth

| körnig | grainy | Gegenlicht, das (-er) | backlight |
| über-, unterbelichtet | overexposed/ underexposed | im Gegenlicht | against the light, into the light |

Media and popular culture

Level 1

General

Medium, das (-dien)	communication medium
Massenmedium, das (-dien)	mass medium
Medienfachfrau, die (-en)	(female) media expert
Medienfachmann, der (-leute)	(male) media expert
Exklusivbericht, der (-e)	exclusive (report)
Nachricht, die (-en)	news
Kurznachrichten, pl.	news in brief; news summary
Nachrichtenagentur, die (-en)	news agency

Print media

Zeitung, die (-en)	newspaper
Tageszeitung, die (-en)	daily paper
Morgen-, Abendzeitung, die (-en)	morning/evening paper
Sonntagszeitung, die (-en)	Sunday paper
Wochenzeitung, die (-en)	weekly paper
Wochenblatt, das ("er)	weekly paper
Monatszeitschrift, die (-en)	monthly
Zeitschrift, die (-en)	magazine, periodical
vierteljährlich erscheinende Zeitschrift	quarterly
Illustrierte, die (-n)	magazine

Magazin, das (-e)	magazine
aktuell	current; up-to-the-minute
Schlagzeile, die (-n)	headline
Herausgeber(in), der/die (-/nen)	editor
Chefredakteur(in), der/die (-e/nen)	editor in chief
Redaktion, die (-en)	editorial office
Nachrichtenredaktion, die (-en)	newsroom
Journalist(in), der/die (-en/nen)	journalist
Reporter(in), der/die (-/nen)	reporter
(über/von) etw berichten	to report (on) sth
Bericht, der (-e)	report
Reportage, die (-n)	reportage
Artikel, der (-)	article
Leitartikel, der (-)	leading article, editorial
Rezension, die (-en)	review
Feuilleton, das (-s)	arts section
Sportteil, der (-e)	sports column
Spalte, die (-n)	column
Klatschspalte, die (-n)	gossip column
Kleinanzeigenspalte, die (-n)	small ads/classified column
Anzeigenspalte, die (-n)	advertising column
Stellenanzeige, die (-n)	job advertisement
Leserbrief, der (-e)	reader's letter, letter to the editor
Nachruf, der (-e)	obituary

Todesanzeige, die (-n)	death notice	Fernbedienung, die (-en)	remote control
die Todesanzeigen, pl.	obituary column/page	Fernsehprogramm, das (-e)	television channel/ programme/guide
Wirtschaftsnach-richten, pl.	business news	Fernsehgebühren, pl.	television licence fee
Wetterbericht, der (-e)	weather forecast	verkabelt	hooked up to cable television
Fortsetzungsroman, der (-e)	serial, serialized novel	Kabelfernsehen, das (no pl.)	cable television
Comicstrip, der (-s)	comic strip	Videorekorder (-recorder), der (-)	VCR
Cartoon, der or das (-s)	cartoon, comic strip	Videokassette, die (-n)	video (cassette tape)
Kreuzworträtsel, das (-)	crossword puzzle	Videothek, die (-en)	video rental store
Rätselecke, die (-n)	puzzle corner	etw aufnehmen	to record sth
Kiosk, der (-e)	newsstand	Sender, der (-)	(radio) station; (television) channel
Buchhandlung, die (-en)	bookshop		
im Buchhandel erhältlich	available from bookshops	etw senden	to broadcast sth
Taschenbuch, das ("er)	paperback	Sendung, die (-en)	broadcast; programme
als Taschenbuch erhältlich	available in paperback	etw übertragen	to broadcast, transmit sth
gebunden	in hardcover	Übertragung, die (-en)	broadcast, transmission
mit festem Einband	in hardcover	Sendepause, die (-n)	intermission
Lexikon, das (-xika)	encyclopaedia	Sportsendung, die (-en)	sports programme
Verlag, der (-e)	publisher	die Sportergebnisse durchsagen	to announce the sports results
Veröffentlichung, die (-en)	publication	Wiederholung, die (-en)	instant replay
etw veröffentlichen	to publish sth	Fernsehmuffel, der (-; coll., hum.)	s.o. who does not like to watch television
erscheinen	to come out, be published	fernsehmüde	tired of watching television
(etw) drucken	to print (sth)	Radio, das, also S, CH: der (-s)	radio (apparatus)
Druckfehler, der (-)	misprint	Radio, das (-s)	radio (broadcasting)
		das Radio auf einen Sender einstellen	to tune the radio to a station
Audiovisual media		Rundfunk, der (no pl.)	radio broadcasting; radio station
Telekommunikation, die (-en)	telecommunication		
Fernseher, der (-)	television (set)	Rundfunkanstalt, die (-en)	broadcasting corporation
Fernsehgerät, das (-e)	television (set)	Hörer(in), der/die (-/nen)	listener
Fernsehen, das (no pl.)	television		
fernsehen	to watch television		
etw einschalten	to turn on sth		

Ansager(in), der/die (-/nen)	announcer
Sprecher(in), der/die (-/nen)	announcer; narrator, anchor
Moderator(in), der/die (-en/nen)	presenter

Advertising

Werbung, die (no pl.)	advertising
für etw Werbung machen	to advertise sth
werben	to advertise
für etw werben	to advertise sth, promote sth
Reklame, die (-n)	advertising; advertisement
Anzeige, die (-n)	advertisement

eine Anzeige inserieren	to place an advertisement
Werbespot, der (-s)	commercial
Werbespruch, der (¨e)	advertising jingle
werbewirksam	effective [advertising]
werbewirksam sein	to be good publicity
in Deutschland hergestellt	made in Germany
Spitzenqualität, die (no pl.)	top quality
Marke, die (-n)	brand, make
Markenname, der (-n)	brand name
Anschlagsäule, die (-n)	advertising pillar
Litfaßsäule, die (-n)	advertising pillar

Level 2

Print media

eine Zeitung im Abonnement beziehen	to subscribe to a newspaper
Abonnementspreis, der (-e)	subscription price
ein Abonnement erneuern	to renew a subscription
Leserschaft, die (no pl.)	readership
Presse, die (no pl.)	press
Pressefreiheit, die (no pl.)	freedom of the press
Pressezensur, die (no pl.)	censorship of the press
Pressebericht, der (-e)	press report
wie verlautet	according to reports
offiziell	on the record
inoffiziell	off the record
Käseblatt, das (¨er; coll., pej.)	rag
Tagespresse, die (no pl.)	daily press
überregionale Presse	national press

Auslandspresse, die (no pl.)	foreign press
Berichterstatter(in), der/die (-/nen)	reporter
Lokalberichterstatter (in), der/die (-/nen)	spot reporter
einen Bericht einsenden	to file a report
Scoop, der (-s)	scoop
Fotoreporter(in), der/die (-/nen)	press photographer
Redaktionsmitglied, das (-er)	staffer
freiberuflich	freelance
Leitartikler(in), der/die (-/nen)	leader writer, editorial-article writer
Kritiker(in), der/die (-/nen)	critic
Sportredakteur(in), der/die (-e/nen)	sports editor
Wirtschaftsredakteur(in), der/die (-e/nen)	business editor
Pressekonferenz, die (-en)	press conference

eine Presseerklärung herausgeben	to release a press statement
Pressestelle, die (-n)	press office
Pressemappe, die (-n)	press kit
Zeitungsausschnitt, der (-e)	press cutting
Presseausweis, der (-e)	press card

Audiovisual media

auf etw umschalten	to switch over to sth
Talkshow, die (-s)	talk show
Frühstücksfernsehen, das (no pl.)	breakfast television
Magazin, das (-e)	magazine programme
Quizsendung, die (-en)	quiz programme
Spielshow, die (-s)	game show
Marathonsendung, die (-en)	telethon
Tagesbericht, der (-e)	daily report
Bildschirm, der (-e)	screen
geteilter Bildschirm	split screen
Münzfernsehen, das (no pl.)	pay television
Werbefernsehen, das (no pl.)	commercial television
Werbekanal, der (¨e)	advertising channel
Kabelkanal, der (¨e)	cable channel
Glotze, die (-n; coll.)	television, telly, box
Glotzkiste, die (-n; coll.)	television, telly, box
Glotzkasten, der (¨; coll.)	television, telly, box
Stubenhocker, der (-)	couch potato
Fernsehstudio, das (-s)	television studio
auf Sendung sein	to be on the air
Sendezeit, die (-en)	broadcasting/air time
zur besten Sendezeit	at peak viewing time
Haupteinschaltzeit, die (-en)	prime time
Einschaltquote, die (-n)	viewing/listening figure
aktuelle Sendung	(news and) current affairs programme

Kommentar, der (-e)	commentary
Teleprompter, der (-)	teleprompter
etw melden	to report sth
wie soeben gemeldet wird	according to reports just coming in
Kurzmeldung, die (-en)	news flash
Meldungen in Kürze, pl.	news headlines
Durchsage, die (-n)	announcement
etw (im Radio/Fernsehen) durchgeben	to announce sth (on the radio/ television)
(Auslands) korrespondent(in), der/die (-en/nen)	(foreign) correspondent
Sonderbericht- erstatter(in), der/die (-/nen)	special correspondent

Advertising

Massenwerbung, die (no pl.)	mass advertising
Werbekampagne, die (-n)	advertising campaign
Werbeagentur, die (-en)	advertising agency
Adressenliste, die (-n)	mailing list
auf etw zielen	to target sth
Werbesendung, die (-en)	advertising mail
Broschüre, die (-n)	brochure
Hochglanzbroschüre, die (-n)	glossy brochure
Prospekt, der (-e)	brochure
Reklamezettel, der (-)	leaflet
Anzeigenbeilage, die (-n)	advertising insert
Warenmuster, das (-)	sample
Warenprobe, die (-n)	sample
Gutschein, der (-e)	coupon, voucher
Anschlagtafel, die (-n)	hoarding, billboard
Anschlagbrett, das (-er)	hoarding, billboard

Level 3

Print media

Auflagenhöhe, die (-n)	circulation
Frontseite, die (-n)	front page
Zeitungskopf, der (¨e)	flag, nameplate
Impressum, das (-pressen)	masthead
Ausgabedatum, das (-ten)	issue date
Bildunterschrift, die (-en)	caption, cutline
Zeile (die [-n]) mit dem Namen des Autors	byline
Lay-out, das (-s)	layout
Layouter(in), der/die (-/nen)	layout artist
Zeitungspapier, das (no pl.)	newsprint
Druckerschwärze, die (no pl.)	printer's ink
Korrekturfahne, die (-n)	galley proof
Korrekturzeichen, das (-)	proofreader's mark
Korrektor(in), der/die (-en/nen)	proofreader
Redaktionsschluss, der (¨e)	press deadline
in Druck gehen	to go to press
die Zeitung ist im Druck	the newspaper has gone to bed
eine Zeitung in Druck geben	to put a newspaper to bed
etw setzen	to typeset sth
Schriftsetzer(in), der/die (-/nen)	typesetter
Tipp, der (-s)	tip-off
Hinweis, der (-e)	tip-off
aus zuverlässiger Quelle	from a reliable source
an der Quelle sitzen	to have access to inside information
etw vertuschen	to hush sth up

Verleumdung, die (-en)	libel
jmdn verleumden	to libel s.o.
Jahrgang, der (¨e)	volume (of a periodical)
Ausgabe, die (-n)	issue
Sensationspresse, die (no pl.)	gutter press
Skandalpresse, die (no pl.)	gutter press
Boulevardpresse, die (no pl.)	gutter press

Audiovisual media

etw im Zeitraffer zeigen	to show sth on fast forward
in (der) Zeitlupe	in slow motion
Zeitlupenwieder-holung, die (-en)	slow motion replay
Satellit, der (-en)	satellite
Satellitenfernsehen, das (no pl.)	satellite television
Kurz-, Langwelle, die (-n)	short/long wave
Amateurfunk, der (no pl.)	amateur radio
Amaterufunker(in), der/die (-/nen)	amateur radio operator, ham
Empfang, der (no pl.)	reception
etw empfangen	to receive sth
Sendersuchlauf, der (¨e)	(automatic) station search
etw stören	to jam sth
Störung, die (-en)	interference
Disk-Jockei (Diskjockei), der (-s)	disc jockey
Piratensender, der (-)	pirate radio station
Schulfunk, der (no pl.)	radio programmes for schools
Übertragungswagen (Ü-Wagen), der (-)	outside broadcast vehicle
Livesendung, die (-en)	live broadcast

Live-Reportage, die (-n)	live/running commentary	Werbegag, der (-s)	advertising gimmick
Filmmaterial, das (-ien)	footage	Markenbild, das (-er)	brand image
Geräuschkulisse, die (-n)	(background) sound effects	Markenwieder-erkennung, die (no pl.)	brand recognition
		Werbeetat, das (-s)	advertising budget
Advertising		Werbeeinkommen, das (-)	advertising revenue
Inserat, das (-e)	advertisement	Anzeigenkonto, das (-s, -ten, or -ti)	advertising account
Reklamerummel, der (no pl.; coll.)	hype	Warenzeichen, das (-)	trademark
etw groß herausbringen	to hype sth (up)	eingetragenes Warenzeichen	registered trademark

---

Exercises

Level 1

1. Welches Wort hat die gleiche oder eine ähnliche Bedeutung? ✓

1. die Illustration
2. das Poster
3. die Skulptur
4. die Statue
5. das Detail
6. die Violine
7. der Hit
8. die Schauspielerin
9. die Komödie
10. der Film
11. die Fotografie
12. die Kamera
13. das Magazin
14. das Radio
15. der Fernsehapparat

2. Ordnen Sie.

das Becken, der Bogen, die Bratsche, das Cello, das Fagott, das Horn, die Klarinette, die kleine Trommel, der Kontrabass, die Oboe, die Pauke, die Pikkoloflöte, die Posaune, die Trompete, die Tuba

Saiteninstrument	Holzblasinstrument	Blechblasinstrument	Schlaginstrument

3. Wie heißt das Substantiv (das Ergebnis des Vorgangs)? ✓

1. malen
2. zeichnen
3. radieren
4. tanzen
5. fotografieren
6. vergrößern
7. berichten
8. senden

4. Welches Verb passt? ✓

a. aufführen, b. blasen, c. drehen, d. hauen, e. klatschen, f. machen,
g. schlagen, h. senden, i. veröffentlichen

1. Beifall	4. für etw Werbung	7. die Trommel
2. ein Schauspiel	5. eine Statue aus Stein	8. einen Roman
3. einen Film	6. die Flöte	9. die Nachrichten

5. Kreuzworträtsel ✓

senkrecht:

 1. Pianistin
 2. die Kunst, zu malen
 3. kleines Orchester
 4. größere Sängergruppe
 5. sehr laute Rockmusik
 7. Horrorfilm
 9. Tragödie
10. kritische Besprechung

12. Reklame
13. populäre U-Musik
15. hervorgehobene Überschriftzeilen
19. Violine
21. eine Art Klavier
23. herabzudrückender Hebel am Klavier
26. mechanischer Sprechgesang

waagerecht:

 1. Musik für wenige Instrumente
 6. Vorstellung
 8. vorbildliche Leistung
11. Fläche, auf die ein Film projiziert wird
14. Unterbrechung
16. altes Tasteninstrument
17. Sprecherin

18. Fabrikat
20. Anschlagsäule
22. Sendung
24. Stand für Zeitungen, Zigaretten usw.
25. Spielleiter
27. jmd, der Kunstwerke schafft
28. Aufzüge

6. Was bedeuten die Wendungen?

1. in die Tasten greifen
2. mir ist der Film gerissen (fig., coll.)
3. über die Bühne gehen (fig., coll.)
4. mach nicht so ein Theater! (fig., coll.)
5. die Szene beherrschen (fig., coll.)
6. ein Tanz auf dem Vulkan (fig.)
7. jmdm die Meinung geigen (fig., coll.)
8. flöten gehen (coll.)

7. Welches Nomen passt nicht? ✓

1. der Blues, der Jazz, der Schocker, der Techno
2. der Bildhauer, die Medienfachfrau, die Regie, der Tubist
3. der Bogen, der Paukenschlegel, der Pinsel, der Schlager
4. die Buchhandlung, der Kiosk, die Redaktion, die Videothek
5. die Ballerina, der Hörer, der Kinobesucher, die Zuschauerin
6. die Chorleiterin, die Dirigentin, die Regisseurin, die Reporterin
7. die Aufführung, die Ausstellung, das Feuilleton, das Konzert
8. die Anzeigenspalte, der Nachruf, das Plakat, der Werbespot
9. die Abendzeitung, der Leserbrief, das Wochenblatt, die Zeitschrift

8. Suchen Sie eine andere Bedeutung.

1. die Skizze
2. die Stimme
3. die Kassette
4. die Handlung
5. der Artikel
6. die Anzeige

9. Falsche Freunde. Ergänzen Sie die Tabelle.

Deutsch	Englisch	Deutsch	Englisch
die Art			art
der Patron			patron
famos			famous
die Kritik			critic
der Rekord			record
der Rest			rest
die Audienz			audience
der Photograf			photograph
aktuell			actual
der Brand			brand
das Pamphlet			pamphlet

10. Übersetzen Sie ins Englische.

Schatten von gestern

Silvio Soldini verfilmt Agota Kristof

Mit der Charakterkomödie „Brot und Tulpen" ist dem italienisch-schweizerischen Regisseur Silvio Soldini sein bisher größter Erfolg gelungen. Sahen bei uns – der Film ist nach wie vor im Kinoeinsatz – bis jetzt mehr als fünfhunderttausend Zuschauer das Werk, rückte es in Italien mit einem Einspielergebnis von mehr als zehn Millionen Mark im Kinojahr 2000 auf die drittbeste Plazierung eines einheimischen Films.

Gegenwärtig arbeitet der Regisseur an seinem neuen Film „Ieri" (Gestern). Die Dreharbeiten zu dem auf dem gleichnamigen Roman der ungarischen Schriftstellerin Agota Kristof basierenden Stoff sind fur das Frühjahr vorgesehen. Das Drehbuch schrieb Soldini wieder zusammen mit Doriana Leondeff.

„Ieri" handelt von einem Jungen namens Tobias, geboren in einem Dorf ohne Namen. Der Sohn einer Diebin, Bettlerin und Landhure führt ein Leben in Armut, mit einer Kindheit zum Vergessen. Als er am ersten Schultag in seinem Lehrer einen regelmäßigen Besucher des elterlichen Zuhauses erkennt und herausfindet, daß jener sein Vater ist, sticht er ihm ein Messer in den Rücken. Eines Tages trifft Tobias auf der Straße eine Schulfreundin, die Tochter des Lehrers. Seine Stiefschwester, Obsession der Vergangenheit und ständige Begleiterin, wird zum Leitmotiv der Geschichte.

Der 1958 in Mailand geborene Regisseur erzählt wie in seinen vier vorangegangenen Spielfilmen von der Suche nach Identität in einer gefühlskalten Welt: „Es sind Geschichten von Menschen, die mit ihrem Leben irgendwie unzufrieden sind, die sich nach etwas sehnen, häufig jedoch, ohne diese Sehnsucht benennen zu können, und die versuchen, ihrem Leben eine Wende zu geben." J.N.

Frankfurter Allgemeine Zeitung, Samstag, 3. März 2001, Nr. 53/9 D, S. 45

Level 2

1. Wie heißt das Gegenteil? ✓

1. das Original
2. die Ateliermalerei
3. abstrakt
4. der Nachspann
5. die Pressefreiheit
6. offiziell
7. gut gestimmt

2. Welches Substantiv passt nicht? ✓

1. die Harfe, die Leinwand, der Malspachtel, die Staffelei
2. die Charge, die Grafikerin, das Redaktionsmitglied, der Platzanweiser
3. das Atelier, die Dunkelkammer, das Fernsehstudio, die Garderobe
4. das Dreibein, die Polka, der Salsa, der Walzer
5. der Auslöseknopf, der Gutschein, das Objektiv, der Sucher
6. der Chargenspieler, die Darstellerin, der Dramaturg, die Leinwandgröße
7. der Vorfilm, der Vorführraum, der Vorhang, der Vorspann

3. Welches Verb passt? ✓

> a. abhalten, b. bekommen, c. einnehmen, d. geben, e. herausgeben,
> f. sein, g. sitzen, h. spielen

1. in Auftrag
2. eine Pose
3. Porträt
4. vom Blatt
5. eine Probe
6. einen Vorhang
7. eine Presseerklärung
8. auf Sendung

4. Bilden Sie mit den Wendungen in Übung 3 je einen Satz.

Beispiel: jmdm Modell stehen: *Sie hat ihm Modell gestanden.*

5. Welches Wort hat die gleiche oder eine ähnliche Bedeutung? ✓

1. das Portrait	6. der Fernseher
2. das Studio	7. die Couchpotato
3. der Tanzboden	8. die Broschüre
4. das Dreibein	9. die Warenprobe
5. die Reporterin	10. die Anschlagtafel

6. Suchen Sie eine andere Bedeutung.

1. verstimmt
2. der Akt
3. die Galerie
4. die Sammlung
5. die Probe
6. das Hackbrett
7. die Ausstattung
8. der Rang
9. der Twist
10. das Gebot

7. Was bedeuten die Wendungen?

1. wissen, was die Glocke geschlagen hat (fig., coll.)
2. aus der Reihe tanzen (fig., coll.)
3. der Bericht ist stark geschminkt (fig.)
4. nicht viel zu melden haben (coll.)
5. das ist wirklich museumsreif
6. ein unbeschriebenes Blatt sein (fig.)

8. Was bedeuten die folgenden Zusammensetzungen?

1. die Presseagentur, der Pressedienst, der Presseempfang, der/die Pressefotograf(in), das Pressegesetz, die Pressekampagne, der/die Pressesprecher(in), die Pressetribüne
2. die Werbeabteilung, die Werbeaktion, der Werbefeldzug, der Werbefunk, das Werbegeschenk, der/die Werbeleiter(in), die Werbesprache
3. der/die Filmamateur(in), das Filmarchiv, das Filmatelier, die Filmausrüstung, das Filmgeschäft, der/die Filmheld(in), die Filmindustrie, der Filmpreis
4. die Kunstausstellung, der Kunstband, der Kunstbesitz, der Kunstdiebstahl, der/die Kunsterzieher(in), der/die Kunstfreund(in), der Kunstführer, die Kunstgeschichte, der/die Kunsthistoriker(in), der/die Kunstkenner(in)

9. Erklären Sie den Unterschied.

1. der Walzer, der Wälzer
2. der Laut, die Laute
3. bieten, bitten
4. der Akkord, das Akkordeon
5. das Register, der Regisseur
6. künstlerisch, künstlich

10. Übersetzen Sie ins Englische.

Wird's was geben

Theater Hagen eröffnet Kinderbühne

Alle Jahre wieder. So war das bisher auch in Hagen. Das obligate Weihnachtsstück war meist schon alles, was für Kinder auf den Spielplan kam. Damit will sich das Theater nicht länger begnügen. Künftig wird es, so der Intendant Rainer Friedemann, ein „geregeltes Angebot" geben: Das Haus, das die Sparten Oper und Tanz, aber kein eigenes Schauspiel unterhält, hat damit begonnen, ein Kinder- und Jugendtheater aufzubauen. An diesem Wochenende geht erstmals der Vorhang auf, gleich drei Inszenierungen haben Premiere: „Max" von Beat Fäh, „Das Herz eines Boxers" von Lutz Hübner und „Rotkäppchen spielen" von Hansjörg Schneider.
  Initiator und Leiter der neuen Bühne ist Werner Hahn, der seit achtzehn Jahren dem Hagener Ensemble als Sänger angehört und für die neue Aufgabe auf eine halbe Stelle wechselt. Da die Stadt für das Kinder- und Jugendtheater keine zusätzlichen Mittel aufbringen kann, muß das Theater es aus seinem laufenden Etat finanzieren. Als Spielstätte dient zunächst das Jugendzentrum

„Globe" in der Konkordiastraße, dessen Bühne jedoch nur für zwei Wochen im Monat zur Verfügung steht. In zwei, drei Jahren, nach der Renovierung des Stadttheaters, sollen dort eigene Räumlichkeiten bezogen werden. Vorgesehen sind vier Produktionen pro Spielzeit, die von theaterpädagogischen Aktivitäten und Mitspielangeboten begleitet werden.

Andreas Rossman

Frankfurter Allgemeine Zeitung, Samstag, 3. März 2001, Nr. 53/9 D, S. 41

Level 3

1. Wie heißt das Adjektiv? ✓

1. der Stein	4. der Marmor
2. das Holz	5. die Bronze
3. das Metall	6. der Ton

2. Wie heißt das Gegenteil? ✓

1. der Vordergrund	8. die Einblendung
2. die Horizontale	9. die Außenaufnahme
3. das Hochrelief	10. der Tonfilm
4. das Kreuz	11. überbelichtet
5. der Auftakt	12. aufblenden
6. das Dur	13. die Kurzwelle
7. der Auftritt	14. der Zeitraffer

3. Wie heißen die Zusammensetzungen? ✓

~~Bunt-~~	werfer	1. *der Buntstift*
Lampen-	punkt	2.
Groß-	klang	3.
Flucht-	aufnahme	4.
Drucker-	wechsel	5.
Bühnen-	~~stift~~	6.
Drei-	schwärze	7.
Schein-	fieber	8.
Kulissen-	anweisung	9.

4. Ergänzen Sie. ✓

1. der Stein – der Meißel : das Holz – _____
2. die Leinwand – die Staffelei : die Noten – _____
3. das Pauspapier – pausen : die Aquarellfarbe – _____
4. der Bauchtanz – bauchtanzen : der Stepptanz – _____

5. der/die Schriftsetzer(in) – setzen : der/die Cutter(in) – _____

6. der/die Maler(in) – der Pinsel : der/die Dirigent(in) – _____

5. Wie heißt das Symbol? ✓

6. Welches Wort hat die gleiche oder eine ähnliche Bedeutung? ✓

1. die Aquarellfarbe   6. der/die Betrachter(in)
2. das Fixativ   7. der Ballettschuh
3. das Pauspapier   8. der/die Statist(in)
4. das Dessin   9. der Tipp
5. das Clair-obscur   10. die Boulevardpresse

7. Was passt wo?

die Blende, der Fingersatz, die Frontseite, die Froschperspektive, die Kastagnette, körnig, die Korrekturfahne, die Livesendung, das Markenbild, der Mollakkord, der Monolog, der Reklamerummel, restaurieren, der Satellit, die Schärfentiefe, schattieren, der Souffleurkasten, das Steppeisen, synchronisieren, taktmäßig, die Totale, das Trikot, der Übertragungswagen, verleumden, das Versatzstück, der Verschnitt, das Warenzeichen

1. die Malerei   2. die Musik   3. der Tanz
a.   a.   a.
b.   b.   b.
c.   c.   c.
4. das Theater   5. der Film   6. die Fotografie
a.   a.   a.
b.   b.   b.
c.   c.   c.
7. die Presse   8. das Fernsehen   9. die Werbung
a.   a.   a.
b.   b.   b.
c.   c.   c.

8. Suchen Sie eine andere Bedeutung.

1. das Kreuz
2. der Prospekt
3. der Ausschnitt

4. die Fahrt
5. die Blende
6. der Ton

9. Schreiben Sie eine Rezension eines Filmes, einer Theateraufführung, einer Fernsehsendung o. Ä. Fassen Sie die Handlung kurz zusammen, besprechen Sie z.B. die Kinematografie, das Drehbuch, die Besetzung, die Beleuchtung, die Musik usw., und bewerten Sie den Film bzw. die Theateraufführung usw.

10. Übersetzen Sie ins Englische.

Die besondere Schönheit des Alltäglichen

Die wenigsten Magazine schaffen es, über Jahre hinweg denselben visuellen Standard zu halten. Viele Designs sind eine Zeit lang gefällig, ja beinahe perfekt. Perfektion jedoch wird meist sehr schnell langweilig.

Bei *i-D* hatte man nie den Eindruck, dass es seinen Machern um Perfektion geht, sondern um ständiges Experimentieren in Sachen Mode, Design, Musik und Style. *Style is nothing you can buy* könnte eine der Maximen des Magazins lauten. So hat *i-D* über Jahre hinweg einen glaubwürdigen Weg vom Street-Fanzine hin zur internationalen Stilbibel beschritten, ohne sich selbst dabei je untreu zu werden.

Als wir Anfang der Neunziger *jetzt*, das Jugendmagazin der *Süddeutschen Zeitung*, gestalteten, hatte *i-D* mit Sicherheit eine Art Vorbildfunktion. Die puristischen, auf angenehme Weise unprätentiösen Gestaltungselemente des Magazins ließen den Inhalten immer genügend Raum. Es war zu spüren, dass hier nie das Werkzeug, der Computer, die Gestaltung bestimmt, sondern der Umgang des Designers mit dem Material – sowie die dem Magazin eigene, besondere Haltung zur Schönheit des Alltäglichen.

Markus Rindermann
34, ArtDirector »GQ«, München

DIE ZEIT, 22. März 2001, Nr. 13, Leben, S. 5

Unit 10

Literature and literary criticism

Level 1

Genres

Gattung, die (-en)	genre
Lyrik, die (no pl.)	lyric poetry
Epik, die (no pl.)	epic poetry, fiction
Dramatik, die (no pl.)	drama
Gedicht, das (-e)	poem
Lied, das (-er)	song
Geschichte, die (-n)	story
Kurzgeschichte, die (-n)	short story
Erzählung, die (-en)	tale, story
Novelle, die (-n)	novella; short story
Märchen, das (-)	fairy tale
Roman, der (-e)	novel
Kriminalroman, der (-e)	detective story, crime novel
Tragödie, die (-n)	tragedy
Komödie, die (-n)	comedy
Lustspiel, das (-e)	comedy
Essay, der or das (-s)	essay
Aufsatz, der (¨e)	essay
Biographie, die (-n)	biography
Auto-, Selbstbiographie, die (-n)	autobiography

Writers

Autor(in), der/die (-en/nen)	author
Schriftsteller(in), der/die (-/nen)	writer, novelist
Erzähler(in), der/die (-/nen)	story-teller
Dramatiker(in), der/die (-/nen)	dramatist
Biograph(in), der/die (-en/nen)	biographer

Structure

Aufbau, der (no pl.)	form, structure, composition
Komposition, die (-en)	composition
Gesamtkomposition, die (-en)	overall structure
(Unter)titel, der (-)	(sub)title
Akt, der (-e)	act
Szene, die (-n)	scene
Figur, die (-en)	character
Haupt-, Nebenfigur, die (-en)	main/secondary character
Rede, die (-n)	speech
Vers, der (-e)	verse
Strophe, die (-n)	verse, stanza
Zeile, die (-n)	line
Reim, der (-e)	rhyme
(Neben)handlung, die (-en)	(sub)plot

es spielt in	it is set in	flüssig	fluent, flowing
Schauplatz, der ("e)	setting	blumig	flowery
		eintönig	monotonous
		langatmig (pej.)	wordy

Style

Stil, der (-e)	style	Gegensatz, der ("e)	contrast
langweilig	dull	Umschreibung,	circumlocution
trocken	dry, uninspiring	die (-en)	
farblos	lifeless	Anspielung, die (-en)	allusion
farbig	colourful	Lautsymbolik, die	sound symbolism
bilderreich	rich in imagery	(no pl.)	
klar	perspicuous, limpid	Dingsymbol, das (-e)	concrete symbol
lebendig	lively	Übertreibung,	exaggeration
schwungvoll	lively	die (-en)	
schwunglos	pedestrian, lacklustre	Nominal-, Verbalstil,	nominal/verbal style
wortreich	wordy	der (no pl.)	

Level 2

Genres

Ballade, die (-n)	ballad	Erziehungsroman,	educational novel
Hymne, die (-n)	hymn	der (-e)	
Sprichwort, das ("er)	proverb	Dissertation,	dissertation
Lehrgedicht, das (-e)	didactic poem	die (-en)	
Fabel, die (-n)	fable	Sachbuch, das ("er)	nonfiction book
Parabel, die (-n)	parable	Tagebuch, das ("er)	diary
Satire, die (-n)	satire	Memoiren, pl.	memoirs
Parodie, die (-n)	parody	Kinderliteratur, die	children's literature
Legende, die (-n)	legend	(no pl.)	
Epos, das (Epen)	epic (poem);	Jugendliteratur, die	teenage fiction
	epos	(no pl.)	
komisches Epos	mock epic	Frauenliteratur, die	literature written by
höfisches Epos	courtly romance	(no pl.)	women
Kriminalgeschichte,	murder mystery	Unterhaltungslektüre,	light reading
die (-n)		die (-n)	
Abenteuergeschichte,	adventure story		
die (-n)		## Writers	
Zeitroman, der (-e)	problem novel	Verfasser(in), der/die	writer, author
Gesellschaftsroman,	social novel	(-/nen)	
der (-e)		Dichter(in), der/die	writer, poet
Entwicklungsroman,	developmental novel	(-/nen)	
der (-e)		Lyriker(in), der/die	lyric poet, lyricist
Bildungsroman,	apprenticeship novel;	(-/nen)	
der (-e)	Bildungsroman	Romanautor(in),	novelist
Künstlerroman,	artist novel	der/die (-en/nen)	
der (-e)		Essayist(in), der/die	essayist
		(-en/nen)	

Structure

Metrik, die (no pl.)	metrics
Verslehre, die (-n)	metrics
Metrum, das (-tren)	metre
Versmaß, das (-e)	metre
Anfangs-, Endreim, der (-e)	initial/end rhyme
Stabreim, der (-e)	alliteration
Kreuzreim, der (-e)	alternate rhyme
Episode, die (-n)	episode
Wendung, die (-en)	twist
Rückwendung, die (-en)	flashback
Rückblende, die (-n)	flashback
Vorausdeutung, die (-en)	foreshadowing
Bewusstseinsstrom, der (¨e)	stream of consciousness
Motiv, das (-e)	motif, theme
Leitmotiv, das (-e)	leitmotiv, central/ dominant theme
der rote Faden	the central theme
(in)direkte Rede	(in)direct speech/ discourse
Einleitung, die (-en)	introduction
Vorwort, das (-e)	preface
Zitat, das (-e)	quotation
Anmerkung, die (-en)	note
Abschnitt, der (-e)	section, part

Style

gehoben	elevated, refined
nüchtern	sober, matter-of-fact
anschaulich	clear, vivid, graphic
knapp	terse, concise, succinct, laconic
präzis	concise, precise

eindringlich	forceful
hölzern	wooden
papieren	wooden
schwerfällig	clumsy
holprig	clumsy
banal	trite
unzusammenhängend	disjointed
zusammenhanglos	disjointed
weit hergeholt	far-fetched
an den Haaren herbeigezogen	far-fetched
bombastisch	bombastic
schwülstig	bombastic, fustian, pompous
Klang-, Lautmalerei, die (-en)	onomatopoeia
lautmalend	onomatopoeic
Rhetorik, die (no pl.)	rhetoric
Redekunst, die (¨e)	rhetoric
rhetorisch	rhetorical
phrasenhaft (pej.)	empty, trite, cliché-ridden
Amtssprache, die (-n)	official language, officialese
Vergleich, der (-e)	simile
Metapher, die (-n)	metaphor
Bandwurmsatz, der (¨e)	interminable sentence
Schachtelsatz, der (¨e)	involved sentence
Kettensatz, der (¨e)	main clause with a chain of subordinate clauses
etw kurz berühren	to touch on sth
etw antippen	to touch on sth
etw hervorheben	to emphasize sth

Level 3

Genres

Rondeau, das (-s)	rondeau
Romanze, die (-n)	romance
Sonett, das (-e)	sonnet
Madrigal, das (-e)	madrigal

Ode, die (-n)	ode
Elegie, die (-n)	elegy
Dithyrambus, der (-ramben)	dithyramb
Sentenz, die (-en)	maxim

Aphorismus, der (-men)	aphorism
Maxime, die (-n)	maxim
Epigramm, das (-e)	epigram
Sinnspruch, der (¨e)	saying
Priamel, die (-n) or das (-)	priamel (late medieval didactic poem)
Spruchgedicht, das (-e)	didactic poem
Gleichnis, das (-se)	exemplum
Travestie, die (-n)	travesty
Saga, die (-s)	saga
Sage, die (-n)	legend
Mythos, der (Mythen)	myth
Schwank, der (¨e)	low burlesque, comic tale
Kalendergeschichte, die (-n)	almanac story
Volksbuch, das (¨er)	chapbook
Schelmenroman, der (-e)	picaresque novel
Staatsroman, der (-e)	utopia
utopischer Roman	utopia
Schlüsselroman, der (-e)	roman à clef
Abhandlung, die (-en)	treatise
Flugblatt, das (¨er)	pamphlet
Belletristik, die (no pl.)	belles-lettres
die schöngeistige Literatur	belletristic literature

Writers

Troubadour, der (-e or -s)	troubadour
Minnesänger, der (-)	minstrel, Minnesinger
Kompilator(in), der/die (-en/nen; elev., pej.)	compiler
Chronist(in), der/die (-en/nen)	chronicler

Structure

innerer Monolog	(direct) interior monologue
erlebte Rede	narrated (indirect interior) monologue
allwissender Erzähler	omniscient author
Gestalt, die (-en)	character
Erzählzeit, die (-en)	narrative time, extrinsic time
erzählte Zeit	narrated time, intrinsic time
Steigerung, die (-en)	rising action, complication
Höhepunkt, der (-e)	climax
fallende Handlung	descending, falling action
Katastrophe, die (-n)	catastrophe
Moment, das (-e)	factor, element
erregendes Moment	exciting force, catalyst
tragisches Moment	tragic force
Peripetie, die (-n)	peripeteia, reversal
retardierendes Moment	retardation, moment of final suspense
Zyklus, der (-klen)	cycle
Takt, der (-e)	foot
Hebung, die (-en)	stressed syllable
Senkung, die (-en)	unstressed syllable
Auftakt, der (-e)	anacrusis
Versfuß, der (¨e)	metrical foot
Knittelvers, der (-e)	rhyming couplets of four-stress lines
Zäsur, die (-en)	caesura
Gesang, der (¨e)	canto
Exkurs, der (-e)	excursus

Style

ein gewandter Stil	an elegant style
gepflegt	cultured, refined
lapidar	succinct, terse
gedrängt	terse, succinct
abgenutzt	hackneyed
abgedroschen	hackneyed
weitschweifig	long-winded
umständlich	long-winded

gestelzt	stilted	Metonymie, die (-n)	metonymy
geschraubt	stilted, affected, pretentious	Stichomythie, die (-n)	stichomythia
gespreizt	affected, unnatural	Parataxe, die (-n)	parataxis
maniert	affected	parataktisch	paratactic
überladen	turgid, over-ornate, flowery	Hypotaxe, die (-n)	hypotaxis
		hypotaktisch	hypotactic
gewunden	convoluted	Anapher, die (-n)	anaphora
rührselig	maudlin	Ellipse, die (-n)	ellipsis
aphoristisch	aphoristic	Präsens historicum, das (no pl.)	historical present
sentenziös	sentential		
Paradoxon, das (-doxa)	paradox	Chiasmus, der (-men)	chiasmus
		Synästhesie, die (-n)	synaesthesia
paradox	paradoxical	Anakoluth, das or der (-e)	anacoluthon
Oxymoron, das (-ra)	oxymoron		

Speaking

Level 1

Conversing

sprechen	to speak, talk
Gespräch, das (-e)	conversation
etw besprechen	to discuss sth
Besprechung, die (-en)	discussion, meeting
reden	to speak, talk
(etw) diskutieren	to discuss (sth)
jmdn anrufen	to call sb up
(mit jmdm) telefonieren	to speak on the telephone (with sb)
jmdn unterbrechen	to interrupt sb
mit jmdm von etw plaudern	to chat with sb about sth

Asking and answering

(etw) fragen	to ask (sth)
jmdn etw fragen	to ask sb sth
nach jmdm/etw fragen	to ask about sb/sth
(jmdm) eine Frage stellen	to ask (sb) a question
jmdn (über etw) befragen	to question sb (about sth)
(jmdm) antworten	to reply (to sb)

auf etw antworten	to reply to sth
etw beantworten	to reply to/answer sth
jmdn um etw bitten	to request sth from sb
jmdn (darum) bitten, etw zu tun	to beg of sb to do sth
etw fordern	to demand/call for sth
etw verlangen	to demand/ask for sth

Explaining

etw erklären	to explain sth
etw klarmachen	to make sth clear
etw definieren	to define sth
jmdn/etw charakterisieren	to characterize sb/sth
etw interpretieren	to interpret sth
etw wiederholen	to repeat sth
etw betonen	to emphasize/stress sth
sich (jmdm) verständlich machen	to make oneself understood (to sb)

Agreeing and disagreeing

einer Meinung sein	to share the same opinion
der gleichen Meinung sein	to be of the same opinion
anderer Meinung (als jmd) sein	to disagree (with sb)
mit jmdm/etw einverstanden sein	to be in agreement with sb/sth
übereinstimmen	to agree
mit jmdm nicht übereinstimmen	to disagree with sb
(sich mit jmdm) streiten	to argue (with sb)
sich über etw streiten	to dispute sth
Streit, der (-e)	quarrel, argument
ein heftiger Streit	a heated argument
jmdm widersprechen	to contradict/argue against sb
Protest, der (-e)	protest
protestieren	to protest
gegen etw sein	to be opposed to sth
Krach haben	to have a row

Informing

etw berichten	to report sth
Bericht, der (-e)	report
einen Bericht geben	to give a report
etw erzählen	to narrate/relate sth
jmdn benachrichtigen	to inform sb
jmdm etw mitteilen	to inform/notify sb about sth
Mitteilung, die (-en)	message
jmdm Bescheid geben/sagen	to let sb know
etw bekannt geben	to announce sth
etw bekannt machen	to make sth public
auf etw hinweisen	to point out sth
etw erwähnen	to mention sth

Asserting and denying

etw sagen	to say sth
etw meinen	to say sth
etw bemerken	to remark
eine Bemerkung machen	to make a remark
etw behaupten	to assert, claim sth
Behauptung, die (-en)	statement, assertion
(jmdm) etw garantieren	to guarantee (sb) sth
etw vorbringen	to advance sth

Calling out

rufen	to call, shout
etw ausrufen	to call out/exclaim sth
Hurra rufen	to cheer
schreien	to shout, cry out, scream, yell, shriek
aufschreien	to yell, scream, shriek, cry out
laut werden	to raise one's voice [get angry]
jmdn beschimpfen	to swear at sb
mit jmdm schimpfen	to rant at sb
herumschimpfen	to rant and rave
(über etw) fluchen	to swear (about sth)
donnern	to thunder on

Praising and complaining

jmdn/etw loben	to praise sb/sth
jmdn ehren	to honour sb
jmdm gratulieren	to congratulate sb
jmdn/etw kritisieren	to criticize sb/sth
schimpfen	to moan, grumble, bitch
sich beklagen	to complain
klagen	to moan, wail; complain

Gossiping and teasing

schwatzen	to gossip
schwatzhaft (pej.)	gossipy
(über jmdn) klatschen (coll., pej.)	to gossip (about sb)
klatschhaft	gossipy
Klatsch, der (no pl.)	gossip

Klatschmaul, das (¨er; coll., pej.)	gossip	Blödsinn reden	to talk rubbish
quatschen	to gossip	reden können	to have the gift of the gab
Schlechtes über jmdn sagen	to speak ill of sb	ohne Unterbrechung reden	to keep up a patter
über jmdn/von jmdm schlecht sprechen	to speak ill of sb	plappern	to chatter, blab
jmdn verspotten	to mock/ridicule sb		
jmdn hänseln	to tease sb		
jmdn veralbern	to make fun of sb		

Miscellaneous

(etw) flüstern	to whisper (sth)
schweigen	to be silent
sich versprechen	to make a slip of the tongue
stottern	to stutter
lispeln	to lisp
etw zurücknehmen	to take sth back
etw aussprechen	to pronounce sth
die Wahrheit sagen	to tell the truth
lügen	to lie
etw vorschlagen	to suggest sth
jmdm raten, etw zu tun	to advise sb to do sth

Rambling and chattering

quatschen	to blather, chatter, blab
schwatzen	to chatter, talk, blab
schwatzhaft (pej.)	talkative, garrulous
plaudern	to chit-chat
gesprächig	talkative
langatmig	long-winded

Level 2

Conversing

sich unterhalten	to talk, converse
Unterhaltung, die (-en)	conversation
etw austauschen	to exchange sth
sich austauschen	to exchange views
über etw Gedanken austauschen	to exchange views about sth
sich an jmdn heranmachen	to chat sb up
mit jmdm ein Gespräch führen	to have a conversation with sb
Dialog, der (-e)	dialogue
Unterredung, die (-en)	discussion, talk
jmdn anreden	to address sb
etw ansprechen	to broach/talk about sth

jmdm ein Loch in den Bauch fragen	to drive sb up the wall with all one's questions
herumfragen (coll.)	to ask around
jmdn wegen etw um Rat fragen	to ask sb for advice about sth
Anfrage, die (-n)	enquiry
anfragen	to inquire, ask
jmdn ausforschen	to question sb
bohren	to keep on (asking)
auf etw eingehen	to go into sth
etw zurückgeben	to retort/rejoin sth
einsilbig antworten	to answer in monosyllables
jmdn inständig/ dringend bitten	to entreat/implore sb

Explaining

mit anderen Worten	in other words
anders gesagt	in other words

Asking and answering

eine Frage an jmdn richten	to put a question to sb

etw begründen	to explain/give reasons for sth	(jmdm über etw) Auskunft geben	to give information (to sb about sth)
sich genauer ausdrücken	to be more specific	jmdn beraten	to advise sb
auf Einzelheiten/ins Detail gehen	to go into detail	jmdm etw versichern	to assure sb (of) sth
		etw darstellen	to depict, portray sth
		etw schildern	to describe sth
		(etw) zitieren	to quote (sth)

Agreeing and disagreeing

ein Streit der Meinungen	a clash of opinions
Streiterei, die (-en)	arguing, quarrelling
Auseinandersetzung, die (-en)	argument, dispute
geteilter Meinung sein	to be in disagreement
Meinungsverschiedenheit, die (-en)	disagreement, difference of opinion
etw bestreiten	to dispute/contest/ challenge sth; deny sth
sich bereit erklären, etw zu tun	to agree to do sth
(es) vereinbaren, dass	to agree that
abmachen, dass	to agree that
jmdm zustimmen	to agree with sb
nicht zustimmen	to dissent
etw angreifen	to attack sth
sich gegen etw aussprechen	to speak out against sth
seine Stimme gegen etw erheben	to speak out against sth
streitlustig, -süchtig	argumentative
einwenden, dass	to object that
etw bezweifeln	to doubt/question sth

Asserting and denying

die Ansicht/ Meinung vertreten, dass	to hold the view that
seine Meinung äußern	to express one's opinion
sich über etw äußern	to give one's view on sth
zu etw Stellung nehmen	to express one's opinion on sth
Stellungnahme, die (-n)	opinion
jmdm etw zusichern	to assure sb of sth
gegen jmdn/vor etw aussagen	to testify against sb/before sth
etw bestätigen	to acknowledge/ confirm sth
etw als unwahr/ falsch bezeichnen	to characterize sth as untrue/wrong
etw verneinen	to answer in the negative; deny/ dispute sth
etw negieren	to deny sth

Informing

etw melden	to report sth
jmdn/sich auf dem Laufenden halten	to keep sb/o.s. informed
jmdn etw wissen lassen	to let sb know sth
jmdn über etw unterrichten	to inform sb about sth

Calling out

brüllen	to shout, roar, yell, bawl, bellow
aufbrüllen	to shout/yell out
jmdn anbrüllen	to bellow at sb
sich heiser schreien	to shout oneself hoarse
jmdm etw zurufen	to shout sth to/ at sb; call sth out to sb
jmdm anfeuernd zurufen	to cheer sb

jubeln	to cheer/shout with joy
jmdm zujubeln	to cheer sb
aufjubeln	to shout (out) with joy
jmdn anfeuern	to spur sb on
jmdn ermutigen	to encourage sb
eine Schimpfkanone loslassen	to rant
mit etw herausplatzen	to blurt sth out

Praising and complaining

von jmdm/etw schwärmen	to enthuse about sb/sth
jmdn würdigen	to pay tribute to sb
jmdn/etw verherrlichen	to glorify, praise, extol sb/sth
jmdn beglückwünschen	to congratulate sb
meckern (coll.)	to moan, bleat, grouse
sich beschweren	to complain
jammern	to wail; moan, yammer
brummen	to grumble, grouch, grouse
jmdm sein Leid/ seinen Kummer klagen	to pour out one's sorrow/grief to sb
jmdm etw vorwerfen	to reproach sb with sth; accuse sb of sth

Gossiping and teasing

über jmdn/etw herziehen	to run sb/sth down; pull sb/sth to pieces
über jmdn losziehen	to pull sb to pieces
jmds Namen mit Schmutz bewerfen	to drag sb's good name through the mud
jmdn in Verruf bringen	to malign sb's character
jmdm Übles nachsagen	to malign sb's character

hetzen	to stir up hatred, say malicious things
gegen jmdn/etw hetzen	to smear sb/agitate against sth
über jmdn/etw lästern	to make malicious remarks about sb/sth
über jmdn/etw spotten	to mock sb/sth; make fun of sb/sth
über jmdn/etw spötteln	to mock sb/sth gently; poke gentle fun at sb/sth
jmdn/etw verhöhnen	to mock, deride, ridicule sb/sth
jmdn mit etw foppen	to make fun of sb with sth
jmdn mit jmdm/etw necken	to tease sb about sb/sth
jmdn mit/wegen etw aufziehen (coll.)	to rib/tease sb about sth

Rambling and chattering

auf etw herumreiten	to go on about sth; harp on sth
sich endlos über etw auslassen	to ramble on about sth
jmdn beschwatzen	to sweet-talk sb
Verkaufsargu- mentation, die (-en)	sales talk
(etw) lallen	to babble/mumble (sth)
(etw) labern	to babble (sth)
blödeln	to make silly jokes
etw brabbeln (coll.)	to mutter/mumble sth
etw brummeln (coll.)	to mumble sth
schwafeln (coll., pej.)	to waffle, blether

Miscellaneous

stillschweigen	to remain silent
sich ausdrücken	to express oneself
sich schlecht ausdrücken können	to be inarticulate
stammeln	to stammer

alles ausplaudern	to spill the beans	jmdm eine Strafpredigt halten	to give sb a lecture
direkt/gleich zur Sache kommen	to get straight to the point	sich einmischen	to butt in
sich jmdm anvertrauen	to confide in sb	etw hinzufügen	to add sth
		jmdn überreden, etw zu tun	to persuade sb to do sth
jmdm etw anvertrauen	to confide sth to sb	auf etw bestehen	to insist on sth

Level 3

Asking and answering

jmdn mit Fragen überschütten	to fire questions at sb
sich nach jmdm/etw erkundigen	to ask after sb/ enquire about sth
jmdn ausquetschen (coll.)	to grill/pump sb
jmdn verhören	to interrogate sb
Verhör, das (-e)	interrogation
etw entgegnen	to reply sth
einer Sache begegnen	to respond to sth
(auf etw) erwidern	to reply (to sth)
scharf erwidern	to retort
etw versetzen	to retort sth
schlagfertig sein	to be quick at repartee
bei jmdm auf den Busch klopfen (coll.)	to sound sb out about sth
jmdn über etw aushorchen	to sound sb out about sth
an jmdn/etw appelieren	to appeal to sb/sth
jmdn anflehen	to entreat/implore sb

Explaining

etw auslegen	to interpret sth
etw deuten	to interpret sth
etw ausdeuten	to interpret sth
etw erläutern	to explain/comment on sth
etw näher erläutern	to clarify sth
etw klarstellen	to clear sth up
etw näher ausführen	to elaborate sth
etw explizieren (elev.)	to explicate sth

Agreeing and disagreeing

sich (mit jmdm) über etw nicht einig sein	to disagree (with sb) about sth
sich darin/darüber einig sein, dass	to be agreed that
sich über etw einig werden	to agree on sth
sich (über etw) einigen	to reach an agreement (about sth)
(sich) zanken	to squabble, bicker
Zank, der (no pl.)	squabble, row
Gezänk, das (no pl.)	quarrelling
Zwietracht, die (no pl.; elev.)	discord
Zwietracht säen	to sow the seeds of discord
etw anfechten	to challenge/dispute sth
spitzfindiges Argument	quibble
einen Einwand (gegen etw) erheben	to raise an objection (to sth)
sich mit jmdm zerstreiten	to fall out with sb
untereinander zerstritten sein	to be at loggerheads
einen Wortwechsel haben	to have/exchange words

einer Sache entgegenhalten, dass	to object to sth that
etw dagegenhalten	to say sth in objection

Informing

(jmdm über etw) Auskunft erteilen	to give information (to sb about sth)
(jmdm) (von etw) Bericht erstatten	to report (to sb) (on sth)
etw referieren	to give a report on sth
etw vermelden	to report/announce sth
etw ankündigen	to announce sth
etw kundtun	to announce sth, make sth known
etw verkünden	to announce sth
etw verkündigen (elev.)	to announce, proclaim sth
etw verlautbaren	to announce sth (officially)
jmdn von etw in Kenntnis setzen	to inform/notify sb of sth
jmdn (über etw) ins Bild setzen	to put sb in the picture (about sth)
jmdn über etw aufklären	to inform sb about sth
etw vermitteln	to pass on/ communicate sth

Asserting and denying

etw beteuern	to affirm/assert sth
sich dafür verbürgen, dass	to vouch that
etw bezeugen	to testify to sth
etw leugnen	to deny sth
etw ableugnen	to deny sth
etw verleugnen	to deny sth
etw in Abrede stellen	to deny/dispute sth
etw abstreiten	to dispute sth; deny sth
etw widerlegen	to refute sth

Calling out

schnauzen (coll.)	to shout
quietschen	to squeal
kreischen	to shriek, squeal
johlen	to howl
jauchzen	to cheer; shout and cheer
(vor etw) aufjauchzen	to shout (out) (with sth)
jubilieren	to rejoice
einen Freuden- schrei/Freudenruf ausstoßen	to give a shout of joy
juchzen	to shriek with delight
aufjuchzen	to whoop with joy
jmdn anspornen	to cheer sb on

Praising and complaining

jmdn/etw rühmen	to praise, extol sb/sth
jmdn/etw preisen	to extol, praise, laud sb/sth
jmdn belobigen	to commend, praise sb
jmdn lobpreisen (elev.)	to praise, glorify sb
maulen (coll.)	to moan
murren	to grumble
jmdn tadeln	to rebuke/reprimand sb

Gossiping and teasing

jmdn verleumden	to slander sb
Verleumder(in), der/die (-/nen)	back-biter
jmdn verunglimpfen (elev.)	to denigrate sb
tratschen	to gossip
jmdn durchhecheln (coll., pej.)	to gossip about sb
jmdn schmähen (elev.)	to revile sb
jmdn wegen einer Sache frotzeln	to tease sb about sth
jmdn verulken (coll.)	to make fun of sb
über jmdn/etw ulken	to make fun of sb/sth

über jmdn witzeln	to joke about sb	radebrechen	to speak pidgin
jmdn anpflaumen (coll.)	to tease sb	kauderwelschen	to talk gibberish; talk jargon; talk a mishmash of languages or dialects

Rambling and chattering

faseln (coll., pej.)	to drivel, blather		
Phrasen dreschen	to spout clichés	seine Worte abwägen	to weigh one's words
quasseln	to chatter		
schnattern (coll.)	to jabber away, chatter	jmdm etw andeuten	to intimate/hint sth to sb
quackeln (coll.)	to chatter	etw verraten	to give sth away
(etw) sabbern/ sabbeln	to chatter on; jabber sth	offen und unverblümt sprechen	to not mince one's words
parlieren (elev.)	to talk away		
salbadern (coll., pej.)	to waffle [pretentiously]	jmdm sein Herz ausschütten	to pour one's heart out to sb
		das Wort ergreifen	to take the floor

Miscellaneous

sich verhaspeln	to stumble over one's words	jmdn in seinen Schranken weisen	to put sb in his place
sich verheddern	to get muddled up	etw verschweigen	to conceal/keep quiet about sth
mit näselndem Tonfall sprechen	to speak with a twang	(etw) dolmetschen	to interpret (sth)

Reading and writing

Level 1

Reading

(etw) lesen	to read (sth)	Unterschrift, die (-en)	signature
jmdm etw vorlesen	to read sth to sb	etw buchstabieren	to spell sth
etw (ganz) durchlesen	to read sth (all the way) through	Rechtschreibung, die (-en)	spelling
etw auslesen	to finish reading sth	etw unterstreichen	to underline sth
die Nase in ein Buch stecken (coll.)	to have one's nose [stuck] in a book	Schreibfehler, der (-)	spelling mistake
		etw entwerfen	to draft sth
mal in etw gucken	to have a read in sth	etw neu schreiben	to rewrite sth
Lektüre, die (-n)	reading; reading matter	etw umschreiben	to rewrite/recast sth
		etw korrigieren	to correct sth
		schriftlich	written, in writing

Writing

(etw) schreiben	to write (sth)		
Handschrift, die (-en)	handwriting		
etw unterschreiben	to sign sth		

Materials

Bleistift, der (-e)	pencil
Kugelschreiber, der (-)	ballpoint pen

Papier, das (-e)	paper	*Types of books*	
Blatt, das (¨er)	sheet of paper	Lehrbuch,	textbook
Schmierpapier,	scrap paper	das (¨er)	
das (no pl.)		Lesebuch, das (¨er)	reader
Heft, das (-e)	notebook	Bilderbuch,	picture book
Zettel, der (-)	note, piece of paper	das (¨er)	
Schreibmaschine,	typewriter	Wörterbuch,	dictionary
die (-n)		das (¨er)	

Level 2

Reading

etw liest sich leicht	sth reads easily
etw genau durchlesen	to peruse sth
in einem Buch nachsehen	to consult a book
in einem Buch blättern	to leaf through a book
etw durchblättern	to leaf through sth
etw überfliegen	to skim through sth
etw diagonal/quer lesen (coll.)	to skim through sth

Writing

eine schöne/ regelmäßige Handschrift	nice/even handwriting
eine schräge Handschrift	slanted writing
etw ausradieren	to erase sth
etw ausstreichen	to cross sth out
sich/jmdm etw aufschreiben	to write sth down
sich etw notieren	to note sth down, make a note of sth
Entwurf (zu einem Roman), der (¨e)	outline/draft (of a novel)
graphisch	graphic
fett(gedruckt)	in bold
Kursivschrift, die (-en)	italics
kursiv (gedruckt)	in italics

Materials

Feder, die (-n)	pen
Füllfederhalter, der (-)	fountain pen
Füller, der (-)	(fountain) pen
Stempel, der (-)	stamp, mark
Radiergummi, der (-s)	eraser
Notizbuch, das (¨er)	notebook
(Notiz)block, der (¨e)	(note) pad
Schreibunterlage, die (-n)	blotter, desk pad

Punctuation

Punkt, der (-e)	full stop, period
Komma, das (-s)	comma
Beistrich, der (-e)	comma
Semikolon, das (-s)	semi-colon
Strichpunkt, der (-e)	semi-colon
Doppelpunkt, der (-e)	colon
Fragezeichen, das (-)	question mark
Ausrufezeichen, das (-)	exclamation mark
Klammer, die (-n)	bracket
Umlaut, der (-e)	umlaut
Zeichensetzung, die (-en)	punctuation
Interpunktion, die (-en)	punctuation

Types of books

Gebetbuch, das (¨er)	prayer book
Messbuch, das (¨er)	missal, mass book
Gästebuch, das (¨er)	visitor's book
Nachschlagewerk, das (-e)	reference book

Band, der (¨e)	volume
dicker Band	tome
Wälzer, der (-; coll.)	hefty tome
Folioband, der (¨e)	folio volume

Level 3

Reading

schmökern (coll.)	to bury oneself in a book
sich in etw vertiefen	to bury oneself in sth
sich in etw versenken	to immerse oneself in/become engrossed in sth
etw verschlingen (coll.)	to devour sth
Bücherwurm, der (¨er)	bookworm

Writing

Blindenschrift, die (-en)	Braille
Punktschrift, die (no pl.)	Braille
etw tilgen (elev.)	to delete/erase sth
Tilgung, die (-en; elev.)	deletion, erasure
Klaue, die (-n; coll.)	scrawl
Gekritzel, das (no pl.)	scribble
(etw) kritzeln	to scribble (sth)
etw hinkritzeln	to scribble sth down

Parts of books

Kapitel, das (-)	chapter
Paragraph, der (-en)	section
Absatz, der (¨e)	paragraph
Spalte, die (-n)	column
Bucheinband, der (¨e)	(book) binding
Inhalt, der (-e)	contents
Schutzumschlag, der (¨e)	dust jacket
Exlibris, das (-)	book plate

Folio, das (-s or Folien)	folio
Anhang, der (¨e)	appendix

Punctuation

Bindestrich, der (-e)	hyphen
Gedankenstrich, der (-e)	dash
Gänsefüßchen, das (-)	quotation mark
Anführungszeichen, das (-)	quotation mark
Akzentzeichen, das (-)	accent mark
Apostroph, der (-e)	apostrophe
runde Klammer	parenthesis, (round) bracket
eckige Klammer	square bracket
spitze Klammer	angle bracket
Schrägstrich, der (-e)	slash, oblique
schiefer Schrägstrich	back slash
Interpunktionszeichen, das (-)	punctuation mark
Satzzeichen, das (-)	punctuation mark

Literacy

nicht lesen und schreiben können	to not be literate
des Lesens und Schreibens (un)kundig	(il)literate
analphabetisch	illiterate
Analphabet(in), der/die (-en/nen)	illiterate person

Exercises

Level 1

1. Was passt zusammen? ✓

> a. die Biographie, b. die Geschichte, c. das Märchen, d. der Roman,
> e. die Strophe, f. die Tragödie

1. der Biograph
2. der Dramatiker
3. die Schriftstellerin
4. die Erzählerin
5. die Gebrüder Grimm
6. das Lied

2. Welches Wort hat die gleiche oder eine ähnliche Bedeutung? ✓

> a. der Aufbau, b. der Aufsatz, c. eintönig, d. der Gegensatz, e. die Geschichte,
> f. die Handlung, g. das Lustspiel, h. reden, i. schwatzen, j. schwungvoll,
> k. die Selbstbiographie, l. verlangen

1. der Essay
2. die Komödie
3. die Autobiographie
4. die Erzählung
5. die Struktur
6. der Plot
7. der Kontrast
8. lebendig
9. monoton
10. sprechen
11. fordern
12. quatschen

3. Welches Verb passt? ✓

> a. bitten, b. geben, c. machen, d. reden, e. sagen, f. stecken, g. stellen

1. jmdm eine Frage
2. jmdn um etw
3. jmdm Bescheid
4. Blödsinn
5. die Nase in ein Buch
6. sich verständlich
7. einen Bericht

4. Wie heißt das Gegenteil? ✓

1. farbig
2. schwungvoll
3. etw fragen
4. der gleichen Meinung sein
5. für etw sein

5. Ergänzen Sie. ✓

1. der Titel – der Untertitel : die Hauptfigur – _____
2. schwatzen – schwatzhaft : klatschen – _____
3. bemerken – die Bemerkung : behaupten – _____
4. kritisieren – loben : lügen – _____
5. streiten – der Streit : protestieren – _____
6. sagen – betonen : schreiben – _____

6. Welche Definition passt? ✓

1. flüstern	a. jmdn verspotten
2. sich versprechen	b. laut rufen
3. jmdn hänseln	c. jmdm etw mitteilen
4. plappern	d. derb schimpfen
5. schreien	e. etw versehentlich anders sagen
6. fluchen	f. etw noch einmal sagen
7. jmdn benachrichtigen	g. fernsprechen
8. etw wiederholen	h. leise sprechen
9. schweigen	i. viel reden und nichts sagen
10. telefonieren	j. still sein

7. Erklären Sie den Unterschied.

1. der Klatsch, das Klatschmaul
2. stottern, lispeln
3. Lyrik, Epik, Dramatik
4. das Ziel, die Zeile

8. Falsche Freunde. Ergänzen Sie die Tabelle.

Deutsch	Englisch	Deutsch	Englisch
die Lektüre			lecture
necken			neck
die Novelle			novel
der Paragraph			paragraph
der Rat			rat
der Roman			Roman
die Sentenz			sentence

9. In jedem Satz fehlt ein Wort. ✓

> beschimpfen, Bleistift, erwähnt, garantieren, klarmachen, Lesebuch, plauderte, Schmierpapier, unterbricht, Unterschrift

1. Er holte sich eine Dose Bier, einen _____ und einen Zettel.
2. Ich gebrauche einseitig gedrucktes Papier als _____.
3. Das Buch eignet sich als Reiseführer, _____ oder Nachschlagewerk.
4. In dem Roman wird sein Name nie _____.
5. Wir _____, dass alle Produkte geliefert werden.
6. Viele grüßen ihn nicht mehr, manche _____ ihn.
7. Wie kann ich es meinen Eltern _____?
8. Seine _____ kann ich nicht lesen.
9. Niemand stört den Redner, keiner _____ ihn.
10. Sie _____ mit den Nachbarn über ihre Reiseerlebnisse.

10. Übersetzen Sie ins Englische.

Luchs des Jahres 2001

Die Jury von ZEIT und Radio Bremen stellt vor: „Malka Mai" von Mirjam Pressler

Wie kommt ein Buch zu einem Literaturpreis? Um mit Astrid Lindgren zu untertreiben: „Es muss gut sein. Ich versichere, dass ich lange und gründlich darüber nachgedacht habe, aber keine andere Antwort darauf weiß als – Es muss gut sein." Vielleicht zählt es zu den erlösendsten Momenten des Kritikers, wenn am Ende aller germanistischen Kriterien und sezierenden Techniken nur eins bleibt: Es ist gut. „Man kann nie sagen: Wie soll ein gutes Kinderbuch sein? Man merkt das, wenn man es liest." Um Superlative zu vermeiden: Mirjam Presslers Roman *Malka Mai* ist ein gutes Buch. Wie klein man wieder wird, wenn die siebenjährige Malka Mai auf der Flucht 1943 von Polen nach Ungarn zurückgelassen wird, wie Angst und Aufatmen abwechseln, wie Poesie und Realismus sich verbinden, wie es ständig um die eigenen Gefühle geht, obwohl diese Zeit so fern liegt.

Doch warum ist dieser Roman besser als die anderen Luchse des Jahres 2001? Warum hat die Jury nicht das engagierte und kluge Jugendsachbuch *GegenPower* (dtv) von Magdalena Köster zum Primus inter Pares gewählt oder das zarte Pflanzensachbuch für Kinder *Über Land und durch die Luft* (Atlantis) von Anne Möller? Warum nicht das wagemutige und poetische Bilderbuch *Warten auf Seemann* (Hammer) von Ingrid Godon und André Sollie oder die großartige kleine Kindergeschichte *Wir alle für immer zusammen* (Oetinger) des Holländers Guus Kuijer? Mit dem Aufzählen kommt die Erinnerung, wird die unglaubliche Goldsucherstory *Der Diener böser Geister* (Hanser) von Roberto Piumini so lebendig wie die mysteriöse Geschichte *Zwischen gestern und morgen* (Ravensburg) aus der Tiefe der Bergwerke in England von David Almond oder der ungewohnte Erzählton des amerikanischen Jugendromans *Ihr kennt mich nicht* (Arena) von David Klass. Drei Bücher kamen der Preisträgerin 2001 numerisch ganz nahe: das lebensfreundliche Bilderbuch *Opas Engel* (Carlsen) von Jutta Bauer, das grandiose Bilderkompendium für Kinder *Die ganze Welt*

(Gerstenberg) von Katy Couprie und Antonin Louchard sowie die Gemäldebiografie für Kinder von Mario Giordano über den Maler Paul Klee: *Der Mann mit der Zwitschermaschine* (Aufbau). Ziemlich unvergleichlich und unvergleichbar.

Vielleicht fiel die Wahl auf *Malka Mai*, weil es von allen das Gute hat. Ein halbes Jahr umfasst dieser Roman, von September 1943 bis März 1944, in dem ein siebenjähriges Kind zu einem Erwachsenen altert und ein Erwachsener wieder ein Kind wird. Panikartig war die jüdische Ärztin Hanna Mai mit ihren beiden Töchtern Malka und Minna über die Berge nach Ungarn geflohen, um einer deutschen „Aktion" zu entkommen ... Es gibt ein Happy End in diesem Roman, der auf einem wahren Schicksal beruht, glücklich ist das Ende nicht. Man bleibt am Leben, das ist genauer. In einer falschen Welt lassen sich keine richtigen Entscheidungen treffen, nur die Geschichten haben Recht. „Früher war ich mal sieben", sagt die Siebenjährige: „Aber das ist lange her."

Astrid Lindgren schreibt: „Dichter erzählen uns von Leben, Tod und Liebe, dem zutiefst Menschlichen, meistens in so schlichten Worten, dass jedes Kind sie verstehen kann – ist dir das schon mal aufgefallen?" Mirjam Pressler schreibt in diesem Ton ihre *Malka Mai*. Sie schreibt seit 20 Jahren Kinder- und Jugendbücher, übersetzt aus dem Niederländischen und Hebräischen, gibt, neben hundert anderen Namen, den Romanen von Uri Orlev ebenso eine deutsche Stimme wie dem *Tagebuch der Anne Frank*, wurde mit dem Deutschen Jugendliteraturpreis ausgezeichnet und für ihre Übertragung von Zeruya Shalevs *Liebesleben* gepriesen. Sie ist eine der Großen, und es bräuchte eigentlich keinen Preis, um ihr zu sagen, wie gut sie ist. Das Buch bekommt den Preis von 5000 Euro, zu dem ihr die Jury aus Amelie Fried, Hilde Elisabeth Menzel, Jens Thiele und Konrad Heidkamp von Herzen gratuliert.   K. H.

DIE ZEIT, 14. Februar 2002, Nr. 8, S. 43

Level 2

1. Ergänzen Sie das deutsche Substantiv und den Artikel.

Artikel	Substantiv	
1.		ballad
2.		hymn
3.		parable
4.		fable
5.		legend
6.		parody
7.		satire
8.		epos
9.		dissertation
10.		memoirs
11.		motif
12.		metaphor

2. Identifizieren Sie die folgenden Beispiele. ✓

> der Anfangsreim, der Endreim, der Kettensatz, der Kreuzreim, der
> Schachtelsatz, der Stabreim

1.
Winterstürme wichen
dem Wonnemond –   (Richard Wagner, „Die Walküre")

2.
Astern, schwälende Tage,
alte Beschwörung, Bann,
Die Götter halten die Waage
Eine zögernde Stunde an.   (Gottfried Benn, „Astern")

3.
Krieg! ist das Losungswort.
Sieg! und so klingt es fort.   (Goethe, „Faust II")

4.
Augen, meine lieben Fensterlein,
Gebt mir schon so lange holden Schein,
Lasset freundlich Bild um Bild herein:
Einmal werdet ihr verdunkelt sein!

                                      (Gottfried Keller, „Abendlied")

5.
Er hätte ihr, da die Kleiderstoffe am Donnerstag, obwohl dieser Tag als Termin festlag, noch
nicht eingefärbt waren, wenigstens Nachricht geben müssen.
                                    (Duden: Richtiges und gutes
Deutsch, S. 743)

6.
Wenn man von dem Rosenhause über den Hügel, auf dem der große Kirschbaum steht,
nordwärts geht, so kommt man in die Wiese, durch welche der Bach fließt, an dem mein
Gastfreund jene Erlengewächse zieht, welche ihm das schöne Holz liefern, das er neben den
andern Hölzern zu seinen Schreinerarbeiten verwendet.   (Stifter)

3. Welche Definition passt? ✓

> a. der Bildungsroman, b. der Gesellschaftsroman, c. der Künstlerroman,
> d. der Zeitroman

1. Roman, in dem die Charakterbildung des Helden geschildert wird
2. Roman, in dem die Entwicklung eines Künstlers geschildert wird
3. Roman, in dem die Probleme einer bestimmten Epoche dargestellt werden
4. Roman, in dem die Probleme und Zustände der Gesellschaft einer Zeit geschildert werden

4. Welches Wort hat die gleiche oder eine ähnliche Bedeutung? ✓

a. etw antippen, b. die Lautmalerei, c. papieren, d. die Redekunst, e. die
Rückblende, f. etw schildern, g. schwerfällig, h. schwülstig, i. die Stellungnahme,
j. streitsüchtig, k. das Tagebuch, l. die Unterredung, m. etw verneinen, n. das
Versmaß, o. zusammenhanglos

1. das Journal
2. die Rückwendung
3. hölzern
4. holprig
5. unzusammenhängend
6. bombastisch
7. die Klangmalerei
8. die Rhetorik
9. etw kurz berühren
10. die Diskussion
11. etw darstellen
12. die Meinung
13. etw negieren
14. das Metrum
15. streitlustig

5. Welches Wort passt nicht? ✓

1. die Essayistin, das Lehrgedicht, die Metrik, der Vers
2. der Abschnitt, die Episode, das Leitmotiv, die Szene
3. bündig, knapp, langatmig, präzis
4. der Dichter, der Liedermacher, der Lyriker, der Romanautor
5. abgedroschen, gehoben, banal, phrasenhaft
6. anfragen, jmdn ausforschen, jmdn beraten, bohren
7. die Auseinandersetzung, die Meinungsverschiedenheit, die Streiterei,
   die Verkaufsargumentation
8. brabbeln, brummeln, jammern, murmeln

6. Welches Verb passt? ✓

a. austauschen, b. blättern, c. bringen, d. erheben, e. führen, f. gehen, g. halten,
h. klagen, i. kommen, j. nehmen, k. richten, l. schreien

1. mit jmdm ein Gespräch
2. eine Frage an jmdn
3. über etw Gedanken
4. seine Stimme gegen etw
5. jmdn auf dem Laufenden
6. zu etw Stellung
7. sich heiser

8. jmdm sein Leid
9. jmdn in Verruf
10. direkt zur Sache
11. auf Einzelheiten
12. in einem Buch

7. *Wie heißen die Zeichen?* ✓
1. ?
2. ,
3. ;
4. !
5. (
6. ¨
7. .
8. :

8. *In jedem Satz fehlt ein Wort.* ✓

> Anfrage, Auskunft, beglückwünscht, bereit, bestätigt, austauschen, einsilbig, ermutigt, gab, geteilter, jubeln

1. Kunden, die eine _____ per E-Mail senden, müssen oft sehr lange auf eine Antwort warten.
2. Deutsche und amerikanische Schüler können sich per E-Mail _____.
3. „Das ist doch mein Recht!", _____ er zurück.
4. „Ja", antwortete er _____ .
5. Die Polizei gab keine _____ darüber.
6. Die Experten sind _____ Meinung.
7. Der König erklärt sich _____ , seinem Bruder die Hälfte seines Reiches zu geben.
8. Der Software-Anbieter hat _____ , dass seine Webseite von Hackern manipuliert wurde.
9. In der sechsten Minute dürfen die Bremer Fans erstmals _____ .
10. Sie hat mich _____ , weiter zu studieren.
11. Sie haben ihn enthusiastisch _____ .

9. *Welches Präfix passt?* ✓
1. Er mischt sich in alles _____.
   a. bei b. ein c. mit d. unter
2. Sie haben ihn wegen seiner abstehenden Ohren _____gezogen.
   a. ab- b. auf- c. los- d. über-
3. Sie haben seine Politik _____gegriffen
   a. ab- b. an- c. ein- d. über-
4. Er hat mich mit Du _____geredet.
   a. ab- b. an- c. auf- d. ein-
5. In diesem Punkt kann ich ihm nicht _____stimmen.
   a. ab- b. an- c. ein- d. zu-

10. Was passt zusammen? ✓

> a. sich etw aufschreiben, b. etw ausradieren, c. etw betonen, d. der Entwurf,
> e. der Füllfederhalter, f. das Gästebuch, g. das Nachschlagewerk, h. der Stempel

1. der Radiergummi
2. kursiv
3. die Frage
4. Besuch
5. Stichworte
6. die Tinte
7. das Stempelkissen
8. der Zettel

11. Übersetzen Sie ins Englische.

Astrid Lindgren: Steine auf dem Küchenbord – Gedanken, Erinnerungen, Einfälle; Verlag Friedrich Oetinger, Hamburg 2000; 88 S., 9,90 €

Dieser schmale Band enthält so viele kluge Zitate, dass jeder damit für den Rest des Lebens gewappnet ist. Natürlich soll man so was nicht machen: Erfundenes und Erfragtes vermischen. Was sich zeigt: Man darf Astrid Lindgren nicht als Kinderbuchautorin preisen, sondern als große Schriftstellerin ohne Präfix. „Man muss leben, damit man sich mit dem Tod anfreundet ... glaube ich, trallala." Am selbstironischen Trallala mangelt es leider manch ernsthaftem Autor.

DIE ZEIT, 7. Februar 2002, Nr. 7, S. 42

Lügen haben lange Nasen

Es bleibt doch einer der schönsten Anfänge: „Es war einmal ..." So lockt uns der nicht eben erfolgreiche Journalist und Schriftsteller Carlo Lorenzini (1826 bis 1890), der sich nach dem toskanischen Städtchen „Collodi" nannte, in seine Geschichte. Ist es ein Märchen? Daran lassen der rituelle Beginn, aber auch die schöne Fee mit den blauen Haaren denken. Ist es eine Fabel? Aus der kommen die Tiere, die, als ob das nichts wäre, sprechen und handeln wie Menschen. Ist es ein Erziehungsroman? Darauf lässt das gute Ende schließen, wenn aus einem Hampelmann „ein richtiger Junge" geworden ist. Ist es eine sanft ironische Parodie auf die Schöpfungsgeschichte? Erschafft doch ein alter Handwerker, wie einst Gott aus einem Klumpen Lehm, aus einem Holzscheit sein Geschöpf. Ist es mit seinen Karikaturen von Onkel Doktor oder Richter nicht eine Satire auf die Gesellschaft?

Dass alle Antworten richtig sein können, erhebt die Abenteuergeschichte in 36 Kapiteln, zu Recht, in den Rang des „berühmtesten Kinderbuchs aller Zeiten", wie der Sprachstempel heißt, ohne den keine neue Ausgabe in allen Sprachen der Welt erscheint.

Inzwischen hat es die Fabelei für die Kleinen in die Literaturgeschichte der Großen geschafft; meint doch Collodis Kollege aus unserer Zeit, Antonio Tabucchi: „Man sollte ‚Pinocchio' als Erwachsener lesen, denn das Buch hat teil am Geist der Tragödie und des Mythos, sein unmittelbarer Gegenstand ist das Leben selbst." In Deutschland wurden Buch und Titelfigur liebend umworben. Das zeigen die vielen Übersetzungs- und Bearbeitungsversuche vom *Zäpfelkern* (Otto Julius Bierbaum) über *Das hölzerne Bengele* bis zu *Kasperle* und *Hampelmann*. Vielleicht ist Heinz Riedts Übersetzung, die jungen und alten Lesern den Namen des Helden im Original zumutet und so sein Geheimnis wahrt, die glücklichste. Die 1960 in Hameln geborene Erzählerin Felicitas Hoppe (*Picknick der Friseure, Pigafrettas Köche*) liest die Abenteuer von der „Insel der fleißigen Bienen" und den „grünen Fischern", von Hund, Esel, Riesenhai und dem Spielzeugland ganz ohne das Raunen einer Märchentante, vielmehr mit frechem Kinderton. Nach Ochs und Esel an der Krippe – ein schöner Ausflug vom Weihnachtsbaum ins Reich der Fantasie, wo die Nase nach jeder Lüge etwas länger wird.

Rolf Michaelis

Carlo Collodi: Pinocchios Abenteuer gelesen von Felicitas Hoppe; Audiobuch Freiburg 2001; 4 CDs; 263 Minuten; 24,90 Euro (ab 8 Jahren und für alle)

DIE ZEIT, 17. Januar 2002, Nr. 4, S. 43

Level 3

1. Wie heißen die Zeichen? ✓

1.]
2. <
3. -
4. –
5. '
6. /
7. \
8. „"
9. ´

2. Welches Wort (welche Wendung) hat die gleiche oder eine ähnliche Bedeutung? ✓

> a. abgenutzt, b. etw auslegen, c. etw leugnen, d. die Punktschrift, e. jmdn rühmen, f. sabbeln, g. das Satzzeichen, h. die Spalte, i. der Staatsroman, j. umständlich, k. etw verkünden, l. jmdn verulken, m. der Zank

1. utopischer Roman
2. abgedroschen
3. weitschweifig
4. etw deuten

5. der Streit
6. etw bekannt geben
7. etw abstreiten
8. jmdn preisen
9. jmdn veralbern
10. sabbern
11. die Blindenschrift
12. die Kolumne
13. das Interpunktionszeichen

3. Identifizieren Sie die folgenden Beispiele. ✓

> die Anapher, der Chiasmus, die Ellipse, die Hypotaxe, das Oxymoron, die Parataxe, das Präsens historicum, die Stichomythie, die Synästhesie

1. Dann fährt er nach Bonn zurück, seine Frau bleibt in Paris.
2. Je länger, je lieber.
3. Sie kannte den Jungen, der über die Straße lief.
4. 1989 fällt die Mauer.
5. Sein Wuchs ist schlank, blond ist sein Haar. (Theodore Fontane, „Gorm Grymme")
6. . . . zogen ihn in der buhlenden Wogen farbig klingenden Schlund. (J. Frh. v. Eichendorf)
7. Hörst du, wie die Brunnen rauschen?
   Hörst du, wie die Grille zirpt?   (Brentano, „Säusle, liebe Myrthe")
8. Antonio: Welch hoher Geist in einer engen Brust!
   Tasso: Hier ist noch Raum, dem Busen Luft zu machen.
   Antonio: Es macht das Volk sich auch mit Worten Luft.
   Tasso: Bist du ein Edelmann wie ich, so zeig es. (Goethe, „Tasso")
9. das tote Leben

4. Welches Verb passt? ✓

> a. ausschütten, b. ausstoßen, c. dreschen, d. erheben, e. erkundigen, f. erstatten, g. klopfen, h. säen, i. setzen, j. stellen

1. bei jmdm auf den Busch
2. sich nach jmdm
3. Zwietracht
4. Einwände gegen etw
5. jmdm von etw Bericht
6. jmdm sein Herz
7. etw in Abrede
8. einen Freudenschrei
9. Phrasen
10. jmdn von etw in Kenntnis

5. Welches Wort passt nicht? ✓

1. die Romanze, das Rondeau, der Schlüsselroman, das Sonett
2. der Aphorismus, das Epigramm, die Maxime, der Schwank
3. der Takt, der Versfuß, die Zäsur, der Zyklus
4. geschraubt, gestelzt, maniert, sentenziös
5. etw entgegnen, etw erläutern, erwidern, etw versetzen
6. jauchzen, johlen, jubilieren, juchzen
7. jmdn anpflaumen, jmdn schmähen, jmdn verleumden, jmdn verunglimpfen

6. Ergänzen Sie das deutsche Substantiv und den Artikel. ✓

	Artikel	Substantiv	
1.			anacoluthon
2.			belles-lettres
3.			catastrophe
4.			compiler
5.			dithyramb
6.			elegy
7.			excursus
8.			madrigal
9.			ode
10.			paradox
11.			peripety
12.			priamel
13.			saga
14.			travesty
15.			troubadour

7. In jedem Satz fehlt ein Wort. ✓

anfechten, angefleht, beteuere, einig, erläutern, kauderwelscht, murren, schlagfertig, überschüttet, verhaspelt

1. Er hat sie mit Fragen _____ .
2. Ich weiß nicht, ob ich so _____ gewesen wäre.
3. Die Mutter hat die Kidnapper _____ , ihre Tochter gesund und heil zurückzugeben.
4. Können Sie das näher _____ ?
5. Sie sind sich nicht _____ und streiten miteinander.
6. Sie will das Urteil _____ .
7. Immer wieder _____ er seine Unschuld.

8. Sie fahren eine Stunde oder mehr mit der S-Bahn, ohne zu _____ .

9. Er stottert und stammelt und _____ sich beim Ankündigen des Programms.

10. Sie _____ im amerikanisch-deutschen Mischmasch.

8. Wie heißt das entsprechende Substantiv? ✓

1. jmdn verhören	
2. sich zanken	
3. etw tilgen	
4. etw kritzeln	
5. etw besprechen	

9. Wie heißt das entsprechende Adjektiv? ✓

1. der Analphabet	
2. das Paradoxon	
3. die Parataxe	
4. die Hypotaxe	
5. der Aphorismus	
6. die Sentenz	

10. Wie heißt das Gegenteil? ✓

1. die Erzählzeit
2. die Steigerung
3. die Hebung
4. die Hypotaxe
5. analphabetisch

11. Schreiben Sie eine Rezension eines Buches. Geben Sie am Anfang der Rezension folgende Informationen an: Author, Titel, Verlag, Erscheinungsort, Erscheinungsdatum, Seitenzahl und Preis. Z.B.,

> Peter Handke: *Der Bildverlust oder Durch die Sierra de Gredos*; Suhrkamp Verlag, Frankfurt am Main 2002; 759 S., 29.90 Euro.

12. Übersetzen Sie ins Englische.

Ehrung geht an Marlene Streeruwitz

AACHEN. Die österreichische Autorin Marlene Streeruwitz erhält den diesjährigen Walter-Hasenclever-Literaturpreis. Die mit 10 000 Euro dotierte Auszeichnung wird am 29. September verliehen. Der 1950 in Baden bei Wien geborenen Schriftstellerin gelang der Durchbruch als Bühnenautorin 1992 mit dem Stück *Waikiki Beach*, 1992 in Köln uraufgeführt. In der Begründung der Jury hieß es, Streeruwitz sei unter strikter Zurückweisung literarischer Moden und gängiger Publikumserwartungen gelungen, ein eigenständiges Werk heranzubilden, das von einer unprätentiösen, ungemein präzisen und doch poetischen Sprache getragen werde. Bisherige Preisträger waren Peter Rühmkorf, George Tabori und Oskar Pastior.   ap

FRANKFURTER RUNDSCHAU, Samstag, 12. Januar 2002, Nr. 10/2, S. 17

Reprinted with the permission of The Associated Press.

13. Lesen Sie den folgenden Text.

Der Herr der Fragezeichen

Der Schriftsteller Peter Handke wandert in die Sierra de Gredos und verirrt sich / Von Ulrich Greiner

Wohin, um Himmels willen, ist Peter Handke mit diesem Buch geraten? In die Sierra de Gredos – und von dort in die Steilhänge der Sinnstifterei, in die Schluchten der Mystifikation, in die Staubwüsten des Schwadronierens. Ihm zu folgen bedeutet qualvolle Entsagung: keine Handlung, die sich erzählen ließe, keine Figur mit Namen, Anschrift und Umriss, keine Dramatik, keine Abenteuer.

Das bleibt Handkes Programm: die Opposition gegen die „Lesefutterknechte", gegen die „Beschreibungsliteratur", gegen das katastrophensüchtige Erzählen. Wer derlei will, liest Stephen King. Der entsagungsgewohnte Handke-Leser aber erhielt doch immer reichlich Ausgleich und schönen Gewinn: statt äußerer Spannung innere Entwicklung, Herzensbildung; anstelle von Liebesaffären und Staatsaktionen „das Wehen der Luft, das Rieseln des Wassers, das Grünen der Erde, das Schimmern der Gestirne", wie es Adalbert Stifter, einer von Handkes Heroen, in der Vorrede zu den *Bunten Steinen* sagt.

In diesem monströsen und voluminösen Roman jedoch ist Handke außer Rand und Band. Nie hat er sich so übermütig, verschroben, haltlos ins Nebulöse hineinfabuliert, sich (und uns!) derart halsbrecherisch all seinen Lieblingstheorien und Marotten ausgeliefert. Man liest, kratzt sich am Kopf, versteht kein Wort, liest weiter, dann wieder geht einem ein Lichtlein auf, man freut sich, aber zu früh, denn plötzlich feixt Handke wie ein Kobold, foppt den Leser, wechselt die Erzählperspektive, Zeit und Ort und Sprache.

Er ist toll – und es ist toll, denn auch hier sieht man, was er kann, auch hier gibt es Passagen leuchtender Intensität, und man erfährt wieder, was vielleicht das Schönste am Handke-Lesen ist, Sehhilfe, Anschauungshilfe, Lebenshilfe, als läse man Dale Carnegies *Sorge dich nicht, lebe*, jetzt aber richtig: Sorge dich nicht, lies und sieh!

Aber ach, wie mühsam ist die Lektüre dieses Mal. Der Text wirkt zuweilen, als habe Handke alles hineingepackt, was ihm einfiel, alles, was er je geschreiben hat, das bereits Gestrichene inbegriffen. Schwer zu sagen, worum es geht. Eigentlich um alles. Das ist, wie man zugeben wird, nicht wenig, es ist die Summe all dessen, was wir bereits kennen: die *Langsame Heimkehr* von der *Niemandsbucht* in *Die Stunde der wahren Empfindung*.

... Die traditionelle Erzählung, die eine Person durch Attribute als besondere vorstellt, kann nicht gelingen, weil sie sich immer schon auf ein vorgegebenes, also fremdbestimmtes Bild bezieht.

Aus dieser Theorie folgert Handke einen bizarren Schluss: Er unterläuft die Fremdbestimmung dadurch, dass er die obligaten Bestimmungen vervielfältigt und neutralisiert. Ein Beispiel: „Unvergleichliches Geräusch des Granitsands unter den Sohlen, weniger ein Knirschen als ein Mahlen und Rauschen der groben Körnermassen, welche einem zugleich die Füße massierten: vordringliches Geräusch auf der iberischen Halbinsel – auch wenn dieses Geräusch einem ähnlich bei einer Alpenüberquerung hätte in den Ohren klingen können, oder in den Anden, oder ihretwegen im Himalaya."

Bis zum Doppelpunkt haben wir eins der für Handke typischen schönen Naturbilder. Danach folgt die Zerstörung des Bildes durch die Auflösung seiner Bestimmtheit. Wenn das Geräusch des Granitsands überall auf der Welt genauso klingt, ist es nicht mehr unvergleichlich. Was hier noch wie eine momentane Selbstparodie klingt, wird durch die Manie der Fragezeichen zum literarischen Prinzip: „Sie stieg und stieg, eine Stunde lang? zwei? einen halben Tag? hinab." Oder: „Einer erklärte ihr: er sei von Tokyo, oder war es Honolulu? oder Kairo? nach Hondareda gereist und habe sich dann da angesiedelt, weil er sich endlich wieder einmal, ‚in einem Zentrum‘ spüren wollte, an einem Ort und in einer Gegend, ‚wo es um etwas ging‘, ‚wo es sich zeigte‘ – was sich zigte? – keine Antwort – aber sie hatte ja auch gar nicht gefragt."

Kann sich denn, so fragt der müde? ungeduldige? unverständige? Leser, der großmächtige Autor nicht verdammt noch mal entscheiden, ob die Frau eine Stunde für den Abstieg benötigt oder zwei, ob der Mann aus Kairo stammt oder aus Tokyo? Und wenn er es nicht weiß, dann soll er aufhören, davon zu faseln. Seiten über Seiten gehen die Fragezeichen-Orgien, oft ellenlange Fragesätze, teils rhetorisch, teils einander aufhebend; dann wieder ganze Salven von Fragezeichen innerhalb eines einzigen Satzes, als ob der Autor an jedem Wort herumfingern müsste, eins hübscher als das andere fände und allesamt stehen ließe, damit der Leser sich eins aussuchen könne ...

Genug. Die Sierra de Gredos, die Handke eindrucksvoll beschreibt (man müsste mal hinfahren), scheint ein derart menschenleeres, unwegsames Gelände zu sein, dass sich sogar ein geübter Wanderer wie Peter Handke darin verirrt hat.

DIE ZEIT, 24. Januar 2002, Nr. 5, S. 41

a. Vokabelübung. Wie heißt das Wort (die Wendung) auf Englisch?

1. schwadronieren
2. außer Rand und Band
3. verschroben
4. fabulieren
5. die Marotte

6. feixen
7. folgern
8. faseln
9. ellenlang
10. die Salve

b. Übersetzen Sie ins Englische die Sätze, die im Text unterstrichen sind.

Unit 11

Leisure

Level 1

Hobbies

Hobby, das (-s)	hobby
basteln	to make things, do crafts
Handarbeit, die (-en)	craft
(etw) stricken	to knit (sth)
(etw) sticken	to embroider (sth)
etw sammeln	to collect sth
Sammlung, die (-en)	collection
Sammler(in), der/die (-/nen)	collector
Briefmarkensammler(in), der/die (-/nen)	stamp collector, philatelist
Briefmarkenalbum, das (-alben)	stamp album
Münze, die (-n)	coin
gärtnern	to garden
angeln	to fish
Angler(in), der/die (-/nen)	angler
wandern	to hike
Wanderer/Wanderin, der/die (-/nen)	hiker
Jagen, das (no pl.)	hunting
Jagd, die (-en)	hunt
Vogelbeobachter(in), der/die (-/nen)	bird watcher

Games

(etw) spielen	to play (sth)
(um Geld) spielen	to gamble
falsch spielen	to cheat
Ball spielen	to play ball
Spiel, das (-e)	game
etw verlieren	to lose sth
(etw) gewinnen	to win (sth)
Karte, die (-n)	card
Karten spielen	to play cards
(etw) mischen	to shuffle (sth)
Rätsel, das (-)	riddle, crossword (puzzle), puzzle
Kreuzworträtsel, das (-)	crossword puzzle
Quiz, das (-)	quiz
Lotto, das (-s)	lottery
(im) Lotto spielen	to do the lottery
Schach, das (no pl.)	chess
Schachbrett, das (-er)	chess board
Damespiel, das (-e)	draughts, checkers
Dame spielen	to play draughts
Damebrett, das (-er)	draughtboard
Spielzeug, das (no pl.)	toy(s)
Spielsachen, pl.	toys
Spielzeugauto, das (-s)	toy car

Spielzeugeisenbahn, die (-en)	toy train
Bauklötzchen, das (-)	building block
Puppe, die (-n)	doll
Teddy, der (-s)	teddy
Teddybär, der (-en)	teddy bear
Schatzsuche, die (no pl.)	treasure hunt
Minigolf, das (no pl.)	miniature golf, putting

Circus and fairs

Zirkus (Circus), der (-se)	circus
Rummelplatz, der (¨e)	fairground
Flohmarkt, der (¨e)	flea market
Jahrmarkt, der (¨e)	(fun-)fair
Jahrmarktsbude, die (-n)	booth/stall at a fairground

Jahrmarktskünst-ler(in), der/die (-/nen)	fairground artist
Clown(in), der/die (-s/nen)	clown
Zauberkünstler(in), der/die (-/nen)	magician, conjurer
Zaubertrick, der (-s)	conjuring trick
Marionette, die (-n)	puppet
Puppenspieler(in), der/die (-/nen)	puppeteer
Akrobat(in), der/die (-en/nen)	acrobat
Berg- und Tal-Bahn, die (-en)	big dipper, roller coaster
Achterbahn, die (-en)	roller coaster
Riesenrad, das (¨er)	Ferris wheel, big wheel
Feuerwerk, das (-e)	fireworks
Umzug, der (¨e)	procession

Level 2

Relaxation

Freizeit, die (no pl.)	free/leisure time
Freizeitzentrum, das (-zentren)	leisure centre
Sauna, die (-s or -nen)	sauna
bummeln	to stroll, wander
sich entspannen	to relax, rest, unwind
sich ausruhen	to rest
relaxen	to take it easy, relax
abschalten	to unwind
sich erholen	to relax, rest
faulenzen	to laze about

Hobbies

Liebhaberei, die (-en)	hobby
Liebhaber(in), der/die (-/nen)	collector
Liebhaberstück, das (-e)	collector's item
Filmliebhaber(in), der/die (-/nen)	film fan

Fingerhut, der (¨e)	thimble
Nadel, die (-n)	needle
Stecknadel, die (-n)	pin
Garnrolle, die (-n)	spool of thread
Stich, der (-e)	stitch
maschinell/mit der Maschine nähen	to machine-stitch
Stickrahmen, der (-)	embroidery frame
etw weben	to weave sth
Webstuhl, der (¨e)	loom
etw spinnen	to spin sth
Töpferei, die (no pl.)	pottery
Töpfer(in), der/die (-/nen)	potter
Bücherfreund(in), der/die (-e/nen)	booklover, bibliophile
Büchernarr, -närrin, der/die (-en/nen)	book-fan, book freak
Buchgemeinschaft, die (-en)	book club

Games

Gesellschaftsspiel, das (-e)	parlour game
Brettspiel, das (-e)	board game
Würfel, der (-)	dice
Würfelbecher, der (-)	shaker
Bingo, das (no pl.)	bingo
Domino spielen	to play dominoes
schachmatt	checkmate
jmdn schachmatt setzen	to checkmate sb
Schachfigur, die (-en)	chessman
Versteckspiel, das (-e)	hide-and-seek
Himmel und Hölle	hopscotch
seilhüpfen	to skip
seilspringen	to skip
Bockspringen spielen	to play leapfrog
Blindekuh (no art.)	blind man's buff
Schaukel, die (-n)	swing
Karussell, das (-s or -e)	merry-go-round
(Kinder)rutschbahn, die (-en)	slide
Rutsche, die (-n)	slide
Schaukelpferd, das (-e)	rocking horse
Plüschtier, das (-e)	soft toy
Malbuch, das (¨er)	colouring book
Zinnsoldat, der (-en)	tin soldier
Drachen, der (-)	kite
Klicker, der (-)	marble
Darts, pl.	darts
Rollbrett, das (-er)	skateboard
Tretroller, der (-)	scooter
Rollschuh, der (-e)	roller skate
Seifenkiste, die (-n)	go-cart

Gokart, der (-s)	go-cart
Hula-Hoop-Reifen, der (-)	hula hoop
Flipper, der (-)	pinball machine
Spielautomat, der (-en)	slot machine
kein Spielverderber sein	to be a good sport
Spielverderber(in), der/die (-/nen)	spoilsport

Circus and fairs

Messe, die (-n)	(trade) fair
Messehalle, die (-n)	fair pavilion
Ausstellung, die (-en)	fair
Freilichtkonzert, das (-e)	open-air concert
Musikpavillon, der (-s)	bandstand
Trapezkünstler(in), der/die (-/nen)	trapeze artist
Seiltänzer(in), der/die (-/nen)	tightrope walker
Kraftmensch, der (-en)	muscle man
Dame mit dem Bart, die (-n)	bearded lady
Schwertschlucker(in), der/die (-/nen)	sword-swallower
Feuerfresser(in), der/die (-/nen)	fire-eater
Feuerschlucker(in), der/die (-/nen)	fire-eater
Knallkörper, der (-)	firecracker
Wunderkerze, die (-n)	sparkler

Level 3

Hobbies

etw heften	to baste sth [sewing]
etw säumen	to hem sth
Abnäher, der (-)	dart
Biese, die (-n)	tuck

Schnittmuster, das (-)	pattern
Schneiderpuppe, die (-n)	tailor's dummy
Stricknadel, die (-n)	knitting needle
Masche, die (-n)	stitch

Maschen aufnehmen	to cast on/increase/ make stitches	Rot, das (–)	hearts [German suit equivalent to hearts]
Maschen abketten	to cast off stitches	Schellen, das (–)	bells [German suit equivalent to diamonds]
eine Masche fallen lassen	to drop a stitch		
Zopfmuster, das (–)	cable stitch	Kreuzdame, die (–n)	queen of clubs
Wollknäuel, das or der (–)	ball of wool	König, der (–e)	king
Philatelie, die (no pl.)	philately	Bube, der (–n)	jack
Philatelist(in), der/die (–en/nen)	philatelist	Ass, das (–e)	ace
		Trumpf, der (¨e)	trump card, trumps
werkeln (S)	to putter around	etw (aus)geben	to deal sth
(herum)hantieren	to tinker/fiddle about	etw austeilen	to deal sth
		Sie geben	it's your deal
		Einsatz, der (¨e)	stake

Games

Glücksspiel, das (–e)	game of chance	mogeln	to cheat
Geschicklichkeits- spiel, das (–e)	game of skill	schummeln	to cheat
		Krocket, das (no pl.)	croquet
sich an Glücksspielen beteiligen	to gamble	Mensch ärgere dich nicht, das (no pl.)	aggravation [game]
wetten	to gamble, bet	Floh(hüpf)spiel, das (–e)	tiddlywinks
bei Pferderennen wetten	to bet on horses		
Spielbank, die (–en)	casino	## Circus and fairs	
Pfänderspiel, das (–e)	forfeits	Kirchweih, die (–en)	fair
Backgammon, das (no pl.)	backgammon	Kirmes, die (–sen; dial.)	fair
Telespiel, das (–e)	video game	Dult, die (–en; Bav.)	fair
Farbe, die (–n)	suit	Marktschreier(in), der/die (–/nen)	hawker
Runde, die (–n)	game	Kartenlegerin, die (–nen)	fortune-teller
seine Karten aufdecken	to show one's hand		
		Liliputaner(in), der/die (–/nen)	dwarf
Blatt, das (¨er)	hand	Riesendame, die (–n)	Fat Lady
Kreuz, das (–)	clubs	Bauchredner(in), der/die (–/nen)	ventriloquist
Pik, das (–)	spades		
Herz, das (–)	hearts	Puppe eines Bauchredners, die (–n)	ventriloquist's dummy
Karo, das (–)	diamonds		
Eicheln, das (–)	acorns [German suit equivalent to clubs]	Jongleur(in), der/die (–e/nen)	juggler
Grün, das (–)	leaves [German suit equivalent to spades]	Kasper(le)theater, das (–)	Punch–and–Judy show

Glücksrad, das (¨er)	wheel of fortune	Sammlerausstellung, die (-en)	collectors' fair
Schießbude, die (-n)	shooting gallery	Antiquitätenmarkt, der (¨e)	antiques market
Schießbudenfigur, die (-en)	Aunt Sally		

Sport

Level 1

Sports

Sport, der (-e; pl. rare)	sport
Sportart, die (-en)	(kind of) sport
Sport treiben	to do sport
Spazierengehen, das (no pl.)	walking
Jogging, das (no pl.)	jogging
Rennen, das (-)	running, racing, race
Gymnastik, die (no pl.)	gymnastics
Turnen, das (no pl.)	gymnastics
Tennis, das (no pl.)	tennis
Tischtennis, das (no pl.)	table tennis
Volleyball, der (no pl.)	volleyball
Fußball, der (no pl.)	football
(American) Football, der (no pl.)	American football
Hockey, das (no pl.)	hockey
Eishockey, das (no pl.)	ice hockey
Golf, das (no pl.)	golf
Basketball, der (no pl.)	basketball
Baseball, der (no pl.)	baseball
Bowling, das (-s)	bowling
Schwimmen, das (no pl.)	swimming
Springen, das (no pl.)	jumping, vaulting, diving
Schießen, das (no pl.)	shooting
Boxen, das (no pl.)	boxing
Rudern, das (no pl.)	rowing
Rudersport, der (no pl.)	rowing
Segeln, das (no pl.)	sailing, yachting
(Pferde)reiten, das (no pl.)	(horseback) riding
Bogenschießen, das (no pl.)	archery
Radfahren, das (no pl.)	biking
Skifahren/Skilaufen, das (no pl.)	skiing
Schlittschuhlaufen, das (no pl.)	ice skating
Rollschuhlaufen, das (no pl.)	roller skating
Autorennen, das (no pl.)	car racing

Premises

Stadion, das (-dien)	stadium
Halle, die (-n)	(sports) hall, gym(nasium)
Fitnesscenter, das (-)	fitness centre
Fitnessstudio, das (-s)	fitness centre
Schwimmbad, das (¨er)	swimming pool
Kabine, die (-n)	booth
Platz, der (¨e)	field
Sportplatz, der (¨e)	sports field, playing field
Fußballplatz, der (¨e)	football (soccer) pitch
Golfplatz, der (¨e)	golf course
Bahn, die (-en)	track, lane
Piste, die (-n)	(ski) slope

Athletes

Athlet(in), der/die (-en/nen)	athlete
Sportler(in), der/die (-/nen)	sportsman/ sportswoman, athlete
Spieler(in), der/die (-/nen)	player
Fußballsspieler(in), der/die (-/nen)	footballer
Läufer(in), der/die (-/nen)	runner
Skiläufer(in), der/die (-/nen)	skier
Jogger(in), der/die (-/nen)	jogger
Schwimmer(in), der/die (-/nen)	swimmer
Turner(in), der/die (-/nen)	gymnast
Boxer(in), der/die (-/nen)	boxer

Equipment

Ball, der (¨e)	ball
Schläger, der (-)	racket, stick, club, bat, paddle, mallet
Tennisschläger, der (-)	tennis racket
Netz, das (-e)	net
Schlagholz, das (¨er)	bat
Rennschuh, der (-e)	track shoe
Spikes, pl.	spiked shoes
Trainingsanzug, der (¨e)	tracksuit
Stirnband, das (¨er)	headband
Schweißband, das (¨er)	wristband
Ski, der (-er)	ski
Skistock, der (¨e)	ski pole/stick
Skianzug, der (¨e)	ski suit
Skilift, der (-e)	ski lift
Schlittschuh, der (-e)	skate
Bogen, der (-; S: ¨)	bow
Pfeil, der (-e)	arrow
Zielscheibe, die (-n)	target

Schießscheibe, die (-n)	target
Helm, der (-e)	helmet
Boxhandschuh, der (-e)	boxing glove
Seile, pl.	ropes
Ringmatte, die (-n)	mat
Segelboot, das (-e)	sailing boat
Segelschiff, das (-e)	sailing ship
Ruderboot, das (-e)	rowing boat

Training and competition

sportlich	sporty
etw üben	to practise sth
Übungen machen	to have a workout
Bodenübung, die (-en)	floor exercise
etw trainieren	to practise sth
Training, das (-s)	training, workout
Trainer(in), der/die (-/nen)	trainer, coach, manager
Fitnesstraining, das (-s)	fitness training
sich qualifizieren	to qualify
Mannschaft, die (-en)	team
Zeitrennen, das (-)	time trial
Wettkampf, der (¨e)	event
Fan, der (-s)	fan
Rückspiel, das (-e)	return match
Wiederholungsspiel, das (-e)	replay
Freundschaftsspiel, das (-e)	friendly match
Heimspiel, das (-e)	home game
Auswärtsspiel, das (-e)	away game
Runde, die (-n)	lap, round
letzte Runde	final round
letztes Spiel	final match
Endrunde, die (-n)	final
Endspiel, das (-e)	final
(Spiel)hälfte, die (-n)	half
Halbzeit, die (-en)	half, halftime
erste/zweite Halbzeit	first/second half
Verlängerung, die (-en)	injury time

ausverkauftes Haus	sellout	Zweitplazierte(r),	runner-up
Mannschaftssport,	team sport	der/die (adj. decl.)	
der (no pl.)		die weiteren	the runners-up
Anstoß, der (¨e)	kick-off	Gewinner, pl.	
Freistoß, der (¨e)	free kick	jmdn angreifen	to tackle sb
Tor, das (-e)	goal	Angriff, der (-e)	tackle
torlos	goalless	Tackling, das (-s)	tackle
Sieger(in), der/die	winner, champion	Foul, das (-s)	foul
(-/nen)		Olympiade, die (-n)	Olympic Games
Verlierer(in), der/die	loser	die Olympischen	the Olympic Games
(-/nen)		Spiele, pl.	
Zweite(r), der/die	runner-up	Weltrekord, der (-e)	world record
(adj. decl.)		den Rekord brechen	to break the record

Level 2

Sports

Leichtathletik,	track and field	Bergsteigen,	climbing,
die (no pl.)	sports, athletics	das (no pl.)	mountaineering
Geländerennen,	cross-country	Klettern, das (no pl.)	climbing
das (-)	running/race	Fallschirmspringen,	parachuting
Aerobic, das (no pl.)	aerobics	das (no pl.)	
Skateboardfahren,	skateboarding	Handball, der	handball
das (no pl.)		(no pl.)	
Abfahrtlaufen, das	(alpine) skiing	Korbball, der	netball
(no pl.)		(no pl.)	
Langlauf, der (no pl.)	cross-country skiing	Polo, das (no pl.)	polo
Snowboarding,	snowboarding	Wasserball, der	water polo
das (-s)		(no pl.)	
Schlittenfahren, das	sledging	Ringen, das (no pl.)	wrestling
(no pl.)		Freistilringen, das	free-style wrestling
Eistanz, der (no pl.)	ice dancing	(no pl.)	
Eiskunstlauf, der	figure skating	Gewichtheben, das	weightlifting
(no pl.)		(no pl.)	
Kanufahren,	canoeing	Krafttraining, das	weight-training
das (no pl.)		(no pl.)	
Surfing, das (no pl.)	surfing	Bodybuilding, das	bodybuilding
Wellenreiten,	surfing	(no pl.)	
das (no pl.)		Billard, das	billiards
Wasserskilaufen,	water-skiing	(-e; AU: -s)	
das (no pl.)		Poolbillard, das	pool
Tauchen, das	diving, scuba diving	(no pl.)	
(no pl.)		Kegelspiel, das (-e)	skittles
Tiefseetauchen,	deep-sea diving	Kricket, das (no pl.)	cricket
das (no pl.)		Rugby, das (no pl.)	rugby

Premises

Turnhalle, die (-n)	gymnasium
Sporthalle, die (-n)	sports hall
Schwimmhalle, die (-n)	indoor swimming pool
Tennishalle, die (-n)	covered tennis court
Umkleideraum, der (¨e)	changing room
Umkleidekabine, die (-n)	changing room
Eisbahn, die (-en)	skating rink
Rollschuhbahn, die (-en)	roller skating rink
Rennbahn, die (-en)	(race)track
Radrennbahn, die (-en)	cycle (racing) track
Bowlingbahn, die (-en)	bowling alley

Athletes

Bergsteiger(in), der/die (-/nen)	climber, mountaineer
Taucher(in), der/die (-/nen)	diver
Ruderer, der (-); Ruderin, die (-nen)	rower
Ringer(in), der/die (-/nen)	wrestler
Bowlingspieler(in), der/die (-/nen)	bowls player
Kegler(in), der/die (-/nen)	bowls/skittle-player

Equipment

Kugel, die (-n)	ball
(Kegel)kugel, die (-n)	bowl
Golfschläger, der (-)	golf club
Tee, das (-s)	tee
Hockeyschläger, der (-)	hockey stick
Puck, der (-s)	puck
Stoppuhr, die (-en)	stopwatch
Zielband, das (¨er)	tape
Sprungstab, der (¨e)	(vaulting) pole
(Sprung)brett, das (-er)	diving board

(Schwimm)flosse, die (-n)	flipper
Tauchmaske, die (-n)	diving mask
Schnorchel, der (-)	snorkel
Taucheranzug, der (¨e)	wetsuit
Gymnastikanzug, der (¨e)	leotard
Geräte, pl.	apparatus
Schwebebalken, der (-)	beam
Pferd, das (-e)	(vaulting) horse
Barren, der (-)	parallel bars
Stufenbarren, der (-)	uneven bars
Reck, das (-e)	horizontal bar
Queue, das (-s)	cue
Billardstock, der (¨e)	cue
Baseballhandschuh, der (-e)	mitt
Mal, das (-e)	base

Training and competition

Sportlichkeit, die (no pl.)	sportsmanship
Fairness, die (no pl.)	fairness
Profi, der (-s)	professional
sich kaputtmachen	to burn o.s. out
Wettlauf, der (¨e)	race
Wettschwimmen, das (no pl.)	(swimming) race
Spielstand, der (no pl.)	score
Spielergebnis, das (-se)	(final) score
Anzeigetafel, die (-n)	scoreboard
Unentschieden, das (-)	draw
das Spiel endete unentschieden/ mit einem Unentschieden	the match ended in a draw
Strafpunkt, der (-e)	penalty point
Schiedsrichter(in), der/die (-/nen)	referee [football, rugby]
Ringrichter(in), der/die (-/nen)	referee [boxing]

Kampfrichter(in), der/die (-/nen)	referee [judo, wrestling]	Pass, der (¨e)	pass
Linienrichter(in), der/die (-/nen)	linesman	Vorlage, die (-n)	forward pass
		auf Mal 2	on second base
Gegner(in), der/die (-/nen)	opponent	Lauf zum ersten Mal, der (¨e)	single [baseball]
Rivale, der (-n); Rivalin, die (-nen)	rival	Homerun, der (-s)	home run
		um alle vier Male laufen	to hit a home run
Sportfest, das (-e)	gala	Inning, das (-s)	innings
Schwimmfest, das (-e)	swimming gala	etw auffangen und zurückwerfen	to field sth
den Rekord halten/innehaben	to hold the record	Balljunge, der (-n); Ballmädchen, das (-)	ball boy; ball girl
Weltrekordinhaber(in), der/die (-/nen)	world record holder		
Weltmeister(in), der/die (-/nen)	world champion	Einzel, das (-)	singles [tennis]
		Doppel, das (-)	doubles [tennis]
Meisterschaft, die (-en)	championship	gemischtes Doppel	mixed doubles
		Hundert-Meter-Lauf (100-Meter-Lauf), der (¨e)	100 metre run
Turnier, das (-e)	tournament, competition, show		
Fackel, die (-n)	torch	Sprint, der (-s)	sprint
Fackelträger(in), der/die (-/nen)	torchbearer	Endspurt, der (-e or -s)	final spurt
Eröffnungsfeier-lichkeiten, pl.	opening ceremony	Handgalopp, der (no pl.)	canter
Vorlauf, der (¨e)	preliminary heat	langsam galoppieren	to canter
Vorkampf, der (¨e)	heat [boxing, etc.]	Galopp, der (-e or -s)	gallop
Ausscheidungskampf, der (¨e)	final heat	galoppieren	to gallop
Einwurf, der (¨e)	throw-in	im gestreckten Galopp	at full gallop

Level 3

Sports

Schussfahrt, die (-en)	schussing	Hochsprung, der (¨e)	high jump
Schussfahren, das (no pl.)	schussing	Stabhochsprung, der (no pl.)	pole vault
Curling, das (no pl.)	curling	Speerwerfen, das (no pl.)	javelin throwing
Bobfahren, das (no pl.)	bobsledding	Kugelstoßen, das (no pl.)	shot put
Rodeln, das (no pl.)	tobogganing	Judo, das (no pl.)	judo
Fünfkampf, der (¨e)	pentathlon	Karate, das (no pl.)	karate
Zehnkampf, der (¨e)	decathlon	Inlineskating, das (no pl.)	in-line skating
Weitsprung, der (¨e)	long jump		

315

Squash, das (no pl.)	squash
Schlagball, der (no pl.)	rounders
Boccia, das (no pl.)	bocce
Snooker(pool), das (no pl.)	snooker
Tauziehen, das (no pl.)	tug-of-war
Federball, der (no pl.)	badminton
Felsenklettern, das (no pl.)	rock climbing
freies Klettern	free climbing
Höhlenforschen, das (no pl.)	caving
Bungeejumping, das (no pl.)	bungee jumping
Drachenfliegen, das (no pl.)	hang-gliding
Segelfliegen, das (no pl.)	gliding
Fechten, das (no pl.)	fencing
Springreiten, das (no pl.)	show jumping
Windhundrennen, das (-)	greyhound racing
Tontaubenschießen, das (no pl.)	clay pigeon shooting

Premises

Badeanstalt, die (-en)	(public) swimming pool
Freibad, das (¨er)	outdoor swimming pool
Tribüne, die (-n)	stand
auf der Tribüne	in the stands
Loipe, die (-n)	cross-country ski run
Rasenplatz, der (¨e)	grass court
Hartplatz, der (¨e)	hard court
Innenfeld, das (-er)	(baseball) diamond
Außenfeld, das (-er)	outfield
Rasenfläche (für Boccia), die (-n)	bowling green (for bocce)

Athletes

Kunstspringer(in), der/die (-/nen)	diver [off springboard]
Turmspringer(in), der/die (-/nen)	diver [off high board]
Kanufahrer(in), der/die (-/nen)	canoeist
Kanute, der (-n); Kanutin, die (-nen)	canoeist
Drachenflieger(in), der/die (-/nen)	hang-glider
Alpinist(in), der/die (-en/nen)	mountaineer
Tormann, -frau, der/die (¨er/en)	goalie
Torhüter(in), der/die (-/nen)	goalkeeper
Torwart(in), der/die (-e/nen)	goalkeeper
Werfer(in), der/die (-/nen)	thrower; bowler [cricket], pitcher [baseball]
Fänger(in), der/die (-/nen)	catcher
Bocciaspieler(in), der/die (-/nen)	bocce player
Springreiter(in), der/die (-/nen)	show-jumper

Equipment

Hantel, die (-n)	dumbbell
Keule, die (-n)	club
Ding(h)i, das (-s)	dinghy
Schlauchboot, das (-e)	rubber dinghy
Kanu, das (-s)	canoe
Schienbeinschützer, der (-)	shin-guard
Torpfosten, der (-)	goal post
Angelgeräte, pl.	fishing tackle
Köder, der (-)	bait, lure
Haken, der (-)	hook
Rolle, die (-n)	reel
Schwimmer, der (-)	cork, float
Watstiefel, pl.	waders

Krockethammer, der (-)	croquet mallet
Krockettor, das (-e)	croquet hoop
Zielpfahl, der (¨e)	stake
Federball, der (¨e)	shuttlecock
Fechtmaske, die (-n)	fencing mask
Florett, das (-e)	foil
Speer, der (-e)	javelin
Sattel, der (¨)	saddle
Zügel, der (-)	rein
Geschirr, das (-e)	harness
Gebiss, das (-e)	bit
Steigbügel, der (-)	stirrup
Zaum, der (¨e)	bridle

Training and competition

Leibesübungen, pl.	physical education
in Führung liegen	to be in the lead
in Führung gehen	to take the lead
seine Führung ausbauen	to extend one's lead
Staffellauf, der (¨e)	relay race
Hürdenlauf, der (¨e)	hurdle race
die Seitenwahl gewinnen/ verlieren	to win/lose the toss
Gedränge, das (no pl.)	scrum [rugby]
Liga, die (Ligen)	league
Abstoß vom Tor, der (¨e)	goal kick
Strafstoß, der (¨e)	penalty
Elfmeter, der (-)	penalty (kick)
im Abseits	offside
Ausgleichstor, das (-e)	equalizing goal
Pokal, der (-e)	cup
das Endspiel um den Pokal	the cup final
sie sind aus dem Pokal ausgeschieden	they're out of the Cup
Fußballweltmeister- schaft, die (-n)	World Cup
Sparring machen	to have a workout [boxing]

Federgewicht, das (no pl.)	featherweight
Federgewichtler(in), der/die (-/nen)	featherweight
Bantamgewicht, das (no pl.)	bantamweight
Mittelgewicht, das (no pl.)	middleweight
Schwergewicht, das (no pl.)	heavyweight
Haken, der (-)	hook [boxing]
Linkshaken, der (-)	left hook
jmdn k.o. schlagen	to knock sb out
Knock-out (K.o.), der (-s)	knockout
jmdn vernichtend schlagen	to trounce sb
Aufschlag, der (¨e)	service
Satz, der (¨e)	set
Satzpunkt, der (-e)	set point
Matchball, der (¨e)	match point
Ballwechsel, der (-)	rally
Aus, das (no pl.)	touch
im Aus	in touch
ins Aus gehen	to go out of play; go into touch
Brustschwimmen, das (no pl.)	breast stroke
Schmetterlingsstil, der (no pl.)	butterfly stroke
Butterfly, der (no pl.)	butterfly stroke
Kraul(stil), der (no pl.)	crawl
Kraulen, das (no pl.)	crawl
kraulen	to do the crawl
Rückenschwimmen, das (no pl.)	backstroke
Seitenschwimmen, das (no pl.)	sidestroke
Doping, das (-s)	drug-taking
Dopingtest, der (-s or -e)	drug test
Dopingsünder(in), der/die (-/nen)	drug-taker
verbotene Substanzen, pl.	banned substances

Exercises

Level 1

1. Was passt zusammen? ✓

a. die Briefmarke, b. der Fisch, c. der Garten, d. Karten, e. das Lotto, f. das Monogramm, g. der Pulli, h. das Rätsel, i. der Rekord, j. der Sport, k. der Wald

1. stricken
2. angeln
3. wandern
4. sammeln
5. sticken
6. spielen
7. lösen
8. mischen
9. gärtnern
10. brechen
11. treiben

2. Wie heißt das Gegenteil? ✓

1. etw verlieren
2. der Sieger
3. das Heimspiel
4. der Bogen
5. fair spielen

3. Ordnen Sie.

die Akrobatin, das Bowling, der Clown, das Damespiel, das Eishockey, der Fußball, das Golf, die Piste, das Schach, das Schlittschuhlaufen, das Skifahren, der Tennisschläger, das Tor

Ballspiele	Wintersport	Brettspiele	Zirkus

4. Welches Wort hat die gleiche oder eine ähnliche Bedeutung? ✓

1. die Zielscheibe
2. etw trainieren
3. das Tackling
4. die Zweite
5. die Spielhälfte
6. die Athletin
7. das Rudern
8. die Gymnastik
9. die Berg- und Tal-Bahn

5. Sportarten. Ergänzen Sie die Zusammensetzungen. ✓

1. der Volley_____
2. das Pferde_____
3. das Bogen_____
4. das Rad_____
5. das Rollschuh_____
6. das Auto_____
7. das Tisch_____
8. der Basket_____

6. Wie heißt jemand, der die folgende Sportart betreibt? ✓

1. das Jogging
2. das Boxen
3. das Turnen
4. das Skifahren
5. der Fußball
6. der Baseball
7. das Schwimmen
8. das Hockey
9. das Tennis

7. Welches Wort passt nicht? ✓

1. der Rennschuh, die Runde, das Schweißband, der Traininganzug
2. die Endrunde, das Rennen, die Ringmatte, der Wettkampf
3. das Bauklötzchen, die Münze, die Puppe, das Spielzeugauto
4. Dame, Hobby, Karten, Lotto
5. die Jagd, der Jahrmarkt, das Riesenrad, der Rummelplatz

8. Welche Definition bzw. welches Synonym passt?

> a. der Anstoß, b. der Boxhandschuh, c. das Endspiel, d. das Foul,
> e. die Mannschaft, f. das Schwimmbad, g. der Umzug, h. der Weltrekord

1. das letzte Wettspiel
2. der erste Schuss
3. die beste Leistung der Welt in einer Sportart
4. Verstoß gegen die Spielregeln
5. zusammengehörige Gruppe von Wettkämpfern
6. gepolsterter Lederhandschuh zum Boxen
7. das Schwimmbecken
8. der Festzug

9. Erklären Sie den Unterschied.

1. das Stadion, das Stadium
2. das Tor, der Tor
3. der Football, der Fußball
4. die Bahn, der Bann
5. der Fan, die Fahne
6. der Schläger, der Schlager
7. die Halle, der Hall

10. Übersetzen Sie ins Englische.

In der Halle

Englands Trainer Sven-Göran Eriksson hat sich als Hallenfan geoutet. „Das ist wahrscheinlich die Zukunft des Fußballs. In 20 Jahren wird es sicher sehr viele solcher Stadien geben." Es gebe keine Sonne, keinen Wind, keinen Regen, nichts störe. „Zudem herrschen angenehme Temperaturen."   sid

Frankfurter Allgemeine Zeitung, Samstag, 8. Juni 2002, Nr. 130/23, S. 38

Völker stolpert, Pechstein findet die schnelle Spur

ERFURT (dpa). Ein Sturz in der letzten Kurve hat am Freitag den neunten nationalen Titel von Sabine Völker verhindert. Die Erfurterin, die zuvor bei den deutschen Mehrkampf-Meisterschaften der Eisschnelläufer in der Gunda-Niemann-Stirnemann-Halle mit Bahnrekorden von 38,4 Sekunden und 1:16,77 Minuten über 500 und 1000 Meter überzeugt hatte, kam im letzten Rennen des Sprint-Vierkampfes in eine Eisrille und wurde aus der Bahn geworfen. Für einen Rekord sorgte auch das Erfurter Publikum. Fast 4000 Besucher kamen an den beiden Tagen in die neue Halle, mehr als je zuvor bei nationalen Titelkämpfen. Allerdings beklagten sich viele Fans und Athleten über mangelnde Information nach dem zwischenzeitlichen Ausfall der Zeitmessung. In Abwesenheit der Titelverteidigerin Monique Garbrecht-Enfeldt aus Berlin errang den Titel im Sprint-Vierkampf überraschend die Pfaffenhofenerin Marion Wohlrab. „Ich ärgere mich furchtbar über den entgangenen Titel. Bis zum Sturz lief alles so gut", sagte Sabine Völker, die vor kurzem einen neuen Weltrekord über 1000 Meter aufgestellt hatte.

Derweil gewann die Berlinerin Claudia Pechstein am Freitag zum dritten Mal nach 1996 und 2000 den Titel im Allround-Mehrkampf. Die Olympiasiegerin über 5000 Meter setzte sich auf allen vier Strecken durch. Bei den Europameisterschaften in einer Woche kommt es in Erfurt zum Duell zwischen Claudia Pechstein und der Inzeller Weltmeisterin Anni Friesinger, die an den nationalen Meisterschaften nicht teilnam. Ihr Bruder Jan stand dafür am Freitag kurz vor seinem ersten Titel im Mehrkampf. Er führte vor dem Lauf über 10 000 Meter (das Rennen war bei Redaktionsschluss dieser Ausgabe noch nicht beendet) deutlich die Gesamtwertung an. Den Sprinttitel sicherte sich der Erfurter Andreas Behr.

Frankfurter Allgemeine Zeitung, Samstag, 29. Dezember 2001, Nr. 302, S. 34

© dpa Deutsche Presse–Agentur GmbH

11. Übersetzen Sie ins Englische.

Wenn der Trainer erst im Foyer steht, gibt es kein Zurück mehr

Fitness-Lehrer sollen Führungskräfte von Schlaflosigkeit und Rückenschmerzen befreien / Von Friederike Böge

Das weiße Hemd und die schwarze Anzughose hat Michael Svoboda locker über die Garderobe geworfen. In kurzer Sporthose und Polo-Shirt steht der Manager in seinem Frankfurter Büro im fünften Stock des Deutsche-Bank-Turms. Es ist vier Uhr. Die grauen Ledersessel, auf denen sonst kleine Konferenzen abgehalten werden, hat er an den Rand geschoben. Auf dem Fußboden ist eine Iso-Matte ausgebreitet – fertig ist der Fitnessraum. Zweimal in der Woche trifft sich Svoboda hier mit seinem persönlichen Trainer, Raimar Hirschmann, der mit seinem Sportrucksack und der Schirmmütze aussieht wie ein Mallorca-Urlauber, der sich in die marmorne Eingangshalle der Deutschen Bank nur verirrt hat.

Das Aufwärmtraining kann beginnen. Arme schwingen, die Knie hoch und auf der Stelle gehen, Kopf kreisen und ausschütteln. Beim Dehnen dient der Schreibtisch als Stütze. Dann kommt das Krafttraining mit den Expandern und schließlich die Bodenübungen: Sit-Ups, einarmige Flugzeuge und Katzenbuckel. Mit ruhiger Stimme gibt Hirschmann Anweisungen und korrigiert die Bewegungsabläufe, damit sie die Gelenke nicht belasten. Nach einer halben Stunde kommt der 54 Jahre alte Manager allmählich ins Schwitzen. Das Telefon hat in dieser Zeit noch kein einziges Mal geklingelt. Alle Anrufe werden im Nebenzimmer abgefangen.

Dann geht es raus in den Park zum Joggen. Eine Mitarbeiterin läuft rot an und murmelt verdattert einen Gruß, als ihr Chef in Shorts in den Aufzug tritt. Dass man im Flur über sein Fitness-Training spricht, stört Svoboda nicht. „Die Mitarbeiter schwätzen natürlich gern. Aber es ist ja nichts Ehrenrühriges daran, Zeit in seinen Körper zu investieren", sagt er und es klingt, als habe er sich selbst erst davon überzeugen müssen. Der Manager, der bei der Deutschen Bank weltweit für Personalpolitik und -entwicklung verantwortlich ist, will ein Beispiel sein. „Ich könnte mir vorstellen, dass wir den persönlichen Trainer zum Kulturbestand der Abteilung machen." Wenn es nach Svoboda ginge, würde im mittleren und oberen Management des Konzerns jedem Mitarbeiter ein persönlicher Fitness-Trainer angeboten. Schließlich sei die Gesundheit von Topmanagern ein teures Gut für das Unternehmen. Und von selbst täten sie dafür nur selten etwas.

Das weiß Svoboda aus eigener Erfahrung. Wie häufig hatte er sich ganz fest vorgenommen, Sport zu treiben. Doch dann kam jedesmal ein Termin dazwischen. Aber wenn der Trainer erst einmal im Haus ist, unten im Foyer, dann gibt es kein Zurück mehr. Wie Besprechungen und Geschäftsessen sind die Trainingseinheiten, zweimal in der Woche neunzig Minuten, zum festen Bestandteil im Terminkalender des Managers geworden. Doch selbst mit dem Trainer hat Svoboda drei Anläufe gebraucht, bis er soweit war. Eine Geschäftsreise reichte aus, um seine Motivation und Fitness zurück auf den Nullpunkt zu bringen. Noch heute fällt es ihm manchmal schwer, einen neuen Anfang zu finden, wenn er nach mehreren Wochen aus dem Ausland zurückkommt. Dann lässt sich wieder einmal kein Termin finden. „Es ist gewöhnungsbedürftig, um vier Uhr nachmittags alles hinter sich zu lassen, egal wieviel Arbeit noch anliegt", sagt Svoboda.

Geduld brauchte er dafür auch. Denn erst nach vier bis sechs Wochen spürte der Banker die ersten Erfolge. Er hatte keine Kopfschmerzen mehr, wie sonst so oft. Dank der Hormone, Adrenalin und des Testosteron, die beim Joggen ausgeschüttet wurden, hatte er mehr Energie und „mehr Lust auf alles". Mit der Zeit habe sich das regelmäßige Training auch auf seine Arbeitsleistung ausgewirkt ...

Frankfurter Allgemeine Zeitung, Samstag, 26. Januar 2002, Nr. 22/4, S. 63

Level 2

1. Welches Wort hat die gleiche oder eine ähnliche Bedeutung? ✓

1. das Hobby
2. seilspringen
3. die Rutsche
4. der Gokart
5. die Feuerfresserin
6. das Surfing
7. das Bergsteigen
8. der Umkleideraum
9. das Queue

2. Welche Definition bzw. welches Synonym passt? ✓

a. der Bergsteiger, b. das Geländerennen, c. der Korbball, d. die Leichtathletik, e. der Linienrichter, f. das Ringen, g. der Ringrichter, h. die Turnhalle

1. der Schiedsrichter beim Boxen
2. Helfer des Schiedsrichters
3. der Querfeldeinlauf
4. Sammelbegriff für Laufen, Hochsprung, Diskuswerfen usw.
5. ein dem Basketball ähnlicher Ballspiel
6. der Turnsaal
7. jmd, der auf Berge steigt
8. waffenloser Zweikampf

3. Welches Wort passt nicht? ✓
1. die Eröffnungsfeierlichkeiten, die Fackelträgerin, der Puppenspieler, die Olympiade
2. der Fingerhut, die Garnrolle, die Nadel, der Webstuhl
3. Blindekuh, der Flipper, Himmel und Hölle, das Versteckspiel
4. die Ausstellung, der Jahrmarkt, die Messe, die Vorlage
5. die Anzeigetafel, der Spielstand, das Unentschieden, das Zielband
6. der Barren, die Kugel, das Pferd, das Reck
7. der Langlauf, das Snowboarding, der Wasserball, das Wellenreiten
8. das Aerobic, das Bodybuilding, das Gewichtheben, das Krafttraining
9. sich ausruhen, sich entspannen, sich erholen, sich kaputtmachen

4. Wie heißt die entsprechende Sportart? ✓
1. die Taucherin   4. die Ruderin
2. der Ringer   5. der Bowlingspieler
3. die Keglerin

5. Ergänzen Sie. ✓
1. der Golfschläger – der Golfball : der Hockeyschläger – _____
2. die Rollschuhbahn – der Rollschuh : die Eisbahn – _____
3. das Schwimmen – die Schwimmhalle : das Bowling – _____
4. galoppieren – der Galopp : langsam galoppieren – _____
5. das Tauchen – der Taucheranzug : das Turnen – _____
6. der Basketball – der Korbball : das Bowling – _____

6. Wie heißen die Zusammensetzungen? ✓

~~Wellen~~	fahren	1. *das Wellenreiten*
Eis	barren	2.
Schlitten	ringen	3.
Tiefsee	punkt	4.
Freistil	~~reiten~~	5.
Stufen	brett	6.
Stopp	tauchen	7.
Sprung	tanz	8.
Straf	uhr	9.

7. Welche Wörter gehören zusammen?

a. das Ballmädchen, b. Darts, c. der Drachen, d. der Einwurf, e. das Karussell, f. der Knallkörper, g. das Malbuch, h. die Sauna, i. die Schachfigur, j. die Schaukel, k. der Spielautomat, l. die Töpferei

1. der Rummelplatz
2. der Baum
3. die Zielscheibe
4. der Wind
5. das Spielen um Geld
6. Silvester

7. die Vase
8. Finnland
9. der Wachsmalstift
10. der König
11. das Tennis
12. der Fußball

8. In jedem Satz fehlt ein Wort. ✓

Bücherfreund, faulenzen, Gesellschaftsspiel, Liebhaberstück, Plüschtiere, schachmatt, Stickrahmen, unentschieden, Wunderkerzen, Würfel

1. Der _____ rollt und zeigt eine Fünf.
2. In 73 Zügen setzte er den IBM-Rechner Deep Blue _____.
3. Aus Holz sind runde und ovale _____ zu haben.
4. Als _____ gibt er jährlich eine größere Summe für Bücher aus.
5. Der Wagen ist richtig alt geworden und wird zum _____.
6. Er meint, dass Monopoly als das beliebteste _____ der Welt gilt.
7. Ihre Leidenschaft für _____ reicht zurück bis in die Kindheit.
8. Nur 50 Prozent der Urlauber wollen am Strand _____ und in der Sonne liegen.
9. Freundschaftsspiele enden am besten _____.
10. Beim ersten Ton aus seiner Kehle verwandelt sich das Stadion in ein Lichtermeer aus Feuerzeugflammen und _____.

9. Übersetzen Sie ins Englische. („WM" = Weltmeisterschaft)

Schaun mer mal

Die Spiele der WM werden in Deutschland in der Kernarbeitszeit übertragen. Und die Zahl der Bildschirmarbeitsplätze wird explodieren

Von Mia Eidlhuber (Text)

Thomas Kellermann, Chefkoch
Mein Fernseher von zu Hause steht jetzt in der Vorbereitungsküche des Portalis. Das muss sein, ich bin mit Fußball groß geworden, mein Vater war Schiedsrichter in der Bundesliga. So kann ich die Deutschlandspiele mitverfolgen – bis der Mittagstrubel losgeht. Der Vormittag ist ohnehin eine komische Zeit für den Fußball. Da fehlt die Nähe. Andererseits ist die frühe Übertragungszeit für mich am besten, da sind noch keine Gäste da. Kommt Deutschland ins Finale, kann ich trotzdem mitfiebern. Denn am Finaltag, dem

Sonntag, ist geschlossen. Da muss ich dann keine Angst haben, dass mir was anbrennt.

Wolfram Sterry, Chefdermatologe am Krankenhaus Charité in Berlin
Wir Ärzte können natürlich nicht einfach die Patienten und unsere Arbeit liegen und stehen lassen. Aber durch die etwas eigenartigen Übertragungszeiten der Spiele aus Japan und Korea, ist für die Fußballfans unter den Ärzten ein kleines Schlupfloch entstanden. Ich werde die tägliche Vormittagsvisite dazu nutzen, um ein bisschen »am Ball« zu bleiben. In den Patientenzimmern, wo ja ohnehin meistens die Fernseher laufen, werde ich mich über die aktuellen Speilstände informieren können und vielleicht so auch die eine oder andere spannende Spielminute mitbekommen. In der Charité sind nicht nur die jüngeren Kollegen glühende Fußballfans, sonder auch viele der älteren Professoren. Wir werden die WM-Spiele nutzen, um mit Patienten einmal für ein, zwei Minuten persönlich ins Gespräch zu kommen – ganz abseits der einzelnen Krankengeschichten.

DIE ZEIT, 29. Mai 2002, Nr. 23, S. 54

10. Übersetzen Sie ins Englische.

Aus „Scrabble", von Sebastian Herzog

Es ist so weit: Drei Wochen vor Beginn des diesjährigen Scrabble-Sommers können wir den Austragungsort des großen *ZEIT*-Scrabble-Turniers 2002 verraten: Horben am Schwarzwald. Das Hotel Luisenhöhe, nur wenige Kilometer von Freiburg im Breisgau entfernt, bietet alles, was Scrabbler brauchen: gemütliche Zimmer, Spielmöglichkeiten in ansprechendem Ambiente und eine Umgebung, die den Teilnehmern in den Turnierpausen angenehme Entspannung bietet. Wenn Sie gern scrabbeln und vom 27. Oktober bis 3. November Zeit haben, sich eine Woche lang mit anderen Scrabblern zu messen, schicken Sie bitte eine E-Mail an scrabble@zeit.de oder eine Postkarte an die Redaktion der *ZEIT*, Stichwort »Scrabble-Turnier«, 20079 Hamburg ...

DIE ZEIT, 29. Mai 2002, Nr. 23, S. 59

Aus „Schach", von Helmut Pfleger

Ex oriente Schach. Vermutlich ist das Schachspiel bald nach der Zeitenwende in Indien entstanden. Weithin bekannt ist die Weizenkornlegende, nach der es ein Brahmane namens Sissa erfunden hat. Dem König gefällt's, Sissa darf sich zur Belohnung etwas wünschen. Dieser, scheinbar bescheiden, bittet um ein Korn auf dem ersten Feld, zwei auf dem zweiten, vier auf dem dritten und so weiter, jeweils die doppelte Anzahl bis zum 64. Feld. Doch der König kann den Wunsch nicht erfüllen, die 18 446 744 073 709 551 651 Körner würden ganz Indien einen Meter hoch bedecken. Der arabische Historiker al-Masudi berichtet um das Jahr 1000 von einer Reise: »Die Inder treiben die Wetten bis zum äußersten. Hat ein Spieler alles verloren, kann es vorkommen, dass er seine Glieder aufs Spiel setzt. In deisem Fall wird in einem kleinen Gefäß eine

Salbe gekocht ... Wenn nun ein Mann in einer Wette einen Finger verliert, schneidet er ihn mit einem Dolch ab, taucht die Hand in die Salbe und brennt so die Wunde aus. Dann spielt er weiter.«

Um dieselbe Zeit erzählt der persische Dichter Firdausi im *Buch der Könige*, wie ein indischer König eine Delegation zum persischen sendet, um von diesem Tribut zu fordern. Es sei denn, diesem gelänge es, die Regeln des mitgebrachten Spiels von je 16 roten und grünen Figuren auf 64 Feldern zu ergründen. Tag und Nacht forschen die Weisen des Landes – und können die Zahlung tatsächlich von ihrem Land abwenden.

In der Neuzeit war es indes ums Schach in seinen Ursprungsländern ziemlich still geworden, in Indien kümmerte es dahin, in Persien war es unter Chomeini sogar verboten. Doch mittlerweile erfreut es sich im Osten (auch in China) wieder großer Beliebtheit, wovon auch die geteilte WM 2000 in Neu-Delhi und Teheran, welche bei den Männern der Inder Anand, bei den Frauen die Chinesin Xie Jun gewann, zeugt ...

DIE ZEIT, 6. Juni 2002, Nr. 24, S. 63

Level 3

1. Spielkarten. ✓

1. Wie heißen die Farben?

   a. ♠

   b. ♣

   c. ♥

   d. ♦

2. Wie heißen die deutschen Farben?

   a. _____

   b. _____

   c. _____

   d. _____

3. Wie heißen die Bildkarten?

   a. _____

   b. _____

   c. _____

   d. _____

2. Welches Wort hat die gleiche oder eine ähnliche Bedeutung? ✓

1. das Badminton
2. die Kanufahrerin
3. der Torwart
4. der Butterfly
5. die Briefmarkensammlerin
6. das Kasino
7. mogeln
8. die Kirmes

3. Welches Verb passt? ✓

| a. aufdecken, b. beteiligen, c. lassen, d. machen, e. liegen, f. schlagen, g. wetten |

1. eine Masche fallen
2. sich an Glückspielen
3. seine Karten
4. bei Pferderennen

5. in Führung
6. jmdn k.o.
7. Sparring

4. Wie heißt das Gegenteil? ✓
1. Maschen aufnehmen
2. das Glücksspiel
3. der Rasenplatz
4. der Werfer
5. das Außenfeld

5. Was gehört zusammen? ✓

| a. der Bauchredner, b. das Florett, c. das Freibad, d. die Hantel, e. der Köder, f. die Loipe, g. die Philatelie, h. säumen, i. der Schienbeinschützer, j. der Steigbügel, k. die Tribüne, l. das Wollknäuel |

1. das Kleid
2. die Stricknadel
3. die Briefmarke
4. die Puppe
5. das Fechten
6. der Sattel

7. der Langlauf
8. das Schwimmen
9. die Zuschauer (pl.)
10. der Kraftmensch
11. der Haken
12. der Fußball

6. Suchen Sie eine andere Bedeutung.
1. das Geschirr
2. das Gebiss
3. der Satz
4. der Haken
5. die Biese

6. die Masche
7. die Keule
8. die Rolle
9. der Schwimmer
10. das Gedränge

7. Welches Wort passt nicht? ✓
1. der Ballwechsel, der Elfmeter, der Matchball, der Satzpunkt
2. die Badeanstalt, das Brustschwimmen, der Kraul, das Seitenschwimmen
3. das Bobfahren, das Curling, der Eiskunstlauf, das Inlineskating
4. das Bergsteigen, das Felsenklettern, das Höhlenforschen, die Watstiefel (pl.)
5. der Federball, das Federgewicht, die Federgewichtlerin, der Mittelgewichtler
6. der Krockethammer, das Krockettor, der Zielpfahl, der Zügel
7. der Hürdenlauf, der Langlauf, der Staffellauf, der Wettlauf

8. In jedem Satz fehlt ein Wort. ✓

Antiquitätenmarkt, Jongleur, Kartenlegerin, Kaspertheater, Krocket,
Schnittmuster, werkelt, wettet, Zopfmuster

1. Sie suchte ein _____ für einen Elefanten aus Stoff.
2. Er _____ an einem Kanu.
3. Sie kaufte sich einen Pullover mit _____ .
4. Sie _____ , dass er seinen Gegner in der dritten Runde k.o. schlagen wird.
5. Die Zuschauer freuten sich über Bogenschießen, Kricket, _____ und Rugby.
6. Er begann als Seiltänzer und _____ und trat fünf Jahre lang beim Zirkus auf.
7. Für die Kinder gibt es um 16 Uhr _____ , für die Erwachsenen Kaffee.
8. Am Samstag wird im Paulanerkeller von 11 bis 18 Uhr ein Sammler- und _____
   veranstaltet.
9. Die _____ legt für 79 Mark pro halbe Stunde die Karten.

9. Schriftliche Übung. Wählen Sie ein Thema.
1. Beschreiben Sie die letzte Minute eines spannenden Fußballspiels.
2. Schreiben Sie einen kurzen Sportbericht über einen Wettlauf.
3. Schreiben Sie einen kurzen Bericht über einen Dopingfall.

10. Übersetzen Sie ins Deutsche. ✓
1. Markus, it's your deal.
2. First I have to baste the hem of this dress.
3. Let's play 'Aggravation'.
4. Skiing, snowboarding and toboganing are popular kinds of winter sports.
5. He won the gold medal in the decathlon at the 1976 Olympic Games in Montreal.
6. She qualified in the long jump with 6.26 metres.
7. He's the world champion in shot put.
8. We followed the game in the stands.
9. The equalizing goal resulted from a penalty kick.
10. He is out of the tournament.

11. Übersetzen Sie ins Englische.

Sport in Kürze

Schwimm-Olympiasiegerin Claudia Poll ist wegen einer positiven
Dopingkontrolle vom internationalen Schwimmverband für vier Jahre
gesperrt worden. Claudia Poll, die 1996 in Atlanta über 200 Meter Freistil die
Goldmedaille vor der Berlinerin Franziska van Almsick gewann, war am 25.
Februar 2002 im Training getestet worden. Im Urin der Schwimmerin fand
sich Norandrosteron, ein Abbauprodukt der unerlaubten
Muskelaufbausubstanz Nandrolon.

Stabhochspringer Danny Ecker hat seinen Start bei der Leichtathletik-Gala
an diesem Samstag in Dortmund wegen eines Längsrisses in der Bizepssehne

der rechten Schulter abgesagt. Auch Hürdenläufer Florian Schwarthoff (Berlin) muss auf das als Europameisterschaftsqualifikation zählende Meeting verzichten. Er leidet an einer Achillessehnenverletzung. Dadurch ist auch die Teilnahme der beiden Leichtathleten an der EM gefährdet.

Frankfurter Allgemeine Zeitung, Samstag, 8. Juni 2002, Nr. 130/23, S. 42

Mein Idol ist auch Oliver Kahn

Oliver Kahns Karriere begann beim Karlsruher SC. Danach wechselte Kahn zum FC Bayern München. Dort erbrachte Kahn Höchstleistungen, wie zum Beispiel im Championsleague-Endspiel gegen FC Valencia. (Bayern kam ins Elfmeterschießen.) Damals gewann der FC Bayern München im Elfmeterschießen durch Oliver Kahns drei Glanzparaden mit 6:5 und wurde zur besten Mannschaft Europas. Sechs Monate später gelang es Oliver Kahn dann sogar zusammen mit dem FC Bayern München den Weltpokal der Vereinsmannschaften zu gewinnen, im Endspiel gegen den Südamerika-Meister aus Buenos Aires. Ferner ist Oliver Kahn im Jahr 2001 zum weltbesten Torwart gewählt worden. Kahn ist auch bei der Weltmeisterschaft in Japan und Südkorea als Torwart der deutschen Nationalmannschaft dabei. Auch in der Bundesliga hat der FC Bayern München Oliver Kahn viel zu verdanken. Zu diesen Verdiensten gehören die deutschen Meisterschaften im Jahre 1999, 2000 und im Jahre 2001.

Daniel Jörg (11 Jahre), Hanau

Frankfurter Rundschau, Samstag, 1. Juni 2002, Nr. 124/22, S. 8

Capriati kämpft sich durch

US-Spitzenspielerinnen bleiben Berliner Publikum erhalten

Das US-Topduo Jennifer Capriati und Serena Williams bleibt den Tennisfans bei den German Open in Berlin am Wochenende erhalten. Während French-Open-Siegerin Capriati, die bei ihren sechs Starts auf der Anlage des LTTC Rot-Weiß am Rande des Grunewaldes nie den Titel gewann, sich beim 6:3, 5:7, 6:4-Sieg in 124 Minuten gegen die auf Sand besonders gefährliche Weltranglistenelfte Sandrine Testud den Einzug ins Halbfinale schwer verdiente, bekam die jüngere Williams-Schwester die Qualifikation für die Runde der letzten Vier geschenkt. Ihre Viertelfinalgegnerin und Titelverteidigerin Amelie Mauresmo aus Frankreich musste wegen Nackenbeschwerden zurückziehen.

Bei Capriati wechselte am Freitag das Spielniveau so schnell wie der tückische Wind auf dem Center Court. Nach souveränem Start mit vielen Vorhand-Gewinnschlägen ließ sie die Zügel schleifen und brachte die kampfstarke Französin zurück ins Spiel. Im dritten Satz lag die von ihrem Vater Stefano betreute Capriati bereits 5:1 in Führung, konnte jedoch drei Matchbälle nicht nutzen. Erst beim 5:4 riss sie sich wieder zusammen und brachte ihren Aufschlag zum Matchgewinn durch. In der Runde der letzten

Vier trifft sie auf Justine Henin (Belgien) oder und Nathalie Dechy (Frankreich).

Nicht zufrieden mit ihrem freien Tag war Serena Williams, die sich in Berlin und Rom auf die French Open (27. Mai bis 9. Juni) vorbereitet. „Ich hätte viel lieber gespielt. Jetzt werde ich etwas trainieren und dann relaxen", sagte sie. Trotz der Favoritenrolle im Halbfinale gegen die Daniela Hantuchova (Slowakei) oder Anna Smashnova (Israel) ist das Traumfinale gegen Capriati noch längst nicht beschlossene Sache. „Wenn man nur an sowas denkt, geht schon der Fokus verloren", analysierte Williams.

Mit Schmerzen und steifem Hals schlich ihre verhinderte Gegnerin über die Anlage. „Ich kann meinen Kopf kaum drehen. Ich habe versucht, ein paar Bälle zu schlagen, aber es ging einfach nicht. Das Problem habe ich schon in Hamburg gehabt, aber dann war es wieder weg", klagte Mauresmo. Dennoch macht sie sich keine Sorgen um einen Start in Paris.   sid

FRANKFURTER RUNDSCHAU, Samstag, 11. Mai 2002, Nr. 108, S. 14

Unit 12

Tourism, travel and transport

Level 1

General

Reise, die (-n)	trip, journey
reisen	to travel
Reisende(r), der/die (adj. decl.)	traveller
Passagier(in), der/die (-e/nen)	passenger
Fahrkarte, die (-n)	ticket
Ausweis, der (-e)	proof of identity, identification
Pass, der (¨e)	passport
Passkontrolle, die (-n)	passport control
durch die Passkontrolle gehen	to go through passport control
Zoll, der (¨e)	customs, duty
Zollkontrolle, die (-n)	customs control
Visum, das (Visa or Visen)	visa
etw packen	to pack sth
etw auspacken	to unpack sth
Ausland, das (no pl.)	foreign country
ins/im Ausland	abroad
Information, die (-en)	information
Auskunft, die (¨e)	information
etw reservieren	to book/reserve sth
etw zweimal reservieren	to double-book sth

Reservierung, die (-en)	reservation
etw buchen	to book sth
Reisescheck, der (-s)	traveller's cheque
Abfahrt, die (-en)	departure
Ankunft, die (no pl.)	arrival
auf dem Weg	en route
(Land)karte, die (-n)	map
Stadtplan, der (¨e)	(street) map
Jetlag, der (-s)	jet-lag

Tourism

Tourist(in), der/die (-en/nen)	tourist
Tourismus, der (no pl.)	tourism
Reisebüro, das (-s)	travel bureau/agency
Saison, die (-s or AU: -en)	season
Ferien, pl.	(school) holidays
Urlaub, der (-e)	vacation, break
Urlaubsort, der (-e)	resort
Ferienort, der (-e)	holiday resort
Skiort, der (-e)	ski resort
Reiseführer, der (-)	travel guide [book]
Tour, die (-en)	tour
Rundfahrt, die (-en)	tour
Stadtrundfahrt, die (-en)	tour of the city
Führung, die (-en)	guided tour

Schloss, das (¨er)	castle
Ansichtskarte, die (-n)	(picture) postcard
Öffnungszeiten, pl.	opening hours

Accommodation and facilities

Hotel, das (-s)	hotel
Motel, das (-s)	motel
Zimmer, das (-)	room
Pension, die (-en)	guest house, boarding house
Gasthaus, das (¨er)	inn
Jugendherberge, die (-n)	youth hostel
Ferienwohnung, die (-en)	holiday flat, vacation apartment
Zelt, das (-e)	tent
Campingplatz, der (¨e)	campsite
Schlafsack, der (¨e)	sleeping bag
Wohnwagen, der (-)	caravan, trailer
Ferien im Wohnwagen, pl.	caravan holiday
Wohnmobil, das (-e)	camper van, RV
Camper, der (-)	camper
frei	free, vacant
„Zimmer frei"	'Vacancies'
belegt	occupied, no vacancies

Entertainment and dining

Show, die (-s)	show
Vorstellung, die (-en)	performance
Disko, die (-s)	disco
Diskothek, die (-en)	discotheque
Fastfoodrestaurant, das (-s)	fast food restaurant
Fischrestaurant, das (-s)	seafood restaurant
Pizzeria, die (-rien or -s)	pizzeria
Cafeteria, die (-rien)	cafeteria
Imbissstube, die (-n)	snack bar
Portion, die (-en)	portion
Kinderportion, die (-en)	child's portion

(etw) bestellen	to order (sth)
etw vorbestellen	to order sth in advance
etw aussuchen	to choose sth
etw empfehlen	to recommend sth
etw servieren	to serve sth
Rechnung, die (-en)	bill
Trinkgeld, das (-er)	tip
Grillparty, die (-s)	barbecue

Personnel

Gast, der (¨e)	guest, visitor, customer
Kellner(in), der/die (-/nen)	waiter/waitress, server
Koch, der (¨e); Köchin, die (-nen)	chef
Barmann, der (¨er)	barman
Barfrau, die (-en)	barmaid
Zimmermädchen, das (-)	chambermaid
Reiseleiter(in), der/die (-/nen)	tour guide
(Reise)führer(in), der/die (-/nen)	(travel) guide

Road transport

Auto, das (-s)	car
Wagen, der (-)	car
Sportwagen, der (-)	sports car
(Auto)bus, der (-se)	bus
Taxi, das (-s)	taxi
Motor, der (-en)	motor
Motorrad, das (¨er)	motor cycle
Moped, das (-s)	motor bike, moped
Traktor, der (-en)	tractor
Führerschein, der (-e)	driving licence
Fahrgast, der (¨e)	passenger
Benzin, das (no pl.)	petrol, gas
Benzintank, der (-s or -e)	petrol tank
Tankstelle, die (-n)	service station
tanken	to fill the tank, tank up
volltanken	to fill up
Unfall, der (¨e)	accident

Panne, die (-n)	puncture, flat (tyre), breakdown
etw parken	to park sth
Parkuhr, die (-en)	parking metre
Hoch-, Tiefgarage, die (-n)	multi-storey/ underground car park
Rad, das (¨er)	wheel
Sitzplatz, der (¨e)	seat
sich anschnallen	to fasten one's seatbelt
etw starten	to start sth
(etw) lenken	to steer/drive sth
Lenkrad, das (¨er)	steering wheel
Steuer, das (-)	steering wheel
Bremse, die (-n)	brake
bremsen	to brake
anhalten	to stop
stoppen	to stop
hupen	to honk, sound the horn
Gang, der (¨e)	gear
der erste Gang	first gear
im ersten Gang	in first gear
umschalten	to change gear
Gas geben	to accelerate, step on the gas
Gas wegnehmen	to decelerate
Nummernschild, das (-er)	number plate
per Anhalter fahren	to hitchhike
trampen	to hitchhike
Anhalter(in), der/die (-/nen)	hitchhiker
Tramper(in), der/die (-nen)	hitchhiker

Rail transport

Bahn, die (-en)	railway, railroad
Eisenbahn, die (-en)	railway, railroad
Deutsche Bundesbahn, die	Federal German Railways
Zug, der (¨e)	train
Lokomotive, die (-n)	locomotive, engine
Wagen, der (-)	carriage, car
Nichtraucher, der (-)	non-smoking car

Schlafwagen, der (-)	sleeping car
Liegewagen, der (-)	sleeping car
Speisewagen, der (-)	restaurant car
Gepäckwagen, der (-)	luggage van, baggage car
Schaffner(in), der/die (-/nen)	ticket inspector
Bahnhof, der (¨e)	train station
Hauptbahnhof, der (¨e)	main railway station
Station, die (-en)	station
umsteigen	to change

Air transport

Flugzeug, das (-e)	plane
Maschine, die (-n)	aeroplane
Hubschrauber, der (-)	helicopter
Flug, der (¨e)	flight
Flughafen, der (¨)	airport
Flugplatz, der (¨e)	airfield, airport
Terminal, der or das (-s)	terminal
Fluggast, der (¨e)	(airline) passenger
Ticket, das (-s)	(plane) ticket
Stand-by-Ticket, das (-s)	stand-by ticket
(Ko)pilot(in), der/die (-en/nen)	(co)pilot
Flugschein, der (-e)	pilot's licence
Kapitän(in), der/die (-e/nen)	captain [also naut.]
Flugbegleiter(in), der/die (-/nen)	flight attendant
Steward(ess), der/die (-s/en)	steward(ess)
starten	to take off
Start, der (-s)	takeoff
landen	to land
Landung, die (-en)	landing
Notlandung, die (-en)	emergency landing
Zwischenlandung, die (-en)	stopover
Start- und Landebahn, die (-en)	runway

Flugzeit, die (-en)	flight time	am Ruder sein	to be at the helm
luftkrank	airsick	Anker, der (-)	anchor
Flugmeilen sammeln	to collect air miles	losmachen	to cast off
		etw festmachen	to moor sth
		Seereise, die (-n)	ocean trip, cruise, voyage

Shipping

Schiff, das (-e)	ship, vessel		
Boot, das (-e)	boat	seekrank	seasick
Motorboot, das (-e)	motorboat	ertrinken	to drown
Ruderboot, das (-e)	rowing boat	jmdn retten	to save sb
Segelboot, das (-e)	sailboat	untergehen	to sink
Fischerboot, das (-e)	fishing boat	sinken	to sink
Rennboot, das (-e)	speedboat	Matrose, der (-n);	sailor
Rettungsboot, das (-e)	lifeboat	Matrosin, die (-nen)	
U-Boot, das (-e)	submarine	Seemann, der	sailor, mariner
Tanker, der (-)	tanker	(Seeleute);	
Öltanker, der (-)	oil tanker	Seefrau, die (-en)	
Deck, das (-s)	deck	Hafen, der (¨)	port, harbour
Paddel, das (-)	paddle	Kanal, der (¨e)	canal, channel
Ruder, das (-)	oar; rudder, helm	vor der Küste	offshore

Level 2

General

verreisen	to go away (on a trip)	einfache Fahrt, die (-en)	single fare, one-way ticket
aus-, einreisen	to leave/enter the country	unterwegs	on the way
Ausreise, die (-n)	leaving the country	Hinfahrt, die (-en)	the way there, outward journey
Einreise, die (-n)	entry	Rückfahrt, die (-en)	return (journey)
Einreisekarte, die (-n)	landing card	Ausflug, der (¨e)	outing, trip, excursion
für etw Zoll bezahlen	to pay duty on sth		
etw verzollen	to pay duty on sth, declare sth	Aufenthalt, der (-e)	stay
		Verspätung, die (-en)	delay, late arrival
etw umbuchen	to change one's booking	Verbindung, die (-en)	connection, link
		Fahrplan, der (¨e)	timetable
etw stornieren	to cancel sth	Lautsprecher, der (-)	loudspeaker
Geschäftsreise, die (-n)	business trip	über Lautsprecher	over the loudspeakers
		Handgepäck, das (no pl.)	hand luggage
Rundreise, die (-n)	round trip		
Tarif, der (-e)	fare	Gepäckausgabe, die (-n)	baggage claim
Fahrkarte erster/ zweiter Klasse, die (-n)	first/second-class ticket	Gepäckaufbewahrung, die (-en)	left luggage office
Rückfahrkarte, die (-n)	round-trip ticket	Zeitunterschied, der (-e)	time difference

Tourism

touristisch	tourist, touristy
Massentourismus, der (no pl.)	mass tourism
Fremdenverkehr, der (no pl.)	tourism
Verkehrsamt, das (¨er)	tourist information office
Vorsaison, die (-s)	early season
Hauptsaison, die (-s)	high season
Nebensaison, die (-s)	off-season
Sehenswürdigkeit, die (-en)	sight
etw besichtigen	to have a look at/ visit/tour sth
Andenken, das (-)	souvenir, keepsake, memento
Souvenir, das (-s)	souvenir
Souvenirladen, der (¨)	souvenir shop
Reiseprospekt, der (-e)	travel brochure
Sommerurlaubsort, der (-e)	summer resort
Wintersportort, der (-e)	winter sports resort
Seebad, das (¨er)	seaside/coastal resort
Kurort, der (-e)	spa, health resort
Urlaub mit dem Fahrrad, der (-e)	cycling holiday

Accommodation and facilities

Unterkunft, die (¨e)	lodging, place to stay, accommodation
Halbpension, die (no pl.)	half board
Vollpension, die (no pl.)	full board
Fremdenzimmer, das (-)	guest room
Schlafsaal, der (¨e)	dormitory [in youth hostel]
Haustausch, der (-e)	home exchange
Chalet, das (-s)	chalet
Villa, die (Villen)	villa
Rezeption, die (-en)	reception

sich anmelden	to check in
abreisen	to check out
Zweibettzimmer, das (-)	room with two twin beds
Einzel-, Doppelzimmer, das (-)	single/double room
Luxushotel, das (-s)	luxury hotel
Hotelkette, die (-n)	hotel chain
Gästeliste, die (-n)	guest list
übernachten	to stay, spend the night
Übernachtung, die (-en)	overnight stay
Weckruf, der (-e)	wake-up call

Entertainment and dining

Gaststätte, die (-n)	restaurant
Weinlokal, das (-e)	wine bar
Weinkarte, die (-n)	wine list
Restaurantkette, die (-n)	restaurant chain
Entertainment, das (no pl.)	entertainment
Unterhaltung, die (-en)	entertainment
während des Fluges	in-flight
Frühstücksbar, die (-s)	breakfast bar
Büfett, das (-s and -e)	bar
kaltes Büfett	cold buffet
Salatbüfett, das (-s)	salad bar
Abendessen mit Tanz, das (-)	dinner dance
Restaurant mit Theatervorführung, das (-s)	dinner theatre
Luxusrestaurant, das (-s)	first-class restaurant
Restaurantführer, der (-)	restaurant guide
jmdn bedienen	to serve/wait on sb
Menü, das (-s)	special; set meal
Tageskarte, die (-n)	menu of the day
Touristenspeisekarte, die (-n)	tourist menu

Spezialität des Küchenchefs, die (-en)	chef's special
Theke, die (-n)	bar
Bierdeckel, der (-)	beer mat

Personnel

Pensionsgast, der ("e)	boarder
Hoteldirektor(in), der/die (-en/nen)	hotel manager
Hoteldiener(in), der/die (-/nen)	hotel porter
Oberkellner(in), der/die (-/nen)	head waiter/waitress
Chefkoch, -köchin, der/die ("e/nen)	head chef
Gastwirt(in), der/die (-e/nen)	restaurant owner/ manager
Bardame, die (-n)	barmaid
Barkeeper(in), der/die (-/nen)	bartender

Road transport

Gebrauchtwagen, der (-)	used car
Automarke, die (-n)	make of car
Baujahr, das (-e)	model year
Benzinverbrauch, der (no pl.)	petrol mileage
Mietwagen, der (-)	hire car
Anhänger, der (-)	trailer
Rückspiegel, der (-)	rear-view mirror
Sicherheitsgurt, der (-e)	safety/seat belt
Reifen, der (-)	tyre
Vorder-, Hinterrad, das ("er)	front/back wheel
Reserverad, das ("er)	spare (wheel)
Kofferraum, der ("e)	boot, trunk
Autobahngebühr, die (-en)	toll
Ein-, Ausfahrt, die (-en)	slip road (entry/exit)
Rastplatz, der ("e)	rest stop
Raststätte, die (-n)	service area, services
Parkscheinautomat, der (-en)	ticket (dispensing) machine

etw anlassen	to start sth [engine]
etw abschalten	to turn off sth [engine]
den ersten Gang ein-legen/einschalten	to engage first gear
auf/in den dritten Gang schalten	to change into third gear
Rückwärtsgang, der ("e)	reverse
im Rückwärtsgang fahren	to (drive in) reverse
im Leerlauf	in neutral
die Orientierung verlieren	to lose one's bearings
sich verfahren	to lose one's way
zurückkehren	to turn back
Verkehr, der (no pl.)	traffic
Stau, der (-s or -e)	traffic jam
Reifenpanne, die (-n)	flat tyre
Pannendienst, der (-e)	breakdown service
etw abschleppen	to tow sth away
Schaden, der (")	damage
etw beschädigen	to damage sth
Werkstatt, die ("en)	garage
Reparatur, die (-en)	repair
Versicherung, die (-en)	insurance
etw versichern	to insure sth
(links/rechts) abbiegen	turn (left/right)
ausrutschen	to skid
Wenden, das (no pl.)	U-turn
zurücksetzen	to back (up)
Tempo, das (-s)	speed
mit hohem Tempo	at a high speed
Strafzettel, der (-)	ticket
Geldstrafe, die (-n)	fine
Fahrschule, die (-n)	driving school
Inspektion, die (-en)	service
ein Auto zur Inspektion geben	to service a car

Rail transport

Lok, die (-s)	engine
Dampflok, die (-s)	steam engine

Lokführer(in), der/die (-/nen)	driver	Bordkarte, die (-n)	boarding pass [also naut.]
Fahrkartenausgabe, die (-n)	ticket office	Besatzung, die (-en)	crew [also naut.]
Fahrkartenschalter, der (-)	ticket counter	Mannschaft, die (-en)	crew [also naut.]
		Direktflug, der (¨e)	direct flight
einfach	one-way	Sitz am Gang, der (-e)	aisle seat
hin und zurück	round trip	Fensterplatz, der (¨e)	window seat
Gleis, das (-e)	platform, track	Kopfhörer, der (-)	headphones
Bahnsteig, der (-e)	platform	Abflug, der (¨e)	takeoff, departure
Abteil, der (-e)	compartment	abfliegen	to take off, leave, depart
Kurswagen, der (-)	through coach		
Kursbuch, das (¨er)	timetable	Abflughalle, die (-n)	departure lounge
D-Zug, der (¨e)	fast train, non-stop train	Warteraum, der (¨e)	departure lounge [for single flight]
Eilzug, der (¨e)	express train	Entführer(in), der/die (-/nen)	hijacker
Intercity (IC), der (-s)	intercity	etw entführen	to hijack sth
Intercityexpresszug (ICE), der (¨e)	intercity express	zur Landung ansetzen	to come in to land
		abstürzen	to crash

Air transport

Jumbo(jet), der (-s)	jumbo jet		
Düsenflugzeug, das (-e)	jet plane	ablegen	to cast off, leave, depart [ship]
Charterflug, der (¨e)	charter flight	anlegen	to come in, arrive [ship]
Inlandflug, der (¨e)	domestic flight		
Passagierflugzeug, das (-e)	passenger aircraft	auslaufen	to leave [ship]
		von Bord gehen	to disembark
Frachtflugzeug, das (-e)	freighter	über Bord	overboard
		Riemen, der (-)	oar
Wasserflugzeug, das (-e)	seaplane	Kompass, der (-e)	compass
		Floß, das (¨e)	raft
Fluglinie, die (-n)	airline	Fähre, die (-n)	ferry
Fluggesellschaft, die (-en)	airline	Autofähre, die (-n)	car ferry
		Containerschiff, das (-e)	container ship
Businessclass, die (no pl.)	business class	Passagierschiff, das (-e)	liner
Touristenklasse, die (no pl.)	economy class	Handelsschiff, das (-e)	merchant ship
einchecken	to check in	Kriegsschiff, das (-e)	warship
Check-in, der or das (-s)	check-in (desk)	Transportschiff, das (-e)	cargo ship
Abfertigungsschalter, der (-)	check-in desk	Jacht, die (-en)	yacht
an Bord	on board [also naut.]	Dampfer, der (-)	steamer
an Bord gehen	to board [also naut.]		

Shipping

Überseedampfer, der (-)	ocean liner	Überfahrt, die (-en)	crossing
auf/unter Deck	on/below deck	Kreuzfahrt, die (-en)	cruise
Ober-, Unterdeck, das (-e or -s)	upper/lower deck	Zahlmeister(in), der/die (-/nen)	purser
Bullauge, das (-n)	porthole	Wrack, das (-s)	wreck
Liegestuhl, der (¨e)	deck chair	Schiffbruch, der (¨e)	shipwreck

Level 3

General

anreisen	to make a journey (here/there)	Kofferanhänger, der (-)	luggage label/tag
abreisen	to depart	Adapter, der (-)	adapter
Anreise, die (-n)	outbound journey, journey here/there	öffentliche Verkehrsmittel, pl.	public transport
Abreise, die (-n)	departure (for the return journey)	öffentlicher Nahverkehr	local public transport
Transitreisende(r), der/die (adj. decl.)	transit passenger	Umsteigefahrschein, der (-e)	transfer ticket
Pendler(in), der/die (-/nen)	commuter	Gruppentarif, der (-e)	group rate
Währung, die (-en)	currency		
Wechselstube, die (-n)	currency exchange office	### *Tourism*	
Wechselkurs, der (-e)	exchange rate	Gürteltasche, die (-n)	money belt
Devisen, pl.	foreign currency	Pauschalreise, die (-n)	package tour
Stornierungsgebühr, die (-en)	cancellation charge	Besichtigung, die (-en)	sightseeing tour; tour
Einwanderungs-behörde, die (-n)	immigration authorities	auf Besichtigungstour gehen	to go sightseeing
Einwanderungs-gesetze, pl.	immigration rules	Denkmal, das (¨er)	monument
Zollbestimmung, die (-en)	customs regulation	historisches Denkmal	historical monument
Einfuhrzoll, der (¨e)	duty	es steht unter Denkmalschutz	it's a listed building
Freigepäck, das (no pl.)	baggage allowance	historisch interessante Stätten, pl.	places of historical interest
Gepäckband, das (¨er)	baggage conveyor belt	die landschaftlich schöne Strecke nehmen	to take the scenic route
Gepäckschließfach, das (¨er)	luggage locker	Tagesausflug, der (¨e)	day trip/excursion
zollfreie Ware, die (-n)	duty-free goods	Tagesausflügler(in), der/die (-/nen)	day tripper
Dutyfreeshop, der (-s)	duty-free shop	Aktivurlaub, der (-e)	activity holiday
Fundbüro, das (-s)	lost property office	Informationstour, die (-en)	study holiday

Safari, die (-s)	safari
Geschenkartikelladen, der (¨)	gift shop
Themenpark, der (-s)	theme park
etw chartern	to charter sth
Rucksacktourist(in), der/die (-en/nen)	backpacker

Accommodation and facilities

Hotel garni, das (-s)	bed and breakfast hotel
Übernachtung mit Frühstück, die (-en)	bed and breakfast
Hotelgewerbe, das (no pl.)	hotel business
Hochzeitssuite, die (-n)	bridal suite
Nebenzimmer, das (-)	adjoining room
angrenzende Zimmer mit Verbindungstür, pl.	connecting rooms
Minibar, die (-s)	minibar
Kaution, die (-en)	deposit
Wohnung auf Timesharingbasis, die (-en)	timeshare
Zimmerservice, der (no pl.)	room service
Wäscheservice, der (no pl.)	laundry service
Einrichtungen, pl.	amenities, facilities
Konferenzein- richtungen, pl.	conference facilities
Zimmervermittlung, die (-en)	room reservation
für Selbstversorger	self-catering
Schlüsselkarte, die (-n)	key card
Hauptschlüssel, der (-)	pass key
Kabine, die (-n)	stateroom
Klappbett, das (-en)	folding bed

Entertainment and dining

Verpflegung, die (no pl.)	food service, meals, catering
Selbstversorgung, die (no pl.)	self-catering
Bedienung, die (no pl.)	service
Selbstbedienung, die (no pl.)	self-service
Partyservice, der (-s)	party catering service
die Speisen und Getränke liefern	to cater
Lieferfirma für Speisen und Getränke, die (-firmen)	caterer
Gaststättengewerbe, das (no pl.)	catering trade
Gastronomie, die (no pl.)	catering trade
etw ausrichten	to arrange, organize sth
Bankett, das (-e)	banquet
Festessen, das (-)	banquet
Festsaal, der (-säle)	banqueting hall
Bankettsaal, der (-säle)	banqueting hall
Lunchpaket, das (-e)	packed lunch
Rastplatz, der (¨e)	picnic area
Beilage, die (-n)	side dish
gutbürgerlich	solid, respectable; good

Personnel

Bedienung, die (-en)	waiter/waitress
Personal, das (no pl.)	personnel, staff
Gastronom(in), der/die (-en/nen)	restaurateur
Hotelier, der (-s)	hotelier
Empfangschef, -dame, der/die (-s/n)	receptionist
Nachtportier, der (-s)	night porter
Zollbeamte, -beamtin, der/die (-n/nen)	customs officer

Dolmetscher(in), der/die (-/nen)	interpreter	Wagenheber, der (-)	jack
		Schraubenschlüssel, der (-)	wrench
Road transport		Kühler, der (-)	radiator
Straßenverkehrsord-nung, die (no pl.)	highway code	Katalysator, der (-en)	catalytic converter
Kraftfahrzeug, das (-e)	motor vehicle	Windschutzscheibe, die (-n)	windscreen
Kraftfahrzeugschein, der (-e)	vehicle registration document	Scheibenwischer, der (-)	windscreen wiper
zugelassen sein	to be registered for road use	Motorhaube, die (-n)	bonnet, hood
		Karosserie, die (-n)	body (work)
TÜV, der (-s)	vehicle validation/inspection; MOT	Stoßstange, die (-n)	bumper
		Stoßdämpfer, der (-)	shock absorber
Lastkraftwagen, der (-)	truck	Scheinwerfer, der (-)	headlight
		Rücklicht, das (-er)	back-up light
LKW, der (-s)	truck	etw abblenden	to dim sth
Kombiwagen, der (-)	station wagon	Fernlicht, das (-er)	high beam
Geländewagen, der (-)	sports utility vehicle	Abblendlicht, das (-er)	dipped headlight, low beam
Kabriolett, das (-s)	convertible	Standlicht, das (-er)	side light
Fließheck, das (-s)	fastback	Spur, die (-en)	lane
Diesel(kraftstoff), der (no pl.)	diesel	Innen-, Überholspur, die (-en)	inside/outside lane
Promillemesser, der (-)	Breathalyzer ®	etw überholen	to pass/overtake sth
Trunkenheit am Steuer, die (no pl.)	drunk driving	die Fahrspur wechseln	to change lanes
		Bankette, die (-n)	hard shoulder
Geschwindigkeit, die (-en)	speed	Seitenstreifen, der (-)	hard shoulder
		Bordstein, der (-e)	kerb
Höchstgeschwin-digkeit, die (-en)	top/maximum speed	Bordkante, die (-n)	kerb
		Mittelstreifen, der (-)	central reservation, median strip
Geschwindigkeits-begrenzung, die (-en)	speed limit	Verkehrsinsel, die (-n)	traffic island
Geschwindigkeits-überschreitung, die (-en)	speeding	**Rail transport**	
		Anschluss, der (¨e)	connection
Tachometer, das (-)	speedometer	Gleisanschluss, der (¨e)	junction
Schalthebel, der (-)	gear lever	Zuschlag, der (¨e)	surcharge
Kupplung, die (-en)	clutch	Platzkarte, die (-n)	seat reservation
Auspufftopf, der (¨e)	silencer, muffler	Bahncard ®, die (-s)	rail card
Abgas, das (-e)	exhaust	Schiene, die (-n)	rail
Beule, die (-n)	dent	Bahndamm, der (¨e)	(railway) embankment
Ersatzteil, der (-e)	spare (part)		

Stellwerkwärter, der (-)	signalman
Eisenbahner(in), der/die (-/nen)	railwayman/woman, railroader
Gepäckträger(in), der/die (-/nen)	porter
Kofferkuli, der (-s)	luggage trolley
Drahtseilbahn, die (-en)	cable car
Güterzug, der (¨e)	freight train
Personenzug, der (¨e)	slow/stopping train; passenger train
Bummelzug, der (¨e)	slow/stopping train
Interregio (IR), der (-s)	regional train
Nahverkehrszug, der (¨e)	local train
Pendlerzug, der (¨e)	commuter train

Air transport

Übergewicht, das (no pl.)	excess baggage
Flugsteig, der (-e)	gate
Sicherheitsmaßnahmen, pl.	safety measures
Leibesvisitation, die (-en)	body search
Abflug-, Ankunftsanzeige, die (-n)	departure/arrivals board
Cockpit, das (-s)	cockpit
Steuerknüppel, der (-)	control column/ stick; joystick
Kabine, die (-n)	cabin [also naut.]
Notausgang, der (¨e)	emergency exit
Schwimmweste, die (-n)	life jacket [also naut.]
Flugzeugrumpf, der (¨e)	fuselage
Flügelspannweite, die (-n)	wingspan
Reisegeschwindigkeit, die (-en)	cruising speed
Reiseflughöhe, die (-n)	cruising altitude

Luftraum, der (¨e)	airspace
Sturzflug, der (¨e)	nosedive
zum Sturzflug ansetzen	to go into a nosedive
Turbulenzen, pl.	turbulence
Luftloch, das (¨er)	air pocket
Ballast, der (-e)	ballast [also naut.]
Flugablaufplan, der (¨e)	flight plan
Bordbuch, das (¨er)	log book
Kontrollturm, der (¨e)	control tower
Fluglotse, -lotsin, der/die (-n/nen)	air-traffic controller
Bodenpersonal, das (no pl.)	ground staff

Shipping

sich (nach etw) einschiffen	to embark (for sth)
etw vertäuen	to moor sth
Schlepper, der (-)	towboat
Frachtkahn, der (¨e)	barge
Flugzeugträger, der (-)	aircraft carrier
Trawler, der (-)	trawler
Kajütboot, das (-e)	cabin boat
Luftkissenboot, das (-e)	hovercraft
Tragflächenboot, das (-e)	hydrofoil
Landungsbrücke, die (-n)	gangway
Reling, die (-s or -e)	(deck) rail
Bug, der (-e or ¨e)	bow
Heck, das (-e)	stern
Schiffskörper, der (-)	hull
Mast, der (-en or -e)	mast
Mastbaum, der (¨e)	mast
Tauwerk, das (no pl.)	rigging
Schornstein, der (-e)	funnel, smokestack
Maschinenraum, der (¨e)	engine room
Schiffsschraube, die (-n)	propeller

Steuermann, der (Steuerleute)	helmsman	Schleuse, die (-n)	lock, sluice, floodgate
		Treidelpfad, der (-e)	towpath
Kielwasser, das (no pl.)	wake	Kai, der (-e or -s)	quay, wharf
		Boje, die (-n)	buoy
Anlegesteg, der (-e)	jetty, landing stage	Ärmelkanal, der (no pl.)	(English) Channel
Landesteg, der (-e)	landing stage	Fahrrinne, die (-n)	shipping channel
Verankerung, die (-en)	anchoring; moorings	Fähnrich zur See, der (-e)	ensign

Exercises

Level 1

1. Wie heißt das Gegenteil? ✓
1. etw packen
2. im Inland
3. die Ankunft
4. die Hochgarage
5. Gas geben
6. landen
7. frei (Zimmer)
8. der Raucher
9. etw festmachen

2. Welches Wort hat die gleiche oder eine ähnliche Bedeutung? ✓
1. die Information
2. etw reservieren
3. die Tour
4. der Camper
5. das Barbecue
6. das Auto
7. das Steuer
8. stoppen
9. der Tramper
10. der Schlafwagen
11. das Flugzeug
12. die Stewardess
13. sinken

3. Ergänzen Sie. ✓
1. der Wagen – der Fahrgast : das Flugzeug – _____
2. der Pass – die Passkontrolle : der Zoll – _____
3. der Kellner – die Kellnerin : der Barmann – _____
4. fahren – der Führerschein : fliegen – _____
5. das Schiff – seekrank : das Flugzeug – _____
6. bremsen – die Bremse : lenken – _____
7. der Zug – der Bahnhof : das Flugzeug – _____

4. Ordnen Sie.
der Anker, die Eisenbahn, die Flugzeit, der Hafen, der Hauptbahnhof, der Hubschrauber, der Matrose, die Notlandung, der Pilot, das Ruder, die Schaffnerin, der Speisewagen, der Tanker

Schienenverkehr	Luftverkehr	Schifffahrt

5. Welche Wörter gehören zusammen? ✓

> a. das Benzin, b. die Diskothek, c. das Fastfoodrestaurant, d. die Parkuhr,
> e. das Rettungsboot, f. das Segelboot, g. der Traktor, h. trampen, i. das Zelt,
> j. das Zimmermädchen

1. der Wind		6. Münzen
2. sinken		7. das Hotel
3. der Daumen		8. das Camping
4. der Bauernhof		9. der Hamburger
5. die Tankstelle		10. tanzen

6. Welches Wort passt nicht? ✓

1. der Ferienort, der Skiort, der Urlaubsort, der Wohnort
2. das Gasthaus, die Imbissstube, die Jugendherberge, das Motel
3. der Ausweis, die Rechnung, das Ticket, das Visum
4. das Motorboot, das Rennboot, das Ruderboot, das U-Boot
5. die Fahrkarte, die Landkarte, der Stadtplan, die Straßenkarte

7. Falsche Freunde. Ergänzen Sie die Tabelle.

Deutsch	Englisch	Deutsch	Englisch
die Pension			pension
das Gas			gas(oline)
das Menü			menu
der Gang			gang
die Lok			lock
das Floß			floss
die Kaution			caution
die Bahn			ban

8. Was bedeuten die Wendungen?

1. wir sitzen alle in einem Boot
2. gute Reise!
3. die letzte Reise antreten
4. ungeladener Gast
5. jmdm an den Wagen fahren
6. er hat ganz schön getankt
7. das fünfte Rad am Wagen sein
8. nicht ganz auf Deck sein

9. Übersetzen Sie ins Deutsche! ✓

1. to miss the boat
2. when my ship comes in
3. to ship water
4. to tour the world
5. the wheels of progress
6. to put on the brakes

10. In jedem Satz fehlt ein Wort. ✓

> Anhalter, Ferienwohnung, hupen, parken, Reisebüro, Sportwagen, Stadtrundfahrt, Tourist, volltanken

1. Als _____ lernt man das Land nur oberflächlich kennen.
2. Er hat seinen Flug im _____ gebucht.
3. Bei einer _____ wurde ihr anschließend Bonn gezeigt.
4. Schon für 600 Mark kann eine Familie mit zwei Kindern eine Woche lang eine _____ an der Nordsee buchen.
5. Sie zeigte eine Vorliebe für schnelle _____.
6. Wer über Ostern nach Frankreich fährt, sollte zuvor sein Auto _____.
7. Wir _____ unsere Wagen in einem Parkhaus am Stadtrand.
8. Autofahrer _____ und versuchen, ein Stückchen weiterzukommen.
9. Sie ist per _____ nach Berlin gefahren.

11. Übersetzen Sie ins Deutsche. ✓

1. A reservation is recommended.
2. During vacation thousands of Berliners leave the city.
3. She sent me a postcard of the snow-covered Alps.
4. He crawls into his sleeping bag and tries to fall asleep.
5. The seafood restaurant is at the other end of the city.
6. I ordered a child's portion.
7. She stopped at the rest stop because of a flat tyre.
8. We have to change (trains) in Göttingen.
9. He was arrested during a stopover in Frankfurt.

12. Übersetzen Sie ins Englische.

Mato Grosso

Beste Reisezeit: Mato Grosso ist tropisch, die Temperaturen liegen zwischen 25 und 30 Grad, Regenfälle sind immer möglich, nicht nur während der Regenzeit von Oktober bis April, sondern auch in der Trockenzeit.

Anreise: Die reine Flugzeit von Frankfurt am Main bis São Paulo und Cuiabá beträgt etwa 15 Stunden; der Flug von Frankfurt am Main nach Cuiabá über São Paulo oder Rio de Janeiro kostet ab 647 Euro zuzüglich Flughafengebühren und Sicherheitszuschlag; eine Nonstop-Verbindung ist geplant. Varig fliegt täglich von Frankfurt nach São Paulo und viermal wöchentlich von Frankfurt nach Rio de Janeiro, vom 15. Juni 2002 an täglich. Wer noch mehr von Brasilien erkunden will, für den ist der „Brasil Airpass" günstig: Er gilt 21 Tage lang, mit ihm können bis zu neun Städten innerhalb Brasiliens angeflogen werden, er kann in Verbindung mit einem internationalen Ticket der Varig oder Lufthansa

erworben werden (je nach Anzahl der Flugcoupons kostet das
Reisepaket zwischen 530 und 930 US-Dollar plus Sicherheitsgebühr) ...

Petra Mies

FRANKFURTER RUNDSCHAU, Samstag, 8. Juni 2002, Nr. 130/23, Magazin,
S. 11

13. Übersetzen Sie ins Englische.

Viel Raum fürs Bein

*Fluggesellschaften und Reisekonzerne buhlen um Geschäftsleute –
Lufthansa setzt auf Extraklasse, TUI auf eine Billig-Airline*

Nur fliegen ist schöner, hieß es einmal in der Autowerbung. Der Spruch
scheint seit dem 11. September keine Gültigkeit mehr zu haben. Im
ersten Quartal 2002 stiegen fünf Prozent weniger Leute ins Flugzeug
als im gleichen Zeitraum ein Jahr zuvor, was einem Minus von 468 300
Passagieren entspricht. Das ist ein Problem für große Fluglinien wie
Lufthansa, deren Einnahmen um knapp acht Prozent auf 2,4 Milliarden
Euro sanken; das ist ein Problem für große Ferienanbieter wie TUI, deren
Flugbuchungen für die Sommersaison 7,9 Prozent unterm Vorjahr
liegen.

Was also tun gegen die Flaute? Lufthansa schreitet mit neuem Konzept
voran und ficht weiter im Kampf um eine kleine, aber feine Gruppe – die
Geschäftsreisenden. Die hatte Lufthansa nach dem Terroranschlag
vernachlässigt, zumindest auf der Strecke Düsseldorf–New York. Sämtliche
Businessflüge waren damals gestrichen worden. Jetzt will man die Strecke
wiederbeleben, weil der Konzern befürchtet, zahlungskräftige
Geschäftskunden zu verlieren. Vom 17. Juni an hebt deshalb ein besonderes
Flugzeug auf dem Düsseldorfer Flughafen an, eine Boeing 737–700,
sechsmal in der Woche. Das ist noch nichts Außergewöhnliches, aber
in dem Flugzeug wird es nur 48 Sitzplätze geben, wo sonst 120 montiert sind.
Viel Beinfreiheit also. »Die Kunden sollen sich wohl fühlen«, sagt
Lufthansa-Sprecherin Amélie Lorenz. Das Essen wird auch nicht auf einem
Wägelchen durch die Reihen gekarrt, sondern wie im Restaurant serviert.
Alles ganz fein. Dass Lufthansa diese Boeing bei der Schweizer Private Air
chartert, habe nichts mit mangelnder Kompetenz im Luxusbusiness zu tun,
sagt Lorenz, aber: »Wir hätten eine unserer Maschinen umbauen müssen, das
wäre teuer geworden.« Und überhaupt sei die neue Strecke kein
Luxusangebot, sagt sie. »Das ist First Class, ein angenehmes Raumgefühl, ein
exklusives Produkt, ja, aber doch kein Luxus.« Denn das exklusive Produkt
kostet genauso viel wie ein normaler Lufthansa-Businessflug von Frankfurt
nach New York: 2880 Euro ...

Franz Lenze

DIE ZEIT, 6. Juni 2002, Nr. 24, S. 66

Level 2

1. Wie heißt das Gegenteil? ✓

1. die Ausreise	7. sich anmelden
2. etw buchen	8. das Hinterrad
3. die Rückfahrt	9. die Einfahrt
4. ablegen	10. etw anlassen
5. das Unterdeck	11. das Passagierflugzeug
6. die Hauptsaison	

2. Welches Verb passt? ✓

> a. abbiegen, b. ansetzen, c. bezahlen, d. einschalten, e. geben, f. gehen, g. verlieren

1. für etw Zoll	5. ein Auto zur Inspektion
2. den zweiten Gang	6. an Bord
3. die Orientierung	7. zur Landung
4. rechts	

3. Welche Wörter gehören zusammen? ✓

> a. die Automarke, b. der Hoteldiener, c. der Liegestuhl, d. der Reiseprospekt,
> e. das Reserverad, f. der Schlafsaal, g. die Sehenswürdigkeit, h. der Stau,
> i. der Strafzettel, j. die Verspätung, k. der Wintersportort

1. warten	7. Porsche
2. das Reisebüro	8. der Kofferraum
3. Skier	9. die Hauptverkehrszeit
4. der Kölner Dom	10. im Parkverbot stehen
5. die Jugendherberge	11. auf Deck
6. das Gepäck	

4. Welches Wort hat die gleiche oder eine ähnliche Bedeutung? ✓

1. der Tourismus	6. das Gleis
2. das Souvenir	7. die Fluglinie
3. das Entertainment	8. der Check-in
4. die Barfrau	9. die Mannschaft
5. die Lokomotive	

5. Welches Wort passt nicht? ✓

1. das Chalet, das Gasthaus, die Gaststätte, das Luxushotel
2. die Reparatur, der Riemen, der Schaden, der Unfall
3. der Fensterplatz, der Inlandflug, die Touristenklasse, das Verkehrsamt
4. der Benzinverbrauch, der Gebrauchtwagen, der Gepäckwagen, der Mietwagen

5. der Abflug, der Abteil, der Direktflug, der Warteraum
6. die Fähre, der Fahrpreis, die Geldstrafe, der Tarif

6. Ordnen Sie.

die Bahn, das Bullauge, die Dampflok, das Einzelzimmer, der Intercity, die Kreuzfahrt, das Kursbuch, die Rezeption, die Seereise, die Überfahrt, die Unterkunft, der Weckruf

Hotel	*Zug*	*Schiff*

7. In jedem Satz fehlt ein Wort. ✓

Aufenthalt, Bierdeckel, Bordkarte, Geschäftsreise, Jacht, Luxusrestaurant,
Rückfahrkarte, Rückspiegel, Vollpension

1. Er wird auf eine längere _____ nach Übersee geschickt.
2. Die _____ zweiter Klasse beträgt 350 Mark.
3. Nach einem zweitägigen _____ in Paris fährt sie nach Wien zurück.
4. Im Preis enthalten sind Fahrt, Unterkunft, _____ und Ausflüge mit dem Bus.
5. Er diniert mit Freunden in einem _____.
6. Er klemmt einen _____ unter den Fuß des wackligen Tisches.
7. Im _____ erscheinen die Dinge näher als sie in Wirklichkeit sind.
8. Bei der Lufthansa soll eine Magnetkarte Flugticket und _____ ersetzen.
9. Sie wollte ihren Urlaub auf einer _____ in der Karibik verbringen.

8. Wie heißen die Zusammensetzungen? ✓

~~Übersee~~	automat	1. *der Überseedampfer*
Pannen	sprecher	2.
Pensions	ort	3.
Schiff	fähre	4.
Laut	flugzeug	5.
Kur	dienst	6.
Abflug	~~dampfer~~	7.
Parkschein	bruch	8.
Auto	gast	9.
Düsen	halle	10.

9. Schriftliche Übung. Wählen Sie ein Thema.

1. Beschreiben Sie Ihre Traumreise.
2. Schreiben Sie einen kurzen Reisebericht.
3. Beschreiben Sie einen Familienurlaub.

10. Reisen. Übersetzen Sie ins Englische.

Sondertarife für Jugendliche legt die Lufthansa auf. Kinder und Jugendliche zwischen 12 und 24 Jahren zahlen für einen Hin- und Rückflug innerhalb Deutschlands 99 Euro inklusive Steuern und Gebühren, Kinder unter 12 Jahren, die in Begleitung eines Erwachsenen fliegen, 55 Euro inklusive Gebühren. Der Tarif gilt bis zum 30. September ...

DIE ZEIT, 13. Juni 2002, Nr. 25, S. 61

Paris mit dem Rad

Radkarte: Die „Mairie de Paris" gibt eine kostenlose Radkarte mit eingezeichneten Radwegen, Reparaturwerkstätten und Leihmöglichkeiten heraus. Die Karte ist im zentralen Rathaus „Hôtel de Ville" am gleichnamigen Platz erhältlich. Zusätzlich sollte man sich die Michelinkarte Nr. 12 Paris 1:10 000 (mit Straßenverzeichnis) anschaffen. Alle im Text genannten Tourenpunkte sind in dieser Karte eingezeichnet.

Mit dem eigenen Rad: Wer mit dem eigenen Rad reist, muss ein sehr stabiles Sicherheitsschloss mitbringen und unbedingt ein Hotel mit Unterstellmöglichkeit buchen.

Radverleih: Zuverlässig und erfahren ist man beim Radverleih Paris Vélo in der Rue du Fer à Moulin, 3. Arrondissement nahe Jardin des Plantes . . . Ein Rad kostet dort pro Tag 14, für drei Tage 33 Euro. Für Gruppen veranstaltet man dort auch geführte Touren zum Beispiel „Paris bei Nacht", „Les Grands Monuments" oder „La Rive Gauche" ...

Claudia Diemar

FRANKFURTER RUNDSCHAU, Samstag, 1. Juni 2002, Nr 124/22, Magazin, S. 12

Information (aus „Unsere kleine Stadt" [Palma de Mallorca])

Anreise: Tägliche Charterflüge von allen deutschen Flughäfen, zum Beispiel von Hamburg mit Hapag Lloyd ab 139 Euro. Linienflüge über Frankfurt oder Barcelona.

Hotels: Hotel San Lorenzo, Carrer Sant Llorenç 14 ... Kleines Vier-Sterne-Hotel mit nur sechs Zimmern nahe dem Llotja-Viertel in der Altstadt, ruhig gelegen, perfekte Zimmer, Hotelgarten mit Swimmingpool. Doppelzimmer von 115 bis 210 Euro.

Hotel Born, Carrer Sant Jaume 3 ... Zwei-Sterne-Hotel in einem Adelspalast in zentraler Lage, schöner Innenhof. Doppelzimmer von 69 bis 114 Euro einschließlich Frühstück.

Restaurants: Restaurante Club Nautico Molinar, Carrer Vicario Joaquin Fuster ... Neu eröffnetes Hafenrestaurant im Stadtteil Es Molinar ... Hauptgerichte ab 8 Euro.
Celler Sa Premsa, Plaça Bisbe Berenguer de Palóu 8 ... Nahe der Fußgängerzone lassen sich zwischen riesigen Weinfässern an derben Holztischen gut und preiswert Tapas essen ...

DIE ZEIT, 6. Juni 2002, Nr. 24, S. 65

11. Fassen Sie den folgenden Text zusammen.

Hinterm wohlgefüllten Teller lugt die Frankfurter Skyline hervor

Nicht nur für Langschläfer: Frühstück und Brunch in der Stadt oder auswärts

Von Barbara Goerlich (www.tafelspitzen.de)

Für Frankfurter scheint es nichts Schöneres zu geben, als am Wochenende auswärts zu frühstücken. Singles, Doubles und Familien mit mehreren Generationen lieben das öffentlich geschmierte Brötchen und den „Kampf" am Brunch-Büffet. Frühstück oder Brunch – kombiniert mit Mittagessen – dürfen sich am Weekend gern bis in den frühen Abend hinziehen. Vor allem Szene-Cafés haben sich darauf eingestellt und tischen – manche ganztags „so lange die Brötchen reichen ..." – Frühstück für Langschläfer auf. Etwa das Café Kante in Nordend, die Wunderbar in Höchst, das Café Klemm in Bockenheim, das Café Karin in der City.
  Auch die großen Hotels setzen auf die hungrige Brunch-Klientel und überbieten sich förmlich mit üppigen Büffets. Für die „Gäste von morgen" geben sie sich bei ihren sonntäglichen Büffets vor allem kinderfrendlich: Das Marriott hat ein „tiefergelegtes" Kinder-Büffet, im Arabella Sheraton Grand speisen Kinder völlig ungestört von den Eltern im separaten „Kinderland", während sie im Waldrestaurant Unterschweinstiege als Mitglied im „Willi-Wildschwein-Club" unterhalten und ebenso gut betreut werden wie im Relexa Hotel im Merton-Viertel. Die Preise für Kinder werden nach Alter oder Größe berechnet, wobei schon mal die Tischkante als Messlatte dient ...

FRANKFURTER RUNDSCHAU, Samstag, 18. Mai 2002, Nr. 114/20, S. 28

Level 3

1. Welches Wort hat die gleiche oder eine ähnliche Bedeutung? ✓

1. die Gastronomie
2. das Bankett
3. der Bordstein
4. der Bummelzug
5. etw festmachen
6. der Propeller

2. Wie heißt die entsprechende Person? ✓

1. der Tagesausflug   4. die Gastronomie
2. pendeln   5. dolmetschen
3. bedienen   6. die Eisenbahn

3. Ordnen Sie.

der Bug, das Fließheck, die Flügelspannweite, der Flugablaufplan, das Kabriolett, die Landungsbrücke, das Luftloch, der Mastbaum, die Reiseflughöhe, der Schlepper, der Stoßdämpfer, der Sturzflug, das Tauwerk, Turbulenzen, der Wagenheber

Auto	Schiff	Flugzeug

4. Was gehört zusammen? ✓

a. der Auspufftopf, b. die Fluglotsin, c. die Geschwindigkeitsüberschreitung, d. die Hochzeitssuite, e. das Kielwasser, f. die Platzkarte, g. der Schalthebel, h. der Scheibenwischer, i. der Scheinwerfer, j. die Schleuse

1. die Kupplung
2. das Abgas
3. die Windschutzscheibe
4. die Geldsstrafe
5. das Ehepaar
6. das Rennboot
7. der Panamakanal
8. der Kontrolturm
9. reservieren
10. die Dunkelheit

5. Wie heißt das Gegenteil? ✓

1. die Anreise   6. die Ankunftsanzeige
2. die Innenspur   7. der Personenzug
3. das Fernlicht

6. Ergänzen Sie. ✓

1. der Geschenkartikelladen – das Geschenk : der Dutyfreeshop – _____
2. das Schiff – das Schiffskörper : das Flugzeug – _____
3. die Wäsche – der Wäscheservice : das Essen – _____
4. der Promillemesser – der Alkoholspiegel : das Tachometer – _____
5. der Zug – die Lokomotive : das Schiff – _____
6. verzollen – der Zoll : stornieren – _____

7. Welche Definition passt? ✓

a. der Aktivurlaub, b. der Bankettsaal, c. die Boje, d. der Frachtkahn, e. das Freigepäck, f. das Fundbüro, g. der Kai, h. der Rucksacktourist, i. die Wechselstube

1. kostenlos transportiertes Gepäck
2. verankerter Schwimmkörper
3. Urlaub und körperliche Betätigung
4. Tourist mit wenig Geld
5. großer Raum für Feste
6. Kahn, der Frachtgut auf Flüssen transportiert
7. Anlegestelle für Schiffe am Ufer
8. Büro für gefundene Sachen
9. Geschäft, in dem man Geld umtauschen kann

8. In jedem Satz fehlt ein Wort. ✓

| Denkmalschutz, Einfuhrzoll, garni, Konferenzeinrichtungen, Mittelstreifen, Nahverkehr, Rücklicht, Währung |

1. Die russische _____ fiel um 5,4 Kopeken auf 28,3283 Rubel je Dollar.
2. Brasilien verlangt 70 Prozent _____ für jedes Auto, das importiert werden soll.
3. Ich möchte in einer Stadt mit gut organisiertem öffentlichen _____ wohnen.
4. Viele Häuser in dieser Gegend stehen unter _____.
5. Wir suchen ein komfortables Hotel _____.
6. Das Haus ist auch mit _____ für Tagungen ausgestattet.
7. Heute besitzt jeder zweite Deutsche ein _____.
8. Das rechte _____ funktioniert nicht.
9. Auf dem _____ steht eine Baumreihe.

9. Suchen Sie eine andere Bedeutung.
1. die Beule
2. der Kühler
3. die Spur
4. das Übergewicht
5. die Schiene
6. die Selbstbedienung

10. Übersetzen Sie ins Englische.

Schweden

Anreise: Mit dem Auto: Bis Puttgarden, dann weiter mit der Fähre nach Rødby (Dänemark) und über die Öresundbrücke nach Schweden. Mit der Bahn: Von Berlin zunächst mit dem Nachtzug nach Sassnitz und dann mit der Fähre nach Trelleborg. Mit dem Flugzeug: Große Airlines bieten Flüge nach Göteborg und Stockholm. Von Frankfurt, Düsseldorf und München geht es im Sommer auch direkt nach Östersund. Preis etwa 380 Euro. Das Dorf Lassekrog ist 210 Kilometer von Östersund entfernt und 395 Kilometer von Stockholm.

Veranstalter: Eine Woche Übernachtung mit Frühstück kostet bei Dertour im Hotel Lassegrog in Lassekrog 277 Euro pro Person (Vollpension: 550 Euro). Zum Angebot von Dertour gehören: Kanutour, Elch- und Bibersafari, Wanderung entlang des Flusses Ljusnan, Wildwasserfahrt mit anschließender Strandsauna am Ljusnan, Ganztagestour „Ins Land der Lappen", alle Transfers.

Ausstattung: Niemals vergessen: Schutzmittel gegen Mücken. Gerade an Seen und Flüssen laufen die Tiere zur Hochform auf. Besonders bewährt hat sich „Djungelolja" ...

Tipps für die Mittsommernacht: Den längsten Tag des Jahres machen die Schweden zum Fest. Sie beginnen in diesem Jahr am 21. Juni. Am Tag danach wird der Midsommerstong aufgestellt, vergleichbar mit dem Maibaum in Deutschland. Kinder und Erwachsene tanzen um den Baum herum, verabreden sich zum Picknick, essen Erdbeerkuchen und Heringe. Das Zeremoniell ist in jedem Ort gleich. Hell bleiben die Nächte bis Anfang August ...

Jörg Hunke

FRANKFURTER RUNDSCHAU, Samstag, 8. Juni 2002, Nr. 130/23, Magazin, S. 15

11. Kraftfahrzeuge. Übersetzen Sie ins Englische.

Ein Isotta Fraschini mit dänischer Karosserie hat bei Christie's in New York den Rekordpreis von 1,38 Millionen Euro erzielt. Erster Eigentümer des 1931 gebauten Wagens des Typs 8B war der damalige dänische Generalkonsul in Stockholm. Er ließ die Karosserie von dem dänischen Designer Viggo Jensen entwerfen und in Kopenhagen bauen. Nur 28 Exemplare des Tipo 8B sind hergestellt worden, es existieren heute nur noch drei. Der Siebenliter-Achtzylinder-Reihenmotor der italienischen Marke leistet 160 PS.

Walter Hönscheidt

Frankfurter Allgemeine Zeitung, Samstag, 25. Mai 2002, Nr. 119/21, S. 63

Die Corvette wird 50: Nur wenige Automodelle erreichen dieses Alter, Chevrolet nimmt es zum Anlass, eine Sonderserie der aktuellen fünften Corvette-Generation aufzulegen. Neben einer auffälligen roten Lackierung und champagnerfarbenen Leichtmetallrädern wird der Innenraum aufgewertet, und die neue elektronische Fahrwerksregelung ist an Bord. Die Stückzahl ist limitiert, verkauft wird die Jubiläums-Corvette als Coupé sowie als Kabrio. Der Verkauf startet im Herbst, das Coupé kostet 65 500 Euro, das Kabrio 71 500. Beide haben einen V8-Motor mit 5,7 Liter Hubraum und 253 kW (344 PS). Gespart wird nicht, das Sondermodell ist rund 4000 Euro teurer.

Boris Schmidt

Frankfurter Allgemeine Zeitung, Samstag, 15. Juni 2002, Nr. 136/24, S. 67

Bus mit 48 Menschen beinahe abgestürzt

BISCHOFSHEIM. Der Ausflug von 48 älteren Menschen in die Rhön hätte am Fronleichnamstag fast mit einer Katastrophe geendet. Ihr Bus konnte in letzter Minute von Feuerwehren gesichert und so verhindert werden, dass der Bus einen Abhang hinunterstürzt.

Nach Angaben der Polizei hatte der 39 Jahre alte Fahrer auf dem Weg vom Kreuzstein zur Wasserkuppe auf einer kleinen Straße bei Bischofsheim (Kreis Rhön-Grabfeld) einen Linienbus das Überholen ermöglichen wollen und war dabei mit seinem Wagen auf die Bankette ausgewichen. Der aufgeweichte Boden gab sofort nach, der Bus geriet in eine gefährliche Schräglage und drohte einen Abhang hinunter zu stürzen. Da sich die Türen nur zu diesem Abhang hin öffnen ließen, konnten die Insassen nicht aussteigen. Die älteren Leute rutschten deswegen alle auf die linke Seite, um so das Fahrzeug zu stabilisieren.

Feuerwehren aus umliegenden Orten, die kurze Zeit später eintrafen, sicherten den Bus zunächst mit Stahlseilen und konnten dann die Senioren in Sicherheit bringen. Sie wurden im Bischofsheimer Feuerwehrhaus versorgt, bevor sie ihren Ausflug am Nachmittag mit einem Ersatzbus fortsetzen konnten.

Andreas Zitzmann

FRANKFURTER RUNDSCHAU, Samstag, 1. Juni 2002, Nr. 124/22, S. 34

Unit 13

Family, birth, death and marriage

Level 1

The family

Familie, die (-n)	family
Mutter, die (¨)	mother
Vater, der (¨)	father
Eltern, pl.	parents
Kind, das (-er)	child
Tochter, die (¨)	daughter
Sohn, der (¨e)	son
Schwester, die (-n)	sister
Bruder, der (¨)	brother
Großvater, der (¨)	grandfather
Großmutter, die (¨)	grandmother
Enkel, der (-)	grandchild; grandson
Enkelkind, das (-er)	grandchild
Onkel, der (-; also coll. -s)	uncle
Tante, die (-n)	aunt
Vetter, der (-)	(male) cousin
Cousin, der (-s)	(male) cousin
Kusine (Cousine), die (-n)	(female) cousin
Neffe, der (-n)	nephew
Nichte, die (-n)	niece
Mama, die (-s)	mum, mummy
Papa, der (-s)	dad, daddy
Familienleben, das (no pl.)	family life

Birth

Geburt, die (-en)	birth
Frühgeburt, die (-en)	premature birth; premature baby
geboren werden	to be born
neugeboren	newborn
Neugeborene(s), das (adj. decl.)	newborn (child)
Baby, das (-s)	baby
Babysitter(in), der/die (-/nen)	babysitter
schwanger	pregnant
im dritten Monat schwanger	three months pregnant
ein Kind kriegen (coll.)	to have a bun in the oven
ein Kind erwarten	to expect a baby
ein Baby zur Welt bringen	to deliver a baby
ledige Mutter	unmarried mother
Familienplanung, die (no pl.)	family planning
Flaschenkind, das (-er)	bottle-fed baby
Pate, der (-n); Patin, die (-nen)	godfather/ godmother
Patenkind, das (-er)	godchild

Death

sterben	to die
umkommen	to get killed
ums Leben kommen	to lose one's life
Lebensgefahr, die (no pl.)	mortal danger
Tod, der (-e)	death
tot	dead
jmdn töten	to kill sb
Mord, der (-e)	murder
morden	to murder, kill
jmdn ermorden	to murder/assassinate sb
Selbstmord, der (-e)	suicide
Selbstmord begehen	to commit suicide
Beerdigung, die (-en)	funeral
jmdn beerdigen	to bury sb
Leichenwagen, der (-)	hearse
Sargträger(in), der/die (-/nen)	pall-bearer
Grab, das (¨er)	grave, tomb
Grabstein, der (-e)	gravestone
Leiche, die (-n)	(dead) body, corpse, cadaver [human]
Asche, die (no pl.)	ashes
Testament, das (-e)	will
(um jmdn) trauern	to mourn for sb
Trauer, die (no pl.)	mourning
Witwer, der (-); Witwe, die (-n)	widow/widower
verwitwet	widowed

Marriage and divorce

ledig	single
verlobt	engaged
sich verloben	to get engaged
Verlobung, die (-en)	engagement
verheiratet	married
(jmdn) heiraten	to marry (sb)
(jmdn) wieder heiraten	to remarry (sb)
sich (mit jmdm) verheiraten	to get married (to sb)
zusammenleben	to cohabit, live together
Braut, die (¨e)	bride
Bräutigam, der (-e)	groom
Hochzeit, die (-en)	wedding
Hochzeits-, Brautkleid, das (-er)	wedding dress
Hochzeitstorte, die (-n)	wedding cake
Hochzeitsreise, die (-n)	honeymoon [trip]
Flitterwochen, pl.	honeymoon
Ehe, die (-n)	marriage
Ehering, der (-e)	wedding ring
Ehemann, -frau, der/die (¨er/en)	husband, wife
(Ehe)paar, das (-e)	(married) couple
Partner(in), der/die (-/nen)	partner
sich trennen	to separate, split up, break up, leave
sich von jmdm trennen	to leave sb
mit jmdm Schluss machen	to break off with sb
sich scheiden lassen	to get divorced
geschieden	divorced
Scheidung, die (-en)	divorce
sich verstehen	to get along
gut zusammenpassen	to be well matched

Level 2

The family

Elternteil, der (-e)	parent
Vati, der (-s; coll.)	dad, daddy
Mutti, die (-s; coll.)	mum, mummy
Schwiegervater, der (¨)	father-in-law
Schwiegereltern, pl.	parents-in-law

Schwiegertochter, die (¨)	daughter-in-law
Schwager, der (¨); Schwägerin, die (-nen)	brother/sister-in-law
Oma, die (-s; coll.)	grandma
Opa, der (-s; coll.)	grandpa
Enkelsohn, der (¨e)	grandson
Enkelin, die (-nen)	granddaughter
Stiefvater, der (¨)	stepfather
Halbbruder, der (¨)	half-brother
verwandt	related
Verwandte(r), der/die (adj. decl.)	relative, relation
brüderlich	fraternal
schwesterlich	sisterly
Geschwister, pl.	siblings
adoptiert	adopted
Adoptivmutter, die (¨)	adopted mother
Adoptivtocher, die (¨)	adopted daughter
Familienname, der (-n)	family name, last name, surname
Vorname, der (-n)	first name, given name
Zwilling, der (-e)	twin
Zwillingsbruder, der (¨)	twin brother
Abhängige(r), der/die (adj. decl.)	dependant

Birth

werdende Mutter	expectant mother
Mutter im Teenageralter	teenage mother
Geburtenkontrolle, die (no pl.)	birth control
Geburtenregelung, die (-en)	birth control
Schwangerschaft, die (-en)	pregnancy
Schwangerschaftstest, der (-s or -e)	pregnancy test
Schwangerschaftsabbruch, der (¨e)	abortion

Abtreibung, die (-en)	abortion
(ein Baby) abtreiben	to abort
Drilling, der (-e)	triplet
Vierling, der (-e)	quadruplet
(un)fruchtbar	(in)fertile
Fruchtbarkeit, die (no pl.)	fertility
Fruchtbarkeitspille, die (-n)	fertility drug
Säugling, der (-e)	infant
an seinem Daumen saugen	to suck one's thumb
Schnuller, der (-)	dummy, pacifier
Hebamme, die (-n)	midwife

Death

ersticken	to suffocate
ertrinken	to drown
hirntot	brain-dead
Tote(r), der/die (adj. decl.)	dead person, fatality, casualty
Todesfall, der (¨e)	death
tödlich	fatal
Totenwache, die (-n)	wake
Begräbnis, das (-se)	burial, funeral
Grabinschrift, die (-en)	epitaph
Nachruf, der (-e)	obituary
Trauer tragen	to be in mourning
Trauer anlegen	to go into mourning
Trauer-, Gedenkgottesdienst, der (-e)	funeral/memorial service
Leichenzug, der (¨e)	funeral procession
Beileid, das (no pl.)	condolences
Todesanzeige, die (-n)	letter announcing sb's death
jmdm etw vererben	to bequeath sth to sb
Nachlass, der (-e or ¨e)	estate
ins Gras beißen (fig., coll.)	to kick the bucket
abkratzen (coll.)	to kick the bucket

Marriage and divorce

sich in jmdn verlieben	to fall in love with sb
sich in jmdn vernarren	to become infatuated with sb
Geliebte(r), der/die (adj. decl.)	lover
Verlobte(r), der/die (adj. decl.)	fiancé(e)
Jungverheiratete(r), der/die (adj. decl.)	newly-wed
Geschiedene(r), der/die (adj. decl.)	divorcee
seine Geschiedene; ihr Geschiedener	his ex-wife; her ex-husband
Junggeselle, der (-n)	bachelor
Trauung, die (-en)	wedding, marriage ceremony
Trauring, der (-e)	wedding ring
Brautschleier, der (-)	bridal veil
Brautstrauß, der (¨e)	bridal bouquet
Brautbukett (-bouquet), das (-e)	bridal bouquet

Brautnacht, die (¨e)	wedding night
Eheversprechen, das (-)	wedding vows
Ehevertrag, der (¨e)	marriage contract
eine glückliche Ehe führen	to have a happy marriage
eheliche Pflichten, pl.	marital duties
Treue, die (no pl.)	fidelity
Ehebruch, der (¨e)	adultery
Ehebruch begehen	to commit adultery
ehebrecherisch	adulterous
Verhältnis, das (-se)	affair
Affäre, die (-n)	affair
jmdn betrügen	to cheat on sb
Eheberatung, die (-en)	marriage guidance
Silberhochzeit, die (-en)	silver wedding (anniversary)
silberne/goldene/ diamantene Hochzeit	silver/golden/ diamond wedding (anniversary)

Level 3

The family

Angehörige(r), der/die (adj. decl.)	relative, relation
Familienangehörige(r), der/die (adj. decl.)	family member
Vorfahr, der (-en)	ancestor
Abstammung, die (no pl.)	ancestry, lineage
Familienstammbaum, der (¨e)	family tree
Vormund(in), der/die (-e or ¨er/nen)	guardian
Familienvorstand, der (¨e; official lang.)	head of the family
ein-, zweieiig	identical/fraternal

Pflegemutter, die (¨)	foster mother
Pflegesohn, der (¨e)	foster son
ein Kind bei jmdm in Pflege geben	to have a child fostered by sb
Kusine zweiten Grades, die (-n)	second (female) cousin
Kind einer Kousine, das (-er)	first cousin once removed
Verwandtschaft, die (-en)	relatives
Nachkomme, der (-n)	descendant
Nachkommenschaft, die (no pl.)	descendants
Erbe, der (-n); Erbin, die (-nen)	heir/heiress
Ernährer(in), der/die (-/nen)	breadwinner

Zuname, der (-n)	family name, surname, last name	hinscheiden	to pass away
		entschlafen	to pass away
mütterlicher-, väterlicherseits	maternal/paternal	selig	late
		verstorben	late, deceased
onkelhaft	avuncular	Sterbeurkunde, die (-n)	death certificate

Birth

Befruchtung, die (-en)	insemination	Bestattung, die (-en; elev.)	interment, burial
künstliche Befruchtung	artificial insemination	Lobesrede, die (-n)	eulogy
		Grabrede, die (-n)	funeral oration
empfangen	to conceive	jmdn beklagen (elev.)	to mourn sb
Empfängnisverhütung, die (-en)	contraception	Klagegesang, der (¨e)	dirge
Fetus (Fötus), der (-se or -ten)	foetus	eine Leiche einäschern	to cremate a body
Wehen, pl.	contractions	Einäscherung, die (-en)	cremation
jmdn gebären	to give birth to sb	sterbliche Überreste, pl.	(mortal) remains
Geburtsurkunde, die (-n)	birth certificate	eine Leiche einbalsamieren	to embalm a body
Erstgeborene(r), der/die (adj. decl.)	first-born	Leichenhalle, die (-n)	mortuary
Fehlgeburt, die (-en)	miscarriage	Leichenbestatter(in), der/die (-/nen)	mortician
Kaiserschnitt, der (-e)	caesarian section	Leichentuch, das (¨er)	shroud
Totgeburt, die (-en)	stillbirth	Totentuch, das (¨er)	shroud
tot geboren	stillborn	(auf) halbmast	at half-mast
Leihmutter, die (¨)	surrogate mother	die Flagge (auf) halbmast setzen	to fly the flag at half-mast
Retortenbaby, das (-s)	test-tube baby		
Samenbank, die (-en)	sperm bank	Grabmal, das (¨er or -e)	tomb
Eugenik, die (no pl.)	eugenics	Staatsbegräbnis, das (-se)	state funeral
jmdn aus der Flasche ernähren	to bottle-feed		
(jmdn) stillen	to breast feed (sb)	Mausoleum, das (-leen)	mausoleum
jmdn zur Adoption freigeben	to put sb up for adoption		

Marriage and divorce

Waise, die (-n)	orphan	Ehestand, der (no pl.)	matrimony
Waisenhaus, das (¨er)	orphanage	Ehevermittlung, die (-en)	marriage broking; marriage bureau

Death

seinen letzten Atemzug tun	to draw one's last breath	Eheberater(in), der/die (-/nen)	marriage counsellor
Todesröcheln, das (no pl.)	death rattle	Ehestifter(in), der/die (-/nen)	matchmaker
die Letzte Ölung	the last rites, extreme unction	ehemündig	of marriageable age

jmdm einen Heiratsantrag machen	to propose to sb	Annulierung, die (-en)	annulment
Aussteuer, die (-n)	trousseau	Scheidungsurteil, das (-e)	decree of divorce
Brautausstattung, die (-en)	trousseau	vorläufiges/endgültiges Scheidungsurteil	decree nisi/absolute
Heiratsgut, das (no pl.)	dowry	Unterhaltszahlung, die (-en)	alimony
Mitgift, die (-en)	dowry	Sorgerecht, das (no pl.)	custody
jmdm den Hof machen	to court sb	ein eheähnliches Verhältnis	a common-law marriage
Ziviltrauung, die (-en)	civil wedding	Lebensgefährte, -gefährtin, der/die (-n/nen)	companion, partner, common-law spouse
standesamtliche Trauung	civil wedding	jmdn dem Bräutigam zuführen	to give sb away (in marriage)
Standesamt, das (¨er)	registry office	Trauzeuge, der (-n)	witness
kirchliche Trauung	church wedding	Trauzeuge des Bräutigams, der (-n)	best man
Mussehe, die (-n)	shotgun wedding		
Gatte, der (-n); Gattin, die (-nen)	spouse		
etw für ungültig erklären	to annul sth	Brautjungfer, die (-n)	bridesmaid
		Herrenabend, der (-e)	stag party

Religion

Level 1

General

Religion, die (-en)	religion
religiös	religious
Religionsfreiheit, die (no pl.)	freedom of worship
Gott, der (¨er); Göttin, die (-nen)	god/goddess
göttlich	divine
heilig	holy, sacred
Heiligkeit, die (no pl.)	holiness
das Heilige Land	the Holy Land
die Heilige Stadt	the Holy City
Heilige(r), der/die (adj. decl.)	saint

Prophet, der (-en)	prophet
Sekte, die (-n)	sect

Religions

Islam, der (no pl.)	Islam
islamisch	Islamic
Muslim(e), der/die (-e/n)	Muslim
Moslem, der (-s); Moslime, die (-n)	Muslim
Judentum, das (no pl.)	Judaism
Judaismus, der (no pl.)	Judaism
jüdisch	Jewish

Jude, der (-n); Jüdin, die (-nen) — Jew/Jewess

Christentum, das (no pl.) — Christianity

christlich — Christian

Christus — Christ

Christ(in), der/die (-en/nen) — Christian

Buddhismus, der (no pl.) — Buddhism

Buddha, der (-s) — Buddha

Buddhist(in), der/die (-en/nen) — Buddhist

buddhistisch — Buddhist(ic)

Hinduismus, der (no pl.) — Hinduism

Hindu, der (-s) — Hindu

Beliefs and doctrines

Glaube, der (no pl.) — belief

Gläubige(r), der/die (adj. decl.) — believer

Hoffnung, die (-en) — hope

Himmel, der (-) — heaven

Hölle, die (no pl.) — hell

Engel, der (-) — angel

Teufel, der (-) — devil

Satan, der (-e) — Satan

Sünde, die (-n) — sin

sündigen — to sin

sündig — sinful

Sünder(in), der/die (-/nen) — sinner

Wahrheit, die (-en) — truth

Bibel, die (-n) — Bible

biblisch — biblical

Moral, die (no pl.) — morality, morals, ethics

ethisch — ethical

jmdm (etw) vergeben — to forgive sb (for sth)

Vergebung, die (no pl.) — forgiveness

Faith and practice

glauben — to believe, have faith

Glaube, der (no pl.) — faith

gläubig — faithful

Gläubige(r), der/die (adj. decl.) — faithful (member of a religion/ congregation)

Kirchgänger(in), der/die (-/nen) — churchgoer

Missionar(in), der/die (-e/nen) — missionary

Mission, die (-en) — mission

Predigt, die (-en) — sermon

(etw) predigen — to preach (sth)

eine Predigt halten — to preach a sermon

Hymne, die (-n) — hymn

sich bekreuzigen — to cross oneself

Gebet, das (-e) — prayer

(für jmdn) beten — to pray (for sb)

Messe, die (-n) — mass

die Messe lesen — to say mass

Gottesdienst, der (-e) — (religious) service

Kommunion, die (-en) — communion [Catholic]

Abendmahl, das (-e) — communion [Protestant], Lord's Supper

das Abendmahl nehmen/empfangen — to take/receive communion

Hostie, die (-n) — host

Taufe, die (-n) — christening, baptism

jmdn taufen — to baptize sb

Sakrament, das (-e) — sacrament

(jmdm etw) beichten — to confess (sth to sb)

Beichte, die (-n) — confession

Konfirmation, die (-en) — confirmation

spenden — to donate, give, contribute

Spende, die (-n) — donation, contribution

Kollekte, die (-n) — collection

fasten — to fast

Evangelist(in), der/die (-en/nen) — evangelist

Anhänger(in), der/die (-/nen) — follower

Jünger, der (-) — disciple

Clergy

Pfarrer(in), der/die (-/nen)	parish priest, pastor, vicar, minister
Pfarrei, die (-en)	parish
Priester(in), der/die (-/nen)	priest/priestess
Pastor(in), der/die (-en/nen)	pastor
Nonne, die (-n)	nun
Bischof, der (¨e); Bischöfin, die (-nen)	bishop
Rabbiner(in), der/die (-/nen)	rabbi
Prediger(in), der/die (-/nen)	preacher
Beichtvater, der (¨)	confessor
Papst, der (¨e)	pope; high priest
Papsttum, das (no pl.)	papacy
Gemeinde, das (-n)	parish, congregation
Guru, der (-s)	guru

Religious buildings and architecture

Kirche, die (-n)	church
Kathedrale, die (-n)	cathedral
Dom, der (-e)	cathedral
Kirchturm, der (¨e)	steeple
Glocke, die (-n)	bell
Glockenturm, der (¨e)	bell tower
Tempel, der (-)	temple
Moschee, die (-n)	mosque
Synagoge, die (-n)	synagogue
Altar, der (¨e)	altar
Kreuz, das (-e)	cross; crucifix

Religious festivals

Feiertag, der (-e)	holiday
kirchlicher Feiertag	religious holiday
Weihnachten, das (-)	Christmas
Weihnachtslied, das (-er)	Christmas carol
Weihnachtsbaum, der (¨e)	Christmas tree
etw schmücken	to decorate sth
Advent, der (-e)	Advent
Adventskalender, der (-)	Advent calendar
Karneval, der (-e or -s)	carnival
Fasching, der (-e or -s; S, AU)	carnival
Ostern, das (-)	Easter

Level 2

General

Theologie, die (no pl.)	theology
theologisch	theological
Konfession, die (-en)	denomination
Kirchensteuer, die (-n)	church tax
Säkularismus, der (no pl.)	secularism
etw säkularisieren	to secularize sth
Antisemitismus, der (no pl.)	anti-Semitism
Fegefeuer, das (no pl.)	purgatory
Garten Eden, der (no pl.)	the Garden of Eden
Sintflut, die (no pl.)	the Flood
das Letzte Abendmahl	the Last Supper

Religions

Katholizismus, der (no pl.)	Catholicism
katholisch	Catholic
Katholik(in), der/die (-en/nen)	Catholic
Protestantismus, der (no pl.)	Protestantism

protestantisch	Protestant
evangelisch	Protestant, Evangelical
Protestant(in), der/die (-en/nen)	Protestant
Mormone, der (-n); Mormonin, die (-nen)	Mormon
mormonisch	Mormon
römisch-katholisch	Roman Catholic
Sikhismus, der (no pl.)	Sikhism
Sikh, der (-s)	Sikh
Taoismus, der (no pl.)	Taoism

Beliefs and doctrines

Lehre, die (-n)	doctrine
Gute, das (adj. decl.)	good
Böse, das (adj. decl.)	evil
böse	wicked
Seele, die (-n)	soul
Gewissen, das (no pl.)	conscience
Todsünde, die (-n)	mortal/deadly sin
die sieben Todsünden	Seven Deadly Sins
Vaterunser, das (-)	Lord's Prayer
Atheismus, der (no pl.)	atheism
Atheist(in), der/die (-en/nen)	atheist
atheistisch	atheistic
Geist, der (-er)	spirit
geistlich	spiritual
Geistlichkeit, die (no pl.)	spirituality
der Heilige Geist	the Holy Spirit/Ghost
Mystiker(in), der/die (-/nen)	mystic
Mystizismus, der (no pl.)	mysticism
Humanismus, der (no pl.)	humanism

Bund, der (¨e)	covenant
der Alte/Neue Bund	the Old/New Testament or Covenant
das Alte/Neue Testament	the Old/New Testament
Gebot, das (-e)	commandment

Faith and practice

etw bereuen	to repent, regret sth
Reue, die (no pl.)	repentance, penitence
reuevoll	repentant
jmdn lossprechen	to absolve sb
Opfer, das (-)	sacrifice
etw opfern	to sacrifice sth
Mitleid, das (no pl.)	pity, sympathy
(nieder)knien	to kneel (down)
(sich) hinknien	to kneel down
Gesangbuch, das (¨er)	hymnal, hymn book
Gesang, der (¨e)	song, hymn
jmdn loben	to praise sb
etw bekennen	to bear witness to sth; confess sth
etw heiligen	to sanctify sth, keep sth holy
Bekehrung, die (-en)	conversion
jmdn zu etw bekehren	to convert sb to sth
sich zu etw bekehren	to convert to sth
zu etw konvertieren	to convert to sth
dem Glauben abschwören	to renounce one's faith
Gemeindemitglied, das (¨er)	parishioner
Chorknabe, der (-n)	choirboy
Andacht, die (-en)	(silent) prayer or worship
Morgen-, Abendandacht, die (-en)	morning/evening prayer
jmdn anbeten	to worship sb
jmdn verehren	to worship sb
Verehrung, die (-en)	worship

jmdn/etw segnen	to bless sb/sth	Abtei, die (-en)	abbey
Segen, der (no pl.)	blessing, benediction	Kirchenportal, das (-e)	main church door
Segnung, die (-en)	blessing, benediction	Kirchenbank, die (¨e)	pew
etw weihen	to consecrate sth	Mittelgang, der (¨e)	aisle
Weihrauch, der (no pl.)	incense	Altarraum, der (¨e)	chancel
(für) etw büßen	to atone for sth	Altarbild, das (-er)	altarpiece
Buße, die (-n)	repentance, penitence	Hochaltar, der (¨e)	high altar
Buße tun	to do penance	Beichtstuhl, der (¨e)	confessional
Pilger(in), der/die (-/nen)	pilgrim	Kanzel, die (-n)	pulpit
pilgern	to make a pilgrimage		

Garments and ceremonial objects

Pilgerfahrt, die (-en)	pilgrimage
aktiv	practising

überzeugt	devout	Kniebank, die (¨e)	kneeler
meditieren	to meditate	Rosenkranz, der (¨e)	rosary
Meditation, die (-en)	meditation	Gebetsperlen, pl.	prayer beads

Clergy

Geistliche(r), der/die (adj. decl.)	(woman) priest, (woman) minister	Gebetsteppich, der (-e)	prayer mat
		Kruzifix, das (-e)	crucifix
Pfarrer/Geistlicher werden	to join/enter the ministry	Weihwasser, das (no pl.)	holy water
Klerus, der (no pl.)	clergy	Weihwasserbecken, das (-)	stoup, holy water font
Mönch, der (-e)	monk		
mönchisch	monastic	Opferstock, der (¨e)	offertory box
klösterlich	monastic/convent	Kelch, der (-e)	chalice, communion cup
jmdn weihen	to ordain sb		
Weihe, die (-n)	consecration, ordination	Rauchfass, das (¨er)	censer
		Priesterkragen, der (-)	clerical collar
Orden, der (-)	order	Nonnenschleier, der (-)	wimple
Kantor(in), der/die (-en/nen)	cantor		

Religious festivals

Kleriker(in), der/die (-/nen)	cleric	Fastenzeit, die (no pl.)	Lent
Abt, der (¨e)	abbot	Fastnacht, die (no pl.)	carnival
Seminarist(in), der/die (-en/nen)	seminarist	Rosenmontag, der (-e)	Monday before Ash Wednesday
Kanoniker/Kanonikus, der (-/ker)	canon	Fastnachtdienstag, der (-e)	Shrove Tuesday

Religious buildings and architecture

		Aschermittwoch, der (-e)	Ash Wednesday
Kapelle, die (-n)	chapel	Karfreitag, der (-e)	Good Friday
Kloster, das (¨)	monastery, convent, cloister	Pfingsten, das (-)	Pentecost
Pfarrhaus, das (¨er)	rectory, vicarage	Allerheiligen, das (no pl.)	All Saints' Day

Heiligabend, der (-e)	Christmas Eve	Nikolaustag, der (-e)	St. Nicholas' Day
Weihnacht, die (no pl.; elev.)	Christmas	Chanukka, die (no pl.)	Hanukkah
		Passah, das (no pl.)	Passover

Level 3

Religions

Messias, der (no pl.)	Messiah
Zionismus, der (no pl.)	Zionism
judäisch	Judaic
Christenheit, die (no pl.)	Christendom
Anglikaner(in), der/die (-/nen)	Anglican
Kalvinist(in) (Calvinist[in]), der/die (-en/nen)	Calvinist
ökumenisch	ecumenical
Fundamentalismus, der (no pl.)	fundamentalism
Fundamentalist(in), der/die (-en/nen)	fundamentalist
Totemismus, der (no pl.)	totemism
Schamanismus, der (no pl.)	shamanism
Heidentum, das (no pl.)	heathenism, paganism
Heide, der (-n); Heidin, die (-nen)	heathen, pagan
Paganismus, der (no pl.)	paganism

Erlösung, die (no pl.)	redemption
Tag des Jüngsten Gerichts, der	Judgment Day
ketzerisch	heretical
Ketzer(in), der/die (-/nen)	heretic
Agnostiker(in), der/die (-/nen)	agnostic
Unfehlbarkeit, die (no pl.)	infallibility
unfehlbar	infallible
Nirwana, das (no pl.)	nirvana
Dreiheiligkeit, die (no pl.)	Trinity
die Heilige Dreiheiligkeit	the Holy Trinity
Kredo, das (-s)	creed, credo
orthodox	orthodox
Talmud, der (no pl.)	Talmud
Pentateuch, der (no pl.)	Pentateuch
Koran, der (-e)	Koran (Qu'ran)
Evangelium, das (-lien)	Gospel
die Heilige Schrift	the Holy Scriptures
Dogma, das (-men)	dogma

Beliefs and doctrines

Gnade, die (-n; pl. rare)	grace, mercy
gnadenvoll	merciful
Barmherzigkeit, die (no pl.)	mercy, compassion
barmherzig	merciful
Nächstenliebe, die (no pl.)	charity
karitativ	charitable

Faith and practice

Ritus, der (Riten)	rite
Ritual, das (-e)	ritual
Pietät, die (no pl.)	piety
fromm	devout, pious
Frömmigkeit, die (no pl.)	religiousness, piousness, piety
Blasphemie, die (-n)	blasphemy
blasphemisch, blasphemistisch	blasphemous

Gotteslästerung, die (-en)	blasphemy
Gotteslästerer, -lästerin, der/die (-/nen)	blasphemer
Laie, der (-n)	layperson
die Laien, pl.	the laity
jmdn laisieren	to unfrock sb
Synode, die (-n)	synod
seelsorgerisch	pastoral
jmdn salben	to anoint sb
jmdn heiligsprechen	to canonize sb
Ordination, die (-en)	ordination
Gesundbeten, das (no pl.)	faith healing
jmdn gesundbeten	to heal sb through prayer
Fürsprache, die (-n)	intercession
das Wort Gottes/das Evangelium verkünden	to preach the word/the gospel
etw sühnen (elev.)	to atone for sth
Sühne, die (-n)	atonement
als Sühne für	in expiation of
Märtyrer(in), der/die (-/nen)	martyr
Märtyrertum, das (no pl.)	martyrdom
Hochamt, das (¨er)	high mass
geistliches Amt	ministry
Eucharistie, die (-n)	Eucharist
Liturgie, die (-n)	liturgy
Matutin, die (-e or -en)	matins
Abendgottesdienst, der (-e)	evensong
Vesper, die (-n)	vespers
Bar-Mizwah, der (-s)	bar mitzvah
Sakrileg, das (-e)	sacrilege
sakrilegisch	sacrilegious
Frevel, der (-)	sacrilege
frevelhaft	sacrilegious
Küster(in), der/die (-/nen)	verger
Novize, der (-n); Novizin, die (-nen)	novice
Kreuzträger(in), der/die (-/nen)	cross-bearer, crucifer
Almosen, das (-)	alms

Clergy

Bistum, das (¨er)	diocese, bishopric
Erzbischof, der (¨e)	archbishop
Prior(in), der/die (-en/nen)	prior/prioress
Priorat, das (-e)	priory
Priesterweihe, die (-n)	holy orders
dem geistlichen Stand angehören	to be in holy orders
die Priesterweihe empfangen	to take holy orders
die niederen/höheren Weihen	minor/major orders
Imam, der (-e or -s)	Imam
Molla (Mulla[h]), der (-s)	Mullah
Ajatollah, der (-s)	Ayatollah
Benediktiner(in), der/die (-/nen)	Benedictine monk/nun
Trappist(in), der/die (-en/nen)	Trappist
Zisterzienser(in), der/die (-/nen)	Cistercian monk/nun
Franziskaner(in), der/die (-/nen)	Franciscan friar/nun
Karmeliter(in), der/die (-/nen)	Carmelite
Postulant(in), der/die (-en/nen)	postulant

Religious buildings and architecture

Baptisterium, das (-rien)	baptistery
Taufkapelle, die (-n)	baptistery
Taufstein, der (-e)	(baptismal) font
Sakristei, die (-en)	vestry
Schrein, der (-e)	shrine, reliquary
Heiligtum, das (¨er)	shrine, sanctuary
(Mittel)schiff, das (-e)	nave

Querschiff, das (-e)	transept
Seitenschiff, das (-e)	aisle
Apsis, die (Apsiden)	apse
Strebebogen, der (-; S, AU, CH: ¨)	flying buttress

Garments and ceremonial objects

Chorhemd, das (-en)	surplice
Chorrock, der (¨e)	surplice
Gewand, das (¨er)	robe, vestment

Talar, der (-e)	cassock
Sutane (Soutane), die (-n)	cassock
Habit, das or der (-e)	habit
Stola, die (Stolen)	stole
Kapuze, die (-n)	cowl
Pluviale, das (-s)	cope
Jarmulke, die (-n)	yarmulke
Schleier, der (-)	yashmak
Monstranz, die (-en)	monstrance

Exercises

Level 1

1. Wie heißt die entsprechende weibliche Person? ✓

1. der Vater	*die Mutter*
2. der Sohn	
3. der Bruder	
4. der Onkel	
5. der Vetter	
6. der Neffe	
7. der Papa	
8. der Pate	
9. der Bräutigam	
10. der Ehemann	
11. der Witwer	

2. Welches Verb passt? ✓

a. begehen, b. bringen, c. erwarten, d. halten, e. kommen, f. lassen, g. lesen, h. machen, i. nehmen, j. trauern

1. ein Baby zur Welt	6. sich scheiden
2. ums Leben	7. ein Kind
3. Selbstmord	8. eine Predigt
4. um jmdn	9. die Messe
5. mit jmdm Schluss	10. das Abendmahl

365

3. Ordnen Sie die folgenden Wörter chronologisch. ✓
1. geschieden, verheiratet, verlobt
2. die Beerdigung, die Geburt, die Hochzeit, die Taufe, der Tod
3. die Beichte, die Sünde, die Vergebung
4. Karneval, Ostern, Weihnachten

4. Wie heißt das Gegenteil? ✓
1. der Himmel
2. geboren werden
3. verheiratet
4. der Teufel
5. staatlicher Feiertag

5. Wie heißen die Angehörigen der folgenden Religionen? ✓

die Religion	der Angehörige	die Angehörige
1. Christentum		
2. Judentum		
3. Islam		
4. Buddhismus		

6. Ergänzen Sie. ✓
1. der Pate – das Patenkind : der Großvater – _____
2. sich verloben – die Verlobung : heiraten – _____
3. der Christ – christlich : der Jude – _____
4. sündigen – der Sünder : glauben – _____
5. das Christentum – Christus : der Buddhismus – _____
6. singen – die Hymne : beten – _____
7. der Pastor – die Pastorin : der Bischof – _____

7. Wie heißt das entsprechende Adjektiv? ✓

	Adjektiv	Bedeutung
1. glauben	gläubig	religiös
2. sündigen		mit Sünden beladen
3. der Gott		von Gott ausgehend
4. die Bibel		die Bibel betreffend
5. der Tod		gestorben
6. scheiden		nicht mehr verheiratet
7. der Witwer/die Witwe		Witwer/Witwe geworden

8. Welche Wörter gehören zusammen? ✓

> a. der Grabstein, b. die Hostie, c. der Jünger, d. die Kollekte, e. die Moschee,
> f. der Pfarrer, g. die Predigerin, h. die Synagoge

1. die Pfarrei   5. die Predigt
2. Judaismus   6. das Abendmahl
3. Islam   7. Christus
4. die Spende   8. das Grab

9. Welches Wort hat die gleiche oder eine ähnliche Bedeutung? ✓

1. das Hochzeitskleid   5. das Abendmahl
2. der Vetter   6. die Kathedrale
3. ums Leben kommen   7. Karneval
4. der Moslem   8. der Teufel

10. In jedem Satz fehlt ein Wort. ✓

> Asche, beerdigt, ermordet, Flaschenkinder, Hochzeitstorte, ledige, Leiche,
> neugeborene, Sargträger, schwanger

1. Das _____ Kind gibt sie zur Adoption frei.
2. Seine Frau ist im fünften Monat _____.
3. Kinder, die von der Mutter gestillt werden, leiden weniger häufig unter Infektionen als _____.
4. Sie war die _____ Mutter eines zwanzigjährigen Sohns.
5. Seine Eltern wurden in Auschwitz _____.
6. Gestern wurde sie im Familiengrab in ihrem Heimatort _____.
7. Ein Flugzeug wird seine _____ über die Wüste verstreuen.
8. Sie haben eine fünfstöckige _____ bestellt.
9. Es war ein Mordfall ohne _____.
10. Er war einer der _____ bei der Beerdigung des Mädchens.

11. Übersetzen Sie ins Englische.

Viele Paare nach Scheidung nicht glücklicher als vorher
CHICAGO, 12. Juli (rtr). Unglückliche Paare erhalten in der Regel viele gute Ratschläge. Eine in den USA veröffentlichte Studie fügt nun einen weiteren hinzu: Trennen Sie sich nicht, stehen Sie die Krise durch! Wissenschaftler der Universität Chicago und anderer Forschungseinrichtungen haben festgestellt, dass fünf Jahre nach der Entscheidung für oder gegen eine Scheidung ungefähr dieselbe Anzahl von Paaren sagt, sie seien inzwischen glücklich. Die Forscher interviewten mehr als 5200 zu Beginn der Untersuchung verheiratete Erwachsene zweimal im Abstand von einem halben Jahrzehnt. Diejenigen, die sich trotz unglücklicher Beziehung fürs Durchhalten entschieden und damit zufrieden seien, stellten der Studie zufolge bei der zweiten Befragung fest, sie

erlebten die Ursachen ihrer damaligen Ehekonflikte als nicht mehr so gravierend.

FRANKFURTER RUNDSCHAU, Samstag, 13. Juli 2002, Nr. 160/28, S. 31

Erneut Tote bei Gefechten in Kaschmir

ISLAMABAD/NEU-DELHI, 14. Juni (dpa/afp). In Kaschmir sind bei neuen Gefechten zwischen Pakistan und Indien erneut mindestens acht Menschen ums Leben gekommen. Das Pakistanische Staatsfernsehen PTV meldete am Freitag, mindestens sechs Zivilisten seien durch indischen Artilleriebeschuss im pakistanischen Teil der Region getötet worden. Bei Erwiderung des Feuers seien 15 indische Soldaten entweder getötet oder verwundet worden. Die Inder meldeten ihrerseits, Gefechte über die Trennungslinie hinweg hätten zwei Menschenleben gekostet ...

FRANKFURTER RUNDSCHAU, Samstag, 15. Juni 2002, Nr. 136/24, S. 2

© dpa Deutsche Presse-Agentur GmbH

Level 2

1. Wie heißen die Koseformen? ✓

1. Vater
2. Mutter
3. Großvater
4. Großmutter

2. Wie heißt die entsprechende weibliche bzw. männliche Person? ✓

1. der Schwiegervater	*die Schwiegermutter*
2. die Schwiegertochter	
3. der Schwager	
4. der Enkelsohn	
5. der Stiefvater	
6. der Halbbruder	
7. die Adoptivmutter	
8. die Adoptivtochter	
9. der Zwillingsbruder	

3. Welches Wort hat die gleiche oder eine ähnliche Bedeutung? ✓

1. die Geburtenkontrolle
2. die Abtreibung
3. die Beerdigung
4. der Ehering
5. das Brautbukett
6. die Affäre
7. protestantisch
8. zu etw konvertieren
9. jmdn anbeten
10. Karneval

4. Welches Verb passt? ✓

a. abschwören, b. abtreiben, c. begehen, d. beißen, e. führen, f. saugen, g. tragen,
h. tun, i. verlieben

1. ein Baby
2. an seinem Daumen
3. Trauer
4. ins Gras
5. sich in jmdn

6. eine glückliche Ehe
7. Ehebruch
8. dem Glauben
9. Buße

5. Falsche Freunde. Ergänzen Sie die Tabelle.

Deutsch	Englisch	Deutsch	Englisch
die Konfession			confession
spenden			spend
absolvieren			absolve
der Born			born
Christ			Christ
fatal			fatal
der Kadaver			cadaver

6. Welche Definition bzw. welches Synonym passt? ✓

a. der Antisemitismus, b. der Atheismus, c. etw bereuen, d. das Passah, e. der Pilger,
f. etw säkularisieren, g. das Alte Testament, h. die Theologie, i. die Todsünde

1. Lehre von der Religion
2. etw verweltlichen
3. Judenfeindschaft
4. Ablehnung der Existenz Gottes
5. Teil der Bibel
6. jüdisches Fest
7. schwere Sünde
8. jemand, der nach einem heiligen Ort wandert
9. etw bedauern

7. Welches Wort passt nicht? ✓
1. die Abtei, die Geistliche, der Kantor, der Mönch
2. Gebetsperlen, der Kanoniker, der Kelch, der Opferstock
3. die Katholikin, die Mormonin, die Protestantin, die Seminaristin
4. die Kanzel, die Kirchenbank, das Mitleid, der Mittelgang

5. das Gebot, der Geist, das Gewissen, die Seele
6. der Drilling, der Feigling, der Vierling, der Zwilling
7. das Beileid, der Nachruf, die Trauer, die Weihe

8. Wie heißt das Gegenteil? ✓

1. das Gute
2. die Morgenandacht
3. fruchtbar
4. der Ehebruch
5. der Vorname

9. Wie heißen die Zusammensetzungen? ✓

Fastnacht	tag	1. *Fastnachtdienstag*
Heilig	kragen	2.
Nikolaus	montag	3.
Ascher	abend	4.
Priester	teppich	5.
Nonnen	mittwoch	6.
Rosen	~~dienstag~~	7.
Weih	schleier	8.
Gebets	bank	9.
Knie	wasser	10.

10. In jedem Satz fehlt ein Wort. ✓

Eheberatung, Hebamme, hirntot, Rosenkranz, Säugling, Segnung, theologisch,
Todesfall, Trauung, Vaterunser

1. Während der Geburt soll eine _____ der Gebärenden zur Seite stehen.
2. Sie wurde als _____ von einer jungen Frau adoptiert.
3. Die Ärzte haben ihn für _____ erklärt.
4. Es ist der neunte _____ der Epidemie.
5. Um 16 Uhr findet heute eine _____ in der Dorfkirche statt.
6. Das Ehepaar geht regelmäßig zur _____.
7. Der Bischof ist _____ konservativ, humorvoll und sehr belesen.
8. Er hält die kirchliche _____ von homosexuellen Paaren für nicht möglich.
9. Wir beten das _____.
10. Er hat einen _____ in der Tasche, den er durch die Finger gleiten lässt.

11. Übersetzen Sie ins Englische.

Zu unserem Artikel „Mutter-Unglück" (Magazin vom 11. Mai 2002)

Über kaum ein Thema rund um Gesundheit gibt es so viele Informationen wie über Schwangerschaft und Geburt. Jede werdende Mutter kann und soll sich daher rechtzeitig über die anstehenden und möglichen Untersuchungen informieren, sie muss die Konsequenzen aus den Ergebnissen tragen. Die pränatale Diagnostik erlaubt es heute den allermeisten Familien, ohne Angst vor Fehlbildungen des wachsenden Kindes der Geburt entgegen zu sehen. Anderen Familien gibt das Wissen vielleicht die Chance, sich rechtzeitig mit einer möglichen Behinderung auseinander zu setzen. Für die meisten Frauen ist gerade das Ultraschallbild ein wichtiger Teil einer schönen Schwangerschaft, und in erstaunlich vielen Familien wird von dem „Embryo" schon mit dem für ihn ausgesuchten Vornamen gesprochen. Von einer Schwangerschaft auf Probe kann hier wohl keine Rede sein. Ich kann mich daher der negativen Berichterstattung über die Pränataldiagnostik nicht anschließen. Nichts desto weniger ist es ein Skandal, wenn Ärzte unfähig sind, ihre Patienten angemessen zu informieren (obwohl eine Biologin, wie ich aus eigener Erfahrung sagen kann, hier in einer noch einigermaßen günstigen Ausgangsposition ist).

Dr. Esther Mietzsch, Mannheim

FRANKFURTER RUNDSCHAU, Samstag, 22. Juni 2002, Nr. 142/25, Magazin, S. 2

Der Duft der heilen Welt

Millionen von Italienern glauben an die wundertätige Wirkung von Pater Pio – jetzt wird er heilig gesprochen

Von Roman Arens (San Giovanni)

Nach zehn Tagen aus dem Koma erwachend, verlangte Matteo Pio Colella sofort ein Eis. Nach drei weiteren Tagen wollte der Junge eine Playstation und besiegte den Arzt, der mit ihm spielte. Matteo war völlig unerklärlich von einer tückischen, eigentlich tödlichen Form der Hirnhautentzündung geheilt. Nur seine Eltern hatten ihn nicht aufgegeben. Sie hatten am Grab eines 1968 gestorbenen Kapuziner-Paters, des inzwischen am meisten verehrten Italieners, um die Rettung gebetet. Padre Pio war gleichzeitig dem Jungen in seinem tiefen Schlaf erschienen und hatte ihn an die Hand genommen.

Dieses Wunder vom Januar 2000 machte einen solchen Eindruck auf die Kongregation für die Angelegenheiten der Heiligen, dass sie den sonst üblichen langwierigen Kanonisierungsprozess sehr schnell über die Runden brachte. Schon an diesem Sonntag kann Johannes Paul II. den religiös und geschäftlich außerordentlich erfolgreichen Mönch heilig sprechen. Erwartungen, dass dazu vielleicht fünfhunderttausend Anhänger des Kapuziners nach Rom kommen, sind nicht unrealistisch ...

FRANKFURTER RUNDSCHAU, Samstag, 15. Juni 2002, Nr. 136/24, S. 3

Wiedereröffnung der Kirche in Rott am Inn

ROTT A. INN Eines der bedeutendsten Bauwerke des Rokoko in Europa, die ehemalige Klosterkirche und jetzige Pfarrkirche St. Marinus in Rott am Inn, steht nach achtjähriger Renovierung wieder für Gottesdienste und für Kunstfreude aus aller Welt offen. Am 30. Juni wird der Münchner Kardinal Friedrich Wetter den Festgottesdienst zur Wiedereröffnung feiern. Dabei wird der von dem Bildhauer Professor Alf Lechner aus Edelstahl geschmiedete neue Altar eingeweiht. Das 1759 auf romanischen Hauptmauern errichtete und 1763 geweihte Gotteshaus war seit 1994 geschlossen und wurde renoviert.

FRANKFURTER RUNDSCHAU, Samstag, 22. Juni 2002, Nr. 142/25, S. 20

Level 3

1. Wie heißt das Gegenteil? ✓

1. der Vorfahr
2. die kirchliche Trauung
3. eine Leiche einbalsamieren
4. der Geistliche
5. die höheren Weihen
6. jmdn aus der Flasche ernähren
7. die Geburtsurkunde

2. Welches Verb passt? ✓

a. empfangen, b. freigeben, c. machen, d. setzen, e. tun, f. verkünden, g. zuführen

1. die Flagge auf halbmast
2. seine letzte Atemzug
3. jmdm einen Heiratsantrag
4. jmdn zur Adoption
5. jmdn dem Bräutigam
6. das Wort Gottes
7. die Priesterweihe

3. Welches Wort hat die gleiche oder eine ähnliche Bedeutung? ✓

a. die Aussteuer, b. die Bestattung, c. der Chorrock, d. die Dreiheiligkeit, e. frevelhaft, f. die Frömmigkeit, g. die Gotteslästerung, h. das Heiratsgut, i. hinscheiden, j. ketzerisch, k. das Leichentuch, l. selig, m. der Talar, n. die Taufkapelle

1. entschlafen
2. verstorben
3. das Totentuch
4. das Begräbnis
5. die Brautausstattung
6. die Mitgift
7. häretisch
8. die Trinität
9. die Blasphemie
10. sakrilegisch
11. das Baptisterium
12. das Chorhemd
13. die Sutane
14. die Pietät

4. Wie heißt die entsprechende männliche Person? ✓

1. die Angehörige	*der Angehörige*
2. die Pflegemutter	
3. die Vormundin	
4. die Erbin	
5. die Gattin	
6. die Lebensgefährtin	
7. die Heidin	
8. die Märtyrerin	
9. die Priorin	
10. die Novizin	

5. Was passt zusammen? ✓

a. die Abstammung, b. die Empfängnisverhütung, c. die Grabrede, d. der Koran,
e. das Mittelschiff, f. die Mussehe, g. das Nirwana, h. der Talmud,
i. die Unterhaltszahlung, j. Wehen

1. die Geburt
2. die Pille
3. der Familienstammbaum
4. die Scheidung
5. der Buddhismus
6. der Judaismus
7. der Islam
8. die Romanische Kirche
9. die Bestattung
10. die Schwangerschaft

6. Welches Wort passt nicht? ✓
1. der Franziskaner, der Gotteslästerer, der Karmeliter, der Trappist
2. der Agnostiker, der Atheist, der Gläubige, der Ketzer
3. der Hinduismus, der Islam, der Sikhismus, der Zionismus
4. die Barmherzigkeit, der Frevel, die Gnade, die Nächstenliebe
5. der Abort, die Fehlgeburt, die Frühgeburt, die Totgeburt
6. das Grabmal, die Leichenhalle, das Mausoleum, das Waisenhaus
7. der Eheberater, der Ehebrecher, der Ehestifter, die Ehevermittlung
8. das Mittelschiff, das Querschiff, das Seitenschiff, das Transportschiff

7. Wie heißen die Zusammensetzungen? ✓

Lobes	röcheln	1. *die Lobesrede*
Todes	schnitt	2.
Leih	rede	3.
Samen	gesang	4.
Trau	mutter	5.
Gesund	trauung	6.
Klage	zeuge	7.
Kaiser	beten	8.
Zivil	bank	9.

8. Wie heißt das Adjektiv? ✓

a. barmherzig, b. fromm, c. gnadenvoll, d. karitativ, e. unfehlbar

1. voller Gnade
2. wohltätig
3. mitleidig und hilfreich
4. niemals irrend
5. gläubig

9. In jedem Satz fehlt ein Wort. ✓

Abendgottesdienst, Almosen, Anglikaner, Ehestand, Evangelium, Fundamentalist, Retortenbaby, Sorgerecht, Staatsbegräbnis

1. 1978 wurde das erste _____ der Welt geboren.
2. Nur für Stresemann und Brandt gab es ein _____.
3. Gestern erschienen sie auf dem Standesamt, um in den _____ zu treten.
4. Seit 1982 kann in der Bundesrepublik das gemeinsame _____ beantragt werden.
5. Die Zahl der _____ wächst in Afrika und Asien, aber in der westlichen Welt geht sie zurück.
6. Ein frommer Muslim ist genausowenig ein _____ wie ein frommer Christ.
7. Die Bekehrten verkünden das _____.
8. Die Apostelkirche veranstaltet einen _____.
9. Er bettelt um _____.

10. Schriftliche Übung. Wählen Sie ein Thema.
1. Beschreiben Sie Ihre Traumhochzeit.
2. Beschreiben Sie Ihr Lieblingsfest (z.B. Weihnachten, Chanukka usw.). Wie feiern Sie dieses Fest?
3. Beschreiben Sie Ihre Familie.

11. Übersetzen Sie ins Englische.

Zahl der Abtreibungen zu Jahresbeginn gesunken

WIESBADEN, 5. Juli (dpa). Die Zahl der Abtreibungen in Deutschland hat sich zu Jahresbeginn leicht verringert. Im ersten Quartal 2002 gab es 35 700 Schwangerschaftsabbrüche, 500 weniger als im Vorjahreszeitraum, wie das Statistische Bundesamt in Wiesbaden mitteilte. 97 Prozent der Abbrüche erfolgten nach der Beratungsregelung. Die übrigen Abtreibungen hatten medizinische Gründe oder waren Folge einer Schwangerschaft nach einer Vergewaltigung. Fast die Hälfte der Frauen waren zum Zeitpunkt der Abtreibung verheiratet, sechs Prozent minderjährig. Die Abtreibungspille Mifegyne wurde bei fünf Prozent der Abbrüche eingesetzt.

FRANKFURTER RUNDSCHAU, Samstag, 6. Juli 2002, Nr. 154/27, S. 5

© dpa Deutsche Presse-Agentur GmbH

Jüngster Erzbischof in Bayerns Diaspora

Weihbischof Ludwig Schick geht nach Bamberg / Erfahrener Kirchenrechtler und beliebter Weihbischof

FULDA/BAMBERG. Was sich lange als Gerücht hielt, ist am Freitagmittag bestätigt worden: der 52-jährige Fuldaer Weihbischof Professor Ludwig Schick wird Erzbischof von Bamberg. Schick tritt damit die Nachfolge des 71-jährigen Bamberger Erzbischofs Karl Braun an, der von 1994 bis 2001 das Bistum geleitet hat und im vergangenen Jahr aus gesundheitlichen Gründen vom Amt „entpflichtet" worden ist. Nach fast zwölfmonatiger Nichtbesetzung des Bischofsstuhls hat die fränkische Stadt damit wieder einen Oberhirten – mit 52 Jahren den Jüngsten in Bayern. Voraussichtlich im September werde er von der Bamberger Diözese „Besitz ergreifen", sagte der neue Erzbischof am Freitagnachmittag in Fulda.

„Ich fühle mich geehrt, Oberhirte dieser alten ehrwürdigen Diözese zu werden", sagte Schick. Trotzdem falle es ihm ein wenig schwer, sein bisheriges Amt in Fulda aufzugeben. „Allein schon wegen des rollenden Rs in meiner Aussprache werde ich in Bamberg mit seinem fränkischen Dialekt schnell meine Heimat finden", sagte Schick augenzwinkernd. Der 52-jährige Kirchenrechtler stammt aus Mardorf (Kreis Marburg-Biedenkopf), studierte in Fulda, Würzburg und Rom und ist 1975 zum Priester geweiht worden. Seit 1981 lehrt er in Fulda und Marburg Kirchenrecht, wurde 1995 Generalvikar der Diözese und im Mai 1998 vom Papst zum zweiten Weihbischof des Bistums Fulda ernannt. Der 52-Jährige war und ist beliebt bei den Fuldaern. Viele hatten gehofft, dass er Nachfolger des im Juli 2000 verstorbenen Erzbischofs Johannes Dyba im Bistum wird. Er galt als ähnlich konsequent, aber moderater im Ton als Dyba. Oberbürgermeister Alois Rhiel (CDU) würdigte Schick als „großen Seelsorger und Sprachrohr der Menschen" und sagte, er werde in Fulda fehlen.

Das Erzbistum Bamberg wurde im Jahre 1007 durch Kaiser Heinrich II. aus Teilen Würzburgs und Eichstätts zum Bistum erhoben. Es ist heute das größte Diasporabistum in Bayern und mit etwa 800 000 Katholiken doppelt so groß wie Fulda. Das Bistumsgebiet mit 367 Pfarreien und Seelsorgestellen umfasst ganz Oberfranken, etwa die Hälfte von Mittelfranken und kleinere Teile von Unterfranken und der Oberpfalz.

Karoline Rübsam, Journalistenbüro Angelstein

FRANKFURTER RUNDSCHAU, Samstag, 29. Juni 2002, Nr. 148/26, S. 33

Unit 14

Education

Level 1

General

Unterricht, der (-e; pl. rare)	teaching, lessons, classes, instruction
(etw) unterrichten	to teach (sth)
jmdn (in etw) unterrichten	to teach sb (sth)
(etw) lehren	to teach (sth)
jmdn etw lehren	to teach sb sth
Kurs, der (-e)	course
einen Kurs belegen	to attend a course
Stunde, die (-n)	lesson, class
etw lernen	to learn sth
(für etw) lernen	to study (for sth)
etw besuchen	to attend sth
sich melden	to put up one's hand
Aufsatz, der (¨e)	essay
Lehrplan, der (¨e)	curriculum, syllabus
Stundenplan, der (¨e)	timetable, schedule
Klassengröße, die (-n)	class size
Talent, das (-e)	talent
Begabung, die (-en)	talent

School

Schule, die (-n)	school
Klasse, die (-n)	class, grade
Klassenzimmer, das (-)	classroom
Pause, die (-n)	break
Schulhof, der (¨e)	playground
Ferien, pl.	holidays

Klassenfahrt, die (-en)	class trip
jmdn bestrafen	to punish sb
Strafe, die (-n)	punishment

Further and higher education

Universität, die (-en)	university
Uni, die (-s)	uni(versity)
Hochschule, die (-n)	college, university
Volkshochschule, die (-n)	adult education centre
etw studieren	to study sth [at a university], read
Studium, das (-dien)	programme of studies
Studienplatz, der (¨e)	place at a university/college
Semester, das (-)	semester
Studentenheim, das (-e)	hall of residence
Mensa, die (-sen)	canteen [of university, college]
Stipendium, das (-dien)	grant, scholarship
Vorlesung, die (-en)	lecture
Vortrag, der (¨e)	lecture, talk
(Pro)seminar, das (-e)	(introductory) seminar
Voraussetzung, die (-en)	prerequisite, requirement
Schein, der (-e)	credit

377

Hörsaal, der (-säle)	lecture hall
Institut, das (-e)	institute, department

Educational materials

Tafel, die (-n)	(black)board
Tafelschwamm, der (¨e)	blackboard sponge, board rubber
Kreide, die (-n)	chalk
Heft, das (-e)	notebook
Bleistift, der (-e)	pencil
Kugelschreiber, der (-)	ballpoint pen
Kuli, der (-s; coll.)	ballpoint
Tinte, die (-n)	ink
Klebestift, der (-e)	glue stick
Kleber, der (-; coll.)	glue
etw kleben	to glue/stick sth
Zeigestock, der (¨e)	pointer
Projektor, der (-en)	projector
Graph, der (-en)	graph
Diagramm, das (-e)	graph, diagram

Staff and students

Lehrer(in), der/die (-/nen)	teacher
Grundschullehrer(in), der/die (-/nen)	primary school teacher
Schuldirektor(in), der/die (-en/nen)	principal
Schulleiter(in), der/die (-/nen)	headmaster/ headmistress; principal
Schüler(in), der/die (-/nen)	pupil, student
Klassenkamerad(in), der/die (-en/nen)	classmate
Klassensprecher(in), der/die (-/nen)	class representative
(Gast)professor(in), der/die (-en/nen)	(visiting) professor
Student(in), der/die (-en/nen)	(university) student
Wissenschaftler(in), der/die (-/nen)	(academic) scientist
Forscher(in), der/die (-/nen)	research scientist
Lehrling, der (-e)	apprentice

Meister(in), der/die (-/nen)	master

Type of school

Kindergarten, der (¨)	kindergarten
Grundschule, die (-n)	elementary school
Realschule, die (-n)	high school
Hauptschule, die (-n)	vocational high school
Gymnasium, das (-sien)	high school (with academic emphasis), grammar school
Gesamtschule, die (-n)	comprehensive school
Sekundarschule, die (-n)	secondary school
Oberschule, die (-n)	secondary school

School and university subjects

Fach, das (¨er)	subject
Haupt-, Nebenfach, das (¨er)	major/minor (subject)
Deutsch, das (no pl.)	German
Englisch, das (no pl.)	English
Geschichte, die (no pl.)	history
Musik, die (-en)	music
Rechnen, das (no pl.)	arithmetic
Mathematik, die (no pl.)	mathematics
Mathe, die (no pl.; school sl.)	maths
Biologie, die (no pl.)	biology
Chemie, die (no pl.)	chemistry
Physik, die (no pl.)	physics
Sport, der (-e; pl. rare)	sport, PE
Turnen, das (no pl.)	gymnastics
Holzarbeit, die (-en)	woodwork
Werken, das (no pl.)	handicrafts

Assessment and qualifications

Arbeit, die (-en)	test, paper
Klassenarbeit, die (-en)	test [at school]
Test, der (-s or -e)	test

schriftlich	written	Schlussexamen, das	final exam
mündlich	oral	(- or -mina)	
richtig	correct, right	Abitur, das	high school diploma
falsch	wrong	(-e; pl. rare)	and university
Fehler, der (-)	mistake		entrance exam
etw korrigieren	to correct sth		(equivalent of A
Korrektur, die (-en)	correction		levels)
Übung, die (-en)	exercise, drill	Note, die (-n)	grade, mark
Diktat, das (-e)	dictation	Zensur, die (-en)	grade
etw diktieren	to dictate sth	Zeugnis, das (-se)	grades, report
jmdn/etw prüfen	to test, examine	etw bestehen	to pass sth
	sb/sth	versetzt werden	to move up (a class)
Prüfung, die (-en)	exam	durchfallen	fail, flunk
Examen, das	exam	sitzen bleiben	to repeat
(- or –mina)			(a year/class)

Level 2

General

Bildung, die (no pl.)	education
Ausbildung, die (-en)	training
jmdn ausbilden	to train sb
ungebildet	uneducated
jmdn erziehen	to educate sb
Erziehung, die (no pl.)	education
erzieherisch	educational
pädagogisch	educational
Einführungskurs, der (-e)	introductory course, foundation course
Grundkurs, der (-e)	basic course
Intensivkurs, der (-e)	intensive course
Abendkurs, der (-e)	evening course
jmdn/sich (irgendwo) anmelden	to enrol sb/[o.s.] (somewhere)
Anmeldung, die (-en)	registration
etw nachholen	to make up sth
Lernstrategie, die (-n)	learning strategy
abwesend	absent
die Schule/ Universität vorzeitig verlassen	to drop out of school

School

Lektion, die (-en)	lesson
Aufgabe, die (-n)	exercise, task
auswendig	by heart
jmdn prügeln	to cane sb
Prügel bekommen	to get the cane
jmdn mit dem Stock schlagen	to cane sb
die Schule schwänzen	to play truant, cut classes
etw schwänzen	to skip sth
(Schul)schwänzer(in), der/die (-/nen)	truant
Schulgeld, das (-er)	school fee, tuition

Further and higher education

sich immatrikulieren	to enrol
Grundstudium, das (no pl.)	basic studies
Aufbaustudium, das (-dien)	post-graduate study
Hochschul(aus)- bildung, die (no pl.)	higher education
Berufsausbildung, die (-en)	vocational training
Berufsschule, die (-n)	vocational college, training college

technische Hochschule	technical college
pädagogische Hochschule	teacher training college
Musikhochschule, die (-n)	college of music
Fachhochschule (FH), die (-n)	higher education institution
medizinische Hochschule	medical school
kaufmännische Fachschule	business school
Stipendiat(in), der/die (-en/nen)	grant-holder
Forschungsstipendium, das (-dien)	research fellowship
Praktikum, das (-ka)	period of practical training
Lehre, die (-n)	apprenticeship
Lehrstelle, die (-n)	apprenticeship
Berufslaufbahn, die (-en)	career
Karriere, die (-n)	career

Educational materials

Füller, der (-)	fountain pen
Filzstift, der (-e)	felt-tipped pen
Leuchtstift, der (-e)	highlighter
Drehbleistift, der (-e)	propelling pencil
kariertes/liniertes Papier	squared/lined paper
Schaubild, das (-er)	chart
Globus, der (-ben or -se)	globe
Dia, das (-s)	slide
Diapositiv, das (-e)	slide
Flussdiagramm, das (-e)	flow-chart
Flipchart, das (-s)	flipchart
Buchzeichen, das (-)	bookmark
Lesezeichen, das (-)	bookmark

Staff and students

Austauschschüler(in), der/die (-/nen)	exchange pupil
Austauschstudent(in), der/die (-en/nen)	exchange student
ehemaliger Schüler/Student	old boy, old student, alumnus
ehemalige Schülerin/Studentin	old girl, old student, alumna
Rektor(in), der/die (-en/nen)	head teacher; principal
Kursleiter(in), der/die (-/nen)	teacher
Kursteilnehmer(in), der/die (-/nen)	course participant, student
Tutor(in), der/die (-en/nen)	tutor
Privatlehrer(in), der/die (-/nen)	tutor
Fachlehrer(in), der/die (-/nen)	specialist teacher
Erzieher(in), der/die (-/nen)	nursery school teacher, kindergarten teacher
Teilzeitstudent(in), der/die (-en/nen)	part-time student
stundenweise unterrichten	to teach part-time
Abiturient(in), der/die (-en/nen)	person who is doing/has done the Abitur
Doktorand(in), der/die (-en/nen)	doctoral student
Sitzenbleiber(in), der/die (-/nen)	repeater (repeating past year's course)
Studienabbrecher(in), der/die (-/nen)	drop-out

Type of school

Vorschule, die (-n)	preschool
Privatschule, die (-n)	private school
staatliche Schule	state school
Sommerschule, die (-n)	summer school
Sonderschule, die (-n)	special school
Behindertenschule, die (-n)	special school (for physically handicapped)

School and university subjects

Wahlfach, das (¨er)	elective subject
Pflichtfach, das (¨er)	compulsory subject
Geographie, die (no pl.)	geography
Erdkunde, die (no pl.)	geography
Religion, die (-en)	religion
Religionsunterricht, der (no pl.)	religious education
Fremdsprache, die (-n)	modern/foreign language
Italienisch, das (no pl.)	Italian
Französisch, das (no pl.)	French
Spanisch, das (no pl.)	Spanish
Kunst, die (¨e)	art
Kunsterziehung, die (no pl.)	art education
Soziologie, die (no pl.)	sociology
Philosophie, die (no pl.)	philosophy
Medizin, die (no pl.)	medicine
Wirtschaftslehre, die (no pl.)	business studies
Hauswirtschaft, die (no pl.)	domestic studies, home economics

Assessment and qualifications

sehr gut	very good (top formal grade)
gut	good
befriedigend	satisfactory
ausreichend	pass
mangelhaft	poor
ungenügend	unsatisfactory (lowest formal grade)
Lernkurve, die (-n)	learning curve
jmdn auf seine Intelligenz testen	test sb's intelligence
jmdn/etw (auf etw) testen	test sb/sth (for sth)
Klausur, die (-en)	test [at a university]
Multiplechoice, das (no pl.)	multiple choice
Leseverständnis, das (-se)	reading comprehension
Hörverständnis, das (-se)	listening comprehension
Antwortbogen, der (-; S: ¨)	answer sheet
Doktor, der (-en)	doctorate
Doktorgrad, der (-e)	doctoral degree
Doktorarbeit, die (-en)	dissertation
begabt	gifted
sprachbegabt	gifted in languages
Zertifikat, das (-e)	certificate
Diplom, das (-e)	degree, diploma
Magister, der (-)	master's degree
Staatsexamen, das (- or -mina)	state examination
etw zensieren	to mark/grade sth
etw benoten	to mark/grade sth

Level 3

General

Allgemeinbildung, die (no pl.)	general education
Pädagoge, der (-n); Pädagogin, die (-nen)	educationalist, educational theorist
Erziehungswissenschaftler(in), der/die (-/nen)	educationalist
Lehrer-Schüler Verhältnis, das (-se)	teacher–pupil ratio
Koedukation, die (no pl.)	coeducation
getrennter Unterricht	single-sex instruction
büffeln (coll.)	to cram
(etw) pauken	to cram (sth)
mogeln	to cheat

durchrutschen	to scrape through	BAföG (Bafög), das	(student) grant
Leistung, die (-en)	achievement	(no pl.)	
Fertigkeit, die (-en)	aptitude	BAföG/Bafög	to get a grant
Förderunterricht,	remedial teaching	kriegen	
der (no pl.)		Erwachsenenbildung,	adult education
Förderkurs, der (-e)	remedial course	die (no pl.)	
Auffrischungskurs,	refresher course	Fort-, Weiterbildung,	further education
der (-e)		die (no pl.)	
Fernkurs, der (-e)	correspondence	Fortbildungskurs,	in-service training
	course	der (-e)	course
fachübergreifend	multidisciplinary	Bildungsweg, der (-e)	course of sb's
interdisziplinär	interdisciplinary		education
Anstellung auf	tenure, appointment	zweiter Bildungsweg	continuing education
Lebenszeit,	to the retiring age	Lehrstuhl, der (¨e)	chair
die (-en)		Fernstudium, das	distance learning
unkündbar angestellt	to have tenure	(no pl.)	
sein		Studiengebühr, die	tuition fee
		(-en)	

School

ausfallen	to not take place, be cancelled
Anwesenheitsliste, die (-n)	attendance list
jmdn von der Schule verweisen	to expel sb from school
Schulpflicht, die (no pl.)	compulsory school attendance
Schulabgangsalter, das (no pl.)	school-leaving age
Umschulung, die (-en)	retraining course
sich umschulen lassen	to retrain
Tyrann(in), der/die (-en/nen)	bully
jmdn tyrannisieren	to bully sb
jmdn schikanieren	to harass/bully sb
Nachsitzen, das (no pl.)	detention
nachsitzen müssen	to be in detention

Kursgebühr, die (-en)	registration fee
Studentenverbindung, die (-en)	sorority/fraternity; students' union
Studentenrat, der (¨e)	student council

Educational materials

Unterrichtsmittel, das (-)	educational equipment
Lehrmittel, das (-)	teaching aid
Folie, die (-n)	transparency
Lernsoftware, die (-s)	educational software
Leihbibliothek, die (-en)	lending library
Leihbücherei, die (-en)	lending library
Katalog, der (-e)	catalogue
Karteikarte, die (-n)	index card
Standortnummer, die (-n)	call number, shelf mark
Literaturliste, die (-n)	reading list
Glossar, das (-e or -rien)	glossary
computergestützt	computer-assisted
Gedächtnishilfe, die (-n)	mnemonic
Eselsbrücke, die (-n; coll.)	mnemonic

Further and higher education

Numerus clausus (NC), der	restricted entry, quota
ZVS (Zentralstelle für die Vergabe von Studienplätzen), die	central clearing house for places on degree courses

Löschpapier, das (-e)	blotting paper
Zeichendreieck, das (-e)	set square
Schmierpapier, das (-e)	rough paper

Staff and students

Dozent(in), der/die (-en/nen)	lecturer
Dozent(in) in höherer Position	senior lecturer
Lehrkraft, die (¨e; formal)	teacher
Lehrerkollegium, das (-gien)	teaching staff [of a school]
Referendar(in), der/die (-e/en)	student teacher
Externe(r), der/die (adj. decl.)	day boy/girl
Internatsschüler(in), der/die (-/nen)	boarder
Kommilitone, der (-n); Kommilitonin, die (-nen)	fellow student [at the university]
Praktikant(in), der/die (-en/nen)	trainee
Auszubildende(r), der/die (adj. decl.)	apprentice, trainee
Azubi, der (-s; coll.)	apprentice, trainee
Schulabgänger(in), der/die (-/nen)	school leaver

Type of school

Kinderkrippe, die (-n)	day care centre
Kindertagheim, das (-e)	preschool
Internat, das (-e)	boarding school
Externat, das (-e)	day school
Fernschule, die (-n)	correspondence school
Klosterschule, die (-n)	convent school
Konfessionsschule, die (-n)	parochial school, church school

School and university subjects

Fakultät, die (-en)	faculty, special field
Fachbereich, der (-e)	special field
Leistungskurs, der (-e)	main subject
Sozialwissenschaften, pl.	social studies
Gemeinschaftskunde, die (no pl.)	social studies
Theologie, die (no pl.)	theology
Geisteswissenschaften, pl.	arts, humanities
Germanistik, die (no pl.)	German (studies)
Anglistik, die (no pl.)	English studies
Amerikanistik, die (no pl.)	American studies
Altphilologie, die (no pl.)	classics
Griechisch, das (no pl.)	Greek
Latein, das (no pl.)	Latin
Rechtswissenschaft, die (no pl.)	law
Jura, pl.	law
Informatik, die (no pl.)	computer science
Wirtschaftswissen-schaften, pl.	economics
Volkswirtschaft, die (no pl.)	economics
Finanzwissenschaft, die (no pl.)	finance
Betriebswirtschaft, die (no pl.)	business management

Assessment and qualifications

Einstufung, die (-en)	assessment
Bewertung, die (-en)	assessment
Prüfungsausschuss, der (¨e)	board of examiners
Prüfungskommission, die (-en)	board of examiners
Prüfling, der (-e)	candidate
Prüfungskandidat(in), der/die (-en/nen)	candidate

Schulabschluss, der ("e)	school-leaving certificate	Eignungsprüfung, die (-en)	aptitude test
Hauptschulabschluss, der ("e)	diploma from a vocational high school	Lehrbefähigung, die (no pl.)	teaching qualification
mittlere Reife, die (no pl.)	diploma from high school	Auszeichnung, die (-en)	distinction, merit
Hochschulreife, die (no pl.)	university entrance qualification	Lesealter, das (no pl.)	reading age
Studienabschluss, der ("e)	BA or BSc.	Lesefähigkeit, die (-en)	reading ability
Aufnahmeprüfung, die (-en)	entrance exam	Lernbehinderung, die (-en)	learning disability
Auswahlprüfung, die (-en)	competitive exam	lernbehindert	learning-disabled, with learning difficulties

Science

Level 1

General

Wissenschaft, die (-en)	science
wissenschaftlich	scientific
Experiment, das (-e)	experiment
ein Experiment durchführen	to carry out an experiment
experimentieren	to experiment
Probe, die (-n)	test
etw untersuchen	to investigate sth
etw entwickeln	to develop sth
Forschung, die (-en)	research
Theorie, die (-n)	theory

Mathematics

Addition, die (-en)	addition
Subtraktion, die (-en)	subtraction
Multiplikation, die (-en)	multiplication
Division, die (-en)	division
etw addieren	to add sth
etw von etw subtrahieren	to subtract sth from sth
etw mit etw multiplizieren	to multiply sth by sth
etw durch etw teilen	to divide sth by sth
plus	plus
minus	minus
mal	times
durch	divided by
zehn weniger fünf ist fünf	ten less five is five
vier mal zwei ist gleich acht	four times two equals eight
zehn geteilt durch zwei	ten divided by two
größer/weniger als	greater/less than
Aufgabe, die (-n)	problem
etw lösen	to solve sth
Lösung, die (-en)	solution
(etw) zählen	to count (sth)
Zahl, die (-en)	number
negativ	negative
positiv	positive
Linie, die (-n)	line
Punkt, der (-e)	point

Prozent, das (-e, after numbers -)	percent

Physical sciences

Gas, das (-e)	gas
gasförmig	gaseous
Flüssigkeit, die (-en)	liquid
flüssig	liquid
Festkörper, der (-)	solid
fest	solid
fest	stable
stabil	stable
Metall, das (-e)	metal
Mineral, das (-e or -ien)	mineral
Materie, die (no pl.)	matter
Stoff, der (-e)	matter
Element, das (-e)	element
Faser, die (-n)	fibre
Alkohol, der (-e)	alcohol
chemisch	chemical
physikalisch	physical
Energie, die (-n)	energy
Erhaltung, die (no pl.)	conservation
Motor, der (-en)	motor
Kraft, die (¨e)	force
Stärke, die (-n)	power
Masse, die (-n)	mass
Mechanik, die (no pl.)	mechanics
Mikrowelle, die (-n)	microwave
Druck, der (¨e)	pressure
Elektrizität, die (no pl.)	electricity
Spannung, die (-en)	voltage
Dampf, der (¨e)	steam
Atom, das (-e)	atom
atomar	atomic
Analyse, die (-n)	analysis
Dichte, die (no pl.)	density
Distanz, die (-en)	distance
reagieren	to react
Reaktion, die (-en)	reaction
Relativität, die (no pl.)	relativity

Relativitätstheorie, die (no pl.)	theory of relativity
Geschwindigkeit, die (-en)	speed

Biological sciences

Zelle, die (-n)	cell
Nukleus, der (Nuklei)	nucleus
organisch	organic
Organismus, der (-men)	organism
Bakterium, das (-rien)	bacterium
Virus, der (Viren)	virus
sich reproduzieren	to reproduce, breed
genetisch	genetic
Genetik, die (no pl.)	genetics
botanisch	botanical

Ecology

Kohle, die (-n)	coal
Erdgas, das (-e)	natural gas
Öl, das (-e)	oil
Erdöl, das (no pl.)	petroleum
Energiequelle, die (-n)	energy source
Energiekrise, die (-n)	energy crisis
Solar-, Sonnenenergie, die (no pl.)	solar energy
Solarzelle, die (-n)	solar cell
Erwärmung, die (-en)	warming
globale Erwärmung	global warming
etw verschmutzen	to pollute sth
Umweltverschmut-zung, die (-en)	pollution
saurer Regen	acid rain
Ozonschicht, die (no pl.)	ozone layer
Ozonloch, das (¨er)	hole in the ozone layer

Space science

Mond, der (-e)	moon

Neu-, Vollmond, der (-e)	new/full moon	Stratosphäre, die (no pl.)	stratosphere
Meteorit, der (-en)	meteorite	schwarzes Loch	black hole
Planet, der (-en)	planet		
Komet, der (-en)	comet		

Scientific instruments

Sonnensystem, das (-e)	solar system	Taschenrechner, der (-)	(pocket) calculator
Sternsystem, das (-e)	galaxy	Mikroskop, das (-e)	microscope
Rakete, die (-n)	rocket, missile	Elektronenmikroskop, das (-e)	electron microscope
Satellit, der (-en)	satellite		
Astronom(in), der/die (-en/nen)	astronomer	Elektromagnet, der (-en)	electromagnet
Astronaut(in), der/die (-en/nen)	astronaut	Batterie, die (-n)	battery
		Laser, der (-)	laser
Lichtjahr, das (-e)	light–year	Filter, der (-)	filter
Weltraum, der (no pl.)	universe	Thermometer, das (-)	thermometer
		Hebel, der (-)	lever

Level 2

General

etw erforschen	to research sth
etw in Frage stellen	to challenge sth
Versuch, der (-e)	experiment
Verfahren, das (-)	procedure, process, method
Datum, das (-ten)	piece of data
Skala, die (Skalen)	dial
Hypothese, die (-n)	hypothesis
Durchbruch, der (¨e)	breakthrough
Forschungspark, der (-s)	research park

Mathematics

(etw) rechnen	to calculate sth/make calculations
etw berechnen	to calculate sth
Berechnung, die (-en)	calculation
etw ausrechnen	to work sth out
etw schätzen	to estimate sth
etw von etw abziehen	to subtract sth from sth
Endsumme, die (-n)	total
Ergebnis, das (-se)	result
Algebra, die (no pl.)	algebra

Geometrie, die (no pl.)	geometry
sphärisch	spherical
Körper, der (-)	solid figure
Fläche, die (-n)	plane
Durchschnitt, der (-)	average
den Durchschnitt nehmen	to take the average
Mitte, die (-n)	medium
Maximum, das (-ma)	maximum
Minimum, das (-ma)	minimum
maximal	maximum (adj.)
bis zu maximal	up to a maximum of
minimal	at least
insgesamt	in total
gerade	even
ungerade	odd
Dezimalzahl, die (-en)	decimal
Komma, das (-s)	decimal point
Ziffer, die (-n)	digit; figure, number
um 10%	by 10%
Prozentsatz, der (¨e)	percentage

Physical sciences

Formel, die (-n)	formula
Gefrierpunkt, der (-e)	freezing point
Siedepunkt, der (-e)	boiling point
Wärmeverlust, der (-e)	heat loss
Verbindung, die (-en)	compound
Zusammensetzung, die (-en)	composition
Eigenschaft, die (-en)	property
anorganisch	inorganic
Säure, die (-n)	acid
sauer	acidic
Alkali, das (-en)	alkali
alkalisch	alkaline
basisch	alkaline, basic
Lackmuspapier, das (no pl.)	litmus paper
sich auflösen	to dissolve
wasserlöslich	water-soluble
(un)löslich	(in)soluble
Emulsion, die (-en)	emulsion
Reibung, die (-en)	friction
Schwerkraft, die (no pl.)	gravity
Schwerpunkt, der (-e)	centre of gravity
Gravitationsgesetz, das (-e)	law of gravity
Welle, die (-n)	wave
Schall, der (-e or ¨e)	sound
Schallwelle, die (-n)	sound wave
Wellenlänge, die (-n)	wavelength
Laserstrahl, der (-en)	laser beam
Lichtstrahl, der (-en)	light beam
Lichtwelle, die (-n)	light wave
Strom, der (¨e)	current
Strömung, die (-en)	current
Stromkreis, der (-e)	circuit
Gleich-, Wechselstrom, der (no pl.)	direct/alternating current
Ladung, die (-en)	charge
etw aufladen	to charge sth
Roboter, der (-)	robot

Akustik, die (no pl.)	acoustics
Aerodynamik, die (no pl.)	aerodynamics
Optik, die (no pl.)	optics
Spektrum, das (-tren or -tra)	spectrum
Elektronik, die (no pl.)	electronics
Hydraulik, die (no pl.)	hydraulics
Metallurgie, die (no pl.)	metallurgy

Biological sciences

Objektträger, der (-)	slide
Mikroorganismus, der (-men)	microorganism
Gewebe, das (-)	tissue
Membran, die (-en)	membrane
Embryo, der (-s or -nen)	embryo
Gen, das (-e)	gene
Genbank, die (-en)	gene bank
mutieren	to mutate
Lebensraum, der (¨e)	habitat
Nahrungskette, die (-n)	food chain

Ecology

Treib-, Kraft-, Brennstoff, der (-e)	fuel
fossile Brennstoffe	fossil fuels
Rohstoff, der (-e)	raw material
Kühlmittel, das (-)	coolant
Energiesparmaß-nahmen, pl.	energy conservation
Energieverbrauch, der (no pl.)	energy consumption
Energiebedarf, der (no pl.)	energy needs
geothermische Energie	geothermal energy
Atom-, Kernenergie, die (no pl.)	atomic energy
Kernkraftwerk, das (-e)	nuclear power station

Wasserkraft, die (no pl.)	hydroelectric power	Mondlandung, die (-en)	moon-landing
Wasserkraftwerk, das (-e)	hydroelectric power plant	Krater, der (-)	crater
Wärmeenergie, die (no pl.)	thermal energy	Kosmonaut(in), der/die (-en/nen)	cosmonaut
Windenergie, die (no pl.)	wind energy	Docking, das (no pl.)	docking
Wellenkraftwerk, das (-e)	wave-power generator	Observatorium, das (-rien)	observatory
etw verunreinigen	to pollute sth	Planetarium, das (-rien)	planetarium
etw verpesten	to pollute sth [atmosphere]	Milchstraße, die (no pl.)	Milky Way
Treibhauseffekt, der (no pl.)	greenhouse effect	Sonnenfleck, der (-e)	sunspot
Ökosystem, das (-e)	ecosystem		

Space science

Umlauf-, Kreisbahn, die (-en)	orbit
Planetenbahn, die (-en)	planetary orbit
Universum, das (no pl.)	universe
Weltall, das (no pl.)	universe
Raumfahrzeug, das (-e)	spacecraft
Raumschiff, das (-e)	spacecraft
Raumkapsel, die (-n)	space capsule
Raumanzug, der (¨e)	spacesuit
Weltraumflug, der (¨e)	space flight

Scientific instruments

Trichter, der (-)	funnel
Scheidetrichter, der (-)	separating funnel
Bunsenbrenner, der (-)	Bunsen burner
Messgerät, das (-e)	gauge
Reagenzglas, das (¨er)	test tube
Reagenzglasgestell, das (-e)	test tube rack
Lupe, die (-n)	magnifying glass
Vergrößerungsglas, das (¨er)	magnifying glass
Becherglas, das (¨er)	beaker
Rührer, der (-)	stirrer
Kühler, der (-)	condenser
Reaktor, der (-en)	reactor

Level 3

General

Verhaltensforschung, die (no pl.)	behavioural science	Biowissenschaften, pl.	biological sciences
angewandte Wissenschaften, pl.	applied sciences	Experimentalwissenschaften, pl.	experimental sciences
exakte Wissenschaften, pl.	exact sciences	reine Wissenschaften, pl.	pure sciences
Naturwissenschaften, pl.	natural sciences	Raumforschung, die (no pl.)	space science
Geowissenschaften, pl.	earth sciences	auf wissenschaftliches Neuland vorstoßen	to push back the frontiers of science

Mathematics

Vektor, der (-en)	vector
Trigonometrie, die (no pl.)	trigonometry
Differentialrechnung, die (no pl.)	differential calculus
Integralrechnung, die (no pl.)	integral calculus
zweistellig	two-digit, two-place
Gleichung, die (-en)	equation
eine Gleichung ersten/zweiten Grades	a linear/quadratic equation
Verhältnis, das (-se)	ratio
im Verhältnis 2 zu 1	in the ratio of 2 to 1
Potenz, die (-en)	power
hoch	to the power of
fünf hoch zwei	five squared
hoch drei	to the third power
Quadratzahl, die (-en)	square
Wurzel, die (-n)	root
die Wurzel aus einer Zahl ziehen	to find the root of a number
Quadratwurzel, die (-n)	square root
zweite Wurzel	square root
Logarithmus, der (-men)	logarithm
Logarithmentafel, die (-n)	logarithm table
Lehrsatz, der ("e)	theorem
Theorem, das (-e)	theorem
Beweis, der (-e)	proof
etw beweisen	to prove sth
deduktiv	deductive
induktiv	inductive
Statistik, die (-en)	statistics
statistisch	statistical

Physical sciences

Periodensystem, das (no pl.)	periodic table
Stickstoff, der (no pl.)	nitrogen
Wasserstoff, der (no pl.)	hydrogen
Chlor, das (no pl.)	chlorine
Jod, das (no pl.)	iodine
Quecksilber, das (no pl.)	mercury
Phosphat, das (-e)	phosphate
Schwefel, der (no pl.)	sulphur
Äther, der (no pl.)	ether
Kohlenstoff, der (no pl.)	carbon
Ammoniak, das (no pl.)	ammonia
Kugellager, das (-)	ball bearing
Getriebe, das (-)	gear
Schmiermittel, das (-)	lubricant
Magnetismus, der (no pl.)	magnetism
Magnetfeld, das (-er)	magnetic field
Geschoss, das (-e)	missile
Reflexion, die (-en)	reflection
Brechung, die (-en)	refraction
Widerstand, der ("e)	resistance
widerstandsfähig	resistant
Elektrode, die (-n)	electrode
Elektron, das (-en)	electron
Spaltung, die (-en)	fission
Verschmelzung, die (-en)	fusion
molekular	molecular
Molekül, das (-e)	molecule
Nuklear-	nuclear
Kern-	nuclear
Nuklearenergie, die (no pl.)	nuclear energy
Kernreaktor, der (-en)	nuclear reactor
Neutron, das (-en)	neutron
(Aus)strahlung, die (-en)	radiation
Quantentheorie, die (no pl.)	quantum theory
Proton, das (-en)	proton
Partikel, das (-)	particle

Biological sciences

etw ausscheiden	to excrete sth
Ausscheidung, die (-en)	excretion
Wachstum, das (no pl.)	growth
Verfall, der (no pl.)	decay
verfallen	to decay
Fotosynthese, die (no pl.)	photosynthesis
Chlorophyll, das (no pl.)	chlorophyll
Desoxyribonukle- insäure (DNS), die (no pl.)	deoxyribonucleic acid (DNA)

Earth sciences

Bergwerk, das (-e)	mine
Steinbruch, der (¨e)	quarry
Schicht, die (-en)	layer
Lehm, der (-e)	loam
Erz, das (-e)	ore
Ablagerung, die (-en)	sediment
Erdreich, das (no pl.)	soil
Gestein, das (-e)	rock stratum
undurchlässiges Gestein	impervious rock
porös	porous
durchlässig	porous
Stalaktit, der (-e or -en)	stalactite
Stalagmit, der (-e or -en)	stalagmite
Verwerfung, die (-en)	fault
Verwerfungslinie, die (-n)	fault line
Erdspalte, die (-n)	fissure
Erdkruste, die (no pl.)	earth's crust
Erdkern, der (no pl.)	earth's core
Kontinentalsockel, der (-)	continental shelf
Kohlenstoffdatierung, die (-en)	carbon dating

Space science

Anziehungskraft, die (¨e)	gravitational pull
Eklipse, die (-n)	eclipse
Finsternis, die (-se)	eclipse
sich verfinstern	to be eclipsed
Asteroid, der (-en)	asteroid
Sonnenwende, die (-n)	solstice
Sternschnuppe, die (-n)	shooting star
Raketenabschuss, der (¨e)	launch
Abschussrampe, die (-n)	launching pad
Mond(lande)fähre, die (-n)	lunar module
in etw wieder eintreten	to re-enter
Wiedereintritt, der (-e)	re-entry
Urknalltheorie, die (no pl.)	big-bang theory
Zeitschleife, die (-n)	time warp
Galaxie, die (-n); Galaxis, die (-xien)	galaxy
galaktisch	galactic

Scientific instruments

Rechenschieber, der (-)	slide rule
Zirkel, der (-)	(pair of) compasses
Glaskolben, der (-)	flask
(Mess)pipette, die (-n)	(graduated) pipette
Messzylinder, der (-)	measuring cylinder
Schmelztiegel, der (-)	crucible
Hahn, der (¨e)	tap, faucet
Mörser, der (-)	mortar
Pistill, das (-e)	pestle
Dreifuß, der (¨e)	tripod
Sonde, die (-n)	probe

Exercises

Level 1

1. Welches Wort hat die gleiche oder eine ähnliche Bedeutung? ✓

1. lehren
2. das Talent
3. der Schuldirektor
4. die Sekundarschule
5. das Examen
6. die Note
7. das Petroleum
8. die Solarenergie
9. die Materie

2. Wie heißen die kurzen Formen der folgenden Wörter? ✓

1. die Universität
2. die Mathematik
3. das Abitur

3. Wie heißt das Gegenteil? ✓

1. schriftlich
2. richtig
3. etw bestehen
4. etw lehren
5. der Meister
6. das Hauptfach
7. die Addition
8. die Division
9. plus
10. mal
11. eine negative Zahl
12. der Vollmond

4. Welche Wörter gehören zusammen? ✓

> a. die Energiekrise, b. der Hörsaal, c. die Korrektur, d. das Lichtjahr, e. die Lösung,
> f. der Schulhof, g. die Spannung, h. das Sternsystem, i. der Tafelschwamm,
> j. die Zensur

1. die Tafel
2. das Zeugnis
3. die Pause
4. die Vorlesung
5. der Fehler
6. die Aufgabe
7. die Elektrizität
8. die Astronomin
9. die Distanz
10. das Öl

5. Wie heißt das passende Verb? ✓

> a. belegen, b. bleiben, c. durchführen, d. multiplizieren, e. subtrahieren, f. teilen,
> g. unterrichten

1. jmdn in etw
2. einen Kurs
3. sitzen
4. ein Experiment
5. etw von etw
6. etw mit etw
7. etw durch etw

6. Welches Wort passt nicht? ✓

1. der Klebestift, die Kreide, der Kugelschreiber, der Kuli
2. das Gymnasium, die Hauptschule, die Hochschule, die Realschule
3. die Arbeit, der Aufsatz, das Diktat, die Dichte
4. das Erdgas, die Kohle, die Mensa, die Sonnenenergie
5. die Holzarbeit, die Klassenarbeit, das Schlussexamen, der Test
6. die Energie, die Kraft, der Hebel, die Stärke

7. Ordnen Sie.

globale Erwärmung, die Geschichte, schwarzes Loch, die Musik, das Ozonloch, der Planet, die Rakete, das Rechnen, saurer Regen, der Satellit, der Sport, die Umweltverschmutzung, der Weltraum

Schulfach	Ökologie	Raumforschung

8. Wie heißt das entsprechende Adjektiv? ✓

1. die Genetik
2. das Atom
3. die Flüssigkeit
4. das Gas
5. der Festkörper
6. die Wissenschaft

9. Was bedeuten die Wendungen?

1. seine gerechte Strafe bekommen
2. Schule machen
3. sich in die Tinte setzen
4. Übung macht den Meister
5. etw Probe fahren

10. In jedem Satz fehlt ein Wort. ✓

experimentiert, Grundschullehrer, Klassengröße, Mikroskop, Proseminar, Relativitätstheorie, Studienplatz, Taschenrechner, Viren

1. Ich addierte die Einnahmen mit dem _____.
2. Unter dem _____ kann man sehen, wie die Zellen ihre Hülle verdicken.
3. Die durchschnittliche _____ liegt an Realschulen bei 27 Schülern.
4. Sein Freund will Medizin studieren, bekommt aber keinen _____.
5. Nicht an jeder deutschen Universität wird in jedem _____ eine Hausarbeit geschreiben.
6. Wer _____ werden möchte, muss Deutsch oder Mathematik als ein Fach wählen.
7. Dort haben Wissenschaftler mit genetisch manipulierten Anthraxbakterien _____.
8. Die allgemeine _____ hat Albert Einstein 1915 formuliert.
9. Gegen _____ sind Antibiotika machtlos.

11. *Übersetzen Sie ins Englische.*

Gib dem Auto Zucker

Glucose könnte demnächst nicht nur unseren Gehirnen, sondern auch
unseren Autos Energie liefern. Wissenschaftler der Universität von Wisconsin
konnten mit einem Platinkatalysator Wasserstoff aus Glucose freisetzen
(*Nature*, Bd. 418, S. 964). Die Ausbeute war groß genug, um gegenüber
bestehenden Verfahren konkurrenzfähig zu sein. Bisher wird zur
Wasserstoffgewinnung Erdgas oder Petroleum verwendet. Da Glucose ein
Hauptbestandteil tierischen und pflanzlichen Materials ist, könnten Bioabfälle
wie Stroh oder Holzbrei diese Quellen ersetzen.

DIE ZEIT, 29. August 2002, Nr. 36, S. 35

Kometenjäger „Contour" meldet sich nicht

PASADENA, 16. August (ap). Die US-Raumfahrtbehörde Nasa hat den
Kontakt zur 158 Millionen Dollar teuren Raumsonde „Contour" verloren, die
mehrere Kometen erforschen sollte. Die Sonde hätte den Angaben zufolge in
225 Kilometern Höhe über dem Indischen Ozean um 10.49 Uhr (MESZ) ihre
Raketen zünden sollen, um aus der Erdumlaufbahn auf den Weg zu den
Kometen zu kommen. Um 11.35 Uhr (MESZ) hätte sie ein Signal zur Erde
senden sollen. Die Empfangsstationen in Kalifornien, Australien und Spanien
hörten aber nichts. „Wir versuchen noch mit der Sonde Kontakt
aufzunehmen", sagte Nasa-Sprecher Don Savage. „Contour" sollte bis 2008
mehrere Kometen treffen.

FRANKFURTER RUNDSCHAU, 17. August 2002, Nr. 190/33, S. 32

Reprinted with permission of The Associated Press.

Ein Feuerwerk aus Sternschnuppen steht bevor

HAMBURG, 9. August (dpa). In den kommenden Nächten erstrahlt ein
Sternschnuppenfeuerwerk am Firmament. Bei klarer Sicht regnen von
Samstag bis Mittwoch bis zu 90 so genannte Laurentiustränen pro Stunde
vom Himmel. Das Maximum erwartet die US-Raumfahrtbehörde Nasa in der
Nacht zu Dienstag. Da die Meteore aus dem Sternbild Perseus zu kommen
scheinen, heißen sie auch Perseiden. Die beste Beobachtungszeit sind die
frühen Morgenstunden, wenn der Perseus hoch im Osten steht. Das anhaltend
schlechte Wetter am Wochenende droht allerdings, das Himmelsschauspiel in
vielen Teilen Deutschlands zu trüben.

   Mit mehr als 200 000 Kilometern pro Stunde sind die Perseiden recht
schnelle Meteore. Dabei tauchen auch besonders helle Objekte auf, so
genannte Feuerkugeln oder Boliden, die mitunter so stark leuchten wie der
Vollmond. In diesem Jahr sind die Voraussetzungen für eine Beobachtung an
sich gut, da kein Mondlicht stört. Am Tag des Maximums verschwindet der
Mond bereits weit vor Mitternacht.

FRANKFURTER RUNDSCHAU, 10. August 2002, Nr. 184/32, S. 32

© dpa Deutsche Presse-Agentur GmbH

Forscher haben entdeckt, dass die Erde dicker wird

WASHINGTON, 2. August (dpa). Die Erde wird platter und legt am Äquator zu. Diese unerwartete Beobachtung haben US-Forscher mit Hilfe von Satelliten-Messungen der Erdanziehungskraft gemacht. Seit 1998 wächst demnach der Bauch unseres Planeten, die Erde wird etwas kürbisförmiger. Als Ursache nehmen die Wissenschaftler eine Umschichtung großer Wassermassen von den Polen bis zum Äquator an, wie die US-Raumfahrtbehörde NASA berichtet.

Warum sich das Wasser neu verteilt, ist allerdings unklar. Die Präzisionsmessungen mit neun Satelliten seit 1979 stellen Christopher Cox von der Firma Raytheon und der NASA-Forscher Benjamin Chao im US-Wissenschaftsjournal *Science* (Bd. 297, S. 831) vom Freitag vor.

FRANKFURTER RUNDSCHAU, 3. August 2002, Nr. 178/31, S. 32

© dpa Deutsche Presse-Agentur GmbH

Bevölkerung spät informiert

Trinkwasser von Fuldabrück mit Koli-Bakterien verseucht

FULDABRÜCK. Im Trinkwasser von Fuldabrück im Kreis Kassel sind Koli-Bakterien festgestellt worden – die Behörden haben die Bevölkerung aber erst sieben Tage später informiert. Die Ursache der Verseuchung ist unklar. Vermutet wird, dass Oberflächenquellen durch starke Regenfälle der vergangenen Wochen und durch gedüngte Felder verschmutzt wurden.

Am 1. August waren die Messergebnisse im Rathaus eingetroffen, doch erst am 7. August stand eine Mitteilung in den amtlichen Bekanntmachungen. Warum die 9000 Einwohner der vier Ortsteile nicht früher informiert wurden?

Man habe sich sofort an das Gesundheitsamt und an die Kasseler Städtischen Werke gewandt, sagte Bürgermeister Wilhelm Müller (SPD) der *FR*. Daraufhin seien die verseuchten Oberflächenquellen und die Leitungen gechlort worden. Und im Kreisgesundheitsamt habe man ihm empfohlen, die Bevölkerung über das amtliche Mitteilungsblatt zu informieren.

Das Kreisgesundheitsamt bestreitet diese Darstellung.

Inzwischen konnte für die Ortsteile Dennhausen, Dittershausen und Dörnhagen Entwarnung gegeben werden. Koli-Bakterien können Durchfall verursachen, was beispielsweise für Kleinkinder und ältere Menschen gefährlich sein kann.

Gundula Zeitz

FRANKFURTER RUNDSCHAU, 10. August 2002, Nr. 184/32, S. 29

Level 2

1. Wie heißt das Gegenteil? ✓

1. der Kursleiter
2. staatliche Schule
3. das Wahlfach
4. gerade Zahl
5. der Gleichstrom
6. organisch

2. Welches Wort hat die gleiche oder eine ähnliche Bedeutung? ✓

1. pädagogisch
2. das Buchzeichen
3. die Tutorin
4. die Geographie
5. die Dissertation
6. etw zensieren
7. die Karriere
8. das Experiment
9. die Friktion
10. der Strom
11. der Treibstoff
12. die Atomenergie
13. der Orbit
14. das Universum
15. das Raumschiff
16. das Vergrößerungsglas

3. Ordnen Sie die folgenden Noten von 1 bis 6. ✓

ausreichend, befriedigend, gut, mangelhaft, sehr gut, ungenügend

4. Welches Wort passt nicht? ✓

1. der Drehbleistift, der Filzstift, der Füller, der Leuchtsstift
2. der Antwortbogen, die Klausur, das Multiplechoice, das Zertifikat
3. das Diplom, der Doktorgrad, der Magister, der Meister
4. die Kunst, die Lektion, der Religionsunterricht, die Wirtschaftslehre
5. das Flussdiagramm, der Graph, das Leseverständnis, das Schaubild
6. etw lösen, etw nachholen, etw rechnen, etw schätzen
7. die Kernenergie, die Wärmeenergie, die Wasserkraft, die Windenergie

5. Welche Definition bzw. welches Synonym passt? ✓

a. der Abiturientin, b. die Austauschstudentin, c. die Erzieherin, d. die Kosmonautin, e. die Rektorin, f. die Sitzenbleiberin, g. die Stipendiatin

1. Empfängerin eines Stipendiums
2. weibliche Person, die die Reifeprüfung ablegen will oder abgelegt hat
3. Kindergärtnerin
4. Raumfahrerin
5. weibliche Person, die wegen eines Austausches im Ausland studiert
6. Leiterin einer Schule (Grund-, Haupt- usw.)
7. Schülerin, die nicht in die nächste Klasse versetzt wird

6. Wie heißt das entsprechende Adjektiv? ✓

1. das Maximum
2. das Minimum
3. die Säure
4. das Alkali
5. die Erziehung
6. die Begabung
7. die Sphäre

7. Welche Wörter gehören zusammen? ✓

a. das Diapositiv, b. die Fläche, c. die Hydraulik, d. der Lichtstrahl, e. der Objektträger, f. die Schallwelle, g. die Schwerkraft, h. verpesten

1. das Gravitationsgesetz
2. das Wasser
3. die Optik
4. die Akustik

5. das Mikroskop
6. die Geometrie
7. die Luft
8. der Projektor

8. Was passt nicht? ✓

1. -kurs: Abend-, Fort-, Grund-, Intensiv-
2. -studium: Aufbau-, Fern-, Grund-, Hinter-
3. -hochschule: Fach-, Musik-, Studium-, Volks-
4. -punkt: Gefrier-, Schwefel-, Schwer-, Siede-
5. -glas: Becher-, Messen-, Reagenz-, Vergrößerungs-
6. Raum-: -anzug, -fahrt, -kapsel, -landung

9. In jedem Satz fehlt ein Wort. ✓

> ausbilden, Austauschschüler, auswendig, Berufsschule, immatrikuliert, Lernstrategien, Sonderschule, Teilzeitstudent

1. An einigen Universitäten werden Kurse über _____ angeboten.
2. Er hat sich zum Schauspieler _____ lassen.
3. Die Verse hat sie _____ gelernt.
4. Wieviele Studenten sind an dieser Uni _____?
5. Dort werden Tischler, Schlosser und Schreiner an der _____ ausgebildet.
6. Er verbrachte ein Jahr als _____ in Deutschland.
7. Das Studium dauert länger, weil er als Berufstätiger nur _____ sein kann.
8. Der Junge geht auf eine _____ für geistig behinderte Kinder.

10. Welches Verb passt? ✓

> a. abziehen, b. bekommen, c. nehmen, d. schwänzen, e. stellen, f. testen, g. verlassen

1. die Universität vorzeitig
2. die Schule
3. Prügel
4. jmdn auf seine Intelligenz
5. etw in Frage
6. etw von etw
7. den Durchschnitt

11. Übersetzen Sie ins Englische.

„Brauchen Frauen eine andere Mathematik?" nennt sich ein internationales, fachübergreifendes Symposion der Hochschule Bremen am 18. und 19. Oktober. Im Mittelpunk stehen Maßnahmen zur Attraktivitätssteigerung technischer Studiengänge für Frauen ...   (dhu.)

Ein deutsch-italienischer Bachelor-Studiengang „Soziologie" beginnt zum Wintersemester an der Katholischen Universität Eichstätt-Ingolstadt (KU) und der Università degli Studie in Trient. Einschreibefrist ist der 2. Oktober ...   (*dhu.*)

An Filmschauspieler richtet sich ein Workshop „Europäische Regisseure arbeiten mit Schauspielern" der Internationalen Filmschule in Köln ...   (*re.*)

Die Abiturientenmesse „Einstieg Abi" findet am 13. und 14. September in Berlin statt. Hochschulen, Unternehmen, private Bildungsträger und Institutionen informieren auf dem Gelände der Messe Berlin ...

Gabriele Hermani

Frankfurter Allgemeine Zeitung, Samstag, 31. August 2002, Nr. 202/35, S. 53

12. Übersetzen Sie ins Englische.

Informatiker brechen am häufigsten ihr Studium ab

Industrie will künftig besser aufklären / Der Bedarf der Branche wird in den kommenden Jahren wachsen / Von Ingrid Hielle

Mehr als jeder zweite Informatik-Student in Deutschland bricht sein Studium ab. Das hat eine neue Untersuchung der Hochschul-Informationssystem GmbH (HIS) in Hannover ergeben. „Die meisten von ihnen scheitern bereits im Vorstudium, ein anderer Teil wird im Hauptstudium abgeworben", beklagt dazu Gerhard Zimmermann, Vorsitzender des Fakultätentages Informatik. Die Autoren der vom Bundesministerium für Bildung und Forschung geförderten Studie führen für die überdurchschnittlich hohe Abbruchquote bei den Informatik-Studenten vor allem den hohen Bedarf der Informationstechnik-Industrie an Computerspezialisten als Begründung an. Sie lockte die Studenten mit hohen Gehaltsversprechungen vorzeitig in die Betriebe.

   Die von HIS berechnete Abbruchquote für Informatik-Studenten setzt sich daraus zusammen, dass im Durchschnitt 37 Prozent aller Studienanfänger des Fachbereichs Informatik die Hochschulen ohne Diplom verlassen. Hinzu kommt eine „Schwundquote" von 16 Prozent – das sind die Informatik-Studenten, die mitten im Studium das Studienfach wechseln. Daraus ergibt sich eine Gesamtabbruchquote von 53 Prozent. Dieser Berechnung liegt ein von HIS schon Anfang der neunziger Jahre entwickeltes Verfahren zugrunde, das auf Bestandsdaten der amtlichen Hochschulstatistik und auf Ergebnisse von bundesweit repräsentativen HIS-Stichprobenuntersuchungen zurückgreift. Daraus geht hervor, dass im Durchschnitt der Studienfächer sowie der Universitäten und Fachhochschulen in Deutschland rund 27 Prozent der Studierenden ein Erststudium ohne Abschlussexamen beenden und auch später nicht wieder aufnehmen. Bei den Universitäten beträgt die durchschnittliche

Abbruchquote 30 Prozent, bei den Fachhochschulen hingegen nur 22 Prozent. Hinzu kommt die „Schwundquote". Sie umfasst alle Studierenden eines Jahrgangs, die keinen Abschluss in dem Bereich erworben haben, in dem sie sich ursprünglich einschrieben, sondern in ein anderes Fach überwechselten. Nicht berücksichtigt werden die Doppeleinschreibungen und die Zahl der „Studienanfänger", die sich eigentlich bereits in einem Zweitstudium immatrikulieren ...

Frankfurter Allgemeine Zeitung, Samstag, 31. August 2002, Nr. 202/35, S. 53

13. Übersetzen Sie ins Englische.

Norwegen stoppt vorerst die Kohlendioxid-Verklappung am Meeresgrund

Unsicherheit über Umweltfolgen und Rechtsaspekte sowie Protest von Greenpeace bewegen Oslo zur Umkehr

Von Hannes Gamillscheg (Kopenhagen)

Als „Sieg der Vernunft" hat die Umweltschutzorganisation Greenpeace den Beschluss der norwegischen Regierung begrüßt, ein internationales Pilotprojekt über die Verklappung von Kohlendioxid (CO_2) am Meeresgrund vorerst zu stoppen. Die Regierung in Oslo behält sich aber weitere Forschung in diese Richtung vor.

Das Experiment hätte zeigen sollen, ob sich die Tiefsee als Kohlendioxid-Abfallstätte eignet. Die Errichtung einer CO_2-Deponie in 800 Metern Meerestiefe zu Testzwecken war zuvor in erster Instanz von der staatlichen Umweltbehörde SFT gebilligt worden. Das norwegische Institut für Wasserforschung sowie Wissenschaftler aus den USA, Kanada, Australien und Japan wollten 5,4 Tonnen flüssiges CO_2 rund 100 Kilometer vor der Küste im Atlantik versenken, um zu testen, wie das Treibhausgas reagiert. Dessen unterseeische Lagerung gilt als mögliche Methode, die CO_2-Emissionen in die Atmosphäre zu verringern.

Doch die Unsicherheit über die Umweltfolgen und die rechtlichen Aspekte wogen schließlich schwerer als ein möglicher kurzfristiger Gewinn für die Klimarechnung. „Die Nutzung des Meeres als CO_2-Lagerstätte ist umstritten", sagte der konservative Umweltminister Börge Brende und verwies darauf, dass die Deponierung gegen internationale Gewässerschutzabkommen verstoßen könne.

Darauf pochte auch Greenpeace und erhob mit anderen Umweltgruppen gegen den SFT-Beschluss Einspruch. „Das Meer ist keine Abfallhalde", sagt Greenpeace-Klimaexperte Truls Gulowsen. „Es ist verboten, sowohl radioaktiven wie giftigen Abfall im Meer zu versenken, und das gilt auch für fossiles CO_2." Die internationale Forschergruppe hatte zuvor versucht, ihr Experiment vor der Küste Hawaiis zu erproben, war aber auch dort auf Ablehnung gestoßen. In Oslo hatte die Umweltbehörde zunächst weniger Bedenken: Von der vorgesehenen Lagerung von 5,4 Tonnen eigens für diesen

Zweck hergestelltem synthetischen Kohlendioxids seien kaum Umweltschäden zu erwarten.

Das bestritt auch Greenpeace nicht, wehrte sich aber aus prinzipiellen Gründen gegen das Experiment. Dieses solle den Weg für die Versenkung von CO_2 in großem Stil bahnen. Geplant ist, das CO_2 von mit fossilen Brennstoffen betriebenen Kraftwerken in Trennanlagen auszusondern und dann in konzentrierter Form durch Pipelines in die Tiefsee zu führen.

Die Forscher gehen davon aus, dass das Gas, mit den Meeresströmen verteilt, wegen seiner Schwere am Meeresboden bleiben werde. Dies könne aber unvorhersehbare negative Folgen für die Meeresökologie bedeuten und berge die Gefahr, dass das Treibhausgas eines Tages doch in die Atmosphäre entweiche, warnt Greenpeace. Die Versenkung von Kohlendioxid schaffe „eine unkontrollierbare Klimabombe für kommende Generationen".

Gänzlich verwerfen will Oslo die Pläne für eine Meeresdeponie als Klimaschutz-Versuch dennoch nicht. Forschung auch in diese Richtung könne nützlich sein, heißt es im Umweltministerium. Zuvor jedoch seien „breitere internationale Diskussionen" erforderlich. Ob eine CO_2-Verklappung gegen die Konvention zum Schutz des Nordost-Atlantiks verstößt, soll vor deren Treffen im Juni 2003 geklärt sein.

Mit unterseeischer Kohlendioxid-Lagerung hat Norwegen Erfahrung aus der Erdgasproduktion: Dabei wird das geförderte Gas von CO_2 getrennt, dieses wird in Brunnen zurückgepumpt. Dabei treibt das CO_2 jedoch nicht frei im Wasser, sondern liegt eingeschlossen viele Kilometer unter dem Meeresgrund im Gesteinsmassiv.

FRANKFURTER RUNDSCHAU, Samstag, 24. August 2002, Nr. 196/34, S. 1

Level 3

1. Wie heißt das Gegenteil? ✓

1. das Internat   4. induktiv
2. der Internatschüler   5. der Stalaktit
3. die Koedukation   6. Geisteswissenschaften

2. Welche Wörter gehören zusammen? ✓

a. die Abschussrampe, b. die Altphilologie, c. das Fernstudium, d. der Kernreaktor, e. die Konfessionsschule, f. das Pistill, g. die Standortnummer, h. die Sternschnuppe

1. das Buch
2. das Griechisch
3. der Fernkurs
4. die Religion
5. die Spaltung
6. der Wunsch
7. die Rakete
8. der Mörser

3. Wie heißen die kurzen Formen der folgenden Wörter? ✓
1. der Auszubildende
2. das Diapositiv
3. das Bundesausbildungsförderungsgesetz

4. Welches Wort hat die gleiche oder eine ähnliche Bedeutung? ✓
1. büffeln
2. jmdn tyrannisieren
3. die Weiterbildung
4. die Leihbibliothek
5. die Gedächtnishilfe
6. die Sozialwissenschaften
7. die Jura
8. die Volkswirtschaft
9. die Prüfungskommission
10. der Prüfling
11. die Pädagogin
12. die Quadratwurzel
13. das Theorem
14. die Nuklearenergie
15. porös
16. die Eklipse

5. Wie heißt das entsprechende Adjektiv? ✓
1. die Lernbehinderung
2. die Statistik
3. die Galaxie
4. das Molekül
5. der Widerstand

6. Welches Wort passt nicht? ✓
1. die Amerikanistik, die Anglistik, die Germanistik, die Informatik
2. das Ammoniak, das Chlor, das Quecksilber, der Stickstoff
3. die Begabung, die Fakultät, die Fertigkeit, die Leistung
4. kariertes Papier, liniertes Papier, das Löschpapier, das Schmierpapier
5. der Beweis, die Gleichung, der Trichter, das Verhältnis
6. die Erdkruste, die Erdspalte, der Verfall, die Verwerfung
7. hoch, die Potenz, die Quadratzahl, der Schall
8. der Raketenabschuss, der Rechenschieber, der Weltraumflug, der Wiedereintritt

7. Wie heißen die Zusammensetzungen? ✓

Integral	tiegel	1. *die Integralrechnung*
Geo	lager	2.
Raum	synthese	3.
Magnet	wissenschaften	4.
Schmelz	system	5.
Kugel	rechnung	6.
Logarithmen	feld	7.
Foto	theorie	8.
Perioden	forschung	9.
Urknall	tafel	10.

8. In jedem Satz fehlt ein Wort. ✓

Anwesenheitsliste, Auszeichnung, Dozent, Erdreich, Glaskolben, Hochschulreife, Kommilitone, Pipette, Praktikant, Schmiermittel

1. Was tut ein _____ während eines Praktikums?
2. Die _____ kann die Studenten oft zwingen, sich in einen Kurs hineinzusetzen.
3. Die Studentensprache unterscheidet sich durch Uni-spezifische Begriffe wie „Mensa" und „_____" von der Alltagssprache.
4. Er ist _____ für Anglistik an der Universität Potsdam.
5. Schon nach elf Jahren erreichen die Engländer die _____.
6. Die Preisträgerin freute sich sehr über die _____.
7. Ein Agrarexperte hat ein umweltfreundliches _____ aus der Canola-Ölpflanze entwickelt.
8. Dadurch waren mehrere tausend Liter Öl ins _____ gelangt.
9. In dem großen _____ befand sich eine undefinierbare Flüssigkeit.
10. Die Laborantin nimmt eine _____ und träufelt einen Tropfen Wasser auf den Punkt.

9. Wie heißen die Wendungen?

1. die Wurzel allen Übels
2. wie aus Erz gegossen dastehen
3. ein Zirkelschluss
4. in Verfall geraten
5. ferngelenktes Geschoss

10. Übersetzen Sie die folgenden Texte ins Englische.

„**Molekulare und strukturelle Produktgestaltung**" bietet die Universität Magdeburg zum Wintersemester an. Das Studienangebot bereitet auf Tätigkeiten in der pharmazeutischen Industrie vor. Bewerbungen sind bis zum 15. September möglich ... (*dhu.*)

Frankfurter Allgemeine Zeitung, Samstag, 31. August 2002, Nr. 202/35, S. 53

„**Internationale Betriebswirtschaftslehre**" bietet die Fachhochschule Darmstadt als berufsbegleitende Weiterbildung an. Anmeldeschluss für das kommende Sommersemester ist der 1. November. Eine Informationsveranstaltung findet am 9. Oktober statt ... (*re.*)

Frankfurter Allgemeine Zeitung, Samstag, 31. August 2002, Nr. 202/35, S. 53

Zahl der Bafög-Empfänger ist stark gestiegen
WIESBADEN, 23. August (dpa). Die Zahl der Empfänger von Leistungen nach dem Bundesausbildungsförderungsgesetz (Bafög) ist im vergangenen Jahr stark gestiegen. Wie das Statistische Bundesamt am Freitag in Wiesbaden mitteilte, erhielten rund 650 000 Lernende und Studierende

Bafög. Das waren 16 Prozent mehr als im Vorjahr. Die Ausgaben des Bundes und der Länder erhöhten sich sogar um 30 Prozent auf 1,65 Milliarden Euro. Grund ist eine Gesetzesänderung, nach der mehr junge Leute gefördert werden.

FRANKFURTER RUNDSCHAU, Samstag, 24. August 2002, Nr. 196/34, S. 5

© dpa Deutsche Presse-Agentur GmbH

Einmalige Potenzen
Was lange währt, wird endlich gut – auch in der Mathematik. Nach nunmehr 150 Jahren hat der Rumäne Preda Mihailescu eine Vermutung von Charles Catalan bewiesen. Er konnte zeigen, dass die Zahlen 8 (gleich 2^3) und 9 (gleich 3^2) die beiden einzigen Potenzen natürlicher Zahlen sind, die sich nur um 1 unterscheiden. Anders gesagt: Die Gleichung $x^m - y^n = 1$ hat nur eine Lösung mit natürlichen Zahlen größer als 1.

DIE ZEIT, 20. Juni, 2002, Nr. 26, S. 33

11. Schreiben Sie eine Zusammenfassung des folgenden Artikels.

Aus dem Beruf heraus ins Ausland zum Studium

Stipendien der CDG fördern die berufliche Weiterbildung in aller Welt / Von Edda von Homeyer

Immer mehr junge Fachkräfte in Deutschland haben Interesse daran, im Ausland Zusatzqualifikationen zu erwerben. Eine interessante Möglichkeit, für Nichtakademiker beispielsweise ein Aufbaustudium im Ausland zu absolvieren, ist, sich für ein spezielles Programm der Carl Duisberg Gesellschaft (CDG) zu bewerben.

Seit Start des Programms 1986 nutzten bislang mehr als 1200 Fachkräfte das Stipendienprogramm „Weiterbildung im Ausland in besonderen Fachgebieten" der Carl Duisberg Gesellschaft und erwarben neue Qualifikationen, zum Beispiel Masterabschlüsse ausländischer Universitäten. Inzwischen fördert die CDG etwa 1000 Berufstätige im Jahr.

Die Voraussetzungen sind folgende: Die Teilnehmer müssen eine abgeschlossene nichtakademische Ausbildung und mindestens ein Jahr Berufserfahrung vorweisen, den Fortbildungsplatz selbst herausfinden und nachweisen, dass eine gleichartige Fortbildung für sie in Deutschland nicht möglich ist. Das Bundesministerium für Bildung und Forschung, das die Stipendienmittel zur Verfügung stellt, möchte damit die berufliche Weiterbildung durch Nutzung ausländischer Angebote erweitern und einen Beitrag zur Gleichwertigkeit der beruflichen Bildung leisten. Gerade für Nichtakademiker mit oft mehrjähriger Berufserfahrung stellt eine theoretische Fortbildung mit starkem Praxisbezug, wie sie etwa in angelsächsischen Ländern üblich ist, eine optimale Zusatzqualifizierung dar.

Die Angehörigen medizinisch-therapeutischer Berufe, die sich insbesondere im englischsprachigen Raum wissenschaftlich fortbilden, stellen zur Zeit mit

41 Prozent die größte Berufsgruppe im Programm, gefolgt von gewerblichen Fachkräften. Grundsätzlich steht das Angebot der Förderung einer drei bis zwölfmonatigen praktischen oder theoretischen Vollzeit-Fortbildung Berufstätigen jeden Alters und aus allen fachlichen Bereichen offen. Frauen nutzen solche Angebote übrigens besonders intensiv: Mit 66 Prozent der Teilnehmer erweisen sie sich klar als der mobilere Teil der Gesellschaft.

Die jungen Fachkräfte gehen mit Mut und Ehrgeiz in die Welt, studieren an Colleges von England bis Australien, kommen mit Master-Abschlüssen und natürlich fließendem Englisch zurück und können sich anschließend trotz angespannter Wirtschaftslage oft unter mehreren Angeboten den besten Job auswählen. Schreiner, Keramikerinnen oder Gärtner qualifizierten sich in Japan, Elektroinstallateure, Logopädinnen oder Kaufleute in Amerika, Buchbinderinnen und Restauratoren aller Richtungen in europäischen Zentren ihres Faches. Da das Programm individuelle Fortbildungen fördert, ist eine Bewerbung jederzeit möglich.

Frankfurter Allgemeine Zeitung, Samstag, 7. September 2002, Nr. 208/36, S. 55

Unit 15

Agriculture

Level 1

Types of farming and farmers

Bauer, der (-n)	farmer
Bäuerin, die (-nen)	farmer, farmer's wife
Landwirtschaft, die (no pl.)	agriculture, farming
Landwirt(in), der/die (-e/nen)	farmer
landwirtschaftlich	agricultural
Landarbeiter(in), der/die (-/nen)	agricultural worker
Milchwirtschaft, die (no pl.)	dairy farming
Zucht, die (no pl.)	breeding
Schweinezucht, die (no pl.; -en)	pig-breeding; pig farm
Schweinezüchter(in), der/die (-/nen)	pig farmer
Rinderzucht, die (no pl.)	cattle breeding
Rinderzüchter(in), der/die (-/nen)	cattle breeder
Schaffarm, die (-en)	sheep farm
Fischzucht, die (no pl.)	fish farming
Fischzüchter(in), der/die (-/nen)	fish farmer
Obstbau, der (no pl.)	fruit-growing
Obstbauer, -bäuerin, der/die (-n/nen)	fruit farmer
Weinbau, der (no pl.)	wine growing
Weinbauer, -bäuerin, der/die (-n/nen)	wine grower

Livestock

Kuh, die (¨e)	cow
Bulle, der (-n)	bull
Kalb, das (¨er)	calf
eine Kuh melken	to milk a cow
Melkkuh, die (¨e)	milch cow
Melkmaschine, die (-n)	milking machine
Milchkanne, die (-n)	milk can; milk churn
Rinder, pl.	cattle
Schwein, das (-e)	pig
Ziege, die (-n)	goat, nanny goat
Hirt(in), der/die (-en/nen)	herdsman/ herdswoman
Ziegenhirt(in), der/die (-en/nen)	goatherd
Huhn, das (¨er)	chicken
Hahn, der (¨e)	rooster
Hähnchen, das (-)	chicken, young rooster
Henne, die (-n)	hen
Ente, die (-n)	duck
Futter, das (no pl.)	feed, fodder
ein Tier füttern	to feed an animal

Hühnerfutter, das (no pl.)	chicken feed	die Ernte einbringen	to bring in the crops
		etw ernten	to harvest sth
Schweinefutter, das (no pl.)	pigswill	etw schneiden	to reap sth
		Mais, der (no pl.)	corn, maize
Pferd, das (-e)	horse	Weizen, der (no pl.)	wheat
Pony, das (-s)	pony	Roggen, der (no pl.)	rye
Schaf, das (-e)	sheep	Stroh, das (no pl.)	straw
Schäfer(in), der/die (-/nen)	shepherd/shepherdess	Heu, das (no pl.)	hay
		heuen	to make hay
Lamm, das (¨er)	lamb	Heuernte, die (-n)	haymaking, hay harvest
Wiese, die (-n)	meadow		
Weide, die (-n)	pasture	Heuhaufen, der (-)	haystack
Weideland, das (no pl.)	pastureland	Heugabel, die (-n)	pitchfork
		Weinbeere, die (-n)	grape
Zaun, der (¨e)	fence	Weintraube, die (-n)	bunch of grapes
Elektrozaun, der (¨e)	electric fence	ein gutes/schlechtes Weinjahr	a good/bad year for wine

Crops

das Land bearbeiten	to work the land
(etw) pflügen	to plough (sth)
Pflug, der (¨e)	plough
Acker, der (¨)	field
Ackerland, das (no pl.)	arable land [being used]
Mist, der (no pl.)	dung, manure
misten	to do the manuring
einen Acker misten	to manure a field
Dung, der (no pl.)	dung, manure
Dünger, der (-)	fertilizer
(etw) düngen	to fertilize (sth)
Mäher, der (-)	mower
etw mähen	to reap sth
Ernte, die (-n)	harvest

Farm buildings

Bauernhof, der, (¨e)	farm
Landwirtschaft, die (-en)	farm
Hof, der (¨e)	farmyard
Stall, der (¨e)	stall, stable
Kuhstall, der (¨e)	cow shed
Pferde-, Rennstall, der (¨e)	stable
Hühnerstall, der (¨e)	henhouse, coop
Kaninchenstall, der (¨e)	rabbit hutch
Schafstall, der (¨e)	(sheep)cote
Schweinestall, der (¨e)	(pig)sty

Level 2

Types of farming and farmers

Kleinbauer, -bäuerin, der/die (-n/nen)	smallholder	Käserei, die (no pl.; -en)	cheese-making; cheese dairy
kleiner Landbesitz	smallholding	Käser(in), der/die (-/nen)	cheese-maker
intensive Landwirtschaft	intensive farming		
		Geflügelfarm, die (-en)	poultry farm
Landwirtschaft betreiben	to farm	Geflügelzucht, die (no pl.)	poultry farming
Molkerei, die (-en)	dairy		

Geflügelzüchter(in), der/die (-/nen)	poultry farmer
Gartenbau, der (no pl.)	horticulture
Gärtner(in), der/die (-/nen)	horticulturalist, market gardener
Bienenzucht, die (no pl.)	beekeeping
Bienenzüchter(in), der/die (-/nen)	beekeeper
Bienenvater, der (¨)	beekeeper
Ackerbau, der (no pl.)	agriculture, farming
Viehzucht, die (no pl.)	(live)stock breeding
Ackerbau und Viehzucht	mixed farming

Livestock

ein Tier schlachten	to slaughter an animal
Schlachthaus, das (¨er)	slaughterhouse
Schlachthof, der (¨e)	slaughterhouse
Schlachtrinder, pl.	beef cattle
Vieh, das (no pl.)	livestock, cattle
Ochse, der (-n)	ox
Joch, das (-e)	yoke
Gespann, das (-e)	team
Esel, der (-)	donkey
Maultier, das (-e)	mule
ein Tier züchten	to breed an animal
Truthahn, -henne, der/die (¨e/n)	turkey
Brut-, Legehenne, die (-n)	sitting hen/layer
Küken, das (-)	chick
Entenküken, das (-)	duckling
Entlein, das (-; poet.)	duckling
Gans, die (¨e)	goose
Gänserich, der (-e)	gander
Gänschen, das (-)	gosling
grasen, weiden	to graze
ein Tier weiden	to put an animal out to graze/pasture
ein Tier auf die Weide treiben	to put an animal out to pasture

Kuhhirt(in), der/die (-en/nen)	cowhand, cowherd
Futterkrippe, die (-n)	manger
Futtertrog, der (¨e)	feeding trough
Tragjoch, das (-e)	yoke [for carrying pails]
ein Tier tränken	to water an animal
ein Pferd putzen	to groom/brush down a horse
den Stall ausmisten	to clean/muck out the stable

Crops

das Land bebauen	to farm the land
bebaubares Land	arable land
bebaut/nicht bebaut sein	to be in/out of crop
das Land bestellen	to till the land
Ackergaul, der (¨e; coll.; pej.)	plough horse
etw umpflügen	to plough sth up
Furche, die (-n)	furrow, rut
Pflugfurche, die (-n)	furrow
Graben, der (¨)	ditch
Düngemittel, das (-)	fertilizer
Kunstdünger, der (-)	chemical fertilizer
Dreschmaschine, die (-n)	thresher
etw dreschen	to thresh sth
Mähdrescher, der (-)	combine harvester
Mähbinder, der (-)	reaper-binder
Getreide, das (no pl.)	grain, cereal
Futtergetreide, das (-)	forage cereal
Hafer, der (no pl.)	oats
Gerste, die (no pl.)	barley
Wurzelgemüse, das (no pl.)	root crop
Frühgemüse, das (-)	early vegetables
Vogelscheuche, die (-n)	scarecrow
Weinlese, die (-n)	grape harvest, vintage
Wimmet, der (no pl.; AU, CH)	grape harvest
Jahrgang, der (¨e)	vintage

Weinpresse, die (-n)	wine press	Nebengebäude, das (-)	outbuilding
Kelter, die (-n)	wine press	Hühnerhaus, das (¨er)	poultry house
Weinbehälter, der (-)	wine vat		
Fass, das (¨er)	cask	Hühnerhof, der (¨e)	chicken-run
Gärung, die (-en)	fermentation	Holzschuppen, der (-)	woodshed
etw in Flaschen abfüllen	to bottle sth	(Futter)silo, das (-s)	(fodder) silo
etw umfüllen	to decant sth	Bienenhaus, das (¨er)	apiary
		Bienenstock, -korb, der (¨e)	beehive

Farm buildings

Bauerngut, das (¨er)	farm(stead)
Bauernhaus, das (¨er)	farmhouse

Level 3

Types of farming and farmers

Bio-Landwirtschafts-betrieb, der (-e)	organic farm	industrieller Viehzuchtbetrieb, der (-e)	factory farm
Bio-Bauer/Bäuerin, der/die (-n/nen)	organic farmer		

Livestock

Gemüseanbaubetrieb, der (-e)	market garden	Eber, der (-)	boar
		Sau, die (¨e)	sow
Gestüt, das (-e)	stud farm	Ferkel, das (-)	piglet
Pächter(in) eines Bauernhofes, der/die (-/nen)	tenant farmer	Widder, der (-)	ram
		Schafbock, der (¨e)	ram
Bauernhof auf Genossenschafts-basis, der (¨e)	cooperative farm	Mutterschaf, das (-e)	ewe
		ein Tier scheren	to shear an animal
Senn, der (-e); Senner, der (-)	Alpine dairyman		
		Wolle (ab)scheren	to shear wool
Senn(er)in, die (-nen)	Alpine dairywoman	Ziegenbock, der (¨e)	billy goat
		Geiß, die (-en; S, AU, CH)	(nanny) goat
Sennerei, die (-en; S, AU)	Alpine dairy	Kicklein, das (-)	kid
Imkerei, die (no pl.)	beekeeping	Färse, die (-n)	heifer
Imker(in), der/die (-/nen)	beekeeper	Huf, der (-e)	hoof
		Euter, das (-)	udder
Legebatterie, die (-n)	battery farm	Zitze, die (-n)	teat
		Fohlen, das (-)	foal; colt; filly
Viehzüchter(in), der/die (-/nen)	stock breeder	Stutfohlen, das (-)	filly
		fohlen	to foal
industriell betriebene Viehzucht, die (no pl.)	factory farming	(Zucht)hengst, der (-e)	(breeding) stallion
		(Zucht)stute, die (-n)	(brood) mare

Hufeisen, das (-)	horseshoe	Saatgut, das (no pl.)	seed(s)
Maul- und Klauenseuche (MKS), die (no pl.)	foot-and-mouth disease	Saatkorn, das (¨er)	seed corn
		Strohballen, der (-)	straw bale
Rinderwahn(sinn) (BSE), der (no pl.)	mad cow disease	Strohballenpresse, die (-n)	straw baler
Grünfutter, das (no pl.)	green fodder	Garbe, die (-n)	sheaf
		Sichel, die (-n)	sickle
Mastfutter, das (no pl.)	(fattening) feed, mast	Ähre, die (-n)	ear [of grain]
		Kolben, der (-)	ear [of corn]
Silage, die (no pl.)	silage	Getreidestoppeln, pl.	stubble
Ölkuchen, der (-)	oil cake	Stoppelfeld, das (-er)	stubble field
ein Tier striegeln	to curry(comb) an animal	etw im Wechsel anbauen	to rotate sth
Geflügel, das (no pl.)	poultry		
Batteriehuhn, das (¨er)	battery hen	Fruchtwechsel, der (no pl.)	crop rotation
etw ausbrüten	to incubate sth	Fruchtfolge, die (no pl.)	crop rotation

Crops

Bewässerung, die (no pl.)	irrigation	Jauche, die (no pl.)	liquid manure
		etw jauchen	to manure sth
Bewässerungskanal, der (¨e)	irrigation canal	Stallmiststreuer, der (-)	manure spreader
Unkrautbekämp-fungsmittel, das (-)	weed killer	brachliegen	to lie fallow
		kalkhaltig	chalky
		lehmig	clayey
Schädling, der (-e)	pest	Rebstock, der (¨e)	(grape)vine
Schädlingsbe-kämpfung, die (no pl.)	crop spraying	Weinrebe, die (-n)	(grape)vine

Farm buildings

Schädlingsbekämp-fungsmittel, das (-)	pesticide	Scheune, die (-n)	barn
		Scheuer, die (-n; Upper German)	barn
Schädlingsbekämp-fungsflugzeug, das (-e)	crop sprayer [plane]	Heuboden, der (¨)	hayloft
		Heubühne, -diele, die (-n; CH)	hayloft
Schädlingsbekämp-fungsfahrzeug, das (-e)	crop sprayer [tractor]	Pferch, der (-e)	pen
		Hürde, die (-n)	pen
Buchweizen, der (no pl.)	buckwheat	Gerät-, Maschinen-schuppen, der (-)	tool/machinery shed
Hanf, der (no pl.)	hemp	Treib-, Kalthaus, das (¨er)	hot/coldhouse
Raps, der (no pl.)	rape		

Industry

Level 1

General

Produkt, das (-e)	product
(Handels)ware, die (-n)	merchandise
Verpackung, die (-en)	packaging, wrapping
vakuumverpackt	vacuum-packed
Ladung, die (-en)	load, batch
Sektor, der (-en)	sector
öffentlicher/privater Sektor	public/private sector
kapital-, arbeitsintensiv	capital/labour-intensive

Industries

Schwer-, Leichtindustrie, die (-n)	heavy/light industry
Autoindustrie, die (-n)	car industry
Chemieindustrie, die (-n)	chemical industry
Metallindustrie, die (-n)	metal industry
Eisenindustrie, die (-n)	iron industry
Stahlindustrie, die (-n)	steel industry
Ölindustrie, die (-n)	oil industry
Tourismusindustrie, die (-n)	tourist industry
Tourismusbranche, die (-n)	tourist industry
Freizeitindustrie, die (-n)	leisure industry
Filmindustrie, die (-n)	film industry
Computerbranche, die (-n)	computer industry
Lebensmittelindustrie, die (-n)	food industry
Fastfoodindustrie, die (no pl.)	fast food industry
Schokoladenindustrie, die (no pl.)	chocolate industry
Kommunikations-industrie, die (-n)	communications industry
Modeindustrie, die (-n)	fashion industry

Personnel

Arbeiter(in), der/die (-/nen)	worker, labourer, blue-collar worker
ungelernt	unskilled
angelernt	semi-skilled
Hilfsarbeiter(in), der/die (-/nen)	unskilled worker
Facharbeiter(in), der/die (-/nen)	skilled worker
Schwerarbeiter(in), der/die (-/nen)	manual worker
Vorarbeiter(in), der/die (-/nen)	foreman/forewoman
Manager(in), der/die (-/nen)	manager
Angestellte(r), der/die (adj. decl.)	(salaried) employee
Büroangestellte(r), der/die (adj. decl.)	office worker, white-collar worker
leitende(r) Angestellte(r), der/die (adj. decl.)	executive
Aufseher(in), der/die (-/nen)	supervisor

Premises and production

Fabrik, die (-en)	factory
Werk, das (-e)	works, factory, plant
Betrieb, der (-e)	factory, works
Autofabrik, die (-en)	car factory

Textilfabrik, die (-en)	textile factory
Wollspinnerei, die (-en)	woollen mill
Baumwollspinnerei, die (-en)	cotton mill
etw spinnen	to spin sth
Weberei, die (-en)	weaving mill
Porzellanfabrik, die (-en)	porcelain factory
Konservenfabrik, die, (-en)	cannery
etw eindosen	to can sth
Schokoladenfabrik, die (-en)	chocolate factory
Druckerei, die (-en)	printing works
Druckerpresse, die (-n)	printing press
etw drucken	to print sth
Eisenwerk, das (-e)	ironworks
Stahlwerk, das (-e)	steelworks
Brauerei, die (no pl.; -en)	brewing; brewery
etw brauen	to brew sth
etw herstellen	to manufacture sth
etw maschinell herstellen	to machine sth
End-, Nebenprodukt, das (-e)	end product/ by-product

Produktion, die (-en)	output
etw automatisieren	to automate sth
Arbeitsplatz, der (¨e)	work place, work station, workspace
Lager, das (-)	warehouse, storeroom, stockroom
Lagerhalle, die (-n)	warehouse

Machinery, tools and equipment

Werkbank, die (¨e)	workbench
Gerät, das (-e)	piece of equipment
(Ersatz)teil, der (-e)	(spare) part
Pumpe, die (-n)	pump
Schalter, der (-)	switch
Werkzeugmaschine, die (-n)	machine tool
(Maschinen)webstuhl, der (¨e)	(automatic) loom
Setzmaschine, die (-n)	typesetting machine
Walzwerk, das (-e)	rolling mill
Kran, der (-e or ¨e)	crane
Kipper, der (-)	dump truck
Betonmischmaschine, die (-n)	cement mixer
Gabelstapler, der (-)	forklift

Level 2

General

Tag-, Nachtschicht, die (-en)	day/night shift
Nachschicht haben	to be on night shift
Früh-, Spätschicht, die (-en)	early/late shift
Unternehmen des privaten Sektors, das (-)	private sector company
etw verstaatlichen	to nationalize sth
etw industrialisieren	to industrialize sth
Patent, das (-e)	patent
etw patentieren lassen	to patent sth

Industries

neue Technologien, pl.	new technologies
Spitzentechnologie, die (-n)	leading-edge technology
High-Tech-Industrie, die (-n)	hi-tech industry
Bergbau, der (no pl.)	mining
Kohlenbergbau, der (no pl.)	coal industry
Forstwirtschaft, die (no pl.)	forestry
Waffenindustrie, die (-n)	armaments/weapons industry

Bauindustrie, die (-n)	building industry
Schiffbau, der (no pl.)	shipbuilding
Raumfahrtindustrie, die (-n)	aerospace industry
Hotelgewerbe, das (no pl.)	hotel industry
Textilindustrie, die (-n)	textile industry
Wollindustrie, die (no pl.)	wool industry
Bekleidungsindustrie, die (-n)	clothing/apparel industry
Hutindustrie, die (no pl.)	millinery industry
Getränkeindustrie, die (-n)	beverage industry
Werbeindustrie, die (-n)	advertising industry
Verlagsindustrie, die (-n)	publishing industry
Medienindustrie, die (-n)	media industry

Personnel

Hersteller(in), der/die (-/nen)	manufacturer
Industrielle(r), der/die (adj. decl.)	industrialist
Techniker(in), der/die (-/nen)	technician
Packer(in), der/die (-/nen)	packer
Aushilfskraft, die (¨e)	temporary worker
Metallarbeiter(in), der/die (-/nen)	metal worker
Schlosser(in), der/die (-/nen)	fitter, metal worker
Weber(in), der/die (-/nen)	weaver
Spinner(in), der/die (-/nen)	spinner

Premises and production

Massenproduktion, die (no pl.)	mass production
Überproduktion, die (no pl.)	overproduction
eine Maschine bedienen	to operate a machine
Fließband, das (¨er)	assembly line
Gießerei, die (-en)	foundry
etw gießen	to cast sth
Töpferei, die (-en)	pottery
etw töpfern	to throw sth, make sth out of clay
Gaswerk, das (-e)	gasworks
Eisenhütte, die (-n)	ironworks
Kohlenrevier, das (-e)	coal field
Grube, die (-n)	mine, pit, colliery
Zeche, die (-n)	coal mine, pit, colliery
Kohlenbergwerk, das (-e)	coal mine
Ölfeld, das (-er)	oil field
Bohrinsel, die (-n)	offshore drilling rig
Raffinerie, die (-n)	refinery
etw raffinieren	to refine sth
Erdölraffinerie, die (-n)	oil refinery
Zuckerraffinerie, die (-n)	sugar refinery
Brennerei, die (-en)	distillery
Kaffeebrennerei, die (-en)	coffee-roasting plant
Ziegelbrennerei, die (-en)	brickworks
Sägewerk, das (-e)	sawmill
etw fräsen	to mill sth
Papierfabrik, die (-en)	paper mill
Papiermühle, die (-n)	paper mill
etw walzen	to mill sth
Munitionsfabrik, die (-en)	munitions factory

Machinery, tools and equipment

Bohrmaschine, die (-n)	drilling machine
Fräse, die (-n)	milling machine
Kettensäge, die (-n)	chainsaw

Vorschlaghammer, der (-)	sledgehammer	Achse, die (-n)	axle
Schweißbrenner, der (-)	welding torch	Träger, der (-)	girder
		Flansch, der (-e)	flange
		Hebebock, der (¨e)	(hydraulic) jack
Treibriemen, der (-)	belt	Rolle, die (-n)	pulley
Zahn, der (¨e)	cog	Winde, die (-n)	windlass
Zahnrad, das (¨er)	cogwheel	Fernsteuerung, Fernlenkung, die (-en)	remote control
Getriebe, das (-)	gears, gearbox, drive, works		

Level 3

General

Klarsichtfolie, die (-n)	shrink-wrap
etw einschweißen	to shrink-wrap sth
das verarbeitende Gewerbe	the manufacturing sector
Betriebskosten, pl.	running costs
Industriespionage, die (no pl.)	industrial espionage
Arbeitsstunde, die (-n)	man-hour
Produktionszeit, die (-en)	lead time
Inventur, die (-en)	stocktaking
Inventur machen	to stocktake

Industries

Grundstoffindustrie, die (-n)	primary industry
verarbeitende Industrie	manufacturing industry
Dienstleistungs-branche, die (-n)	service industry
Vergnügungsindustrie, die (-n)	entertainment industry
Luxusgüterindustrie, die (-n)	luxury goods industry
Hochbau, der (no pl.)	structural engineering
Tiefbau, der (no pl.)	civil engineering [excluding construction of buildings]

Hoch- und Tiefbau	civil engineering
Maschinenbau, der (no pl.)	mechanical engineering
Elektrotechnik, die (no pl.)	electrical engineering
Pharmaindustrie, die (-n)	pharmaceuticals industry
Präzisionswerk-zeugindustrie, die (no pl.)	precision tool industry
Rüstungsindustrie, die (-n)	armaments industry
Munitionsindustrie, die (no pl.)	munitions industry
Kernindustrie, die (-n)	nuclear industry
Heimindustrie, die (-n)	cottage industry
Wachstumsindustrie, die (-n)	growth industry
Zulieferindustrie, die (-n)	ancillary industry

Personnel

Monteur(in), der/die (-e/nen)	fitter
Nieter(in), der/die (-/nen)	riveter
Schweißer(in), der/die (-/nen)	welder
Gießer(in), der/die (-/nen)	caster, founder

Former(in), der/die (-/nen)	molder	Flöz, das (-e)	seam
Dreher(in), der/die (-/nen)	turner	Grubengas, das (no pl.)	firedamp
Brauer(in), der/die (-/nen)	brewer	Belüftung, die (no pl.)	ventilation
Lagerist(in), der/die (-en/nen)	stockman/stockwoman	Grubenlampe, die (-n)	safety lamp
Gerber(in), der/die (-/nen)	tanner	(Korn)mühle, die (-n)	flour mill
		etw mahlen	to grind sth, mill sth
Wollkämmer(in), der/die (-/nen)	wool-carder	Kiesgrube, die (-n)	gravel pit
		Zementwerk, das (-e)	cement works
		Spannbeton, das (no pl.)	prestressed concrete
		(Schiffs)werft, die (-en)	shipyard

Premises and production

Produktionsstätte, die (-n)	shop floor
Maschinenhalle, die (-n)	machine shop
Montagehalle, die (-n)	assembly shop
Lackiererei, die (-en)	paint shop
Kantine, die (-n)	canteen
Versandabteilung, die (-en)	shipping department
Expedition, die (-en)	shipping department
Aufbereitungsanlage, die (-n)	processing plant
Schlackenhalde, die (-n)	slag heap
Legierung, die (-en)	alloy
Spritzgussverfahren, das (-)	diecasting
Hochofen, der (¨)	blast furnace
Sprengarbeiten, pl.	blasting

Machinery, tools and equipment

Schraubstock, der (¨e)	vice
Gehrungswinkel, der (-)	bevel
Gehrmaß, das (-e)	bevel
Schraubzwinge, die (-n)	clamp
Drehbank, die (¨e)	lathe
Punze, die (-n)	punch
batteriebetrieben	battery powered
mit Netzanschluss, für Netzbetrieb	mains powered
Kurbel, die (-n)	crank
Kurbelwelle, die (-n)	crankshaft
Ratsche, die (-n)	ratchet
Dichtung, die (-en)	gasket
Stromkreisunterbrecher, der (-)	circuit breaker

Exercises

Level 1

1. Wie heißt das Gegenteil? ✓

1. die Schwerindustrie
2. ungelernter Arbeiter
3. die Kuh
4. der private Sektor
5. arbeitsintensiv

2. Welches Wort hat die gleiche oder eine ähnliche Bedeutung? ✓
1. die Tourismusindustrie
2. die Fabrik
3. der Bauer
4. der Dung
5. die Farm

3. Wie heißt das passende Verb? ✓

> a. brauen, b. drucken, c. düngen, d. einbringen, e. ernten, f. melken, g. spinnen

1. eine Kuh   5. Bücher
2. einen Acker   6. Garn
3. die Ernte   7. Heu
4. Bier

4. Welches Wort passt nicht? ✓
1. der Bergbau, die Fischzucht, der Obstbau, die Schweinezucht
2. der Hahn, die Henne, der Hohn, das Huhn
3. das Hühnerhaus, der Pferdestall, der Schafstall, der Stahl
4. der Artikel, das Lager, das Produkt, die Ware
5. die Aufseherin, die Managerin, die Schwerarbeiterin, die Vorarbeiterin
6. die Baumwollspinnerei, die Druckerei, die Textilfabrik, die Weberei
7. der Gabelstapler, die Heugabel, der Kran, der Kipper

5. Welche Wörter gehören zusammen? ✓

> a. die Autofabrik, b. der Hirt, c. die Konservenfabrik, d. der Maschinenwebstuhl,
> e. die Modeindustrie, f. die Setzmaschine, g. die Weintraube

1. die Weberei   5. der Weinbau
2. die Druckerei   6. Rinder
3. die Dose   7. der Wagen
4. Kleider

6. Wie heißt das junge Tier? ✓
1. die Kuh
2. der Hahn
3. das Schaf

7. Bauer oder Züchter? ✓
1. Schweine_____
2. Rinder_____
3. Wein_____
4. Obst_____
5. Fisch_____

8. Wie heißen die Wendungen?

1. Schwein haben
2. mit ihm kann man Pferde stehlen
3. einen Streit vom Zaun brechen
4. die Ernte seines Fleißes
5. Stroh im Kopf haben
6. Geld wie Heu haben

9. In jedem Satz fehlt ein Wort. ✓

> Büroangestellte, düngen, Landwirtschaft, mähen, Milchkanne, Nebenprodukt, pflügen, Schweinestall, Weide

1. Jeder 8. Arbeitsplatz hängt von der _____ ab.
2. Mit der _____ holte man die Milch direkt beim Bauern.
3. Frühmorgens zieht er mit seiner Herde allein auf die _____.
4. Die Bauern glauben, dass sie mehr ernten können, wenn sie intensiver _____.
5. Bauern in Niedersachsen dürfen nicht mehr mit Gülle, Jauche und flüssigem Geflügelkot _____.
6. Die Bauern _____ ihre Wiesen fast immer von außen nach innen.
7. Der kräftige Geruch in der Luft stammt aus dem nahen _____.
8. Jeden Tag sendet und empfängt der typische _____ sechszig E-Briefe.
9. Als _____ kommt Schlacke aus Hochofen und Stahlwerk.

10. Suchen Sie eine andere Bedeutung.

1. die Zucht   5. der Hof
2. die Ziege   6. das Werk
3. die Ente   7. die Pumpe
4. der Mist   8. der Schalter

11. Übersetzen Sie ins Englische.

Mistmanagement

SYDNEY, 27. September (afp). Aus Wut über verweigerte Lohnerhöhungen sind die Wärter des Zoos von Sydney in einen geruchsintensiven Bummelstreik getreten: Sie wollen so lange den Dung der Tiere nicht mehr wegkarren, bis ihnen das Management doch noch die geforderten drei Prozent mehr bezahlt, wie ihre Gewerkschaft am Freitag verkündete.

Besonders erbost sind die Wärter darüber, dass das Management sich selbst eine Gehaltsverbesserung genehmigte, bei den Arbeitern aber mit dem Argument hart blieb, sie leisteten nicht genug. „Etwas stinkt hier zum Himmel, und das soll auch das Publikum merken", sagte dazu der Sprecher des australischen Gewerkschaftsbunds, Russ Collison. Die Regierung des australischen Bundesstaats New South Wales hatte die Anhebung der Löhne für den gesamten öffentlichen Dienst bereits bewilligt.

FRANKFURTER RUNDSCHAU, Samstag, 28. September 2002, Nr. 226/39, S. 1

Elektro-Industrie muss alte Geräte entsorgen

Umweltminister Trittin feiert Kompromiss über EU-Richtlinie als Durchbruch

FRANKFURT A. M. Im jahrelangen Streit über den Umgang mit Elektroschrott haben EU-Ministerrat und Europäisches Parlament einen Kompromiss gefunden, der das Einsammeln und Verwerten gebrauchter Waschmaschinen, Kühlschränke, Computer, Fernseher, Telefone und weiterer Geräte von 2005 an europaweit einheitlich regelt. Zufrieden zeigt sich Bundesumweltminister Jürgen Trittin (Bündnis 90 / Die Grünen): „Dies ist der entscheidende Schritt zur Durchsetzung der Produktverantwortung in einem Bereich, der bisher von stetig steigenden Abfallmengen gekennzeichnet war."

Von einem „Etappensieg" spricht der hiesige Branchenverband ZVEI. Nun komme es darauf an, wie die EU-Vorgabe national umgesetzt werde. Zwar werde die Verwertung in Deutschland pro Jahr zwischen 350 und 500 Millionen Euro kosten, schätzt ZVEI-Hauptgeschäftsführer Gotthard Graß. Doch positiv wertet er, dass eine „Sippenhaftung" der Branche abgewendet worden sei. Stattdessen gelte das Prinzip der individuellen Verantwortung jedes Anbieters für die eigenen Produkte. Für alte Geräte, die vor Inkrafttreten der Richtlinie auf dem Mark waren, soll die Industrie eine gemeinsames Modell entwerfen, das die Finanzierung dieser Aufgabe sichert.

Umweltminister Trittin hebt in seiner Erklärung hervor, dass ein verbindliches Sammelziel von mindestens vier Kilogramm Elektroschrott pro Einwohner und Jahr festgelegt wurde. Zudem müsse die Industrie bei der Verwertung festgelegte Quoten erfüllen. Außerdem ist sie laut Trittin verpflichtet, die Sammlung ab den Rücknahmestellen sowie die umweltgerechte Entsorgung zu bezahlen.

Die kommunalen Sammelstellen, die in Deutschland seit langem vielerorts etabliert sind, dürfen weiter betrieben werden, wobei offen gelassen wird, ob Industrie oder Städte und Gemeinden die Kosten für diese Dienstleistung tragen. Diese Entscheidung bleibt dem nationalen Gesetzgeber überlassen. Die Industrie-Lobby ZVEI will freilich „deutliche Signale der Politik" empfangen haben, dass die Wirtschaft hier aus der Pflicht genommen wird.

Die geplante Richtlinie tritt 2003 in Kraft, wenn Ministerrat und Europäisches Parlament jeweils dieses Ergebnis, das der Vermittlungsausschuss beider Institutionen erzielt hat, bestätigen.

Markus Sievers

FRANKFURTER RUNDSCHAU, Samstag, 12. Oktober 2002, Nr. 237/41, S. 9

Level 2

1. Wie heißt das junge Tier? ✓
1. das Huhn
2. die Ente
3. die Gans

2. Wie heißt das Gegenteil? ✓

1. die Nachtschicht
2. die Frühschicht
3. der Truthahn
4. die Gans
5. bebaut sein

3. Welches Wort hat die gleiche oder eine ähnliche Bedeutung? ✓

1. die Fernsteuerung
2. der Bienenzüchter
3. grasen
4. die Weinlese
5. die Weinpresse
6. der Bienenstock
7. das Schlachthaus
8. die Papierfabrik

4. Wie heißt das passende Verb? ✓

> a. abfüllen, b. ausmisten, c. bebauen, d. bedienen, e. betreiben, f. putzen,
> g. raffinieren, h. töpfern, i. treiben, j. verstaatlichen

1. Landwirtschaft
2. ein Tier auf die Weide
3. ein Pferd
4. den Stall
5. das Land
6. den Wein in Flaschen
7. Privatbetriebe
8. eine Maschine
9. eine Vase
10. Zucker

5. Wie heißen die Zusammensetzungen? ✓

~~Brut~~	drescher	1. *die Bruthenne*
Futter	rinder	2.
Pflug	tier	3.
Mäh	gang	4.
Vogel	~~henne~~	5.
Schlacht	furche	6.
Jahr	hirt	7.
Wein	scheuche	8.
Maul	trog	9.
Kuh	behälter	10.

6. Welches Wort passt nicht? ✓

1. die Furche, das Getriebe, der Graben, die Grube
2. die Bekleidungsindustrie, die Textilindustrie, die Werbeindustrie, die Wollindustrie
3. der Metallarbeiter, der Packer, der Schlosser, der Schweißer
4. die Käserei, die Konditorei, die Milchwirtschaft, die Molkerei

5. die Gerste, das Getreide, der Hafen, der Hafer
6. das Eisenwerk, die Fräse, die Kettensäge, das Sägewerk
7. der Bergbau, das Kohlenbergwerk, der Schiffbau, die Zeche

7. Ergänzen Sie das deutsche Substantiv und den Artikel. ✓

Artikel	Substantiv	
1.		aerospace industry
2.		beverage industry
3.		building industry
4.		coal industry
5.		hotel industry
6.		millinery industry
7.		publishing industry
8.		armaments (weapons) industry

8. Welche Definition passt? ✓

1. der Hersteller	a. tragender Balken
2. die Aushilfskraft	b. Fabrik, in der Metall gegossen wird
3. der Träger	c. Käsemacher
4. die Brennerei	d. kleine, junge Ente
5. die Gießerei	e. jmd, der aushilft
6. der Käser	f. chemisch hergestellter Dünger
7. die Viehzucht	g. jmd, der etw herstellt
8. das Entlein	h. Gärfutterbehälter
9. der Kunstdünger	i. Betrieb für die Herstellung von Branntwein
10. das Silo	j. Zucht von Nutzvieh

9. In jedem Satz fehlt ein Wort. ✓

Bienenzucht, Dreschmaschine, Eisenhütte, Fließband, Gärung, Geflügelzüchter, Kleinbauer, Massenproduktion, Vorschlaghammer

1. Er ist _____, der nur zwei Hektar Land besitzt.
2. Von billigerem Getreide werden Schweine- und _____ profitieren.
3. Viele Imker betreiben die _____ als Hobby.
4. Die _____ bläst die Spreu auf die Felder.
5. Die alkoholische _____ kann mehrere Wochen dauern.
6. Mit dem mechanischen Webstuhl wurde die _____ möglich.
7. Sein Vater arbeitet am _____ des Automobilkonzerns.

8. Das Panzerglas hat er mit einem _____ zertrümmert.
9. Er will die älteste Fabrik in der Stadt übernehmen, eine alte _____.

10. *Schriftliche Übung. Beschreiben Sie eine Industrie in Deutschland, z. B. die Schokoladenindustrie, das Autoindustrie, die Getränkeindustrie.*

11. *Übersetzen Sie ins Deutsche.* ✓
1. We slaughter 500 pigs per week.
2. The ox pulls a plough very slowly.
3. Many farmers breed pigs on the side.
4. They can put their sheep out to graze wherever they want.
5. He bought himself a small farmstead.
6. The fire broke out in a woodshed.
7. Unfortunately he didn't patent his discovery.
8. In the area of leading-edge technology, Germany lies far behind the USA.
9. The culprits opened the safe with a welding torch.
10. He was an industrialist and one of the richest men in Europe.

12. *Übersetzen Sie ins Englische.*

Hessens Bauern fahren weniger in die Scheune, ein

Backweizen soll im Preis eher stabil bleiben, bei Kartoffeln gehen die Preise leicht zurück / Neue Trends bei Tomaten und Gurken

Von Stephan Börnecke

Geringere Erträge, manchmal mangelnde Qualität, zum Teil unbefriedigende Preise – für Hessens Getreidebauern fiel die Ernte dieses Jahr durchweg magerer aus als die Rekordernte vor einem Jahr. Bei Obst und Gemüse hingegen gibt es deutlicher als in früheren Jahren extreme regionale Unterschiede. Mancherorten blieb die Befruchtung aus, da die Bienen im kalten April und Mai kaum flogen.

FRANKFURT A.M. Noch Anfang Juni, sagt Lothar Kölner, Getreidechef bei der Raiffeisen Warenzentrale Rhein-Main, „haben wir gedacht, wohin mit diesen riesigen Mengen, die da auf den Feldern heranreifen. Wo können wir das alles einlagern?" Doch nur wenige Wochen später war klar: Von der erhofften Rekordernte beim Weizen blieb nur wenig übrig. Denn es folgten heiße Wochen, in denen die Ähren nur wenig schwerer wurden. „Das hat dem Weizen nicht sehr gut getan." Von „Schmachtkorn" sprechen die Landwirte dann.

Vor allem in den neuen Bundesländern und Niedersachsen machten später im Jahr dann noch Regenfälle es unmöglich, das schon reife Korn zu ernten. Weiter im Westen und Süden und damit auch in Hessen habe es zwar auch „ein paar Schläge" gegeben, doch sei hier zu Lande das Mengen-Ergebnis erheblich besser. Besser war dran, wer früh ernten konnte, denn eine spätere Ernte führte auch in Hessen angesichts der Regenperioden zu Ausfällen.

„Mit einem blauen Auge davongekommen", sagt Kölner, doch es gibt Abstriche: Denn nur etwa 80 Prozent der bei der Warenzentrale aufgekauften Ernte sei auch mühlenfähig. Nicht immer stimmt die Backqualität – eine Folge vor allem des trockenen Junis, einer Zeit also, in der das Korn Eiweiß anreichert. Zwar werden nur 38 Prozent des Weizens in Deutschland zu Mehl vermahlen; das Gros geht in die Stärke- oder Kraftfutterproduktion oder landet gleich im Trog. Doch weil vor allem Elite-Sortimente fehlen, könnte es partiell Engpässe geben.

Dass trotz dieser Situation die Preise für Backweizen nicht uferlos steigen, sondern eher stabil bleiben bis moderat wachsen, erklärt Kölner mit der internationalen Lage. Die EU-Kommission habe es zugelassen, dass nach Deutschland immer mehr Getreide aus Osteuropa komme; darunter zunehmend Spitzenqualitäten – und zwar zu niedrigen Preisen. So versucht der Händler die Hoffnungen der Bauern auf allzu heftige Aufschläge bei den Topqualitäten zu dämpfen. Allerdings gehen sowohl Experten in Hessen als auch das Bundeslandwirtschaftsministerium wegen einer weltweit geringeren Ernte von einem insgesamt steigenden Weizenpreis aus. Je nach Qualität gibt es derzeit zwischen acht und zwölf Euro je Doppelzentner. „Da kommt im Frühjahr noch ein Euro drauf", sagt Ernst-August Hildebrandt vom Hessischen Dienstleistungszentrum für Landwirtschaft, Naturschutz und Gartenbau ...

FRANKFURTER RUNDSCHAU, Samstag, 12. Oktober 2002, Nr. 237/41, S. 28

Level 3

1. Ergänzen Sie die Tabelle. ✓

männlich	weiblich	jung
1. der Widder		
2.	die Sau	
3. der Ziegenbock		
4.		das Fohlen

2. Welches Wort hat die gleiche oder eine ähnliche Bedeutung? ✓

1. der Fruchtwechsel
2. die Weinrebe
3. die Heubühne
4. die Hürde
5. die Bienenzucht
6. die Scheune
7. die Expedition
8. das Gehrmaß

3. Welche Wörter gehören zusammen? ✓

a. die Garbe, b. das Gestüt, c. der Gießer, d. der Kolben, e. die Legebatterie, f. der Raps, g. die Sennerei, h. die Sichel

1. Pferd	5. das Stroh
2. die Kuh	6. der Mais
3. die Henne	7. mähen
4. das Öl	8. das Eisen

4. Welches Wort passt nicht? ✓

1. die Freizeitindustrie, die Heimindustrie, die Luxusgüterindustrie, die Vergnügungsindustrie
2. die Munitionsindustrie, die Rüstungsindustrie, die Waffenindustrie, die Zulieferindustrie
3. etw einschweißen, die Klarsichtfolie, die Schlackenhalde, die Verpackung
4. der Gerber, der Monteur, der Nieter, der Schweißer
5. das Batteriehuhn, das Geflügel, die Legehenne, die Legierung
6. die Färse, das Grünfutter, der Ölkuchen, die Silage
7. die Drehbank, das Flöz, die Schraubzwinge, der Schraubstock
8. die Elektrotechnik, der Gartenbau, der Hochbau, der Maschinenbau

5. Wie heißt das passende Verb? ✓

> a. abscheren, b. ausbrüten, c. jauchen, d. machen, e. mahlen, f. striegeln

1. Inventur
2. Kaffee
3. Wolle
4. ein Pferd
5. Eier
6. ein Feld

6. Wie heißt das Gegenteil? ✓

1. der Hochbau
2. batteriebetrieben
3. die Sennerin
4. bebaut sein
5. die Zuchtstute

7. In jedem Satz fehlt ein Wort. ✓

> Arbeitsstunde, Betriebskosten, Bio-Bauern, Buchweizen, Industriespionage, Produktionszeit, Saatgut, Schädling

1. Das Rindfleisch der deutschen _____ ist BSE-frei.
2. Dieser Mais ist gegen den _____ „Maiszünsler" widerstandsfähig.
3. Zu den alternativen Getreidearten zählen Amaranth, _____ und Quinoa.
4. Wie die anderen Bauern erhielt sie vom Roten Kreuz _____.
5. Das Flugzeug soll der Fluggesellschaft jährliche _____ von 150 Mio. DM sparen.
6. Letztes Jahr gab es über 1000 Fälle von _____.
7. Im Jahre 1992 mussten in Deutschland für eine _____ rund 30 DM bezahlt werden.
8. Die _____ dieses Weihnachtskuchens dauert ungefähr 30 Stunden.

8. Suchen Sie eine andere Bedeutung.

1. die Dichtung
2. die Ratsche
3. der Dreher
4. die Mühle

9. Übersetzen Sie ins Englische.

Aventis streicht Arbeitsplätze
Die französische Gewerkschaft CGT berichtet, der deutsch-französische
Pharmahersteller Aventis plane, in Pariser Forschungszentren 545 Stellen zu
streichen. Das habe das Management Arbeitnehmervertretern gesagt.

FRANKFURTER RUNDSCHAU, Samstag, 19. Oktober 2002, Nr. 243/42, S. 10

Brüssel will Klage gegen Südkorea erheben

BRÜSSEL (rtr). Der Streit über Schiffbau-Subventionen zwischen der
Europäischen Kommission und Südkorea eskaliert. Nach monatelangen
Verhandlungen hat die Brüsseler Behörde die Gespräche mit den Ostasiaten
für gescheitert erklärt. „Es gibt fundamentale Meinungsverschiedenheiten
über die Preise für koreanische Schiffe", sagte die Sprecherin von
EU-Handelskommissar Pascal Lamy, der Südkorea bezichtigt, Preisdumping
zu betreiben. Wiederholte Aufforderungen, diese Praktiken einzustellen,
waren von der Gegenseite abgelehnt worden.

Damit gilt als sicher, dass die Kommission Klage vor der
Welthandelsorganisation WTO gegen Korea erheben wird. Die Sprecherin
kündigte diesen Schritt bis Ende Oktober an. Gleichzeitig können Europas
Werften vom 1. Oktober an wieder auf Subventionen hoffen. Über beide
Punkte wird der Ministerrat am Montag entscheiden.

FRANKFURTER RUNDSCHAU, Samstag, 28. September 2002, Nr. 226/39,
S. 11

Der Zeitgeist holt auch den Öko-Bäcker ein

**Bei Mulinbeck in Düdelsheim gibt es nicht mehr nur
Vollkornprodukte/ Inhaber Udo Kilb setzt auf Getreide aus der
direkten Umgebung**

Von Stephan Börnecke

BÜDINGEN. Der Mann ist gelernter Bäcker – vom Elternhaus her. Doch 60
Stunden in der Mainflinger Backstube stehen, wie ihm das schon als
18-Jährigem widerfuhr, und sich vom Vater „knechten" lassen, das war die
Sache von Udo Kilb nicht. „Wir wollten ökologisch produzieren und auch
ökologisch arbeiten." Mit Abstrichen, das zeigt die fast 20-jährige Geschichte
der Bio-Bäckerei Mulinbeck aus Büdingen-Düdelsheim, scheint das gelungen.

Kilb, heute 52 Jahre alt, fragt lachend seinen Bäckermeister Heiko Gessner,
der vor dem immer wieder ausgebauten und vergrößerten Fachwerkbau hockt

und raucht: „Kann man mit Öko Geld verdienen?" Klar, strahlt der junge
Mann mit der vermehlten Igelfrisur, „das kann man."

120 Tonnen Bio-Getreide werden in der kleinen Bäckerei in einer
Nebenstraße der Wetterau-Kommune heute verarbeitet, eine Menge, wie sie
auf knapp 50 Hektar Bio-Ackern wächst. 30 Wiederverkäufer, Läden zwischen
Gießen und Frankfurt, verkaufen Land-, Kamut-, Dinkel-, Roggen- und
Weizenbrot sowie Kuchen und neuerdings auch Weizenbrötchen, dazu
kommen Stände auf Wochenmärkten und zwei eigene Geschäfte. 1,2
Millionen Euro setzt das Unternehmen mit seinen 23 Beschäftigten heute um.
Tendenz: weiter steigend. Pro Jahr wachse der Umfang noch um sechs bis acht
Prozent. Am Freitag nach dem Tag der Deutschen Einheit begannen die
Bäcker morgens um kurz nach Mitternacht, sonst stehen die Kollegen von
zwei Uhr an in der Stube. In eineinhalb Schichten wird gearbeitet, und selbst
stonntags steht ein Bäcker an den Bottichen, um den Vorteig anzusetzen ...

FRANKFURTER RUNDSCHAU, Samstag, 12. Oktober 2002, Nr. 237/41, S. 29

10. Lesen Sie den folgenden Text.

„Gen-Mais als Silage verfüttern"

WÖLFERSHEIM/GIESSEN. Der in der Wetterau illegal angebaute gentechnisch
veränderte Mais kann nach einer Anordnung des Gießener
Regierungspräsidiums (RP) als Silage verfüttert werden. Ob der Landwirt von
dieser Möglichkeit Gebrauch macht, liegt allerdings nach Mitteilung des
hessischen Umweltministeriums in seiner Entscheidung. Der Mais dürfe
ausschließlich an die Tiere des betroffenen Hofes verfüttert werden, sagte eine
RP-Sprecherin am Freitag in Gießen.

Außerdem sei dem Landwirt zur Auflage gemacht worden, die Pflanzen
zuvor zu silieren, um sie keimunfähig zu machen. Gegen den Bauern sei ein
Bußgeldverfahren eingeleitet worden, teilte das Umweltministerium mit. Er
hatte keinen Nachweis über die wissenschaftliche Begleitung des Mais-Anbaus
vorweisen können.

Gegen die Herstellerfirma Syngenta war bereits im Juli ein
Ordnungswidrigkeitsverfahren wegen Verletzung der Aufsichtspflicht
eingeleitet worden. Damals war bereits ein Feld mit Gen-Mais bei dem
Landwirt entdeckt worden. Der Bauer hatte dieses Feld abgemäht und das
Grünzeug untergepflügt.

Die Umweltschutzorganisation Greenpeace, die mehrfach gegen den Anbau
des gentechnisch veränderten Maises in Mittelhessen protestiert hatte, forderte
die Vernichtung der Pflanzen. Verbraucherschutzministerin Renate Künast
(Grüne) dürfe nicht tatenlos zusehen, wenn illegaler Mais verfüttert werde.

Der Gen-Mais BT-176 des schweizerischen Konzerns Syngenta darf nach
Darstellung des Regierungspräsidiums nur unter der Auflage angebaut
werden, dass die Pflanzen gleichzeitig wissenschaftlich erforscht werden. Der
Mais hat nach Angaben des Herstellers zwei fremde Erbinformationen: Er
produziert ein Eiweiß, das die Raupen des Maiszünslers tötet, und ist
unempfindlich gegen ein Antibiotikum. Der Maiszünsler richtet jedes Jahr die
großen Schäden auf Maisfeldern an.

Greenpeace hatte im September berichtet, auf drei Feldern bei Wölfersheim werde Gen-Mais angebaut. Der betroffene Landwirt hatte erklärt, konventionelles Saatgut sei in seinem Betrieb unabsichtlich mit gentechnisch verändertem Saatgut verunreinigt worden.   lhe

FRANKFURTER RUNDSCHAU, Samstag, 5. Oktober 2002, Nr. 231/40, S. 28

a. Vokabelübung. Wie heißt das Wort (die Wendung) auf Englisch?
1. der in der Wetterau illegal angebaute gentechnisch veränderte Mais
2. jmdm etw zur Auflage machen
3. silieren
4. keimunfähig
5. die Umweltschutzorganisation
6. Verbraucherschutzministerin
7. die Erbinformation

b. Fassen Sie den Text kurz zusammen.

Unit 16

Business and commerce

Level 1

General

Handel, der (no pl.)	commerce, trade
Import/Export, der (-e)	import/export
Ein-, Ausfuhr, die (-en)	import/export
in Mengen einkaufen	buy in bulk
Konkurrenz, die (-en)	competition
Konkurrent(in), der/die (-en/nen)	competitor
Monopol, das (-e)	monopoly
Logo, das (-s)	logo

The firm

Firma, die (Firmen)	firm
Betrieb, der (-e)	business, concern, operation, office
Geschäft, das (-e)	business, store; deal, transaction
Filialgeschäft, das (-e)	branch
Unternehmen, das (-)	enterprise, company
Gesellschaft, die (-en)	company
etw begründen	to found sth
Fusion, die (-en)	merger
fusionieren	to merge
Arbeitsgemeinschaft, die (-en)	working party
Arbeitsgruppe, die (-n)	working party

Ownership, management and personnel

Arbeitnehmer(in), der/die (-/nen)	employee
Arbeitgeber(in), der/die (-/nen)	employer
Management, das (-s)	management
Führung, die (no pl.)	management
Leitung, die (no pl.)	management
Leiter(in), der/die (-/nen)	manager, department head
Chef(in), der/die (-s/nen)	boss
Direktor(in), der/die (-en/nen)	director
Mitarbeiter(in), der/die (-/nen)	employee, worker
(Senior)partner(in), der/die (-/nen)	(senior) partner
Teilhaber(in), der/die (-/nen)	joint partner
Nachfolger(in), der/die (-/nen)	successor
Personal, das (no pl.)	personnel
Personal-Management, das (no pl.)	personnel management

Krisenmanagement, das (no pl.)	crisis management
mittleres Management	middle management
Vertreter(in), der/die (-/nen)	agent
persönlicher Assistent; persönliche Assistentin	personal assistant

Production and consumption

Produzent(in), der/die (-en/nen)	producer
Verbraucher(in), der/die (-/nen)	consumer
Reihe, die (-n)	range [of products]
Marke, die (-n)	brand
Produkteinführung, die (-en)	product launch
etw einführen	to launch sth
Käufer-, Verkäufer-markt, der (¨e)	buyer's/seller's market
Marktführer, der (-)	market leader
Spitzenqualität, die (-en)	top-of-the-range
einfach	bottom-of-the-line

Marketing and sales

(Export)marketing, das (no pl.)	(export) marketing
ein (neues) Produkt auf den Markt bringen	to market a (new) product
Marktanalyse, die (-n)	market analysis
Marktforschung, die (no pl.)	market research
Verkauf, der (no pl.)	sales [department]
Kunde, der (-n); Kundin, die (-nen)	customer
Rechnung, die (-en)	invoice

eine Rechnung ausstellen	to issue an invoice
etw liefern	to deliver sth
Lieferung, die (-en)	delivery
Liefertermin, der (-e)	delivery date
Lieferung gratis	free delivery
Lieferschein, der (-e)	delivery note
Lieferzeit, die (-en)	delivery time
Ladeplatz, der (¨e)	loading bay
Muster, das (-)	sample
etw führen	to stock sth
ausverkauft	out of stock
das Geschäft geht schlecht	business is slack
Discountgeschäft, das (-e)	discount store
Verkaufsstelle, die (-n)	sales outlet
Zollgebühr, die (-en)	customs duty
zollfrei	duty-free

Prices and profit

Kauf-, Verkaufspreis, der (-e)	purchase/selling price
Herstellungspreis, der (-e)	cost price
Listenpreis, der (-e)	list price
Ladenpreis, der (-e)	retail price
Einführungspreis, der (-e)	introductory price
Inklusivpreis, der (-e)	all-in price
Preiskrieg, der (-e)	price war
Preisindex, der (-e, -indizes, or -indices)	price index
Preisliste, die (-n)	price list
Preiskontrolle, die (-n)	price control
Preissenkung, die (-en)	price cut

Level 2

General

Binnenhandel, der (no pl.)	home trade
Außenhandel, der (no pl.)	foreign trade
Großhandel, der (no pl.)	wholesale trade
Großhändler(in), der/die (-/nen)	wholesaler
Einzelhandel, der (no pl.)	retail trade
Einzelhändler(in), der/die (-/nen)	retailer
Einzelhandelsgeschäft, das (-e)	retail outlet
Balkendiagramm, das (-e)	bar chart
Kreisdiagramm, das (-e)	pie chart
Flussdiagramm, das (-e)	flow chart
unlauterer Wettbewerb	unfair competition

The firm

Vorstand, der (¨e)	board of directors
Betriebsrat, der (¨e)	works council
Zweigniederlassung, die (-en)	branch
Zweigstelle, die (-n)	branch office
Muttergesellschaft, die (-en)	parent company
Schwestergesellschaft, die (-en)	affiliated company
Tochtergesellschaft, die (-en)	subsidiary (company)
Konsortium, das (-tien)	consortium, syndicate
Mischkonzern, der (-e)	conglomerate
Franchise, der (no pl.)	franchise
Übernahme, die (-n)	take-over, buy-out
etw übernehmen	to take over sth

| Übernahmeangebot, das (-e) | take-over bid |

Departments

Verkaufsabteilung, die (-en)	sales department
Personalabteilung, die (-en)	personnel department
Kundendienstabteilung, die (-en)	customer service department
Beschwerdeabteilung, die (-en)	complaints department
Buchhaltung, die (-en)	accounts department
Exportabteilung, die (-en)	export department
Kostenbuchhaltung, die (-en)	costing department
Versandsabteilung, die (-en)	forwarding department
Spedition, die (-en)	forwarding department

Ownership, management and personnel

Beschäftigte(r), der/die (adj. decl.)	employee
Belegschaft, die (-en)	staff
mit einer zu großen Belegschaft	overmanned
eine zu große Belegschaft haben	to be overmanned
Stellvertreter(in), der/die (-/nen)	deputy
Alleinvertreter(in), der/die (-/nen)	sole agent
bevollmächtigter Vertreter; bevollmächtigte Vertreterin	accredited agent
Provisionsvertreter(in), der/die (-/nen)	commission agent
Verkaufsleiter(in), der/die (-/nen)	sales manager

Verkaufsleitung, die (no pl.)	sales management	Markttendenzen, pl.	market trends
Personalleiter(in), der/die (-/nen)	personnel manager	Marktgelegenheiten, pl.	market opportunities
Produktionsleiter(in), der/die (-/nen)	production manager	Zielmarkt, der ("e)	target market
		Verkaufsziel, das (-e)	sales target
Abteilungsleiter(in), der/die (-/nen)	department manager, department head	ein Ziel setzen	to set a target
		gezielte Aktion, die (-en)	targeted campaign
Geschäftsleitung, die (no pl.)	senior management	Marktfähigkeit, die (-en)	marketability
Geschäftsführer(in), der/die (-/nen)	managing director	marktfähig	marketable
		absetzbar	marketable
Hauptgeschäfts- führer(in), der/die (-/nen)	chief executive officer	Haustürverkauf, der ("e)	door-to-door selling
		Telefonverkauf, der ("e)	telesales
Franchisegeber(in), der/die (-/nen)	franchiser	einen Auftrag erteilen	to place an order
Franchisenehmer(in), der/die (-/nen)	franchisee	Auftragsbuch, das ("er)	order book

Production and consumption

Rohmaterial, das (-ien)	raw material	Bestellnummer, die (-n)	order number
Rohstoff, der (-e)	raw material	Bestellformular, das (-e)	order form
Fertigerzeugnisse, pl.	finished goods	eine Bestellung widerrufen	to cancel an order
Markenartikel, der (-)	proprietary brand		
Markenbild, das (-er)	brand image	Waren auf Probe, pl.	goods on approval
Markenbewusstsein, das (no pl.)	brand awareness	Versand, der (no pl.)	shipment

Prices and profit

Qualitätsnorm, die (-en)	quality standard	Preisklasse, die (-n)	price range
Qualitätskontrolle, die (-n)	quality control	Preislage, die (-n)	price range
		Preis ab Werk, der (-e)	factory price, ex-works price
Produktdesign, das (-s)	product design	Preiskartell, das (-e)	price ring; cartel
Warentest, der (-s or -e)	product testing	wettbewerbs-, konkurrenzfähig	competitive
		Strichkode, der (-s)	bar code

Marketing and sales

Aus-, Räumungs- verkauf, der ("e)	clearance sale	Strichkodeleser, der (-)	bar-code reader
Schlussverkauf, der ("e)	(end-of-season) sale	Reingewinn, der (-e)	net profit
		Nettoertrag, der ("e)	net profit
im (Sonder)angebot	on sale	Gesamtgewinn, der (-e)	gross profit
Marktuntersuchung, die (-en)	market survey	Bruttogewinn, der (-e)	gross profit

Wiederverkaufswert, der (-e)	resale value	Hauptbuch, das (¨er)	ledger
		Steuerjahr, das (-e)	fiscal year
		Startkosten, pl.	start-up costs
Accounts and costs		Fixkosten, pl.	fixed costs
Buchhaltung, die (-en)	book-keeping	veränderliche Kosten, pl.	variable costs
Buchprüfung, die (-en)	audit	Preise treiben	to profiteer
etw prüfen	to audit sth	Profitmacher(in), der/die (-/nen)	profiteer

Level 3

The firm

Hauptverwaltung, die (-en)	head office
Bezirksbüro, das (-s)	area office
etw eintragen lassen	to register sth
eingetragene Firma	registered company
handelsgerichtlich eingetragene Gesellschaft	registered company
multinationales Unternehmen	multinational corporation
Aktiengesellschaft (AG), die (-en)	joint stock company
Gesellschaft mit beschränkter Haftung (GmbH), die (-en)	limited company
Holding-Gesellschaft, die (-en)	holding company
Personengesellschaft, die (-en)	partnership
Trust, der (-s or -e)	trust company
Treuhandvertrag, der (¨e)	trust agreement
Aufkauf, der (¨e)	buy-out
etw aufkaufen	to buy out sth
etw auflösen	to dissolve, wind up sth
Unternehmenspolitik, die (-en)	company policy

Ownership, management and personnel

stellvertretender Leiter	assistant manager
Regionalleiter(in), der/die (-/nen)	area manager
Vertriebsleiter(in), der/die (-/nen)	sales manager, marketing director
Leiter(in) der Finanzabteilung, der/die (-/nen)	finance director
Fachgebietsleiter(in), der/die (-/nen)	line manager
Aktionär(in), der/die (-e/nen)	shareholder
etw verkleinern	to downsize sth
freie Kapazität	idle capacity
Vorsitzende(r), der/die (adj. decl.)	chairperson
bei einer Sitzung den Vorsitz führen	to chair a meeting
Führungsstil, der (-e)	management style
Unternehmensbe-rater(in), der/die (-/nen)	management consultant
Gesellschaftsrecht-ler(in), der/die (-/nen)	company lawyer
Hausjurist(in), der/die (-en/nen)	company/in-house lawyer
Headhunter(in), der/die (-/nen)	head hunter

Nachwuchsführungs-kraft, die (¨e)	trainee manager
Mitbestimmung, die (no pl.)	worker participation
Zeiteinteilung, die (-en)	time management
Büroverwaltung, die (-en)	office management

Production and consumption

Konsumgüter, pl.	consumer goods
Konsumgesellschaft, die (-en)	consumer society
Verbraucherschutz, der (no pl.)	consumer protection
Verbrauchsge-wohnheiten, pl.	consumer habits
Angebot und Nachfrage	supply and demand
Produktionsziel, das (-e)	production target
Wachstumsmarkt, der (¨e)	growth market
maßgefertigt, speziell angefertigt	custom-made
individuell aufmachen	to customize
Verfallsdatum, das (-ten)	sell/use-by date
Wegwerf-	disposable
Wegwerfgesellschaft, die (-en)	throwaway society

Marketing and sales

Nachfrage erzeugen	to create a market
einen Markt erschließen	to tap a market
Umsatz, der (¨e)	sales volume, turnover
guten Absatz finden	to find a ready market
Absatzgebiet, das (-e)	market outlet
Marktnische, die (-n)	market niche
Marktanteil, der (-e)	market share
der Markt ist flau	the market is slack
Vorrat, der (¨e)	stocks

einen geringen Vorrat haben	to run low
etw vorrätig haben	to have sth in stock
mit gutem Sortiment	well-stocked
frachtfrei	carriage paid, shipping included, shipping paid
Frachtgebühr, die (-en)	carriage, shipping charge
Kundentreue, die (no pl.)	customer loyalty
Kundschaft, die (no pl.)	clientele
(Kosten)voranschlag, der (¨e)	estimate
einen Kostenvoranschlag einholen	to get an estimate
Zollabfertigung, die (-en)	customs clearance
Zollerklärung, die (-en)	customs declaration
Einfuhrzoll, der (¨e)	import duty
den Markt sättigen	to saturate the market
den Markt überschwemmen	to flood the market
den Markt monopolisieren	to corner the market
aggressive/weiche Verkaufstaktik	hard/soft sell

Prices and profit

Rabatt, der (-e)	discount
Skonto, das or der (-s)	cash discount
Bar(zahlungs)preis, der (-e)	cash price
Barzahlung bei Lieferung	cash on delivery
Niedrigstpreise, pl.	rock-bottom prices
zu Schleuderpreisen	cut-price, throwaway prices
zu verbilligtem Tarif	cut-rate
den Preis radikal herabsetzen	to slash the price

risikoreich	high risk	allgemeine	overheads
rentabel	profit-making	Geschäftskosten,	
Gewinnspanne,	profit margin	pl.	
die (-n)		Ladekosten, pl.	handling charges
keinen Gewinn	non-profit	kostendeckend	to break even
anstrebend		arbeiten	
Verlust, der (-e)	loss	Gewinnbeteiligung,	profit-sharing
etw wieder	to recoup sth	die (-en)	scheme
gutmachen		Reisespesen, pl.	travel expenses
		Risikoanalyse,	risk analysis

Accounts and costs
		die (-n)	
Grenzkosten, pl.	marginal costs	kosteffizient	cost-effective
Betriebskosten, pl.	running costs	Kalkulation, die (-en)	costing

Employment

Level 1

General

Arbeit, die (-en)	employment
(Arbeits)kollege(in),	work mate
der/die (-en/nen)	
die arbeitende	the working
Bevölkerung	population
schwarzarbeiten	to do illicit work,
	moonlight
Berufskrankheit,	occupational illness
die (-en)	
beruflich	to further one's
vorankommen	career

Application and training

Stelle, die (-n)	job, position
offene Stelle	vacancy
Stellung, die (-en)	job, position
eine Stelle suchen	to look for a job
Arbeitssuchende(r),	jobseeker
der/die (adj. decl.)	
sich um eine Stelle	to apply for a job
bewerben	
Bewerbung, die (-en)	job application
Lebenslauf, der ("e)	curriculum vitae,
	résumé
Arbeitsamt, das ("er)	employment office

Praktikum, das (-ka)	practical training
jmdn beschäftigen	to employ sb
Qualifikationen, pl.	qualifications
Arbeitsvertrag,	employment contract
der ("e)	
Probezeit, die (-en)	trial period
auf Probe angestellt	to be employed for a
sein	probationary
	period

Salary and conditions

Lohn, der ("e)	wage
Garantielohn,	guaranteed minimum
der ("e)	wage
Gehalt, das ("er)	salary
Grundgehalt,	basic salary
das ("er)	
Arbeitszeit, die (-en)	working hours
Kaffeepause, die (-n)	coffee break
Mittagspause,	lunch break
die (-n)	
Krankengeld, das	sickness benefit
(no pl.)	
Kindergeld, das	child benefit
(no pl.)	
Stechuhr, die (-en)	time clock

Stechkarte, die (-n)	time card
Stelle ohne Zukunft, die (-n)	job with no prospects
jmdn versetzen	to transfer sb
Versetzung, die (-en)	transfer
Mutter-, Vaterschafts- urlaub, der (-e)	maternity/paternity leave
einen Tag frei bekommen	to have a day off
Genesungsurlaub, der (-e)	sick leave
bezahlter/unbezahlter Urlaub	paid/unpaid leave
Schichtarbeit, die (no pl.)	shift work
Schichtarbeiter(in), der/die (-/nen)	shift worker
Schicht arbeiten	to do shift work
Zeitarbeit, die (-en)	temporary work
freiberuflich	freelance
Freiberufliche(r), der/die (adj. decl.)	freelancer

Termination of employment

jmdm kündigen	to give sb notice, dismiss sb
kündigen	to hand in one's notice, resign
Kündigung, die (-en)	termination; notice to quit, resignation
jmdn rausschmeißen (coll.)	to sack sb
jmdn feuern (coll.)	to fire sb
arbeitslos	unemployed
Arbeitlosigkeit, die (no pl.)	unemployment
Arbeitslose(r), der/die (adj. decl.)	unemployed person

Jobs, trades and professions
(see also Units 3, 15 and 17)

Verkäufer(in), der/die (-/nen)	salesperson
Kaufmann, -frau, der/die (-leute/en)	businessman/ businesswoman

Geschäftsmann, -frau, der/die (-leute/en)	businessman/ businesswoman
Banker(in), der/die (-/nen)	banker
Journalist(in), der/die (-en/nen)	journalist
Fotograf(in), der/die (-en/nen)	photographer
Techniker(in), der/die (-/nen)	technician
Chemiker(in), der/die (-/nen)	chemist
Assistent(in), der/die (-en/nen)	assistant
Politiker(in), der/die (-/nen)	politician
Dolmetscher(in), der/die (-/nen)	interpreter
Briefträger(in), der/die (-/nen)	postman/woman
Polizist(in), der/die (-en/nen)	police officer
Beamte(r), der (adj. decl.); Beamtin, die (-nen)	civil servant
Architekt(in), der/die (-en/nen)	architect
Erzieher(in), der/die (-/nen)	nursery school teacher, kindergarten teacher
Ingenieur(in), der/die (-e/nen)	engineer
Bäcker(in), der/die (-/nen)	baker
Fleischer(in), der/die (-/nen)	butcher
Metzger(in), der/die (-/nen; S, W, CH)	butcher
Schlachter(in), der/die (-/nen; N)	butcher
Konditor(in), der/die (-en/nen)	confectioner
Zuckerbäcker(in), der/die (-/nen)	confectioner

Süßwarenver-käufer(in), der/die (-/nen)	confectioner	Gärtner(in), der/die (-/nen)	gardener
Lebensmittelhänd-ler(in), der/die (-/nen)	grocer	Handwerker(in), der/die (-/nen)	craftsman/woman; (skilled) manual worker
Fischhändler(in), der/die (-/nen)	fishmonger, fish dealer	Tischler(in), der/die (-/nen)	joiner, carpenter
Käsehändler(in), der/die (-/nen)	cheese merchant	Möbeltischler(in), der/die (-/nen)	cabinet maker
Gemüsehändler(in), der/die (-/nen)	greengrocer, vegetable supplier	Schreiner(in), der/die (-/nen)	carpenter
Obsthändler(in), der/die (-/nen)	fruit merchant	Schneider(in), der/die (-/nen)	tailor, dressmaker
Straßenhändler(in), der/die (-/nen)	costermonger, street hawker	Damenschneider(in), der/die (-/nen)	dressmaker
Blumenhändler(in), der/die (-/nen)	florist	Unternehmer(in), der/die (-/nen)	entrepreneur, employer

Unions and industrial action

Milchhändler(in), der/die (-/nen)	dairyman/ dairywoman
Milchmann, -frau, der/die (¨er/en)	milkman/dairywoman
Mechaniker(in), der/die (-/nen)	mechanic
Friseur, der (-e); Friseuse, die (-n)	hairdresser
Gastarbeiter(in), der/die (-/nen)	guest worker
Wanderarbeiter(in), der/die (-/nen)	migrant worker
Wirt(in), der/die (-e/nen)	owner of restaurant, innkeeper
Koch, der (¨e); Köchin, die (-nen)	cook
Kellner(in), der/die (-/nen)	waiter/waitress
Zimmermädchen, das (-)	chamber maid
Hoteljunge, der (-n)	bell boy
Tellerwäscher(in), der/die (-/nen)	dishwasher
Telefonist(in), der/die (-en/nen)	telephone operator, telephonist
Soldat(in), der/die (-en/nen)	soldier
Sozialarbeiter(in), der/die (-/nen)	social worker

Gewerkschaft, die (-en)	trade union
Industriegewerkschaft, die (-en)	industrial union
Gewerkschaftsmitglied, das (-er)	union member
Gewerkschaft(l)er(in), der/die (-/nen)	trade unionist
einer Gewerkschaft beitreten	to join a union
in eine Gewerkschaft eintreten	to join a union
einer Gewerkschaft angehören	to belong to a union
Gewerkschaftsbe-wegung, die (no pl.)	trade unionism
Streik, der (-s)	strike
Streikende(r), der/die (adj. decl.)	striker
streiken	to strike, be on strike, go on strike
Streit, der (-e)	dispute
Demonstration, die (-en)	demonstration
Diskriminierung, die (-en)	discrimination

Level 2

Application and training

Bewerber(in), der/die (-/nen)	applicant
(Bewerbungs)formular, das (-e)	application form
Bewerbungsschreiben, das (-)	letter of application
Bewerbungsgespräch, das (-e)	(job) interview
jmdn einstellen	to recruit sb; appoint sb
Einstellung, die (-en)	recruiting
Zeugnisse, pl.	credentials
Ausbildung, die (-en)	training
Ausbildungskurs, der (-e)	training course
Ausbildungsprogramm, das (-e)	training programme
Auszubildende(r), der/die (adj. decl.)	trainee
Management-Ausbildung, die (-en)	management training
Berufsberatung, die (-en)	careers guidance
Berufsberater(in), der/die (-/nen)	careers officer

Salary and conditions

Lohnempfänger(in), der/die (-/nen)	wage-earner
Gehaltsempfänger(in), der/die (-/nen)	salary-earner
Einkommensklasse, die (-n)	income bracket
Nettolohn, der (¨e)	take-home pay
Mindestlohn, der (¨e)	minimum wage
Gehaltspaket, das (-e)	salary package
Lohn-, Gehaltsliste, die (-n)	payroll
Lohn-, Gehaltsstreifen, der (-)	pay slip

Prämie, die (-n)	bonus
Zuschlag, der (¨e)	bonus
stempeln	to clock in
stechen	to clock out
Stundenzettel, der (-)	time sheet
Überstunden, pl.	overtime
Kurzarbeit, die (no pl.)	short time
kurzarbeiten	to be on short shift/time
Gleitzeit, die (no pl.)	flexitime
beurlaubt sein	to be on leave of absence
jmdn befördern	to promote sb
jmdn degradieren	to demote sb
Zufriedenheit am Arbeitsplatz, die (no pl.)	job satisfaction
Sicherheit des Arbeitsplatzes, die (no pl.)	job security
Firmenwagen, der (-)	company car
pendeln	to commute
jmdn anders einsetzen	to redeploy sb
Umzug, der (¨e)	relocation

Termination of employment

jmdn entlassen	to let sb go, dismiss sb, fire sb, lay sb off
Entlassung, die (-en)	dismissal
fristlos	without notice
fristgerecht	with proper notice
Arbeitslosenhilfe, die (no pl.)	unemployment benefit
Arbeitslosenzahlen, pl.	unemployment figures
Arbeitslosenquote, die (-n)	unemployment rate
Frührente, die (-n)	early retirement
in Frührente gehen (coll.)	to take early retirement

Jobs, trades and professions

(see also Units 3, 15 and 17)

Reinemachefrau, die (-en)	cleaner
Gebäudereiniger(in), der/die (-/nen)	cleaner
Fensterputzer(in), der/die (-/nen)	window cleaner
Müllfahrer(in), der/die (-/nen)	dustman, garbage man/woman
Straßenkehrer(in), der/die (-/nen)	street sweeper
Zeitungshändler(in), der/die (-/nen)	newsagent, news dealer
Drucker(in), der/die (-/nen)	printer
Buchhändler(in), der/die (-/nen)	bookseller
Verleger(in), der/die (-/nen)	publisher
Bibliothekar(in), der (-e/nen)	librarian
Kunsthändler(in), der/die (-/nen)	art dealer
Juwelier(in), der/die (-e/nen)	jeweller
Schmuckhändler(in), der/die (-/nen)	jeweller
Goldschmied(in), der/die (-e/nen)	goldsmith
Landarbeiter(in), der/die (-/nen)	farmhand
Stallbursche, der (-n)	stable lad
Förster(in), der/die (-/nen)	forester
Matrose, der (-n); Matrosin, die (-nen)	sailor
Eheberater(in), der/die (-/nen)	marriage guidance counsellor
Fahrlehrer(in), der/die (-/nen)	driving instructor
Verkehrspolizist(in), der/die (-en/nen)	traffic police officer

Last(kraft)wagenfahrer(in), der/die (-/nen)	lorry/truck driver
Tankwart(in), der/die (-e/nen)	petrol station attendant
Bahnarbeiter(in), der/die (-/nen)	railway worker
Dachdecker(in), der/die (-/nen)	roofer
Maurer(in), der/die (-/nen)	bricklayer
Laborant(in), der/die (-en/nen)	lab technician
Meister(in), der/die (-/nen)	master (craftsman/craftswoman)
(Bilder)rahmer(in), der/die (-/nen)	framer
Töpfer(in), der/die (-/nen)	potter
Anstreicher(in), der/die (-/nen)	(house) painter; painter and decorator
Hausmeister(in), der/die (-/nen)	caretaker
Fahrstuhlführer(in), der/die (-/nen)	elevator attendant
Gebrauchtwarenhändler(in), der/die (-/nen)	second-hand dealer
Lieferant(in), der/die (-en/nen)	delivery man/woman; supplier
Schlosser(in), der/die (-/nen)	locksmith
Tabak(waren)händler(in), der/die (-/nen)	tobacconist
Kassierer(in), der/die (-/nen)	cashier
Rechtsanwalt, -anwältin, der/die (¨e/nen)	lawyer, attorney
Buchhalter(in), der/die (-/nen)	bookkeeper
Wirtschaftsprüfer(in), der/die (-/nen)	accountant

Buchprüfer(in), der/die (-/nen)	auditor	Warnstreik, der (-s)	token strike
Theateragent(in), der/die (-en/nen)	theatrical agent	wilder Streik	wildcat strike
		spontaner Streik	lightning strike
Modeschöpfer(in), der/die (-/nen)	fashion designer	Sympathiestreik, der (-s)	sympathy strike
Designer(in), der/die (-/nen)	designer	in den Streik treten	to go on strike
Polsterer, der (-); Polsterin, die (-nen)	upholsterer	Streikbrecher(in), der/die (-/nen)	strike breaker
		Streikkasse, die (-n)	strike funds
		Streikgeld, das (no pl.)	strike pay

Unions and industrial action

industrielle Arbeitsbeziehungen, pl.	industrial relations	Gewerkschaftsführer(in), der/die (-/nen)	union leader
Rassendiskriminierung, die (-en)	racial discrimination	Gewerkschaftsvertreter(in), der/die (-/nen)	union representative
Diskriminierung auf Grund des Geschlechts, die (-en)	sexual discrimination	gewerkschaftsgebundene Firma, die (Firmen)	closed shop
Lohn-, Gehaltsforderung, die (-en)	pay claim		

Level 3

General

Vollbeschäftigung, die (no pl.)	full employment
Arbeitsbeschaffung, die (no pl.)	job creation
Arbeitskräftemangel, die (-n)	labour shortage
sich seinen Lebensunterhalt verdienen	to earn one's living
Arbeitswütige(r), der/die (adj. decl.)	workaholic
Arbeitssüchtige(r), der/die (adj. decl.)	workaholic
Arbeitstier, das (-e)	workaholic
arbeitsscheu	work shy
Drückeberger(in), der/die (-/nen)	shirker
sich vor etw drücken	to shirk sth

Application and training

Kleinanzeige, die (-n)	classified ad
eine Stelle inserieren	to advertise a job
Stellenbeschreibung, die (-en)	job description
Stellenvermittlung, die (-en)	employment agency
Referenz, die (-en)	referee; reference; testimonial
jmdn als Referenz angeben	to give sb as a referee
jmdm als Referenz dienen	to be a referee for sb
Beurteilung, die (-en)	appraisal
Stellenangebot, das (-e)	job offer
Ausbildung am Arbeitsplatz, die (-en)	on-the-job training

innerbetriebliche Ausbildung	on-the-job training	Gewerkschaftsbeitrag, der (¨e)	union dues
hausinterne Ausbildung	in-house training	Arbietsplatzteilung, die (-en)	job sharing
jmdn zu etw ernennen	to appoint sb sth	Berufsrisiko, das (-ken)	occupational hazard
		Gefahrenzulage, die (-n)	danger money

Salary and conditions

Lohnskala, die (-skalen)	wages scale	Leistungszulage, die (-n)	incentive bonus payment
Gehaltsskala, die (-skalen)	salary scale	Anreizsystem, das (-e)	incentive scheme
Lohnstopp, der (-s)	wage freeze		

Termination of employment

Gehalts-, Lohnfortzahlung, die (-en)	sick pay	Arbeitsplatzabbau, der (no pl.)	job cuts
Nachzahlung, die (-en)	back pay	Kündigungsschutz, der (no pl.)	protection against wrongful dismissal
Essensmarke, die (-n)	luncheon voucher		
indexgebunden	index-linked	Kündigungsfrist, die (-en)	period of notice
Bezahlung in Naturalien, die (-en)	payment in kind	goldener Handschlag	golden handshake
zusätzliche Leistungen, pl.	fringe benefits	Abfindung, die (-en)	severance pay
Arbeitsbedingungen, pl.	conditions of employment	Erwerbsunfähig-keitsrente, die (-n)	disability pension
Arbeitslast, die (-en)	workload	freiwillige Arbeitslosigkeit	voluntary redundancy
Reisekostenvergütung, die (-en)	travel expense reimbursement	Arbeitsgericht, das (-e)	industrial tribunal
Spesenkonto, das (-s, -ten, or -ti)	expense account		

Jobs, trades and professions
(see also Units 3, 15 and 17)

Beurlaubung wegen einer dringenden Famileinangele-genheit, die (-en)	compassionate leave	Gastronom(in), der/die (-en/nen)	caterer
Vergünstigung, die (-en)	perk	Schornsteinfeger(in), der/die (-/nen)	chimney sweep
Abzüge, pl.	deductions	Schuster(in), der/die (-/nen)	shoemaker
Beitrag, der (¨e)	contribution		
Rentenversiche-rung, die (-en)	pension plan	Sattler(in), der/die (-/nen)	saddler
Rentenversicherungs-beitrag, der (¨e)	pension scheme contribution	Korbflechter(in), der/die (-/nen)	basket maker
Sozialversicherung, die (-en)	social security	Kesselflicker(in), der/die (-/nen)	tinker

Installateur(in), der/die (-e/nen)	plumber	Meldefahrer(in), der/die (-/nen)	dispatch rider
Klempner(in), der/die (-/nen)	plumber	Auskunftsbeamte(r), der (adj. decl.); Auskunftsbeamtin, die (-nen)	information officer
Elektroinstallateur(in), der/die (-e/nen)	electrician		
Gasinstallateur(in), der/die (-e/nen)	gas-fitter	Zollbeamte(r), der (adj. decl.); Zollbeamtin, die (-nen)	customs officer
Steinmetz(in), der/die (-en/nen)	stone mason		
Stuckateur(in), der/die (-e/nen)	plasterer	Militärangehörige(r), der/die (adj. decl.)	serviceman/ servicewoman
Fliesenleger(in), der/die (-/nen)	tiler	Kustos, der (Kustoden); Kustodin, die (-nen)	curator
Eisenschmied(in), der/die (-e/nen)	blacksmith		
Eisen(waren)- händler(in), der/die (-/nen)	ironmonger, hardware dealer	Aufseher(in), der/die (-/nen)	attendant [museum]; guard [prison]
Schrotthändler(in), der/die (-/nen)	scrap merchant	Aufsichtsbeamt(r), der (adj. decl.); Aufsichtsbeamtin, die (-nen)	attendant [museum]; guard [prison]
Grundstücks- makler(in), der/die (-/nen)	(real) estate agent		
Immobilienmakler(in), der/die (-/nen)	(real) estate agent	Gefängniswärter(in), der/die (-/nen)	prison officer
Devisenhändler(in), der/die (-/nen)	foreign exchange dealer	Sicherheitsbeamte(r), der (adj. decl.); Sicherheits- beamtin, die (-nen)	security guard
Steuerbeamte(r), der (adj. decl.); Steuerbeamtin, die (-nen)	tax officer		
Versicherer, der (-); Versicherin, die (-nen)	underwriter	Wächter(in), der/die (-/nen)	guard
		Nationalpark- wächter(in), der/die (-/nen)	national park ranger
Versicherungsver- treter(in), der/die (-/nen)	insurance agent	Leibwächter(in), der/die (-/nen)	bodyguard
Versicherungs- makler(in), der/die (-/nen)	insurance broker	(Schaufenster)deko- rateur(in), der/die (-e/nen)	window dresser
		Fußpfleger(in), der/die (-/nen)	chiropodist
Börsenmakler(in), der/die (-/nen)	stockbroker	Handelsvertreter(in), der/die (-/nen)	commercial traveller

Reeder(in), der/die (-/nen)	ship owner	Streit um den Zuständigkeits- bereich, der (-e)	demarcation dispute
Bestatter(in), der/die (-/nen)	undertaker	Streikposten, der (-)	picket
Landvermesser(in), der/die (-/nen)	surveyor	Streikpostenkette, die (-n)	picket line
Antiquitäten- händler(in), der/die (-/nen)	antique dealer	eine Streikpostenkette durchbrechen	to cross a picket line
Antiquar(in), der/die (-e/nen)	second-hand bookseller	Dienst nach Vorschrift machen	to work to rule
Reiseveranstalter(in), der/die (-/nen)	travel agent	Verlangsamung, die (-en)	slowdown
Möbelspediteur(in), der/die (-e/nen)	furniture remover	Stilllegung, die (-en)	stoppage
Pförtner(in), der/die (-/nen)	porter, doorman/ doorwoman	Arbeitskampf- maßnahmen, pl.	industrial action
Nachtpförtner(in), der/die (-/nen)	night porter	Verhandlungstisch, der (-e)	bargaining table
Platzanweiser(in), der/die (-/nen)	usher	Tarifverhandlungen, pl.	collective bargaining
Hausierer(in), der/die (-/nen)	door-to-door salesperson	Schlichtungskom- mission, die (-en)	conciliation board
Hostess, die (-en)	escort	vor eine Schlich- tungskommission gehen	to go to arbitration

Unions and industrial action

Beschwerdepunkt, der (-e)	grievance	die Basis der Gewerkschaft	the rank and file
Arbeitsstreitigkeit, die (-en)	industrial dispute	die einfachen Gewerkschafts- mitglieder, pl.	the rank and file

---

Exercises

Level 1

1. Wie heißt das Gegenteil? ✓
1. die Einfuhr
2. die Arbeitgeberin
3. der Käufermarkt
4. der Kaufpreis
5. der Mutterschaftsurlaub

2. Wie heißt die entsprechende Person? ✓

	männlich	*weiblich*
1. die Konkurrenz		
2. die Leitung		
3. die Schichtarbeit		
4. die Arbeitslosigkeit		
5. die Gewerkschaft		
6. der Streik		

3. Welches Wort hat die gleiche oder eine ähnliche Bedeutung? ✓

1. das Geschäft
2. der Export
3. die Arbeitsgruppe
4. das Management
5. der Konsument
6. die Stelle
7. jmdn feuern
8. der Fleischer (S und N)
9. die Konditorin
10. der Florist
11. die Milchfrau
12. die Kauffrau

4. Ordnen Sie.

das Arbeitsamt, das Gehalt, der Kellner, die Köchin, der Lebenslauf,
der Möbeltischler, die Polizistin, der Schreiner, der Soldat, der Tellerwäscher,
der Tischler, der Wirt

das Restaurant	*die Bewerbung*	*Möbel*	*Sicherheitskräfte*

5. Welches Verb passt? ✓

a. arbeiten, b. ausstellen, c. begründen, d. bringen, e. einkaufen, f. eintreten,
g. suchen

1. eine Stelle
2. ein Geschäft
3. ein neues Produkt auf den Markt
4. eine Rechnung
5. in Mengen
6. Schicht
7. in eine Gewerkschaft

6. Welches Wort passt nicht? ✓

1. die Dolmetscherin, der Journalist, die Fotografin, der Schneider
2. die Architektin, die Erzieherin, die Ingenieurin, die Technikerin
3. der Gemüsehändler, der Käsehändler, der Obsthändler, der Schmuckhändler
4. die Firma, die Gesellschaft, die Überführung, das Unternehmen
5. der Herstellungspreis, der Ladenpreis, der Listenpreis, der Verkaufspreis
6. der Genesungsurlaub, die Kaffeepause, die Mittagspause, unbezahlter Urlaub

7. Falsche Freunde. Ergänzen Sie die Tabelle.

Deutsch	Englisch	Deutsch	Englisch
der Unternehmer			undertaker
die Konkurrenz			concurrence
der Chef			chef
die Marke			mark
das Muster			muster
der Lohn			loan

8. Was passt nicht? ✓
1. Liefer-: -ent, -schein, -termin, -ung
2. -händler: Brief-, Fisch-, Lebensmittel-, Straßen-
3. Gewerkschafts-: -bewegung, -führer, -ler, -mitglied
4. Markt-: -analyse, -forschung, -führer, -senkung
5. Preis-: -gebühr, -index, -krieg, -liste

9. In jedem Satz fehlt ein Wort. ✓

> ausverkauft, gekündigt, Kindergeld, Krisenmanagement, Preissenkung, Probezeit, Seniorpartner, versetzt, zollfrei

1. Er ist ein hoch angesehener _____ einer erfolgreichen Anwaltssozietät.
2. Das _____ der Regierung klappte nicht reibungslos.
3. Die EU kann ihre Produkte _____ in der Türkei verkaufen.
4. Das Buch ist in Deutschland ein Bestseller und seit Wochen _____.
5. Die _____ hat man ursprünglich für die Zeit vor Weihnachten geplant.
6. Ohne eine _____ wollte er ihn nicht einstellen.
7. Die Grünen wollen das _____ auf 300 DM anheben.
8. Dem Mitarbeiter wurde fristlos _____.
9. Sie wird in eine andere Abteilung _____.

10 Übersetzen Sie ins Englische.

Richter kippen Montis drittes Fusionsverbot

„Analysemängel, Begründungsfehler, Beweismangel" / Wettbewerbskommissar baut Behörde um

FRANKFURT/BRÜSSEL, 25. Oktober. Zum dritten Mal hintereinander haben die Luxemburger Europarichter ein Fusionsverbot von Binnenmarktkommissar Mario Monti gekippt. Das Europäische Gericht erster Instanz (EuG) erklärte eine Entscheidung für nichtig, mit der Monti den Zusammenschluss zwischen einer Tochtergesellschaft des skandinavischen Tetra Laval, dem Weltmarktführer für Kartonverpackungen, und dem französischen Unternehmen Sidel untersagt hatte. Auch diesmal warfen die

Richter Montis Kontrollbehörde „verschiedene Analysemängel, Begründungsfehler und mangelnde Beweise" vor ...

Joachim Jahn, Peter Hort, und Bettina Bonde

Frankfurter Allgemeine Zeitung, Samstag, 26. Oktober 2002, Nr. 249/43, S. 11

Generalstreik in Italien
ROM, 18. Oktober. Mit einem Generalstreik hat die größte italienische Gewerkschaft CGIL nicht nur Teile des Landes lahmgelegt, sondern auch heftige Diskussionen unter den Arbeitnehmerorganisationen und den Parteien der Linken verursacht. Während die CGIL den Streik als Mittel des Widerstands gegen Berlusconis Wirtschaftspolitik und Staatshaushalt verteidigte, zeigten sich die anderen Gewerkschaften kritisch und beurteilten ihn allein als rein politische Veranstaltung.

Tobias Piller

Frankfurter Allgemeine Zeitung, Samstag, 19. Oktober 2002, Nr. 243/42, S. 1

Banken-Tarifstreit geht weiter
In den festgefahrenen Tarifstreit des Bankgewerbes kommt wieder Bewegung. Nach monatelanger Pause wollen Arbeitgeber und die Gewerkschaft Verdi am 7. November in Frankfurt erstmals wieder verhandeln. Wie Verdi mitteilte, gibt es in der besonders umstrittenen Frage einer variablen Vergütung von Vertriebsmitarbeitern „möglicherweise eine Einigungschance". Verdi hatte ursprünglich 6,5 Prozent mehr Lohn und Gehalt gefordert, ist inzwischen aber zu einem niedrigeren Abschluss bereit. Der Bankenverband hatte seinen Mitgliedern eine freiwillige Anhebung der Gehälter um 3,1 Prozent empfohlen.

Frankfurter Allgemeine Zeitung, Samstag, 19. Oktober 2002, Nr. 243/42, S. 12

© dpa Deutsche Presse-Agentur GmbH

Level 2

1. Wie heißt das Gegenteil? ✓
1. der Außenhandel
2. der Gesamtgewinn
3. die Fixkosten
4. jmdn befördern
5. fristlos

2. Welches Wort hat die gleiche oder eine ähnliche Bedeutung? ✓
1. marktfähig
2. die Preisklasse
3. konkurrenzfähig
4. der Barcode
5. das Konglomerat
6. die Spedition
7. das Rohmaterial
8. die Prämie
9. stempeln
10. der Räumungsverkauf

3. Wie heißt die entsprechende Person? ✓

	männlich	*weiblich*
1. der Großhandel		
2. der Einzelhandel		
3. die Verkaufsleitung		
4. die Bewerbung		
5. die Berufsberatung		
6. die Buchhaltung		

4. Welches Verb passt?

a. erteilen, b. prüfen, c. setzen, d. treten, e. treiben

1. ein Ziel
2. einen Auftrag
3. Preise
4. die Bücher
5. in den Streik

5. Ergänzen Sie. ✓
1. der Lohn – der Lohnempfänger : das Gehalt – _____
2. der Elternteil – das Kind : die Muttergesellschaft – _____
3. das Telefon – der Telefonverkauf : die Beine – _____
4. etw bestellen – das Bestellformular : sich um eine Stelle bewerben – _____
5. krank – das Krankengeld : arbeitslos – _____

6. Welche Wörter gehören zusammen? ✓

a. die Anstreicherin, b. die Bibliothekarin, c. der Eheberater,
d. der Fahrstuhlführer, e. die Juwelierin, f. der Kassierer, g. der Kunsthändler,
h. der Matrose, i. die Maurerin, j. die Polsterin, k. der Schlosser, l. der Stenotypist,
m. der Straßenkehrer, n. der Tankwart, o. die Töpferin

1. Bücher
2. der Besen
3. das Gemälde
4. die Kette
5. die See
6. der Lift
7. der Ton
8. der Streit
9. der Schlüssel
10. das Sofa
11. das Benzin
12. der Backstein
13. die Schreibmaschine
14. die Farbe
15. das Geld

7. Kreuzworträtsel ✓

senkrecht:

1. alle Beschäftigten einer Firma
2. Gegensatz: brutto
4. Kurzarbeit leisten
7. Fabrikat
8. Rechnungsbuch für die Schlussbilanz
9. kurzfristiger Streik
10. Warenverkehr
11. vorzeitig gezahlte Rente
12. Buchdrucker
14. das Umziehen
16. Kürzel von Firmennamen
18. Import
19. festes Einkommen
20. berufliche Tätigkeit

waagerecht:

1. Gesamtertrag
3. Arbeitseinstellung
5. weibliche Fachkraft für Laborarbeiten
6. Ausfuhr
7. Minimallohn
9. Handelsgut
13. einzige Vertreterin
15. gleitende Arbeitszeit
17. Sortiment
21. jemand, der Bücher veröffentlicht
22. illegal arbeiten
23. Abteilung für kaufmännische Rechnungsführung
24. Hafner

8. In jedem Satz fehlt ein Wort. ✓

Arbeitslosenquote, Firmenwagen, Gebäudereiniger, Markenbewusstsein, Nettolohnes, Sonderangebot, Streikbrecher, unlauteren, Vorstand, wilder

1. Es handelt sich um einen Verstoß gegen das Gesetz gegen _____ Wettbewerb.
2. Der _____ dankt ihm für seine langjährigen Dienste für die Firma.
3. Der Lebensmittelhersteller profitiert mit seinen Marken vom _____ der Verbraucher.
4. Ein Liter Bier kostet im _____ oft weniger als eine Mark.
5. Die _____ sank von 9,3 auf 8,7 Prozent.
6. Den _____ darf er auch privat fahren.
7. Die _____ werden in zwei Schichten arbeiten.
8. Das Unternehmen hat _____ eingestellt und Lohnzahlungen an Streikende gestoppt.
9. Ein _____ Streik ist rechtswidrig.
10. Das Streikgeld liegt bei rund der Hälfte eines _____.

9. Zeichnen Sie die folgenden Diagramme:
1. ein Balkendiagramm
2. ein Flussdiagramm
3. ein Kreisdiagramm

10. Übersetzen Sie ins Englische.

Gute Kontakte zahlen sich aus

Jobverlust: Der typische Outplacement-Kandidat ist Mitte Vierzig

Wenn in Deutschland ein qualifizierter Mitarbeiter seinen Job verliert, so braucht er durchschnittlich fünfeinhalb Monate, um einen neuen zu finden. Weltweit beträgt die durchschnittliche Zeit der Jobsuche dagegen nur etwas mehr als drei Monate. Dies ist eines der Ergebnisse der Studie „Career choices and challenges in transition" von Drake, Beam Morin (DBM), New York. Der internationale Personalberater bringt jährlich eine globale Studie heraus, die Erfahrungen von Personen sammelt, die ihren Job verloren und einen neuen durch Beratung (Outplacement) gefunden haben. Für Deutschland beteiligt sich von Rundstedt und Partner an dieser Studie. Im vergangenen Jahr wurde die Erfahrung von 14 338 Arbeitnehmern abgefragt, die in 35 Ländern der Erde eine Outplacement-Beratung durch DBM erhalten haben. 71 Prozent der Studienteilnehmer waren männlich, 29 Prozent weiblich. Der typische Outplacement-Kandidat ist demnach Anfang bis Mitte 40 Jahre alt, war durchschnittlich 9 Jahre bei seinem Arbeitgeber, bevor er seine Kündigung erhielt, und in der Regel eine Führungskraft, Manager oder eine Fachkraft. Der überwiegende Teil der Befragten verlor seinen Job durch Fusionen, Restrukturierungen, Rücktritte, Pensionierungen. Nur etwa zwei Prozent gaben ein Fehlverhalten als Grund an. Die Studie hebt die Bedeutung guter Netzwerke hervor: In den meisten Fällen wurde der neue Job durch Kontakte gewonnen. Deutlich wurde auch, dass durch Kontaktpflege die Suchzeit verkürzt werden konnte.

Fachleute, die älter als 50 Jahre sind, entschieden sich eher für die Selbständigkeit, was häufig als letzte Chance einzuschätzen ist. Mit 30 Prozent wechselt eine große Zahl nicht nur die Branche, sondern auch die Funktion, und zwar bei gleichem oder sogar höherem Gehalt als im vorherigen Job. Frauen fanden in der Regel schneller einen neuen Arbeitgeber als Männer, und zwar mit einer höheren Wahrscheinlichkeit, die Höhe des Gehaltes zu halten und zu verbessern, und dies sogar eher als im Vergleich zu den männlichen Befragten.

Der Düsseldorfer Outplacement-Fachmann Eberhard von Rundstedt empfiehlt vom Jobverlust Betroffenen, auch „offen für alternative Lösungen zu sein". Obwohl man bei dem Thema Karriere immer von der Vorstellung eines Vollzeitjobs ausgehe, würden flexible Arbeitszeit, Teilzeit, Job-Sharing, freie Mitarbeit oder die projektbezogene Selbständigkeit mehr und mehr akzeptiert.

Gabriele Hermani

Frankfurter Allgemeine Zeitung, Samstag, 28. September 2002, Nr. 226/39, S. 49

Mehrsprachig, kommunikationsfähig und selbständig

Wer im Ausland arbeiten will, braucht interkulturelle Kompetenz

In fernen Ländern und anderen Kulturen zu leben ist reizvoll. Die Möglichkeiten hierfür steigen, denn immer mehr Unternehmen arbeiten global und suchen auch deutsche Mitarbeiter, die für lange oder kurze Zeit ins Ausland gehen. „Wer das Ziel hat, im Ausland zu arbeiten, sollte schon während seines Studiums mehrere Praktika dort absolvieren. Dies schütz davor, eine Auslandstätigkeit anzunehmen und danach erst festzustellen, dass es doch nichts für einen selbst ist", erklärt Michael Ibach, Geschäftsführer der Sycor Asia in Singapur. Der 39 Jahre alte Forstwirt weiß, wovon er spricht: Nach seinem Hochschulstudium arbeitete er zunächst für ein forstwirtschaftliches Beratungsunternehmen in Westafrika ... Seit 1998 lebt und arbeitet Ibach nun in Singapur.

Sein Arbeitgeber, Sycor Asia, unterstützt asiatische Tochterunternehmen deutscher Chemie- und Pharmaproduzenten sowie asiatische Unternehmen beim elektronischen Dokumentenmanagement ...

Die Göttinger Muttergesellschaft wird ... zukünftig auch eigene IT-Fachleute zeitlich begrenzt nach Singapur entsenden. Das Anforderungsprofil hierfür ist klar gefasst, wie Jochen Kuhl, Mitglied der Sycor-Geschäftsleitung, darlegt: „Wer für uns in Asien – aber auch in den Vereinigten Staaten – tätig sein will, muss das Talent zur Vielsprachigkeit, Kommunikationsfähigkeit und Selbständigkeit mitbringen. Wir können zwar den notwendigen fachlichen Support geben – vor Ort muss der Mitarbeiter jedoch eigenständig mit den unterschiedlichsten Herausforderungen klarkommen", sagt Kuhl. Auf den Auslandsaufenthalt bereitet das Unternehmen seine Mitarbeiter mit Sprachunterricht und englischsprachigen Kursen beispielsweise zu den Themen „Kundenorientierung" und „Konfliktmanagement" vor ... (*jgö.*)

Frankfurter Allgemeine Zeitung, Samstag, 26. Oktober 2002, Nr. 249/43, S. 55

Level 3

1. Welches Wort hat die gleiche oder eine ähnliche Bedeutung? ✓

1. die Gesellschaftsrechtlerin
2. speziell angefertigt
3. der Arbeitssüchtige
4. die Ausbildung am Arbeitsplatz
5. der Installateur
6. die Immobilienmaklerin

2. Welche Wörter gehören zusammen? ✓

a. die Antiquarin, b. der Bestatter, c. der Gefängniswärter, d. die Kustodin,
e. der Leibwächter, f. der Platzanweiser, g. der Reeder, h. die Sattlerin,
i. der Schuster, j. der Stuckateur

1. das Theater   6. die Wand
2. die Leiche   7. das Schiff
3. das Museum   8. der Gefangene
4. das Pferd   9. der Staatspräsident
5. der Schuh   10. Bücher

3. Ordnen Sie die folgenden Ausdrücke nach dem Ausmaß, der Geschwindigkeit usw. ✓

1. den Markt monopolisieren, den Markt sättigen, den Markt überschwemmen
2. Dienst nach Vorschrift, die Stilllegung, die Verlangsamung
3. kostendeckend, rentabel, Verlust bringend
4. der Arbeiter, der Arbeitssüchtige, der Drückeberger

4. Wie heißen die folgenden Ausdrücke auf Deutsch? ✓

a. company/Gesellschaft
  1. holding company
  2. joint-stock company
  3. limited company
  4. partnership

b. manager/Leiter
  1. area manager
  2. assistant manager
  3. line manager
  4. finance director

c. costs/Kosten
  1. handling charges
  2. marginal costs
  3. overheads
  4. running costs

5. Welches Verb passt? ✓

> a. dienen, b. durchbrechen, c. einholen, d. eintragen lassen, e. erschließen, f. finden,
> g. führen, h. herabsetzen, i. verdienen

1. eine Firma
2. den Vorsitz
3. einen Markt
4. einen Kostenvoranschlag
5. guten Absatz
6. den Preis radikal
7. sich seinen Lebensunterhalt
8. jmdm als Referenz
9. eine Streikpostenkette

6. Welches Wort passt nicht? ✓
1. die Abfindung, die Einstellung, die Kleinanzeige, die Stellenbeschreibung
2. der Aufsichtsbeamte, die Sicherheitsbeamtin, die Steuerbeamtin, der Wächter
3. Abzüge, der Einfuhrzoll, die Frachtgebühr, der Vorrat
4. die Börsenmaklerin, der Devisenhändler, die Bankerin, der Pförtner
5. der Gewerkschaftsbeitrag, die Lohnfortzahlung, die Nachzahlung, die Reisekostenvergütung
6. die Arbeitsstreitigkeit, das Berufsrisiko, der Beschwerdepunkt, die Gehaltsforderung

7. In jedem Satz fehlt ein Wort. ✓

> Abfindung, Arbeitsbeschaffung, erzeugen, flau, inserieren, Konsumgüter,
> Kündigungsschutz, Skonto, Stellenangebot, vorrätig

1. Die Preise für _____ bleiben stabil.
2. Das Medikament war in der Apotheke nicht _____.
3. Im Sommer läuft das Geschäft _____.
4. Die vorgeschlagenen Programme zur _____ werden viel Geld kosten.
5. Die meisten Grundstücksmakler _____ nicht nur in den Zeitungen.
6. Jeder Arbeitslose soll nach spätestens einem Jahr ein _____ bekommen.
7. Damit _____ sie eine Nachfrage.
8. Wo man bar bezahlen kann, bekommt man _____.
9. Schwangere genießen einen besonderen _____.
10. Je geringer das Einkommen, desto geringer die Steuer auf die _____.

8. Übersetzen Sie ins Deutsche. ✓
1. The trust agreement remains valid.
2. It isn't a buy-out, but rather a merger.
3. The previous company policy will not change.
4. He has been chair of the board of directors of the airline since 1986.
5. In order to reach the production target, we have to do overtime.
6. Unfortunately we have become a throwaway society.

7. With a market share of 15 percent, the PC producer is one of the market leaders.
8. Everything is being sold at giveaway prices.
9. The customer has to assume (agree to pay) the travel expenses.

9. *Schriftliche Übung. Schreiben Sie einen Geschäftsbrief. Wählen Sie eins der folgenden Themen.*

1. Produktanfrage
2. Bestellung
3. Beschwerde
4. Bewerbungschreiben
5. Referenz

10. *Übersetzen Sie ins Englische.*

Kunert baut noch mehr Stellen ab

Kunert AG, Immenstadt im Allgäu. Der Strumpfhersteller Kunert wird sein Umsatzziel in diesem Jahr nicht erreichen und kündigt einen zusätzlichen Personalabbau an. Aufgrund des schwachen Geschäftsverlaufs im dritten Quartal rechnet das Unternehmen nicht mehr damit, einen Erlös auf dem Niveau des Vorjahres von 155,3 Millionen Euro zu erzielen. Erwartet wird nun ein Rückgang um 9 Prozent für Kunert, während für die Branche eine Einbuße um 10 Prozent vorhergesagt wird. Das Ziel eines kleinen Gewinns gebe das Unternehmen nicht auf, doch müsse mit einer verschärften Kostensenkung darum gerungen werden, sagte ein Sprecher. Dafür sei auch ein zusätzlicher Personalabbau notwendig, über den mit dem Betriebsrat verhandelt werde. Im Kreis der Arbeitnehmer heißt es, es gehe um 100 Stellen. Seit längerem plant Kunert, die Zahl der Mitarbeiter bis Ende 2002 auf rund 2000 zu verringern. Anfang 2001 waren es noch 2900 Beschäftigte gewesen. Das Unternehmen teilte mit, der Aufsichtsrat habe Finanzvorstand Hubert Nopper zum Vorstandssprecher ernannt, da seinem Ressort eine besondere Verantwortung zukomme. Seit dem Rücktritt des Vorstandschefs Helmut Gilbert im August 2000 hatte es in der Unternehmensleitung keinen Vorsitzenden gegeben.

Joachim Herr

Frankfurter Allgemeine Zeitung, Samstag, 26. Oktober 2002, Nr. 249/43, S. 14

Dell wieder Marktführer bei Personalcomputern

FRANKFURT, 18. Oktober. Der texanische Computerhersteller Dell hat im dritten Quartal 2002 die Führung auf dem Weltmarkt für Personalcomputern (PC) zurückerobert. Nach der Fusion mit Compaq war Mitbewerber Hewlett Packard vor einem halben Jahr an die Spitze aufgerückt. Dell steigerte nach Erhebungen des amerikanischen Marktforschungsunternehmen IDC die Auslieferungen im Vergleich zum Vorjahresquartal um 23 Prozent auf 5,2 Millionen PC. Mit einem Weltmarktanteil von 16 Prozent ist Dell damit führend. HP rutschte mit 5 Millionen PC (minus 5 Prozent) und einem Marktanteil von 15,5 Prozent auf den zweiten Platz. Erstmals seit fünf

Quartalen wurde laut IDC zudem der Abwärtstrend auf dem Weltmarkt für PC beendet. Von Juli bis September stiegen die Auslieferungen im Vergleich zum selben Zeitraum des Vorjahres um 3,8 Prozent auf 32,6 Millionen Stück. „Das Wachstum bleibt begrenzt, aber wenigstens bewegt sich der Markt in die richtige Richtung", erklärte IDC-Analystin Loren Loverde. Die Investitionen der Unternehmen seien weiterhin schwach und auch die Nachfrage der Endverbraucher verbessere sich nur schrittweise.

Sabine Krömer

Frankfurter Allgemeine Zeitung, Samstag, 19. Oktober 2002, Nr. 243/42, S. 17

Unit 17

The office and computing

Level 1

Personnel

Sekretär(in), der/die (-e/nen)	secretary
etw tippen	to type sth
etw mit der Maschine schreiben	to type sth
Maschine schreiben	to type
Büroangestellte(r), der/die (adj. decl.)	office worker
Büroleiter(in), der/die (-/nen)	office manager
Programmierer(in), der/die (-/nen)	computer programmer
Laufbursche, -junge, der (-n)	errand boy, office boy

Offices

Büro, das (-s)	office
Informationsbüro, das (-s)	information office
Büroparty, die (-s)	office party
Sekretärinnenzimmer, das (-)	secretary's office
Schreibzimmer, das (-)	(typist's) office
Warteraum, der (¨e)	waiting room
Öffnungszeiten, pl.	office hours

Office equipment and materials

Computer, der (-)	computer
Fotokopierer, der (-)	photocopier
Kopie, die (-n)	photocopy
etw kopieren	to photocopy sth, duplicate sth
Briefpapier, das (-e)	stationery
(Brief)umschlag, der (¨e)	envelope
Schreibmaterial, das (-ien)	writing material, stationery
Schreibmaschinen-papier, das (-e)	typing paper
Schreibpapier, das (-e)	(typing) paper, writing paper
Kopierpapier, das (-e)	copy paper
Druckpapier, das (-e)	printing paper
Büromöbel, pl.	office furniture
Schreibtisch, der (-e)	desk
Schreibtischlampe, die (-n)	desk lamp
Drehstuhl, der (¨e)	swivel chair
Papierkorb, der (¨e)	waste-paper basket
Trennwand, die (¨e)	partition (wall)
Anschlagbrett, das (-er)	notice board, bulletin board
Hefter, der (-)	stapler
Heftklammer, die (-n)	staple
Gummiband, das (¨er)	rubber band
Tesafilm, der (-e; trademark)	Scotch tape ®, Sellotape ®

(Bleistift)spitzer, der (-)	pencil sharpener	Mausmatte, die (-n)	mouse mat/pad
Schredder, der (-)	shredder	(Maus)klick, der (-s)	(mouse) click
(Papier)schneidema- schine, die (-n)	paper cutter	(doppel)klicken	to (double-)click
		etw anklicken	to click on sth
Brieföffner, der (-)	letter opener, paper knife	Diskette, die (-n)	diskette
		etw formatieren	to format sth
Briefwaage, die (-n)	letter scale	vorformatiert	preformatted
Tischkalender, der (-)	desk diary	kaputt	corrupt
Terminkalender, der (-)	appointments diary	nicht lesbar	corrupt
		etw kaputt/nicht lesbar machen	to corrupt sth
Briefbeschwerer, der (-)	paperweight	Dokument, das (-e)	document
Akte, die (-n)	file, record	Datei, die (-en)	file
(Akten)ordner, der (-)	document file	im Gebrauch	active [file]
Aktendeckel, der (-)	folder	Dateiname, der (-n)	file name
Ringbuch, das (¨er)	ring binder	Modem, das (-e)	modem
Aktenschrank, der (¨e)	filing cabinet	E-Mail, die (-s)	e-mail
		sich einloggen	to log on/in
Kartei, die (-en)	card file, card index	sich ausloggen	to log off/out
Karteikarte, die (-n)	file card, index card	Passwort, das (¨er)	password
Karteikasten, der (¨)	file-card box	Hardware, die (no pl.)	hardware
Visitenkarte, die (-n)	business card	Software, die (-s)	software
Original, das (-e)	original	Software für Computerspiele, die (-s)	games software
(Tele)fax, das (-e)	fax; fax machine		
(Tele)faxgerät, das (-e)	fax machine	Zeichen, das (-)	character
		Schrift, die (-en)	font
(etw) (tele)faxen	to fax (sth)	Kleinbuchstabe, der (-n)	lower-case letter
Diktiergerät, das (-e)	dictating machine		
Diktiermaschine, die (-n)	dictating machine	Großbuchstabe, der (-n)	capital letter
		gepunktete Linie	dotted line
jmdm etw diktieren	to dictate sth to sb	Unterstreichung, die (-en)	underlining

Computing and typing

Personalcomputer (PC), der (-)	personal computer (PC)	Tippfehler, der (-)	typing mistake, typo
auf/per Computer	on/by computer	Suchmaschine, die (-n)	search engine
Desk-, Laptop, der (-s)	desktop/laptop computer	etw suchen	to search for sth
		Suchergebnisse, pl.	search results
(Farb)monitor, der (-en or -e)	(colour) monitor	(Computer)programm, das (-e)	(computer) program
Bildschirm, der (-e)	screen	etw programmieren	to program sth
Drucker, der (-)	printer	Programmieren, das (no pl.)	programming
Tastatur, die (-en)	keyboard		
Eingabetaste, die (-n)	enter key	ein Programm ablaufen lassen	to run a program
Maus, die (¨e)	mouse		

Hilfe, die (-n)	help	Internet, das (no pl.)	internet
Online-Hilfe, die (-n)	on-line help	hacken	to hack
Menü, das (-s)	menu	Hacker(in), der/die	hacker
scrollen	to scroll	(-/nen)	
Cursor, der (-s)	cursor	Computervirus, der	virus
Fenster, das (-)	window	or das (-viren)	

Level 2

Personnel

Fremdsprachense- kretär(in), der/die (-e/nen)	bilingual secretary	das Protokoll aufnehmen	to take the minutes
		Formbrief, der (-e)	form letter
Herr/Dame am Empfang, der/die (-en/n)	receptionist	Sprechanlage, die (-n)	intercom
		Konferenztisch, der (-e)	conference table
Empfangssekretär(in), der/die (-e/nen)	receptionist	persönliches/ individuelles Briefpapier	personalized letterhead
Kurzschrift, die (-en)	shorthand	fein liniertes Papier	narrow-ruled paper
Stenografie, die (-n)	shorthand	unliniertes Papier	plain paper
Stenotypist(in), der/die (-en/nen)	shorthand typist	Toner, der (-)	toner
		Tonerpatrone, die (-n)	toner cartridge
stenografieren	to write shorthand		
Büropersonal, das (no pl.)	clerical staff	Tonerkassette, die (-n)	toner cassette
Schreibkraft, die (¨e)	clerical worker, copy typist	Farbband, das (¨er)	ribbon
		Datumsstempel, der (-)	date stamp
Bürokraft, die (¨e)	clerical worker		
		etw mit Datumsstempel versehen	to date stamp sth

Offices

Vorzimmer, das (-)	receptionist's office, outer office	Unterschriftstempel, der (-)	signature stamp
Chefzimmer, das (-)	executive's office	Stempel-, Farbkissen, das (-)	ink pad
Konferenzsaal, der (-säle)	conference room		
Sitzungssaal, der (-säle)	board room	gefütterter Briefumschlag	padded envelope
Poststelle, die (-n)	mailroom	Versandtasche, die (-n)	padded envelope
Bürogebäude, das (-)	office building		
Bürohaus, das (¨er)	office block	selbstklebend	self-sealing
		gummiert	gummed [envelope]

Office equipment and materials

Mitteilung, die (-en)	memo	etw zukleben	to seal sth
Protokoll, das (-e)	minutes	Fensterbriefumschlag, der (¨e)	window envelope

453

Adressenaufkleber, der (-)	address label	etw auf Diskette sichern/abspeichern	to save sth to disk
Büroklammer, die (-n)	(small) paper clip	Datenbank, die (-en)	data bank, database
Aktenklammer, die (-n)	(large) paper clip	Datenverarbeitung, die (-en)	data processing
Locher, der (-)	punch	elektronische Datenverarbeitung (EDV)	electronic data processing, computing
Korrekturflüssigkeit, die (-en)	correcting fluid		
Akten ordnen/ anlegen	to file	etw sortieren	to sort sth
etw zu den Akten legen	to file sth away	Textverarbeitung, die (-en)	word processing
etw unter B ablegen	to file sth under 'B'	Textverarbeitungsanlage, die (-n)	word processor
bei den Akten	on file	etw mit Textverarbeitung schreiben	to word-process sth
Reißwolf, der (¨e)	shredder		
etw in den Reißwolf geben	to shred sth	Text(verarbeitungs)programm, das (-e)	word processor [software]
Frankiermaschine, die (-n)	franking machine	Textverarbeitungssoftware, die (-s)	word-processing software
etw frankieren	to frank sth	maschinenlesbar	machine-readable
Geschäftsbuch, das (¨er)	accounts book	Computersprache, die (-n)	computer language
Kassenbuch, das (¨er)	cash book	Leertaste, die (-n)	space bar
sich schriftlich beschweren	to write a letter of complaint	Umschalttaste, die (-n)	shift key [typewriter]
sich schriftlich entschuldigen	to write a letter of apology	Shifttaste, die (-n)	shift key [computer]
Begleitbrief, der (-e)	cover(ing) letter	Caps-Lock-Taste, die (-n)	caps lock key
		Netzwerk, das (-e)	network

Computing and typing

Arbeitsplatzstation, die (-en)	work station	Farbdrucker, der (-)	colour printer
		Laserdrucker, der (-)	laser printer
Büroautomatisierung, die (-en)	office automation	Matrixdrucker, der (-)	dot-matrix printer
Computerisierung, die (-en)	computerization	Tintenstrahldrucker, der (-)	inkjet printer
benutzer-, anwenderfreundlich	user-friendly	Bubblejet Drucker, der (-)	bubble-jet printer
sich mit Computern auskennen	to be computer literate	Papiervorschub, der (¨e)	paper feed
laden	to boot up	Druckvorschau, die (-en)	print preview
etw laden	to (up)load sth	Hard Copy, die (-s)	hard copy
etw herunterladen	to download sth	Ausdruck, der (-e)	printout
etw sichern	to save sth	Speicher, der (-)	memory
		Byte, das (-s)	byte

CD-ROM, die (-s)	CD-ROM	etw eingeben	to input sth
CD-ROM-Laufwerk, das (-e)	CD-ROM drive	etw markieren	to highlight sth
		etw löschen	to delete sth
Diskettenlaufwerk, das (-e)	disk drive	Text ausschneiden und einfügen	to cut and paste text
Rechtschreibprüfung, die (-en)	spell-checker	Clip-Art, die (-s)	clip art
		Icon, das (-s)	icon
Grammatikprüfung, die (-en)	grammar checker	Symbolleiste, die (-n)	toolbar
		Verzeichnis, das (-se)	directory
Speicherschreib- maschine, die (-n)	memory typewriter	etw (ein)scannen	to scan sth (in)
		Scanner, der (-)	scanner

Level 3

Personnel

Aushilfskraft, die (¨e)	temp
Bürogehilfe, -gehilfin, der/die (-n/nen)	office junior
Fonotypist(in), der/die (-en/nen)	audiotypist
Texterfasser(in), der/die (-/nen)	keyboard operator
Textverarbeiter(in), der/die (-/nen)	word processor
Systemanalytiker(in), der/die (-/nen)	systems analyst
Kurier(in), der/die (-e/nen)	courier
Servicemechaniker(in), der/die (-/nen)	service engineer
PR-Mann, -Frau, der/die (¨er/en)	PR man/woman

Offices

Büro der Bauleitung, das (-s)	site office
Kanzlei, die (-en)	office [of lawyer, notary]
Vorstandsetage, die (-n)	executive suite
Sekretariat, das (-e)	secretariat
Bürorangeleien, pl.	office politics
Großraumbüro, das (-s)	open-plan office

Geschäftsräume, pl.	business premises
Vorverkaufstelle, die (-n)	(advance) booking office

Office equipment and materials

Büroartikel, pl.	office supplies
Bürobedarf, der (no pl.)	office supplies
etw vervielfältigen	to duplicate sth
etw kollationieren	to collate sth
in doppelter Ausfertigung	in duplicate
Klebstreifenhalter, der (-)	adhesive tape dispenser
Klebstreifenrolle, die (-n)	roll of adhesive tape
Schreibunterlage, die (-n)	desk pad
Ablagekorb, der (¨e)	letter tray
Ablage für Ein-, Ausgänge, die (-n)	in/out-tray
(Brief)kuvert, das (-s)	envelope
Ries, das (-e)	ream
2 Ries Papier	2 reams of paper
selbstdurchschrei- bendes Papier	carbonless paper
Durchschlag, der (¨e)	carbon copy
Geschäfts(brief)papier, das (-e)	letterhead
Kanzleipapier, das (-e)	foolscap

Dünndruckpapier, das (-e)	India paper
Florpost, die (no pl.)	bank paper, onionskin paper
Hartpostpapier, das (-e)	bond(ed) paper
chlorfrei gebleichtes Papier	paper bleached without chlorine
ungebleicht	unbleached [paper]
verziert	crested [notepaper]
glänzend	glossy [paper]
geprägt	embossed [paper]
Folio, das (-s)	folio
DIN-Format, das (-e)	German standard paper size
Post-it, der (-s; trademark)	Post-it ®
Haftnotiz, die (-en)	self-stick note
Auftragsbuch, das (¨er)	order book
Pro-forma-Rechnung, die (-en)	pro forma invoice
Portokasse, die (-n)	petty cash
etw abzeichnen	to initial sth
etw nach Sachgebieten anordnen	to arrange sth by subject area
Ablagesystem, das (-e)	filing system
Leitz-Ordner, der (-; trademark)	lever-arch file
Hängeordner, der (-)	hanging file
Karteireiter, der (-)	index tab
Urkunde, die (-n)	document, deed, title deed
eine Urkunde (über etw) ausstellen/ ausfertigen	to draw up a document (about sth)
Entwurf, der (¨e)	draft
Firmenverzeichnis, das (-se)	trade directory

Computing and typing

computergestützt	computer-aided
Tabellenkalkulations- programm, das (-e)	spreadsheet
Anwendungspaket, das (-e)	application package
Tutorial, das (-s)	tutorial
interaktiv	interactive
Seriendruck, der (-e)	mail merge
Benutzerunterstützung, die (-en)	user support
Desktop-Publishing, das (no pl.)	desktop publishing
Fuß-, Kopfzeile, die (-n)	footer/header
Fuß-, Endnote, die (-n)	footnote/endnote
Rand, der (¨er)	margin
der obere/untere/ rechte Rand	the upper/lower/ right margin
Einzug, der (¨e)	indent
hängender Einzug	hanging indent
Lineal, das (-e)	ruler
links-, rechtsbündig	left/right-justified
zentriert	centred
Zeilenabstand, der (¨e)	line spacing
Seitenumbruch, der (¨e)	page break
Tabulator, der (-en)	tab
Tabulatortaste, die (-n)	tab key
Control-Taste, die (-n)	control key
Funktionstaste, die (-n)	function key
Pfeiltaste, die (-n)	arrow key
Resettaste, die (-n)	reset button
Lichtgriffel, der (-)	light pen
geschweifte Klammer	curly bracket
Bruchstrich, der (-e)	slash
Fehlermeldung, die (-en)	error message
Absturz, der (¨e)	crash
etw abbrechen	to abort sth
Notepad, das (-s)	notepad computer
elektronisches Notizbuch	personal organizer
Festplatte, die (-n)	hard disk
Datensichtgerät, das (-e)	visual display unit (VDU)

Speicherkapazität, die (-en)	memory capacity	auf etw zugreifen	to access sth
		Zugriff, der (no pl.)	access
Dateimanager, der (-)	file manager	Zugriff verweigert	access denied
		Autosave, das (no pl.)	autosave
Stammdatei, die (-en)	master file	automatische Speicherung, die (-en)	automatic save
Dialogfeld, das (-er)	dialogue box		
Zwischenablage, die (-n)	clipboard	Sicherungskopie, die (-n)	back-up copy
etw rückgängig machen	to undo sth	rücksetzen	to reset
Eingabeaufforderung, die (-en)	prompt	Computerjargon, der (-s)	computerese

Post and telecommunications

Level 1

Post

Post, die (no pl.)	post, mail, post office
Postamt, das ("er)	post office
Luftpost, die (no pl.)	airmail
per Luftpost	by air(mail)
Brief, der (-e)	letter
Briefschreiber(in), der/die (-/nen)	correspondent
Unterschrift, die (-en)	signature
Privatbrief, der (-e)	personal letter
Paket, das (-e)	package, parcel
Päckchen, das (-)	small package, parcel
Briefmarke, die (-n)	stamp
Absender(in), der/die (-/nen)	sender, sender's name and address
Adresse, die (-n)	address
Anschrift, die (-en)	address
Telegramm, das (-e)	telegram
Empfänger(in), der/die (-/nen)	addressee
Briefkasten, der (")	mailbox
Postkarte, die (-n)	postcard
etw schicken	to send sth
etw senden	to send sth
etw aufgeben	to have sth sent
Briefsammeltasche, die (-n)	collection bag

etw leeren	to empty sth
etw stempeln	to stamp/cancel sth
Bundespost, die (no pl.)	Federal Post Office
Poststempel, der (-)	postmark
mit der ersten Post kommen	to come with/in the first post
Telebrief, der (-e)	fax sent via the post office
Briefbombe, die (-n)	letter bomb
Postzug, der ("e)	mail train
Postwagen, der (-)	mail car/van

Telephone

Telefon, das (-e)	telephone
Fernsprecher, der (-)	telephone
Fernsprechapparat, der (-e)	telephone
das Telefon läutet/klingelt	the telephone is ringing
am Apparat	on the phone
bleiben Sie am Apparat!	hold the line! stay on the line!
Auf Wiederhören!	Goodbye.
Handy, das (-s)	mobile phone, cell(ular) phone

Telefonbuch, das (¨er)	telephone book	den Hörer auflegen/einhängen	to hang up the phone
sie steht im Telefonbuch	she's in the book	jmdn anrufen	to call sb
eine Nummer wählen	to dial a number	mit jmdm telefonieren	to speak with sb on the phone
Hörer, der (-)	receiver	telephonieren	to make a phone call
den Hörer abnehmen	to answer the phone	jmdn zurückrufen	to call sb back
ans Telefon gehen	to answer the phone	Telefonzelle, die (-n)	telephone booth

Level 2

Post

Postdienst, der (no pl.)	postal service
Postmeister(in), der/die (-/nen)	post master/mistress
Postfach, das (¨er)	box number, post office box
Postleitzahl, die (-en)	post code, zip code
Postgebühr, die (-en)	postage
Porto, das (-s or -ti)	postage
Brief-, Paketgebühr, die (-en)	letter/parcel rate
porto-, gebührenfrei	postage paid
freigemacht, frankiert	postage paid [envelope]
Briefkarte, die (-n)	letter card
Drucksache, die (-n)	printed matter
Post auf dem Landweg/Seeweg	surface mail
Eilbrief, der (-e)	express letter
Einschreiben, das (-)	certified mail, recorded delivery
vertraulich	confidential
Einladungsschreiben, das (-)	(official) invitation
Gratulationsschreiben, das (-)	letter of congratulation
Glückwunsch-schreiben, das (-)	letter of congratulation
Dankschreiben, das (-)	thank-you letter
Todesanzeige, die (-n)	death announcement

Geburtsanzeige, die (-n)	birth announcement
offener Brief	open letter
Neujahrskarte, die (-n)	New Year card
Anschriftenliste, die (-n)	mailing list
Rundschreiben, das (-)	circular
Kurierdienst, der (-e)	courier service
Postskript, das (-e)	postscript
Postskriptum, das (-te or -ta)	postscript

Telephone

durchwählen	to dial direct
sich verwählen	to misdial, dial the wrong number
ich habe mich verwählt	I've got the wrong number
Vorwahl, die (-en)	area code
Besetztzeichen, das (-)	busy signal
Rufzeichen, das (-)	ringing tone
Wählton, der (¨e)	dial tone
sich melden	to answer
Autotelefon, das (-e)	car phone
ein mobiles Telefon	a mobile phone
ein schnurloses Telefon	a cordless phone
ein tragbares Telefon	a portable phone
Kartentelefon, das (-e)	card telephone
Telefonkarte, die (-n)	telephone card

Fernsehtelefon, das (-e)	videophone	Anrufbeantworter, der (-)	answering machine
ein Gespräch vermitteln	to put a call through	Bandansage, die (-n)	recorded message
jmdn (mit jmdm) verbinden	to put sb through (to sb)	Signal-, Pfeifton, der (¨e)	beep
ein Gespräch unterbrechen	to disconnect a call	hinterlassen Sie Ihren Namen und Ihre Nummer nach dem Signalton	leave your name and number after the beep
ich/sie etc. war falsch verbunden	it was a wrong number	Telefongebühren, pl.	telephone rates

Level 3

Post

Zollerklärung, die (-e)	customs declaration	Karte mit Gene-sungswünschen, die (-n)	get-well card
Wertangabe, die (-n)	declaration of value	Versandhauskatalog, der (-e)	mail-order catalogue
Postanweisung, die (-en)	postal/money order	Versandhaus, das (¨er)	mail-order house
Einlieferungsschein, der (-e)	receipt of posting	Versandgeschäft, das (-e)	mail-order firm
Postwertzeichen, das (-)	stamp	frankierter Rückumschlag	prepaid return envelope
versiegelt	sealed	Antwortkarte, die (-n)	reply card
Adressat(in), der/die (-en/nen)	addressee	Antwortschein, der (-e)	(international) reply coupon
postlagernd	general delivery	postwendend	by return (of post)
Postbote, -botin, der/die (-n/nen)	letter carrier	Unterzeichner(in), der/die (-/nen)	signatory
Nachgebühr, die (-en)	excess, postage due		
Strafporto, das (-s or -ti)	excess, postage due	Rechts-, Links-unterzeichnete(r), der/die (adj. decl.)	right/left signatory
Rückporto, das (-s or -ti)	return postage	etw gegenzeichnen	to countersign sth
Einführungsschreiben, das (-)	letter of introduction	Empfehlungszettel, der (-)	compliments slip
Traueranzeige, die (-n)	death announcement	beiliegend	enclosed
Trauerbrief, der (-e)	letter announcing sb's death	dem Brief beigelegt	enclosed with/in the letter
Kondolenzbrief, der (-e)	letter of condolence	hiermit	herewith
Beileidsschreiben, das (-)	letter of condolence	in Beantwortung Ihres Briefes	in reply to your letter

Telephone

Fern(sprech)amt, das (¨er)	(telephone) exchange
Vermittlungsstelle, die (-en)	telephone exchange; switchboard
Fernsprechauskunft, die (¨e)	directory assistance
Orts-, Ferngespräch, das (-e)	local/long-distance call
Zeitunterschied, der (-e)	time difference
Zeitzone, die (-n)	time zone
R-Gespräch, das (-e)	reverse-charge call
ein R-Gespräch führen	to reverse the charges
Nebenanschluss, der (¨e)	extension
Apparat 2738	extension 2738
Münzfernsprecher, der (-)	coin-operated phone
Fernschreiber, der (-)	teleprinter
Funkrufempfänger, der (-)	pager
nicht verzeichnet	unlisted
es knackt in der Telefonleitung	the telephone is crackling
eine Telefonleitung anzapfen	to tap a phone line
die Leitung wird abgehört	the wires are tapped
faseroptisches Kabel	fibre-optic cable

Exercises

Level 1

1. Welches Wort hat die gleiche oder eine ähnliche Bedeutung? ✓

1. die Diktiermaschine
2. der Laufjunge
3. die Post (Gebäude)
4. die Adresse
5. etw senden
6. das Telefon
7. etw tippen

2. Wie heißt das Gegenteil? ✓

1. sich einloggen
2. die Software
3. der Kleinbuchstabe
4. den Hörer abnehmen
5. lesbar
6. die Absenderin
7. der Desktop
8. die Kopie

3. Ergänzen Sie die Tabelle. ✓

Maschine	Papier
1. die Schreibmaschine	
2.	das Kopierpapier
3. der Drucker	
4.	das Faxpapier

4. Welches Verb passt? ✓

> a. aufgeben, b. bleiben, c. einhängen, d. formatieren, e. gehen, f. klicken,
> g. leeren, h. wählen

1. ans Telefon	5. mit der Maus
2. eine Nummer	6. eine Diskette
3. den Briefkasten	7. am Apparat
4. einen Brief	8. den Hörer

5. Welches Wort passt nicht? ✓
1. der Aktenschrank, der Schreibtisch, die Telefonzelle, die Trennwand
2. die Postkarte, der Privatbrief, der Telebrief, die Visitenkarte
3. die Büroangestellte, die Büroleiterin, die Büroparty, das Büropersonal
4. der Fernsprecher, der Hacker, der Hefter, der Spitzer
5. der Aktendeckel, der Brieföffner, die Schneidemaschine, der Schredder

6. Welche Wörter gehören zusammen? ✓

> a. der Bildschirm, b. die Heftklammer, c. der Karteikasten, d. die Luftpost,
> e. die Mausmatte, f. der Ordner, g. der Poststempel, h. der Umschlag

1. der Brief
2. die Karteikarte
3. die Maus
4. der Monitor
5. der Hefter
6. die Briefmarke
7. das Flugzeug
8. die Akte

7. Wie heißen die Zusammensetzungen? ✓

~~Ring~~	raum	1. *das Ringbuch*
Eingabe	zeiten	2.
Dreh	waage	3.
Papier	taste	4.
Warte	brett	5.
Brief	korb	6.
Tipp	stuhl	7.
Öffnungs	~~buch~~	8.
Anschlag	fehler	9.

8. In jedem Satz fehlt ein Wort. ✓

> Datei, Gummiband, Handy, kopieren, Päckchen, scrollen, Suchergebnisse,
> Tastatur, Telefonbuch, Terminkalender, Unterschrift, zurückrufen

1. Er setzte seine _____ unter das Dokument.
2. Das Porto für _____ und Pakete wird vom 1. Juli an steigen.
3. Jeder dritte Deutsche besitzt schon ein _____.
4. Ich stehe nicht im _____.
5. Kann Herr Meier Sie _____?
6. In Bibliotheken kann jeder Bücher ausleihen und _____.
7. Der Umschlag war mit einem _____ umwickelt.
8. Sie beschwert sich über den vollgestopften _____.
9. Der PC wird mit _____ und Maus ausgeliefert.
10. Man sollte verdächtige E-mail löschen und auf keinen Fall die angehängte _____ öffnen.
11. Die _____ werden in einem kleinen Fenster wiedergegeben.
12. Bei sehr großen Seiten muss man manchmal weit hinunter _____.

9. Übersetzen Sie ins Englische.

Computer allgegenwärtig

Die meisten Unternehmen in Deutschland nutzen Computer. Inzwischen stehen sie bei 71 Prozent der Firmen, und 58 Prozent haben Zugang zum Internet. Wie das Statistische Bundesamt mitteilt, werden weitere vier Prozent bis zum Jahresende einen Anschluss haben. Fast alle Unternehmen mit mehr als 20 Beschäftigten setzen Computer ein.

FRANKFURTER RUNDSCHAU, Samstag, 23. November 2002, Nr. 273/47, S. 10

Internet weist den Weg zur Tankstelle

Gas geben – und das im wahrsten Sinne des Wortes wollen viele Autofahrer: Weil es umweltfreundlicher ist und weil es sich für sie rechnet, steigen sie auf Erdgas getriebene Autos um. Deren höheren Anschaffungskosten stellen sie in ihrer persönlichen Bilanz die erfreulich niedrigen Preise an den Tankstellen gegenüber.

Nur – das Netz der Erdgastankstellen ist noch längst nicht so dicht geknüpft wie das der Benzin- und Dieselstationen. Im Gegenteil: Oft genug stresst die Suche nach der nächstgelegenen Auffüllstelle die Fahrer von Erdgasautos gewaltig.

Damit könnte jetzt Schluss sein, wenn die Chauffeure über eine Verbindung ins Internet verfügen. Denn das Web-Angebot *www.erdgasfahrzeuge.de* weist ihnen kostenlos den direkten Weg zur nächsten Erdgastankstelle.

Dafür ist auf der genannten Website zuerst die Rubrik „Tankstellenfinder" anzuklicken. Die verweist auf den „Routenplaner", der für jede Tour innerhalb Deutschlands die entlang der Strecke liegenden Erdgastankstellen anzeigt und beschreibt, wie sie zu erreichen sind.

Der Menüpunkt „Umkreissuche" listet nach Eingabe der Adresse des Suchers alle in der Nähe befindlichen Stationen sowie die Entfernung und den günstigsten Anfahrtweg dorthin auf. Angezeigt werden darüber hinaus Öffnungszeiten, Telefonnummern, Zahlungsmodalitäten und Betreiber der Erdgastankstellen.

Werner Balsen

FRANKFURTER RUNDSCHAU, Samstag, 23. November 2002, Nr. 273/47, S. 10

Level 2

1. Welches Wort bzw. welche Wendung hat die gleiche oder eine ähnliche Bedeutung? ✓

1. die Stenografie
2. die Bürokraft
3. das Farbkissen
4. Akten ordnen
5. die Versandtasche
6. benutzerfreundlich
7. die Postgebühr
8. gebührenfrei
9. das Gratulationsschreiben
10. frankiert
11. der Signalton
12. persönliches Briefpapier

2. Welches Verb passt? ✓

> a. ablegen, b. abspeichern, c. aufnehmen, d. beschweren, e. frankieren, f. geben, g. herunterladen, h. legen, i. versehen, j. zukleben

1. das Protokoll
2. etw mit Datumsstempel
3. ein Schreiben zu den Akten
4. etw in den Reißwolf
5. sich schriftlich
6. etw auf Diskette
7. eine Akte unter F
8. einen Umschlag
9. einen Brief
10. eine Datei aus dem Internet

3. Wie heißt das Gegenteil? ✓

1. die Geburtsanzeige
2. liniertes Papier
3. ein Gespräch vermitteln
4. die Soft Copy
5. etw eingeben
6. das Besetztzeichen

4. Welches Wort passt nicht? ✓

1. etw eingeben, etw einscannen, etw laden, etw suchen
2. der Ausdruck, die Druckkabine, der Matrixdrucker, der Tintenstrahldrucker
3. die Empfangssekretärin, der Programmierer, das Sekretärinnenzimmer, der Stenotypist
4. etw ausschneiden, etw einfügen, etw freimachen, etw markieren

5. der Fernsprechauftragsdienst, der Geleitdienst, der Kurierdienst, der Postdienst
6. die Drucksache, der Eilbrief, das Einschreiben, das Schreibmaterial

5. Was bedeuten die folgenden Zusammensetzungen?
1. die Briefgebühren, die Paketgebühren, die Telefongebühren
2. das Chefzimmer, das Schreibzimmer, das Vorzimmer
3. der Datumsstempel, der Poststempel, der Unterschriftstempel
4. das Dankschreiben, das Einladungsschreiben, das Rundschreiben
5. das Autotelefon, das Fernsehtelefon, das Kartentelefon

6. In jedem Satz fehlt ein Wort. ✓

Bürogebäude, Büroklammer, Datenbank, entschuldigt, Konferenzsaal, Leertaste, maschinenlesbarer, Mitteilung, Reißwolf, Signalton, Tonerkassetten, verwählt

1. Die Sitzung wird im _____ staatfinden.
2. Im _____ im sechsten Stock erwartete ihn seine Assistentin.
3. Wie es in einer _____ vom Montag hieß, wird das Unternehmen den Gewinn in diesem Jahr mehr als verzehnfachen können.
4. Wie wird das umweltschädliche Druckerzubehör – z.B. Farbbänder, _____ – entsorgt?
5. Sie hat sich schriftlich _____.
6. Die Dokumente sind im _____ gelandet.
7. Die _____ wird ständig aktualisiert und erweitert.
8. Die Daten müssen in _____ Schrift eingetragen werden.
9. In Online-Manuals kann man einfach mit der _____ weiterblättern.
10. Hinterlassen Sie bitte eine Nachricht nach dem _____.
11. Entschuldigung, ich habe mich _____.
12. Das Foto hat sie mit einer _____ angeheftet.

7. Ordnen Sie.
der Adressenaufkleber, der Anrufbeantworter, die Bandansage, der Begleitbrief, die Druckvorschau, der Fensterbriefumschlag, der Fernsprechapparat, die Frankiermaschine, die Rechtschreibprüfung, der Speicher, die Symbolleiste, die Telefonkarte, die Textverarbeitung, der Wählton

der Brief	der Computer	das Telefon

8. Schriftliche Übung. Schreiben Sie einen Brief. Wählen Sie eins der folgenden Themen.
1. das Dankschreiben
2. die Geburtsanzeige
3. das Glückwunschschreiben

9. *Übersetzen Sie ins Englische.*

Auch O$_2$ verlangt hohe Wechselgebühr

FRANKFURT A.M. Handy-Besitzer, die zu einem anderen Mobilfunkbetreiber wechseln und dabei ihre Nummer behalten wollen, müssen tief in die Tasche greifen. Wer seinen Vertrag bei O$_2$ (früher Viag Interkom) kündigt, muss für die Mitnahme der Rufnummer zu einem anderen Anbieter 22,50 Euro zahlen. Und damit liegen die Münchner, wie sie gestern verkündeten, noch deutlich unter den bisher veröffentlichten Gebühren der Konkurrenz.

E-Plus fordert nach eigenen Angaben 25,95 Euro. Die beiden großen Betreiber T-Mobile und Vodafone hatten zuvor angekündigt, sie wollten rund 25 Euro respektive 30 Euro für die „Rufnummern-Portierung" verlangen, die von Anfang November an möglich sein soll. O$_2$ und E-Plus hatten zunächst auf branchenweit deutlich niedrigere Gebühren gehofft, doch spielten die Marktführer nicht mit. Sie müssen eher als die kleineren Wettbewerber die Abwanderung von Kunden durch die Möglichkeit der Nummernmitnahme fürchten.

Von ihr verspricht sich O$_2$-Manager Erwin Schmietow mehr neue Kunden, die von anderen Netzbetreibern kommen. Sein Haus lockt Wechselwillige vorerst bis Jahresende mit einem Guthaben von 25 Euro. Sie können damit die Portierungsgebühr, die sie ihrem alten Betreiber zahlen müssen, ganz oder teilweise ausgleichen.

Hans Georg Schröter

FRANKFURTER RUNDSCHAU, Samstag, 26. Oktober 2002, Nr. 249/43, S. 10

Post-Chef will nicht am neuen Porto rütteln

FRANKFURT A.M., 27. Dezember. Post-Vorstandschef Klaus Zumwinkel will auf einen Konter gegen die vom Regulierer angeordnete Portosenkung verzichten. Zwar hält er die vom 1. Januar an gültigen Preisabschläge „nach wie vor für nicht vertretbar". Der Manager schließt im Interview mit der *Frankfurter Rundschau* jedoch aus, dass der Konzern bei der Behörde beantragt, die Gebühren wieder anzuheben. „Keine der beteiligten Parteien möchte noch einmal durch solche schwierigen Verfahren gehen", signalisiert Zumwinkel, dass er einen neuen Porto-Streit vermeiden will. „Auf lange absehbare Zeit" sehe er „hier keine Bewegung".

Zu Neujahr sinken – erstmals – die Gebühren für zahlreiche Postsendungen. Für Standardbriefe in Europa verlangt die Post dann 0,55 (statt 0,56) Euro, für Postkarten 0,45 (statt 0,51) Euro. Zugleich erhöht sie aber die Preise für Zusatzdienste wie Nachnahmesendungen. Auch werden Nachsendeanträge kostenpflichtig.

Zumwinkel bekräftigte, dass der Konzern nach weiteren Engagements im Ausland Ausschau hält: „Wenn eine Postgesellschaft privatisiert wird, sind wir interessiert."

Detlef Fechtner

FRANKFURTER RUNDSCHAU, Samstag, 28. Dezember 2002, Nr. 301/52, S. 1

Level 3

1. Wie heißt das Gegenteil? ✓

1. die Ablage für Eingänge
2. gebleichtes Papier
3. die Kopfzeile
4. der untere Rand

5. linksbündig
6. die Floppy Disk
7. das Ferngespräch

2. Ordnen Sie. ✓

der Briefschreiber, der Fernschreiber, der Dateimanager, der Karteireiter, der Postmeister, der Servicemechaniker, der Texterfasser

Gegenstand	Mensch

3. Welche Wörter gehören zusammen?

> a. der Funkrufempfänger, b. der Hängeordner, c. die Kanzlei, d. die Karte mit Genesungswünsche, e. der Klebstreifenhalter, f. der Münzfernsprecher, g. die Vermittlungsstelle

1. der Rechtsanwalt
2. die Klebstreifenrolle
3. der Aktenschrank
4. die Krankheit

5. die Telefonistin
6. die Telefonzelle
7. die Ärztin

4. Welches Wort hat die gleiche oder eine ähnliche Bedeutung? ✓

1. der Bürobedarf
2. etw kopieren
3. der Briefumschlag
4. die Briefmarke
5. die Nachgebühr
6. die Todesanzeige

7. der Kondolenzbrief
8. das Versandhaus
9. der Empfänger
10. die Briefträgerin
11. das Autosave

5. Welches Verb passt? ✓

> a. abbrechen, b. abzeichnen, c. anordnen, d. anzapfen, e. ausfertigen, f. führen, g. machen, h. zugreifen

1. ein R–Gespräch
2. eine Telefonleitung
3. eine Mitteilung
4. ein Programm

5. auf ein Dokument
6. eine Urkunde
7. eine Operation rückgängig
8. ein Verzeichnis nach Sachgebieten

6. Welches Wort passt nicht? ✓

1. das Dünndruckpapier, die Florpost, das Geschäftspapier, die Postanweisung
2. die Aushilfskraft, der Bürogehilfe, das Sekretariat, der Textverarbeiter
3. die Büroangeleien, das Büro der Bauleitung, das Großraumbüro, das Informationsbüro
4. der Adressenaufkleber, der Durchschlag, die Haftnotiz, der Post-it
5. geprägt, glänzend, lockig, verziert
6. der Einzug, die Endnote, der Seitenumbruch, die Wertangabe

7. Welches Wort passt? ✓

a. die Fonotypist, b. das Kanzleipapier, c. der Kurier, d. das Ries, e. das Rückporto,
f. der Scanner, g. der Unterzeichner, h. die Zeitzone

1. Gebiet, in dem die gleiche Zeit gilt
2. jmd, der etw unterzeichnet hat
3. Porto für die Rücksendung von Postsachen
4. Maschinenschreiber, der nach einem Diktiergerät schreibt
5. ein Gerät, das Dokumente in digitale Signale umsetzt
6. der Bote
7. Papiermaß
8. Schreibpapier in DIN-Format 21 × 27,9 cm

8. In jedem Satz fehlt ein Wort. ✓

Ausfertigung, Fehlermeldung, Hartpostpapier, Schreibunterlage, Sicherungskopie,
Systemanalytiker, Tabellenkalkulationsprogramm, Tabulatortaste, Zeilenabstand

1. Zur Verstärkung ihrer Abteilung Softwareentwicklung suchen sie einen _____.
2. Dem Antrag hat sie einen Lebenslauf in doppelter _____ beigefügt.
3. Wir drucken Briefbogen überwiegend auf _____.
4. Ein _____ ist ein Programm, mit dem Daten in Tabellenform dargestellt und ausgewertet werden können.
5. Der _____ in diesem Text ist zu groß.
6. Die _____ verschiebt den Cursor nach rechts.
7. Wir erhalten dauernd die folgende _____ beim Öffnen des Programms.
8. Man sollte täglich eine _____ erstellen.
9. Sie können diese Weltkarte als _____ gebrauchen.

9. Übersetzen Sie ins Englische.

Call-by-Call im Ortsnetz erst später

Regulierer schiebt Verpflichtung auf / Telefonanschluss nicht teurer

Bonn, 29. November. Telefonkunden können vom 1. Dezember an doch nicht den Betreiber für Ortsgespräche frei wählen (Call-by-Call). Die

Regulierungsbehörde für Telekommunikation und Post hat wie erwartet die Verpflichtung zur Einführung von Call-by-Call jetzt offiziell bis Ende Februar 2003 ausgesetzt. Außerdem hat die Behörde den Antrag der Deutschen Telekom abgelehnt, die Neueinrichtung eines Telefonanschlusses dem Kunden nach Aufwand abzurechnen. Die hätte zu deutlich höheren Preisen geführt.

Nach Einschätzung der Telekom wie der Wettbewerber sei die Einführung von Call-by-Call und der Betreibervorauswahl (Preselection) am 1. Dezember technisch nicht möglich, teilte die Behörde mit. Die kurze Zeit seit der Gesetzesänderung habe nicht ausgereicht, um die Software für die Vermittlungsstellen zu entwickeln. Zum Zeitbedarf wird das Amt die Beteiligten jetzt anhören. Die Telekom hält die Einführung von Call-by-Call frühestens am 24. April 2003 und von Preselection am 8. Juli 2003 für realisierbar. Nach der Entscheidung der Aufsichtsbehörde muss die Telekom künftig für die Bereitstellung analoger Telefonanschlüsse ein Pauschalentgelt verlangen. Zum Schutz der Kunden vor einem Preismissbrauch könnten „grundsätzlich nur kalkulierte, einheitliche Entgelte in Betracht kommen", heißt es in der Entscheidung. Bisher verlangt das Unternehmen 51,57 Euro als einmalige Gebühr bei Neueinrichtung. Dieser Preis könne die Kosten für Arbeiten in den Räumen des Kunden nicht abdecken, argumentiert die Telekom. Deshalb wollte sie je Viertelstunde praktischer Arbeit 14,83 Euro und zusätzlich 47,45 Euro Fahrtkosten je Arbeitstag verlangen.

Heinz Stüwe

Frankfurter Allgemeine Zeitung, Samstag, 30. November 2002, Nr. 279/48, S. 12

Unit 18

Law

Level 1

Crime

jmdn töten	to kill sb
jmdn ermorden	to kill/murder sb
Mord, der (-e)	murder
Massenmord, der (-e)	mass murder
Mörder(in), der/die (-/nen)	murderer
Serienmörder(in), der/die (-/nen)	serial murderer
einbrechen	to break in
Einbrecher(in), der/die (-/nen)	burglar
Einbruch, der (¨e)	breaking and entering
Verbrecher(in), der/die (-/nen)	criminal
streiten	to fight
kämpfen	to fight
sich (mit jmdm) schlagen	to fight (with sb)
Schlägerei, die (-en)	fight, brawl
Dieb(in), der/die (-e/nen)	thief
etw stehlen	to steal sth
Diebstahl, der (¨e)	theft, larceny
Autodiebstahl, der (¨e)	car theft
einfacher/schwerer Diebstahl	petty/grand larceny
Einbruchsdiebstahl, der (¨e)	burglary
Taschendiebstahl, der (¨e)	purse snatching
Überfall, der (¨e)	mugging, raid, holdup
jmdn überfallen	to mug sb
etw überfallen	to raid sth
Bande, die (-n)	gang
jmdn ausrauben	to rob sb
Raub, der (no pl.)	robbery, theft
Raubüberfall, der (¨e)	robbery
bewaffneter Raubüberfall	hold-up, armed robbery
bewaffnet	armed
ausbrechen	to escape [from prison]
Schwindel, der (no pl.)	swindle, fraud, con
Terrorist(in), der/die (-en/nen)	terrorist
(etw) schmuggeln	to smuggle (sth)
Waffenschmuggler(in), der/die (-/nen)	gun runner
Drogenhändler(in), der/die (-/nen)	drug dealer
Dealer(in), der/die (-/nen)	drug pusher
Drogenhandel, der (no pl.)	drug-trafficking
Verbrechen, das (-)	crime

organisiertes Verbrechen	organized crime	Wachhund, der (-e)	guard dog
Kriminalität, die (no pl.)	crime; crime rate	Informant(in), der/die (-en/nen)	informer
Mafia, die (no pl.)	Mafia, mob	jmdn befragen	to question sb
Unterwelt, die (no pl.)	underworld	Identifikation, die (-en)	identification
Gangster(in), der/die (-/nen)	gangster	Beschreibung, die (-en)	description
Gewalt, die (no pl.)	violence	Todesursache, die (-n)	cause of death
Opfer, das (-)	victim	Alibi, das (-s)	alibi
Blutbad, das (¨er)	blood bath	Fingerabdruck, der (¨e)	fingerprint
jmdn kidnappen	to kidnap sb	Lösegeld, das (-er)	ransom
Kidnapper(in), der/die (-/nen)	kidnapper	Belohnung, die (-en)	reward
		sich ergeben	to give o.s. up
		sich stellen	to give o.s. up

Police and investigation

Polizei, die (no pl.)	police
Verkehrspolizei, die (no pl.)	traffic police
Polizist(in) (in Zivil), der/die (-en/nen)	(plain-clothes) police officer
außer Dienst	off duty
(Privat)detektiv(in), der/die (-e/nen)	(private) detective
Polizeichef(in), der/die (-s/nen)	chief of police
Polizeipräsident(in), der/die (-en/nen)	chief of police
Kommissar(in), der/die (-e/nen)	inspector, commissioner, superintendent
(vor jmdm) flüchten	to escape (from sb)
jmdn fangen	to catch sb
jmdn festnehmen	to arrest sb
jmdn verhaften	to arrest sb
Verhaftung, die (-en)	arrest
Untersuchung, die (-en)	inquiry, investigation
Durchsuchung, die (-en)	search
etw nach etwas durchsuchen	to search sth for sth
Durchsuchungsbefehl, der (-e)	search warrant
Polizeihund, der (-e)	police dog

Justice

Gesetz, das (-e)	law
gesetzlich	legal
Paragraf, der (-en)	section, paragraph
Gericht, das (-e)	court
Gerichtssaal, der (-säle)	courtroom
vor Gericht erscheinen	to appear in court
Prozess, der (-e)	case, trial, litigation
Beweis, der (-e)	evidence, proof
etw beweisen	to prove sth
Anspruch, der (¨e)	claim, right
Recht, das (-e)	right
Rechtshilfe, die (-n)	legal aid
Richter(in), der/die (-/nen)	judge
Friedensrichter(in), der/die (-/nen)	justice of the peace, magistrate
Rechtsanwalt, -anwältin, der/die (¨e/nen)	solicitor, barrister; lawyer, attorney
Staatsanwalt, -anwältin, der/die (¨e/nen)	public prosecutor, district attorney
Verteidiger(in), der/die (-/nen)	defence lawyer
jmdn verteidigen	to defend sb

Schuld, die (no pl.)	guilt	elektrischer Stuhl	electric chair
(un)schuldig	(not) guilty	lebenslänglich	to receive a life
sich (un)schuldig	to plead (not) guilty	bekommen	sentence, get life
bekennen		Anklage, die (-n)	charge
jmdn beschuldigen	to charge/accuse sb	jmdn (wegen etw)	to accuse/charge sb
jmdn für	to find sb. (not) guilty	anklagen	(with sth)
(un)schuldig		Klage, die (-n)	suit, complaint
befinden		gegen jmdn auf etw	to sue sb for sth
Strafe, die (-n)	punishment, fine,	klagen	
	sentence	Fall, der (¨e)	case
Geldstrafe, die (-n)	fine	Motiv, das (-e)	motive
Strafzettel, der (-)	ticket	in Notwehr handeln	to act in self-defence
jmdn bestrafen	to sentence/punish	Wahrheit, die (-en)	truth
	sb	Gerechtigkeit, die	justice
jmdn verurteilen	to sentence sb	(no pl.)	
Freiheitsstrafe,	prison sentence	gerecht	just, fair
die (-n)		Kaution, die (-en)	bail
Gefängnis, das (-se)	prison	Kaution stellen	to stand bail
Urteil, das (-e)	sentence, judgment	jmdn gegen Kaution	to release sb on bail
einstimmig	unanimous	freilassen	
Todesurteil,	death sentence	jmdn gegen Kaution	to bail sb out
das (-e)		freibekommen	
Hinrichtung,	execution	Abschreckungseffekt,	deterrent effect
die (-en)		der (-e)	

Level 2

Crime

Totschlag, der	manslaughter,	schwere	grievous bodily harm
(no pl.)	homicide	Körperverletzung	
Killer(in), der/die	killer, hit-man/	Rechtsbrecher(in),	law-breaker
(-/nen)	woman	der/die (-/nen)	
jmdn killen (sl.)	to bump sb off, kill sb	Wiederholungs-	persistent offender
Auftragsmord,	contract killing	täter(in), der/die	
der (-e)		(-/nen)	
Entführer(in),	kidnapper	Gewohnheitstäter(in),	habitual offender
der/die (-/nen)		der/die (-/nen)	
etw/jmdn entführen	to hi-jack sth,	Straftat, die (-en)	offence
	kidnap/abduct sb	strafbar	punishable
Angreifer(in),	assailant	etw begehen	to commit sth
der/die (-/nen)		Ladendiebstahl,	shoplifting
jmdn erstechen	to stab sb to death	der (¨e)	
jmdn vergiften	to poison sb	Deckname, der (-n)	alias
Körperverletzung,	bodily injury, assault	Betrug, der (no pl.)	fraud
die (-en)	(and battery)	Bestechung, die (-en)	bribery
		jmdn bestechen	to bribe sb

Verbrechenswelle, die (–n)	crime wave
Drogenmissbrauch, der (no pl.)	drug abuse
Drogenabhängige(r), der/die (adj. decl.)	drug addict
Schusswaffe, die (–n)	firearm
Verkehrsverstoß, der (¨e)	traffic offence/ violation
Verwarnung, die (–en)	caution, warning
gebührenpflichtige Verwarnung	fine
mit etw schieben (coll.)	to traffic in sth
jmdn anführen	to hoax sb
jmdn hereinlegen	to hoax sb
Störung des Friedens, die (–en)	disturbance of the peace
Kleinkriminalität, die (no pl.)	petty crime
Anstifter(in), der/die (–/nen)	instigator
aus kürzester Entfernung/Distanz	at point-blank range
jmdm entkommen	to escape from sb
Häftling, der (–e)	prisoner
entflohener Häftling	escapee
Krawall, der (–e)	riot
jmdn verpfeifen (coll.)	to grass on sb
der Polizei einen Tipp/Wink geben	to tip off the police
mit jmdm eine alte Rechnung begleichen	to settle a score with sb
wildern	to poach
Wilderer, der (–); Wilderin, die (–nen)	poacher
über die Grenze fliehen	to flee/skip the country
auf der Flucht	on the run
Flüchtling, der (–e)	fugitive
Kinderpornografie, die (no pl.)	child pornography
Geldbuße, die (–n)	fine
Bußgeld, das (–er)	fine [driving]

Police and investigation

Spur, die (–en)	clue, trail
Reifenspuren, pl.	tyre tracks
die Polizei ist ihm auf der Spur	the police are on his trail
Spürhund, der (–e)	sleuth
jmdm etw anhängen	to frame sb for sth
Polizeispitzel(in), der/die (–/nen)	police informer
nach Angaben des Zeugen	according to (the testimony of) the witness
Überwachung, die (–en)	stakeout
jmdn überwachen	to keep sb under surveillance
Beschatter(in), der/die (–/nen; coll.)	tail
jmdn beschatten lassen	to put a tail on sb
etw abhören	to bug sth, listen in on sth [conversation]
Bullen, pl. (sl.)	fuzz
Polyp, der (–en; coll., hum.)	cop
Polizeirevier, das (–e)	police station
Gefangene(r), der/die (adj. decl.)	prisoner
Handschelle, die (–n)	handcuff
jmdm Handschellen anlegen	to handcuff sb
Vermisste(r), der/die (adj. decl.)	missing person
Streifenwagen, der (–)	patrol car, panda car
nicht gekennzeichnet	unmarked [police car]
Straßensperre, die (–n)	roadblock
Radarfalle, die (–n)	speed trap
Überfallkommando, das (–s)	riot police

Schutzschild, der (-e)	riot shield	Zeugenstand, der (no pl.)	witness stand
Razzia, die (-zien)	raid	Beklagte(r), der/die (adj. decl.)	defendant [in civil cases]
Knüppel, der (-)	baton, truncheon		
Tränengas, das (no pl.)	teargas	Angeklagte(r), der/die (adj. decl.)	accused, defendant
kugelsicher	bulletproof	Kläger(in), der/die (-/nen)	claimant, plaintiff
Funksprechgerät, das (-e)	two-way radio		
Sicherheitsdienst, der (-e)	security firm	Geschworene(r), der/die (adj. decl.)	juror
		die Geschworenen, pl.	the jury

Justice

gegen etw verstoßen	to offend/violate sth	Geschworenenbank, die (¨e)	jury box
gegen jmdn Anklage erheben	to bring charges against sb	Protokollführer(in), der/die (-/nen)	Clerk of the Court
Anklageschrift, die (-en)	indictment	Protokoll, das (-e)	transcript
eine Klage gegen jmdn einrei-chen/erheben	to institute proceedings against sb	jmdn freisprechen	to acquit sb
		Freispruch, der (¨e)	acquittal
Vorladung, die (-en)	summons	jmdn (ins Gefängnis) einsperren	to jail sb
jmdn verhören	to cross-examine/ interrogate sb	Haftung, die (-en)	(legal) liability/ responsibility
Verhör, das (-e)	examination, interrogation	eine Lücke im Gesetz	a loophole in the law
		Fehlurteil, das (-e)	miscarriage of justice
unzulässig	inadmissible	ein Urteil über jmdn/etw fällen	to pass judgment on sb/sth
belastend	incriminating		
Aussage, die (-n)	statement	die Beweise reichen nicht aus	there isn't enough evidence
eine eidliche/ schriftliche Aussage	a sworn/written statement	aus Mangel an Beweisen	for lack of evidence
eine Aussage machen	to make a statement, give evidence	jmdn entlassen	to discharge sb
		Einzelhaft, die (no pl.)	solitary confinement
gegen/für jmdn aussagen	to testify against/for sb	Haftentlassung, die (no pl.)	release from prison
Einspruch, der (¨e)	objection		
Einspruch erheben	to object	bedingte Haftentlassung	parole
ich erhebe Einspruch	objection!	zivilrechtlich	civil
Einspruch abgelehnt/ stattgegeben	objection overruled/ sustained	Zivilprozess, der (-e)	civil action
(Augen)zeuge, -zeugin, der/die (-n/nen)	(eye)witness	Gerichtshof, der (¨e)	court (of justice), law court
		Oberster Gerichtshof	Supreme Court (of Justice)
Zeuge/Zeugin der Verteidigung/der Anklage, der/die (-n/nen)	witness for the defence/ prosecution	Auslieferung, die (-en)	extradition
		jmdn ausliefern	to extradite sb

Level 3

Crime

Straffällige(r), der/die (adj. decl.)	offender
straffällig werden	to commit a criminal offence
Straftäter(in), der/die (-/nen)	offender, criminal
jugendlicher Straftäter; jugendliche Straftäterin	juvenile delinquent
Ersttäter(in), der/die (-/nen)	first offender
etw fälschen	to forge sth
Fälschung, die (-en)	forgery
Delikt, das (-e)	offence, crime
Bagatelldelikt, das (-e)	petty/minor offence
Vergehen, das (-)	crime, offence
etw unterschlagen	to embezzle sth
Unterschlagung, die (-en)	embezzlement
Erpressung, die (-en)	extortion, blackmail
jmdn erpressen	to blackmail sb
Geld erpressen	to extort money
Geisel, die (-n)	hostage
Zuhälterei, die (no pl.)	pimping, procuring
Zuhälter(in), der/die (-/nen)	pimp, procurer
Hehler(in), der/die (-/nen)	fence, receiver of stolen goods
Hehlerei, die (-en)	receiving
etw hehlen	to receive [stolen goods]
Verleumdung, die (-en)	slander
gedungener Mörder; gedungene Mörderin	hired assassin
Meineid, der (-e)	perjury
einen Meined leisten	to commit perjury
einen Tresor knacken (sl.)	to crack a safe
ein Schloss knacken (sl.)	to pick a lock
Attentat, das (-e)	assassination
ein Attentat auf jmdn verüben	to assassinate sb; make an attempt on sb's life
Attentäter(in), der/die (-/nen)	assassin
Kinderschänder(in), der/die (-/nen)	child molester
Kindesmisshandlung, die (-en)	child abuse
misshandelt	battered
Spanner, der (-; coll.)	peeping Tom
Herumtreiber(in), der/die (-/nen)	prowler
unsittliches Verhalten	act of indecency
Komplize, der (-n); Komplizin, die (-nen)	accomplice
Brandstiftung, die (-en)	arson
Brandstifter(in), der/die (-/nen)	arsonist
Bombenanschlag, der (¨e)	bomb attack
Brandanschlag, der (¨e)	arson attack
jmdn belästigen	to harass sb
Prostituierte(r), der/die (adj. decl.)	prostitute
Nutte, die (-n; pej.)	hooker
jmdn vergewaltigen	to rape sb
Vergewaltiger, der (-)	rapist
vorbestraft sein	to have a criminal record
nicht vorbestraft sein	to have a clean record
gesetzestreu	law-abiding

Police and investigation

die Polizei verständigen	to notify the police
Anzeige, die (-n)	report

Anzeige gegen jmdn erstatten	to report sb to the authorities	Gerichtsdiener(in), der/die (-/nen)	bailiff
Verdacht, der (no pl.)	suspicion	Untersuchungshaft (U-Haft), die (no pl.)	custody, detention
Wanze, die (-n)	bug		
etw verwanzen	to bug sth		
das Zimmer ist verwanzt	the room is bugged	in Untersuchungs-haft	on remand, in detention
Phantombild, das (-er)	Identikit®/Photofit® picture	jmdn weiterhin in Untersuchungs-haft behalten	to remand sb in custody
Haftbefehl, der (-e)	arrest warrant		
einen Haftbefehl gegen jmdn ausstellen	to issue a warrant for sb's arrest	Berufung, die (-en)	appeal
		Berufung einlegen	to appeal
		Berufungsgericht, das (-e)	court of appeal
Fahndung, die (-en)	search, manhunt		
nach etw fahnden	to search for sth	Berufungsinstanz, die (-en)	court of appeal
jmdm hart auf den Fersen folgen	to be in hot pursuit of sb	eine Anklage zurückziehen	to withdraw a charge
Tarnung, die (no pl.)	cover		
getarnt als	under cover as	ein Verfahren niederschlagen	to dismiss a case
jmdn enttarnen	to blow sb's cover	außergerichtliche Einigung	out-of-court settlement
Ermittlung, die (-en)	investigation		
Ermittlungen anstellen	to make inquiries	Schadenersatz, der (no pl.)	damages
Ermittler(in), der/die (-/nen)	investigator	jmdn auf Schadenersatz verklagen	to sue sb for damages
verdeckter Ermittler	undercover investigator		
jmdn ertappen	to catch sb	Schadenersatz zugesprochen bekommen	to be awarded damages
etw beschlagnahmen	to seize sth		
Drogenfahndungs-behörde, die (-n)	drug squad	als Kronzeuge auftreten	to turn King's evidence
Sittenpolizei, die (no pl.)	vice squad	Geständnis, das (-se)	confession
etw leugnen	to deny sth	etw gestehen	to confess sth
jmdn vernehmen	to question sb	verminderte Zurech-nungsfähigkeit	diminished responsibility; insanity
forensisch, gerichtlich	forensic		
Verbrechensverhü-tung, die (no pl.)	crime prevention	nicht zurechnungsfähig	unfit to plead
Verbrechensbekämp-fung, die (no pl.)	combating crime	mildernde Umstände, pl.	extenuating circumstances
		Indizienbeweis, der (-e)	circumstantial evidence

Justice

(Handlungs)vollmacht, die (-en)	power of attorney	Vorsatz, der (¨e)	premeditation, intent
		mit Vorsatz	with intent
Mandant(in), der/die (-en/nen)	(lawyer's) client	Eid, der (-e)	oath

einen Eid ablegen/ schwören/leisten	to take/swear an oath	Verfahren, das (-)	proceedings
		Wiederaufnahme-verfahren, das (-)	retrial
Plädoyer, das (-s)	address to the jury, summation	Nachsicht, die (no pl.)	leniency
Milde, die (no pl.)	clemency	Verhandlung, die (-en)	trial, hearing; plea bargaining
Begnadigung, die (-en)	pardon	eine Gefängnisstrafe verbüßen	to serve a prison sentence
Strafaufschub, der (¨e)	suspension of sentence, reprieve	eine Freiheitsstrafe in eine Geldstrafe umwandeln	to commute a prison sentence to a fine
Vollstreckungs-aufschub, der (¨e)	stay of execution		
ein Urteil aufheben	to reverse/quash a judgment	Straferlass, der (¨e)	remission (of a sentence)
Bewährung, die (no pl.)	suspension, probation	Übergangshaus, das (¨er)	halfway house
jmdm (ein Jahr) Bewährung geben	to put sb on probation (for a year)	Strafkolonie, die (-n)	penal colony
		Sträfling, der (-e)	prisoner
Bewährungshelfer(in), der/die (-/nen)	probation officer	Zuchthäusler(in), der/die (-/nen)	convict
auf Bewährung Freigelassene(r), der/die (adj. decl.)	offender on probation, probationer	Knast, der (no pl.; sl.)	clink
		Knast schieben (sl.)	to do time, do porridge
eine Strafe zur Bewährung aussetzen	to impose a suspended sentence	Knastbruder, der (¨; coll.)	jailbird

Finance

Level 1

General

sich etw leisten	to afford sth	Finanzmarkt, der (¨e)	financial market
Inflation, die (-en)	inflation	Geldgeber(in), der/die (-/nen)	financial backer
Deflation, die (-en)	deflation		
Rezession, die (-en)	recession	*Money*	
Kapital, das (-ien or -e)	capital	Geld, das (no pl.)	money
		Mark, die (-)	mark
einen Preis nennen	to quote a price	Euro, der (- or -s)	euro
Weltbank, die (no pl.)	World Bank	Pfennig, der (-e)	pfennig
Finanzier(in), der/die (-s/nen)	financier	Schein, der (-e)	banknote, bill
		Dollar, der (- or -s)	dollar
Finanz-, Geschäftsjahr, das (-e)	financial year	Bargeld, das (no pl.)	cash
		Kleingeld, das (no pl.)	change, coin

Payment and purchasing

zahlen	to pay
etw bezahlen	to pay for sth
etw (in) bar bezahlen	to pay cash for sth
Bezahlung, die (-en)	payment
etw ausgeben	to spend sth
Ausgabe, die (-n)	expense, expenditure
Scheck, der (-s)	cheque
Bankscheck, der (-s)	bank cheque
mit einem Scheck bezahlen	to pay by cheque
Kreditkarte, die (-n)	charge card; credit card

Profit and loss

Marktwert, der (-e)	market value
Gewinn, der (-e)	profit
profitabel	profitable
Gewinn/Profit bringend	profitable
(mit etw) einen Profit/Gewinn machen	to make a profit (on/out of sth)
Verlust, der (-e)	loss
Verluste machen	to make a loss
Verlust bringend	loss-making
Bankrott, der (-e)	bankruptcy
Bankrott gehen/machen	to become/go bankrupt

Credit and debt

Kredit, der (-e)	credit; loan
sie hat bei der Bank Kredit	her credit is good with the bank
Kreditgrenze, die (-n)	credit limit
Schulden, pl.	debt
Schulden machen	to run up debts
jmdm etw schulden	to owe sb sth
Rechnung, die (-en)	bill, invoice
Kreditgeber(in), der/die (-/nen)	creditor
Gläubiger(in), der/die (-/nen)	creditor
Schuldner(in), der/die (-/nen)	debtor

das Konto überziehen	to overdraw one's account
etw zurückzahlen	to pay back sth
Darlehen, das (-)	loan
Darlehensgeber(in), der/die (-/nen)	lender
Darlehensnehmer(in), der/die (-/nen)	borrower
Hypothek, die (-en)	mortgage
zahlungs(un)fähig	(in)solvent

The market

Börse, die (-n)	stock market
an der Börse spekulieren	to play the market
Börsenanalytiker(in), der/die (-/nen)	stock analyst
Markt, der (¨e)	market, trade
fallender Markt	falling market
fester Markt	firm market
Geldmarkt, der (¨e)	money market
Aktie, die (-n)	share
Aktienhandel, der (no pl.)	equity trading
Aktienindex, der (-e, -dizes, or -dices)	share index
Makler(in), der/die (-/nen)	broker
Börsenmakler(in), der/die (-/nen)	stock broker, floor broker
Maklergeschäft, das (-e)	brokerage
Maklerfirma, die (-firmen)	brokerage firm
sinken	to fall, drop [price]
Marktwirtschaft, die (no pl.)	market economy
Börsenkrach, der (¨e)	stock market crash

Banks and bank staff

Bank, die (-en)	bank
Banker(in), der/die (-/nen)	banker
Bankier(in), der/die (-s/nen)	banker
Schalter, der (-)	counter

477

Kassierer(in), der/die (-/nen)	teller, cashier	Geldautomatenkarte, die (-n)	cash card
Bankangestellte(r), der/die (adj. decl.)	bank clerk	Geheimzahl, die (-en)	PIN, personal identification number
Bankkaufmann, -frau, der/die (-leute/en)	(qualified) bank clerk	einen Scheck (aus)schreiben	to write (out) a cheque
Sparkasse, die (-n)	savings bank	einen Scheck einlösen	to cash a cheque

Banking and investment

(Bank)konto, das (-s, -ten, or -ti)	(bank) account	Reisescheck, der (-s)	traveller's cheque
ein Konto eröffnen	to open an account	Kasse, die (-n)	cash point, cash desk
ein Konto löschen/auflösen	to close an account	etw investieren	to invest sth
Geld (auf ein Konto) einzahlen	to deposit money (into an account)	Investition, die (-en)	investment

Taxation

Einzahlung, die (-en)	deposit	Steuer, die (-n)	tax
Einzahler(in), der/die (-/nen)	depositor	Steuern bezahlen	to pay taxes
Einzahlungsschein, der (-e)	deposit slip	Steuerzahler(in), der/die (-/nen)	tax-payer
Geld (von einem Konto) abheben	to withdraw money (from an account)	Lohn-, Einkommen(s)steuer, die (-n)	income tax
Geld auf dem Konto haben	to be in credit	Steuergruppe, -klasse, die (-n)	tax bracket
Kontonummer, die (-n)	account number	besteuerbar	taxable
Gemeinschaftskonto, das (-s, -ten, or -ti)	joint account	steuerfrei	tax-free
		Finanzamt, das (¨er)	tax office
Transaktion, die (-en)	transaction	Steuererklärung, die (-en)	tax return

Insurance

Geld überweisen	to transfer money	Versicherung, die (-en)	insurance
Überweisung, die (-en)	transfer	Versicherungsgesellschaft, die (-en)	insurance company
etw sparen	to save sth	Krankenversicherung, die (-en)	health insurance
für/auf etw sparen	to save for sth		
Sparkonto, das (-s, -ten, or -ti)	savings/deposit account	Lebensversicherung, die (-en)	life insurance
Sparbuch, das (¨er)	bankbook; passbook	Feuerversicherung, die (-en)	fire insurance
Zins, der (-en)	interest		
Zinsen tragen/ bezahlen	to carry/pay interest	Kraftfahrzeugversicherung, die (-en)	car insurance
auflaufen	to accrue		
Schalterstunden, pl.	banking hours	Arbeitslosenversicherung, die (-en)	unemployment insurance
Geldautomat, der (-en)	cash machine, automatic teller		

| Versicherungs-nehmer(in), der/die (-/nen) | insured (party), policy holder | Versicherungsgeber(in), der/die (-/nen) | insurer, underwriter |
| | | versichert (bei) | insured (with/by) |

Level 2

General

Einnahmen und Ausgaben, pl.	accounts
Eigenkapital, das (no pl.)	equity
Startkapital, das (-ien or -e)	starting capital
Wie viel haben sie dafür verlangt?	How much did they quote for that?
Abwertung, die (-en)	devaluation
etw abwerten	to devalue sth
Unterschuss, der (¨e)	deficit
Überschuss, der (¨e)	surplus
Defizit, das (-e)	deficit
Finanzierungsge-sellschaft, die (-en)	financial company
Finanzberater(in), der/die (-/nen)	financial consultant
inflationär, inflationistisch	inflationary

Money

Münze, die (-n)	coin
Wechselgeld, das (no pl.)	change
Falschgeld, das (-er)	counterfeit money
Groschen, der (-)	penny
Rappen, der (-)	Swiss centime
Schilling, der (- or -e)	(Austrian) schilling
(Schweizer) Franken, der (-)	(Swiss) franc
Rück-, Zahlseite, die (-n)	tails
Kopfseite, die (-n)	heads

Payment and purchasing

umsonst	free
Barzahlung, die (-en)	cash payment
Bargeldtransfer, der (-s)	cash transaction

auf Kredit kaufen	to buy on credit
Rate, die (-n)	instalment
eine Rate für etw zahlen	to make a payment on sth
Teilzahlungskauf, der (¨e)	instalment plan
Anzahlung, die (-en)	down payment
etw abbezahlen	to pay off sth
Zurückzahlung, die (-en)	repayment

Profit and loss

Einnahme, die (-n)	takings
den Haushalt ausgleichen	to balance the budget
den Bankrott anmelden/ ansagen/erklären	to declare/file for bankruptcy
eingehen (coll.)	to fold
blank sein (coll.)	to be broke
pleite (coll.)	broke [person], bust [business]
einen Verlust erleiden	to incur a loss
Nettoverlust, der (-e)	net loss

Credit and debt

kreditfähig, kreditwürdig	creditworthy
Kreditwürdigkeit, die (no pl.)	credit rating
jmds Kreditwürdigkeit überprüfen	to run a credit check on sb
Kreditbrief, der (-e)	letter of credit
verschuldet sein	to be in debt
sich verschulden	to get into debt
Kontoüberziehung, die (-en)	overdraft
Überziehungskredit, der (-e)	overdraft provision

etw abdecken	to cover sth [debts]
etw decken	to cover sth [loan]
Kreditvereinbarungen, pl.	credit arrangements
Kreditbedingungen, pl.	credit terms
Zinssatz, der (¨e)	interest rate; lending rate
(Darlehen)zinssatz, der (¨e)	lending rate
Hypothekenzinssatz, der (¨e)	mortgage rate
eine Hypothek aufnehmen	to take out a mortgage
zinslos, -frei	interest-free
Vorschuss, der (¨e)	advance
Überbrückungskredit, der (-e)	bridging loan

The market

Hausse, die (-n)	boom, bull market
Baisse, die (-n)	slump, bear market
Baissemarkt, der (¨e)	bear market
Haussemarkt, der (¨e)	bull market
Anfangs-, Eröffnungskurs, der (-e)	opening price
Schlusskurs, der (-e)	closing price
Börsenschluss, der (no pl.)	close of the stock market
Immobilienmarkt, der (¨e)	property/real estate market
Devisenmarkt, der (¨e)	currency market
Devisenkontrolle, die (-n)	exchange control
Bondmarkt, der (¨e)	bond market
Terminmarkt, der (¨e)	futures market
Wechselkurs, der (-e)	exchange rate
Börsensturz, der (¨e)	collapse of the market
Maklergebühr, die (-en)	brokerage fee, broker's commission

Banks and bank staff

Handelswesen, das (no pl.)	banking
Handelsbank, die (-en)	merchant/commercial bank
Handelsbankier(in), der/die (-s/nen)	merchant banker
Anlagebank, die (-en)	investment bank
Investitionsbankier(in), der/die (-s/nen)	investment banker
Postsparkasse, die (-n)	Girobank, Post Office Savings Bank
Filialleiter(in) (einer Bank), der/die (-/nen)	branch manager
Bankfiliale, die (-n)	branch of a bank
Kreditgenossenschaft, die (-en)	credit union [US]
Bankleitzahl, die (-en)	bank code

Banking and investment

Mittel, pl.	funds
Spareinlagen, pl.	savings
laufendes Konto	current account
ruhendes Konto	dormant account
Kontoinhaber(in), der/die (-/nen)	account holder
ein Konto belasten	to charge an account
ein Konto ausgleichen	to balance an account
einen Betrag von einem Konto abbuchen	to debit a sum to an account
Kontostand, der (¨e)	balance
Kontoauszug, der (¨e)	bank statement
Auslandsinvestition, die (-en)	foreign investment
Investmentgesellschaft, die (-en)	investment company
Anlageberater(in), der/die (-/nen)	investment advisor
Kapitalanleger(in), der/die (-/nen)	investor
Kapitalanlage, die (-n)	investment of capital

etw auf der Rückseite unterschreiben	to endorse sth
einen Scheck (auf jmdn) ausstellen	to make out a cheque (payable to sb)
Scheckkarte, die (-n)	banker's card, cheque identification card
Nachtsafe, der (-s)	night safe
Banksafe, der (-s)	safe-deposit box
Dividende, die (-n)	dividend
Extradividende, die (-n)	bonus
Wertpapiere, pl.	securities
Wertsteigerung, die (-en)	appreciation
Wertverlust, der (-e)	depreciation
Zinsen berechnen	to charge interest
Zinseszins, der (-en)	compound interest
Emission, die (-en)	issue [of shares, banknotes]
Ausgabe, die (-n)	issue [of shares, banknotes]
Liquiditätsprobleme, pl.	cash-flow problems
einen Scheck verrechnen	to clear a cheque
Verrechnung, die (-en)	clearing
gedeckter Scheck	cleared cheque; certified cheque
elektrischer Geldverkehr	electronic banking

Taxation

etw versteuern	to pay tax on sth
versteuerte Waren, pl.	taxed goods
etw besteuern	to tax sth

Steuersatz, der (¨e)	rate of taxation
Arbeitseinkommen, das (-)	earned income
Vermögenssteuer, die (-n)	property tax
Steuerparadies, das (-e)	tax haven
Steuerhinterziehung, die (-en)	tax evasion
Steuerhinterzieher(in), der/die (-/nen)	tax dodger
Steuerflucht, die (no pl.)	tax exile

Insurance

eine Versicherung (gegen etw) abschließen	to take out insurance (against sth)
Vermögensversicherung, die (-en)	property insurance
Hausratversicherung, die (-en)	household contents insurance
Invalidenversicherung, die (-en)	disability insurance
Unfallversicherung, die (-en)	industrial insurance
Ernteversicherung, die (-en)	crop insurance
Versicherungsvertreter(in), der/die (-/nen)	insurance agent
im Unrecht sein	to be at fault
Sachschaden, der (¨)	material damage
Personenschaden, der (¨)	personal injury
Körperschaden, der (¨)	physical injury

Level 3

General

jmdn (für etw) entschädigen	to compensate sb (for sth)
eingefrorenes Kapital	frozen assets
brachliegendes Kapital	idle capital

Währungspolitik, die (no pl.)	monetary policy
Schwankung, die (-en)	fluctuation
Barreserve, die (-n)	cash reserve

Pauschalsumme, die (-n)	lump sum
Internationaler Währungsfonds	International Monetary Fund
Bruttosozialprodukt, das (no pl.)	gross national product
Abrechnungszeitraum, der (¨e)	accounting period
Kassenwart(in), der/die (-e/nen)	treasurer
Geldwäsche, die (no pl.; coll.)	money laundering

Money

Währung, die (-en)	currency
harte Währung	hard currency
Nennwert, der (-e)	denomination
Devisen, pl.	foreign currency
etw prägen	to mint sth
etw in Umlauf bringen	to put sth into circulation
etw aus dem Verkehr ziehen	to take sth out of circulation
gesetzliches Zahlungsmittel	legal tender

Payment and purchasing

Kaufkraft, die (no pl.)	purchasing power
etw verschwenden	to squander/waste sth
Begleichung, die (-en)	payment
vollständige/teilweise Begleichung	payment in full/partial payment
Frist, die (-en)	deadline
eine Zahlung leisten	to make a payment
Zahlungstermin, der (-e)	payment deadline
Zahlungsbedingungen, pl.	terms of payment
die Einkäufe auf seine Rechnung setzen	to charge the purchases to his account
einen Scheck sperren	to stop a cheque

Profit and loss

Verdienst, der (-e)	profit, earnings
Rentabilität, die (no pl.)	profitability
Rendite, die (-n)	return on capital
Ertragsrate, die (-n)	rate of return
etw liquidieren	to liquidate sth
etw auflösen	to wind up sth [company]
Liquidierung, die (-en)	liquidation
in Konkurs gehen	to go into receivership
Konkursverwalter(in), der/die (-/nen)	receiver

Credit and debt

Bürge, der (-n); Bürgin, die (-nen)	guarantor
für etw bürgen	to guarantee sth
Bürgschaft, die (-en)	surety
jmdm einen Kredit gewähren	to grant sb credit/a loan
einen Kredit sperren	to freeze credit
hypothekarisch belastet	mortgaged
Hypothekengläu-biger(in), der/die (-/nen)	mortgagee
Hypotheken-schuldner(in), der/die (-/nen)	mortgager
entlasteter/ rehabilitierter Konkursschuldner	discharged bankrupt
Außenstände, pl.	outstanding debts
Schulden begleichen	to discharge debts
zusätzliche Sicherheit	collateral
ein Darlehen kündigen	to foreclose on a loan
säumig sein	to default
Säumige(r), der/die (adj. decl.)	defaulter
Inkassobeauftragte(r), der/die (adj. decl.)	debt collector

Kredithai, der (-e; coll.)	loan shark	Einzugsermächtigung, die (-en)	direct debit instruction
Wucherzinsen, pl.	extortionate interest rates	Verrechnungsscheck, der (-s)	non-negotiable cheque
Festzinsanleihe, die (-n)	fixed-interest loan	Blankoscheck, der (-s)	blank cheque
		Überbringer(in), der/die (-/nen)	bearer (of a cheque)

The market

Warenbörse, die (-n)	commodity exchange	Zahlungsempfänger(in), der/die (-/nen)	payee
Wertpapierbörse, die (-n)	stock exchange		
börsennotierte Aktie	listed share, listed stock	Bezogene(r), der/die (adj. decl.)	drawee
Aktienzertifikat, das (-e)	share certificate, stock certificate	hoch verzinslich	high-interest [account]
liquide Mittel, pl.	liquid assets	Leitzins, der (-en)	base rate
Nenn-, Nominalwert, der (-e)	face value/nominal value	gängig	going [rate]
		üblich	going [rate]
Kurswert, der (-e)	market value	Zahlungsanweisung, die (-en)	money order
Goldwährung, die (no pl.)	gold standard	Offshorebankgeschäfte, pl.	offshore banking
sich an der Börse versuchen	to dabble on the stock market	Clearinghaus, das (¨er)	clearing house
Nachbörse, die (no pl.)	after-hours trading	Verrechnungsstelle, die (-n)	clearing house
Bezugsrecht, das (-e)	option	Schuldschein, der (-e)	promissory note
Abwärtstrend, der (-s)	downtrend	Aktionär(in), der/die (-e/nen)	shareholder
zurückgehen	to take a downturn		
abflauen	to take a downturn	Obligation, die (-en)	bond
Insiderhandel, der (no pl.)	insider trading	Obligationär(in), der/die (-e/nen)	bond-holder
Kapitalaufnahme durch Emission von Aktien, die (-n)	flotation	Rentenfonds, der (-)	fixed-income fund
		Schuldverschreibung, die (-en)	debenture bond

Banking and investment

Saldo, der (-s, di, or -den)	balance	Staatsanleihe, die (-n)	government bond
		erstklassig	blue-chip
Saldoübertrag, -vortrag, der (¨e)	balance brought forward	ertragsstark	high-yield
		indexgebunden	index-linked
Aufgliederung der Zahlen, die (-en)	breakdown of figures	Kapitalgewinn, der (-e)	capital gain
Einzugsauftrag, der (¨e)	direct debit	Kapitalverlust, der (-e)	capital loss

floaten	to float	*Insurance*	
floatender/frei schwankender Wechselkurs	floating exchange rate	Versicherungspolice, die (-n)	insurance policy
		Versicherungsprämie, die (-n)	insurance premium
fester Wechselkurs	fixed exchange rate	Begünstigte(r), der/die (adj. decl.)	beneficiary
Taxation		Haftpflichtversi- cherung, die (-en)	liability insurance; third-party insurance
Kapitalerträge, pl.	investment income		
Mehrwertsteuer, die (no pl.)	value added tax	Pauschalversicherung, die (-en)	comprehensive insurance
Freibetrag, der (¨e)	tax allowance		
steuerlich absetzbar	tax-deductible	Leibrente, die (-n)	life annuity
Steuervergünstigung, die (-en)	tax relief	unbeschränkte Haftung	unlimited liability
Steueranreiz, der (-e)	tax incentive	Teilkaskoversicherung, die (-en)	third-party, fire and theft insurance
Erbschaftssteuer, die (-n)	inheritance tax; estate taxes; death duties	Vollkaskoversicherung, die (-en)	fully comprehensive insurance
Kapitalverkehrssteuer, die (-n)	capital transfer tax	Versicherung auf Gegenseitigkeit, die (-en)	mutual insurance
Körperschaftssteuer, die (-n)	corporation tax		
Einkommenssteuer einbehalten	to deduct income tax at source	Schadenssachver- ständige(r), der/die (adj. decl.)	insurance adjuster, loss adjuster

---

Exercises

Level 1

1. Wie heißt das Gegenteil? ✓

1. schwerer Diebstahl
2. schuldig
3. die Inflation
4. der Gewinn
5. die Darlehensgeberin
6. ein Konto eröffnen
7. Geld einzahlen
8. der Versicherungsnehmer
9. zahlungsfähig

2. Welches Wort hat die gleiche oder eine ähnliche Bedeutung? ✓

1. kämpfen
2. jmdn festnehmen
3. sich ergeben
4. profitabel
5. der Kreditgeber
6. das Investment

3. Welches Verb passt? ✓

a. bekennen, b. bekommen, c. bezahlen, d. erscheinen, e. freilassen, f. handeln, g. machen, h. nennen, i. spekulieren, j. überziehen

1. vor Gericht
2. sich unschuldig
3. lebenslänglich
4. in Notwehr
5. jmdn gegen Kaution

6. einen Preis
7. etw bar
8. Bankrott
9. das Konto
10. an der Börse

4. Wie heißt die entsprechende Person? ✓

	männlich	*weiblich*
1. einbrechen		
2. jmdn ermorden		
3. jmdn verteidigen		
4. jmdm etw schulden		
5. Geld einzahlen		
6. etw schmuggeln		
7. jmdn kidnappen		

5. Welches Wort passt nicht? ✓

1. der Dieb, der Drogenhändler, der Makler, der Terrorist
2. der Banker, der Bankkaufmann, der Kassierer, der Schalter
3. der Beweis, der Fingerabdruck, die Kaution, das Motiv
4. der Dollar, der Euro, die Mark, der Pfennig
5. die Bank, der Dealer, der Geldautomat, die Kasse

6. Welche Wörter gehören zusammen? ✓

a. der Börsenmakler, b. die Geldautomatenkarte, c. der Gerichtssaal, d. die Hypothek, e. der Informant, f. die Krankenversicherung, g. der Raubüberfall, h. das Sparkonto, i. der Verbrecher

1. die Unterwelt
2. die Pistole
3. die Richterin
4. die Belohnung
5. das Grundstück

6. Aktien
7. die Geheimzahl
8. die Patientin
9. der Zins

7. Welche Definition (welches Synonym) passt? ✓

> a. das Alibi, b. die Ausgabe, c. der Geldgeber, d. die Geldstrafe, e. der Polizist,
> f. die Rezession, g. die Schlägerei, h. der Schwindel, i. der Taschendiebstahl,
> j. die Untersuchung, k. das Urteil

1. Prügelei
2. Diebstahl von Dingen aus Taschen
3. Betrug
4. Geldbuße
5. Polizeibeamte
6. Aufklärung

7. Nachweis, dass man nicht am Tatort zur Tatzeit war
8. Richterspruch
9. Rückgang
10. jemand, der etw finanziert
11. Zahlung

8. In jedem Satz fehlt ein Wort. ✓

> anklagen, Bargeld, bewaffnet, Durchsuchungsbefehl, Einkommensteuer,
> Feuerversicherung, Lösegeld, Maklerfirma, Privatdetektiv, Scheck, sparen,
> steuerfrei, Überweisung

1. Ohne _____ durften die Beamten die Zimmer nicht betreten.
2. Sie bezahlte einen _____, um ihn zu beobachten.
3. Seine Familie bezahlte fünf Millionen Mark _____ für seine Freilassung.
4. Er muss sie entweder _____ oder freilassen.
5. Ein Dieb zwingt die Besitzer des Geschäfts, die Kasse zu leeren, und die Kunden, Schmuck und _____ herzugeben.
6. Sie waren mit Pistolen und Dolchen _____.
7. Er unterschreibt einen _____ über 700 Mark.
8. Sein Vater gründete 1960 in Berlin eine _____.
9. Die bestellten Produkte können die Kunden per _____ oder mit Kreditkarte bezahlen.
10. Die Bundesregierung plant keine weitere Reform der _____.
11. Die _____ versichert Schäden durch Feuer.
12. Er muss die Aktien mindestens sechs Jahre halten, damit sie _____ bleiben.
13. Er arbeitet dort, um Geld für ein neues Auto zu _____.

9. Übersetzen Sie ins Englische.

Bombenanschlag folgt auf Hinrichtung in USA

KARATSCHI, 15. November (dpa). Bei einem Bombenanschlag im Süden Pakistans sind am Freitag mindestens zwei Menschen getötet und weitere neun verletzt worden. Nach Polizeiangaben ereignete sich die Explosion in einem Bus in der Stadt Hyderabad. Die Bombe sei unter einem Sitz versteckt gewesen.

Der Anschlag ereignete sich nur rund zwei Stunden, nachdem im US-Bundesstaat Virginia ein 38-jähriger Pakistaner wegen der Ermordung von zwei CIA-Mitarbeitern hingerichtet worden war. Hunderte protestierten

in der Heimat des Gehenkten gegen die Vollstreckung des Todesurteils. Die
US-Regierung hatte die Befürchtung geäußert, dass es nach der Hinrichtung
zu Racheakten kommen könnte.

FRANKFURTER RUNDSCHAU, Samstag, 16. November 2002, Nr. 267/46, S. 6

© dpa Deutsche Presse-Agentur GmbH

10. Lesen Sie den folgenden Text.

Aus „Am Rand der Deflation" von Mario Müller

Was für Aussichten: Das Glas Bier in der Kneipe kostet wieder so viel wie vor
der Einführung des Euro-Bargelds, Obst und Gemüse sind für'n Appel und'n
Ei zu haben, die Auto-Hersteller locken mit permanenten
Super-Sonder-Rabatten, der Hausbesitzer geht mit der Miete runter.
  Alles nur ein schöner Traum? Nicht unbedingt, meinen namhafte Experten.
Sie rechnen damit, dass die Preise auf breiter Front sinken könnten. Doch was
die meisten Bürger zunächst als Wohltat empfänden, halten Ökonomen für ein
großes Übel. Denn dieser Prozess – Deflation genannt – wäre noch
verheerender als sein Gegenpart, die Inflation.
  Das D-Wort hat Konjunktur. Die Zeiten, da die Hauptsorge in vielen
westlichen Industrieländern dem starken Preisauftrieb galt, sind längst vorbei.
Allenthalben weisen die Lebenshaltungskosten nur noch relativ bescheidene
Steigerungsraten auf. Dafür gibt es mehrere Gründe. Neben einer rigideren
Geldpolitik spielt auch die Globalisierung eine wichtige Rolle: Die
zunehmende internationale Konkurrenz engt die Spielräume von
Unternehmen und Beschäftigten für Preis- und Lohnaufschläge ein.
  Bislang schien allerdings nur Japan in echte Schwierigkeiten geraten zu sein.
Dort herrscht schon seit mehreren Jahren Deflation. Doch inzwischen geht
das Gespenst auch anderen Orts um. In den USA wird Stephen Roach,
einflussreicher Ökonom der New Yorker Investmentbank Morgan Stanley,
nicht müde, das Menetekel fallender Preise an die Wand zu malen. Die
Vereinigten Staaten hätten ein „Date", eine Verabredung, mit der Deflation,
fürchtet auch Brad DeLong, Wirtschaftsprofessor an der Universität von
Kalifornien in Berkley. Hier zu Lande stimmt inzwischen Professor Norbert
Walter, Chefvolkswirt der Deutschen Bank, in den Kassandra-Chor ein ...
  Selbst Geldpolitiker sind aufgeschreckt. „Angesichts ihres niedrigen
Ausgangsniveaus könnte die Inflation sogar in eine Deflation umschlagen",
warnt die Bank der Notenbanken, die BIZ, in Basel. Und die
US-Währungsbehörde Fed ließ kürzlich untersuchen, welche Lehren aus dem
Fall Japan gezogen werden könnten.
  Die Mahnungen gründen im Wesentlichen auf folgenden Überlegungen:
Seit dem Ende des New-Economy-Booms und dem Kurssturz an den
internationalen Börsen befindet sich die Weltwirtschaft in einem prekären
Zustand. Die Krise an den Kapitalmärkten dämpft nicht nur die Kauflust der
privaten Verbraucher, sie erschwert auch die Finanzierung von Investitionen
durch die Unternehmen. Viele von ihnen, vor allem in der
Telekommunikationsbranche, hatten in ihrer Wachstumseuphorie gewaltige
Überkapazitäten aufgebaut und sind nun wegen der schrumpfenden Nachfrage
gezwungen, die Preise zu senken, um im Geschäft zu bleiben. Da die Firmen

wegen der geringeren Gewinne ihre Investitionen in neue Maschinen und Anlagen zurückschrauben und Arbeitsplätze abbauen, sinken die Einkommen. Kurz: Mit der Konjunktur geht es in immer schnellere Fahrt bergab ...

FRANKFURTER RUNDSCHAU, Samstag, 26. Oktober 2002, Nr. 249/43, S. 9

a. Vokabelübung I. Welche Definition passt? ✓

> a. katastrophal, b. kleiner werdend, c. mäßig, d. Preiserhöhung, e. Preisnachlass, f. Warnung, g. Warnungszeichen, h. Wirtschaftslage

1. der Rabatt   5. das Menetekel
2. verheerend   6. der Preisaufschlag
3. Konjunktur   7. die Mahnung
4. bescheiden   8. schrumpfend

b. Vokabelübung II. Wie heißt das Wort (die Wendung) auf Englisch?

1. der Preisauftrieb   6. die Kauflust
2. Lebenshaltungskosten   7. die Überkapazität
3. die Steigerungsrate   8. abbauen
4. der Kassandrachor   9. bergab
5. der Kurssturz

c. Fassen Sie den Text kurz zusammen.

Level 2

1. Welches Wort hat die gleiche oder eine ähnliche Bedeutung? ✓
1. der Kidnapper   4. pleite
2. jmdn anführen   5. kreditfähig
3. das Defizit   6. die Emission

2. Wie heißt das Gegenteil? ✓
1. Einspruch abgelehnt
2. der Beklagte
3. der Unterschuss
4. die Zahlseite
5. die Hausse
6. der Schlusskurs
7. die Wertsteigerung

3. Welches Verb passt? ✓

> a. anlegen, b. anmelden, c. aufnehmen, d. ausgleichen, e. ausstellen, f. begehen, g. begleichen, h. erheben, i. erleiden, j. fällen, k. fliehen

1. über die Grenze
2. ein Verbrechen
3. jmdm Handschellen
4. mit jmdm eine alte Rechnung
5. gegen jmdn Anklage
6. ein Urteil über jmdn
7. den Haushalt
8. den Bankrott
9. einen Verlust
10. eine Hypothek
11. einen Scheck auf jmdn

4. Wie heißen die Zusammensetzungen? ✓

1. drug addict: d___ Drogen_____
2. secret service: d___ Geheim_____
3. bodily injury: d___ Körper_____
4. traffic violation: d___ Verkehrs_____
5. petty crime: d___ Klein_____
6. tyre tracks: d___ Reifen_____
7. solitary confinement: d___ Einzel_____
8. roadblock: d___ Straßen_____
9. habitual offender: d___ Gewohnheits_____
10. eye witness: d___ Augen_____
11. police informer: d___ Polizei_____
12. civil action: d___ Zivil_____

5. Welches Wort passt nicht? ✓

1. der Groschen, der Krawall, die Münze, der Rappen
2. die Anzahlung, die Rate, der Teilzahlungskauf, die Verrechnung
3. die Ernteversicherung, die Hausratversicherung, die Spurensicherung, die Unfallversicherung
4. der Flüchtling, der Gefangene, der Häftling, der Spürhund
5. das Attentat, der Auftragsmord, die Razzia, der Totschlag

6. Suchen Sie eine andere Bedeutung.

1. der Polyp
2. die Spur
3. der Knüppel
4. das Protokoll
5. die Mittel (pl.)

7. In jedem Satz fehlt ein Wort. ✓

> Bestechung, Decknamen, eidliche, entkommen, Freispruch, Haftentlassung, kugelsichere, Streifenwagen, überwachen, verhören, Vorladung, Wiederholungstäter

1. Als _____ wurde er lebenslänglich gesperrt.
2. In Rom lebte Goethe unter dem _____ Johann Philipp Möller.
3. Er wurde zu drei Jahren Haft wegen _____ von mehreren Beamten verurteilt.
4. Sein Komplize konnte der Polizei _____.
5. Leider ist es nicht einfach, verdächtige Straftäter zu _____.
6. Als Abschreckung ist stets ein _____ in der Nähe.
7. Bis heute Nacht um zehn können wir Zeugen _____.
8. Er hat keine Aussicht auf eine _____ nach 15 Jahren.

9. Mindestens ein Jahr Freiheitsstrafe steht auf _____ Falschaussage.

10. Die Verteidigung hat auf _____ plädiert.

11. Ein Privatdetektiv hat ihr eine _____ im Scheidungskrieg präsentiert.

12. Sie hatten Schusswaffen und trugen _____ Westen.

8. Ergänzen Sie. ✓

1. der Mensch – der Personenschaden : der Gegenstand – _____

2. Inland – die Steuerhinterziehung : Ausland – _____

3. der Zins – der Zinssatz : die Steuer – _____

4. Termingeschäfte – der Terminmarkt : Devisen – _____

5. die Handelsbank – die Handelsbankierin : die Anlagebank – _____

6. killen – der Killer : wildern – _____

9. Übersetzen Sie ins Englische.

Russischer Statthalter übt Kritik an Moskaus Razzien

MOSKAU, 15. November (ap/dpa). Der von Russland eingesetzte Verwaltungschef für Tschetschenien hat die verstärkten Razzien der Streitkräfte in der Kaukasusrepublik kritisert. Nach der Geiselnahme tschetschenischer Rebellen in Moskau seien allein in seinem Heimatdorf Zentoroi in dieser Woche neun Bewohner verschwunden, sagte Achmed Kadyrow am Freitag der Moskauer Nachrichtenagentur Interfax. Es sei unmöglich, Informationen über ihren Verbleib zu erhalten.

Mutmaßliche tschetschenische Verbrecher zündeten in einem vollbesetzten Bus in Inguschetien eine Granate, töteten dabei vier Menschen und verletzten neun. Nach Angaben der Polizei vom Freitag ereignete sich der Überfall am Vorabend auf dem Busbahnhof der Stadt Malgobek.

Nach Angaben der russischen Nachrichtenagentur Itar-Tass wollten die Tschetschenen zwei Passagiere des Busses entführen.

FRANKFURTER RUNDSCHAU, Samstag, 16. November 2002, Nr. 267/46, S. 6

Reprinted with permission of The Associated Press.

© dpa Deutsche Presse-Agentur GmbH

7000 Euro Strafe wegen Bestechung

Eine Geldstrafe von 7000 Euro wegen Bestechung von zwei Kfz-Prüfern beim Frankfurter TÜV hat das Amtsgericht Frankfurt am Mittwoch festgesetzt. Der verurteilte 44-jährige Gebrauchtwagenhändler hatte nach Feststellung des Gerichts im Jahr 1999 in 57 Einzelfällen den Prüfern Schmiergelder ab 20 Mark gezahlt. Sein Ziel war es, dass Mängel bei den von ihm vorgeführten Gebrauchtwagen nicht festgestellt wurden.

Die Gesamtsumme der Schmiergelder betrug rund 1500 Mark (rund 750 Euro). Unabhängig von der minimalen Höhe der Schmiergelder lag laut Urteil der Tatbestand der Bestechung eindeutig vor. Wegen Korruption beim

Frankfurter TÜV in gravierenderen Fällen hat es am Landgericht Frankfurt seit dem vergangenen Jahr mehrere Verfahren gegeben.

Dabei ging es um Bestechungssummen in fünfstelliger DM-Höhe. Mehrere bestochene TÜV-Prüfer und zahlende Kfz-Vorführer wurden zu Haftstrafen bis zu zwei Jahren auf Bewährung und zusätzlichen Geldbußen bis zu umgerechnet 9000 Euro verurteilt.   lhe

FRANKFURTER RUNDSCHAU, Samstag, 23. November 2002, Nr. 273/47, S. 6

© dpa Deutsche Presse-Agentur GmbH

Visa und Mastercard drohen Milliarden-Strafen

NEW YORK (afp). Die gegen die Kreditkartenanbieter Visa und Mastercard klagenden US-Handelskonzerne sind optimistisch, den Prozess zu gewinnen. Nun bei Gericht eingereichte Dokumente belegten eindeutig, dass beide Gesellschaften ihre dominierende Stellung auf dem Markt für bargeldlose Zahlungsmittel ausgenutzt hätten, um überhöhte Provisionen bei so genannten Debit Cards zu verlangen, erklärte Kläger-Anwalt Lloyd Constantine. Eigentlich sei nur noch unklar, wie scharf das Urteil ausfalle.

Kläger in dem Verfahren sind unter anderem die Einzelhandelsriesen Wal-Mart, Sears und Safeway. Sie verlangen eine Strafe in zweistelliger Milliardenhöhe. Visa und Mastercard sollen beim Einsatz von Debit Cards, bei denen anders als bei Kreditkarten der bezahlte Betrag direkt vom Kundenkonto abgebucht wird, überhöhte Gebühren verlangt haben. Diese lägen bei 1,49 Dollar je 100 Dollar Rechnungssumme. Dagegen würden andere Anbieter lediglich neun Cent kassieren.

Da Visa und Mastercard den Markt für bargeldloses Bezahlen dominierten, entstünden den Einzelhändlern Jahr für Jahr Mehrkosten in Milliardenhöhe, die letztlich über höhere Preise auf die Kunden überwälzt werden müssten, klagen die Einzelhandelskonzerne.

Visa und Mastercard hatten Debit Cards vor einem Jahrzehnt eingeführt. Beide Gesellschaften zwangen den Klägern zufolge die mit ihnen vertraglich verbundenen Händler seinerzeit, neben den Kreditkarten auch ihre Debit Cards zu akzeptieren. Andernfalls wurde laut Anklage mit dem Ausschluss aus dem Kreditkartennetz der Finanzdienstleister gedroht.

FRANKFURTER RUNDSCHAU, Samstag, 16. November 2002, Nr. 267/46, S. 10

Level 3

1. Welches Wort hat die gleiche oder eine ähnliche Bedeutung? ✓

1. der Straffällige
2. das Clearinghaus
3. das Delikt
4. forensisch
5. das Berufungsgericht
6. der Gewinn

2. Welches Verb passt? ✓

a. ausstellen, b. einlegen, c. folgen, d. gehen, e. gewähren, f. leisten, g. setzen, h. verbüßen, i. verklagen, j. versuchen

1. einen Haftbefehl gegen jmdn
2. jmdn auf Schadenersatz
3. jmdm hart auf den Fersen
4. Berufung
5. einen Eid
6. eine Gefängnisstrafe
7. sich an der Börse
8. in Konkurs
9. die Einkäufe auf seine Rechnung
10. jmdm einen Kredit

3. Wie heißt das Gegenteil? ✓
1. Geld in Umlauf bringen
2. der Hypothekenschuldner
3. der Kapitalgewinn
4. vorbestraft sein
5. zurechnungsfähig
6. teilweise Begleichung
7. frei schwankender Wechselkurs

4. Ergänzen Sie. ✓
1. die Bombe – der Bombenanschlag : das Feuer – _____
2. das Konto – der Kontoinhaber : die Obligation – _____
3. das Vermögen – die Vermögenssteuer : die Erbschaft – _____
4. die Zuhälterei – der Zuhälter : die Hehlerei – _____
5. das Geld – das Falschgeld : der Eid – _____

5. Wie heißt ein umgangssprachliches Synonym? ✓
1. das Gefängnis
2. eine Gefängnisstrafe absitzen
3. die Prostituierte
4. der Voyeur
5. einen Tresor mit Gewalt öffnen

6. Wie heißen die Zusammensetzungen? ✓
1. lump sum: d___ _____summe
2. gross national product: d___ _____produkt
3. money laundering: d___ Geld_____
4. monetary policy: d___ _____politik
5. rate of return: d___ _____rate
6. extortionate interest rates: d___ _____zinsen

7. share certificate: d__ _____zertifikat

8. down trend: d__ _____trend

9. promissory note: d__ _____schein

10. tax relief: d__ Steuer_____

11. liability insurance: d__ _____versicherung

12. commodity exchange: d__ _____börse

7. Welche Definition (welches Synonym) passt? ✓

a. Blankoscheck, b. Leibrente, c. Mehrwertsteuer, d. Saldovortrag,
e. Verrechnungsscheck, f. Versicherungspolice, g. Zahlungsanweisung

1. Übertragung des Saldos auf die neue Rechnung
2. Scheck ohne Betrag
3. Umsatzsteuer
4. Scheck, der nicht in bar ausgezahlt wird
5. Urkunde über den Abschluss einer Versicherung
6. lebenslängliche Rente
7. Anweisung für eine Zahlung

8. In jedem Satz fehlt ein Wort. ✓

begleichen, beschlagnahmen, Begnadigung, Brandstiftung, bürgen, enttarnen,
Geiseln, Mandant, Unterschlagung, Verdacht, Währung, Zahlungstermin

1. Der Direktor der Bank wurde wegen _____ zu zehn Jahren Gefängnis verurteilt.
2. Es ist ihnen gelungen, die _____ zu befreien.
3. Da der Brand an mehreren Stellen ausgebrochen ist, könnte es sich um eine _____ handeln.
4. Sie steht im _____, ihren Mann vergiftet zu haben.
5. Die Polizei konnte nur einen sehr kleinen Teil des geschmuggelten Kokains _____.
6. Der Verteidiger versuchte, nachzuweisen, dass sein _____ niemals am Tatort gesehen wurde.
7. Sie versuchen seit einem Jahr, den Spion zu _____.
8. Über 70 Prozent der Bürger sind gegen eine _____ der früheren Diktator.
9. Der Kurs der russischen _____ verbesserte sich.
10. Handwerker stellen Rechnungen meist mit einem festen _____ aus.
11. Er ist nicht bereit, für zusätzliche Kredite persönlich zu _____.
12. Ihm bleibt nichts anderes übrig, als die Schulden seines Sohnes zu _____.

9. Übersetzen Sie ins Englische.

Entlassener tötet Freundin

LÜNEBURG (afp). Zu langsam arbeitende Mühlen der Justiz haben einem
Mann aus Lüneburg die Freiheit beschert, die dieser zur Tötung seiner

Lebensgefährtin nutzte. Wie das Justizministerium in Hannover mitteilte, gestand der 47-Jährige die Tat. Er war kurz zuvor nur deshalb aus Untersuchungshaft entlassen worden, weil eine Hauptverhandlung wegen des Vorwurfs der Vergewaltigung vom zuständigen Gericht nicht termingerecht binnen sechs Monaten eröffnet worden war. Der Mann war zudem bereits 1982 wegen eines Tötungsdelikts zu lebenslanger Haft verurteilt worden und erst im Jahr 2000 auf Bewährung entlassen worden.

FRANKFURTER RUNDSCHAU, Samstag, 16. November 2002, Nr. 267/46, S. 36

Erpressungsversuch mit Insulin

Gegenüber der Firma Aventis hat es im Sommer einen Erpressungsversuch gegeben, wie erst jetzt bekannt wurde. Die Täter drohten, Insulin-Präparate zu vertauschen, und verlangten 20 Millionen Euro von dem Unternehmen. Drei Tatverdächtige wurden festgenommen und sitzen seitdem in Untersuchungshaft.

Aventis habe den Erpressungsversuch verschwiegen, um „keine Nachahmer" auf den Plan zu rufen, wie Firmensprecherin Kerstin von Aretin sagte. Der Fall wurde jetzt bekannt, weil der Prozess vor dem Landgericht gegen die mutmaßlichen Täter terminiert ist.

Nach Angaben des ermittelnden Staatsanwalts Justus Koch ging in den ersten Juni-Tagen bei dem Unternehmen ein Umschlag mit acht Insulin-Ampullen aus Aventis-Produktion ein. Die Päparate seien manipuliert worden, um ein „Drohpotenzial" aufzubauen, sagte Koch ...

Kurz nach dem Eingang des Umschlags haben sich der Staatsanwaltschaft zufolge die Täter bei Aventis gemeldet und gedroht, weitere Ampullen zu manipulieren, wenn das Unternehmen nicht 20 Millionen Euro zahle. Die Firma schaltete nach Angaben ihrer Sprecherin sofort die Polizei ein, die mit umfangreichen Ermittlungen begann.

Am 12. Juni sollten die 20 Millionen Euro in Eppstein übergeben werden. Dabei wurden zwei der drei mutmaßlichen Erpresser gefasst. Deren Komplizen nahm die Polizei wenig später in einer Wohnung fest ... Der Prozess gegen die drei Männer beginnt im Februar vor dem Landgericht Frankfurt.

Volker Mazassek

FRANKFURTER RUNDSCHAU, Samstag, 16. November 2002, Nr. 267/46, S. 28

Ein Euro ist wieder einen Dollar wert

FRANKFURT A.M. Erstmals seit Juli wechselte der Euro an den internationalen Devisenmärkten gestern für mehr als einen Dollar den Besitzer. Am späten Nachmittag notierte die Einheitswährung bei 1,0003 Dollar und pendelte anschließend um die Parität. Die Europäische Zentralbank hatte zuvor den Referenzkurs mit 0,9974 (Donnerstag: 0,9864) Dollar festgelegt.

Händler interpretieren die Aufwertung des Euro vor allem als Schwäche des Dollar. Der sei unter Druck geraten, weil aktuelle Konjunkturdaten etwas ungünstiger ausfielen als erwartet. So ist die Zahl der US-Beschäftigten außenhalb der Landwirtschaft im Oktober um 5000 gesunken. Die Arbeitslosenquote stieg leicht auf 5,7 (September: 5,6) Prozent. Die Durchschnittslöhne der US-Arbeiter kletterten zwar im Berichtsmonat um 0,2 Prozent. Volkswirte hatten aber mit einem höheren Plus gerechnet. Die Kennziffern vom Arbeitsmarkt verstärkten die Ängste, die Konsumnachfrage der Amerikaner könnte bald schon merklich sinken.

Mit wenig erfreulichen Nachrichten wartete auch das Institute for Supply Management auf. Dessen viel beachteter Einkaufsmanagerindex fiel erneut und signalisierte damit ein rückläufiges Geschäft der US-Industrie.

Detlef Fechtner

FRANKFURTER RUNDSCHAU, Samstag, 2. November 2002, Nr. 255/44, S. 10

Unit 19

Geography, history, war and peace

Level 1

Geography

Geografie, die (no pl.)	geography
geografisch	geographical
Geograf(in), der/die (-en/nen)	geographer
Erde, die (-n)	earth, world, ground
Boden, der (¨)	ground, soil; seabed
Land, das (¨er)	country
Landkarte, die (-n)	map
Gegend, die (-en)	area
Region, die (-en)	region
Gebiet, das (-e)	area, territory
Kontinent, der (-e)	continent
kontinental	continental
Schelf, der or das (-e)	continental shelf
Erdteil, der (-e)	continent
Breite, die (-n)	latitude
Länge, die (-n)	longitude
Kompass, der (-e)	compass
nach dem Kompass	by the compass
Norden, der (no pl.)	north
Süden, der (no pl.)	south
Osten, der (no pl.)	east
Westen, der (no pl.)	west
nördlich	north(ern)
südlich	south(ern)
östlich	east(ern)
westlich	west(ern)
Pol, der (-e)	pole
Polarkreis, der (-e)	polar circle
südlicher Polarkreis	Antarctic circle
nördlicher Polarkreis	Arctic circle
Äquator, der (no pl.)	equator
äquatorial	equatorial
Tropen, pl.	tropics
Wüste, die (-n)	desert
Geologe, der (-n); Geologin, die (-nen)	geologist
Geologie, die (no pl.)	geology

Geographical names and peoples

Europa, das (no pl.)	Europe
Europäer(in), der/die (-/nen)	European
Nordamerika, das (no pl.)	North America
Südamerika, das (no pl.)	South America
Amerikaner(in), der/die (-/nen)	American
Afrika, das (no pl.)	Africa
Afrikaner(in), der/die (-/nen)	African
Asien, das (no pl.)	Asia
Asiat(in), der/die (-en/nen)	Asian
Australien, das (no pl.)	Australia
Antarktika, die (no pl.)	Antarctica

Deutschland, das (no pl.)	Germany	Schweden, das (no pl.)	Sweden
Bundesrepublik Deutschland (BRD), die (no pl.)	Federal Republic of Germany	Schwede, der (-n); Schwedin, die (-nen)	Swede
Frankreich, das (no pl.)	France	Norwegen, das (no pl.)	Norway
Franzose, der (-n); Französin, die (-nen)	Frenchman; Frenchwoman	Norweger(in), der/die (-/nen)	Norwegian
Belgien, das (no pl.)	Belgium	Finnland, das (no pl.)	Finland
Niederlande, pl.	Netherlands	Island, das (no pl.)	Iceland
Niederländer(in), der/die (-/nen)	Dutch	Monaco, das (no pl.)	Monaco
Holländer(in), der/die (-/nen)	Dutch	Monegasse, der (-n); Monegassin, die (-nen)	Monegasque
Spanien, das (no pl.)	Spain	Andorra, das (no pl.)	Andorra
Portugal, das (no pl.)	Portugal	Andorraner(in), der/die (-/nen)	Andorran
Portugiese, der (-n); Portugiesin, die (-nen)	Portuguese	Tschechische Republik, die (no pl.)	the Czech Republic
Schweiz, die (no pl.)	Switzerland	Tscheche, der (-n); Tschechin, die (-nen)	Czech
Italien, das (no pl.)	Italy		
Italiener(in), der/die (-/nen)	Italian	Polen, das (no pl.)	Poland
Liechtenstein, das (no pl.)	Liechtenstein	Pole, der (-n); Polin, die (-nen)	Pole
Österreich, das (no pl.)	Austria	Slowakei, die (no pl.)	Slovakia
Luxemburg, das (no pl.)	Luxembourg	Slowake, der (-n); Slowakin, die (-nen)	Slovak
Irland, das (no pl.)	Ireland	Ungarn, das (no pl.)	Hungary
Ire, der (-n); Irin, die (-nen)	Irishman/woman	Ungar(in), der/die (-n/nen)	Hungarian
England, das (no pl.)	England	Rumänien, das (no pl.)	Romania
Schottland, das (no pl.)	Scotland	Rumäne, der (-n); Rumänin, die (-nen)	Romanian
Großbritannien, das (no pl.)	Great Britain		
Nordirland, das (no pl.)	Northern Ireland	Bulgarien, das (no pl.)	Bulgaria
Dänemark, das (no pl.)	Denmark	Bulgare, der (-n); Bulgarin, die (-nen)	Bulgarian
Däne, der (-n); Dänin, die (-nen)	Dane	Slowenien, das (no pl.)	Slovenia

Slowene, der (-n); Slowenin, die (-nen)	Slovene	Russe, der (-n); Russin, die (-nen)	Russian
Kroatien, das (no pl.)	Croatia	Türkei, die (no pl.)	Turkey
Kroate, der (-n); Kroatin, die (-nen)	Croatian	Türke, der (-n); Türkin, die (-nen)	Turk
Bosnien, das (no pl.)	Bosnia	Syrien, das (no pl.)	Syria
Albanien, das (no pl.)	Albania	Irak, der (no pl.)	Iraq
Albaner(in), der/die (-/nen)	Albanian	Iran, der (no pl.)	Iran
		Jordanien, das (no pl.)	Jordan
Jugoslawien, das (no pl.)	Yugoslavia	Israel, das (no pl.)	Israel
Jugoslawe, der (-n); Jugoslawin, die (-nen)	Yugoslav	Israeli, der (- or -s); Israelin, die (-nen)	Israeli
Mazedonien, das (no pl.)	Macedonia	Libanon, der (no pl.)	Lebanon
		Libanese, der (-n); Libanesin, die (-nen)	Lebanese
Serbien, das (no pl.)	Serbia	Kuwait, das (no pl.)	Kuwait
Serbe, der (-n); Serbin, die (-nen)	Serbian	Saudi-Arabien, das (no pl.)	Saudi Arabia
Griechenland, das (no pl.)	Greece	Saudiaraber(in), der/die (-/nen)	Saudi
Grieche, der (-n); Griechin, die (-nen)	Greek	Katar, das (no pl.)	Qatar
		Vereinigte Arabische Emirate, pl.	United Arab Emirates
Estland, das (no pl.)	Estonia	Oman, das (no pl.)	Oman
Este, der (-n); Estin, die (-nen)	Estonian	Jemen, der (no pl.)	Yemen
Lettland, das (no pl.)	Latvia	Jemenit, der (-en); Jemenitin, die (-nen)	Yemeni
Lette, der (-n); Lettin, die (-nen)	Latvian	Kasachstan, das (no pl.)	Kazakhstan
Litauen, das (no pl.)	Lithuania	Georgien, das (no pl.)	Georgia
Litauer(in), der/die (-/nen)	Lithuanian	Armenien, das (no pl.)	Armenia
Belorussland, das (no pl.)	Belarus	Aserbaidschan, das (no pl.)	Azerbaijan
Belorusse, der (-n); Belorussin, die (-nen)	Belarussian	Mongolei, die (no pl.)	Mongolia
Ukraine, die (no pl.)	Ukraine	Mongole, der (-n); Mongolin, die (-nen)	Mongolian
Ukrainer(in), der/die (-/nen)	Ukrainian		
Moldawien, das (no pl.)	Moldova	China, das (no pl.)	China
Russland, das (no pl.)	Russia	Chinese, der (-n); Chinesin, die (-nen)	Chinese

Japan, das (no pl.)	Japan	Vietnamese, der (-n); Vietnamesin, die (-nen)	Vietnamese
Süd-, Nordkorea, das (no pl.)	South/North Korea	Kambodscha, das (no pl.)	Cambodia
Koreaner(in), der/die (-/nen)	Korean	Kambodschaner(in), der/die (-/nen)	Cambodian
Taiwan, das (no pl.)	Taiwan	Philippinen, pl.	Philippines
Taiwanese, der (-n); Taiwanesin, die (-nen)	Taiwanese	Filipino, der (-s); Filipina, die (-s)	Filipino; Filipina
Kirgisistan, das (no pl.)	Kirghizstan	Malaysia, das (no pl.)	Malaysia
Kirgise, der (-n); Kirgisin, die (-nen)	Kirghiz	Malaysier(in), der/die (-/nen)	Malaysian
Tadschikistan, das (no pl.)	Tajikistan	Indonesien, das (no pl.)	Indonesia
Afghanistan, das (no pl.)	Afghanistan	Neuseeland, das (no pl.)	New Zealand
Afghane, der (-n); Afghanin, die (-nen)	Afghan	Marokko, das (no pl.)	Morocco
Pakistan, das (no pl.)	Pakistan	Marokkaner(in), der/die (-/nen)	Moroccan
Indien, das (no pl.)	India	Algerien, das (no pl.)	Algeria
Inder(in), der/die (-/nen)	Indian	Tunesien, das (no pl.)	Tunisia
Nepal, das (no pl.)	Nepal	die westliche Sahara	the Western Sahara
Nepalese, der (-n); Nepalesin, die (-nen)	Nepalese	Mauretanien, das (no pl.)	Mauretania
Bhutan, das (no pl.)	Bhutan	Mali, das (no pl.)	Mali
Bangladesch, das (no pl.)	Bangladesh	Libyen, das (no pl.)	Libya
Birma, Burma, das (no pl.)	Burma	Libyer(in), der/die (-/nen)	Libyan
Birmane, der (-n); Birmanin, die (-nen)	Burmese	Ägypten, das (no pl.)	Egypt
Burmese, der (-n); Burmesin, die (-nen)	Burmese	Ägypter(in), der/die (-/nen)	Egyptian
Thailand, das (no pl.)	Thailand	Senegal, das (no pl.)	Senegal
Laos, das (no pl.)	Laos	Guinea, das (no pl.)	Guinea
Laote, der (-n); Laotin, die (-nen)	Laotian	Guineer(in), der/die (-/nen)	Guinean
Vietnam, das (no pl.)	Vietnam	Sierra Leone, das (no pl.)	Sierra Leone
		Liberia, das (no pl.)	Liberia
		Liberianer(in), der/die (-/nen)	Liberian
		Côte d'Ivoire, die (no pl.)	Côte d'Ivoire
		Elfenbeinküste, die (no pl.)	Ivory Coast

Ivorer(in), der/die (-/nen)	Ivorian	Ruander(in), der/die (-/nen)	Rwandan
Ghana, das (no pl.)	Ghana	Tansania, das (no pl.)	Tanzania
Togo, das (no pl.)	Togo	Tansanier(in), der/die (-/nen)	Tanzanian
Benin, das (no pl.)	Benin		
Niger, das (no pl.)	Niger	Burundi, das (no pl.)	Burundi
Nigrer(in), der/die (-/nen)	person from Niger	Angola, das (no pl.)	Angola
Nigeria, das (no pl.)	Nigeria	Angolaner(in), der/die (-/nen)	Angolan
Nigerianer(in), der/die (-/nen)	Nigerian	Sambia, das (no pl.)	Zambia
Tschad, der (no pl.)	Chad	Sambier(in), der/die (-/nen)	Zambian
Sudan, der (no pl.)	Sudan	Mosambik, das (no pl.)	Mozambique
Eritrea, das (no pl.)	Eritrea		
Eritreer(in), der/die (-/nen)	Eritrean	Malawi, das (no pl.)	Malawi
Zentralafrikanische Republik, die (no pl.)	Central African Republic	Simbabwe, das (no pl.)	Zimbabwe
Äthiopien, das (no pl.)	Ethiopia	Simbabwer(in), der/die (-/nen)	Zimbabwean
Dschibuti, das (no pl.)	Djibouti	Botsuana, das (no pl.)	Botswana
Somalia, das (no pl.)	Somalia	Botsuaner(in), der/die (-/nen)	Botswanan
Somalier(in), der/die (-/nen)	Somali	Namibia, das (no pl.)	Namibia
Kenia, das (no pl.)	Kenya	Namibier(in), der/die (-/nen)	Namibian
Kenianer(in), der/die (-/nen)	Kenyan	Südafrika, das (no pl.)	South Africa
Uganda, das (no pl.)	Uganda	Madagaskar, das (no pl.)	Madagascar
Ugander(in), der/die (-/nen)	Ugandan	Madagasse, der (-n); Madagassin, die (-nen)	Madagascan
die Demokratische Republik Kongo	the Democratic Republic of Congo	Guatemala, das (no pl.)	Guatemala
die Volksrepublik Kongo	the People's Republic of Congo	Guatemalteke, der (-n); Guatemaltekin, die (-nen)	Guatemalan
Kongolese, der (-n); Kongolesin, die (-nen)	Congolese	Belize, das (no pl.)	Belize
Gabun, das (no pl.)	Gabon	El Salvador, das (no pl.)	El Salvador
Kamerun, das (no pl.)	Cameroon	Salvadorianer(in), der/die (-/nen)	El Salvadorian
Äquatorialguinea, das (no pl.)	Equatorial Guinea	Honduras, das (no pl.)	Honduras
Ruanda, das (no pl.)	Rwanda		

Honduraner(in), der/die (-/nen)	Honduran	Ecuadorianer(in), der/die (-/nen)	Ecuadorian
Nicaragua, das (no pl.)	Nicaragua	Guyana, das (no pl.)	Guyana
Nicaraguaner(in), der/die (-/nen)	Nicaraguan	Guyaner(in), der/die (-/nen)	Guyanese
Costa Rica, das (no pl.)	Costa Rica	Surinam, das (no pl.)	Surinam
Costa-Ricaner(in), der/die (-/nen)	Costa Rican	Französisch-Guayana, das (no pl.)	French Guiana
Panama, das (no pl.)	Panama	Französich-Guayaner(in), der/die (-/nen)	French Guianan
Panamene, der (-n); Panamenin, die (-nen)	Panamanian	Brasilien, das (no pl.)	Brazil
		Brasilianer(in), der/die (-/nen)	Brazilian
Panamese, der (-n); Panamesin, die (-nen)	Panamanian	Peru, das (no pl.)	Peru
		Peruaner(in), der/die (-/nen)	Peruvian
Bahamas, pl.	Bahamas	Bolivien, das (no pl.)	Bolivia
Bahamaer(in), der/die (-/nen)	Bahamian	Bolivianer(in), der/die (-/nen)	Bolivian
Kuba, das (no pl.)	Cuba	Paraguay, das (no pl.)	Paraguay
Kubaner(in), der/die (-/nen)	Cuban	Chile, das (no pl.)	Chile
Jamaika, das (no pl.)	Jamaica	Chilene, der (-n); Chilenin, die (-nen)	Chilean
Jamaikaner(in), der/die (-/nen)	Jamaican		
Haiti, das (no pl.)	Haiti	Argentinien, das (no pl.)	Argentina
Haitianer(in), der/die (-/nen)	Haitian	Grönland, das (no pl.)	Greenland
Dominikanische Republik, die (no pl.)	Dominican Republic	Kanada, das (no pl.)	Canada
		Kanadier(in), der/die (-/nen)	Canadian
Dominikaner(in), der/die (-/nen)	Dominican	die Vereinigten Staaten, pl.	the United States
Puerto Rico, das (no pl.)	Puerto Rico	Mexiko, das (no pl.)	Mexico
Puerto-Ricaner(in), der/die (-/nen)	Puerto Rican	Mexikaner(in), der/die (-/nen)	Mexican
Venezuela, das (no pl.)	Venezuela		

History

Venezolaner(in), der/die (-/nen)	Venezuelan
Kolumbien, das (no pl.)	Columbia
Ecuador, das (no pl.)	Ecuador

Geschichte, die (-n)	history
geschichtlich	historical, historic
Geschichte machen	to make history
vorgeschichtlich	prehistoric
Vorgeschichte, die (no pl.)	prehistory

Historiker(in), der/die (-/nen)	historian
historisch	historical, historic
König(in), der/die (-e/nen)	king/queen
Prinz(essin), der/die (-en/nen)	prince/princess
Krone, die (-n)	crown
jmdn krönen	to crown sb
Kaiser(in), der/die (-/nen)	emperor/empress
Revolution, die (-en)	revolution
etw entdecken	to discover sth
Entdeckung, die (-en)	discovery
Schreiber(in), der/die (-/nen)	scribe

War

Krieg, der (-e)	war
Kampf, der (¨e)	battle, fight, combat
kämpfen	to fight
Konflikt, der (-e)	conflict
Explosion, die (-en)	blast, explosion
Front, die (-en)	front
an der Front	at the front
im Krieg sein/stehen	to be at war
im Krieg fallen/bleiben	to be killed in the war/in action
Wunde, die (-n)	wound
jmdn verwunden	to wound sb
jmdn verletzen	to wound sb
jmdn angreifen	to attack sb
Angriff, der (-e)	attack
schießen	to shoot
marschieren	to march
etw sprengen	to blow sth up

Military

Militär, das (no pl.)	military
Militär, der (-s)	(army) officer
Armee, die (-n)	army; (armed) forces
Heer, das (-e)	army
Luftwaffe, die (-n)	air force
(Kriegs)marine, die (-n)	navy
Truppe, die (no pl.)	army; troops
Truppen, pl.	troops

Friedenstruppen, pl.	peace-keeping forces
General, der (-e or ¨e)	general
Offizier(in), der/die (-e/nen)	officer
Unteroffizier(in), der/die (-e/nen)	noncommissioned officer (NCO)
Stabsoffizier(in), der/die (-e/nen)	staff officer
Soldat(in), der/die (-en/nen)	soldier
Matrose, der (-n); Matrosin, die (-nen)	sailor
Uniform, die (-en)	uniform
Kaserne, die (-n)	barracks
Opfer, das (-)	casualty

Weapons

Waffe, die (-n)	weapon
Schusswaffe, die (-n)	gun
Pistole, die (-n)	pistol
Revolver, der (-)	revolver
Gewehr, das (-e)	rifle
Kugel, die (-n)	bullet
Kanone, die (-n)	cannon, gun
Rakete, die (-n)	rocket, missile
Atombombe, die (-n)	atomic bomb
Bomber, der (-)	bomber [aircraft]
feuern	to fire
Autobombe, die (-n)	car bomb
Handgranate, die (-n)	hand grenade
Radar, der or das (no pl.)	radar

Peace

Frieden, der (-)	peace
friedlich	peaceful
Freiheit, die (-en)	freedom
Friedensbewegung, die (-en)	peace movement
Pazifist(in), der/die (-en/nen)	pacifist
Friedenskämpfer(in), der/die (-/nen)	pacifist
Pazifismus, der (no pl.)	pacifism
Menschenrechte, pl.	human rights

Level 2

Geography

Erdbeben, das (-)	earthquake
Vulkan, der (-e)	volcano
tätig/untätig	active/dormant
(Vulkan)krater, der (-)	(volcanic) crater
Ausbruch, der (¨e)	eruption
ausbrechen	to erupt
Geysir, der (-e)	geyser
Fuß, der (¨e)	bottom [mountain], foot
Grund, der (¨e)	bottom [canyon, body of water]
Gelände, das (-)	(open) country, terrain
Territorium, das (-rien)	territory
territorial	territorial
Vaterland, das (¨er)	native country
Heimatland, das (¨er)	native country
Hemisphäre, die (-n)	hemisphere
Halbkugel, die (-n)	hemisphere
Breiten-, Längengrad, der (-e)	(degree of) latitude/longitude
es liegt (auf/unter) 20 Grad nördlicher Breite	it lies 20 degrees north
Himmelsrichtung, die (-en)	direction
die vier Himmelsrichtungen	the four points of the compass
Vermessung, die (-en)	survey
etw vermessen	to survey sth
Meereskunde, die (no pl.)	oceanography
Meereskundler(in), der/die (-/nen)	oceanographer
meereskundlich	oceanographic
Archipel, der (-e)	archipelago
Klimatologie, die (no pl.)	climatology
Klimaforscher(in), der/die (-/nen)	climatologist
Geochemie, die (no pl.)	geochemistry
Geophysik, die (no pl.)	geophysics
Geopolitik, die (no pl.)	geopolitics

Geographical names and peoples

Atlantik, der (no pl.)	Atlantic
der Antlantische Ozean	the Atlantic Ocean
Pazifik, der (no pl.)	Pacific
der Pazifische Ozean	the Pacific Ocean
der Stille Ozean	the Pacific Ocean
der Arktische Ozean	the Arctic Ocean
der Antarktische Ozean	the Antarctic Ocean
der Indische Ozean	the Indian Ocean
das Adriatische Meer	the Adriatic Sea
das Ägäische Meer	the Aegean Sea
das Tote Meer	the Dead Sea
das Schwarze Meer	the Black Sea
Ostsee, die (no pl.)	Baltic Sea
Nordsee, die (no pl.)	North Sea
das Chinesische Meer	the China Sea
das Karibische Meer	the Caribbean Sea
Karibe, der (-n); Karibin, die (-nen)	Carib
Mittelmeer, das (no pl.)	the Mediterranean Sea
das Kaspische Meer	the Caspian Sea
das Rote Meer	the Red Sea

History

Höhepunkt, der (-e)	peak, pinnacle, apex
zu Fall kommen	to collapse [government]
Sturz, der (¨e)	fall, overthrow
verfallen	to fall into decline [empire]
Untergang, der (¨e)	decline [empire]; ruin [person]
untergehen	to collapse [civilization]

in die Geschichte eingehen	to go down in history	jmdn/etw verteidigen	to defend sb/sth
Altertum, das (no pl.)	antiquity	etw zerstören	to destroy sth
Neuzeit, die (no pl.)	modern age	siegen	to win
Zeitalter, das (-)	period	jmdn besiegen	to defeat sb
Epoche, die (-n)	epoch	Sieger(in), der/die (-/nen)	winner, victor
Ära, die (Ären)	era		
durch alle Zeiten	through the ages	Sieg, der (-e)	victory
Eiszeit, die (-en)	Ice Age	Niederlage, die (-n)	defeat
Steinzeit, die (-en)	Stone Age	jmdn erschießen	to shoot (and kill) sb
Bronzezeit, die (no pl.)	Bronze Age	jmdn/etw beschießen	to fire at sb/sth
Eisenzeit, die (no pl.)	Iron Age	Schuss, der (¨e)	shot
Jungsteinzeit, die (no pl.)	Neolithic age	zusammenstoßen	to clash
Altsteinzeit, die (no pl.)	Palaeolithic age	jmdn/etw überfallen	to attack, raid, invade sb/sth
Sozialhistoriker(in), der/die (-/nen)	social historian	jmdn gefangen nehmen	to capture sb
Kriegshistoriker(in), der/die (-/nen)	military historian	jmdn gefangen halten	to hold sb prisoner
Geschichtsschreibung, die (no pl.)	historiography	Rückzug, der (¨e)	retreat
		den Rückzug antreten	to retreat
Geschichtsschreiber(in), der/die (-/nen)	historian, historiographer	Schutz, der (no pl.)	protection
		jmdn/etw (vor/gegen etw) schützen	to protect sb/sth (from/against sth)
Archäologe, der (-n); Archäologin, die (-nen)	archaeologist	Schlacht, die (-en)	battle
		Schlachtfeld, das (-er)	battlefield
Archäologie, die (no pl.)	archaeology	Seeschlacht, die (-en)	naval battle
Ausgrabung, die (-en)	excavation	etw besetzen	to occupy sth
		Besetzung, die (-en)	occupation
		Blockade, die (-n)	blockade
War		Mobilmachung, die (-en)	mobilization
den Krieg erklären	to declare war	Truppen mobilisieren	to mobilize troops
totaler Krieg	all-out war		
heiliger Krieg	holy war	Truppen kriegsbereit machen	to mobilize troops
Atomkrieg, der (-e)	nuclear/atomic war		
ausbrechen	to break out [war]	kampfbereit	ready for combat
Feind(in), der/die (-e/nen)	enemy	Offensive, die (-n)	offensive
		eine Offensive (gegen jmdn/etw) starten	to mount an offensive (against sb/sth)
Gegner(in), der/die (-/nen)	enemy		
feindlich	enemy, hostile	jmdn/etw evakuieren	to evacuate sb/sth
Kampfgebiet, das (-e)	battle zone	etw räumen	to evacuate sth
Luftangriff, der (-e)	air raid	vermisst	missing in action

auf-, untertauchen	to surface/submerge	Veteran(in), der/die (-en/nen)	veteran
Propaganda, die (no pl.)	propaganda	Streitkräfte, pl.	armed forces
Taktik, die (-en)	tactics	die Zahl der in Deutschland stationierten Streitkräfte	the number of troops deployed in Germany
Kriegsverbrechen, das (-)	war crime		
Kriegsverbrecher(in), der/die (-/nen)	war criminal	Verstärkung, die (-en)	reinforcements
Verwundete(r), der/die (adj. decl.)	wounded man/woman	Verbündete(r), der/die (adj. decl.)	ally
Gefallene(r), der/die (adj. decl.)	soldier killed in action	Alliierten, pl.	allies
Rebell(in), der/die (-en/nen)	rebel	Rang, der (¨e)	rank
Widerstand, der (¨e)	resistance	Kriegsminister(in), der/die (-/nen)	Secretary of State for War
Widerstand leisten	to resist	Admiral(in), der/die (-e/nen)	admiral
Untergrundbewegung, die (-en)	underground movement	Flotte, die (-n)	fleet
Aufruhr, der (-e; pl. rare)	riot	Einheit, die (-en)	unit
		Regiment, das (-e)	regiment
Aufstand, der (¨e)	rebellion, revolt, insurrection	Bataillon, das (-e)	battalion
		Infanterie, die (no pl.)	infantry
Unruhen, pl.	unrest		
Massaker, das (-)	massacre	Infanterist(in), der/die (-en/nen)	foot soldier, infantry-man/woman

Military

		Kompanie, die (-n)	company
Bundeswehr, die (no pl.)	Federal Army	Zug, der (¨e)	platoon
		Kommando, das (-s)	commando
Wehrpflicht, die (no pl.)	conscription, compulsory military service	Sonderkommando, das (-s)	special unit, detachment
		Kavallerie, die (-n)	cavalry
Wehrpflichtige(r), der/die (adj. decl.)	conscript, draftee	Schwadron, die (-en)	squadron
		Konvoi, der (-s)	convoy
Wehrdienst, der (no pl.)	military service	Brigade, die (-n)	brigade
jmdn einberufen	to draft/conscript/call up sb	Brigadegeneral(in), der/die (-e or ¨e/nen)	brigadier, brigadier general
Nationalgarde, die (-n)	National Guard [USA]	Hauptmann, der (-leute)	captain
Zivilist(in), der/die (-en/nen)	civilian	Major(in), der/die (-e/nen)	major
ein gemeiner Soldat	a common soldier	Leutnant, der (-s)	(second) lieutenant
Reservist(in), der/die (-en/nen)	reservist	Oberstleutnant, der (-s)	lieutenant colonel
Sanitäter(in), der/die (-/nen)	orderly	Oberst, der (-en)	colonel
		Wache haben	to be on watch
Sanitätskorps, der (-)	medical corps	Wachposten, der (-)	sentry, look-out

Deserteur(in), der/die (-e/nen)	deserter
Verräter(in), der/die (-/nen)	traitor
Militärgericht, das (-e)	court martial
Kriegsgericht, das (-e)	(wartime) court martial

Weapons

Maschinenpistole, die (-n)	submachine gun
Maschinengewehr, das (-e)	machine gun
Abzug, der (¨e)	trigger
Artillerie, die (-n)	artillery
etw laden	to load sth
auf etw zielen	to aim at sth
die chemische Kriegsführung	chemical warfare
chemische Waffe	chemical weapon
biologische Waffe	biological weapon
bakteriologische Waffe	bacteriological weapon
konventionelle Waffe	conventional weapon
zu den Waffen greifen	to take up arms
Waffenhandel, der (no pl.)	arms trade
Raketenwerfer, der (-)	rocket launcher
Flammenwerfer, der (-)	flame thrower
Giftgas, das (-e)	poison gas
Nervengas, das (-e)	nerve gas
Gasangriff, der (-e)	gas attack
Flugabwehr, die (no pl.)	air defence
Flugabwehrrakete, die (-n)	anti-aircraft missile
Jagdflugzeug, das (-e)	fighter plane
Düsenjäger, der (-)	jet fighter
Flugzeugträger, der (-)	aircraft carrier
Kriegsschiff, das (-e)	warship

Zerstörer, der (-)	destroyer [ship]
etw außer Dienst nehmen	to decommission sth
Torpedo, der (-s)	torpedo
torpedieren	to torpedo
Panzer, der (-)	tank
(Plastik)sprengstoff, der (-e)	(plastic) explosive
Sprengkörper, der (-)	explosive device
atomarer Sprengkörper	nuclear device
Munition, die (no pl.)	ammunition
Minenfeld, das (-er)	minefield
Minensuchboot, das (-e)	mine sweeper
Minenwerfer, der (-)	mortar
jmdn/etw bombardieren	to bombard sb/sth
Wasserstoffbombe, die (-n)	H-bomb
Neutronenbombe, die (-n)	neutron bomb

Peace

den Frieden schließen	to make peace
Frieden stiften	to make peace
Friedensstifter(in), der/die (-/nen)	peacemaker
Friedensplan, der (¨e)	peace plan
Friedensnobelpreis, der (-e)	Nobel peace prize
Friedenspolitik, die (-en)	policy of peace
Zivildienst, der (no pl.)	community service [alternative to military service]
Zivildienstleistende(r), der/die (adj. decl.)	person doing community service
Zivi, der (-s; coll.)	person doing community service
Friedensforschung, die (no pl.)	peace studies
Friedensdemonstrant(in), der/die (-en/nen)	peace protester

Level 3

Geography

Erschütterung, die (-en)	tremor
Spalte, die (-n)	fissure, crevice
Verwerfung, die (-en)	fault
(Boden)falte, die (-n)	fold
Schicht, die (-en)	layer, stratum
Flöz, das (-e)	seam
Muttergestein, das (-e)	bedrock
Eruptivgestein, das (-e)	igneous rock
Sediment, das (-e)	sediment
Becken, das (-)	basin
Mulde, die (-n)	trough
Senke, die (-n)	valley
Vertiefung, die (-en)	depression
Gletscher, der (-)	glacier
Gletscherspalte, die (-n)	crevasse
Wasserscheide, die (-n)	watershed
Grundwasserspiegel, der (-)	water table
Atlant, der (-en)	atlas
Höhenlinie, die (-n)	contour line
Höhenlinienkarte, die (-n)	contour map
Kartografie, die (no pl.)	cartography
Topografie, die (no pl.)	topography
Demografie, die (-n)	demography
Meridian, der (-e)	meridian
Breitenkreis, der (-e)	parallel
Datumsgrenze, die (-n)	dateline

Geographical names and peoples

Azoren, pl.	Azores
Bermudas, pl.	Bermudas
Bermuder(in), der/die (-/nen)	Bermudan
Orkneyinseln, pl.	Orkneys
Shetlandinseln, pl.	Shetland Islands
Kanarische Inseln, pl.	Canary Islands
Kanarier(in), der/die (-/nen)	Canary Islander
Färöer, pl.	Faroe Islands
Färöer(in), der/die (-/nen)	Faroese
Falklandinseln, pl.	Falkland Islands
Neufundland, das (no pl.)	Newfoundland
Jungferninseln, pl.	Virgin Islands
Bahrein, das (no pl.)	Bahrain
Sri Lanka, das (no pl.)	Sri Lanka
Sri-Lanker(in), der/die (-/nen)	Sri Lankan
Korfu, das (no pl.)	Corfu
Korfiot(in), der/die (-en/nen)	Corfiot
Korsika, das (no pl.)	Corsica
Korse, der (-n); Korsin, die (-nen)	Corsican
Kreta, das (no pl.)	Crete
Kreter(in), der/die (-/nen)	Cretan
Zypern, das (no pl.)	Cyprus
Zypriot(in), der/die (-en/nen)	Cypriot
Malta, das (no pl.)	Malta
Malteser(in), der/die (-/nen)	Maltese
Sizilien, das (no pl.)	Sicily
Sizilianer(in), der/die (-/nen)	Sicilian
Aleuten, pl.	Aleutian Islands
Fidschi, das (no pl.)	Fiji
Fidschianer(in), der/die (-/nen)	Fijian
Hawaii, das (no pl.)	Hawaii
Hawaii(an)er(in), der/die (-/nen)	Hawaiian
Marshallinseln, pl.	Marshall Islands

Marshaller(in), der/die (-/nen)	Marshallese
Samoa, das (no pl.)	Samoa
Samoaner(in), der/die (-/nen)	Samoan
Tahiti, das (no pl.)	Tahiti
Tahiti(an)er(in), der/die (-/nen)	Tahitian

History

geschichtsträchtig	steeped in history
geschichtslos	with no history; with no historical records
Chronist(in), der/die (-en/nen)	chronicler, annalist
Archivar(in), der/die (-e/nen)	archivist
Archiv, das (-e)	archives
Paläograf(in), der/die (-en/nen)	palaeographer
Handschriftenkunde, die (no pl.)	palaeography
vorsintflutlich	antediluvian
byzantinisch	Byzantine
hellenisch	Hellenic
Römerreich, das (no pl.)	Roman Empire
plebejisch	plebeian
Plebejer(in), der/die (-/nen)	plebeian
Mittelalter, das (no pl.)	Middle Ages
feudal	feudal
Feudalsystem, das (-e)	feudal system
mittelalterlich	medieval
Mediävist(in), der/die (-en/nen)	medievalist
Kreuzzug, der (¨e)	crusade
einen Kreuzzug führen	to (go on) crusade
Kreuzfahrer(in), der/die (-/nen)	crusader
Pest, die (no pl.)	plague, pestilence
die Bauernkriege, pl.	Peasant War(s)

Renaissance, die (-n)	Renaissance
Reformation, die (no pl.)	Reformation
Barock, das or der (no pl.)	Baroque
der Dreißigjährige Krieg	the Thirty Years' War
Pilgerväter, pl.	Pilgrim Fathers
amerikanischer Unabhängig- keitskrieg	American War of Independence
Sklaverei, die (no pl.)	slavery
die Konföderierten Staaten von Amerika	the Confederacy (USA)
Abolition, die (-en)	abolition
die Aufklärung	the Enlightenment
der Siebenjährige Krieg	the Seven Years' War
die industrielle Revolution	the industrial revolution
die Französische Revolution	the French Revolution
der Amerikanische Bürgerkrieg	the American Civil War
das Deutsche Reich	the German Reich
Kaiserreich, das (-e)	empire
der Erste Weltkrieg	the First World War
die Weimarer Republik	the Weimar Republic
Frauenstimmrecht, das (no pl.)	women's suffrage
die Weltwirtschafts- krise	the Depression
Prohibition, die (-en)	Prohibition
das Dritte Reich	the Third Reich
Nationalsozialismus, der (no pl.)	National Socialism
Nationalsozialist(in), der/die (-en/nen)	National Socialist
Nazi, der (-s)	Nazi
Konzentrationslager (KZ), das (-)	concentration camp
die Schutzstaffel (SS)	the SS
Kristallnacht, die (no pl.)	Crystal Night, 'Night of Broken Glass'

Braunhemd, das (-en)	Brownshirt	jmdn/etw vernichten	to annihilate/ destroy/crush sb/sth
Holocaust, der (no pl.)	Holocaust		
der Zweite Weltkrieg	the Second World War	Hinterhalt, der (-e)	ambush
		Feldzug, der (¨e)	campaign
Luftbrücke, die (-n)	airlift	verheerend	devastating
die Nürnberger Prozesse, pl.	the Nuremberg (war crime) Trials	ethnische Säuberung, die (-en)	ethnic cleansing
		jmdn abwehren	to fend/ward sb off
Warschauer Pakt	Warsaw Pact	etw erobern	to conquer sth
die Berliner Mauer	the Berlin Wall	jmdn/etw im Sturm erobern	to take sb/sth by storm
der Eiserne Vorhang	the Iron Curtain		
Ostblock, der (no pl.)	the Eastern Block	Eroberung, die (-en)	conquest, overthrow
Vietnamkrieg, der (no pl.)	the Vietnam War	etw patrouillieren	to patrol sth
		Manöver, das (-)	manoeuvre
Wiedervereinigung, die (no pl.)	reunification	Kriegshetze, die (no pl.)	war-mongering
Wende, die (-n)	major political change	Gefecht, das (-e)	battle, encounter, skirmish
Golfkrieg, der (-e)	Gulf War	Feindseligkeiten, pl.	hostilities
		Belagerung, die (-en)	siege
War		etw belagern	to besiege sth
Waffenruhe, die (no pl.)	cease-fire	jmdn in die Flucht schlagen	to rout sb
Waffenstillstand, der (no pl.)	truce; armistice	Schlagkraft, die (¨e)	strike power
		(de)eskalieren	to (de-)escalate
Verteidigungskrieg, der (-e)	defensive war	Stadtguerilla, die (-s or –rillen)	urban guerrilla warfare
Guerillakrieg, der (-e)	guerrilla warfare	Blutzoll, der (no pl.)	toll (of lives)
Blitzkrieg, der (-e)	blitzkrieg	sich ergeben	to surrender
kalter Krieg	cold war	***Military***	
kriegsbeschädigt, -versehrt	war-disabled	Guerilla, der (-s)	guerrilla
		Guerillakämpfer(in), der/die (-/nen)	guerrilla
Grabenkampf, der (¨e)	trench warfare	Freischärler(in), der/die (-/nen)	guerrilla
Schützengraben, der (¨)	trench	Scharfschütze, -schützin, der/die (-n/nen)	sharpshooter, marksman/ markswoman
Schützenloch, das (-¨er)	foxhole		
Repressalien, pl.	reprisals	Bogenschütze, -schützin, der/die (-n/nen)	archer
Luftschutzbunker, der (-)	air-raid shelter		
Luftschutzkeller, der (-)	air-raid shelter	Bombenräumkommando, das (-s)	bomb squad

Bombenräumer(in), der/die (-/nen)	bomb disposal expert	Kaplan, der (¨e)	chaplain
Freiwilligenheer, das (-e)	volunteer army	Nachrichtenoffizier(in), der/die (-e/nen)	intelligence officer
sich freiwillig melden	to volunteer		
Rekrut(in), der/die (-en/nen)	recruit; rookie	**Weapons**	
Kampfanzug, der (¨e)	battle dress	Rüstung, die (no pl.)	arms
Patronengurt, der (-e)	cartridge-belt	aufrüsten	to build up arms
		Wettrüsten, das (no pl.)	arms race
Ärmelstreifen, der (-)	stripe	Massenvernichtungs- waffen, pl.	weapons of mass destruction
Epaulett, das (-en), Epaulette, die (-n)	epaulette	Leuchtrakete, die (-n)	signal rocket
Miliz, die (-en)	militia	Leuchtkugel, die (-n)	flare
Militionär(in), der/die (-e/nen)	militiaman/ militiawoman	Leuchtgeschoss, das (-e)	flare
Söldner(in), der/die (-/nen)	mercenary	Notrakete, die (-n)	distress rocket
		Salve, die (-n)	volley
Grenadier, der (-e)	grenadier; infantryman	Granate, die (-n)	shell
		Schrapnell, das (-e or -s)	shrapnel
Legionär, der (-e)	legionnaire		
Patrouille, die (-n)	patrol	Entlaubungsmittel, das (-)	defoliant
Vor-, Nachhut, die (-en)	vanguard/rearguard	Stacheldraht, der (¨e)	barbed wire
(in Reih und Glied) antreten	to fall in	(Stand)armbrust, die (-e or ¨e)	crossbow
ins Glied treten	to fall in [one soldier]	Schrotflinte, die (-n)	shotgun
wegtreten	to fall out	Bajonett, das (-e)	bayonet
Feldwebel(in), der/die (-/nen)	sergeant	Brandsatz, der (¨e)	incendiary compound
Oberfeldwebel(in), der/die (-/nen)	first sergeant [army]; master sergeant [air force]	Lenkwaffe, die (-n)	guided missile
		Luft-Boden-Rakete, die (-n)	air-to-surface missile
Hauptfeldwebel(in), der/die (-/nen)	(company) sergeant major	Langstreckenrakete, die (-n)	long-range missile
Gefreite(r), der/die (adj. decl.)	private first class	Interkontinetalrakete, die (-n)	intercontinental missile
Fallschirmjäger(in), der/die (-/nen)	paratrooper	Cruisemissile, das (-s)	cruise missile
Artillerist, der (-en)	artilleryman	Nuklearsprengkopf, der (¨e)	nuclear warhead
Kanonier(in), der (-e/nen)	gunner		
Fernmelder(in), der/die (-/nen)	signaller	Fall-out, der (-s)	fallout
Kundschafter(in), der/die (-/nen)	scout	**Peace**	
		Abrüstung, die (no pl.)	disarmament

abrüsten	to disarm
Friedenskundgebung, die (-en)	peace rally
etw vermitteln	to arrange/mediate/ negotiate sth
über den Frieden verhandeln	to hold peace negotiations
Verhandlung, die (-en)	negotiation
Friedensverhand-lungen, pl.	peace talks
Friedensbedin-gungen, pl.	peace terms

Friedensbewegte(r), der/die (adj. decl.)	peace activist
Kriegsdienstver-weigerer, -verweigerin, der/die (-/nen)	conscientious objector
Kriegsdienstver-weigerung, die (no pl.)	refusal to fight in a war
den Kriegsdienst verweigern	to be a conscientious objector

Exercises

Level 1

1. Ergänzen Sie die Tabelle. ✓

1. der Norden	
2.	
3.	
4.	westlich

2. Welches Wort (welche Wendung) hat die gleiche oder eine ähnliche Bedeutung? ✓

1. der Kontinent
2. die Gegend
3. die Armee
4. im Krieg bleiben
5. der Holländer
6. die Burmesin
7. der Panamese
8. historisch

3. Geographiequiz. ✓

1. Wie heißen die sieben Kontinente?
2. Wie heißen die neun Nachbarländer der BRD?
3. Welches Land liegt nicht in Südamerika? Chile, Guyana, Nicaragua, Peru, Surinam?
4. Welcher Staat ist kein Inselstaat? Haiti, Jamaika, Japan, Laos, Madagaskar?
5. Welches Land liegt nicht in Afrika? Eritrea, Ghana, Kirgise, Mali, Marokko?

4. Ergänzen Sie die Tabelle.

Land	Mann	Frau
1.		die Portugiesin
2. Irland		
3.	der Schwede	
4.		die Norwegerin
5. Slowakei		
6.	der Kroate	
7.		die Bulgarin
8. Andorra		
9.	der Serbe	
10.		die Jugoslawin
11. Griechenland		
12.	der Lette	
13.		die Türkin
14. Israel		
15.	der Jemenit	

5. Welche Wörter gehören zusammen? ✓

a. die Autobombe, b. der Kaiser, c. die Kaserne, d. die Krone, e. die Luftwaffe, f. der Matrose, g. der Revolver, h. die Tropen

1. die Marine
2. die Explosion
3. schießen
4. Truppen
5. der König
6. Rom
7. das Flugzeug
8. der Äquator

6. Regelmäßig abgeleitete Einwohnernamen. ✓
die Schweiz: der Schweizer, die Schweizerin
Spanien: der Spanier, die Spanierin
England: der Engländer, die Engländerin

Wie heißen die Einwohnernamen?
1. Kuwait, Malawi, Oman, Pakistan, Senegal, Togo
2. Armenien, Bosnien, Georgien, Indonesien, Jordanien, Moldawien, Syrien
3. Finnland, Island, Schottland

7. Länder und Hauptstädte. ✓

Land	Hauptstadt	Land	Hauptstadt
1. Deutschland	Berlin	11.	Amsterdam
2.	Rom	12.	Budapest
3.	Moskau	13.	Kiev
4.	Bagdad	14.	Teheran
5.	Beirut	15.	Beijing
6.	Kathmandu	16.	Hanoi
7.	Kairo	17.	Nairobi
8.	Pretoria	18.	Luanda
9.	Caracas	19.	Bogota
10.	Lima	20.	Santiago

8. In jedem Satz fehlt ein Wort. ✓

> entdeckt, Friedensbewegung, friedliche, gesprengt, Gewehr, Krieg,
> Menschenrechte, Unteroffizier, vorgeschichtliche, Wunde

1. Er begeistert sich für die _____ Archäologie.
2. Kolumbus hat Amerika _____ .
3. Er schildert den _____ aus der Perspektive eines einfachen Soldaten.
4. Er dient als _____ bei der Bundeswehr.
5. Die Terroristen haben im Sommer in Ulster ein Hotel in die Luft _____ .
6. Er erhielt eine tödliche _____ .
7. Fast jeder hier hat ein _____ für die Jagd.
8. Der Roman gibt Auskunft über das kriegerische und das _____ Leben im Norden.
9. Sie engagiert sich seit Jahren in der _____ .
10. Die Ziele und Werte der Vereinten Nationen sind Frieden, _____ , Freiheit, Gerechtigkeit und Entwicklung.

9. Übersetzen Sie ins Englische.

Die in Kolumbien verschleppte Politikerin Ingrid Betancourt ist für ihren Einsatz für den Frieden in ihrer Heimat mit dem Petra-Kelly-Preis ausgezeichnet worden. Der Ehemann der Politikerin nahm die Auszeichnung der Heinrich-Böll-Stiftung am Freitag in Berlin stellvertretend für seine Frau entgegen. (AFP)

Frankfurter Allgemeine Zeitung, Samstag, 14. Dezember 2002, Nr. 291/50, S. 6

US -Kritik an Indiens Raketentest

WASHINGTON (dpa). Die USA haben den jüngsten indischen Raketentest kritisiert. Der Sprecher des Außenministeriums, Richard Boucher, erklärte, es sei „enttäuschend", dass Indien eine Rakete abgefeuert habe, die Atombomben tragen kann.

FRANKFURTER RUNDSCHAU, 11. Januar 2003, Nr. 9/2, S. 6

© dpa Deutsche Presse-Agentur GmbH

Marine testet Uran-Munition

SEATTLE (rtr). Die US-Marine hat vor der Pazifik-Küste des Bundesstaates Washington uranhaltige Munition getestet. Eine Sprecherin der Marine wies am Donnerstag in Seattle zugleich aber Kritik zurück, die radioaktive Munition gefährde Menschen und die Umwelt.

FRANKFURTER RUNDSCHAU, 11. Januar 2003, Nr. 9/2, S. 6

Level 2

1. Welches Wort (welche Wendung) hat die gleiche oder eine ähnliche Bedeutung? ✓
1. das Vaterland
2. die Hemisphäre
3. der Pazifische Ozean
4. den Frieden schließen
5. der Militärdienst

2. Wie heißt das Gegenteil? ✓
1. der Breitengrad
2. der Arktische Ozean
3. die Neuzeit
4. der Freund
5. der Sieg
6. der Soldat
7. untertauchen

3. Welches Verb passt? ✓

> a. antreten, b. eingehen, c. greifen, d. haben, e. kommen, f. leisten, g. nehmen, h. starten

1. zu Fall
2. in die Geschichte
3. jmdn gefangen
4. den Rückzug
5. eine Offensive gegen jmdn
6. Widerstand
7. Wache
8. zu den Waffen

4. Ergänzen Sie. ✓
1. der Ozean – die Meereskunde : die Witterung – _____
2. die Infanterie – der Infanterist : der Zivildienst – _____
3. das Regiment – das Bataillon : die Kavallerie – _____

4. Seestreitkräfte – der Admiral : die Brigade – _____
5. die Luft – die Rakete : das Wasser – _____
6. das Maschinengewehr – konventionelle Waffe : das Giftgas – _____
7. das Meer – der Grund : der Berg – _____

5. Ordnen Sie die Meere und Länder einander zu. ✓

a. Algerien, b. Griechenland, c. Großbritannien, d. Israel, e. Italien, f. Polen,
g. Puerto Rico, h. Taiwan

1. das Adriatische Meer
2. das Ägäische Meer
3. das Tote Meer
4. die Ostsee
5. die Nordsee
6. das Chinesische Meer
7. das Karibische Meer
8. das Mittelmeer

6. Welches Wort passt nicht? ✓
1. die Front, das Kampfgebiet, das Kriegsverbrechen, das Schlachtfeld
2. der Aufruhr, der Aufstand, der Rebell, die Unruhen
3. die Bronzezeit, die Eiszeit, die Eisenzeit, die Steinzeit
4. der Ausbruch, der Geysir, der Krater, der Vulkan
5. der Fall, der Gefallene, der Sturz, der Untergang
6. angreifen, behüten, schützen, verteidigen

7. Welche Definition passt? ✓

a. die Archäologie, b. die Flotte, c. die Himmelsrichtung, d. die Jungsteinzeit, e. die
Kompanie, f. die Meereskundlerin, g. der Sanitäter, h. die Schlacht, i. Streitkräfte,
j. das Territorium, k. die Wehrpflicht, l. das Zeitalter

1. Gebiet
2. Süden
3. Ozeanografin
4. Epoche
5. Neolithikum
6. Altertumskunde
7. Kampf
8. Verpflichtung zum Wehrdienst
9. Krankenpfleger
10. Truppen
11. alle Schiffe eines Staates
12. kleinste Infanterieeinheit

8. In jedem Satz fehlt ein Wort. ✓

> Archipel, Archäologe, Erdbeben, Flugzeugträger, Friedensnobelpreis, heiligen,
> Militärgericht, Panzer, Sprengstoff, Waffenhandel

1. Die katastrophalen _____ in der Türkei zeigen, dass die Erde noch sehr aktiv ist.
2. Die kleinen Inseln bilden einen _____.
3. Ein chinesischer _____ stieß 1962 auf eine Siedlung aus der jüngeren chinesischen Steinzeit.
4. Man spricht vom „_____ Krieg" und meint das arabische Wort „Gihad".
5. Ein _____ hat den Deserteur verurteilt.
6. In einer Wohnung hatte die Polizei 100 Kilogramm _____, zwei Maschinenpistolen und Gewehre gefunden.
7. Deutschland sollte keine _____ an die Türkei liefern, solange die dortige Regierung Menschenrechte verletzt.
8. Großbritannien beorderte einen _____ in die Golfregion.
9. Die Ausbreitung von _____ im Internet ist möglich, da das Internet nicht kontrollierbar ist.
10. Die internationale Hilfsorganisation „Ärzte ohne Grenzen" hat 1999 den _____ erhalten.

9. Übersetzen Sie ins Englische.

Der Vulkan Stromboli bleibt unruhig. Am Freitag lösten sich abermals größere Gesteinsmassen und stürzten ins Meer. Vor wenigen Tagen hatte ein Ausbruch des Vulkans auf der gleichnamigen süditalienischen Insel erhebliche Schäden angerichtet und die Bewohner in Angst versetzt. Noch immer wächst von Tag zu Tag die Furcht vor weiteren Eruptionen, Lavaausstößen und Steinabbrüchen. Die Fährverbindungen zu der Insel nördlich von Sizilien wurden wiederaufgenommen, doch bestehen nach wie vor Einschränkungen für Touristen.

Heinz-Joachim Fisher

Frankfurter Allgemeine Zeitung, Samstag, 4. Januar 2003, Nr. 3/1, S. 7

10. Fassen Sie den folgenden Text zusammen.

UN erwarten mit Spannung irakische Waffenliste
NEW YORK / BAGDAD, 6. Dezember (dpa/afp/ap/D). Die Vereinten Nationen rechnen damit, dass die Überprüfung der für Samstag erwarteten irakischen Waffendeklaration Wochen dauern kann. Einzelheiten des Prozesses wollte der UN-Chefinspektor, Hans Blix, am Freitag mit dem UN-Sicherheitsrat erörtern. Nach Angaben seines Sprechers hält sich ein Team von 15 Experten in New York bereit, um Bagdads Aufstellung möglicher chemischen und biologischen Waffenmaterials und der Raketensysteme mit der Datenbank der UN zu vergleichen. Dabei war ungewiss, ob die irakische Regierung ihre Liste in arabischer oder englischer Sprache übermitteln wird – und in welchem Umfang. Laut Berichten aus Bagdad soll die Liste etwa 13 000

Seiten umfassen. Allein die Übersetzung könnte Wochen dauern. Die Regierungen in Washington und London erwarten den Bericht mit Skepsis.

Angesichts der bislang ergebnislos verlaufenen Suche der UN-Kontrolleure nach Massenvernichtungswaffen wollen die USA offenbar die Kooperation irakischer Rüstungswissenschaftler erzwingen. Nach den Plänen der US-Regierung sollten die UN-Inspektoren die irakischen Experten notfalls auch gegen deren Willen zur Ausreise bewegen, damit sie außer Landes mögliche Waffenverstecke verraten könnten, berichtete die *New York Times* am Freitag unter Berufung auf ungenannte UN- und US-Vertreter. Im Gegenzug wolle Washington ihnen Asyl anbieten. Einer Umfrage zufolge glauben 80 Prozent der US-Bürger nicht an eine Zusammenarbeit Iraks mit den Inspektoren. 57 Prozent sprachen sich für einen Krieg aus, sollte Irak die Arbeit der UN behindern.

Für den Kriegsfall erbaten die USA logistische, finanzielle und militärische Hilfe von den Nato-Mitgliedsstaaten. Washington erwarte aber keine „unmittelbare militärische Beteiligung" der Allianz, sagte Nato-Generalsekretär George Robertson. Ein Krieg gegen Irak könnte die USA über die kommenden zehn Jahre hinweg zwischen 99 Milliarden und gut 1,9 Billionen Dollar kosten. Das ist das Ergebnis einer Studie der Amerikanischen Akademie für Künste und Wissenschaften.

Die USA schickten derweil einen weiteren Flugzeugträger los. Die „USS Truman" soll die im Mittelmeer stationierte „USS Washington" ablösen, teilte das Verteidigungsministerium mit.

FRANKFURTER RUNDSCHAU, 7. Dezember 2002, Nr. 285/49, S. 6

Reprinted with permission of The Associated Press.

© dpa Deutsche Presse-Agentur GmbH

Level 3

1. Ergänzen Sie die Tabelle. ✓

Land	Mann	Frau
1.	der Bermuder	
2.		die Färöerin
3. Sri Lanka		
4.	der Korse	
5.		die Hawaiierin
6. Samoa		
7.	der Malteser	
8.		die Korfiotin
9. Kreta		
10.	der Tahitianer	

2. Welches Wort hat die gleiche oder eine ähnliche Bedeutung? ✓
1. die Paläografie
2. der Luftschutzbunker
3. der Guerillakämpfer
4. kriegsbeschädigt
5. die Leuchtkugel
6. die Mulde

3. Wie heißt das Gegenteil? ✓
1. die Vorhut
2. antreten
3. geschichtslos
4. aufrüsten
5. der Veteran

4. Ordnen Sie die folgenden Ausdrücke nach dem Rang, chronologisch usw. ✓
1. der Feldwebel, der Hauptfeldwebel, der Oberfeldwebel
2. die Aufklärung, das Barock, die Reformation, die Renaissance
3. das Deutsche Reich, das Dritte Reich, das Pharaonenreich, das Römerreich
4. der Amerikanische Bürgerkrieg, der amerikanische Unabhängigkeitskrieg, der Dreißigjährige Krieg, der Erste Weltkrieg, der Golfkrieg, der Siebenjährige Krieg
5. byzantinisch, mittelalterlich, vorsintflutlich

5. Welche Wörter gehören zusammen? ✓

a. die Abolition, b. das Eruptivgestein, c. das Feudalsystem, d. das Flöz, e. der Gletscher, f. das Konzentrationslager, g. der Ostblock, h. die Verwerfung, i. die Wende

1. das Mittelalter
2. die Sklaverei
3. der Holocaust
4. die Wiedervereinigung
5. der Eiserne Vorhang
6. die Spalte
7. die Schicht
8. Magma
9. das Eis

6. Welches Verb passt? ✓

a. erobern, b. führen, c. melden, d. schlagen, e. verhandeln, f. verweigern

1. jmdn in die Flucht
2. jmdn im Sturm
3. sich freiwillig
4. über den Frieden
5. den Kriegsdienst
6. einen Kreuzzug

7. Wie heißt die entsprechende Person? ✓

Instrument / Interesse	männliche Person	weibliche Person
1. die Kanone		
2. der Fallschirm		
3. das Archiv		
4. das Mittelalter		
5. der Nationalsozialismus		
6. der Kreuzzug		
7. der Sold		

8. In jedem Satz fehlt ein Wort. ✓

> Belagerung, Blutzoll, Datumsgrenze, Friedensbewegten, Friedensverhandlungen, Granaten, Langstreckenrakete, Massenvernichtungswaffen, Nachrichtenoffizier, Stacheldraht, Waffenstillstand

1. Der 180er Meridian, der durch den Pazifik verläuft, bildet die _____.
2. Es ist nicht ein Blitzkrieg, sondern eine _____.
3. In den nächsten Wochen wird ein weiterer Test einer _____ erwartet.
4. Ein _____ wurde in der Nähe eines Sperrgebietes von einem russischen Wachposten erschossen.
5. Die Mauer und der _____ trennen Deutschland nicht länger in zwei Teile.
6. Er hat die Explosion von _____ und das Feuer automatischer Waffen gehört.
7. Der _____ auf beiden Seiten war unbeschreiblich.
8. Syrien ist zu _____ mit Israel bereit.
9. Die UN-Inspekteure sollen in Irak nach versteckten _____ suchen.
10. Seit 1990 herrscht ein _____.
11. Die _____ haben auf dem Luisenplatz einen Informationsstand errichtet.

9. Übersetzen Sie ins Englische.

Kämpfe in Kongo vertreiben Tausende

LONDON, 3. Januar (epd). Die neuen Kämpfe im Nordosten Kongos haben in den vergangenen Wochen angeblich mehr als 100 000 Menschen in die Flucht getrieben. Hilfsorganisationen berichteten von „Panik" unter den vertriebenen Zivilisten, meldete der britische Rundfunksender BBC am Freitag.

Die Kämpfe zwischen rivalisierenden Rebellengruppen in der rohstoffreichen Gegend um die Stadt Beni waren kurz nach Unterzeichnung des Kongo-Friedensabkommens am 17. Dezember ausgebrochen. Hilfsorganisationen versorgen die Menschen mit Nahrung und Medikamenten. Unter den Flüchtlingen seien auch viele Pygmäen, die aus ihrer Heimat in den tropischen Wäldern vertrieben worden seien, berichtete die Hilfsorganisation „Ärzte ohne Grenzen".

Nach ihren Angaben dauerten die Kämpfe trotz eines am Montag vereinbarten Waffenstillstandes für die Region nahe der Grenze zu Uganda an.

In dem von Regierung, Rebellengruppen und Opposition unterzeichneten Friedenvertrag war die Entwaffnung der zahlreichen bewaffneten Gruppen nicht explizit geregelt worden. Besonders der Nordosten gilt weiter als Spannungsherd.

Frankfurter Rundschau, 4. Januar 2003, Nr. 3/1, S. 6

Raketenwerfer

Die Ermittler in Kenia sind sich einig, dass der gescheiterte Anschlag auf die israelische Chartermaschine mit russischen Boden-Luft-Raketen verübt wurde. Damit kommen vier Modelle in Frage, die zur Bekämpfung von niedrig fliegenden Flugzeugen gedacht sind.

Das jüngste Modell ist die „SA-18 Grouse Igla", die wiederum eine Weiterentwicklung der „SA-16 Gimlet Igla-1" ist. Bei beiden Waffen handelt es sich um mobile Werfer, mit denen Raketen von der Schulter aus abgefeuert werden. Sie haben eine Reichweite von rund fünf Kilometern und suchen sich mit Hilfe eines Wärme- und eines Ultraviolett-Sensors ihr Ziel selbstständig ...

Weltweit verbreitet und damit für Terroristen leichter zu beschaffen sind die „SA-14 Gremlin Strela 3" und das Vorgängermodell „SA-7 Grail Strela 2". Letztere ist unter anderen Namen auch bei der chinesischen, der pakistanischen und der ägyptischen Armee eingeführt. Die SA-7 wurde seit 1959 von der russischen Rüstungsindustrie entwickelt und zählt mit 50 000 produzierten Einheiten zu den meistverbreiteten Raketenwerfern weltweit.

Vor allem die SA-7 gilt als anfällig. Der Wärmesucher steuert den rund ein Kilogramm schweren Sprengkopf in das wärmste Ziel innerhalb eines Radius von 5,5 Kilometern. Schon die warme Sonne oder der erwärmte Boden können den Wärmesensor auf die falsche Fährte locken. Die Nachladezeit für den Raketenwerfer beläuft sich auf etwa zehn Sekunden.

Daniel Herrmann

Frankfurter Rundschau, 30. November 2002, Nr. 279/48, S. 6

Friedensorganisationen rufen zu Protestgang auf

Friedensorganisationen, die sich unter dem Namen „Resist" zusammengeschlossen haben, machen am heutigen Samstag, 14. Dezember, „gegen einen drohenden Irak-Krieg" mobil. Die Teilnehmer treffen sich um 13 Uhr am Bahnhof Zeppelinheim zu einem „Protestgang", der um 14.30 Uhr mit einer Kundgebung vor der Airbase am Flughafen endet. Auf der Rednerliste stehen Andreas Buro – Komitee für Grundrechte und Demokratie; Jochen Stay – Anti-Atom-Bewegung; Janelle Flory – Internationaler Versöhnungsbund; Elke Steven – resist und Horst-Eberhard Richter, Ehrenvorsitzender der Ärzte zur Verhütung eines Atomkrieges. „Resist" kündigt bei einem Irak-Krieg „Aktionen zivilen Ungehorsams" vor Militäreinrichtungen und diplomatischen Vertretungen der USA an.

Hans-Jürgen Biedermann

Frankfurter Rundschau, 14. Dezember 2002, Nr. 291/50, S. 25

Unit 20

Politics and international relations

Level 1

General

Macht, die (no pl.)	power, might
(Super)macht, die (¨e)	(super) power
an die Macht kommen	to come to power
politisch (un)korrekt	politically (in)correct
politische Korrektheit	political correctness
autonom	autonomous
jmdn verfolgen	to persecute sb
jmdn/etw unterdrücken	to repress sb/sth
etw zensieren	to censor sth

Political systems and ideologies

Sozialismus, der (no pl.)	socialism
Kommunismus, der (no pl.)	communism
Marxismus, der (no pl.)	Marxism
Kapitalismus, der (no pl.)	capitalism
Faschismus, der (no pl.)	fascism
Demokratie, die (-n)	democracy
Republik, die (-en)	republic
Monarchie, die (-n)	monarchy
Nationalismus, der (no pl.)	nationalism

Patriotismus, der (no pl.)	patriotism
Linke(r), der/die (adj. decl.)	left-winger
Rechte(r), der/die (adj. decl.)	right-winger

Political parties

Partei, die (-en)	party
liberal	liberal
konservativ	conservative
sozialistisch	socialist
kommunistisch	communist
Mitglied, das (-er)	member
Regierungspartei, die (-en)	ruling party
Oppositionspartei, die (-en)	opposition party
Koalitionspartei, die (-en)	coalition party
Koalition, die (-en)	coalition
Parteisprecher(in), der/die (-/nen)	party spokesperson
Parteichef(in), der/die (-s/nen)	party boss
Parteiführer(in), der/die (-/nen)	party leader

Elections

Wahl, die (-en)	election

Parlamentswahl, die (-en)	parliamentary election	Abgeordnete(r), der/die (adj. decl.)	representative, member of parliament
Wähler(in), der/die (-/nen)	voter	Kongress, der (-e)	congress
Stimme, die (-n)	vote	Senator(in), der/die (-en/nen)	senator
seine Stimme abgeben	to cast one's vote	Senat, der (-e)	senate
jmdm/einer Partei seine Stimme geben	to vote for sb/a party	Sprecher(in), der/die (-/nen)	speaker
jmdn/etw wählen	to vote for/elect sb/sth	Unter-, Oberhaus, das (no pl.)	Lower/Upper House
für/gegen jmdn stimmen	to vote for/against sb	Politiker(in), der/die (-/nen)	politician
Kandidat(in), der/die (-en/nen)	candidate	Gesetz, das (-e)	law, bill
		Grundgesetz, das (-e)	basic law
Parteiprogramm, das (-e)	party platform	Verfassung, die (-en)	constitution
		Sitz, der (-e)	seat
Fernsehdebatte, die (-n)	televised debate	Haushalt, der (-e)	budget
Wahltag, der (-e)	election day		
zur Wahl gehen	to go to the polls		
Stimmzettel, der (-)	ballot paper		
etw (nach)zählen	to (re)count sth		

Government

Staat, der (-en)	state, government
Regierung, die (-en)	government
(jmdn/etw) regieren	to rule/govern (sb/sth)
herrschen	to rule
Regierungschef(in), der/die (-s/nen)	head of the government
Kanzler(in), der/die (-/nen)	chancellor
Kabinett, das (-e)	cabinet
Ministerium, das (-rien)	ministry
Minister(in), der/die (-/nen)	(cabinet) minister
Präsident(in), der/die (-en/nen)	president
Ministerpräsident(in), der/die (-en/nen)	prime minister, Minister President
Parlament, das (-e)	parliament
parlamentarisch	parliamentary

Political activity

Politik, die (-en)	politics; policy
politisch	political
Rede, die (-n)	speech
Redner(in), der/die (-/nen)	speaker
demonstrieren	to demonstrate
Demonstrant(in), der/die (-en/nen)	demonstrator
(etw) organisieren	to organize (sth)
(gegen etw) protestieren	to protest (against sth)
politische Aktionsgruppe, die (-n)	political action committee [USA]
Sitzung, die (-en)	sitting, session
Komitee, das (-s)	committee
Ausschuss, der (¨e)	committee
Reform, die (-en)	reform
Reformer(in), der/die (-/nen)	reformer
Kompromiss, der (-e)	compromise
zu einem Kompromiss kommen	to come to a compromise
jmdn konsultieren	to consult sb
jmdn delegieren	to delegate sb

International relations

internationale Beziehungen, pl.	international relations
Diplomatie, die (no pl.)	diplomacy
Diplomat(in), der/die (-en/nen)	diplomat
diplomatisch	diplomatic
Botschaft, die (-en)	embassy
Botschafter(in), der/die (-/nen)	ambassador
Konsulat, das (-e)	consulate
Konsul(in), der/die (-n/nen)	consul
Außenpolitik, die (no pl.)	foreign policy
Auslandshilfe, die (no pl.)	foreign aid
Fahne, die (-n)	flag
Embargo, das (-s)	embargo
Boykott, der (-s or -e)	boycott
Sanktion, die (-en)	sanction
Nothilfe, die (no pl.)	emergency aid

Spying

Spion(in), der/die (-e/nen)	spy, mole
spionieren	to spy
Spionage, die (no pl.)	spying, espionage
Spionageflugzeug, das (-e)	spy plane
Doppelagent(in), der/die (-en/nen)	double agent
Geheimagent(in), der/die (-en/nen)	secret agent
Geheimdienst, der (-e)	secret service
versteckte Aktivitäten, pl.	covert activities

Immigration and asylum

Ein-, Auswanderung, die (-en)	immigration/ emigration
Ein-, Auswanderer, der (-); Ein-, Auswanderin, die (-nen)	immigrant/emigrant
Abwanderung, die (-en)	migration
Gastarbeiter(in), der/die (-/nen)	immigrant/foreign worker
Asyl, das (-e)	asylum
um Asyl bitten	to apply for asylum
Asylant(in), der/die (-en/nen)	asylum seeker
Exil, das (-e)	exile
ins Exil gehen	to go into exile

Level 2

General

Behörde, die (-n)	authorities
Behördensprache, die (-n)	officialese
Schmiergelder, pl.	slush fund
Redefreiheit, die (no pl.)	freedom of speech
Versammlungsfreiheit, die (no pl.)	freedom of assembly
gemeinsinnig	public-spirited
Gemeinschaftssinn, der (no pl.)	community spirit
an die Macht gelangen (elev.)	to come to power
Staatsstreich, der (-e)	coup (d'état)
Völkermord, der (-e)	genocide
Menschenrechtler(in), der/die (-/nen)	human rights activist

Political systems and ideologies

Ideologie, die (-n)	ideology
Konservatismus, der (no pl.)	conservatism
Konservative(r), der/die (adj. decl.)	conservative
Liberalismus, der (no pl.)	liberalism

Liberale(r), der/die (adj. decl.)	liberal
Mitte, die (-n)	centre
die linke/rechte Mitte	centre-left/right
Imperialismus, der (no pl.)	imperialism
Extremist(in), der/die (-en/nen)	extremist
Radikalismus, der (no pl.)	radicalism
(Militär)diktatur, die (-en)	(military) dictatorship
Polizeistaat, der (-en; pej.)	police state

Political parties

Sozialdemokratische Partei Deutschlands (SPD), die (no pl.)	(German) Social Democratic Party
Sozialdemokrat(in), der/die (-en/nen)	Social Democrat
Christlich-Demokratische Union (CDU), die (no pl.)	Christian Democratic Union
Christdemokrat(in), der/die (-en/nen)	Christian Democrat
Christlich-Soziale Union (CSU), die (no pl.)	Christian Social Union
Christsoziale(r), der/die (adj. decl.)	member of the CSU
die Grünen, pl.	the Greens
Grüne(r), der/die (adj. decl.)	Green
Freie Demokratische Partei (FDP), die (no pl.)	Free Democratic Party
Partei des Demokratischen Sozialismus, (PDS), die (no pl.)	Party of Democratic Socialism
die Demokratische Partei (USA)	the Democratic Party
die Republikanische Partei (USA)	the Republican Party
Labour Party, die (no pl.; Brit.)	Labour Party
die Konservative Partei (Brit.)	the Conservative Party
die liberal-demokratische Partei (Brit.)	the Liberal Democrat Party

Elections

wahlberechtigt	entitled to vote
Wahlrecht, das (-e)	right to vote, franchise, suffrage
das allgemeine Wahlrecht	universal suffrage
Wahlkampf, der (¨e)	election campaign
den Wahlkampf führen	to campaign
sich zur Wahl stellen	to run [for an office], stand
Kundgebung, die (-en)	rally
Wahlwerbung machen	to canvas
Wahlhelfer(in), der/die (-/nen)	canvasser
Wahlwerber(in), der/die (-/nen)	campaign worker
Meinungsumfrage, die (-n)	opinion poll
Abstimmung, die (-en)	vote, ballot, poll
Abstimmungsergebnis, das (-se)	result of the vote
Wahllokal, das (-e)	polling station
Wahlkabine, die (-n)	polling booth
Wahlurne, die (-n)	ballot box

Government

Bundesregierung, die (-en)	federal government
Bundesrat, der (¨e)	Bundesrat, upper house
Bundestag, der (no pl.)	Bundestag, lower house

Rat, der (¨e)	council
Ratsmitglied, das (-er)	councillor
Gemeinderat, der (¨e)	district council
Stadtrat, der (¨e)	town/city council
Bürgermeister(in), der/die (-/nen)	mayor
Amt, das (¨er)	department, (political) office
Beamte, der (adj. decl.); Beamtin, die (-nen)	civil/public servant
Innenministerium, das (-rien)	Home Office, Ministry of the Interior, Department of the Interior (USA)
Innenminister(in), der/die (-/nen)	Home Secretary, Minister of the Interior, Secretary of the Interior (USA)
Außenministerium, das (-rien)	Foreign Office, Foreign Ministry, State Department (USA)
Außenminister(in), der/die (-/nen)	Foreign Secretary, Foreign Minister, Secretary of State (USA)
Finanzminister(in), der/die (-/nen)	Chancellor of the Exchequer; Minister of Finance, Treasury Secretary (USA)
Verteidiungs-minister(in), der/die (-/nen)	Secretary of State for/Minister of Defence
Landwirtschafts-minister(in), der/die (-/nen)	Secretary of State for/Minister of Agriculture
Gesundheits-minister(in), der/die (-/nen)	Secretary of State for/Minister of Health
Arbeitsminister(in), der/die (-/nen)	Employment Secretary, Labor Secretary (USA)
Umweltminister(in), der/die (-/nen)	Secretary of State/Minister for the Environment
Handelsminister(in), der/die (-/nen)	Trade Secretary, Secretary of Commerce (USA)
Justizminister(in), der/die (-/nen)	Minister of Justice, Justice Minister
Kultusminister(in), der/die (-/nen)	Minister of Education and the Arts

Political activity

Flugblatt, das (¨er)	leaflet, flyer
etw verteilen	to distribute sth
Bürgerinitiative, die (-n)	citizens' action group
Ad-Hoc-Ausschuss, der (¨e)	ad hoc committee
gemischter Ausschuss	joint committee
Tagesordnung, die (-en)	agenda
Änderung, die (-en)	amendment
Antrag, der (¨e)	motion
einen Antrag stellen	to move/make a motion
Probeabstimmung, die (-en)	straw vote
über etw verhandeln	to negotiate/bargain about sth
Unterhändler(in), der/die (-/nen)	negotiator
Veto, das (-s)	veto
sein Veto gegen etw einlegen	to veto sth
von etw zurücktreten	to resign/step down from sth
Rücktritt, der (-e)	resignation
etw durchführen/ ausführen	to implement sth

International relations

Vertrag, der (¨e)	agreement, treaty
einen Vertrag abschließen	to enter into/ conclude a treaty
Abkommen, das (-)	agreement, treaty

Verhandlungen wieder aufnehmen	to resume negotiations	Einreise-, Ausreisevisum, das (-visa or -visen)	entrance/exit visa
sich einigen	to reach a settlement	Arbeitserlaubnis, die (-se)	work permit
Entwicklungsland, das (¨er)	developing country	multikulturelle Gesellschaft	multicultural society
Entwicklungshilfe, die (no pl.)	foreign aid	Multikulti, das (no pl., coll.)	multiculturalism
Entwicklungs-helfer(in), der/die (-/nen)	VSO worker, Peace Corps worker (USA)		
das Rote Kreuz	the Red Cross	*Europe*	
Hilfsorganisation, die (-en)	relief organization	überstaatlich	supranational
		eurozentrisch	eurocentric
Hilfsgüter, pl.	relief supplies	jmdn europäisieren	to Europeanize sb
Goodwillreise, die (-n)	good-will mission	Eurotunnel, der (no pl.)	Eurotunnel
Goodwilltour, die (-en)	good-will tour	Kanaltunnel, der (no pl.)	Channel Tunnel
Staatsbesuch, der (-e)	state visit	Eurovision, die (no pl.)	Eurovision
Staatssicherheit, die (no pl.)	national security	europäische Norm	European standard
		Europäische Union (EU), die (no pl.)	European Union (EU)
Immigration and asylum		Europäische (Wirtschafts)ge-meinschaft (EG), die (no pl.)	European (Economic) Community (EC)
Staatsbürgerschaft, die (-en)	citizenship		
Staatsangehörigkeit, die (-en)	citizenship	Gemeinsamer Markt	Common Market
Herkunftsland, das (¨er)	country of origin	Europäische Zentralbank	European Central Bank
Reiseziel, das (-e)	destination	die Nato/NATO (no pl.)	NATO
Flüchtling, der (-e)	refugee		
Flüchtlingslager, das (-)	refugee camp		

Level 3

General

Verschwörung, die (-en)	conspiracy, plot	die Basis (coll.)	(those at) the grass roots
sich zu etw verschwören	to conspire to do sth, plot sth	basisdemokratisch	grass roots
		alte Garde	old guard
die Macht ergreifen/erringen	to seize/gain power	autark	self-sufficient
		eine abwartende Haltung einnehmen	to adopt a policy of wait-and-see
jmdn vereidigen	to swear in sb		

Political systems and ideologies

der linke/rechte Flügel	left/right wing
linksradikal, -extrem	far left
rechtsradikal, -extrem	far right
Föderalismus, der (no pl.)	federalism
Aristokratie, die (-n)	aristocracy
Aristokrat(in), der/die (-en/nen)	aristocrat
Autokratie, die (-n)	autocracy
Despotismus, der (no pl.)	despotism
Tyrannei, die (-en)	tyranny
Totalitarismus, der (no pl.)	totalitarianism
Absolutismus, der (no pl.)	absolutism
Anarchie, die (-n)	anarchy
Anarchist(in), der/die (-en/nen)	anarchist

Political parties

Bündnis 90, das (no pl.)	Alliance 90
Sozialistische Einheitspartei Deutschlands (SED), die (no pl.; of GDR)	(German) Socialist Unity Party
Republikaner(in) (REP), der/die (-/nen)	Republican
Deutsche Volksunion (DVU), die (no pl.)	German People's Union
Nationaldemokratische Partei Deutschlands (NPD), die (no pl.)	German National Democratic Party
Kommunistische Partei Deutschlands (KPD), die (no pl.)	German Communist Party
Fraktion, die (-en)	congressional or parliamentary party
Splitterpartei, die (-en)	splinter party
Splittergruppe, die (-n)	splinter group
Ampelkoalition, die (-en)	coalition of SPD, FDP and the Greens
große/kleine Koalition	grand/little coalition
zu einer anderen Partei übergehen	to switch to another party
parteipolitisch	party political
parteilos	independent, nonparty
Parteilinie, die (-n)	party line
auf die Parteilinie einschwenken	to toe the party line

Elections

Wahlkreis, der (-e)	constituency
um einen Wahlkreis kämpfen	to contest a seat
Nachwahl, die (-en)	by-election
Wechselwähler(in), der/die (-/nen)	floating voter
Stammwähler(in), der/die (-/nen)	loyal voter
Volksentscheid, der (-e)	referendum
die abgegebenen Stimmen, pl.	the votes cast
stellvertretend abgegebene Stimme	proxy vote
eine geheime Abstimmung	a secret ballot
mit knapper Mehrheit gewählt werden	to be elected by a narrow majority
ausschlaggebende Stimme	deciding vote
Wählerschaft, die (-en)	electorate
über etw abstimmen lassen	to put sth to the vote

527

eine Wahl durch Handaufheben	a vote by a show of hands
etw manipulieren	to rig sth

Government

Exekutive, die (-n)	executive branch
Judikative, die (-n)	judiciary
Legislative, die (-n)	legislature
gesetzgebend	legislative
Mehrheits-, Minderheitsregierung, die (-en)	majority/minority rule
Verwaltung, die (-en)	administration
Beschluss, der (¨e)	decision, resolution
einen Beschluss fassen	to pass a resolution
Vorschrift, die (-en)	regulation, rule
in Kraft treten	to come into force
Gesetzentwurf, der (¨e)	(draft) bill
Erlass, der (¨e)	decree, edict
Amtsmissbrauch, der (¨e)	abuse of one's position
Stellvertreter(in), der/die (-/nen)	deputy, representative
jmdn zu etw ernennen	to appoint sb sth
Landesregierung, die (-en)	government of a state
eine provisorische Regierung	a provisional government
Amtsinhaber(in), der/die (-/nen)	officeholder
Vorsitzende(r), der/die (adj. decl.)	chair
Lordsiegelbewahrer(in), der/die (-/nen)	Lord Chancellor (GB)
ein souveräner Staat	a sovereign nation

Political activity

Schlichtungsausschuss, der (¨e)	arbitration/conciliation commission
ständiger Ausschuss	standing committee
auf die Abgeordneten Einfluss nehmen	to lobby

ziviler Ungehorsam	civil disobedience
die Vertrauensfrage stellen	to ask for a vote of confidence
Tadelsantrag, der (¨e)	vote of censure
Ombudsmann, -frau, der/die (¨er/en)	ombudsman/ombudswoman
Schattenkabinett, das (-e)	shadow cabinet
Kommunalpolitik, die (-en)	local government politics
Gipfeltreffen, das (-)	summit meeting
Intrige, die (-n)	intrigue
Unterschriftenliste, die (-n)	petition
Unterschriften (für/gegen etw) sammeln	to get up a petition (for/against sth)
etw ratifizieren	to ratify sth
etw umbilden	to reshuffle sth
sich politisch betätigen	to be involved in politics
etw (an jmdn) abgeben	to relinquish sth (to sb)

International relations

Immunität, die (no pl.)	diplomatic immunity
Gesandte(r), der/die (adj. decl.)	envoy
Attaché, der (-s)	attaché
diplomatisches Korps	diplomatic corps
ein Land diplomatisch anerkennen	to recognize a country diplomatically
Protokoll, das (no pl.)	protocol
Beschwichtigung, die (no pl.)	appeasement
die Vereinten Nationen (UN)	United Nations (UN)
Sicherheitsrat, der (no pl.)	Security Council
die Weltgesundheitsorganisation (WGO)	World Health Organization (WHO)
Bündnis, das (-se)	alliance
unilateral, einseitig	unilateral
bilateral	bilateral

multilateral	multilateral	politische(r) Gefangene(r) (adj. decl.)	political prisoner
gemeinsamer Beschluss	joint resolution	Rassenkrawalle, pl.	ethnic violence

Spying

Gegenspionage, die (no pl.)	counter-espionage	Xenophobie, die (no pl.)	xenophobia
Spionage treiben	to spy, carry on espionage	xenophob	xenophobic

Europe

Spionageabwehr, der (no pl.)	counter-intelligence
etw chiffrieren	to encypher/code sth
Chiffreschrift, die (-en)	cypher, code
etw entziffern	to decipher sth
Verschlusssache, die (-n)	classified document
konspirative Wohnung	safe house

Europe

Europäisches Parlament	European Parliament
Europarat, der (no pl.)	Council of Europe
Ministerrat, der (¨e)	Council of Ministers (of EC)
Europäische Kommission	European Commission
Europäischer Gerichtshof (EuGH)	European Court of Justice
Europäische Währungsunion	European Monetary Union
die OECD	OECD
Europäische Freihandelszone	European Free Trade Association
Eurobond, der (-s)	Eurobond
Euroskeptiker(in), der/die (-/nen)	Eurosceptic
Eurokrat(in), der/die (-en/nen)	Eurocrat
Europol, die (no pl.)	Europol

Immigration and asylum

asylberechtigt	entitled to political asylum
Asyl gewähren	to grant asylum
Aufenthaltsgeneh- migung, die (-en)	residence permit
jmdn einbürgern	to naturalize sb
Einbürgerung, die (no pl.)	naturalization
jmdn ausbürgern	to expatriate sb
im Ausland Lebende(r), der/die (adj. decl.)	expatriate

Public services, social and environmental issues

Level 1

Social services

Sozialdienst, der (-e)	social service	staatliche Unterstützung	state aid
Sozialarbeit, die (no pl.)	social work	Behinderung, die (-en)	disability
Sozialarbeiter(in), der/die (-/nen)	social worker	(schwer/leicht) behindert	(severely/partially) disabled
Unterstützung, die (no pl.)	assistance, aid	Sozialhilfe, die (no pl.)	income support, welfare (aid)

Sozialamt, das (¨er)	social security office
Heilsarmee, die (no pl.)	Salvation Army

Poverty and homelessness

arm	poor
Armut, die (no pl.)	poverty
Not, die (¨e)	need, poverty
betteln	to beg
Bettler(in), der/die (-/nen)	beggar
schmutzig	dirty
dreckig	filthy, squalid
Schuld, die (-en)	debt
verschuldet sein	to be in debt
obdachlos	homeless
Obdachlose(r), der/die (adj. decl.)	homeless person
Sozialwohnung, die (-en)	council flat, state-subsidized apartment
Innenstadt, die (no pl.)	inner city
Slum, der (-s)	slum
Überfüllung, die (no pl.)	overcrowding
überfüllt	overcrowded
Volksküche, die (-n)	soup kitchen

Alcohol and drugs

Alkohol, der (-e)	alcohol
Alkoholiker(in), der/die (-/nen)	alcoholic
unter Alkohol stehen	to be under the influence of alcohol
unter Alkoholeinfluss	under the influence of alcohol
Alkoholismus, der (no pl.)	alcoholism
Droge, die (-n)	drug
harte/weiche Droge	hard/soft drug
Rehabilitation, die (-en)	rehabilitation
Rehabilitationszentrum, das (-zentren)	rehabilitation centre

Marihuana, das (no pl.)	marijuana
Kokain, das (no pl.)	cocaine
Heroin, das (no pl.)	heroin
Speed, das (-s)	speed
LSD, das (no pl.)	LSD
Acid, das (no pl.)	acid
Ecstasy, das (no pl.)	ecstasy
high	high
Trip, der (-s; coll.)	trip

Environment

Umwelt, die (no pl.)	environment
etw verschmutzen	to pollute sth
verschmutzt	dirty, polluted
Umweltverschmutzung, die (-en)	pollution
Luftverschmutzung, die (-en)	air pollution
Wasserverschmutzung, die (-en)	water pollution
etw recyclen	to recycle sth
Recycling, das (no pl.)	recycling
Müll, der (no pl.)	rubbish, garbage, refuse
Abfall, der (no pl.)	rubbish, garbage, refuse
Abfälle, pl.	litter
Abfall wegwerfen	to litter
etw schaden	to damage sth
Smog, der (no pl.)	smog
Umweltschutz, der (no pl.)	environmental protection
Umweltschützer(in), der/die (-/nen)	environmentalist
ökologisch	ecological
Ökologie, die (no pl.)	ecology
umweltfreundlich	environmentally friendly
autofreier Sonntag	car-free Sunday
aussterben	to become extinct
Umweltkatastrophe, die (-n)	environmental disaster

Level 2

Social services

Fürsorge, die (no pl.)	welfare, relief, assistance
Sozialfürsorge, die (no pl.)	welfare
Kinderfürsorge, die (no pl.)	child welfare
Kindergeld, das (no pl.)	child benefit
Arbeitslosengeld, das (-er)	unemployment benefit
Wohngeld, das (-er)	housing benefit
Mutterschaftsgeld, das (-er)	maternity benefit
Sozialversicherung, die (-en)	social security, national insurance
Sozialversicherungs-ausweis, der (-e)	social security card
soziale Einrichtungen, pl.	welfare services

Poverty and homelessness

abgebrannt (coll.)	broke
pleite (coll.)	broke
heruntergekommen	down-and-out
elend	squalid, wretched
erbärmlich	pitiful, wretched
Obdachlosigkeit, die (no pl.)	homelessness
Obdachlosenheim, das (-e)	homeless shelter
Wohungsnot, die (no pl.)	housing shortage
Elendsviertel, das (-)	slums, slum area
Elendsquartier, das (-e)	slum dwelling
Sanierung, die (-en)	renovation
Hausbesetzer(in), der/die (-/nen)	squatter
etw besetzen	to squat in sth
Minimallohn, der (¨e)	subsistence wage, minimum wage
einkommensschwach	low-income
Unterschicht, die (-en)	underclass

Alcohol and drugs

Überbevölkerung, die (-en)	overpopulation
Rauschgift, das (-e)	drug, narcotic
Rauschmittel, das (-)	intoxicant
Alkoholsucht, die (no pl.)	alcohol addiction
alkoholsüchtig	addicted to alcohol
Drogenbenutzer(in), der/die (-/nen)	drug user
Drogenmissbrauch, der (¨e)	drug abuse
Drogensucht, die (¨e)	drug addiction
Drogenabhängigkeit, die (no pl.)	drug addiction
drogensüchtig, -abhängig	addicted to drugs
Drogensüchtige(r), der/die (adj. decl.)	drug addict
Drogenabhängige(r), der/die (adj. decl.)	drug addict
Fixer(in), der/die (-/nen)	junkie
Junkie, der (-s)	junkie
Grass, das (no pl.)	marijuana, grass
Joint, der (-s)	joint
Koks, der (no pl.; coll.)	coke
Crack, das (no pl.)	crack
Amphetamin, das (-e)	amphetamine

Environment

Schadstoff, der (-e)	pollutant
schädlich	damaging
Abwasser, das (¨)	sewage
Abgas, das (-e)	exhaust, emissions
Auspuffgase, pl.	exhaust fumes
Sondermüll, der (no pl.)	hazardous waste
Giftmüll, der (no pl.)	toxic waste
Atommüll, der (no pl.)	nuclear waste
Industriemüll, der (no pl.)	industrial waste

Chemiemüll, der (no pl.)	chemical waste	Altöl, das (-e)	used oil
Hausmüll, der (no pl.)	household waste	Spraydose, die (-n)	aerosol can
Öko, der (-s; coll.)	Green	Abfalldeponie, die (-n)	rubbish/garbage dump
Öko-	eco-; ecological	Giftmülldeponie, die (-n)	toxic waste dump
etw wiederverwerten	to recycle sth		
wiederverwertbar	recyclable	saurer Regen	acid rain
Altglascontainer, der (-)	bottle bank		

Level 3

Social services

Sozialleistungen, pl.	social security benefits
Sozialhilfeempfänger(in), der/die (-/nen)	recipient of income support/welfare
Sozialhilfeempfänger(in) sein	to be on social security
schmarotzen	to sponge, scrounge, freeload
Schmarotzer(in), der/die (-/nen)	sponger, scrounger, freeloader
Zuschuss, der (¨e)	subsidy, grant
Beihilfe, die (-n)	financial assistance
Anleihe, die (-n)	loan
Wohlfahrtsorganisation, die (-en)	charity
Wohlfahrtstaat, der (-en)	welfare state

Poverty and homelessness

Armut leiden	to be poverty-stricken
mittellos	destitute
bettelarm	utterly destitute
die Bedürftigen (adj. decl.)	the needy
unterprivilegiert	underprivileged
die Unterprivilegierten (adj. decl.)	the underprivileged
G(h)etto, das (-s)	ghetto
baufällig	dilapidated

verfallen	dilapidated
verlassen	deserted
verwahrlost	neglected
mit Ratten verseucht sein	to be rat-infested
etw von/bei jmdm abstauben (coll.)	to bum sth off/from sb
etw schnorren	to cadge/scrounge sth
die Abfalleimer plündern	to scavenge in the bins/trash cans
Stadtstreicher(in), der/die (-/nen)	vagrant
Penner(in), der/die (-/nen; coll.)	tramp, bum, down-and-out
oberhalb/unterhalb/ an der Armutsgrenze leben	to be above/ below/on the poverty line
Existenzminimum, das (no pl.)	subsistence level

Alcohol and drugs

Aufputschmittel, das (-)	stimulant
Opiat, das (-e)	opiate
eine radikale Entziehungskur machen	to come off drugs cold turkey
sofortiger Totalentzug	a cold-turkey cure
Anonyme Alkoholiker, pl.	Alcoholics Anonymous

Kokainlinie, die (-n)	line of cocaine	Pestizid, das (-e)	pesticide
		Phosphat, das (-e)	phosphate
Drogenkonsument(in), der/die (-en/nen)	druggie	phosphatfrei, -haltig	phosphate-free/ containing phosphates
Drogi, der (-s; coll.)	druggie		
Schnüffler(in), der/die (-/nen)	glue-sniffer	Bodenschätze, pl.	mineral resources
		Bodenerosion, die (-en)	soil erosion
schnüffeln	to sniff [glue, drugs]		
etw sniffen	to sniff sth; snort sth [cocaine]	Abholzung, die (-en)	deforestation
		Entwaldung, die (-en)	deforestation
etw spritzen	to inject/shoot sth [heroin, etc.]		
		Wiederaufforstung, die (-en)	reforestation
sich einen antörnen (sl.)	to get stoned		
		Waldsterben, das (no pl.)	forest dieback
halluzinieren	to hallucinate		
halluzinogen	hallucinogenic	bleifreies Benzin	unleaded petrol
verschreibungs- pflichtige Medikamente, pl.	controlled drugs	Null-Emission, die (-en)	zero emission
		Ölteppich, der (-e)	oil slick
vom Heroin runterkommen (coll.)	to kick heroin	Dunstglocke, die (-n)	pall of smog
es sich abgewöhnen	to kick the habit	Wegwerfgesellschaft, die (-en)	throwaway society
Environment		Schrottplatz, der (¨e)	scrapyard
Beseitigung, die (no pl.)	disposal		
		Verschwendung, die (no pl.)	wastefulness
Entsorgung, die (no pl.)	(waste) disposal		
		biologisch abbaubar	biodegradable
etw belasten	to negatively affect/ pollute sth	Treibhauseffekt, der (no pl.)	greenhouse effect
Unkrautbekämp- fungsmittel, das (-)	weed killer	Ozonloch, das (¨er)	hole in the ozone layer

Exercises

Level 1

1. Wie heißt das Gegenteil? ✓

1. der Linke
2. liberal
3. die Oppositionspartei
4. das Unterhaus
5. umweltfeindlich

6. die Einwanderin
7. reich
8. der Reichtum
9. harte Droge
10. politisch korrekt

2. Welches Verb passt? ✓

a. abgeben, b. bitten, c. gehen, d. kommen, e. stehen, f. stimmen, g. wegwerfen

1. an die Macht   5. für jmdn
2. um Asyl   6. Abfall
3. seine Stimme   7. zur Wahl
4. unter Alkohol

3. Wie heißen die Zusammensetzungen? ✓
1. super power: d___ Super_____
2. coalition party: d___ _____partei
3. party leader: d___ Partei_____
4. televised debate: d___ _____debatte
5. parliamentary election: d___ Parlaments_____
6. basic law: d___ Grund_____
7. foreign policy: d___ _____politik
8. secret agent: d___ _____agentin
9. inner city: d___ _____stadt
10. air pollution: d___ _____verschmutzung

4. Welche Wörter gehören zusammen? ✓

a. die Demokratie, b. der Faschismus, c. der Kapitalismus, d. der Kommunismus,
e. der Marxismus, f. die Monarchie, g. der Patriotismus, h. der Sozialismus

1. Gütergemeinschaft
2. der Diktator
3. soziale Gerechtigkeit
4. der Klassenkampf
5. das freie Unternehmertum
6. die Volksherrschaft
7. der König
8. die Vaterlandsliebe

5. Ergänzen Sie. ✓
1. wählen – der Wähler : betteln – _____
2. der Senat – der Senator : das Parlament – _____
3. die Botschaft – die Botschafterin : das Konsulat – _____
4. kommunistisch – der Kommunist : obdachlos – _____
5. die Sozialarbeit – der Sozialarbeiter : die Diplomatie – _____

6. Welches Wort hat die gleiche oder eine ähnliche Bedeutung? ✓
1. die Regierung   4. die Armut
2. der Müll   5. das Acid
3. das Komitee

7. Welche Definition passt? ✓

a. der Alkoholismus, b. der Kandidat, c. der Kanzler, d. der Minister, e. das Recycling, f. die Rehabilitation, g. der Slum, h. das Speed, i. die Unterstützung

1. Amphetamin
2. Wiedereingliederung in die Gesellschaft
3. Wiederverwertung von Abfallstoffen
4. Trunksucht
5. Elendsviertel
6. geldliche Hilfe
7. jemand, der gewählt werden will
8. Regierungschef
9. Leiter eines Ministeriums

8. In jedem Satz fehlt ein Wort. ✓

Aktionsgruppe, Demonstrant, Gastarbeiter, konsultieren, Nothilfe, Parteiprogramm, Politik, Politiker, Spionage, zensieren

1. Der Staat lässt Bücher aus dem Ausland _____.
2. Sein Vater war ein einflussreicher _____.
3. Die SPD wird ihr _____ weiterentwickeln und neu formulieren.
4. Er möchte wieder in die _____ einsteigen.
5. Mindestens ein _____ wurde festgenommen, einer wurde mit leichten Verletzungen ins Krankenhaus gebracht.
6. Dies war die medienwirksamste politische _____ der achtziger und neunziger Jahre in den USA.
7. Er wollte die Nato-Partner vorher noch einmal _____.
8. Die Vereinten Nationen haben um _____ für mindestens 300 000 Menschen in Mosambik gebeten.
9. Er wurde wegen _____ zu lebenslanger Haft verurteilt.
10. Die ersten _____ wurden in den 50er Jahren nach Deutschland eingeladen.

9. Übersetzen Sie ins Englische.

Große Koalition wieder belebt

KOPENHAGEN, 17. Januar. Mit der Bildung einer großen Koalition zwischen der sozialdemokratischen Siumut-Partei und der konservativen Atassut endete am Freitag die Regierungskrise in Grönland. Damit behielt Regierungschef Hans Enoksen (Siumut), dessen Abgang vor wenigen Tagen noch alle anderen Parteien gefordert hatten, die bei den Wahlen vor fünf Wochen eroberte Macht.

Damals hatte Enoksen eine Koalition mit der linken IA-Partei gebildet, die aber rasch scheiterte. IA-Chef Josef Motzfeldt warf Enoksen „Vetternwirtschaft" bei der Besetzung hoher Verwaltungsposten vor. Auch bezichtigte er Enoksen des Okkultismus. Grund war eine „Vertreibung böser

Geister" aus den Regierungsgebäuden, die der mittlerweile entlassenen Verwaltungsdirektor Jens Lyberth veranlasst hatte.

Motzfeld strebte dann selbst ein Bündnis mit der Atassut an. Doch es gelang Enoksen den Partnertausch zu vollziehen und er ging nun wieder jene große Koalition ein, deren Scheitern die Dezember-Wahlen erst ausgelöst hatte. „Diesmal hält die Zusammenarbeit. Wir glauben an eine handlungsfähige Regierung für die nächsten vier Jahre", sagte die Atassut-Vorsitzende Augusta Salling, die noch vor einer Woche die Beendigung der Siumut-Vorherrschaft gefordert hatte, die seit Erringung der Autonomie vor 22 Jahren andauert. Der Wiedereinstieg der Konservativen in die Koalition bremst die Selbstständigkeitsbestrebungen in Grönland, die der IA wichtig waren. Für Atassut ist die Bewahrung der engen Beziehungen zum Mutterland Dänemark eine Kernfrage.

Johannes Gamillscheg

FRANKFURTER RUNDSCHAU, 18. Januar 2003, Nr. 15/3, S. 5

Botschafter verwendet sich für inhaftierte Kubaner

BERLIN, 10. Januar (FR). Der kubanische Botschafter in Berlin, Marcelino Medina, hat sich für fünf Landsleute eingesetzt, die in den USA inhaftiert sind. Das Verfahren sei unfair gewesen und müsse wieder aufgenommen werden, forderte auch der Präsident der Internationalen Anwaltskammer in Havanna, Rodolfo Davalos Fernandez. Als Grund wird genannt, dass das Verfahren in Miami stattgefunden habe, wo die Fünf wegen des hohen Anteils von Exilkubanern schon vorverurteilt gewesen seien. Die Fünf waren wegen Spionage verurteilt worden. Sie hatten sich in exilkubanische Organisationen in Florida eingeschlichen und Dossiers über deren Arbeit an die Regierung in Havanna weitergegeben. Ihr Ziel sei es gewesen, „geplante Terroraktionen dieser Gruppen" zu verhindern, sagte der Botschafter.

FRANKFURTER RUNDSCHAU, 11. Januar 2003, Nr. 9/2, S. 7

Level 2

1. Wie heißt das Gegenteil? ✓
1. der Liberalismus
2. die linke Mitte
3. die Demokratische Partei
4. der Bundestag
5. das Innenministerium
6. das Einreisevisum
7. die Oberschicht

2. Welches Verb passt? ✓

a. abschließen, b. einlegen, c. führen, d. geben, e. gelangen, f. machen, g. stellen, h. verteilen

1. an die Macht
2. den Wahlkampf
3. sein Veto gegen etw
4. sich zur Wahl

5. einen Vertrag
6. einer Partei seine Stimme
7. Wahlwerbung
8. Flugblätter

3. Wofür sind die folgenden Abkürzungen? ✓

1. CDU
2. CSU
3. SPD
4. FDP

5. PDS
6. EU
7. EG

4. Ordnen Sie die Minister und Angelegenheiten einander zu. ✓

> a. die Außenministerin, b. der Finanzminister, c. die Innenministerin,
> d. der Justizminister, e. die Kultusministerin, f. der Landwirtschaftsminister,
> g. die Umweltministerin, h. der Verteidigungsminister

1. Umweltschutz
2. Angelegenheiten innerhalb des Staates
3. Ackerbau und Viehzucht
4. auswärtige Angelegenheiten

5. das Geldwesen
6. Streitkräfte
7. das Rechtswesen
8. kulturelle Angelegenheiten

5. Welches Wort hat die gleiche oder eine ähnliche Bedeutung? ✓

1. der Vertrag
2. der Eurotunnel
3. abgebrannt
4. erbärmlich
5. die Droge
6. die Drogenabhängigkeit

7. drogenabhängig
8. der Junkie
9. das Marihuana
10. der Grüne
11. etw recyclen

6. Wie heißen die Zusammensetzungen? ✓

1. hazardous waste: d ___ _____ müll
2. chemical waste: d ___ _____ müll
3. household waste: d ___ _____ müll
4. industrial waste: d ___ _____ müll
5. toxic waste: d ___ _____ müll
6. nuclear waste: d ___ _____ müll

7. Ergänzen Sie. ✓

1. das Wasser – das Abwasser : das Gas – _____
2. reden – die Redefreiheit : sich versammeln – _____
3. der Obdachlose – das Obdachlosenheim : der Flüchtling – _____
4. SPD – Sozialdemokrat : CDU – _____
5. die Bürgerinitiative – der Bürger : der Rat – _____
6. das Kokain – der Koks : der Multikulturalismus – _____
7. Kinder – das Kindergeld : die Wohnmiete – _____

8. In jedem Satz fehlt ein Wort. ✓

> Diktatur, Probeabstimmung, Schmiergelder, Staatsstreich, Stadtrat, Tagesordnung

1. Zwei Manager der Bahn sollen _____ von einem Bauunternehmer angenommen haben.
2. Die Regierung von Mexiko verurteilte den _____ als illegalen Sturz einer gewählten Regierung.
3. In einer _____ werden Menschenrechte zumindest teilweise außer Kraft gesetzt.
4. Der _____ dieser Stadt wird in freier und geheimer Wahl für sechs Jahre gewählt.
5. Wir müssen zur _____ übergehen.
6. Bei der _____ bekam der Antrag aber nur 25 von 35 nötigen Stimmen.

9. Übersetzen Sie ins Englische.

Paris und Berlin gleichen Verfahren an

PARIS, 13. Dezember (dpa/afp). Deutschland und Frankreich wollen bei der Ausweisung illegal Einwandernder stärker zusammenarbeiten, bestätigte ein Sprecher des französischen Innenministeriums am Freitag. Eine neue Vereinbarung über die Aufnahme illegal Eingewanderter sei zur Zeit in Arbeit. Vorgesehen sei eine engere Zusammenarbeit über die Kontrolle von Ausweispapieren, Visa und Aufenthaltsgenehmigungen, um die Verfahren zu harmonisieren.

Derweil begannen die Abbrucharbeiten im französischen Flüchtlingslager Sangatte an der Kanalküste. Nach Angaben des Roten Kreuzes warteten am Freitag noch rund 200 Flüchtlinge auf ihre Ausreise nach Großbritannien. London und Paris hatten in der vergangenen Woche die vorzeitige Schließung des Lagers besiegelt. Seit Anfang November hatten die französischen Behörden neu Ankommenden die Aufnahme in Sangatte verweigert.

FRANKFURTER RUNDSCHAU, 14. Dezember 2002, Nr. 291/50, S. 5

© dpa Deutsche Presse-Agentur GmbH

10. Fassen Sie den folgenden Text zusammen.

Aus „Geduldig reihen sich die Kenianer ein" von Christoph Link (Nairobi)

In Kenias Hauptstadt Nairobi herrschte eine ungewohnte Stille. Geschäfte und Märkte blieben geschlossen, die Straßen der City waren menschenleer, nur ein Polizeilastwagen mit schwer bewaffneten Uniformierten der „Anti-Krawall-Einheit" preschte durch die Gassen.

In der Nacht zuvor war im Kibera-Slum ein junger Mann erstochen worden, er hatte mit anderen vergeblich versucht, Porträts des Kandidaten der Regierunspartei Kanu, Uhuru Kenyatta, aufzuhängen. Kibera gilt wie ganz Nairobi als Hochburg der Opposition.

Diszipliniert und in bis zu 500 Meter langen Schlangen warteten viele der 10,5 Millionen Wahlberechtigten mitunter stundenlang auf den Zugang zu den Wahltischen. In nobleren Stadtteilen wie Kileleshwa erinnerten die Zustände an die Ordentlichkeit einer deutschen Bundestagswahl. Ein Dutzend örtlicher Beobachter der Parteien wachte über ein korrektes Geschehen im Wahllokal, an einem Tisch mit Beisitzern wurden die Personalien geprüft und selbst die Warteschlangen waren abgesperrt und mit Nummern versehen.

Dennoch klagten viele, dass ihre Namen nicht in den Wählerverzeichnissen eingetragen waren. Die Opposition beschuldigte die Regierung der Wahlmanipulation: 20 Prozent aller Wahlberechtigten seien ausgeschlossen worden. In mehreren Dörfern wurden Gruppen von Wählern beobachtet, die auf und ab gingen und auf eine Bezahlung durch Parteien warteten. Im Wahlbezirk Changamwe in Mombasa verhaftete die Polizei zwei Personen, weil sie Wählern 100 Schillingen (1,25 Euro) dafür geboten haben sollen, für die Regierung zu stimmen.

Der seit 24 Jahren regierende Präsident Daniel Arap Moi durfte aus Verfassungsgründen nicht wieder kandidieren. Den 42-jährigen Sohn von Staatsgründer Jomo Kenyatta hatte er zum offiziellen Bewerber der Kanu-Partei emporgehoben. Uhuru Kenyatta stimmte in seinem Heimatort Gatundu ab und erklärte, er sei zuversichtlich, die Wahlen zu gewinnen.

Gegen Kenyatta trat der 71-jährige Oppositionsführer Mwai Kibaki an. Kibaki stimmte in seiner Heimat Othaya im Auto sitzend ab, da er immer noch an den Folgen eines Unfalls laboriert. Kibaki appellierte an die Kenianer, ruhig zu bleiben und Vertrauen in den Sieg seiner „Regenbogen-Allianz" zu haben. Das Endergebnis wird Sonntag oder Montag erwartet.

FRANKFURTER RUNDSCHAU, 28. Dezember 2002, Nr. 301/52, S. 6

Level 3

1. Wie heißt das Gegenteil? ✓
1. die Spionage
2. etw chiffrieren
3. der linke Flügel
4. der Stammwähler
5. die Mehrheitsregierung
6. phosphatfrei
7. der Unitarismus
8. jmdn einbürgern

2. Wofür sind die folgenden Abkürzungen? ✓
1. SED   5. NPD
2. REP   6. UN
3. DVU   7. WGO
4. KPD

3. Welches Verb passt? ✓

a. einschwenken, b. fassen, c. gewähren, d. herunterkommen, e. kämpfen, f. lassen, g. nehmen, h. sammeln, i. stellen, j. treiben, k. treten

1. Spionage
2. auf die Parteilinie
3. über etw abstimmen
4. um einen Wahlkreis
5. auf die Abgeordneten Einfluss
6. einen Beschluss

7. in Kraft
8. die Vertrauensfrage
9. Unterschriften
10. Asyl
11. vom Heroin

4. Welches Wort hat die gleiche oder eine ähnliche Bedeutung? ✓

1. verfallen
2. sniffen
3. linksradikal
4. die Alleinherrschaft

5. das Plebiszit
6. unilateral
7. der Drogenkonsument

5. Welche Definition passt? ✓

a. die Aristokratie, b. autark, c. die Basis, d. bettelarm, e. der Europol, f. der Despotismus, g. die Parteilinie, h. die Wählerschaft, i. der Zuschuss

1. zusätzliche Zahlung
2. sehr arm
3. die einfachen Mitglieder einer Partei
4. selbständig
5. Adelsherrschaft

6. System der Gewaltherrschaft
7. Ideologie einer Partei
8. die Gesamtheit der Wähler
9. europäisches Kriminalamt

6. Welche Wörter gehören zusammen? ✓

a. die Anarchie, b. der Gesandte, c. die Immunität, d. der Ministerrat, e. der Sicherheitsrat, f. spritzen, g. die Xenophobie

1. Heroin
2. Gesetzlosigkeit
3. Diplomaten
4. der Attaché

5. UN
6. Angst und Ablehnung
7. EG

7. Ergänzen Sie. ✓
1. die gesetzgebende Gewalt = _____
2. die richterliche Gewalt = _____
3. die vollziehende Staatsgewalt = _____

8. Welches Adjektiv passt? ✓

a. biologisch abbaubar, b. bleifrei, c. geheim, d. halluzinogen, e. ständig, f. zivil

1. Abstimmung
2. LSD
3. Benzin
4. Ausschuss
5. Waschmittel
6. Ungehorsam

9. In jedem Satz fehlt ein Wort. ✓

> Ampelkoalition, Armutsgrenze, Entsorgung, Europarat, Euroskeptiker, Gerichtshof, geschnorrt, Sozialhilfeempfänger, Splitterpartei, Totalentzug, umbilden, verschwören

1. Er glaubt, das andere sich gegen ihn _____
2. Eine _____ mit den Grünen schließt er aus.
3. Duisburg ist die Heimat einer rechtsextremen _____.
4. Frankreichs Ministerpräsident will Frankreichs Regierung _____.
5. Die _____ halten Europa für noch nicht reif für eine gemeinsame Währung.
6. Die Zahl der _____ nimmt andauernd zu.
7. Zwei Millionen Jugendliche leben unter der _____.
8. Der _____ wurde 1949 gegründet und zählt heute 44 Mitgliedstaaten.
9. Er hat sich ein paar Zigaretten _____.
10. Der Europäische _____ besteht aus 15 Richtern und wird von 9 Generalanwälten unterstützt. [Januar 2002]
11. Nach einem sofortigen _____ ist er nicht mehr rauschgiftsüchtig.
12. Die Frage der _____ des radioaktiven Abfalls ist noch nicht gelöst.

10. Übersetzen Sie ins Englische.

Verband setzt sich für Behindertenwerkstätten ein

FRANKFURT A. M., 27 Dezember (dpa). Der Paritätische Wohlfahrtsverband hat mehr Geld gefordert, um neue Arbeitsplätze in Werkstätten für Menschen mit Behinderung zu schaffen. Es sei ein „sozialer Skandal", dass die Bundesanstalt für Arbeit die Einrichtung von mehr als 5000 neuen Arbeitsplätzen blockiere, kritisierte die Verbandsvorsitzende Barbara Stolterfoth am Freitag in Frankfurt. Das Bundesministerium für Gesundheit und Soziales habe bereits 149 Projekte als förderungswürdig anerkannt.

Die Bundesanstalt für Arbeit, die sich an den Investitionen beteiligen müsse, habe für 2003 lediglich 26,1 Millionen Euro im Haushalt eingeplant. „Diese Summe reicht in keinem Fall, um die vom Sozialministerium anerkannten Projekte zu realisieren", sagte Stolterfoth. Die Absicht, Arbeitsplätze für Menschen mit Behinderung zu schaffen, dürfe bei der Hartz-Reform nicht unter die Räder kommen.

FRANKFURTER RUNDSCHAU, 28. Dezember 2002, Nr. 301/52, S. 4

© dpa Deutsche Presse-Agentur GmbH

Schröder und Bökel attackieren Roland Koch

KASSEL. Mit Bundeskanzler Gerhard Schröder, ihrem Spitzenkandidaten Gerhard Bökel und dessen Schattenkabinett haben die hessischen Sozialdemokraten am Donnerstagabend in der Kasseler Stadthalle die heiße Phase des Landtagswahlkampfes eingeleitet. Schröder und Bökel gaben sich vor rund 800 Zuhörern siegesgewiss. „Lasst Euch nicht beirren durch Umfragen", beschwor Bökel die Genossen. „Lasst doch die anderen die Umfragen gewinnen, wenn wir dann die Wahl gewinnen", sagte Schröder. Beide Politiker gingen mit der schwarz-gelben Landesregierung ins Gericht: Vier Jahre Roland Koch hätten Hessen geschadet. Die SPD werde nach einem Wahlsieg die Familien-, Beschäftigungs- und Bildungspolitik in den Mittelpunkt stellen.

Gundula Zeitz

FRANKFURTER RUNDSCHAU, 11. Januar 2003, Nr. 9/2, S. 31

Aus „Fieber steigt nicht mehr" von Stephan Börnecke

HOFHEIM. Umweltminister Wilhelm Dietzel (CDU) sagte in Hofheim, er sei „zufrieden", dass die Forscher eine weitere leichte Erholung der Wälder hätten feststellen können. Er hoffe, dass sich dieser insgesamt positive Trend in den folgenden Jahren fortsetze. Die aktuelle Entwicklung zeige ihm, so der Christdemokrat, dass die Politik aufgrund der heftigen Diskussionen um das Waldsterben in den achtziger Jahren „die richtigen politischen Entscheidungen getroffen" habe. Dazu zählten vor der Einbau von Filtern bei Industrie und Kraftwerken sowie die Einführung des Katalysators in den Autos ...

FRANKFURTER RUNDSCHAU, 26. Oktober 2002, Nr. 249/43, S. 28

Key to exercises

Words and word formation

A. Nouns

1. -er, -in; 'female letter writer'
2. Fehl-, -ung; 'bad planning'
3. Ge-, -e; 'knocking'
4. Grund-; 'basic rule'
5. -heit; 'prettiness'
6. -e; 'lawn care'
7. Schein-, -schaft; 'false pregnancy'
8. -ität; 'stability'
9. Ur-; 'original source'
10. -lein; 'little fence'

B. Adjectives

1. -lich; 'plump (somewhat fat)'
2. -haft; 'full of gaps'
3. -los; 'moonless'
5. -mäßig; 'according to rank'
6. un-, -bar; 'unsolvable'

C. Verbs

1. ab-; 'to tear off'
2. an-; 'to partly tear'
3. auf-; 'to scratch open'
4. be-; 'to shade'
5. ent-; 'to undress'
6. über-; 'to overheat'
7. um-; 'to surround with a wall'
8. ver-; 'to thin down', 'to dilute'
9. zer-; 'to divide into pieces'
10. zu-; 'to button up'

D. Adverbs

1. -weise; 'by the bucketful', 'in bucketfuls'
2. -halber; 'for reasons of health'
3. -erweise; 'cleverly', 'wisely'
5. -maßen; 'to be consistent'
6. -weise; 'on a trial basis'

Dictionary use

1.

	Gender	Genitive singular ending	Plural form
a.	masculine	-s	Bagger
b.	masculine	-s	no plural form
c.	masculine	-s	Kästen
d.	feminine	no ending	Pusteln
e.	masculine	-n	Löwen
f.	none (only plural)	none (only plural)	Niederlande
g.	neuter	-ens	Herzen

2.

a. harrt   harrte   hat geharrt

b. birgt   barg   hat geborgen

c. flieht   floh   ist geflohen

d. kommt um   kam um   ist umgekommen

e. durchleuchtet   durchleuchtete   hat durchleuchtet

3.

a. Staat

b. Post

c. Journal

d. backen

e. Stadt

4.

a. transitive

b. intransitive

c. transitive and intransitive

d. reflexive

e. reflexive

5.

a. ein Buch besprechen/rezensieren

b. eine Entscheidung treffen

c. mit jemandem ausgehen

d. einen Schluss ziehen

e. etwas berücksichtigen/bedenken

Unit 1 Towns and buildings; household; gardens

Level 1

1.

1. f 2. i 3. h 4. b 5. g 6. d 7. c 8. a 9. e

2.

1. der Gehweg 2. der Vergnügungspark 3. die Bibliothek 4. der Dom 5. der Laden 6. der Aufzug
7. der Dachboden 8. der Flur 9. das Sofa 10. das Bettlaken

4.

1. jäten 2. anbauen 3. Gartenbank 4. Obstgarten 5. Kissen 6. Schaukelstuhl 7. Schublade
8. Veilchen 9. Ampel 10. Sehenswürdigkeit

5.

1. j 2. k 3. a 4. f 5. d 6. n 7. m 8. e 9. c 10. l 11. b 12. i 13. g 14. h

6.

1. die Kerze 2. die Kneipe 3. der Besen 4. die Bettwäsche 5. die Umgebung 6. das Regal
7. das Messer 8. die Kaffeekanne 9. das Blumenbeet

Level 2

1.

1. das Geschäftsviertel 2. der Trödelmarkt 3. der Stock 4. die Brandleiter 5. die Einrichtung
6. der Geschirrspüler 7. der Müll 8. der Rechen 9. die Flammenblume 10. die Gartenwicke

3.

1. der Vermieter 2. die Vorstädterin 3. der Wasserkrug 4. der Salzstreuer 5. das Backblech
6. der Nagel 7. der Bohnerwachs 8. etw schmirgeln 9. der Handrasenmäher

4.

1. h 2. p 3. f 4. i 5. e 6. g 7. b 8. n 9. m 10. o 11. l 12. j 13. a 14. d 15. c 16. k

6.

1. Waage- 2. Kuchen- 3. Deckel- 4. Tor- 5. Deserteur- 6. Stecken- 7. Armbinde- 8. Rot-
9. Zigaretten- 10. -teller

7.

1. zentral 2. möbliert 3. geräumig 4. begehbar 5. zusammenklappbar 6. verschiebbar 7. drehbar

8.

1. Fußgängerzone 2. Wohngemeinschaft 3. Fußgängerüberweg 4. Dachfenster 5. Allzweckraum
6. Gegensprechanlage 7. Raumteiler 8. Fertighaus 9. Speisekammer 10. Tiefkühlfach

9.

2. das Bleichmittel 3. die Kaffeemühle 4. das Einbaumöbel 5. der Luftverbesserer
6. der Elektroherd 7. das Abtropfsieb 8. der Staubsauger 9. der Abfalleimer
10. der Kerzenleuchter

11a.

1. pur 2. Tristesse 3. Rankpflanze 4. gedeihen 5. Accessoires 6. behaglich 7. montieren

Level 3

1.

1. die Unterführung 2. der Ausgang 3. die Ausfahrt 4. der Verkäufermarkt 5. jmdm etw
verpachten 6. der kurzflorige Teppich 7. der Warmwassergriff 8. eine Schraube herausdrehen
9. das stumpfe Messer

2.

1. g 2. f 3. b 4. h 5. e 6. i 7. d 8. a 9. c

4.

1. der Kreis 2. der Dachvorsprung 3. der Geschirrschrank 4. das Parkett 5. das Klosett
6. die Stielkasserolle 7. die Lackfarbe 8. der Spross 9. etw umpflanzen

5.

O	H	E	R	Z	L	I	L	I	E	R	A	L	Ö	B
G	L	A	D	I	O	L	E	A	K	E	L	E	I	R
H	O	L	A	V	E	N	D	E	L	O	P	F	R	E
Z	I	N	N	I	E	R	I	Z	E	S	E	E	F	N
D	A	H	L	I	E	S	S	I	N	E	N	U	O	N
I	M	S	T	A	F	Ö	T	E	N	E	V	I	R	N
K	A	P	U	Z	I	N	E	R	K	R	E	S	S	E
L	G	Ä	L	A	V	E	L	G	R	O	I	L	Y	S
E	N	U	P	L	E	L	Ü	R	O	S	L	U	T	S
M	O	H	E	E	C	K	G	A	K	E	C	P	H	E
A	L	O	E	E	T	E	Ü	S	U	I	H	I	I	L
T	I	S	H	O	R	T	E	N	S	I	E	N	E	Ä
I	E	L	Ö	W	E	N	Z	A	H	N	E	E	U	
S	C	H	N	E	E	G	L	Ö	C	K	C	H	E	N
F	T	R	Ä	N	E	N	D	E	S	H	E	R	Z	O

6.

1. Sack- 2. -panne 3. Blau- 4. Decken- 5. Spül-

7.

1. f (die) 2. g (der) 3. j (die) 4. e (der) 5. l (der) 6. k (das) 7. b (die) 8. i (die) 9. h (die) 10. d (die)
11. a (der) 12. c (die)

8.

1. Panoramafenster 2. Dachrinne 3. Glockenturm 4. Tünche 5. Nebenkosten 6. Korbmöbel
7. Teppichboden 8. Badewanne 9. Hausapotheke 10. Grashalm

Unit 2 The physical world; the animal world; weather

Level 1

1.

1. das Hochgebirge 2. das Süßwasser 3. flaches Wasser 4. zahm 5. die Katze
6. die Temperatur sinkt 7. wolkig 8. die Kälte 9. schmelzen 10. nass

2.

1. der Urwald 2. das Meer 3. das Kriechtier 4. etw angeln 5. der Kakerlak 6. wehen 7. der Sturm

3.

1. gebirgig 2. sonnig 3. warm 4. heiß 5. wolkig 6. neblig 7. regnerisch 8. schneeig 9. frostig 10. windig 11. stürmisch

4.

1. e 2. f 3. b 4. i 5. h 6. g 7. c 8. a 9. d

7.

1. das Maul 2. miauen 3. der Schnabel 4. kriechen 5. das (Hunde)junge 6. schneien 7. der Strom 8. der Bach 9. das Ufer 10. der Vogel 11. die Kaulquappe

Level 2

1.

1. j 2. h 3. d 4. a 5. i 6. c 7. f 8. g 9. b 10. e

2.

1. die Lichtung 2. das Hochwasser 3. die Gischt 4. der Deich 5. die Spitze 6. der schottische Schäferhund 7. der Dackel 8. die Beutelratte 9. der Stieglitz 10. das Krustentier 11. das Glühwürmchen 12. das Naturschutzgebiet

3.

1. der Fels 2. der Schlamm 3. das Klima 4. der Dunst 5. die Schneeglätte 6. das Gewitter

4.

1. die Flut 2. der Nadelbaum 3. die Quelle 4. der Süßwasserfisch 5. regenreich 6. die Höchsttemperatur 7. sich bewölken 8. leicht bewölkt 9. die Kaltfront

5.

1. die Hundehütte 2. der Kaninchenbau 3. der Fuchsbau 4. der Biberbau 5. die Löwenhöhle 6. der Maulwurfshügel 7. das Nest 8. der Ameisenhaufen

6.

1. b 2. e 3. c 4. f 5. a 6. d

8.

E	T	Ü	M	M	L	E	R	H	S	T	A	R	S	M	E
Z	E	C	K	E	S	C	H	O	P	I	L	Ä	N	A	I
W	Ü	S	T	E	N	S	P	R	I	N	G	M	A	U	S
E	R	H	B	R	E	C	U	N	K	T	R	H	C	L	V
B	B	A	R	S	C	H	M	I	A	E	A	E	H	W	O
E	R	B	A	C	N	I	A	S	B	N	S	I	T	U	G
R	F	I	U	H	Ü	M	R	S	E	F	M	L	I	R	E
K	L	C	N	W	N	P	V	E	L	I	Ü	B	G	F	L
N	A	H	B	E	R	A	B	E	J	S	C	U	A	A	L
E	M	T	Ä	I	C	N	E	A	A	C	K	T	L	M	E
C	I	S	R	N	E	S	H	N	U	H	E	T	L	S	R
H	N	E	I	C	H	E	L	H	Ä	H	E	R	N	E	Ö
T	G	T	I	H	E	R	M	E	L	I	N	O	N	L	N
R	O	T	K	E	H	L	C	H	E	N	R	O	B	B	E
I	T	E	Ä	N	K	E	R	F	A	L	K	E	T	T	R
S	C	H	W	A	L	B	E	N	S	C	H	W	A	N	Z

9.

1. flattert 2. Nieselregen 3. beschnüffeln 4. Schneegestöber 5. Walfang 6. Wettervorhersage
7. Durchschnittstemperatur 8. Aufheiterung 9. piepen 10. Glatteis 11. brüllt 12. Tauwetter

10.

2. der Windstoß 3. die Gewitterfront 4. der Hagelschauer 5. der Gefrierpunkt 6. die Kältewelle
7. das Nebelhorn 8. der Pulverschnee 9. die Sturzflut 10. der Erdrutsch

Level 3

1.
1. i 2. f 3. h 4. e 5. a 6. b 7. j 8. g 9. d 10. c

2.
1. die Zitterpappel 2. der Tümpel 3. der Vorstehhund 4. der Schweißhund 5. der Schwimmfuß
6. die Schar 7. transpirieren 8. verhangen 9. sprühen 10. nachlassen 11. der Wirbelsturm
12. die Flaute

3.
1. der Wurf 2. der Schakal 3. der Salamander 4. die Bucht 5. die Anhöhe 6. die Ulme
7. der Windhund 8. der Mungo 9. die Aufheiterung

4.
1. a 2. g 3. e 4. f 5. b 6. h 7. c 8. d

5.
1. der (Rau-)reif 2. die Graupel 3. die Lawine 4. läufig werden 5. die Schlangenhaut
6. die Bartfäden 7. die Schwanzflosse 8. das Schneckenhaus 9. das Seepferdchen

8.
1. krähen 2. quaken 3. gurren 4. kollert 5. Krallen 6. Tierrechtler 7. Robbenfang 8. Tierversuch
9. Maden 10. Kokon 11. Torf

9.
1. c 2. f 3. g 4. h 5. a 6. b 7. e 8. d

Unit 3 The human body and health; the health service and medicine
Level 1
1.
1. d 2. c 3. f 4. a 5. g 6. e 7. h 8. b

2.
1. die Backe 2. der Schnupfen 3. der Brechreiz 4. der Kopfweh 5. der Herzanfall
6. (sich) erbrechen 7. der Schwangerschaftsabbruch 8. die Heilkunde 9. die Ärztin
10. die Krankenpflegerin 11. das Mittel 12. die Tablette 13. der Gummi 14. der Verband
15. der Sanitätskasten 16. die Plombe 17. der Bruch

3.
1. f 2. d 3. i 4. l 5. b 6. a 7. h 8. k 9. e 10. m 11. g 12. c 13. j

4.
1. i 2. b 3. d 4. j 5. g 6. f 7. a 8. e 9. h 10. c

7.
1. der Kinderarzt, die Kinderärztin 2. der Frauenarzt, die Frauenärztin 3. der Chirurg, die
Chirurgin 4. der Psychiater, die Psychiaterin 5. der Augenarzt, die Augenärztin 6. der Zahnarzt,
die Zahnärztin

8.
1. Er geht mir auf die Nerven.
2. Sie war außer Atem.
3. Er hat eine Leiche im Keller.
4. Er ist nur noch Haut und Knochen.
5. Sie hat ihn in die Rippen gestoßen. / Sie stieß ihn in die Rippen.
6. Ich habe mich erkältet. / Ich erkältete mich.
7. Der Arzt hat ihr in den Hals geschaut. / Der Arzt schaute ihr in den Hals.
8. Sie hat tief Atem geholt. / Sie holte tief Atem.

10.
1. c 2. g 3. h 4. b 5. a 6. d 7. e 8. f

Level 2

1.

1. der Gehörsinn 2. das Sehvermögen 3. der Geruchssinn 4. der Geschmackssinn
5. der Gefühlssinn

2.

Finger: 2. der Zeigefinger 3. der Mittelfinger 4. der Ringfinger 5. der kleine Finger
Zehen: 2. die zweite Zehe 3. die Mittelzehe 4. die vierte Zehe 5. die kleine Zehe

3.

1. b 2. e 3. a 4. d 5. c

4.

1. die Schlagader 2. die Blutader 3. die Achselhöhle 4. die Geschwulst 5. die Gelenkentzündung
6. die Arznei 7. die Blutwäsche 8. der Schieber 9. die Kinderlähmung 10. ohnmächtig
11. die Kehle

5.

1. g 2. d 3. b 4. f 5. c 6. h 7. a 8. i 9. e

6.

1. gesund 2. ausatmen 3. der Dünndarm 4. jmdn entlassen 5. der Unterarm 6. bösartig

7.

1. das Stießbein 2. der Busen 3. die Schiene 4. der Blinddarm 5. die Hebamme
6. der Physiotherapeut 7. die Achsel 8. das Hörrohr 9. Wehen 10. die Krankenbahre

8.

1. bewusstlos 2. blutarm 3. schmerzhaft 4. allergisch 5. zuckerkrank 6. krampfartig 7. schwindlig

9.

1. Ohrläppchen 2. Schlüsselbein 3. Beruhigungsmittel 4. Brustkorb 5. Impfung 6. Gipsverband
7. Krankengymnastik 8. Intensivstation 9. Ermüdung 10. Lebensmittelvergiftungen
11. Chiropraktikerin 12. Homöopathie

Level 3

1.

1. kanzerogen 2. die Demenz 3. der Hautausschlag 4. der Milzbrand 5. sich etw ausrenken
6. prickelnd 7. das Linderungsmittel 8. die Knopflochchirurgie 9. die Strahlenbehandlung
10. die Zahnfäule 11. die Regenbogenhaut 12. der Leib 13. die Bluterkrankheit

3.

1. der Urologe, die Urologin 2. der Geriater, die Geriaterin 3. der Virologe, die Virologin
4. der Onkologe, die Onkologin 5. der Rheumatologe, die Rheumatologin 6. der HNO-Arzt, die
HNO-Ärztin 7. der Hämatologe, die Hämatologin 8. der Endokrinologe, die Endokrinologin

5.
1. b 2. d 3. e 4. f 5. a 6. c

6.
1. der Fußrücken 2. die Wurzel 3. das Oberschenkelbein 4. das Schienbein 5. der Pathologe
6. die Gewebsverpflanzung 7. der Dialyseapparat 8. die Zahnspange 9. das Beatmungsgerät

7.
1. autistisch 2. inkontinent 3. schizophren 4. epileptisch 5. querschnittsgelähmt 6. deprimiert
7. geisteskrank

8.
1. das Hühnerauge 2. der Kropf 3. die Warze 4. die Milz 5. die Naht 6. der Ultraschall
7. die Antidepressivum 8. das Kreuzbein 9. der Eiter

Unit 4 Physical appearance; gesture and movement

Level 1

1.
1. dünn 2. klein 3. zunehmen 4. ein schmales Gesicht 5. weiche Gesichtszüge 6. helle Hautfarbe
7. fettige Haut 8. eine niedrige Stirn 9. feuchte Lippen 10. ein spitzes Kinn 11. helles Haar
12. langes Haar 13. dichtes Haar 14. fettiges Haar 15. eine schlechte Haltung haben 16. lange
Beine 17. lange Finger 18. dünne Finger 19. unschön 20. unattraktiv

2.
1. c 2. b 3. d 4. e 5. i 6. f 7. h 8. a 9. g

3.
1. blass 2. strähnig 3. aufrecht 4. runzelig 5. schlank

4.
1. ein strahlendes Gesicht 2. die Miene 3. zarte Haut 4. eine gekrümmte Haltung 5. nach oben
gehen 6. hinfallen 7. sich beeilen 8. etw umrühren 9. den Kopf senken

5.
1. b 2. i 3. f 4. e 5. h 6. a 7. g 8. d 9. j 10. c

6.
1. Gesten 2. schieben 3. Sprung 4. winken 5. Zusammenstoß 6. anfassen 7. klopfte 8. schütteln
9. nicken 10. beugte 11. Arme

7.
1. h 2. a 3. g 4. c 5. d 6. i 7. j 8. f 9. b 10. e

Level 2

2.
1. wohlbeleibt 2. mollert 3. missgestaltet 4. abgemergelt 5. ein gebräuntes Gesicht 6. der Teint
7. volles Haar 8. eine strammige Haltung 9. bezaubernd 10. niedersinken 11. sich regen
12. rasen 13. herumtollen 14. gegen etw rammen 15. sich vor Lachen biegen 16. mit den Augen
zwinkern

3.
1. breitschultrig 2. fleischig 3. rotblond 4. fettleibig 5. abstoßend 6. graben 7. schwenken

4.
1. ein ausdrucksloses Gesicht 2. glattes Haar 3. glatte Haut 4. hellhäutig 5. linkshändig 6. her
7. seine Schritte verlangsamen 8. wackelig auf den Beinen

5.
1. d 2. g 3. k 4. j 5. l 6. f 7. i 8. c 9. b 10. h 11. e 12. a

6.
1. c 2. i 3. a 4. g 5. d 6. e 7. h 8. b 9. f

7.
1. winzig, schmal, rundlich, dickleibig, fettleibig
2. tiefschwarzes Haar, angegrautes Haar, graues Haar, silbernes Haar, schlohweißes Haar
3. sich im Schneckentempo bewegen, schlendern, eilen, rennen, sausen, sprinten
4. ein kreidebleiches Gesicht, ein bleiches Gesicht, ein gerötetes Gesicht, ein hochrotes Gesicht
5. glattes Haar, welliges Haar, lockiges Haar, krauses Haar

8.
2. der, treten 3. der, schreiten 4. der, vorbeimarschieren 5. der, hinaufsteigen 6. die, gestikulieren
7. die, wandern 8. die, ankommen 9. die, paradieren 10. der, springen 11. der, zusammenstoßen
12. die, zurückkehren 13. der, marschieren

9.
1. k 2. c 3. i 4. f 5. b 6. e 7. a 8. d 9. j 10. g 11. h

Level 3

1.
1. b 2. c 3. g 4. e 5. d 6. f 7. a

2.
1. der Schubs 2. der Sturz 3. die Ersteigung 4. die Senkung 5. der Trab 6. die Ohrfeige

3.
1. der Dickwanst 2. ein hageres Gesicht 3. ein schwermütiges Gesicht 4. einen Schmollmund
machen 5. struppliges Haar 6. der Spliss 7. ihr sträuben sich die Haare 8. O-Beine

9. auf etw zusteuern 10. trotten 11. zockeln 12. jmdn zwicken 13. schwingen 14. stolzieren
15. onkeln 16. jmdm einen Schock versetzen 17. jmdn windelweich hauen 18. zwinkern

4.
1. grazil 2. flink 3. zersaust 4. wallend 5. pausbackig 6. füllig 7. kraus

5.
1. i 2. b 3. c 4. g 5. f 6. h 7. a 8. e 9. d

6.
1. vollbusig 2. ein fliehendes Kinn 3. spärliches Haar 4. lockeres Haar 5. x-beinig

7.
1. unbewegter 2. schmerzverzerrtem 3. abgespannt 4. markantes 5. Pausbacken 6. Tränensäcke
7. Stupsnase 8. Wuschelkopf 9. zappelig 10. plumpsen 11. wimmelt 12. sputen

8.
1. b 2. h 3. e 4. g 5. f 6. a 7. d 8. i 9. c

9.
2. das Pferdegesicht 3. die Hakennase 4. die Mandelaugen 5. das Händeschütteln
6. die Zehenspitze 7. die Kniebeuge 8. der Purzelbaum 9. die Duldermiene
10. der Schmollmund

Unit 5 Personality and human behaviour
Level 1

2.
1. unmoralisch 2. ein schlechtes Gewissen haben 3. unehrlich 4. taktvoll 5. unfreundlich
6. schlechte Manieren haben 7. intolerant 8. unzufrieden 9. unaufmerksam 10. inaktiv
11. kraftlos

3.
1. unanständig 2. eifersüchtig 3. streng 4. treu 5. verdächtig 6. großzügig 7. hilfsbereit
8. selbstsüchtig 9. gefühllos 10. nervös 11. wahnsinnig 12. bescheiden

4.
1. d 2. j 3. f 4. c 5. a 6. i 7. b 8. h 9. k 10. l 11. g 12. e

5.
1. streng 2. bescheiden 3. respektlos 4. launisch 5. eingebildet 6. feige 7. apatisch 8. tüchtig

6.
1. b 2. a 3. c 4. f 5. h 6. d 7. g 8. e

8.
1. f 2. g 3. e 4. a 5. c 6. d 7. b

9.
1. Wut 2. selbstsicher 3. klug 4. unhöflich 5. gierig 6. liebevolles 7. enttäuscht 8. Laune
9. Gewissensbisse 10. glaubwürdig

Level 2

1.
1. sittlich 2. redlich 3. jmdn hereinlegen 4. etw entstellen 5. unbeirrbar 6. unschlüssig
7. die Habgier 8. gerecht 9. verschlossen 10. der Reiz 11. stur 12. spießig 13. unbefangen
14. unartig 15. beglückt 16. betrübt 17. schwarzseherisch 18. jmdn hänseln 19. schwermütig
20. gewalttätig

2.
1. hochbeglückt 2. todunglücklich 3. hochgelehrt 4. hochgeistig 5. überempfindlich 6. übereifrig
7. überbelastet 8. rücksichtslos 9. sittenlos 10. schamlos 11. kompromisslos 12. sorgenfrei
13. teilnahmslos

3.
1. die Geilheit, lechery 2. die Bedenkenlosigkeit, unscrupulousness 3. die Selbstgerechtigkeit,
self-righteousness 4. die Leichtgläubigkeit, gullibility 5. die Entschlossenheit, determination
6. die Hartnäckigkeit, obstinacy 7. der Geiz, miserliness 8. die Menschenfreundlichkeit,
philanthropy 9. das Entgegenkommen, obligingness 10. die Unvoreingenommenheit,
impartiality 11. die Unverschämtheit, impudence 12. die Niederschlagenheit, despondency
13. die Empfindlichkeit, sensitivity 14. die Nachlässigkeit, carelessness

4.
1. geistlos 2. unfähig 3. missvergnügt 4. unbefangen 5. einfallslos 6. rücksichtslos 7. irresolut
8. indiskret 9. unaufrichtig

5.
1. e 2. h 3. f 4. c 5. a 6. b 7. g 8. d

7.
1. c 2. a 3. b 4. a 5. a 6. b 7. b 8. b

8.
1. beschränkt 2. scheinheilig 3. unbeständig 4. bedrückt 5. schwärmerisch

9.
1. hinterlistig 2. abgespannt 3. leidenschaftliche 4. weitblickend 5. aufbrausend 6. gefasster
7. glückstrahlend 8. dicke

10.
1. ehr- 2. Jung- 3. liebe- 4. -losig 5. einsicht-

Level 3

1.

1. b 2. h 3. j 4. f 5. i 6. a 7. c 8. e 9. d 10. g

2.

1. quietschvergnügt 2. putzmunter 3. fuchsteufelswild 4. tollkühn 5. tugendhaft 6. dünkelhaft

3.

1. gehörig 2. verdienstvoll 3. freimütig 4. wohltätig 5. knickerig 6. schweigsam 7. mitteilsam
8. griesgrämig 9. gleichmütig 10. standhaft 11. gefügig 12. kühn 13. gerissen 14. trödelig
15. heldenhaft 16. siegesgewiss 17. umgänglich 18. rüpelhaft

5.

1. keusch 2. schäbig 3. der Prahler 4. verdrießlich 5. dämlich 6. geistesgegenwärtig 7. waghalsig
8. couragiert

6.

1. Sinnen 2. umnachtet 3. Eifersucht 4. Wutanfall 5. unzurechnungsfähig 6. selig
7. zuvorkommend 8. ungebärdiges 9. aufdringlich 10. schelmisch

Unit 6 Clothes, accessories and grooming; food and drink
Level 1

2.

1. das Haarwaschmittel 2. der Haartrockner 3. der Strumpf 4. der Schlafanzug 5. gebraucht
6. die Schuhgröße 7. kostbar 8. die Nahrungsmittel (pl.) 9. die Speise 10. der Pilz
11. das Plätzchen

3.

1. f 2. c 3. e 4. d 5. h 6. b 7. g 8. a 9. i

5.

1. das Nachthemd 2. der Kamm 3. das Bügeleisen 4. die Bürste 5. der Krapfen 6. der Saft
7. der Bonbon

7.

1. die Krawatte 2. etw bügeln 3. die Kartoffel 4. der Blumenkohl 5. die Tomate 6. der Rettich
7. der Kohl 8. die Pflaume 9. die Apfelsine 10. die Sahne 11. das Eis 12. der Nachtisch
13. das Butterbrot 14. das Brötchen 15. der Imbiss 16. die Fleischerei 17. das Abendessen

8.

1. jmdm einen Schlag unter die Gürtellinie versetzen 2. den Gürtel enger schnallen 3. reg dich
nicht auf! 4. etw in die eigene Tasche stecken 5. von jmdm abhängig sein 6. die Klappe halten
7. in jmds Haut stecken 8. ein alter Hut 9. auf der Stelle 10. jmdn rausschmeißen 11. jmdn zu
Tode erschrecken 12. jmdn unvorbereitet treffen 13. das war knapp! 14. das wird sich alles
klären

10.

1. b 2. f 3. e 4. c 5. a 6. g 7. d

11.

1. Stoff zum Nachdenken 2. kneifen 3. Tacheles reden 4. weder Fisch noch Fleisch 5. (über etw) meckern 6. sich über etw den Kopf zerbrechen 7. (im eigenen Saft) schmoren 8. leichtes Geld machen 9. Pfirsichhaut 10. ein Traumjob 11. sich wie ein Ei dem anderen gleichen 12. (jmdm gegenüber) aus der Schule plaudern 13. jmdm Honig um den Mund/Bart schmieren

Level 2

1.

1. der tiefe Kleidausschnitt 2. der Schnürsenkel 3. der Schuhlöffel 4. die kurze Hose
5. das Dörrobst 6. der Kartoffelbrei 7. die Teigwaren 8. der Lebkuchen 9. das Milchmixgetränk
10. etw vermengen

2.

Bäckerei: die Brezel, das Vollkornbrot
Drogerie: das Deo, die Feuchtigkeitscreme, das Haarfärbemittel
Fleischerei: das Brühwürstchen, das Hackfleisch, das Kotelett, der Speck
Juweliergeschäft: der Armreif, die Brosche, das Ohrgehänge, die Perlenkette
Milchladen: die Dickmilch, der Hartkäse, saure Sahne
Schuhgeschäft: der Pumps, der Schnürschuh

3.

1. der Rolli 2. die Manschette 3. die Gesäßtasche 4. der Rollmops 5. die Rosine 6. sauer
7. schälen

5.

1. Latzhose 2. Trainingsanzug 3. Wickelrock 4. Hosenträger 5. Sakko 6. Twinset 7. Schürze
8. Anorak

6.

2. die Sonnencreme 3. die Dauerwelle 4. der Rennschuh 5. der Trauring 6. die Brusttasche
7. die Nagelfeile 8. das Schaumbad 9. das Rasierwasser 10. der Lockenwickler 11. der Edelstein
12. das Schultertuch

7.

1. Eis- 2. Mandel- 3. Kittel- 4. Hut- 5. Fertig- 6. Braun- 7. Brei- 8. Espresso- 9. Beutel-
10. Leicht-

Level 3

1.

1. etw kürzer machen 2. etw auslassen 3. sich stark schminken 4. zäh 5. durch 6. lieblich
7. nüchtern 8. schwarzer Kaffee 9. kohlensäurehaltig 10. altbacken

3.
1. g 2. e 3. a 4. d 5. i 6. b 7. j 8. c 9. h 10. f

5.
1. –keule 2. Beiz– 3. Smok– 4. Rosa– 5. Bären– 6. –zehe 7. Saum–

6.
1. d 2. g 3. k 4. a 5. h 6. i 7. e 8. c 9. b 10. f

7.
1. Die Soße 4 bis 6 Minuten kochen lassen.
2. Pochierte Eier werden entweder auf Toast zu würzigen Soßen gegessen oder aber in einer warmen Senfsoße zu Salzkartoffeln oder Kartoffelbrei.
3. Die Soße über das Fleisch gießen, den Deckel aufsetzen und 30 Minuten im Backofen schmoren lassen.
4. Die Eier in eine Tasse schlagen.
5. Den Maissalat mit der Petersilie bestreuen.
6. Den Speck in Würfel schneiden. Die Zwiebel schälen und in Würfel schneiden.
7. Die Bohnen abgießen und mit den Speckwürfeln, den Paprikastreifen, den Zwiebelwürfeln, dem Salz, dem Pfeffer, dem Knoblauchpulver und dem Essig mischen.
8. Den Gurkensalat mit den Eischeiben garnieren.

8.
1. die Schrittlänge 2. die Wimperntusche 3. der Schaft 4. der Abnäher 5. die Paspel
6. der Zierstich 7. der Pantoffel 8. die Muskatnuss 9. der Most

Unit 7 Perception; colour and light; materials and textures
Level 1

1.
1. etw schwärzen 2. etw weißen 3. etw röten 4. etw bläuen 5. grauen 6. bräunen 7. sich röten
8. blauen 9. grünen

2.
1. dunkel 2. leise 3. sauer 4. bunt 5. das Weichholz 6. die Dunkelheit 7. hart

3.
2. das Grün 3. das Gelb 4. das Rot 5. das Rosa 6. das Braun

4.
1. c 2. a 3. d 4. b 5. d

5.
1. grün 2. blau 3. rot 4. gelb 5. weiß

6.

1. der Geruch 2. der Gestank 3. der Blick 4. der Klang 5. der Pfiff 6. der Lärm 7. der Strahl
8. der Geschmack 9. der Krach

7.

1. klingeln 2. rauschen 3. klicken 4. hämmern 5. hupen 6. schweigen 7. lärmen

8.

1. Schwarz, Rot, Gold 2. Blau, Gelb, Rot 3. tiefblau 4. grüne Weihnachten, weiße Weihnachten
5. schwarz, weiß 6. Rote 7. Blau 8. Orange 9. goldene 10. silberne

9.

1. i 2. c 3. h 4. f 5. b 6. d 7. a 8. e 9. g

11.

2. weißlich, die Weiße 3. bläulich, die Bläue 4. rötlich, die Röte

12.

1. f 2. c 3. i 4. d 5. e 6. j 7. a 8. h 9. b 10. k 11. g

13.

1. Er ist ganz grau geworden.
2. Der Junge, der im Rollstuhl sitzt, möchte nicht angestarrt werden.
3. Keineswegs sollte man die Sonnenfinsternis ungeschützt beobachten.
4. Ungeduldig blickte er auf seine Uhr.
5. Der Himmel verdunkelte sich vor dem Gewitter.
6. Nervös trommelte er mit den Fingern auf dem Tisch.
7. Der faulige Geruch verbreitete sich im Flur.
8. Käse aus pasteurisierter Milch ist sicherer, aber leider schmeckt er nicht nach Käse.
9. Sie hat vor Aufregung einen roten Kopf bekommen.
10. Die Treppen müssen noch betoniert werden.

Level 2

1.

1. grau 2. braun 3. rot 4. blau 5. gelb 6. grün 7. grau 8. gelb 9. blau 10. rot 11. grün

2.

1. c 2. n 3. g 4. o 5. j 6. a 7. d 8. e 9. f 10. k 11. b 12. m 13. h 14. l 15. i

4.

1. die Zellwolle 2. der Kattun 3. das Spanholz 4. das Bügeleisen 5. jmdn verbläuen 6. läuten
7. glühen 8. blaurot

5.

1. f 2. i 3. g 4. a 5. d 6. b 7. j 8. c 9. h 10. e

6.
1. g 2. c 3. e 4. d 5. f 6. b 7. h 8. a

7.
1. f 2. h 3. g 4. l 5. e 6. b 7. c 8. i 9. d 10. j 11. k 12. a

8.
1. heftete 2. Dämmerung 3. Blick 4. verklingen 5. zugeknallt 6. kreischen 7. sahnige
8. appetitlich 9. lackiert 10. flaschengrün 11. errötete 12. Kaschmirwolle

9.
1. g 2. d 3. h 4. i 5. c 6. b 7. e 8. a 9. f

10.
1. Sie hat Augen vorn und hinten.
2. Er hat sie forschend angesehen.
3. Ich habe sie nicht zu Gesicht bekommen.
4. Er hat mich finster angestarrt.
5. Dein Vorschlag hört sich gut an.
6. Es raschelt im Stroh.
7. Der Schokoladenkuchen hat einfach köstlich geschmeckt.
8. Heute möchte ich eine Pause machen und den Duft der Rosen genießen.
9. Anderen Bewohnern des Wohnblocks war der stechende Geruch aufgefallen.
10. Er trug eine weinrote Bomberjacke und weiße Jeans.
11. Palmen umgeben pastellfarbene Häuser.
12. Der schönste Farbton für Lippen und Nägel ist ein kräftiges Rosa.

Level 3

1.
1. c 2. e 3. g 4. d 5. h 6. f 7. i 8. j 9. a 10. b

2.
1. g 2. m 3. j 4. c 5. k 6. f 7. h 8. a 9. i 10. l 11. e 12. d 13. b

3.
1. stockdunkel 2. pech(raben)schwarz 3. hochrot 4. zappenduster 5. der Heidenlärm
6. der Mordskrach 7. der Höllenspektakel

4.
1. die Schlacke 2. der Schrott 3. der Kitt 4. die Kordel 5. der Nessel 6. der Teer
7. der Schmirgel 8. das Gewühl

5.
1. h 2. b 3. c 4. a 5. f 6. d 7. e 8. g

6.

1. grau 2. rot 3. grün 4. gelb 5. weiß 6. blau 7. schwarz

7.

1. c 2. e 3. f 4. b 5. d 6. a

8.

1. Chemiefaser 2. Steifleinen 3. Tüll 4. knorrig 5. gemasertem 6. düster 7. verblichen 8. flackert
9. spähen 10. beäugen 11. schweifen 12. säuerliche

Unit 8 Shapes and patterns; size and quantity; containers; time
Level 1

1.

1. f 2. d 3. b 4. g 5. h 6. e 7. a 8. c

2.

1. krumm 2. klein 3. kurz 4. leer 5. wenig 6. nah 7. abnehmen 8. nichts 9. hier 10. die Breite
11. die Nacht 12. spät 13. selten

3.

1. j 2. b 3. g 4. d 5. c 6. f 7. i 8. k 9. a 10. e 11. h

4.

1. b 2. f 3. c 4. e 5. a 6. d

5.

1. der Eimer 2. der Blumentopf 3. der Hängekorb 4. kariert 5. der Meter 6. der Anstieg
7. die Entfernung 8. der Monat 9. die Frühe 10. die Uhr

6.

1. sieben 3. zehn nach sieben 4. Viertel nach sieben 5. zwanzig nach sieben 6. fünf vor halb acht
7. halb acht 8. fünf nach halb acht 9. zwanzig vor acht 10. Viertel vor acht 11. zehn vor acht
12. fünf vor acht

7.

1. i 2. f 3. h 4. b 5. c 6. a 7. j 8. e 9. d 10. g

9.

2. das Parfümfläschchen 3. der Schlafsack 4. die Badewanne 5. die Papiertüte 6. das Bierfass
7. die Thermosflasche 8. das Spülbecken 9. der Teebeutel 10. die Streichholzschachtel

10.

1. Grenze 2. viereckig 3. ovales 4. Pyramide 5. gestreiftes 6. Zwischenraum 7. gepunktete
8. Gesamtzahl 9. Hauptteil

Level 2

1.

1. senkrecht 2. asymmetrisch 3. schmal 4. die Tiefe 5. die Minderheit 6. das Maximum
7. an Wert gewinnen 8. stumpf 9. die Pfandflasche 10. unregelmäßig 11. zuletzt 12. nachher

2.

1. g 2. h 3. d 4. a 5. c 6. f 7. b 8. e

3.

1. die Parallele 2. die Diagonale 3. die Gerade 4. der Querstreifen 5. die Spirale 6. das Dreieck
7. das Quadrat

4.

1. l 2. h 3. o 4. m 5. p 6. c 7. j 8. g 9. f 10. n 11. b 12. e 13. d 14. a 15. i 16. q 17. k

5.

2. sieben Uhr abends 3. neun Uhr morgens 4. zwölf Uhr nachts 5. zwölf Uhr mittags
6. drei Uhr nachmittags 7. sechs Uhr morgens 8. neun Uhr abends 9. zwei Uhr nachts

6.

senkrecht:
1. Henkel 2. Ausguss 3. Pappkarton 4. Ration 5. Geigenkasten 8. Tabaksbeutel
11. Karteikasten 15. Milliliter 18. Spüle 19. Rest 20. Dosis

waagerecht:
6. Karo 7. Aktentasche 9. knapp 10. Geldschrank 12. Vase 13. Kübel 14. Karaffe
16. Zigarrenkiste 17. Müllbeutel 21. Milchtüte 22. Schnitte 23. Quadratkilometer

7.

1. g 2. b 3. a 4. d 5. c 6. f 7. e

8.

1. sich verengen 2. die Strecke 3. der Inhalt 4. die Thermosflasche 5. das Waschbecken
6. die Kreisbahn 7. lediglich 8. die Brieftasche 9. der Jahrgang 10. der Feiertag

9.

1. morgen Abend 2. heute Nachmittag 3. gestern Abend 4. letzte Nacht 5. heute Abend
6. morgen früh 7. morgen Nachmittag 8. übermorgen 9. gestern Morgen 10. vorgestern

10.

1. Fläche 2. Fahrradständer 3. Schulranzen 4. Kerzenständer 5. Schirmständer
6. Gepäckablagen 7. Abfalleimer 8. Sandkasten

Level 3

1.

1. b 2. d 3. f 4. c 5. e 6. a 7. g

2.

1. die Unmenge 2. die Unzahl 3. das Übermaß 4. die Überfülle

3.

2. morgig 3. heutig 5. jährlich 6. monatlich 7. wöchentlich

4.

1. e 2. o 3. g 4. h 5. b 6. m 7. d 8. a 9. f 10. n 11. c 12. k 13. p 14. l 15. i 16. j

5.

1. i 2. g 3. f 4. a 5. c 6. h 7. d 8. e 9. k 10. b 11. j

6.

1. der Tragekorb 2. die Anschwellung 3. der Nistkasten 4. die Vitrine 5. der Sitzsack
6. der Umlauf 7. sich vermindern 8. der Umriss 9. der Maßstab

7.

1. d 2. e 3. c 4. b 5. a

8.

1. der Zoll, der Fuß, das Yard, die Meile
2. die Unze, das Pint, der Liter, die Gallone
3. das Gramm, das Pfund, das Kilo, der Zentner
4. spärlich, ansehnlich, unzählig
5. die Streichholzschachtel, der Federkasten, das Handschuhfach, die Mülltonne
6. viertel zwei, halb zwei, dreiviertel zwei, zwei
7. vorig, gegenwärtig, künftig
8. längst, neuerdings, demnächst

10.

1. melierten 2. geädert 3. Fischgrätmuster 4. Nieten 5. Labyrinth 6. Krümmung 7. wellig
8. Gestalt 9. knollige 10. Frist 11. Zeitraum

11.

1. f 2. c 3. g 4. a 5. d 6. e 7. b

Unit 9 Visual and performing arts; media and popular culture

Level 1

1.

1. die Abbildung 2. das Plakat 3. die Bildhauerei 4. das Standbild 5. die Einzelheit 6. die Geige
7. der Schlager 8. die Darstellerin 9. das Lustspiel 10. der Streifen 11. das Lichtbild
12. der Fotoapparat 13. die Zeitschrift 14. der Rundfunk 15. der Fernseher

3.

1. das Gemälde 2. die Zeichnung 3. die Radierung 4. der Tanz 5. das Foto 6. die Vergrößerung
7. der Bericht 8. die Sendung

4.

1. e 2. a 3. c 4. f 5. d 6. b 7. g 8. i 9. h

5.

senkrecht:

1. Klavierspielerin 2. Malerei 3. Kapelle 4. Chor 5. Punk 7. Gruselfilm 9. Trauerspiel
10. Rezension 12. Werbung 13. Pop 15. Schlagzeilen 19. Geige 21. Flügel 23. Taste 26. Rap

waagerecht:

1. Kammermusik 6. Aufführung 8. Meisterwerk 11. Leinwand 14. Pause
16. Cembalo 17. Ansagerin 18. Marke 20. Litfaßsäule 22. Übertragung 24. Kiosk 25. Regisseur
27. Künstler 28. Akte

7.

1. der Schocker 2. die Regie 3. der Schlager 4. die Redaktion 5. die Ballerina 6. die Reporterin
7. das Feuilleton 8. der Nachruf 9. der Leserbrief

Level 2

1.

1. die Fälschung 2. die Freilichtmalerei 3. anschaulich 4. der Vorspann 5. die Pressezensur
6. inoffiziel 7. verstimmt

2.

1. die Harfe 2. die Charge 3. die Garderobe 4. das Dreibein 5. der Gutschein 6. der Dramaturg
7. der Vorhang

3.

1. d 2. c 3. g 4. h 5. a 6. b 7. e 8. f

5.

1. das Bildnis 2. das Atelier 3. die Tanzfläche 4. das Stativ 5. die Berichterstatterin 6. die Glotze
7. der Stubenhocker 8. der Prospekt 9. das Warenmuster 10. das Anschlagbrett

Level 3

1.

1. steinern 2. hölzern 3. metallen 4. marmorn 5. bronzen 6. tönern

2.

1. der Hintergrund 2. die Vertikale 3. das Flachrelief 4. das B 5. der Niederschlag 6. das Moll
7. der Abgang 8. die Ausblendung 9. die Atelieraufnahme 10. der Stummfilm 11. unterbelichtet
12. abblenden 13. die Langwelle 14. die Zeitlupe

3.

2. das Lampenfieber 3. die Großaufnahme 4. der Fluchtpunkt 5. die Druckerschwärze
6. die Bühnenanweisung 7. der Dreiklang 8. der Scheinwerfer 9. der Kulissenwechsel

4.

1. der Beitel 2. der Notenständer 3. aquarellieren 4. steppen 5. montieren 6. der Taktstock

5.

1. das B 2. der Bassschlüssel 3. die ganze Note 4. die Sechzehntelnote 5. das Auflösungszeichen 6. die Viertelpause 7. die Achtelnote 8. die ganze Pause 9. der Violinschlüssel 10. das Kreuz 11. die punktierte halbe Note 12. die Tonartvorzeichnung

6.

1. die Wasserfarbe 2. das Fixiermittel 3. das Transparentpapier 4. der Entwurf 5. das Helldunkel 6. der/die Beschauer(in) 7. der Spitzenschuh 8. der Komparse, die Komparsin 9. der Hinweis 10. die Sensationspresse

Unit 10 Literature and literary criticism; speaking; reading and writing

Level 1

1.

1. a 2. f 3. d 4. b 5. c 6. e

2.

1. b 2. g 3. k 4. e 5. a 6. f 7. d 8. j 9. c 10. h 11. l 12. i

3.

1. g 2. a 3. e 4. d 5. f 6. c 7. b

4.

1. farblos 2. schwunglos 3. etw beantworten 4. anderer Meinung sein 5. gegen etw sein

5.

1. die Nebenfigur 2. klatschhaft 3. die Behauptung 4. die Wahrheit sagen 5. der Protest 6. unterstreichen

6.

1. h 2. e 3. a 4. i 5. b 6. d 7. c 8. f 9. j 10. g

9.

1. Bleistift 2. Schmierpapier 3. Lesebuch 4. erwähnt 5. garantieren 6. beschimpfen 7. klarmachen 8. Unterschrift 9. unterbricht 10. plauderte

Level 2

1.

1. die Ballade 2. die Hymne 3. die Parabel 4. die Fabel 5. die Legende 6. die Parodie 7. die Satire 8. das Epos 9. die Dissertation 10. die Memoiren (pl.) 11. das Motiv 12. die Metapher

2.

1. der Stabreim 2. der Kreuzreim 3. der Anfangsreim (auch der Endreim) 4. der Endreim 5. der Schachtelsatz 6. der Kettensatz

3.
1. a 2. c 3. d 4. b

4.
1. k 2. e 3. c 4. g 5. o 6. h 7. b 8. d 9. a 10. l 11. f 12. i 13. m 14. n 15. j

5.
1. die Essayistin 2. das Leitmotiv 3. langatmig 4. der Romanautor 5. gehoben 6. jmdn beraten
7. die Verkaufsargumentation 8. jammern

6.
1. e 2. k 3. a 4. d 5. g 6. j 7. l 8. h 9. c 10. i 11. f 12. b

7.
1. das Fragezeichen 2. das Komma 3. das Semikolon 4. das Ausrufezeichen 5. die Klammer
6. der Umlaut 7. der Punkt 8. der Doppelpunkt

8.
1. Anfrage 2. austauschen 3. gab 4. einsilbig 5. Auskunft 6. geteilter 7. bereit 8. bestätigt
9. jubeln 10. ermutigt 11. beglückwünscht

9.
1. b 2. b 3. b 4. b 5. d

10.
1. b 2. c 3. g 4. f 5. d 6. e 7. h 8. a

Level 3

1.
1. eckige Klammer 2. spitze Klammer 3. der Bindestrich 4. der Gedankenstrich
5. der Apostroph 6. der Schrägstrich 7. schiefer Schrägstrich 8. die Anführungszeichen (pl.)
9. das Akzentzeichen

2.
1. i 2. a 3. j 4. b 5. m 6. k 7. c 8. e 9. l 10. f 11. d 12. h 13. g

3.
1. die Parataxe 2. die Ellipse 3. die Hypotaxe 4. das Präsens historicum 5. der Chiasmus
6. die Synästhesie 7. die Anapher 8. die Stichomythie 9. das Oxymoron

4.
1. g 2. e 3. h 4. d 5. f 6. a 7. j 8. b 9. c 10. i

5.
1. der Schlüsselroman 2. der Schwank 3. der Zyklus 4. sentenziös 5. etw erläutern 6. johlen
7. jmdn anpflaumen

6.
1. das Anakoluth 2. die Belletristik 3. die Katastrophe 4. der/die Kompilator(in)
5. der Dithyrambus 6. die Elegie 7. der Exkurs 8. das Madrigal 9. die Ode 10. das Paradoxon
11. die Peripetie, 12. die Priamel 13. die Saga 14. die Travestie 15. der Troubadour

7.
1. überschüttet 2. schlagfertig 3. angefleht 4. erläutern 5. einig 6. anfechten 7. beteuerte
8. murren 9. verhaspelt 10. kauderwelscht

8.
1. das Verhör 2. der Zank 3. die Tilgung 4. das Gekritzel 5. die Besprechung

9.
1. analphabetisch 2. paradox 3. parataktisch 4. hypotaktisch 5. aphoristisch 6. sentenziös

10.
1. erzählte Zeit 2. fallende Handlung 3. die Senkung 4. die Parataxe 5. des Lesens und
Schreibens kundig

Unit 11 Leisure; sport

Level 1

1.
1. g 2. b 3. k 4. a 5. f 6. e 7. h 8. d 9. c 10. i 11. j

2.
1. etw gewinnen 2. der Verlierer 3. das Auswärtsspiel 4. der Pfeil 5. falsch spielen

4.
1. die Schießscheibe 2. etw üben 3. der Angriff 4. die Zweitplazierte 5. die Halbzeit
6. die Sportlerin 7. der Rudersport 8. das Turnen 9. die Achterbahn

5.
1. ball 2. rennen 3. schießen 4. fahren 5. laufen 6. rennen 7. tennis 8. ball

6.
1. der Jogger 2. der Boxer 3. der Turner 4. der Skiläufer 5. der Fußballspieler
6. der Baseballspieler 7. der Schwimmer 8. der Hockeyspieler 9. der Tennisspieler

7.
1. die Runde 2. die Ringmatte 3. die Münze 4. Hobby 5. die Jagd

8.
1. c 2. a 3. h 4. d 5. e 6. b 7. f 8. g

Level 2

1.

1. die Liebhaberei 2. seilhüpfen 3. die Rutschbahn 4. die Seifenkiste 5. die Feuerschluckerin
6. das Wellenreiten 7. das Klettern 8. die Umkleidekabine 9. der Billardstock

2.

1. g 2. e 3. b 4. d 5. c 6. h 7. a 8. f

3.

1. der Puppenspieler 2. der Webstuhl 3. der Flipper 4. die Vorlage 5. das Zielband 6. die Kugel
7. der Wasserball 8. das Aerobic 9. sich kaputtmachen

4.

1. das Tauchen 2. das Ringen 3. das Kegelspiel 4. das Rudern 5. das Bowling

5.

1. der Puck 2. der Schlittschuh 3. die Bowlingbahn 4. der Handgalopp 5. der Gymnastikanzug
6. das Kegelspiel

6.

2. der Eistanz 3. das Schlittenfahren 4. das Tiefseetauchen 5. das Freistilringen
6. der Stufenbarren 7. die Stoppuhr 8. das Sprungbrett 9. der Strafpunkt

7.

1. e 2. j 3. b 4. c 5. k 6. f 7. l 8. h 9. g 10. i 11. a 12. d

8.

1. Würfel 2. schachmatt 3. Stickrahmen 4. Bücherfreund 5. Liebhaberstück
6. Gesellschaftsspiel 7. Plüschtiere 8. faulenzen 9. unentschieden 10. Wunderkerzen

Level 3

1.

1. a. Pik b. Kreuz c. Herz d. Karo
2. a. Grün b. Eicheln c. Rot c. Schellen
3. a. der Bube b. die Dame c. der König d. das Ass

2.

1. der Federball 2. die Kanutin 3. der Torhüter 4. der Schmetterlingsstil 5. die Philatelistin
6. die Spielbank 7. schummeln 8. die Kirchweih

3.

1. c 2. b 3. a 4. g 5. e 6. f 7. d

4.

1. Maschen abketten 2. das Geschicklichkeitsspiel 3. der Hartplatz 4. der Fänger
5. das Innenfeld

5.

1. h 2. l 3. g 4. a 5. b 6. j 7. f 8. c 9. k 10. d 11. e 12. i

7.

1. der Elfmeter 2. die Badeanstalt 3. das Inlineskating 4. die Watstiefel (pl.) 5. der Federball
6. der Zügel 7. der Langlauf

8.

1. Schnittmuster 2. werkelt 3. Zopfmuster 4. wettet 5. Krocket 6. Jongleur 7. Kaspertheater
8. Antiquitätenmarkt 9. Kartenlegerin

10.

1. Markus, du gibst.
2. Zuerst muss ich den Saum dieses Kleides heften.
3. Spielen wir „Mensch ärgere dich nicht"!
4. Skifahren, Snowboarding und Rodeln sind beliebte Wintersportarten.
5. Er gewann bei den Olympischen Spielen 1976 in Montreal die Goldmedaille im Zehnkampf.
6. Sie hat sich im Weitsprung mit 6,26 Metern qualifiziert.
7. Er ist Weltmeister im Kugelstoßen.
8. Wir verfolgten das Spiel auf der Tribüne.
9. Das Ausgleichstor resultierte aus einem Elfmeter.
10. Er ist aus dem Turnier ausgeschieden.

Unit 12 Tourism, travel and transport

Level 1

1.

1. etw auspacken 2. im Ausland 3. die Abfahrt 4. die Tiefgarage 5. Gas wegnehmen 6. starten
7. belegt 8. der Nichtraucher 9. losmachen

2.

1. die Auskunft 2. etw buchen 3. die Rundfahrt 4. das Wohnmobil 5. die Grillparty 6. der Wagen
7. das Lenkrad 8. anhalten 9. der Anhalter 10. der Liegewagen 11. die Maschine
12. die Flugbegleiterin 13. untergehen

3.

1. der Fluggast 2. die Zollkontrolle 3. die Barfrau 4. der Flugschein 5. luftkrank 6. das Lenkrad
7. der Flughafen

5.

1. f. 2. e 3. h 4. g 5. a 6. d 7. j 8. i 9. c 10. b

6.

1. der Wohnort 2. die Imbissstube 3. die Rechnung 4. das Ruderboot 5. die Fahrkarte

9.

1. den Anschluss verpassen 2. wenn ich das große Los ziehe 3. leck sein 4. eine Weltreise machen 5. der Fortschritt 6. bremsen

10.

1. Tourist 2. Reisebüro 3. Stadtrundfahrt 4. Ferienwohnung 5. Sportwagen 6. volltanken
7. parken 8. hupen 9. Anhalter

11.

1. Eine Reservierung wird empfohlen.
2. In den Ferien verlassen tausende Berliner die Stadt.
3. Sie hat mir eine Ansichtskarte von den verschneiten Alpen geschickt.
4. Er kriecht in seinen Schlafsack und versucht einzuschlafen.
5. Das Fischrestaurant liegt am anderen Ende der Stadt.
6. Ich habe eine Kinderportion bestellt.
7. Sie hat wegen einer Panne auf dem Rastplatz gestoppt.
8. Wir müssen in Göttingen umsteigen.
9. Er wurde bei einer Zwischenlandung in Frankfurt festgenommen.

Level 2

1.

1. die Einreise 2. etw stornieren 3. die Hinfahrt 4. anlegen 5. das Oberdeck 6. die Nebensaison
7. abreisen 8. das Vorderrad 9. die Ausfahrt 10. etw abschalten 11. das Frachtflugzeug

2.

1. c 2. d 3. g 4. a 5. e 6. f 7. b

3.

1. j 2. d 3. k 4. g 5. f 6. b 7. a 8. e 9. h 10. i 11. c

4.

1. der Fremdenverkehr 2. das Andenken 3. die Unterhaltung 4. die Bardame 5. die Lok
6. der Bahnsteig 7. die Fluggesellschaft 8. der Abfertigungsschalter 9. die Besatzung

5.

1. die Gaststätte 2. der Riemen 3. das Verkehrsamt 4. der Gepäckwagen 5. der Abteil
6. die Fähre

7.

1. Geschäftsreise 2. Rückfahrkarte 3. Aufenthalt 4. Vollpension 5. Luxusrestaurant
6. Bierdeckel 7. Rückspiegel 8. Bordkarte 9. Jacht

8.

2. der Pannendienst 3. der Pensionsgast 4. der Schiffbruch 5. der Lautsprecher 6. der Kurort
7. die Abflughalle 8. der Parkscheinautomat 9. die Autofähre 10. das Düsenflugzeug

Level 3

1.

1. die Gaststättengewerbe 2. das Festessen 3. die Bordkante 4. der Personenzug 5. etw vertäuen
6. die Schiffsschraube

2.

1. der/die Tagesausflügler(in) 2. der/die Pendler(in) 3. die Bedienung 4. der/die
Gastronom(in) 5. der/die Dolmetscher(in) 6. der/die Eisenbahner(in)

4.

1. g 2. a 3. h 4. c 5. d 6. e 7. j 8. b 9. f 10. i

5.

1. die Abreise 2. die Überholspur 3. das Abblendlicht 4. die Abfluganzeige 5. der Güterzug

6.

1. die zollfreie Ware 2. der Flugzeugrumpf 3. der Zimmerservice 4. die Geschwindigkeit
5. der Maschinenraum 6. die Stornierungsgebühr

7.

1. e 2. c 3. a 4. h 5. b 6. d 7. g 8. f 9. i

8.

1. Währung 2. Einfuhrzoll 3. Nahverkehr 4. Denkmalschutz 5. garni
6. Konferenzeinrichtungen 7. Kraftfahrzeug 8. Rücklicht 9. Mittelstreifen

Unit 13 Family, birth, death and marriage; religion

Level 1

1.

2. die Tochter 3. die Schwester 4. die Tante 5. die Kusine 6. die Nichte 7. die Mama 8. die Patin
9. die Braut 10. die Ehefrau 11. die Witwe

2.

1. b 2. e 3. a 4. j 5. h 6. f 7. c 8. d 9. g 10. i

3.

1. verlobt, verheiratet, geschieden
2. die Geburt, die Taufe, die Hochzeit, der Tod, die Beerdigung
3. die Sünde, die Beichte, die Vergebung
4. Karneval, Ostern, Weihnachten

4.
1. die Hölle 2. sterben 3. ledig 4. der Engel 5. kirchlicher Feiertag

5.
1. der Christ, die Christin 2. der Jude, die Jüdin 3. der Muslim, die Muslime 4. die Buddhist, die Buddhistin

6.
1. das Enkelkind 2. die Ehe 3. jüdisch 4. der Gläubige 5. Buddha 6. das Gebet 7. die Bischöfin

7.
2. sündig 3. göttlich 4. biblisch 5. tot 6. geschieden 7. verwitwet

8.
1. f 2. h 3. e 4. d 5. g 6. b 7. c 8. a

9.
1. das Brautkleid 2. der Cousin 3. umkommen 4. der Muslim 5. die Kommunion 6. der Dom
7. der Fasching 8. der Satan

10.
1. neugeborene 2. schwanger 3. Flaschenkinder 4. ledige 5. ermordet 6. beerdigt 7. Asche
8. Hochzeitstorte 9. Leiche 10. Sargträger

Level 2
1.
1. Vati 2. Mutti 3. Opa 4. Oma

2.
2. der Schwiegersohn 3. die Schwägerin 4. die Enkelin 5. die Stiefmutter 6. die Halbschwester
8. der Adoptivvater 9. der Adoptivsohn 10. die Zwillingsschwester

3.
1. die Geburtenregelung 2. der Schwangerschaftsabbruch 3. das Begräbnis 4. der Trauring
5. der Brautstrauß 6. das Verhältnis 7. evangelisch 8. sich zu etw bekehren 9. jmdn verehren
10. die Fastnacht

4.
1. b 2. f 3. g 4. d 5. i 6. e 7. c 8. a 9. h

6.
1. h 2. f 3. a 4. b 5. g 6. d 7. i 8. e 9. c

7.
1. die Abtei 2. der Kanoniker 3. die Seminaristin 4. das Mitleid 5. das Gebot 6. der Feigling
7. die Weihe

8.

1. das Böse 2. die Abendandacht 3. unfruchtbar 4. die Treue 5. der Familienname

9.

2. der Heiligabend 3. der Nikolaustag 4. der Aschermittwoch 5. der Priesterkragen
6. der Nonnenschleier 7. der Rosenmontag 8. das Weihwasser 9. der Gebetsteppich
10. die Kniebank

10.

1. Hebamme 2. Säugling 3. hirntot 4. Todesfall 5. Trauung 6. Eheberatung 7. theologisch
8. Segnung 9. Vaterunser 10. Rosenkranz

Level 3

1.

1. der Nachkomme 2. die standesamtliche Trauung 3. eine Leiche einäschern 4. der Laie
5. die niederen Weihen 6. jmdn stillen 7. die Sterbeurkunde

2.

1. d 2. e 3. c 4. b 5. g 6. f 7. a

3.

1. i 2. l 3. k 4. b 5. a 6. h 7. j 8. d 9. g 10. e 11. n 12. c 13. m 14. f

4.

2. der Pflegevater 3. der Vormund 4. der Erbe 5. der Gatte 6. der Lebensgefährte 7. der Heide
8. der Märtyrer 9. der Prior 10. der Novize

5.

1. j 2. b 3. a 4. i 5. g 6. h 7. d 8. e 9. c 10. f

6.

1. der Gotteslästerer 2. der Gläubige 3. der Zionismus 4. der Frevel 5. die Frühgeburt
6. das Waisenhaus 7. der Ehebrecher 8. das Transportschiff

7.

2. das Todesröcheln 3. die Leihmutter 4. die Samenbank 5. der Trauzeuge 6. das Gesundbeten
7. der Klagegesang 8. der Kaiserschnitt 9. die Ziviltrauung

8.

1. c 2. d 3. a 4. e 5. b

9.

1. Retortenbaby 2. Staatsbegräbnis 3. Ehestand 4. Sorgerecht 5. Anglikaner 6. Fundamentalist
7. Evangelium 8. Abendgottesdienst 9. Almosen

Unit 14 Education; science

Level 1

1.
1. unterrichten 2. die Begabung 3. der Schulleiter 4. die Oberschule 5. die Prüfung
6. die Zensur 7. das Erdöl 8. die Sonnenenergie 9. der Stoff

2.
1. die Uni 2. die Mathe 3. das Abi

3.
1. mündlich 2. falsch 3. durchfallen 4. etw lernen 5. der Lehrling 6. das Nebenfach
7. die Subtraktion 8. die Multiplikation 9. minus 10. durch 11. eine positive Zahl
12. der Neumond

4.
1. i 2. j 3. f 4. b 5. c 6. e 7. g 8. h 9. d 10. a

5.
1. g 2. a 3. b 4. c 5. e 6. d 7. f

6.
1. der Klebestift 2. die Hochschule 3. die Dichte 4. die Mensa 5. die Holzarbeit 6. der Hebel

8.
1. genetisch 2. atomar 3. flüssig 4. gasförmig 5. fest 6. wissenschaftlich

10.
1. Taschenrechner 2. Mikroskop 3. Klassengröße 4. Studienplatz 5. Proseminar
6. Grundschullehrer 7. experimentiert 8. Relativitätstheorie 9. Viren

Level 2

1.
1. der Kursteilnehmer 2. die Privatschule 3. das Pflichtfach 4. ungerade Zahl
5. der Wechselstrom 6. anorganisch

2.
1. erzieherisch 2. das Lesezeichen 3. die Privatlehrerin 4. die Erdkunde 5. die Doktorarbeit
6. etw benoten 7. die Berufslaufbahn 8. der Versuch 9. die Reibung 10. die Strömung
11. der Brennstoff 12. die Kernenergie 13. die Kreisbahn 14. das Weltall 15. das Raumfahrzeug
16. die Lupe

3.
sehr gut, gut, befriedigend, ausreichend, mangelhaft, ungenügend

4.

1. Drehbleistift 2. das Zertifikat 3. der Meister 4. die Lektion 5. das Leseverständnis
6. etwas nachholen 7. die Kernenergie

5.

1. g 2. a 3. c 4. d 5. b 6. e 7. f

6.

1. maximal 2. minimal 3. sauer 4. alkalisch 5. erzieherisch 6. begabt 7. sphärisch

7.

1. g 2. c 3. d 4. f 5. e 6. b 7. h 8. a

8.

1. Fort- 2. Hinter- 3. Studium- 4. Schwefel- 5. Messen- 6. -landung

9.

1. Lernstrategien 2. ausbilden 3. auswendig 4. immatrikuliert 5. Berufsschule
6. Austauschschüler 7. Teilzeitstudent 8. Sonderschule

10.

1. g 2. d 3. b 4. f 5. e 6. a 7. c

Level 3

1.

1. das Externat 2. der Externe 3. getrennter Unterricht 4. deduktiv 5. der Stalagmit
6. Naturwissenschaften

2.

1. g 2. b 3. c 4. e 5. d 6. h 7. a 8. f

3.

1. der Azubi 2. das Dia 3. das BAföG

4.

1. pauken 2. jmdn schikanieren 3. die Fortbildung 4. die Leihbücherei 5. die Eselsbrücke
6. die Gemeinschaftskunde 7. die Rechtswissenschaft 8. die Wirtschaftswissenschaften
9. der Prüfungsausschuss 10. der Prüfungskandidat 11. die Erziehungswissenschaftlerin
12. die zweite Wurzel 13. der Lehrsatz 14. die Kernenergie 15. durchlässig 16. die Finsternis

5.

1. lernbehindert 2. statistisch 3. galaktisch 4. molekular 5. widerstandsfähig

6.

1. die Informatik 2. das Quecksilber 3. die Fakultät 4. das Löschpapier 5. der Trichter
6. der Verfall 7. der Schall 8. der Rechenschieber

7.
2. die Geowissenschaften (pl.) 3. die Raumforschung 4. das Magnetfeld 5. der Schmelztiegel
6. das Kugellager 7. die Logarithmentafel 8. die Fotosynthese 9. das Periodensystem
10. die Urknalltheorie

8.
1. Praktikant 2. Anwesenheitsliste 3. Kommilitone 4. Dozent 5. Hochschulreife
6. Auszeichnung 7. Schmiermittel 8. Erdreich 9. Glaskolben 10. Pipette

Unit 15 Agriculture; industry

Level 1

1.
1. die Leichtindustrie 2. der Facharbeiter 3. der Bulle 4. der öffentliche Sektor 5. kapitalintensiv

2.
1. die Tourismusbranche 2. der Betrieb 3. der Landwirt 4. der Mist 5. der Bauernhof

3.
1. f 2. c 3. d 4. a 5. b 6. g 7. e

4.
1. der Bergbau 2. der Hohn 3. der Stahl 4. das Lager 5. die Schwerarbeiterin 6. die Druckerei
7. die Heugabel

5.
1. d 2. f 3. c 4. e 5. g 6. b 7. a

6.
1. das Kalb 2. das Hähnchen 3. das Lamm

7.
1. züchter 2. züchter 3. bauer 4. bauer 5. züchter

9.
1. Landwirtschaft 2. Milchkanne 3. Weide 4. pflügen 5. düngen 6. mähen 7. Schweinestall
8. Büroangestellte 9. Nebenprodukt

Level 2

1.
1. das Küken 2. das Entenküken 3. das Gänschen

2.
1. die Tagschicht 2. die Spätschicht 3. die Truthenne 4. der Gänserich 5. nicht bebaut sein

3.

1. die Fernlenkung 2. der Bienenvater 3. weiden 4. der Wimmet 5. die Kelter 6. der Bienenkorb
7. der Schlachthof 8. die Papiermühle

4.

1. e 2. i 3. f 4. b 5. c 6. a 7. j 8. d 9. h 10. g

5.

2. der Futtertrog 3. die Pflugfurche 4. der Mähdrescher 5. die Vogelscheuche
6. die Schlachtrinder (pl.) 7. der Jahrgang 8. der Weinbehälter 9. das Maultier 10. der Kuhhirt

6.

1. das Getriebe 2. die Werbeindustrie 3. der Packer 4. die Konditorei 5. der Hafen
6. das Eisenwerk 7. der Schiffbau

7.

1. die Raumfahrtindustrie 2. die Getränkeindustrie 3. die Bauindustrie 4. der Bergbau
5. das Hotelgewerbe 6. die Hutindustrie 7. die Verlagsindustrie 8. die Waffenindustrie

8.

1. g 2. e 3. a 4. i 5. b 6. c 7. j 8. d 9. f 10. h

9.

1. Kleinbauer 2. Geflügelzüchter 3. Bienenzucht 4. Dreschmaschine 5. Gärung
6. Massenproduktion 7. Fließband 8. Vorschlaghammer 9. Eisenhütte

11.

1. Wir schlachten 500 Schweine pro Woche.
2. Der Ochse zieht ganz langsam einen Pflug.
3. Viele Bauern züchten nebenher Schweine.
4. Sie können ihre Schafe weiden, wo immer sie wollen.
5. Er kaufte sich ein kleines Bauerngut.
6. Das Feuer ist in einem Holzschuppen ausgebrochen.
7. Leider hat er seine Erfindung nicht patentieren lassen.
8. Im Bereich der Spitzentechnologie liegt Deutschland weit hinter den USA.
9. Die Täter öffneten den Safe mit einem Schweißbrenner.
10. Er war Industrieller und einer der reichsten Männer Europas.

Level 3

1.

1. das Mutterschaf, das Lamm 2. der Eber, das Ferkel 3. die Geiß, das Kicklein 4. der Hengst,
die Stute

2.

1. die Fruchtfolge 2. der Rebstock 3. der Heuboden 4. der Pferch 5. die Imkerei 6. die Scheuer
7. die Versandabteilung 8. der Gehrungswinkel

3.

1. b 2. g 3. e 4. f 5. a 6. d 7. h 8. c

4.

1. die Heimindustrie 2. die Zulieferindustrie 3. die Schlackenhalde 4. der Gerber
5. die Legierung 6. die Färse 7. das Flöz 8. der Gartenbau

5.

1. d 2. e 3. a 4. f 5. b 6. c

6.

1. der Tiefbau 2. mit Netzanschluss 3. der Senner 4. nicht bebaut sein 5. der Zuchthengst

7.

1. Bio-Bauern 2. Schädling 3. Buchweizen 4. Saatgut 5. Betriebskosten 6. Industriespionage
7. Arbeitsstunde 8. Produktionszeit

Unit 16 Business and commerce; employment

Level 1

1.

1. die Ausfuhr 2. die Arbeitnehmerin 3. der Verkäufermarkt 4. Verkaufspreis
5. der Vaterschaftsurlaub

2.

1. der Konkurrent, die Konkurrentin 2. der Leiter, die Leiterin 3. der Schichtarbeiter, die
Schichtarbeiterin 4. der Arbeitslose, die Arbeitslose 5. der Gewerkschaftler, die
Gewerkschaftlerin 6. der Streikende, die Streikende

3.

1. der Betrieb 2. die Ausfuhr 3. die Arbeitsgemeinschaft 4. die Führung 5. der Verbraucher
6. die Stellung 7. jmdn rausschmeißen 8. der Metzger, der Schlachter 9. die Zuckerbäckerin
10. der Blumenhändler 11. die Milchhändlerin 12. die Geschäftsfrau

5.

1. g 2. c 3. d 4. b 5. e 6. a 7. f

6.

1. der Schneider 2. die Erzieherin 3. der Schmuckhändler 4. die Überführung
5. der Herstellungspreis 6. unbezahlter Urlaub

8.

1. -ent 2. Brief- 3. -ler 4. -senkung 5. -gebühr

9.

1. Seniorpartner 2. Krisenmanagement 3. zollfrei 4. ausverkauft 5. Preissenkung 6. Probezeit
7. Kindergeld 8. gekündigt 9. versetzt

Level 2

1.

1. der Binnenhandel 2. der Reingewinn 3. veränderliche Kosten 4. jmdn degradieren
5. fristgerecht

2.

1. absetzbar 2. die Preislage 3. wettbewerbsfähig 4. der Strichkode 5. der Mischkonzern
6. die Versandsabteilung 7. der Rohstoff 8. der Zuschlag 9. stechen 10. der Ausverkauf

3.

1. der Großhändler, die Großhändlerin 2. der Einzelhändler, die Einzelhändlerin
3. der Verkaufsleiter, die Verkaufsleiterin 4. der Bewerber, die Bewerberin 5. der Berufsberater,
die Berufsberaterin 6. der Buchhalter, die Buchhalterin

4.

1. c 2. a 3. e 4. b 5. d

5.

1. der Gehaltsempfänger 2. die Tochtergesellschaft 3. der Haustürverkauf
4. das Bewerbungsformular 5. die Arbeitslosenhilfe

6.

1. b 2. m 3. g 4. e 5. h 6. d 7. o 8. c 9. k 10. j 11. n 12. i 13. l 14. a 15. f

7.

senkrecht:
1. Belegschaft 2. netto 4. kurzarbeiten 7. Marke 8. Hauptbuch 9. Warnstreik
10. Markt 11. Frührente 12. Drucker 14. Umzug 16. Logo 18. Einfuhr 19. Gehalt 20. Arbeit
waagerecht:
1. Bruttogewinn 3. Streik 5. Laborantin 6. Export 7. Mindestlohn 9. Ware
13. Alleinvertreterin 15. Gleitzeit 17. Reihe 21. Verleger 22. schwarzarbeiten 23. Buchhaltung
24. Töpfer

8.

1. unlauteren 2. Vorstand 3. Markenbewusstsein 4. Sonderangebot 5. Arbeitslosenquote
6. Firmenwagen 7. Gebäudereiniger 8. Streikbrecher 9. wilder 10. Nettolohnes

Level 3

1.

1. die Hausjuristin 2. maßgefertigt 3. das Arbeitstier 4. innerbetriebliche Ausbildung
5. der Klempner 6. die Grundstücksmaklerin

2.

1. f 2. b 3. d 4. h 5. i 6. j 7. g 8. c 9. e 10. a

3.

1. den Markt sättigen, den Markt überschwemmen, den Markt monopolisieren
2. Dienst nach Vorschrift, die Verlangsamung, die Stilllegung
3. Verlust bringend, kostendeckend, rentabel
4. der Drückeberger, der Arbeiter, der Arbeitssüchtige

4.

a. 1. Holding-Gesellschaft 2. Aktiengesellschaft 3. Gesellschaft mit beschränkter Haftung
   4. Personengesellschaft
b. 1. Regionalleiter 2. stellvertretender Leiter 3. Fachgebietsleiter 4. Leiter der Finanzabteilung
c. 1. Ladekosten 2. Grenzkosten 3. allgemeine Geschäftskosten 4. Betriebskosten

5.

1. d 2. g 3. e 4. c 5. f 6. h 7. i 8. a 9. b

6.

1. die Abfindung 2. die Steuerbeamtin 3. der Vorrat 4. der Pförtner 5. der Gewerkschaftsbeitrag
6. das Berufsrisiko

7.

1. Konsumgüter 2. vorrätig 3. flau 4. Arbeitsbeschaffung 5. inserieren 6. Stellenangebot
7. erzeugen 8. Skonto 9. Kündigungsschutz 10. Abfindung

8.

1. Der Treuhandvertrag bleibt gültig.
2. Es ist kein Aufkauf, sondern eine Fusion.
3. Die bisherige Unternehmenspolitik wird sich nicht ändern.
4. Seit 1986 ist er Vorsitzender des Vorstands der Fluggesellschaft.
5. Um das Produktionsziel zu erreichen, müssen wir Überstunden leisten.
6. Leider sind wir eine Wegwerfgesellschaft geworden.
7. Mit einem Marktanteil von 15 Prozent ist der PC-Hersteller einer der Marktführer.
8. Alles wird zu Schleuderpreisen verkauft.
9. Der Kunde muss die Reisespesen übernehmen.

Unit 17 The office and computing; post and telecommunications
Level 1

1.

1. das Diktiergerät 2. der Laufbursche 3. das Postamt 4. die Anschrift 5. etw schicken
6. der Fernsprecher 7. etw mit der Maschine schreiben

2.

1. sich ausloggen 2. die Hardware 3. der Großbuchstabe 4. den Hörer auflegen 5. nicht lesbar
6. die Empfängerin 7. der Laptop 8. das Original

3.
1. das Schreibmaschinenpapier 2. der Fotokopierer 3. das Druckpapier 4. das Faxgerät

4.
1. e 2. h 3. g 4. a 5. f 6. d 7. b 8. c

5.
1. die Telefonzelle 2. die Visitenkarte 3. die Büroparty 4. der Hacker 5. der Aktendeckel

6.
1. h 2. c 3. e 4. a 5. b 6. g 7. d 8. f

7.
2. die Eingabetaste 3. der Drehstuhl 4. der Papierkorb 5. der Warteraum 6. die Briefwaage
7. der Tippfehler 8. die Öffnungszeiten (pl.) 9. das Anschlagbrett

8.
1. Unterschrift 2. Päckchen 3. Handy 4. Telefonbuch 5. zurückrufen 6. kopieren
7. Gummiband 8. Terminkalender 9. Tastatur 10. Datei 11. Suchergebnisse 12. scrollen

Level 2

1.
1. die Kurzschrift 2. die Schreibkraft 3. das Stempelkissen 4. Akten anlegen 5. der gefütterte
Briefumschlag 6. anwenderfreundlich 7. das Porto 8. portofrei 9. das Glückwunschschreiben
10. freigemacht 11. der Pfeifton 12. individuelles Briefpapier

2.
1. c 2. i 3. h 4. f 5. d 6. b 7. a 8. e 9. j 10. g

3.
1. die Todesanzeige 2. unliniertes Papier 3. ein Gespräch unterbrechen 4. die Hard Copy
5. etw löschen 6. das Rufzeichen

4.
1. etw suchen 2. die Druckkabine 3. das Sekretärinnenzimmer 4. etw freimachen
5. der Geleitdienst 6. das Schreibmaterial

6.
1. Konferenzsaal 2. Bürogebäude 3. Mitteilung 4. Tonerkassetten 5. entschuldigt 6. Reißwolf
7. Datenbank 8. maschinenlesbarer 9. Leertaste 10. Signalton 11. verwählt 12. Büroklammer

Level 3

1.
1. die Ablage für Ausgänge 2. ungebleichtes Papier 3. die Fußzeile 4. der obere Rand
5. rechtsbündig 6. die Festplatte 7. das Ortsgespräch

2.
Gegenstand: der Dateimanager, der Fernschreiber, der Karteireiter
Mensch: der Briefschreiber, der Postmeister, der Servicemechaniker, der Texterfasser

3.
1. c 2. e 3. b 4. d 5. g 6. f 7. a

4.
1. Büroartikel 2. etw vervielfältigen 3. der Kuvert 4. das Postwertzeichen 5. das Strafporto
6. die Traueranzeige 7. das Beileidsschreiben 8. das Versandgeschäft 9. der Adressat
10. die Postbotin 11. die automatische Speicherung

5.
1. f 2. d 3. b. 4. a 5. h 6. e 7. g 8. c

6.
1. die Postanweisung 2. das Sekretariat 3. die Büroangeleien 4. der Durchschlag 5. lockig
6. die Wertangabe

7.
1. h 2. g 3. e 4. a 5. f 6. c 7. d 8. b

8.
1. Systemanalytiker 2. Ausfertigung 3. Hartpostpapier 4. Tabellenkalkulationsprogramm
5. Zeilenabstand 6. Tabulatortaste 7. Fehlermeldung 8. Sicherungskopie 9. Schreibunterlage

Unit 18 Law; finance

Level 1

1.
1. einfacher Diebstahl 2. unschuldig 3. die Deflation 4. der Verlust 5. die Darlehensnehmerin
6. ein Konto löschen 7. Geld abheben 8. der Versicherungsgeber 9. zahlungsunfähig

2.
1. sich schlagen 2. jmn verhaften 3. sich stellen 4. Gewinn bringend 5. der Gläubiger
6. die Investition

3.
1. d 2. a 3. b 4. f 5. e 6. h 7. c 8. g 9. j 10. i

4.
1. der Einbrecher, die Einbrecherin 2. der Mörder, die Mörderin 3. der Verteidiger, die
Verteidigerin 4. der Schuldner, die Schuldnerin 5. der Einzahler, die Einzahlerin
6. der Schmuggler, die Schmugglerin 7. der Kidnapper, die Kidnapperin

5.
1. der Makler 2. der Schalter 3. die Kaution 4. der Pfennig 5. der Dealer

6.
1. i 2. g 3. c 4. e 5. d 6. a 7. b 8. f 9. h

7.
1. g. 2. i 3. h 4. d 5. e 6. j 7. a 8. k 9. f 10. c 11. b

8.
1. Durchsuchungsbefehl 2. Privatdetektiv 3. Lösegeld 4. anklagen 5. Bargeld 6. bewaffnet
7. Scheck 8. Maklerfirma 9. Überweisung 10. Einkommensteuer 11. Feuerversicherung
12. steuerfrei 13. sparen

10 a.
1. e 2. a 3. h 4. c 5. g 6. d 7. f 8. b

Level 2

1.
1. der Entführer 2. jmdn hereinlegen 3. der Unterschuss 4. blank 5. kreditwürdig 6. die Ausgabe

2.
1. Einspruch stattgegeben 2. der Kläger 3. der Überschuss 4. die Kopfseite 5. die Baisse
6. der Eröffnungskurs 7. der Wertverlust

3.
1. k 2. f 3. a 4. g 5. h 6. j 7. d 8. b 9. i 10. c 11. e

4.
1. der /die Drogenabhängige 2. der Geheimdienst 3. der Körperschaden 4. der Verkehrsverstoß
5. die Kleinkriminalität 6. die Reifenspuren (pl.) 7. die Einzelhaft 8. die Straßensperre
9. der Gewohnheitstäter, die Gewohnheitstäterin 10. der Augenzeuge, die Augenzeugin
11. der Polizeispitzel, die Polizeispitzelin 12. der Zivilprozess

5.
1. der Krawall 2. die Verrechnung 3. die Spurensicherung 4. der Spürhund 5. die Razzia

7.
1. Wiederholungstäter 2. Decknamen 3. Bestechung 4. entkommen 5. überwachen
6. Streifenwagen 7. verhören 8. Haftentlassung 9. eidliche 10. Freispruch 11. Vorladung
12. kugelsichere

8.
1. der Sachschaden 2. die Steuerflucht 3. der Steuersatz 4. der Devisenmarkt
5. die Investitionsbankierin 6. der Wilderer

Level 3

1.
1. der Straftäter 2. die Verrechnungsstelle 3. das Vergehen 4. gerichtlich 5. die Berufungsinstanz
6. der Verdienst

2.
1. a 2. i 3. c 4. b 5. f 6. h 7. j 8. d 9. g 10. e

3.
1. Geld aus dem Verkehr ziehen 2. der Hypothekengläubiger 3. der Kapitalverlust 4. nicht
vorbestraft sein 5. nicht zurechnungsfähig 6. vollständige Begleichung 7. fester Wechselkurs

4.
1. der Brandanschlag 2. der Obligationär 3. die Erbschaftssteuer 4. der Hehler 5. der Meineid

5.
1. der Knast 2. Knast schieben 3. die Nutte 3. der Spanner 4. einen Tresor knacken

6.
1. die Pauschalsumme 2. das Bruttosozialprodukt 3. die Geldwäsche 4. die Währungspolitik
5. die Ertragsrate 6. die Wucherzinsen (pl.) 7. das Aktienzertifikat 8. der Abwärtstrend
9. der Schuldschein 10. die Steuervergünstigung 11. die Haftpflichtversicherung
12. die Warenbörse

7.
1. d 2. a 3. c 4. e 5. f 6. b 7. g

8.
1. Unterschlagung 2. Geiseln 3. Brandstiftung 4. Verdacht 5. beschlagnahmen 6. Mandant
7. enttarnen 8. Begnadigung 9. Währung 10. Zahlungstermin 11. bürgen 12. begleichen

Unit 19 Geography, history, war, and peace

Level 1

1.
1. nördlich 2. der Süden, südlich 3. der Osten, östlich 4. der Westen

2.
1. der Erdteil 2. das Gebiet 3. das Heer 4. im Krieg fallen 5. der Niederländer 6. die Birmanin
7. der Panamene 8. geschichtlich

3.
1. Europa, Nordamerika, Südamerika, Afrika, Asien, Australien, Antarktika
2. Frankreich, Belgien, die Niederlande, Dänemark, Polen, die Tschechische Republik,
   Österreich, die Schweiz, Luxemburg
3. Nicaragua
4. Laos
5. Kirgise

4.

1. Portugal, der Portugiese 2. der Ire, die Irin 3. Schweden, die Schwedin 4. Norwegen, der Norweger 5. der Slowake, die Slowakin 6. Kroatien, die Kroatin 7. Bulgarien, der Bulgare, 8. der Andorraner, die Andorranerin 9. Serbien, die Serbin 10. Jugoslawien, der Jugoslawe 11. der Grieche, die Griechin 12. Lettland, die Lettin 13. die Türkei, der Türke 14. der Israeli, die Israelin 15. Jemen, die Jemenitin

5.

1. f 2. a 3. g 4. c 5. d 6. b 7. e 8. h

6.

1. der Kuwaiter, die Kuwaiterin; der Malawier, die Malawierin; der Omaner, die Omanerin; der Pakistaner, die Pakistanerin; der Senegaler, die Senegalerin; der Togoer, die Togoerin
2. der Armenier, die Armenierin; der Bosnier, die Bosnierin; der Georgier, die Georgierin; der Indonesier, die Indonesierin; der Jordanier, die Jordanierin; der Moldawier, die Moldawierin; der Syrier, die Syrierin
3. der Finnländer, die Finnländerin; der Isländer, die Isländerin; der Schottländer, die Schottländerin

7.

2. Italien 3. Russland 4. Irak 5. Libanon 6. Nepal 7. Ägypten 8. Südafrika 9. Venezuela 10. Peru 11. die Niederlande 12. Ungarn 13. die Ukraine 14. Iran 15. China 16. Vietnam 17. Kenia 18. Angola 19. Kolumbien 20. Chile

8.

1. vorgeschichtliche 2. entdeckt 3. Krieg 4. Unteroffizier 5. gesprengt 6. Wunde 7. Gewehr 8. friedliche 9. Friedensbewegung 10. Menschenrechte

Level 2

1.

1. das Heimatland 2. die Halbkugel 3. der Pazifik 4. Frieden stiften 5. der Wehrdienst

2.

1. der Längengrad 2. der Antarktische Ozean 3. das Altertum 4. der Feind 5. die Niederlage 6. der Zivilist 7. auftauchen

3.

1. e 2. b 3. g 4. a 5. h 6. f 7. d 8. c

4.

1. die Klimatologie 2. der Zivildienstleistende 3. die Schwadron 4. der Brigadegeneral 5. der Torpedo 6. chemische Waffe 7. der Fuß

5.

1. e 2. b 3. d 4. f 5. c 6. h 7. g 8. a

6.
1. das Kriegsverbrechen 2. der Rebell 3. die Eiszeit 4. der Geysir 5. der Gefallene 6. angreifen

7.
1. j 2. c 3. f 4. l 5. d 6. a 7. h 8. k 9. g 10. i 11. b 12. e

8.
1. Erdbeben 2. Archipel 3. Archäologe 4. heiligen 5. Militärgericht 6. Sprengstoff 7. Panzer
8. Flugzeugträger 9. Waffenhandel 10. Friedensnobelpreis

Level 3

1.
1. die Bermudas, die Bermuderin 2. die Färöer, der Färöer 3. der Sri-Lanker, die Sri-Lankerin
4. Korsika, die Korsin 5. Hawaii, der Hawaiier 6. der Samoaner, die Samoanerin 7. Malta, die
Malteserin 8. Korfu, der Korfiot 9. der Kreter, die Kreterin 10. Tahiti, die Tahitianerin

2.
1. die Handschriftenkunde 2. der Luftschutzkeller 3. der Freischärler 4. kriegsversehrt
5. das Leuchtgeschoss 6. die Senke

3.
1. die Nachhut 2. wegtreten 3. geschichtsträchtig 4. abrüsten 5. der Rekrut

4.
1. der Feldwebel, der Oberfeldwebel, der Hauptfeldwebel
2. die Renaissance, die Reformation, das Barock, die Aufklärung,
3. das Pharaonenreich, das Römerreich, das Deutsche Reich, das Dritte Reich
4. der Dreißigjährige Krieg, der Siebenjährige Krieg, der amerikanische Unabhängigkeitskrieg,
   der Amerikanische Bürgerkrieg, der Erste Weltkrieg, der Golfkrieg
5. vorsintflutlich, byzantinisch, mittelalterlich

5.
1. c 2. a 3. f 4. i 5. g 6. h 7. d 8. b 9. e

6.
1. d 2. a 3. c 4. e 5. f 6. b

7.
1. der Kanonier, die Kanonierin 2. der Fallschirmjäger, die Fallschirmjägerin 3. der Archivar,
die Archivarin 4. der Mediävist, die Mediävistin 5. der Nationalsozialist, die Nationalsozialistin
6. der Kreuzfahrer, die Kreuzfahrerin 7. der Soldat, die Soldatin

8.
1. Datumsgrenze 2. Belagerung 3. Langstreckenrakete 4. Nachrichtenoffizier 5. Stacheldraht
6. Granaten 7. Blutzoll 8. Friedensverhandlungen 9. Massenvernichtungswaffen
10. Waffenstillstand 11. Friedensbewegten

Unit 20 Politics and international relations; public services, social and environmental issues

Level 1

1.
1. der Rechte 2. konservativ 3. die Regierungspartei 4. das Oberhaus 5. umweltfreundlich
6. die Auswanderin 7. arm 8. die Armut 9. weiche Droge 10. politisch unkorrekt

2.
1. d 2. b 3. a 4. e 5. f 6. g 7. c

3.
1. die Supermacht 2. die Koalitionspartei 3. der Parteiführer 4. die Fernsehdebatte
5. die Parlamentswahl 6. das Grundgesetz 7. die Außenpolitik 8. die Geheimagentin
9. die Innenstadt 10. die Luftverschmutzung

4.
1. d 2. b 3. h 4. e 5. c 6. a 7. f 8. g

5.
1. der Bettler 2. der Abgeordnete 3. die Konsulin 4. der Obdachlose 5. der Diplomat

6.
1. der Staat 2. der Abfall 3. der Ausschuss 4. die Not 5. das LSD

7.
1. h 2. f 3. e 4. a 5. g 6. i 7. b 8. c 9. d

8.
1. zensieren 2. Politiker 3. Parteiprogramm 4. Politik 5. Demonstrant 6. Aktionsgruppe
7. konsultieren 8. Nothilfe 9. Spionage 10 Gastarbeiter

Level 2

1.
1. der Konservatismus 2. die rechte Mitte 3. die Republikanische Partei 4. der Bundesrat
5. das Außenministerium 6. das Ausreisevisum 7. die Unterschicht

2.
1. e 2. c 3. b 4. g 5. a 6. d 7. f 8. h

3.
1. die Christlich-Demokratische Union 2. die Christlich-Soziale Union
3. die Sozialdemokratische Partei Deutschlands 4. die Freie Demokratische Partei
5. die Partei des Demokratischen Sozialismus 6. die Europäische Union
7. die Europäische Wirtschaftsgemeinschaft

4.
1. g 2. c 3. f 4. a 5. b 6. h 7. d 8. e

5.
1. das Abkommen 2. der Kanaltunnel 3. pleite 4. elend 5. das Rauschgift 6. die Drogensucht
7. drogensüchtig 8. der Fixer 9. das Grass 10. der Öko 11. etw wiederverwerten

6.
1. der Sondermüll 2. der Chemiemüll 3. der Hausmüll 4. der Industriemüll 5. der Giftmüll
6. der Atommüll

7.
1. das Abgas 2. die Versammlungsfreiheit 3. das Flüchtlingslager 4. der Christdemokrat
5. das Ratsmitglied 6. das Multikulti 7. das Wohngeld

8.
1. Schmiergelder 2. Staatsstreich 3. Diktatur 4. Stadtrat 5. Tagesordnung 6. Probeabstimmung

Level 3

1.
1. die Gegenspionage 2. etw entziffern 3. der rechte Flügel 4. der Wechselwähler
5. die Minderheitsregierung 6. phosphathaltig 7. der Totalitarismus 8. jmdn ausbürgern

2.
1. die Sozialistische Einheitspartei Deutschlands 2. die Republikaner 3. die Deutsche
Volksunion 4. die Kommunistische Partei Deutschlands 5. die Nationaldemokratische Partei
Deutschlands 6. die Vereinten Nationen 7. die Weltgesundheitsorganisation

3.
1. j 2. a 3. f 4. e 5. g 6. b 7. k 8. i 9. h 10. c 11. d

4.
1. baufällig 2. schnüffeln 3. linksextrem 4. die Autokratie 5. der Volksentscheid 6. einseitig
7. der Drogi

5.
1. i 2. d 3. c 4. b 5. a 6. f 7. g 8. h 9. e

6.
1. f 2. a 3. c 4. b 5. e 6. g 7. d

7.
1. die Legislative 2. die Judikative 3. die Exekutive

8.

1. c 2. d 3. b 4. e 5. a 6. f

9.

1. verschwören 2. Ampelkoalition 3. Splitterpartei 4. umbilden 5. Euroskeptiker
6. Sozialhilfeempfänger 7. Armutsgrenze 8. Europarat 9. geschnorrt 10. Gerichtshof
11. Totalentzug 12. Entsorgung